Paths Out of Dixie

PRINCETON STUDIES IN AMERICAN POLITICS

HISTORICAL, INTERNATIONAL, AND COMPARATIVE PERSPECTIVES
Ira Katznelson, Eric Schickler, Martin Shefter, and Theda Skocpol,
Series Editors

A list of titles in this series appears at the back of the book

Paths Out of Dixie

The Democratization
of Authoritarian Enclaves
in America's Deep South, 1944–1972

Robert Mickey

Princeton University Press

Princeton and Oxford

Copyright © 2015 by Princeton University Press
Published by Princeton University Press,
41 William Street, Princeton, New Jersey 08540
In the United Kingdom: Princeton University Press,
6 Oxford Street, Woodstock, Oxfordshire OX20 1TW

press.princeton.edu
Jacket Art: Ben Shahn, 1898–1969. *Break Reaction's Grip*, 1946, offset lithograph, 411/4 x
29 in. (104.8 x 73.7 cm) Smithsonian American Art Museum, Gift of Leslie, Judy and Gabri
Schreyer, and Alice Schreyer Batk 2000.75.5. Courtesy of Art Resource/The Estate of Ben
Shahn/VAGA, NY. Cover art © Estate of Ben Shahn/Licensed by Vaga, New York, NY.

ISBN 978-0-691-13338-6

ISBN (pbk.) 978-0-691-14963-9

Library of Congress Control Number: 2014956071

British Library Cataloging-in-Publication Data is available

This book has been composed in Sabon Next LT Pro

1 3 5 7 9 10 8 6 4 2

For Anita Mickey and to the memory of Bob Mickey
PROUD AUSTINITES AND DEMOCRATIZERS IN THEIR OWN WAY

Contents

CHAPTER EIGHT
"No, Not One"

PART FOUR: Modes of Democratization and Their Legacies since 1964   *257*

CHAPTER NINE
The Deathblows to Authoritarian Rule
The Civil and Voting Rights Acts and

CHAPTER TEN

CHAPTER ELEVEN

Illustrations and Tables

Illustrations

Tables

Preface and Acknowledgments

Paths Out of Dixie DEVELOPS A NEW interpretation of the political transformation of the U.S. South. It views southern states from the late nineteenth century until the early 1970s as pockets of authoritarian rule trapped within, and sustained by, a federal democracy. These enclaves—devoted to maintaining a dependable supply of cheap agricultural labor and "white supremacy"—were established by conservative Democrats to protect their political careers and their clients' interests. Relying on several defenses, they ruled their polities without serious threat for half a century. Beginning with the abolition of the whites-only Democratic primary in 1944 and continuing up through the national party reforms of the early 1970s, enclaves were battered and destroyed by a series of democratization pressures from without by federal actors and the national party, and from within by domestic insurgencies. This book focuses on three similarly situated Deep South states—Georgia, Mississippi, and South Carolina—and describes and explains how their rulers attempted to elude successive democratization pressures and then minimize federal oversight of their dismantling of segregation and suffrage restriction. It then suggests that the different ways in which these rulers navigated their polity's transition to democracy produced important political and economic consequences that reverberate today. While I hope the book advances our understanding of these states' political history, this is not its primary purpose. Rather, the book is intended as a contribution to a few different conversations among political scientists, historians, and other scholars.

First, the book is meant to jump-start a conversation about America's democratic development that explicitly takes note of differences in governance across and even within the states. In my view, the United States consolidated its democratization—the process by which it became (in most understandings of the term) a democracy across its entire territory—quite recently. The hows and whys of this long, drawn-out process—and in particular the ways in which America's political parties encouraged democratic rule in some areas and moments, and aided and abetted its opponents in others—is something we don't understand very well. This phenomenon is not limited to the states that formed the Confederacy, but the South is a good place to start. I focus largely on enclave rulers, their governance challenges, and the monumental tasks faced by their adversaries. External interventions alone would not suffice in defeating these enclaves, a fact reflected in the book's cover, which features a poster by famed artist-agitator Ben Shahn that announced the Congress of Industrial Organization's 1946 drive to unionize southern workers. Enclave rulers at first successfully repelled this effort—which also featured voter registration campaigns—to "Break Reaction's Grip." But, capitalizing on other external pressures, black and Hispanic insurgents and their white allies in the South ultimately helped destroy enclaves and build democratic institutions, and thereby forced America to deliver on its democratic promise. This is a tale of a triumph, the magnitude of which has not been fully acknowledged. But it is also a story about democratization's meager fruits, and the enduring influence of enclave rulers and their clients. Understanding better the many consequences of America's strange democratic development is vital.

Second, the book is meant to help advance the study of southern history by viewing the transformation of twentieth-century southern politics seriously in terms of regime change—a change in the mode of governance. These states really are polities in their own right, and they should be studied as such. I have tried to describe and explain democratizations of three similarly situated Deep South states, but much is left to do, both with respect to these states and the experiences of other southern states (leaving open, too, a discussion of what constitutes "the South"). Additionally, I hope *Paths Out of Dixie* supports the recent effort among historians to understand the diversity among southern rulers from Redemption until the 1970s, and also the implications of this diversity for apprehending the South today.

Third, and a bit more implicitly, I hope this book is a useful contribution to burgeoning research by students of comparative politics on subnational political change. Edward Gibson and others have begun to think through how and why states or provinces around the world sometimes constitute enclaves of authoritarian rule or of democratic rule, as well as what effects these undemocratic holdouts or incubators of democracy have on national-level politics. In my view, the United States provides (at least) eleven new cases for comparison.

I should be clear about what this book is *not*. It is certainly not a comprehensive political history of the South, or even of three Deep South states, over the twentieth century. Several excellent such texts already exist. The book also does not narrate the civil rights movement. This has been done before—especially for the region at large but also at the state level—and often in eloquent and moving ways. Public historians and earlier generations of scholars advanced the view of a single movement, characterized as an effort to secure full citizenship, which flourished during the years between *Brown v. Board of Education* in 1954 and the Voting Rights Act in 1965. More recently, historians have urged us to see instead a "long civil rights movement" that begins much earlier and continues on through the 1970s, and that concerns economic justice as much as the securing of civil and political rights. On this second view, earlier contentious politics by blacks, Hispanics, poorer whites, and others had important legacies (viewed as both positive and negative) for the 1950s, 1960s, and beyond. My work accords with this longer perspective, but departs from it somewhat, too. As I suggest in chapter 1, in answering certain questions, there are advantages in not framing this period from a "social movements" perspective. This book throughout retains a focus on southern state Democratic parties and their responses to similarly timed democratization pressures from within and without. Finally, the book does not narrate the region's race relations. This is not its purpose, in part because to do so, I think, obscures the achievements of generations of southerners in founding democratic governance in their region. Moreover, "race relations"—a concept that forces a group psychology frame upon much thinking, popular and scholarly, about the politics of racial and ethnic division—may mislead us more than it helps us understand these phenomena. We might do better by avoiding it, or at least acknowledging its limitations.

There's a small issue regarding terminology that's worth addressing now. Martin Luther King's father, Reverend Martin Luther ("Daddy") King, Sr., was campaigning in South Carolina on behalf of the Democratic gubernatorial candidate in 1970. State Democratic party official Don Fowler was charged with driving him around Columbia and then hustling him to the airport to catch the day's final flight back to Atlanta. King insisted on a last-minute visit to Maurice's Piggy Park, a well-known barbeque joint. Fowler noted the late time; King repeated his request. Fowler told King that the Piggy Park's owner, Maurice Bessinger, was an outspoken white supremacist who had not exactly mourned the death of King's son two years before. King made himself clear: "*We are going to the Piggy Park.*" I relate this story not just because it brings together two southern passions, politics and barbeque. I hope it also helps explain why I don't follow a common practice of reserving the term "southerners" for whites. Blacks, whatever their status in the polity, economy, and society, have long made and remade the South. Viewing "southerners" as meaning only "whites" writes blacks out of a region they helped forge and, I argue here, ultimately democratize. Blacks are southerners, too. "Daddy" King went to Maurice's.

Should any trees remain after the environmental norms I violated with the help of Proquest Historical Newspapers, I partly atone here by omitting a bibliography. For a link to my sources please see http://press.princeton .edu/titles/9469.html.

◆——▶

Let's get the first V. O. Key quotation out of the way: "Of books about the South there is no end." My family, friends, and colleagues can be forgiven for thinking that there'd be no end to this one. I hope I can begin to repay these people somehow for all of their insights, encouragement, and patience. Without them, there'd be no book at all. Furthermore—without them, there'd be no dissertation, and no long Michigan winters to survive (hold on a sec!).

Working backward: First, I'd like to thank Chuck Myers, Eric Crahan, Brigitte Pelner, and others at Princeton University Press, and copyeditor Linda Truilo, for making this book happen. I'm very grateful to Chuck and Eric for all they did to help make this a better book, and for the Press's herculean patience. Thanks, too, to Cambridge University Press and the editors of *Studies in American Political Development* for allowing me to incorporate some material that first appeared in its pages, and to Jim Reische and two anonymous reviewers for University of Michigan Press.

Upon arriving at Michigan, I worried about how I would fit in doing historically inflected political science at the home of the study of party identification and all of that psychology stuff. Luckily, I could not have been more wrong. I received expert advice and encouragement from so many colleagues, including two of Georgia's native sons, Matt Lassiter and the late, great Hanes Walton; Pam Brandwein; Nancy Burns; Tony Chen; Anna Grzymała-Busse; Rick Hall; Don Kinder; Skip Lupia; and Liz Wingrove. I'm very grateful to Anna G-B for her feedback, encouragement, and productive impatience, and for organizing a manuscript workshop that featured valuable advice from Bill Clark, Rick Hall, and Ken Kollman, all valued friends. At moments when my health faltered, departmental chairs Don Kinder and Chuck Shipan went above and beyond the call to help out. And at a critical juncture, when I was frustrated enough to give up, friends in Ann Arbor and beyond bailed me out. Jake, Cara, Peggy, and especially Orit and Rob never gave me any useful suggestions on the manuscript; their help was infinitely more valuable than that.

I have received many great suggestions and encouragement over the years from scholars far and wide. Manuscript reviewers at Princeton and at University of Michigan Press provided great feedback. I am extremely grateful to Kim Johnson, Matt Lassiter, David Smith, and Elizabeth Mann, who gave me very constructive comments on the entire manuscript. Related material received excellent suggestions from two anonymous reviewers, as well as the editors, at *Studies in American Political Development*. I've lost count of this book's flaws, but it has been much improved because of this help. Indeed, it would be better still if I had done a better job of incorporating their ideas.

My debts to Morgan Kousser and Rick Valelly will be obvious to readers of the endnotes. In real life they have been equally helpful and very generous with their time and advice. I am extremely lucky to have gotten to exchange ideas with them, as well as with other scholars whose work has inspired me, including Richard Bensel, Charles Bullock, Charles Payne, Jim Cobb, the late John Egerton, Ira Katznelson, Liz Sanders, Byron Shafer, and Gavin Wright. I also had helpful conversations and encouragement from the late Howard Reiter, Dan Carpenter, Devin Caughey, Joe Crespino, Jim Glaser, and Joe Luders. For their very sharp suggestions, I thank Ira Katznelson, Alan Brinkley, Greg Wawro, and other participants at Columbia University; David Waldner, Gerard Alexander, Sid Milkis, and others at the University of Virginia; and discussants and audiences at Mexico's ITAM, UC-Berkeley, Vanderbilt, Yale, and the annual meetings of the Southern, Western, Midwestern, and American Political Science Associations.

I am extremely grateful to the Robert Wood Johnson Foundation for including me in its Scholars in Health Policy Research program. Besides giving me valuable time to work on this and other projects, RWJ introduced me to Naomi Murakawa, Chris Parker, Jim Morone, John Ellwood, Aaron Panofsky, and several other folks at the program's UC-Berkeley site—I'm all the better for it. Naomi and Chris gave me a lot of smart feedback on this book as well. (And I am eternally grateful to RWJ for helping me meet my wife, Jenny.)

I had heard tell of the hospitality of southern archivists, and was not disappointed. Across the region, they provided very generous, inventive help that was invaluable, and I offer a woefully incomplete acknowledgment of them here. In Georgia, senior archivist Dale Couch and others at the Georgia Department of Archives and History, and Jill Severn and her staff at the Richard B. Russell Library at the University of Georgia were wonderful. Similar treatment was accorded at Atlanta University Center, Special Collections at the Woodruff Library at Emory, the Southern Regional Council, and the Auburn Avenue Research Library on African American Culture. Most of all, many thanks to my dear sister Elizabeth and her amazing family for their generosity in hosting me while I was in Georgia. In Mississippi, I am particularly grateful to the archivists and staff at the Mississippi Department of Archives and History and Jackson State University, and to Jan Hillegas and her Freedom Information Service Archives. My four months in Mississippi were made even more memorable by getting to spend some time with legendary journalist Bill Minor, and by the hospitality of D'Andra Orey as well as King Edward and everybody else down at the Subway Lounge. In South Carolina, the incredibly generous and expert help of Herb Hartsook, Kate Moore, and others at South Carolina Political Collections at USC made all the difference, as did conversations with Don Fowler (Sr.), Tom Terrill, Cole Blease Graham, Jr., James McLawhorn, and John Hammond Moore.

At Vanderbilt, Richard Pride helped put a roof over my head, and the archivists at the Heard Library's Southern Politics Collection helped me march through the papers of V. O. Key. A lunch with former Chancellor Alexander Heard, conductor of the vast majority of interviews on which Key's *Southern Politics* is based, was a real treat. At various other archives and the National Archives in College Park, Maryland, I received warm welcomes. The incredibly knowledgeable Allen Fisher and Tina Houston confirmed the LBJ Presidential Library's reputation as the country's researcher-friendliest. Closer to home, expert librarians at Michigan's Hatcher Graduate Library and the particularly forgiving staff of its Interlibrary Loan office earned my deep gratitude.

This book stands on the shoulders of giants in the study of southern political history, but not just them. While the empirical contribution of the book is based predominantly on archival materials and newspapers, I cite close to one thousand works of scholarship, many of them excellent dissertations never published. This book couldn't have been written without them. Thanks, too, to the archivists who have developed digitized collections of materials, including those at the University of Southern Mississippi, Mississippi State University, and the University of North Carolina-Chapel Hill.

I was also greatly helped by several research assistants, including Nnamudi Amobi, Jared Ellias, Susan Goldis, Fenlene Hsu, Duncan Hwang, Brandi Jans, Ellen Kersten, Derrick Lam, Maura McNulty, Veronica Melendez, Raghav Murali, Jasel Panchal, Nisha Patel, Tyra Saechao, Jess Steinberg, Courtney Taymour, Laurie Thompson, Michael Tomsky, and Alton Worthington. A special thanks goes to David Smith, a colleague from his first day in graduate school who is now getting paid like one. Talks with him were immensely helpful. Jim Alt, Ken Andrews, and Manfred Berg very generously shared their data with me.

This book began as a dissertation at Harvard. My dissertation committee was chaired by the inimitable Theda Skocpol, who introduced me to the study of American political development. More than any single act of mentoring—and Lord knows there have been many—I'll always be grateful for the chance to witness her brilliance and determination, both of which continue to inspire. The other committee members—John Aldrich, Dan Kryder, and Paul Pierson—were incredibly generous in their advice and encouragement. John reprised his role as the nicest person in the discipline, providing enthusiasm, great feedback, and, along with the program on Democratic Institutions and Political Economy, a base camp at Duke while I roamed about the South. Dan, a fellow southerner and southernist, offered expertise, detailed feedback, unflagging, patient support, and great friendship, and I continue to learn from him. Paul broadened my intellectual horizons and remains a valued advice-giver and friend. I'm very grateful to

Glenn Loury for letting me spend a year at his Institute on Race & Social Division at Boston University, where Glenn, Rebeccah Welch, Mia Bay, and Chris Winship provided such a stimulating atmosphere. Big thanks to Steve Teles for helping make this (and much else) possible, as well as for his input and encouragement. Eric Schickler, Bruce Cain, and the much-missed Nelson Polsby offered a carrel, sage advice, and tea most afternoons during a wonderful stay at Berkeley's Institute of Governmental Studies.

Even earlier, the first ideas animating this book appeared in a conference paper. At the Western Political Science Association meeting an embarrassing number of years ago, Amy Bridges reassured me that thinking about southern political development in terms of democratization was both not crazy and potentially useful. Early on, I hadn't quite figured out how to reconcile a democratization approach to the South with the fact that southern states weren't sovereign nation-states (my home state of Texas, of course, excepted). A meeting with Ed Gibson came at a wonderful time, as he helped me reckon with U.S. federalism and see these states as authoritarian enclaves. His help is reflected in the book's title and most of its pages, and his encouragement over the years has been critical; I hope it can be repaid.

In Boston and beyond, an amazing group of people—both students and (in Tony Soprano's term) "citizens"—kept me in one piece. I'm indebted to so many, from (A)aron Belkin to (Z)ahavah and everyone in between, including Sue Aaron, Gabe Aguilera, Landis Armstrong, Ben Berger, Fenway ticket scalper Sean (surname withheld), Sasha K. Dass, Anna Greenberg, Britt Guerrina, Konrad Huber, Jodi Hullinger, Bert Johnson, Kern, Steve Marshall, Pedro Martínez, Andy Molinsky, Nancy Hopkins and Bruce McKinney, Tommy Ort, Alejandro Poiré, Eric Rosenthal, Steve Rochlin, Guillermo Rosas, Alex Samuel, Meredith Seidel, Steve Teles, Van Houweling, and Keith Wexelblatt.

Five years spent in Prague just after the revolutions of 1989 sparked my interests in democratization and in racial and ethnic conflict. I'm grateful to Stephen Heintz for bringing me aboard the EastWest Institute, which gave me the chance to travel, learn, and meet an amazing cast of characters across East Central Europe and the Balkans. A few such characters—Adam Smith Albion, Karla Brom, Lenka Nováková, Kate Storm Steel, Jonathan Stein, Jenny Zales, and, especially, Jonathan Zimmerman—stand out for their love and friendship.

Before Cambridge and Prague, there was Providence, where the late Eric Nordlinger tried to teach me how to think clearly, and Austin, where Laura Camp encouraged my interest in politics and history. Two other Austinites did the same—my parents. I dedicate this book to my mother, Anita, and to the memory of my father, Bob. She worked for LBJ in the late 1950s (is it a coincidence that Robert Caro finally starts to say nice things about him in these years?). He phone-banked for Nixon in 1960, and soon decided that all politicians are crooks (now I know where I got the tendency to over-learn from a single case). They raised me in an enclave's enclave, and for that and so much else I am grateful. And ever since I left home for distant lands, they've sustained me in every way imaginable. If there's any value in the pages that follow, they are to be thanked. In any case, I am thankful for them every day.

My dad passed away as this book went to press. If he were still with us when it arrived, he would have—as always—expressed his pride in me, and he would have had the good sense not to read it. Both of those reactions make me proud to be his son.

I am glad that this project won't bother daughter Rachel or son Sam the way it burdened my parents. Or Jenny. I tried but failed to finish it before she got caught up in it. I am so very lucky that she has stuck with me. Any future endeavors are hereby dedicated in advance to her. And to Rachel and Sam, if they promise to be good.

PART ONE

Deep South Enclaves, 1890–1940

CHAPTER ONE

Southern Political Development in Comparative Perspective

What is the State? It is the Democratic party. . . . Whenever there were political questions involved, . . . we looked to the interests of the party, because they are the interests of the State.

—*Judge Thomas J. Semmes*, delegate at Louisiana's constitutional convention (1898)

The conversion of the South into a democracy in the sense that the mass of people vote and have a hand in their governance poses one of the most staggering tasks for statesmanship in the modern world.

—*Valdimer Orlando Key, Jr.* (1949)

ON JANUARY 11, 1961, Charlayne Hunter and Hamilton Holmes desegregated the University of Georgia in Athens. Their first afternoon of classes complete, Hunter settled in her dorm room, while Holmes returned to an off-campus residence. Much of the campus—and the state capitol in nearby Atlanta—was abuzz with talk of that night's scheduled disturbance. Politicians from north Georgia pleaded with Governor Ernest Vandiver to dispatch the state highway patrol to ensure that the court-ordered desegregation occurred peacefully. Advisers from south Georgia disagreed; some secretly helped riot leaders in their bid to make the campus unsafe for Hunter and Holmes and safe again for white supremacy. By ten o'clock, a crowd of some two thousand students and locals set upon Hunter's dormitory, where they hurled bricks and bottles and set fires nearby. After Athens cops fended off the crowd with tear gas and fire hoses, state troopers arrived—two hours after police requested help from the vacillating governor. National papers showed U.S. marshals rushing a distraught Hunter to safety. North Georgia politicians were chagrined by the disorder; those from south Georgia fumed at the state's capitulation.[1]

On a late September morning in 1962, U.S. marshals escorted James Meredith across the University of Mississippi campus to the Lyceum—the school's main administrative building—where a taciturn registrar awaited. Oxford's air still stung with tear gas; stray bullets had pockmarked the statues of Confederate fallen. The group proceeded down a bloodstained corridor past exhausted U.S. marshals slumped against the walls, gas masks still strapped to their jaws. A pitched battle had just resulted in two deaths and hundreds of injuries. Alternately encouraged, discouraged, and repressed by confused state and county law enforcement, two thousand rampaging white supremacists had attacked the marshals. U.S. troops numbering 31,000—more than were stationed in South Korea—detained hundreds of civilians and restored order. Mississippi's "occupation" had begun.[2]

Four months later, aspiring architect Harvey Gantt, stepping dapper out of a Buick sedan, strolled confidently across the campus of South Carolina's Clemson College in his dark pinstripe suit, checked coat, and hat. As he did, jostling and commotion ensued. The first stirrings of a riot here in America's last bastion of segregation? No, just shutterbugs jockeying for position. A polite meeting with the registrar, a quick press conference, a few curious onlookers.... Where was the angry white mob? Northern journalists left dejected. State politicians had foiled white supremacists' planned disorder. The *New York Times* cried, "Bravo, Clemson.... What a contrast to Mississippi!" President Kennedy applauded, too, and discussed doubling South Carolina's defense contracts.[3]

These confrontations among black insurgents, white crowds, state authorities, and federal officials varied greatly, ranging from the breakdown of order in Mississippi to South Carolina's much-lauded "integration with dignity." This book situates these crises as important moments in a much longer process—the democratization of southern authoritarian enclaves. Having begun in the 1940s, these transitions from authoritarian rule concluded by the early 1970s in the successful democratization of the eleven states of the former Confederacy. However, statesmen had converted them in sharply different ways. They differed in their ability to minimize outside interference with their dismantling of disfranchisement and "Jim Crow" social practices, to make peace with national Democrats, and to attract business investment. In part because they beat different paths out of Dixie, these states today differ in their politics and economics. Apprehending the contemporary South means coming to terms with the legacies of its democratizations.

In the 1890s leaders of the eleven states of the old Confederacy founded stable, one-party authoritarian enclaves under the "Democratic" banner. Having secured a conditional autonomy from the central state and the national party, these rulers curtailed electorates, harassed and repressed opposition parties, and created and regulated racially separate—and significantly unfree—civic spheres. State-sponsored violence enforced these elements in a system that ensured cheap agricultural labor and white supremacy. These regimes were effectively conflations of the state apparatus with those institutions regulating political ambition. The state apparatus oversaw the hegemonic Democratic party, while the party staffed, exploited, and guided local, county, and state governments. Given the strength of these regimes, their most serious challenges would emanate from without, not within. Enclaves capitalized on their influence in Congress and the national Democratic party—as well as national indifference—to shield themselves from those who might violate their "sovereignty." For a half-century, they succeeded.

Beginning with the U.S. Supreme Court's abolition of the "white only" Democratic primary in 1944, black insurgents, mostly in the South, inspired, compelled, and capitalized on federal judicial rulings, national legislation, and national party reforms that battered these enclaves. By the early 1970s, a variety of actors—federal authorities, domestic insurgents, and their allies "abroad"—had defeated southern authoritarians. In the process, the central state had supervised the dismantling of disfranchisement, segregation, and state repression, while national Democrats ordered southern parties to incorporate racial minorities.

But the devil, as usual, was in the details. Across the South, officeholders sought to minimize federal supervision of state compliance with civil and voting rights legislation and scores of judicial directives, ranging from school desegregation to legislative reapportionment, from electoral systems to lunch counters. In many ways, minimizing oversight could lower the costs of democratization for incumbents and their clients. How successful were these resisters in doing so? How much autonomy did they manage to preserve? Were they able to democratize on their own terms, or was the process out of their hands? Once the guarantor of southern authoritarianism, an emboldened national Democratic party had begun to interfere with the manner in which state parties treated black voters, nominated candidates, and selected presidential delegates. Did southern Democrats reform racial practices and normalize relations, or did they bicker with the national party, file for "divorce," and then walk away?

Across the region, the eleven enclaves differed in the nature of their compliance with federal directives; the pace and scope of black incorporation into the state Democratic party; and the timing and nature of their reconciliation with the national party. Different configurations of these factors constituted distinct modes of democratization (table 1.1). In one, enclaves quickly submitted to pressures to democratize, or even preempted some of them through "indigenous" reforms. Falling into line with federal and national party directives, these enclaves—usually in the Outer South— experienced an *acquiescent democratization*.[4] Others sought to delay change, control the pace of democratizing reforms, and minimize the consequences of black incorporation into the Democratic party.[5] To do so, they needed to walk a tight wire from angry defiance to lawful compliance without inducing disorder (and the breaches of "sovereignty" that might follow). Some successfully implemented this strategic accommodation, and thereby secured a *harnessed democratization*. Others failed, triggering enclave intransigence, massive interventions, and fractured national party relations, and experienced a *protracted democratization*.

Surprisingly, this variation existed even within the Deep South—a region that remains relatively undifferentiated in the popular imagination and academic mind. As the transitions began in the 1940s, these enclaves featured similar demographics, political economies, modes of governance, partisan dynamics, and commitments to white supremacy. Over time, rulers' responses to democratization pressures propelled these states onto different paths. South Carolina managed a harnessed democratization, Mississippi stumbled through a protracted democratization, and Georgia experienced a bifurcated democratization, in which sectional conflict led north and south Georgia to come to different terms with the feds and the national party.

These different paths generated important legacies that still shape the present. Those enclaves that accommodated democratization pressures garnered greater success in capital accumulation and accelerated their state's economic growth. Conversely, those enclaves unable to do so suffered greatly on this score. Ironically, however, by managing to incorporate blacks and reconcile with the national party smoothly, enclave rulers doomed state Democrats over the long run. Where rulers failed to accommodate strategically to democratization pressures, they unintentionally benefited state Democrats over the coming decades.

Southern regime change has never been examined. This study—a comparative historical analysis of democratization in Georgia, Mississippi, and South Carolina—seeks to explain one important element of this change: the processes of democratization undergone by Deep South states. It argues that elite cohesion, and the institutions of party and state that equipped and constrained these elites, help account for differences in modes of democratization across the Deep South. (Regime elites are discussed further in chapter 2. For now, by *elites* I mean powerful authorities in party or state institutions, and other important resource-holders within the regime.) *Elite cohesion* refers to the degree to which regime politicians and other resource-holders agree that the party remains the best vehicle for pursuing political careers and policy goals, and agree broadly on a strategy to resist democratization pressures. *Party-state capacity* refers to the degree of fit between, on the one hand, the institutions regulating political ambition and those of the state apparatus, and, on the other, elites' efforts to undertake various governance tasks—especially those necessary for maintaining enclave rule.[6] By

TABLE 1.1
Modes of Democratization

	Outer South	South Carolina	Mississippi	Georgia
State compliance with federal directives	Preemptive	Superficial and tranquil	Delayed and violent	Split by region
Black incorporation into state party	Early and extensive	Early and managed	Late and divisive	Split by region
Reconciliation with national party	Earliest and preemptive	Early 1960s and smooth	Late (mid-1970s) and turbulent	Split by region (early 1970s)
Type of democratization process	Acquiescent	Harnessed	Protracted	Bifurcated

the early 1960s, enclaves differed on these two dimensions, and thus varied in how they navigated mounting democratization pressures.

The South's democratization—a complex macrohistorical process occurring amid great social, cultural, and economic change—is the most important development in American politics since World War II. It has contributed to the ideological and racial polarization of the national parties, altered the dimensions on which the parties compete, redrawn the map of presidential elections, and transformed Congress. Moreover, today millions of Americans now practice an entirely different mode of politics. Whereas blacks were once shut out of electoral politics, some six thousand black elected officials now serve southern constituencies. More than 73 million southern adults, native-born and newly arrived, may participate freely in a competitive, two-party system. Whereas Democrats once occupied about 95 percent of all elective offices, Republicans now claim more than one-half of the region's federal and state offices.[7] Thus, understanding how the recent past shapes contemporary U.S. politics requires illuminating the political development of the American South.

This study offers an optic for focusing on the region, and on the United States, in cross-national perspective. The remainder of this chapter describes some of the principal approaches to southern political change, outlines the one used here, describes the study's research design, and summarizes the findings to come. This book is *not* a study of the emergence of a two-party South—the object of most scholarly and popular attention. However, as a study of Deep South democratizations, it will illuminate how Republican party advancement was in part both a consequence *and* a cause of these democratization processes.

Alternative Perspectives
on Postwar Southern Politics

Scholars have tackled several different facets of the South's recent political transformation. Most political scientists interpret it in terms of electoral politics and in particular seek to trace the contours of Republican advancement across the region and over time.[8] Other social scientists and historians have sought to understand several momentous changes, from the reenfranchisement of blacks and poorer whites to the desegregation of southern schools to the destruction of Jim Crow to the growth of black political power, and so on. In doing so, their explanations have centered on three main types of causes: political culture, political economy, and social movements. While scholars have not studied the post–World War II South in terms of the region's democratization, I review these families of explanations—as well as related arguments by scholars of comparative politics—to see what light they might shed on variation within the region in modes of democratization. Each generates crucial insights, and each points to important differences between the Outer South and Deep South. But none alone suffices to explain the surprising variation within the latter.

Political Culture

Many scholars focus on the period as one of a growing convergence in political cultures between the South and the rest of the country. Here, the region's elites and masses are seen as undergoing great change—especially in terms of white racial attitudes.[9] There are at least two different routes by which political culture may matter for my purposes. First, rapid changes in *mass* beliefs and attitudes about politics can fuel political change. A variant of modernization theory argues that changing mass values and attitudes can be critical for stimulating public demand for political reforms.[10] In fact, the leading work in political science on postwar southern politics, Earl Black and Merle Black's *Politics and Society in the South*, offers a modernization account. It and other studies explain the pace and location of Republican advancement by emphasizing the importance of growing southern white incomes, industrialization, urbanization, and other changes—particularly the influx of nonnative whites to the region. These factors produced profound cultural changes, including a white electorate both less devoted to white supremacy and less loyal to the Democratic party, which spurred the growth of white Republican voting. Second, the beliefs, attitudes, and bearings of political *elites* can often help explain political change, especially short, turbulent periods in which elite agency is thought to be crucial in explaining outcomes.[11]

An emphasis on mass political culture would suggest that states' experiences during the civil rights era might differ given growing levels of the familiar components of modernization: urbanization, education, income, and exposure to national mass culture and communications. As these components increased, the commitment of white publics to white supremacy would weaken, and middle-class whites would pressure authorities to embark on liberalizing political reforms. By the same token, changing white mass attitudes might enable officeholders to embark on political projects they preferred but had shied away from in the past. And urbanization and educational attainment might help empower and embolden blacks and their white allies to mount more serious challenges to the political status quo, and thereby raise the costs for both white elites and publics of maintaining it. Thus, states that modernized earlier—such as those in the more urbanized Outer South—would experience earlier political change. And this change would likely be more peaceful, as pressure on authorities to respond to black insurgency with repression would be diminished. In fact, some Outer South states might enact reforms before ordered by the federal government to do so.[12]

Southern historians often explain the momentous events of the 1950s and 1960s with reference to elite political culture. Political elites are thought to have ranged widely, from North Carolina's "progressive plutocrats" and Virginia's aristocrats to Louisiana's "buffoons," from the "redneck" leadership of Mississippi to the "dignified" politicians of South Carolina.[13] Even if they did differ sharply across states, the explanatory power of these differences is not obvious; nor are there clear predictions to be made either between the Outer South and Deep South or within the Deep South. As chapter 7 details, for example, in the 1950s South Carolina's "dignified" authorities responded to black mobilizations after *Brown v. Board of Education* with sufficient viciousness to cast doubt on this approach. Still, if elite agency is especially important in explaining concentrated periods of major political change, perhaps cross-state differences among elite styles of governance might help explain modes of democratization.[14]

The Political Economy of Southern Political Change

Differences in political economies may also help explain the diversity of states' experiences during the turbulent civil rights period. Two approaches are most relevant here: modernization theory and the politics of labor-repressive agriculture. The economic variant of modernization theory holds that economic growth promotes changes in a society's class structure that hasten the emergence of popular demands for liberalizing political change, usually because various classes develop new preferences and outlooks but, locked out of existing political institutions, cannot secure policies consistent with them. In some versions, middle classes are the chief protagonists; in others, the working classes are.[15] Applied to the South, the approach suggests that those states in which incomes began to catch up more quickly to the national average would be more likely to feature rising middle classes impatient with the political status quo—especially those in the "Sunbelt" suburbs that began to emerge in the 1950s.[16]

Other political economists emphasize less the political and cultural effects of economic modernization than the relative political influence of various sectors of the economy. Most relevant is the prevalence of "labor-repressive agriculture."[17] Here, a polity's economy is substantially driven by large landowners who adopt public policies and rely on state-sponsored coercion of agricultural workers in order to guarantee a steady supply of farm labor. Labor-dependent landed elites are more likely to fear democracy, because their primary asset—land—is fixed and thus more easily taxed by politically empowered lower classes, and generally because the political and economic arrangements sustaining the status quo are vulnerable to abolition in a democracy.[18] In the South, large landowners dominated the "Black Belt," the wide swath of counties running from east Texas to southern Virginia that were both rich in fertile soil and often majority-black (as reflected in figure 1.1). These elites estimated the costs of democracy to be even higher because they lived in more densely black areas, where the reenfranchisement of blacks would threaten local elites' domination of municipal and county-level offices.[19] As in authoritarian regimes everywhere, suffrage would have to be "conquered, not granted."[20]

Broad postwar economic change, particularly the mechanization of southern agriculture, is often cited as attenuating the ferocity with which powerful economic interests—whether planters or their coalition partners among the region's merchants and industrialists—defended the status quo.[21] As the "Bulldozer Revolution" commenced after World War II, and southern states became more reliant on nonagrarian sectors, politicians linked to these sectors could then enact political and social reforms necessary to enhance their state's labor force through human capital investment and to attract foreign direct investment.[22]

Comparativists suggest that the structure of the authoritarian political economy has great bearing not only on the preferences of economic elites for democracy but also on the turbulence of transition periods that may occur. When rulers are choosing between conceding to democratization pressures and repression, landowners—particularly those in highly unequal, labor-repressive agrarian societies—are more likely to favor repression than are industrialists. They consider the costs of repression to be lower, in part because they attach less value to their polity's reputation as an orderly, peaceful, and attractive site of external capital investment.[23]

Both political-economic approaches predict that substantial political reforms—such as the reenfranchisement of blacks and poorer whites—should occur earlier and in a more orderly manner in the more industrialized Outer South than in the Deep South. Still, a few matters give us pause here. First, prominent landowners and firms cannot always easily convert their economic influence into political power. Political institutions can refract economic interests in strange ways; for instance, as chapter 3 describes, Georgia's bizarre electoral system blunted for decades the influence of Atlanta's economic modernizers in state politics. Second, as economic historian Gavin Wright has recently shown, white middle-class southerners and elected officials—including those relatively autonomous from their economic clients—had no trouble squaring rapid economic and metropolitan growth with their own preference for retaining segregated civic, social, and economic spheres. Third, when powerful interests clash, it is more difficult to predict which interests will carry the day. Fourth, a focus only on labor-repressive agriculture misses out on possible conflict and repression due to employment competition among blacks and working-class whites. As Joseph Luders suggests, when the latter is present, "society-led" repression (opposed by economic elites and authorities) or even "full intransigence" (when economic elites, the clients of public authorities, still rely on black labor) is possible.

Thus, political-economic approaches suggest that there may be variation within southern states, not broad distinctions between them.[24] Thus, while possibly helpful in explaining broad differences between the Outer South and the more agrarian Deep South, political economy scholarship suggests that we bring in the interaction of political economy and institutions of party and state to reckon with variations in the Deep South.[25]

Black Insurgency and Southern Political Change

Finally, sociologists and historians have often treated black insurgency as the main driver of southern political change. Here, the region's political transformation is narrated in large part through the development and cresting of a social movement, with its attendant triumphs and limits. In his seminal work on black insurgency, sociologist Doug McAdam explains the emergence, development, and decline of black movement organizations, rather than the outcomes of conflicts between black claimants and white political authorities and economic elites. Nevertheless, this approach implicitly offers some predictions about variation in the latter.

McAdam agrees with the political-economic perspective that the decline of "King Cotton" was significant for southern political development, but suggests an additional reason. Besides altering the strategies and relative influence of major economic sectors, this change enhanced the capacity of black protest and weakened opposition to it. The mechanization of agriculture pushed blacks off the land and into southern cities, where potential activists held advantages over their rural counterparts. These included greater physical safety, denser associational networks, more aggressive churches, a larger critical mass of blacks economically independent of white employers, and black colleges and other useful sites for organizing. For McAdam, the demise of King Cotton facilitated black protest via a cultural channel (the development of a rising black militant consciousness) and an infrastructural one (as movement activities themselves became safer and better organized).[26] On this view, black insurgency would develop earlier, and more successfully, in the more urbanized Outer South. McAdam suggests that urbanization would also account for differences within states in the development and behavior of insurgencies.

However, the social movement approach leaves unclear how the emergence and development of black insurgency helps us to understand the eventual outcomes of clashes with adversaries. The implicit assumption is that stronger movements face lower levels of white repression; since strength is based on the goals and tactics of black groups, the choices of black insurgents are paramount in explaining outcomes. But, as McAdam acknowledges, the relative strength of black insurgencies across the South did not determine interactions with authorities and others (such as white supremacist organizations). As I will show in chapter 7, South Carolina's black protest declined sharply in the 1950s even as the structural conditions thought to foster this protest—education, urbanization, and so on—improved. Despite these advantages, the movement in South Carolina—the Deep South state with the least turbulent civil rights period—never approached the size, or experienced the frequency of contentious events or statewide dispersion, of those that emerged elsewhere. While movement strength, strategy, and tactics are critical to any explanation of outcomes, authorities' preferences and behavior must join the explanation in a more comprehensive way.[27]

In sum, explanations of various facets of the South's transformation drawing on political culture, political economy, and social movements capture essential features of the South's recent political development. Moreover, they overlap and support one another, particularly through a modernization perspective on political change. And they converge on a prediction that, broadly speaking, Outer South states experienced earlier and less tumultuous modes of democratization. However, these accounts are less useful for explaining the surprising variation within the Deep South, where states shared common values on identified causal forces, but political outcomes differed—often sharply.

These accounts are also theoretically unsatisfying for their inattention to political authority. While social and economic forces certainly shape politics, Ruth Berins Collier and David Collier write, "the political arena is not simply fluid, constantly responding to socioeconomic change. Instead, because of an autonomous political logic and vested interests, it may be resistant to change over significant periods of time," and "may to some degree follow its own pattern and pace of change that at times take a highly discontinuous form."[28] Which public authorities were more likely to deter, neutralize, preempt, or adapt to their challengers, why, and with what institutional endowments constraining and enabling their ability to carry out these strategies?

To the extent that regime actors emerge in the analysis, they do so as clients of political-economic interests or as politicians infected by different strains of racist ideology. However, they do not appear as public authorities rooted in institutions and forced to manage their governance responsibilities while enmeshed in relations among localities, counties, and state and federal governments. Indeed, while histories of the civil rights period often compare localities, state government—its institutions, resources, and warrants of authority and responsibility—often go missing.[29] With it, the starring actors of Key's *Southern Politics*—southern Democratic politicians—have been shooed away. Many scholars appreciate the South's democratizers, yet democracy's resisters remain poorly understood.[30] To understand differences within the Deep South, we must beckon these actors back on stage. I propose to do this through viewing these states as authoritarian enclaves under assault.

Authoritarian Enclaves and Their Democratization

Most observers see the pre-1970s South as democratically governed and racist. Is the South really better viewed as a set of enclaves of authoritarian rule somehow allowed to exist within a federal democracy? I think so. To earn the moniker, democracies must feature free and fair elections, the safeguarding of rights necessary to sustain such elections—such as freedoms of assembly, association, and speech—and a state apparatus sufficiently responsive to election winners and autonomous from social and economic forces that these elections are meaningful. By this standard, which I defend and deploy in chapter 2, southern enclaves were clearly undemocratic and different in kind from nonsouthern states—diverging even from those marked by electoral fraud and unfair ballot laws or the corrupt practices of machines and other urban regimes. Here, I introduce the phenomenon of authoritarian enclaves and offer some intuitions about how they might be democratized.

Subnational Authoritarianism

Today, most of the world's regimes are authoritarian. Moreover, those in which a single political party rules through less than free and fair elections are the most common form of authoritarian governance, and comprise fully one-third of all regimes. The share of these "electoral authoritarian" regimes is growing. Since World War II, elections and universal suffrage have become normative worldwide. The most dedicated autocrats understand that their regimes benefit from the appearance of elections.[31] Additionally, electoral authoritarian regimes are the most durable brand of authoritarianism. Far from hastening the demise of a regime's incumbents, regularly held unfree and unfair elections often serve the interests of rulers. They provide valuable (if imperfect) information about the preferences of their subjects and thereby help them respond to popular demand, co-opt opponents, and pay off supporters; they also shore up the regime's legitimacy.[32]

However, sometimes authoritarian regimes stumble and a transition ensues. Although the most common form of regime transition occurs from one form of authoritarianism to another, many transitions result in a nascent democracy. Even if democratic rule is consolidated, however, there often remains substantial variation in political practices across a country's territory.[33] In democratic polities, authoritarian enclaves are areas—usually states or provinces within a federal polity—that feature the absence of the aforementioned components of democracy. Such enclaves now exist in Argentina, Brazil, Mexico, Russia, and elsewhere.[34]

Of course, authoritarian enclaves are not sovereign polities. Usually ruled by hegemonic state-level parties, enclaves are variably constrained by national state institutions and policies—especially constitutions, public finance disbursements, and the regulation of elections, administration, and so on. Additionally, as Edward Gibson argues in his pioneering work, national parties limit, to varying degrees, the extent to which their state-level counterparts can maneuver. Challenges may emanate "bottom-up" from indigenous movements, "top-down" from reformers within the ruling party, or through the imposition of central state authority. To forestall challenges, rulers seek to limit outside involvement in local affairs.[35]

Paradoxically, doing so requires projecting their power onto national-level politics, and monopolizing linkages between provincial-level actors and both the central state and national party. These linkages include institutions regulating intergovernmental relations on such matters as "revenue flows between center and periphery, communication flows, and service delivery between levels of government," as well as rules that determine the balance of power between the national party and its subnational units. Conversely, in order to weaken the regime, domestic opponents reach out across enclave boundaries for assistance from supportive central state officials, allies in the national party, and other "outside agitators."[36]

Since enclaves lack actual sovereignty, they depend on the unwillingness or inability of the central state and national party to intervene against them. Often their ability to deter such intervention is achieved through deals between local elites and national-level politicians. Whether seeking to build a new national coalition or secure national-level political or economic reforms, federal politicians often turn to enclave rulers for their votes in the national legislature or their help within the national party. In exchange, they offer rulers warrants of autonomy over province-level politics, greater influence within the party, or financial or other resources. Even national officials sympathetic to the subjects of enclave rule usually decide that the costs of challenging them outweigh the benefits. Rulers also benefit from a national-level judiciary that does not disturb repression and that does not challenge often-arbitrary law enforcement. Once established, enclaves "are extremely difficult to dislodge in the absence of outside intervention."[37]

Despite recent waves of democratizations worldwide, authoritarian enclaves are increasingly common. Transitions to democracy have been frequently accompanied by decentralization, or the devolution of power and key governance tasks from the national government to subnational units. Decentralization has provided local elites with opportunities to maintain (or even build anew) authoritarian rule over their states or provinces. Thus, in some Mexican states, local *caciques* have made "full use of local clientelistic networks, economic resources, and political machines to consolidate provincial authoritarian projects."[38] Additionally, national democratizers are usually not preoccupied with dynamics at the local level. Rather, they are focused on securing power, advancing large-scale political and economic reforms, and accomplishing other tasks that require national coalitions. These coalitional needs leave national leaders indebted to subnational politicians who can exert reliable control over voters and legislators, giving these regional rulers additional political leverage over the center.[39] Clearly, the fate of authoritarian enclaves hinges on much more than the particular characteristics of states or provinces—rather, the dynamic interaction between and among national and subnational polities is decisive.

Subnational Democratization

Why do authoritarian enclaves collapse, and in what ways? At the national level, the process of dismantling authoritarian regimes differs widely, even within the same region.[40] Explaining the causes—and consequences—of different modes of democratization is difficult. Usually, modes of national-level democratization have been distinguished by the identity of the actor initiating the challenge to the regime ("soft-liners" and "hardliners" within the regime, "moderates" and "radicals" among its opponents, and so forth), the relative importance of particular socioeconomic classes as initiators, and the degree of confrontation that ensues among the transition's major actors.[41] Many observers have preferred so-called "pacted" transitions, in which an agreement is hammered out among a limited set of actors, to revolutions from below or other types of transitions that feature greater popular participation. On their view, the latter will provoke additional repression from rulers, sparking greater disorder and violence. Even if democracy then takes hold, they anticipate long-term negative consequences for democratic stability.[42] While there is no consensus on how to classify or explain modes of national democratization, many scholars agree that the manner in which a country democratizes generates durable legacies for the future, even independent of the larger forces that first brought the country to the brink of a regime transition.[43]

Scholarship on modes of democratization at the national level points to the importance of initiating actors, dynamics among contestants, and the likelihood that different paths out of authoritarian rule generate their own important political, economic, and social legacies. That said, as Edward Gibson argues, subnational democratization is not national democratization cast in miniature. While maintaining focus on the identities of initiating actors, he points to the vertical dynamics between subnational and national actors as most important. Gibson distinguishes broadly between "party-led" and "center-led" modes of subnational democratization. In the former, party allies at the national level assist embattled partisans within an enclave, who then triumph via the ballot box. Party-led democratizations, as in Mexico, are thus only possible where enclave electoral practices are not so onerous as to prevent this pathway. In contrast, in situations in which enclaves have greater autonomy relative to the center, only a center-led transition is possible. Here, enclave insurgents must depend on the central state to oversee and effectively sponsor the enclave's democratization. A third broad mode of democratization—a largely indigenous or self-imposed democratization in which external pressures and resources are not crucial—is highly unlikely given the severe imbalance of power within the enclave. Given this imbalance, "authoritarian incumbents prevail when the scope of conflict is localized. They are threatened when provincial conflict becomes nationalized," as opponents build alliances with national-level actors and exploit new resources to destroy enclave rule.[44]

Another major difference between national and subnational democratizations is that the variation among cases of the latter is likely to be truncated, especially when they occur within the same nation-state. In this situation, they are likely to be brought about by many of the same national-level forces, whether the national party, the central state, or both. Moreover, they are also likely to be subject to similar types of oversight as they transition. Relatedly, the major concern regarding the possible legacies of different modes of national democratization—a turbulent democratization imperils subsequent democratic consolidation—is lessened. Subnational democratization is likely to be a centralizing phenomenon. Given the fact that these subnational units are not sovereign and are now weaker relative to the center, "backsliding" into authoritarian rule is unlikely—or at least much less likely than is true for democratic transitions of nation-states.

The distinction between party- and center-led transitions is helpful, both in classifying different paths out of subnational authoritarianism and in pointing to how we might explain variation across cases. There still remains variation within these broad types. The eleven cases of the U.S. South, for example, are of the center-led mode, but they still differ in important respects. How can we explain the differences among them? And what might the legacies be of their different democratizations? Some of the thoughts below draw in part upon the narratives to follow; thus, this study should be treated only as a work of theory-building, not theory-testing.

Dimensions of Subnational Democratization: Compliance with Federal Directives, Political Incorporation, and Reconciliation with the National Party

As Ruth Berins Collier writes, "[I]f democracy is understood as a particular set of institutions, democratization, in turn, is understood as the introduction, adoption, or installation of those institutions." Because authoritarian enclaves are likely to be ruled by a hegemonic political party that is conflated with the state apparatus, democratization must involve upending both halves of these "party-states."[45] Three dimensions of subnational democratization are particularly important: the compliance of enclave regimes with new federal policies and with orders to reform their state apparata; the incorporation of new voters and groups into the polity; and the nature of the ruling party's reconciliation with the national party.

Compliance with federal directives to institutionalize democratic rule is, of course, essential, in two ways. First, the destruction of authoritarian institutions and the installation of democratic ones require this compliance. In the southern cases and likely others, this involves not merely federal statutes but also new federal regulations and judicial decrees. Second, rapid, orderly, and complete compliance is vital for moving toward national, democratic standards of the rule of law. Whether this compliance emerges early or late, or is orderly or turbulent and even violent, may alter democratization paths and their subsequent legacies. State- and local-level compliance hinges not merely on the preferences of authorities but also on their capacity and willingness to employ state policing institutions. And—besides their own ideological commitments—the nature of demands for compliance in various arenas by domestic insurgencies significantly shapes authorities' behavior. With respect to the southern cases, major indicators of compliance include responses by authorities to the Civil and Voting Rights Acts, to judicial desegregation decrees aimed at county and local school officials, and—less well publicized—to federal statutes, regulations, and court orders requiring the desegregation of the southern public sectors.

Political incorporation of voters and politicians is usually a central dimension of democratization. Whether directly, through suffrage restrictions against citizens of particular groups, or indirectly, through the effects of elections that are less than free or fair, one-party rule restricts political contestation and often distributes participation rights unequally. Democratization is thus often accompanied by the mobilization of voters, activists, and ambitious politicians into existing parties and political organizations. In the U.S. South, this generally meant blacks, Hispanics, and poorer whites. Elsewhere, incorporation has meant the inclusion of rural areas, working classes, unions, and so forth. The timing and thoroughness of incorporation can each generate their own important political legacies.[46]

Political incorporation requires the involvement of both motivated ruling party officials and empowered ones. Incorporation episodes are, in the words of Martin Shefter, "products of serious and unbridgeable conflicts dividing the political elite," as well as the goals and strategies of those demanding incorporation. Elites motivated to effect the incorporation of the previously excluded must actually be empowered within party and state institutions to make it happen. Attention here is placed on the timing and extensiveness of the incorporation of black voters and candidates into state Democratic parties, the ruling parties of southern authoritarianism. (This eventual incorporation, as opposed to other possible sites of black political mobilization, must be explained, not assumed, and the state-level narratives to come will do so). Indicators include statutes and regulatory changes governing access to the voting booth, to candidacy filings, and to local and state-level party organizations. Party incorporation should also be reflected in nontrivial levels of black participation in local and state party conventions and officeholding, in shifts in party position-taking, and in the election and appointment of black legislators and officials. Additionally, major policy shifts, such as changes in resource flows to groups and regions, usually accompany substantial new incorporations.[47]

Ruling parties' reconciliation with the national party is also likely to be a critical component of subnational democratization. During stable enclave rule, ruling parties often benefit from their influence within the national party. As democratization challenges emerge and a transition begins, relations between national and state parties are placed under great stress. In enclaves where their reconciliation occurs earlier and more smoothly, subsequent democratization may be more orderly. This reconciliation has several possible indicators, including these: state party endorsement of democratization and acceptance of any national party reforms; some convergence in party platforms and position-taking; and the timely reappearance or acceptance as members in good standing of enclave parties in national party decision-making bodies. With respect to the South, this would mean the timing of southern state Democratic parties' reappearance at presidential nominating conventions, the racial integration of delegations to these conventions, and the full acceptance of party reforms ordered by the national Democratic party in the early 1970s.

The timing and nature of reconciliation with the national party is likely to be shaped by a few factors. The first is the regime challengers' own choices about whether to mobilize supporters in a new party or other movement, or to seek incorporation in the ruling party. Second, the relative strength of factions within the regime is critical. Disagreements among them on reconciliation may emerge because of ideological commitments, electoral vulnerability, or additional careerist concerns. Additionally, institutions within the party may affect its maneuverability for those favoring reconciliation. Third, the timing of any incorporation into the ruling party may be closely related to reconciliation. If this incorporation occurs early, earlier reconciliation is also likely, as those in the ruling party opposing reconciliation will exit it more quickly. The more quickly this sorting dynamic occurs, the smoother reconciliation is likely to be.

The foregoing discussion has repeatedly pointed to two causal forces that may shape modes of subnational democratization: elite cohesion within the ruling party, and the fit of party and state institutions with enclaves' preferred responses to democratization challenges. Because politicians of hegemonic subnational parties are likely to rule enclaves, subnational authoritarian regimes are effectively party-states, a term I use interchangeably with "regime" in order to emphasize this conflation of party and state apparatus.

Elite Cohesion and Enclave Responses to Democratization Challenges

Durable regimes, according to Karen Orren and Stephen Skowronek, hold "together in the same orbit interests and ambitions that in other circumstances could be expected to be regularly at loggerheads." Thus, there is always some degree of elite conflict within a ruling party over policy choices and the distribution of resources. A critical factor here is that the losers of these conflicts are not tempted to exit the party. At the onset of democratization challenges, ruling parties seek to deter, defeat, or at least defer them indefinitely. After all, "threats from below"—a good description of black activists' exploiting external democratization challenges—are, as Robert Kaufman writes, the "most important bond of cohesion" in authoritarian regimes.[48] Whatever differences may exist within the ruling party, there is an initial, strong disposition toward the status quo.

Over time, interventions and responses to them can shift the factional balance and affect rulers' ability to implement their preferred strategies.[49] Some elites associated with particular social groups, economic interests, or regions may seek to liberalize civil society and expand opportunities for political participation, and may no longer value the party's ideological commitments.[50] Others, whether for ideological reasons or because liberalization and eventual democratization are expected to exact higher costs, may prefer above all to honor these historic commitments, if necessary through repression of regime opponents. Those not prevailing in these debates may now face the loss of their elite status or their core goals (or both), and the temptation to defect grows, as they conclude that the ruling party is no longer the most effective means to advance their goals. As this exit option becomes more attractive, elite cohesion declines, and the prospects for effective collective action by the regime diminish. Given this dynamic, the degree to which elites remain committed to the party as the best vehicle for pursuing political careers and policy goals, while agreeing broadly on a strategy to resist challenges to the regime, is extremely important. While the dominance of a particular faction may enable an enclave to respond more coherently and effectively to a democratization challenge, a severe split may stymie such a response. Indeed, low levels of elite cohesion raise the likelihood of confusion, miscalculations, tangled lines of authority (both horizontally across the polity and vertically between state and local officials), and poorly executed responses. In this study, elite cohesion is ascertained largely through the use of archival materials, which help depict the degree of factionalism and the relative strength of different factions, as well as the preferences and beliefs about the future of key elites and of their clients.[51]

Party-State Institutions and Enclave Responses to Democratization Challenges

As democratization challenges begin, the shape of party institutions can facilitate or frustrate elites' abilities to enact their preferred strategies. These institutions affect the quality of information rulers use to update their beliefs and strategies, and their capacity to act quickly and decisively. A party's ability to block the exit of valuable individuals and resources is also critical. Some parties promise longer-term careers for individuals or deploy other carrots or sticks to induce party discipline. These parties may be able to induce loyalty, swing the balance of power to their pragmatists, and thereby adapt more skillfully during a transition. Generally, the shape of its institutions may affect a party's flexibility, informational needs, and ability to discipline those who wield its label as officeholders, office seekers, and activists.

In three key respects, rulers may be frustrated by a poor fit between their preferred responses to democratization challenges and state institutions responsible for implementing these responses.[52] First, authorities must secure and maintain order. These party-state officials, whatever their ideological preferences, are distinguished from other actors because they *rule*—they must order the polities they govern. In transition periods, rulers face uncertain environments, perhaps with social disturbances, organized or spontaneous violence, and other threats to order. In certain circumstances it matters greatly whether a state's repressive capacity is centralized, professional, projected across the entire polity, and capable of deterring, minimizing, or committing cost-effective violence and avoiding the excessive use of force. As suggested earlier, these issues become important during the college desegregation crises. Second, state institutions in enclaves differ in their administrative or fiscal capacities to develop and implement programs to co-opt potential reactionaries and insurgents, or to develop new bases of support.[53]

Third, in a more general way, the degree to which public authority is centralized is likely to affect the range of possible responses to democratization challenges. Within federal polities, states vary in their authorities and responsibilities, as they empower different actors at different levels of the polity to accomplish different tasks. Subnational polities do as well; this is especially true with regard to southern states, where county jurisdictions have often long been invested with powerful authority and resources. Rulers who frame policy responses at the state level, for example, may be unable to wrest authority from officials within county and municipal governments. In the management of crises—when temporal constraints prevent institutional innovations—these vertical distributions of authority within enclaves are likely to influence outcomes. This last issue points to an interesting and perhaps unique feature of southern democratizations: they unfolded slowly relative to other democratizations (national or subnational). As the narratives demonstrate, rulers had time to anticipate future challenges and respond by adapting existing institutions or creating new ones to better meet these challenges. As with elite cohesion, this fact forces us to consider party-state institutions as moving targets rather than as static background conditions to explain outcomes in a straightforward way. But, as Orren and Skowronek note, "[C]hange confronts political authority already on the scene." Party-state institutions developed often decades earlier for quite different purposes could block rulers' efforts to adapt their institutional toolkit for new challenges.[54]

Research Design

This book has a few goals. First, it attempts to demonstrate that political institutions and elite behavior, not merely antecedent conditions such as political culture and political economy, best account for variation in modes of democratization in the Deep South. Second, it seeks to probe the plausibility of the historical interpretation advanced at greater length in the next chapter—that by aiding and then abetting subnational authoritarian enclaves, U.S. democracy was consolidated only very recently. To make this case requires detailed evidence married to theories and concepts from comparative politics. A third goal, building on this last point, is to chip away at the parochialism of the book's home subfield of American Political Development. The frequent choice not to draw upon concepts and theories of comparative politics leads to many missed opportunities.[55]

In the tradition of comparative historical analysis, scholars tackle large-scale processes and outcomes that unfold over long stretches of time. A small number of similarly situated cases is used to identify configurations of causal forces that help explain puzzling differences among these cases. Such research is often used to develop new concepts and generate theories that can be tested on additional cases. The effort to describe and explain in a systematic and detailed way particular historical outcomes usually exacts costs concerning the testing of highly general causal propositions.[56]

This study fits into that tradition. To explain how different processes of democratization unfold, this study constructs and compares three narratives of enclave demise in the Deep South. To discipline the narratives, the study periodizes a regionwide, southern transition consisting of highly similar and effectively simultaneous external challenges to enclave rule. The narratives describe and explain the consequences of major democratization challenges. They then trace how these pressures conditioned enclaves to absorb subsequent challenges, culminating in different modes of exit from authoritarian rule. The book's close discusses how some of the legacies of these different experiences help explain divergent patterns of partisan and economic change.[57]

The comparison of richly detailed narratives has some important disadvantages. One is that it cannot suffice as a testing ground for theories. The theoretical approach sketched in this chapter is in part informed by the narratives; the narratives cannot then be said to test this account.[58] Another is that narratives resist replication, in part because they are not assembled from systematically collected datasets. Rather, this study relies on process tracing to describe and explain democratization challenges and their consequences. Process tracing, as David Waldner describes, is often used in case-study research and draws upon "multiple types of evidence for the verification of a single inference." Through the assemblage of these "causal process observations," the analyst asserts the existence of a "causal chain" in which, given some fact patterns, causal claims, and causal mechanisms, "one event constrain[s] future events such that a subsequent event [is] bound to happen, or at least [more likely to occur]."[59] The comparison of three narratives thus puts a premium on internal validity, but at the expense of external validity. Despite these (and other) problems, this brand of research is appropriate given our state of knowledge on subnational authoritarian politics. Research on subnational authoritarianism is at an early stage with respect to concepts, theories, and measurements, and subnational democratization is even less well understood. Theory generation remains a priority, and this research design advances this goal.[60]

Telling Time in the South

As with other work of comparative historical analysis, this study is preoccupied with issues of temporality. Here I touch on a few: the periodization of the transition and the exogenous "shocks" that structure it; whether and how critical junctures demarcate time during the transition; and the presence of path-dependent properties in the narratives to follow.[61]

This study periodizes a regionwide, southern democratic transition period occurring from 1944 until 1972 (see chapter 2 for a defense of this periodization). A succession of external interventions challenged southern rulers by strengthening their opponents, withholding valuable regime resources, and making the ruling party's historic project less viable. These were the Supreme Court's abolition of the white primary in 1944; national Democrats' embrace of racial equality in 1948; the Supreme Court's invalidation of state-mandated segregation in schools and other public sites in 1954 and the important college desegregation crises that the decision spawned; the Court's invalidation of gross legislative malapportionment in 1962; the Civil and Voting Rights Acts of 1964 and 1965; and the national party reforms of 1968–72. As democratic transitions go, this is a fairly long one. Some individual enclaves moved through this period more quickly than others, and the relative importance of particular external challenges for them varied.[62]

Were these democratization pressures really external? If they were not emanating from outside the enclave and were not of roughly similar substance and timing, structuring the comparison of enclaves as I have described might be problematic. As we will see, none of these pressures could have emanated from within, but they were not perfectly "exogenous" to the behavior of rulers and challengers within enclaves—certainly not when compared to the impact of, say, World War II on Latin America.[63] The central state institution most isolated from enclave influence, the U. S. Supreme

Court, cast a large shadow over the southern transition. But even its pressures were not perfectly exogenous. First, they did not strike their targets at exactly the same time. Some did in a shallow sense. Supreme Court rulings applied to the entire region, of course, were announced just once, and President Harry S. Truman's rhetorical commitment of the national party to racial equality in early 1948 reverberated through the South at the same moment. But federal judicial implementation decrees—the moments when a particular state (or locality) was ordered to take some action—differed. Enclave rulers' own strategies and choices, such as their desire and ability to stall mandated change through seemingly endless legal challenges—influenced when these moments came. The choices of domestic insurgents to devote resources to attacking some parts of enclave rule and not others also mattered. In this sense, the timing of these shocks was often not quite the same for all enclaves. Second, federal judges, legislators, and agency officials crafted rulings, statutes, and regulations with likely levels of resistance weighing heavily on their minds. Enclaves could influence the substance of democratization pressures, such as when their rulers warned the Court and others that mass bloodshed might follow an onerous ruling. And enclave opponents clearly affected the timing and substance of democratization pressures, whether through their own efforts in federal courts or through the use of nonviolent direct action to compel Congress to act. I raise these issues in the narratives.

Comparative historical analyses commonly invoke much-debated concepts such as "critical juncture" and "path dependence." Used together, they have, as Waldner notes, "come to mean moments in which structural constraints have been relaxed so that political actors exercise greater agency and their actions during the critical juncture have highly enduring legacies."[64] While the narratives in this book highlight college desegregation crises as important moments in long democratic transitions, I am generally skeptical about the presence of critical junctures and path-dependent processes, for a couple of reasons. First, common uses of "critical juncture" suggest that its origins are to be explained with reference to structural forces, not human agency. On the contrary, my narratives of the first two decades of the transition emphasize the importance of the choices of institutionally situated politicians. Second, analyses relying on a critical juncture framework, especially when combined with path dependence, typically argue that agency is much less important after the critical juncture, as the range of both possible options for actors and possible historical trajectories is narrowed.[65] Of course, some moments *are* more important than others. As I discuss in chapter 4, the politics unleashed by the abolition of the white primary in 1940s Georgia almost ushered in massive change. Likewise, there are many types of processes at work in these narratives, and some would be termed "path-dependent"—such as the back-and-forth sorting of many elites and voters into different parties after the Voting Rights Act.[66] Still, there is a good deal of continuity—in institutions, in actors' preferences, in distributions of power, and in the importance of human agency—that, according to Wolfgang Streeck and Kathleen Thelen, extends "through and in spite of historical break points."[67] I return to these matters while discussing the operation of historical legacies in chapter II.

Case Selection and Evidence

At an early stage in research programs, when work is intended to generate testable hypotheses, qualitative scholars commonly select cases for intensive analysis that are similar in terms of those characteristics thought to explain outcomes, but are diverse—and puzzlingly so—with respect to outcomes of interest.[68] The South is helpful in this regard. As V. O. Key insists, the South was never as "solid" as outsiders believed.[69] Most importantly, Deep South states—Alabama, Georgia, Louisiana, Mississippi, and South Carolina—shared a number of characteristics that distinguished them from the states of the Outer South.[70]

For most of the twentieth century, the populations of the Deep South states were more rural and featured a greater share of blacks, their economies were more dominated by labor-repressive agriculture and were less industrialized, their polities were marked by almost a total absence of Republican or other ruling party challengers, their white populations seemed the most committed to white supremacy, and they had the weakest infrastructure for black insurgency. Just as important, they differed in their subsequent modes of democratization (table 1.1). Thus, the five Deep South states provide an excellent subset of cases for analysis, as they satisfy both case selection criteria.

Among the Deep South states, Georgia, Mississippi, and South Carolina have been chosen for study. They are especially similar to one another even among the Deep South states. In contrast, Alabama's much earlier industrialization sets the state apart from its neighbors, and Louisiana's parish system and reliance on the Napoleonic code introduces complications that frustrate comparisons of county governance.[71] Finally, all three boast excellent secondary literatures that help corroborate inferences drawn from primary sources.[72]

Several measures bear out the similarities among the Deep South states under study as well as their differences with those in the Outer South. For instance, as figure 1.1 illustrates, these states stand apart in their greater share of blacks.

Second, Deep South political economies were marked by labor-intensive agricultural production (for which the share of black sharecroppers among all farm operators is a good proxy). As table 1.2 demonstrates, these states—

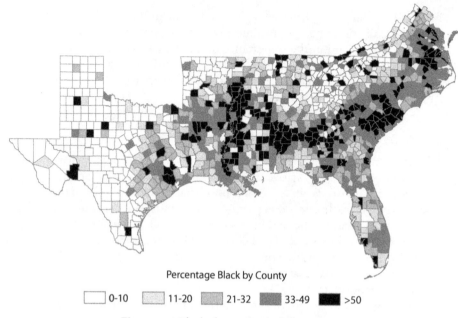

Percentage Black by County

☐ 0-10 ☐ 11-20 ☐ 21-32 ☐ 33-49 ■ >50

Figure 1.1. Black share of population, 1940
(Source: University of Virginia Historical Census Bureau)

all substantial growers of cotton (as chapter 2 discusses, a classic "reactionary crop")—were at least three times more reliant on this mode of production on the eve of the transition period than the average in other southern
states.[73]

TABLE 1.2
Enclave Reliance on Labor-Intensive Agriculture, 1945

	Black sharecroppers as percentage of all farm operators
Georgia	16
Mississippi	31
South Carolina	19
Remainder of Census South[a]	6

Source: Bureau of the Census, *United States Census of Agriculture, 1945*, vol. 2: *General
Report* (Washington, D.C.: Government Printing Office, 1947), chap. 3, "Color and Tenure
of Farm Operator."
[a] Includes the eleven states of the ex-Confederacy (excluding Georgia, Mississippi, and
South Carolina), plus Delaware, Maryland, Oklahoma, Kentucky, and West Virginia.

Third, these states' electorates throughout the period of stable enclave rule (1890s–40s) were highly demobilized. Figure 1.2 demonstrates the share of their voting-age populations participating in presidential elections. Fourth, these states were highly devoted to the national Democratic ticket, even relative to the Outer South (see figure 1.3).

Chapter 3 discusses other important commonalities among Deep South enclaves that cast doubt on the political cultural, political economic, and social movement approaches discussed earlier.

The main advantage of focusing on the Deep South is that it allows for investigating the claim that differences in modes of democratization were substantially shaped by the actions of institutionally situated rulers. This is because similarities in these states' structural features (such as their political economies) provide something like "controls" that cast at least initial doubt on plausible alternative explanations. There are disadvantages, too, of course, which I discuss in chapter 11.[74] One potentially problematic question should be addressed now: do these three states really constitute independent cases? Whether due to preference, skill, or luck, some enclaves successfully delayed the absorption of particular shocks and thus experienced them later than other enclaves. This could allow late-movers to learn and benefit from others' experiences, and this in turn endangers the assumption that the cases under study are truly independent of one another. For instance, as I will show in chapters 6 and 7, the fact that South Carolina's

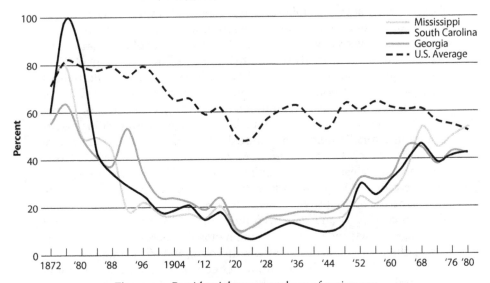

Figure 1.2. Presidential voters as share of voting-age population, 1872–1980

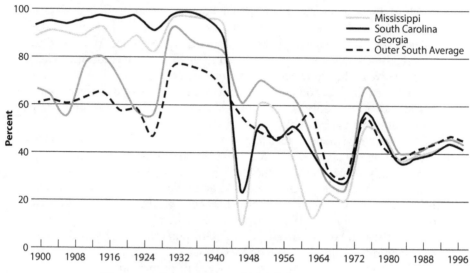

Figure 1.3. Democratic presidential vote, 1900–2000

rulers could experience that state's main college desegregation crisis a few months later than Mississippi meant that they could learn valuable lessons. Moreover, regionwide collective action helped these enclaves emerge as well as endure, and also existed during their transitions. This issue, which I discuss in the narratives that follow, is a real concern. However, it is not unique to the South but is in fact common in recent waves of regime transitions.[75]

To trace the ways in which external challenges, elite cohesion, and party-state institutions interacted over time to produce different paths out of Dixie, several types of evidence are required. On the basis of archival collections of state parties and important politicians, contemporaneous elite interviews, oral histories, newspaper accounts, and memoirs, I make inferences concerning the beliefs, preferences, and relative influence within ruling parties of various actors. Transcripts of hundreds of interviews conducted by Alexander Heard for V. O. Key's *Southern Politics*—rarely exploited by scholars—are especially valuable, as are other interviews conducted in the 1940s, 1970s, and thereafter.[76] Official records in state archives, records of state parties, newspaper accounts, private papers, interviews, and other sources capture the impact of party and state institutions on rulers' responses to external challenges. Newspapers, both local and national, situate discussions of electoral politics and intraelite conflict, as do voting and officeholding data.[77]

Various collections of papers from presidential libraries, official histories of administrative agencies, and publications of federal agencies help capture the nature of federal interventions and the degree of compliance with them in areas such as voting, the desegregation of public sector employment, public accommodations and schooling, and law enforcement. Official papers of national- and state-level black protest groups (such as Congress of Racial Equality [CORE], the National Association for the Advancement of Colored People [NAACP], and the Student Non-Violent Coordinating Committee [SNCC]) and of southern nongovernmental organizations (such as the Southern Regional Council [SRC]), as well as oral histories with black and white activists, help describe insurgents' goals, strategies, and decision-making. Finally, this study relies on many excellent, unpublished works that offer a range of evidence on enclave rule. A bibliography available online provides a complete list of sources used and archives consulted.[78]

Summary of Findings

Given differences in elite cohesion and party-state institutions, rulers' responses to early interventions buffeted Deep South enclaves in different ways, positioning them differently to meet later ones. By the early 1960s, they had different reputations in the eyes of federal authorities, national black protest organizations, and national party officials. These reputations shaped rulers' ability to minimize outside interference in their dismantling of authoritarian states and parties, and thus harness political change. By the 1970s, Deep South enclaves had been democratized differently; the legacies of these different modes of democratization contributed to divergent patterns of Republican growth and economic development.

After some two decades of forthright resistance to any racial reforms, of attacks on white civil society, and of black protest, South Carolina's rulers capitalized on cohesive elite networks and an effective coercive apparatus to navigate safely the desegregation crisis at Clemson. This outcome made rulers' strategic accommodation to democratization pressures more likely. They capitalized on the state's external reputation to maintain order, deter interventions by national black protest organizations, and, where possible, limit federal oversight of party-state compliance with federal directives. By doing so, rulers accelerated the exit of white supremacist activists from the ruling party, and sped the party's incorporation of blacks and its reconciliation with the national party. Limiting the disruptive effects of democratization in the short term, South Carolina successfully harnessed the revolution. For South Carolina's rulers of the 1960s and early 1970s, this outcome was a salutary one, for it helped them retain their offices, pursue further ambitions within the national party, and exploit the state's reputation as a dignified, orderly site for capital investment and firm relocation. In the long run, however, South Carolina's harnessed revolution would be disastrous for the Democratic party.

Mississippi also resisted early democratization pressures. However, during the 1950s the state's decentralization of authority stymied reformers' attempts to overhaul the state's policing apparatus and pursue other institutional reforms. The party faction's dominance by White Citizens' Council (WCC) forces, coupled with the state's disorganized law enforcement, resulted in the debacle at Oxford. The federal military intervention exacerbated a white supremacist backlash to the university's desegregation that further corroded law enforcement and induced a massive intervention from national black protest organizations. An ensuing spiral of interventions and disorder resulted in substantial federal oversight of Mississippi's compliance with federal directives. An incredibly quick mobilization of black Mississippi occurred, but it did so outside of the confines of the ruling party. In the ensuing chaos of a fissured state Democratic party, relations with the national party became estranged and remained so into the mid-1970s. In sum, Mississippi's rulers stumbled through the 1960s. By failing to deter white supremacist violence, they unwittingly induced the violations of Mississippi "sovereignty" against which they had long railed. Ironically, however, this chaotic transition would reap benefits for future wielders of the Democratic party label, while slowing the state's economic development.

Finally, Georgia's white supremacist rulers narrowly escaped a collapse of the ruling party in the late 1940s. Securing the dominance of the segregationist Talmadge faction, they pursued a massive resistance to democratization pressures through the 1950s. In doing so, they damaged statewide networks of black protest. By the time black direct action movements swept the state, many of the forces of black protest in Atlanta—the likely engine of statewide black insurgency—had accommodated corporate interests by trading critical support in mayoral elections for meager policy benefits. This accommodation weakened statewide networks of black insurgency. Georgia's Black Belt activists were left largely on their own to deal with powerful county interests, violence, and intimidation. Atlanta's carefully developed reputation as a "dignified," compliant city reaped benefits for north Georgia, and helped deter substantial interventions by black protest organizations and the federal government in south Georgia. The two Georgias quickly diverged, as north Georgia experienced a harnessed revolution and south Georgia a protracted democratization.

This study argues that interactions between rulers and challengers produced different democratization processes, which generated important legacies for these states' politics and economics. Three types of objections might be raised here. First, rulers' agency and party-state institutions during transitions may have little effect on the democratizations that ensue; rather, differences in antecedent conditions may bear all the causal weight.[79] Second, politicians' agency at alleged key moments in the narratives may not be important. Rather, emerging secular differences in economic development, black insurgency, or other potential causal forces since the beginning of the long transition may swamp the importance of rulers' responses to democratization pressures. Third, even if these forces do matter, ensuing modes of democratization may fail to produce important legacies for politics and economics. Differences since the 1970s in partisan change and economic development are due to longstanding (pretransition) differences across cases or have proximate sources. Chapters 10 and 11 wrestle with these issues.

This book, like the democratization of the South itself, unfolds slowly. The next chapter makes the case for interpreting the post-1890s South as a set of stable enclaves of authoritarian rule, and describes their founding and maintenance until serious democratization challenges began in the 1940s. Chapter 3 introduces Deep South enclaves as polities in their own right, describing their intraparty factions, party-state institutions, political economies, and prospects for black insurgency on the eve of the transition. Chapters 4 and 5 analyze the democratization challenges of the 1940s—the Supreme Court's abolition of the whites-only primary and President Harry Truman's commitment of the national Democratic party to the cause of racial equality—and compares the responses to them by Deep South enclaves. After a prologue that discusses *Brown v. Board of Education* and the region's "massive resistance" that followed, chapters 6, 7, and 8 assess how each enclave navigated the challenges of the 1950s and its chief college desegregation crisis in the early 1960s. Chapter 9 traces how the federal government and black protest organizations intervened in different ways in these enclaves. Chapter 10 compares how these enclaves experienced different modes of democratization in light of the deathblows of federal legislation, domestic insurgencies, and national party reform in the 1960s and early 1970s. In chapter 11, the book closes with a discussion of the legacies of these different paths out of Dixie and of the research agendas that emerge if a democratization approach to understanding the twentieth-century South is adopted.

Once called "not quite a nation within a nation, but the next thing to it," the South has long captured the imaginations of Americans. This fascination can be a problem. The region has long retained a mystical status over many writers, whose usual unadorned prose lapses into poetic imageries: Spanish moss, wisteria, fire hoses and police dogs, "strange fruit," and so on. By advancing a southern exceptionalism, the South can be pushed further out of analytical reach. Even when not romanticizing the region, many social scientists code observations that fall within the South with a "dummy" variable—the statistical equivalent of a shrug regarding *how* the South is different. The region becomes an undifferentiated, unexplored mass that, even worse, renders "normal" the politics of another such mass: the "non-South." The South must be reckoned with as distinctive, but should be approached with familiar tools of comparative historical analysis. In so doing, we can link the region—and its component parts—to other cases past and present.[80]

By framing the political development of the South as one of regime change, this book returns the study of American political development to the belated and uneven nature of the country's consolidation of democratic rule. The United States has long seen itself as "*the* democratic nation." Scholars have instead seen a democracy with limited, if constantly expanding, voting rights.[81] In contrast, I argue that the United States was not a fully democratic polity until preparations were well under way for the celebration of the bicentennial of the Declaration of Independence. Instead, it was a federal polity of representative democracy at the national level with durable enclaves of authoritarian rule. This fact is not principally "about" the South and its distinctive characteristics. Rather, authoritarian enclaves exist at the pleasure of the democracies in which they are allowed to form and endure. Over the lifespan of America's enclaves, their host opened global trade routes, established colonies, won world wars, split atoms, visited the moon, prevailed in a geopolitical competition with the Soviet Union, and exported models for economics and politics throughout the world. While most of what follows concerns politics within three Deep South states, the broader story is most importantly one of *America's* political development.[82]

CHAPTER TWO

The Founding and Maintenance of Southern Enclaves, 1890–1940

The New South presents a perfect Democracy, the oligarchs leading in the popular movement—a social system compact and closely knitted, less splendid on the surface, but stronger at the core.

—*Henry Grady*, "New South" booster (1886)

Side by side with that warm human quality called "Southern" stands the grim fact that right here beside you, laughing easily with you and shaking your hand cordially, are men who hunt men: who hunt and kill in packs, at odds of a hundred to one under cover of night. They have lynched five hundred Negroes in forty years; they have killed un-numbered white men. There must be living and breathing in Georgia today at least ten thousand men who have taken human life, and ten times that number who have connived at it.

—*W.E.B. Du Bois* (1925)

Southern politics . . . is deadly serious business that is sometimes carried on behind a droll façade.

—*V. O. Key* (1949)

Everybody knows there is no fineness or accuracy of suppression; if you hold down one thing, you hold down the adjoining.

—*Saul Bellow* (1953)

FOR MOST OF THE TWENTIETH CENTURY, southern states are best understood as eleven enclaves of authoritarian rule. Here I justify this interpretation and argue that it is superior to the common view that the South of this period was a region of "herrenvolk" democracy—democracy for whites but not for blacks. I describe enclaves' emergence in the 1890s as well as their means of defense from internal and external threats, and briefly outline the key challenges that made up the southern transition period that began in the 1940s. In rendering the South in broad brushstrokes, this portrayal draws on the impressive literature on southern political history.[1]

Beyond lacking features of democratic polities, southern enclaves—like all stable, authoritarian polities—should be given their due as political achievements. They reconciled the interests of urban elites, "New South" boosters, industrialists, and large landowners in a single regime, and equipped it with institutions to demobilize white electorates, extrude blacks from electoral politics, and forestall workers' challenges to state institutions and policies. Enclave rulers carefully protected their polity's conditional autonomy and skillfully deployed federal officeholders to block potential interference, especially concerning voting rights and state-sponsored violence. That is, they successfully completed key tasks required of modern polities, including maintaining order, regulating political ambition, delivering minimal economic performance, and balancing diverse interests. While nonsouthern whites often viewed southern politics as a comic opera, it was, as Key writes, "deadly serious business."

It is first necessary to define a much-debated term: "the South." Definitions differ depending on one's purposes and on the period under examination. Political scientists usually view the South as the eleven states of the former Confederate States of America, as I do here. Recently, Ira Katznelson and colleagues have argued that the South of the mid-twentieth century should be viewed as these eleven states plus six others that featured state-mandated segregation by race in schooling and other institutions: a seventeen-state region marked by "a long-standing compulsory racial order of white supremacy." Across the United States, however, many states, counties, and municipalities featured various modes of racial segregation. By one estimate, until the late 1940s, more than four in ten of the country's primary and secondary school students were racially or ethnically segregated across twenty-nine of forty-eight states (in addition to the District of Columbia). For my purposes, a definition of the region should be based on the characteristics that made its politics distinctive. The eleven former states of the Confederacy featured state-mandated segregation but also massive suffrage restriction and unfair political contestation, and these attributes rendered these states fundamentally different from those featuring democratic competition.[2]

In this study, I employ a proceduralist conception of democracy. Democratic regimes are defined by their political processes, not the policies they produce. They must feature "regular free and fair elections, universal suffrage, accountability of the state's administrative organs to the elected representatives, and effective guarantees for freedom of expression and association as well as protection against arbitrary state action." The core here is free elections. Universal suffrage and the ability to organize on behalf of these elections without fear or impediment make them free; some amount of accountability of the state apparatus to the winners makes them meaningful.[3] Dichotomous conceptions of democracy such as this one are common but come with costs. When regimes are placed on a continuous spectrum, after all, additional information is preserved; we are able to note differences between, say, the type of authoritarianism found in 1980s Mexico and in North Korea (as well as between democracies that seem barely to warrant the label and those that shine on all dimensions). Still, I stick with the dichotomous approach. The study of authoritarian enclaves is in its infancy, and first I must argue for their presence in the United States. Also, the narratives to come contain a good deal of information on a range of dimensions that analysts might highlight in developing continuous conceptualizations of subnational regimes.[4]

Of course, before the South's democratization in the early 1970s, areas outside the South also violated democracy's requirements. Most important here, of course, is the barring of women from almost all of America's voting booths.[5] Also, other jurisdictions—in particular cities—often featured electoral fraud and sometimes-serious suffrage restrictions.[6] Still, these latter practices were not as enduring and did not exist statewide, as was true of those in the South. For these reasons, southern politics is distinctive.

In contemporary social science, the South's distinctiveness is assumed and implied but rarely described. When it is, scholars sometimes view the South as a "dual system" or a "partial," "restricted," or herrenvolk democracy. The terms suggest the coexistence of an egalitarian democratic polity for citizens identified as members of a race atop that society's racial hierarchy alongside the exclusion of another group (or groups) from civic and political spheres. This is a confused and confusing concept, and not merely because several enclaves at the time of their founding were majority-black or very close to it. As historian Michael R. West argues, "[B]ecause segregation did not create two societies or nations, disfranchisement cannot have created a democracy for [only those whites whose suffrage rights were protected]." As the remainder of this chapter seeks to demonstrate, until recently southern politics has been simply undemocratic.[7]

The Birth of Southern Enclaves

Before the period of enclave rule, the South had never featured stable, durable democratic politics. On the other hand, even after Emancipation, it took about three decades for stable subnational authoritarianism to appear. It emerged from a coordinated, regionwide movement by state-level Democratic party leaders in the mid-1890s to develop institutions that could guarantee political hegemony for them and their clients. Prior to this moment, there had been no such guarantees.

The South before the Civil War

Southern states have long been politically diverse. Parts or all of several of them began as colonies, each with its own "proto-constitution," laws, and institutions. This diversity continued to some degree after the ratification of the U. S. Constitution. While southern constitutions in general differed little from nonsouthern constitutions, those adopted in younger southern states provided for more popular participation and influence than did their older counterparts. By the early 1800s the South featured basically unfettered white male political participation and vibrant interparty competition. Some states allowed free blacks to vote.[8]

From the perspective of owners of land and capital, the central question in the South from the founding of the first European settlements had been how to solve their labor shortage. This question was answered with inducements to European settlers, indentured servitude, and bondage. Slavery arrived in the eventual United States in the 1560s, meaning that slavery was three centuries old by the time of the Civil War.[9] After 1800 the South and North began to diverge economically because of their different reliance on slavery. Slaveowners held a large and growing share of their wealth in (mobile) slaves rather than (fixed) land, giving them little incentive to encourage physical and human capital investment or build towns, much less approve of investments to develop other regions of a state. Combined with lower savings rates, this meant that slavery slowed the South's economic growth relative to that of the North. This economic divergence encouraged political divergence as well.[10]

Of course, agrarian politics per se is not authoritarian. But the labor requirements and attendant economies of scale of some crops generate political-economic interests that ultimately associate these crops with different modes of politics. Sugar and cotton, for example, have long been considered "reactionary crops," in part because they were usually cultivated on large plots of land by gang labor surveilled by overseers; small, independent farmers could not compete with these operations. The successful cultivation of cotton, which required two labor peaks each year, meant that its growers were especially concerned with a regular supply of reliable labor.[11] By the early decades of the 1800s, as greater and greater shares of southern wealth were tied up in both cotton production and in slaves themselves, southern politicians' defense of slavery against opponents inside and outside the region became more intense. This defense included mounting restrictions on the civil liberties of whites as well as slaves and free blacks, including censorship and restrictions on the press.[12]

Some southern states prohibited criticism of slavery—a crime punishable even by death. Whites were restricted from various behaviors "considered subversive in [their] influence on slaves," such as educating them and trading with them.[13] Soon, Democrats seeking to hold together a fragile, bisectional national party moved even further and nationalized some restrictions on civil society. Best known here are the "gag rules" put in place in the U. S. House and Senate to limit discussion of slavery's abolition.[14] Additionally, the federal postmaster censored the mails in an effort to prevent antislavery literature from flooding the South. While antislavery societies proliferated in the border states and Outer South, these measures had a chilling effect on freedoms of speech and association—as did deadly mob violence against suspected abolitionists. As slavery's guardians increasingly felt under siege beginning in the 1820s, the result was "an arc of southern unfreedom spiraling outward," from slaves to free blacks and then to whites.[15]

In sum, southern politics before the Civil War does not fully support historian George Frederickson's characterization of it as a herrenvolk democracy. After secession, a new regionwide regime was founded. The Confederate States of America featured nominally democratic institutions, but from the start was too fragile to be considered stably democratic—even in a herrenvolk manner.[16] A push for a real democratization of the South would have to wait for Emancipation and Reconstruction.

Reconstruction and What It Left Unresolved

Reconstruction marks both a brief, tumultuous historical era and a dizzying array of projects undertaken by central state authorities, southern public officials, civic groups, political organizations, and individuals. These were inspired by humanitarian and moral aims as well as economic, partisan, and other objectives. Many of them succeeded, and some urgent questions posed by secession and war—particularly about federal-state relations and citizenship—were resolved. But many of these projects failed, including the effort to consolidate democratic governance in the newly readmitted southern states.[17]

After Emancipation, the overarching political-economic question in the region remained whether, and how, large landowners would develop a reliable supply of labor. They soon chose to pursue their goals through state Democratic parties. Given powerful resistance from most southern white elites and officeseekers—especially those associated with Democrats—the consolidation of democratic rule at the state level required, among other things, the rapid development of competitive state Republican parties. These parties would be the key agents in the drafting and ratification of state constitutions and in the passage and implementation of democratizing statutes. Vibrant Republican parties would require the mobilization and electoral participation of freedmen and a substantial number of southern white men. And this political activity would in turn require the safeguarding of voting rights, officeholding rights, competent

and fair election administration, and reliable freedoms of association sufficient for mobilizing voters.

Many of these conditions were met. Occupying military forces helped
oversee voter registration and elections. Freedmen and freedwomen launched
an incredible, and incredibly quick, civic and political mobilization that
drew on black and Republican newspapers, perhaps two thousand local
Union Leagues, churches, and an impressive Republican party-building initiative underwritten in part by national officials. Black voter registration
ranged from 85 to 94 percent in the Deep South, and almost *one million*
freedmen were voting throughout the region within three years of the war's
end. These voters and their white Republican counterparts helped elect
some two thousand freedmen, most of them in majority-black jurisdictions.
More than three-quarters served local and county jurisdictions, and they delivered fairer law enforcement and more extensive public schooling. Scores
drafted constitutions and legislation as state legislators. Fourteen served in
the U. S. House and two in the U. S. Senate, where their voting ranked them
as their chambers' most liberal members.[18]

Democratizers benefited from overreach by conservative white elites.
The latter's resistance to changes preferred by Radical Republicans in
Congress—and in particular the conservatives' passage of draconian "Black
Codes" that attempted to reintroduce physical and economic coercion of
blacks that differed little from slavery—backfired. In response, Radical Republicans passed much more stringent civil rights legislation, and required
the ratification of state constitutions providing for much greater popular
influence in politics as the prerequisite for readmission to the Union and
the halls of Congress. The resulting constitutions differed markedly from
those written immediately after the South's surrender. Indeed, they were
quite modern in their endorsement of individual rights, their requirements
for voting and office-holding, their provision of public education and social
welfare, and so on.[19]

The high-water mark of Reconstruction for black and southern Republican power came in 1872, a full century before the completion of the region's
democratization. Battling Klan insurgencies in South Carolina, the Grant
administration even suspended habeas corpus in nine counties. Still, by this
year Union troop levels in southern states had begun a sharp decline. The
fabled Bureau of Refugees, Freedmen, and Abandoned Lands (Freedmen's
Bureau) never managed to assign on average even one agent per southern
county. Republican gains in southern state legislatures were ephemeral,
for a number of reasons. Chief among them was political—and especially
electoral—violence against Republican voters, black and white, as well as
officeseekers and officeholders. Networks of armed white supremacists,
often sponsored by Democratic elites, managed to organize in one-quarter
of southern counties—an impressive feat. They murdered some Republi-

can candidates and banished others. Some of this violence and disorder occurred on a large scale. A "successful military coup" toppled Louisiana's Republican governor, and more than eleven thousand men battled for control of New Orleans. In South Carolina, rival armed governments faced off against one another. Political violence dampened black political participation regionwide, and heightened growing perceptions of futility on the part of whites predisposed to vote against Democrats (or "Conservatives," as they sometimes preferred to be called). Supreme Court decisions and the return to power of Democrats in Congress in 1875 both hampered efforts to wield central state authority against purveyors of political violence. Factional differences among national Republicans worsened the problems caused by violent resistance by Democrats and their supporters and by the federal government's declining legal, administrative, and military assistance.[20]

By the eve of the contested presidential election of 1876 and the Hayes-Tilden Compromise of 1877 that settled it, Republicans had already lost control of nine southern statehouses, and more than three-quarters of the region's congressional seats. Southern Democrats had signaled to national Republicans, federal authorities, and northern publics that the costs of "reconstructing" the South were very high. The withdrawal of most of the region's federal troops, whose presence had boosted Republican turnout, preceded the settlement. Thus, the Compromise ratified, rather than precipitated, declining federal support for freedmen and their white allies. Southern Democrats—sometimes styling themselves as "Redeemers" (and this period as "Redemption") for having restored the region's honor by beating back the scurrilous Reconstruction—seemed to have prevailed.[21]

Still, the Compromise did not settle the South's political future. Intense conflict continued, both within the region and between the national parties. Each side continued to allocate serious political resources in an effort to win the struggle over whether voting rights were to be nationally or subnationally regulated. Meanwhile, these rights remained insecure. The Fifteenth Amendment was interpreted as not conferring positive rights in voting; rather, it only forbade suffrage restrictions that explicitly invoked race.[22]

Consolidating democratic rule in the South had been a very tall order, and for a few reasons the region's democratizers came up short. These included the effectiveness of political violence and disorder in raising the perceived (and real) costs of continued northern investment in safeguarding rights and rights-bearers; growing splits among northern Republicans, caused in part by emerging differences among leading economic sectors and their concerns about a sustained, costly military occupation; and fatigue and eventually inattention on the part of nonsouthern white publics (themselves often hostile to blacks in their own communities). The long-term viability of Reconstruction, many argued (then and now), would remain imperiled without substantial change in the southern agricultural economy. On this view, the distribution of confiscated lands to blacks was a necessary condition for the unfettered exercise of political rights by freedmen, whose dependence on white landowners would, lacking federal guarantees, render them politically unfree.[23]

Within two decades of the war's end, labor arrangements stabilized among large landowners and black and white farmworkers. They varied given the ability of the worker to secure credit and purchase the means of production (short of land itself). True tenants effectively rented only the use of the land, worked independently, and even held legal title in the crop. As workers had less access to cash or credit, these arrangements became increasingly unfavorable. Sharecroppers furnished only their own labor, while owners provided tools, seed, cash advances, and other necessities. By harvest time, when sharecroppers and owners split the crop, the sharecroppers were often even deeper in debt to owners or nearby merchants. Especially for those whites and blacks without land—and those who soon would be without it, after falling cotton prices and indebtedness took their toll—sharecropping made political engagement even more difficult to envision and undertake, before and after the founding of enclave rule.[24]

Had Reconstruction been a critical juncture in southern political development? Yes, in part. The failure to consolidate democratic rule was arguably a necessary but not sufficient condition for the emergence of southern authoritarian enclaves. Much else was up in the air, and the eventual founding—more than two decades later—of stable enclave rule was not a foregone conclusion. For the purposes of this study, the central fact about Reconstruction is that, while it failed to remake the region as democratic, neither did it establish stable authoritarian politics. Those seeking to reconstruct the South—southern blacks, southern whites opposed to the Democrats, and national Republican party leaders seeking to build a dominant, nationwide party—all had good reason to continue the struggle, and did so. Similarly, as Pamela Brandwein has recently shown, Supreme Court jurists had also not yet abandoned the cause of developing doctrine that could support a range of rights required for democratic rule in the South. Moreover, southern Democrats' own policies and a difficult economic environment—in particular, collapsing commodity (especially cotton) prices, coupled with deflation and the crop lien system—helped fuel farmers' increasingly radical protest against the Redeemers.[25]

For the next two decades, despite substantial electoral fraud and violence, and despite Redeemers' impressive ability to build coalitions and alliances that co-opted potential opponents and demobilized voters likely to back these opponents, black and anti-Democratic whites continued to organize, and vote, in large numbers.[26] Moreover, Republican presidents and strategists remained motivated to nurture southern Republicanism and the perception that its growth was possible. The Department of Justice (DOJ) brought more than one thousand cases against southern officials regarding the violation of federal elections statutes. After Democrats gutted the statutes Republicans had used to punish and deter southern election fraud and voter intimidation, House Republicans contested elections to "maintain a southern presence." From 1881 to 1901, more than one-third of fifty-eight Republican seats in the South came about because of election contests.[27]

In 1890 the Lodge Elections Bill (termed by southern Democrats the "Force Bill") won the support of the House, President Benjamin Harrison, and a Senate majority, but was narrowly defeated by a southern filibuster. The legislation might have altered the course of southern politics, as it would have provided federal—even, if necessary, military—oversight of local compliance with voter registration and electoral administration in national elections. Given that the timing of most state elections coincided with congressional and presidential elections, this would effectively mean the end of subnational control over election administration.[28] The bill's failure, coupled with the emergence of major party-building opportunities in western states, increasing gains elsewhere, and worsening southern suffrage restriction, meant that by 1896, national Republican leaders had neither a strong need to build southern state Republican parties nor much hope that continued investments in them would bear fruit. In that year the Republican party's national platform removed its longstanding demand for free and fair elections in the South.[29]

Still, southern Democrats continued to face substantial electoral volatility and uncertainty. Moreover, the costs of intermittently using violence and disorder to win elections were increasingly at odds with the efforts of some "New South" boosters to attract capital investment. Indeed, when combined, southern states outnumbered those in the rest of the country in their deployment of state militias, with which authorities quelled racial violence that they themselves as candidates had often fomented.[30] Before the 1890s, they had not yet established the main features of enclave rule: one-party politics, racially segregated public spheres, and the political exclusion of blacks and many whites.

Enclave Foundings

In the 1880s and 1890s agrarian movements challenged conservative control from inside Democratic parties and from outside, and electoral politics grew more chaotic. Protest organizations built local branches throughout the South. Most important here was the Farmers' Alliance, which soon clashed with state and national Democratic parties on major economic issues, including debt relief for farmers and the regulation of business. A Colored Farmers' Alliance grew rapidly as well, and held out the possibility of biracial coalition-building. Republicans along with Populists and other third parties experimented with different coalitions of partially incorporated freedmen and agrarian radicals while often using white supremacist rhetoric to attract other voters. Populists and Republicans agreed to support common lists of candidates for state and local offices in Alabama, Georgia, North Carolina, and Texas, even as Populists supported the national Democratic ticket. In major gubernatorial elections in the 1880s, white turnout surpassed 75 percent in six states, and in nine states a majority of eligible blacks voted. In 1894 electoral gains for anti-Democrats coincided with serious violence in Alabama, Georgia, and Louisiana. Despite the repression of their opponents, nowhere did Democrats ever win the support of 40 percent of the voting-age population.[31]

North Carolina in the 1890s made clear the danger of successful anti-Democratic coalitions. After a fusion ticket of Republicans, Populists, and others captured the state legislature and governor's mansion, this coalition decentralized authority to elected officials at the county level. Blacks and white anti-Democrats captured some of these offices and redirected local and county public administration. The state legislature produced immediate policy benefits for farmworkers and poorer farmowners, black and white, and also lowered barriers to voting. Democratic elites and their main clients—large landowners and their urban allies—responded with paramilitary organizations and other tools to suppress their opponents' turnout and boost their own in the 1898 elections. They stoked fears of Reconstruction, co-opted Populists, and intimidated opposing candidates. On election day, the state's Republican governor narrowly escaped a Democratic lynch-mob. In Republican-controlled Wilmington, Democratic notables launched a wave of violence and killings of Republicans and their supporters, black and white, to take back the state's largest city; hundreds fled for good. Some of the state's congressional delegation pleaded to the McKinley administration for assistance but none came. A "coup" had occurred in North Carolina.[32]

Their interests persistently endangered by this uncertain electoral environment, planters and a growing number of urban boosters, merchants, and "New South" industrialists organized for collective action through Democratic channels in what amounted to a "public conspiracy." In each state, they alternately co-opted and repressed Populists, seized control of the state apparatus, and effectively ended credible partisan competition. They first used violence and fraud to weaken the electoral influence of blacks and poorer whites, and then achieved substantial suffrage restriction via legislative statute. Constitutional revision—especially via a constitutional convention—posed much greater risks than achieving suffrage restriction through statute. Once such a convention began, its agenda might be altered to include issues that those well served by the status quo preferred to remain untouched. Thus, Democrats shrank their electorates before calling such conventions and selecting delegates for them. Either constitutional revision or the drafting and ratification of a new constitution was typically the final step in completing suffrage restriction. By the mid-1890s, Democrats had fashioned a new southern constitutional order, and had founded subnational authoritarian regimes.[33]

These new constitutions completed the political extrusion of blacks and many whites through several techniques. All states adopted the poll tax, which dampened poor whites' political participation as well as that of blacks. Seven adopted literacy requirements, and four used property qualifications. All of these devices delegated substantial discretion to local officials, who could choose whether to disfranchise potential voters because of race, factional loyalty, or other criteria. If most white anti-Democrats had backed disenfranchisement, the herrenvolk interpretation might gain support, since suffrage restriction would seem to have been supported even by those whites whose voting it curtailed. Instead, as historian J. Morgan Kousser shows, suffrage restriction was a *partisan* project that Democrats strongly backed but was strongly opposed by the "vast majority" of Republicans, third-party politicians, and black activists.

These constitutions also weakened local governments, converted many elective offices into appointive positions controlled by the governor or state legislature, and further insulated state judiciaries from popular input. Apportionment schemes benefited Black Belt counties, home to leading planters, and cities erected their own barriers to voting for and electing opposition candidates. Additionally, partly in an effort to prevent locally elected blacks and other anti-Democrats from making fiscal and policy changes opposed by Democratic interests, these constitutions greatly limited the ability of localities to borrow and spend.[34]

The restriction of suffrage had partisan aims and consequences. It significantly raised the entry costs of opponents, especially by eliminating the possibility of building opposition parties through appeals to blacks and poorer whites. Turnout rates and support for opposition forces were high before, and declined precipitously after, this wave of suffrage restriction. Afterward, candidates for statewide offices could often win election with the support of less than 10 percent of the voting-age population. Following suffrage restriction, southern Democrats adopted the direct (and white-only) primary, which further convinced ambitious politicians that there was no hope in pursuing careers through alternative vehicles. They also passed laws designed to disadvantage opposition party-builders, and they helped one another across state lines devise these safeguards.[35]

Southern Republican parties now posed no risk to enclave rule. Indeed, until the 1960s, contested general elections in many areas of the South were rare; successful Republican candidacies were, in most states, events to behold. Pockets of Republicanism existed in the "upland" (or mountain) regions of North Carolina, Tennessee, and Virginia. Mountain Republicans were mostly white yeoman farmers and others near the Appalachian mountain chain who had been economically and culturally isolated from the southern plantation economy. For decades they opposed Black Belt Democrats' calls for secession, and war, and later backed anti-Democratic candidates before and after the founding of enclave rule.[36]

However, these and other Republicans were too few in number to threaten Democratic control of state or federal offices. The often-chaotic state of southern Republican parties was largely a legacy of the vacillating policies of Republican presidents and aspirants in the three decades after Reconstruction.[37] Most states had at least a "lily-white" and a "black-and-tan" faction. The former were the residue of the strategy by these national Republicans to reorient the party away from black voters and toward whites. For most of the first five decades of enclave rule, the latter were larger, principally because so few white politicians could be persuaded to use the Republican party as the vehicle for their ambitions. Factions warred over legal control of the party and fought for recognition by the national party in order to be seated at conventions. Once there, they traded their votes for patronage in the form of control over federal appointments. By 1916 the national party, now having halted any real efforts to stimulate southern Republican growth, cut substantially the number of seats offered southern Republicans at these conventions. By the late 1920s white Republicans began pushing blacks out of leadership positions, and black patronage machines in most states had weakened considerably.[38]

For the dean of southern historians, C. Vann Woodward, this generation of southern Democrats "laid the lasting foundations in matters of race, politics, economy, and laws for the modern South." From the turn of the century until the early 1960s, politicians used a "Democrat" identifier. Controlling virtually all offices, state Democratic parties regulated political ambition and staffed the state apparatus. In the words of Thomas J. Semmes, a prominent Louisiana judge and constitutional expert, "The State . . . is the Democratic party. [T]he interests of the party . . . are the interests of the State."[39]

Doubly embedded in a federal state and a confederal national party, enclaves could not openly disavow mass political participation—those outside enclaves would not countenance a blanket rejection of democracy. Elites had to advance the party project within a polity featuring substantial popular control of officeholding. Lacking interparty competition, Democrats did not develop partisan, vote-seeking operations, usually did not hold issue-oriented campaigns, and often lacked durable factions. State party machinery had no role in channeling resources among primary nominees. Thus, for Key, southern Democratic "parties" did not merit the moniker; the one-party South "really ha[d] no political parties."[40]

Since campaign resources were not needed for general elections, they flowed outside party channels to support primary candidacies, often through networks of "friends and neighbors." State parties provided an institutional apparatus for distributing elective and appointed positions, constrained the position-taking of all contestants through incantations of "White Supremacy," and brought the phrase to life by conflating statehood with party— and party disloyalty with state treason.[41] Indeed, Key's charge that southern Democratic parties were really "no-parties" better suits the region's Republican parties, which rarely resembled teams of politicians and activists seeking to win offices and secure preferred policies.

After an increasingly tumultuous antebellum period, the agonies of war and a humiliating Reconstruction, and the continued uncertainties of Redemption and agrarian revolt, southern politics was—finally—not merely undemocratic but stable. Thus, it was now more effectively geared toward producing outcomes sought by key economic clients and ambitious party politicians. Enclaves were truly impressive achievements. But what were they geared to produce?

flipped to Mon economics

The Project of Southern "Democracy"

Dominating officeholding channels and policymaking required some unity of purpose. Until 1966, the ballot of the Democratic party of South Carolina offered one such purpose with its seal, "White Supremacy—For the Right." In response to the question "*Which* whites' supremacy?" V. O. Key answers that, by the 1940s, the counties of the Black Belt had "managed to subordinate the entire South to the service of their particular needs."[42] For southern elites, white supremacy and political repression were inextricably bound up with concerns about guaranteeing a steady supply of cheap labor, a favorable distribution of landownership, and low taxes.[43] Especially (but by no means only) in the Deep South, accomplishing these goals meant relying on sharecropping and tenancy, state policies that supported these institutions, and fashioning paternalistic (or patron-client) relationships with workers. Planters exchanged in-kind benefits (such as medical and legal assistance, and even protection from violent white supremacists) and access to credit for workers' loyalty and outward displays of deference.[44]

Meeting these goals also required blocking policies that might threaten their labor supply, such as substantial investments in schooling and federal interventions into southern labor practices.[45] In 1905, nine of ten North Carolina farmers surveyed opposed compulsory education for blacks because it rendered them "valueless as farm laborers." Wherever nonagricultural jobs could be found, blacks found their path blocked, both directly— through firms' refusals to hire them (or promote them from the most menial positions)—and indirectly, through the state's paltry investment in their education. While the "have-nots" (in Key's language) prefer democracy since it provides a more equal sphere within which to pursue their material-ist goals, southern rulers, and especially those involved in or representing the interests of labor-intensive agriculture, preferred to pursue their goals within authoritarian polities.[46]

In this study, *elites* refers to important resource-holders within the re-gime and those who had nontrivial influence over them. Thus, powerful public authorities and party officials are joined with large landowners and firm-owners who were important clients of the party, important opinion leaders (such as newspaper publishers), and leaders of civic organizations affiliated with party factions (such as "good-government" groups like the League of Women Voters, or the network of authoritarian White Citizens' Councils). Whether local and county-level authorities deserve being called elites depends on the context. For instance, when seekers of statewide office appealed less to voters than to county courthouse cliques of the "banker-merchant-farmer-lawyer-doctor governing class" who exerted influence over white farmworkers and small landowners, members of these cliques—such as V. O. Key, Sr.—would warrant the label. I use *rulers* when referring to those public authorities with the most influence over enclave responses to democratization pressures.[47]

With the founding of southern enclaves, Black Belt elites and emerging New South boosters, town-builders, and industrialists developed and main-tained mutually beneficial policies in a wide range of areas, such as state subsi-dies for attracting low-wage manufacturing. As historian James Cobb argues, "So long as industrial-development initiatives posed no threat to white su-premacy, labor control, fiscal conservatism, and political stability, the interests of the region's planters were in no danger of compromise."[48] Indeed, over the coming decades, southern white progressives accepted suffrage restriction, segregation, wage discrimination, antiunionism, and other policies in the ser-vice of industrial and capital recruitment. Rural elites secured manufacturing plants in nonfarm rural areas and small towns. Thus, the

> ongoing pattern of industrial expansion . . . not only retarded urbanization, but left the region's urban businessmen heavily dependent on trade with the agricul-tural countryside and wedded them to [its] *status quo*. . . . [D]espite the expanded role of government as an agent of modernization, economic decentralization helped to preserve political decentralization and a conservative style of govern-ment that served the needs of the industrialist without damaging the interests of the planter.[49]

By the early 1930s the planter-industrialist alliance seemed "impregnable."[50] And the South remained poor. Home to almost thirty million Americans (then one-quarter of the U. S. population), more than thirteen million were tenants or sharecroppers. The region held one-tenth of the country's wealth.[51]

From the 1890s until the New Deal, southern Democrats stood almost alone as reliable members of the national party, but earned little beyond noninterference. In fact, U. S. tariffs and federal spending patterns since Reconstruction constituted what Richard Bensel calls a "twofold tax" on the region: southern wealth was transferred to the northern core directly, in the form of tariff revenues, and indirectly in the form of higher prices for protected northern manufacturers. Moreover, the interplay of national party competition, sectional preferences regarding foreign economic and security policies, and the international economy produced major defeats in Congress for leading southern economic sectors. For instance, pursuing the interests of cotton and tobacco producers—who had traditionally exported their goods to Europe and for whom better access to markets in the Pacific held no allure—southern congressional representatives opposed but failed to halt the development of American imperialism and military expansion.[52]

Southern politics was stable but not frozen in place. Black and white workers, farmers, and community leaders agitated sporadically against the main elements of enclave rule. And occasional disputes among elites rose to comic, if dangerous, levels. In the Deep South enclaves under study, standoffs among governors, legislators, and highway departments in the 1930s featured troopers with Tommy guns, the deployment of National Guards, the imposition of martial law, and even the beatings of political opponents by governors' plainclothes thugs.[53]

But southern enclaves were built on much more than caricatures of the demagogic officeholder, sadistic sheriff, and gentlemanly plantation owner. In particular, white progressives played an important role in shoring up enclave rule. Like those elsewhere, white middle-class reformers organized hundreds of local and state-level projects to reconcile "progress and tradition" in the region. They improved the region's public health infrastructure and provision of city services, and sponsored industrial and vocational education to make the region more attractive to capital investment. Many were also motivated to stabilize social relations and secure a racial peace—especially after white-on-black pogroms and riots swept across the nation during World War I.[54] They viewed "the great race settlement" (suffrage restriction and Jim Crow segregation) as a rational, modern innovation beneficial to all. Later, they often advocated reforms that would improve its functioning. Some of these progressives, under the banner of the Commission on Interracial Cooperation, encouraged regular discussions among community leaders of both races, and sponsored annual events like "Race Relations Sunday." Generally, white progressives championed black progress in ways that did not threaten enclave rule.[55]

Organized labor also continued and expanded through the early part of the century. Emerging in some parts of the South after the Civil War, unions were hamstrung. One-party politics, legislative malapportionment favoring planters over cities, and restricted freedoms of association for biracial or leftist gatherings all took their toll. To secure gains at the state level, such as workers' compensation, they were forced to work within Democratic party channels. Always weakest in the South, the country's least industrialized region, unions continually targeted cotton textiles, its largest manufacturing sector. The structural features of the sector made its firms especially hostile to unionization efforts. Still, in 1934, 170,000 textile workers went on strike at hundreds of mills scattered throughout the southeast. Owners and governors dispatched about 23,000 armed personnel to head off and eventually halt the strikes. By decade's end, only about 7 percent of southern millworkers remained union members. Given the barriers in place, other efforts were surprisingly successful, such as Communist organizing of black and white workers in Alabama, and the biracial Southern Tenant Farmers' Union, which peaked at 35,000 members in the Delta in the late 1930s and achieved unlikely wage gains. Five times throughout the first three decades of enclave rule in Alabama, interracial groups of coal miners went on strike, and twice they triggered invocations of martial law in Birmingham.[56] But on the eve of the transition in the 1940s, it seemed unlikely that organized labor would develop enough of a foothold in the region to challenge the status quo.[57] Additionally, the region's intrepid white liberals and radicals occasionally produced important reforms, but these activists were too few in number and their organizations were too vulnerable to repression to mount much of an assault.[58]

The Maintenance of Enclave Rule

The turn-of-the-century foundings of southern enclaves exploited propitious national political conditions, including Republican success in other regions that weakened the party's incentive to challenge southern Democrats, and the country's preoccupation with the turbulent politics of industrialization. For the next half-century, enclave rulers relied on two chief sets of supports. First, southern influence "abroad" in central state institutions and the national party greatly reduced the potential for interference with enclave politics. Second, various institutions and practices at "home" lowered threats of interparty competition, mass insurgencies, social disorder, and potentially debilitating fissures within the ruling party.

External Supports of Enclave Rule

The foundings of enclave rule relied on a particular mode of federalism—the distribution of warrants of authority and responsibility across levels of the polity. It is difficult to imagine authoritarian enclaves in the absence of the decision at the country's founding to allow states to decide whether to grant property rights in humans.[59] Otherwise, there would not have been a politics of statehood centered on whether a state would be "slave" or "free." By providing constitutional protections to diverse political economies—rooted in different property rights regimes—cross-state differences in governance could accelerate. The additional protections provided to states, not cities, also made it more likely that pockets of subnational authoritarianism, were they to emerge, would be constituted as state polities.[60]

Of course, the parchment constitution alone would not suffice. Enclaves were possible only because by the 1890s the region had "won a special constitutional status." Friendly interpretations of the Fourteenth and Fifteenth Amendments did not award them complete autonomy—the U.S. Constitution would continue to set the parameters for southern political practices. But as long as southern state actors did not craft suffrage restriction devices that explicitly discriminated on grounds of race, judicial readings of these amendments would provide these politicians with great leeway. Seven years after affirming state-mandated segregation in *Plessy v. Ferguson*, the Supreme Court did the same for suffrage restriction. Associate Justice Oliver Wendell Holmes's majority opinion in *Giles v. Harris* (1903) acknowledged that Alabama's voting laws constituted "a great political wrong," but declared that remedies could come only from Congress or the White House. The Court would not interfere. For legal historian Richard Pildes, *Giles* removed "democracy from the agenda of constitutional law."[61] The Court occasionally hemmed in southern policymaking on issues such as spatial segregation and vagrancy laws and the practice of peonage, but basically stood aside for a half-century.[62]

However, the Constitution seemed to offer at least two important resources for enclave opponents. First, it guarantees to states "a Republican form of Government." On a plain reading of the Guarantee Clause, subnational authoritarianism seems impossible—or at the very least highly unlikely. But in an 1849 decision, the Supreme Court decided that only Congress, not the Court, was fit to judge what constituted republican governance.[63] Second, section 2 of the Fourteenth Amendment penalized states' representation in Congress if they denied or abridged the "right to vote" held by adult males in federal elections. Southern suffrage restriction never triggered it, meaning that, on one estimate, enclave rulers were allowed to hold some twenty-five additional U.S. House seats (and thus twenty-five additional votes in the Electoral College), and therefore garnered more influence in both Congress and the national party. Black activists and groups such as the NAACP frequently called for its use, and House Republicans repeatedly introduced legislation—echoed by the 1904 Republican platform—to enforce section 2, all to no avail. Southern Democrats' influence within the central state and national party blocked this path.[64]

The Court's timorousness was shaped by two powerful currents in elite opinion. First, at the turn of the century elites expressed substantial skepticism toward democracy and universal suffrage. As the era of the initiative, the referendum, the direct primary, and women's suffrage, the Progressive period was hardly one of generalized opposition to greater popular participation in politics. Still, nonsouthern white publics and elites reacted to enclave foundings with little outrage. In fact, many elites viewed the attempt to enfranchise southern blacks and poorer whites as a mistake. Authorities in the North and West replaced the color-coded ballots distributed by parties—which facilitated voting by illiterates informed of the color or symbols of their preferred party—with the "Australian" ballot distributed by the state. This ballot required that voters be literate (and understand English) in order to select the names of their preferred candidates. Officials also tightened voter registration and voting requirements, all of which dampened turnout by immigrants, and passed laws preventing fusion tickets as a means of weakening the threat of third parties.[65]

Second, Presidents William McKinley, Theodore Roosevelt, and Howard Taft and other influential authorities began to devote much attention and verbiage to the cause of sectional reconciliation, and Republican and Progressive party position-taking on suffrage restriction and related issues reflected this cause. Attacks by the federal government on the new enclaves would have been out of step with reconciliation.[66] As Woodrow Wilson wrote, with the "abandonment of federal interference with elections, the 'southern question' fortunately lost its [national] prominence."[67]

After their founding, the *maintenance* of enclaves required substantial influence in three domains: Congress, the executive branch, and the national party. First, southern representatives developed extraordinary influence in Congress through a large, powerful, and usually unified delegation. One-party politics, in concert with southern members' interest in congressional careers and both chambers' seniority norms, meant outsized enclave influence. From 1896 to 1932, southerners made up two-thirds of the Democratic House caucus; from 1933 to 1953, their share never slipped below 40 percent (figure 2.1). Southern unity in the Senate—a chamber much more amenable to the interests of well-organized minorities—was also impressive.[68]

Despite dominating the ranks of the Democratic party leadership for most of the New Deal period, the South's sway over Congress lay primarily in its dominance of powerful committees, most especially the Rules Com-

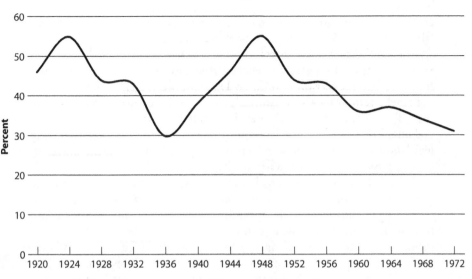

Figure 2.1. Southern share of Democratic House Caucus, 1920–72

mittee of the House, which controlled the floor agenda, length of debate, and the rules for bill consideration.[69] There, enclave influence manifested itself primarily in successful efforts to block harmful legislation but also occasionally in advancing a positive legislative agenda. In the Senate—once called "the South's unending revenge upon the North for Gettysburg"— longstanding southern members became expert in the use of parliamentary procedure, particularly with respect to dilatory tactics such as the filibuster.[70] Congressional hearings offered one way in which enclave opponents could bypass southern politicians' "monopolization" of their linkages with the central state. Decades before Congress empowered the U.S. Commission on Civil Rights to adopt the role, it investigated the worst excesses of southern labor relations, such as peonage, the leasing of convicts to private firms, and chain gangs, and even condemned the "evils" of sharecropping and tenancy.[71]

In general, however, Congress served as a bulwark for enclave rule. As discussed earlier, before the Depression, southern members of Congress achieved little more than this. With the advent of the New Deal, however, they brought home substantial amounts of financial assistance.[72] They also participated in New Deal programs that had often-profound effects across the southern landscape. For instance, through the extremely popular Rural Electrification Act, the share of farms across the Deep South that had electricity increased by factors of six to eight.[73] Just as important, they modified federal social and labor policy—through both statutory revision and influence over federal agencies—in order to maintain control over agricultural labor and southern labor markets more generally (see chapters 4 and 5).

And southerners in Congress continued to stifle passage of federal interventions that could destabilize enclave rule. No Democrat in Congress—southern or otherwise—voted for civil rights or voting rights legislation in the nineteenth century, and few would do so until the early 1940s. In the late 1930s, President Franklin D. Roosevelt complained that if he supported federal interference in southern law enforcement—in the form of antilynching legislation—southern committee chairs would "block every bill I ask Congress to pass to keep America from collapsing."[74]

Second, southern politicians began to exert influence in, and over, the executive branch. In 1913 newly elected President Woodrow Wilson—overseeing the first Democratic administration since the founding of enclave rule—consolidated this rule in two ways. In doing so, he and his southern-majority cabinet squared off against the recently founded NAACP. Wilson worked with the relevant congressional committees to segregate the District of Columbia. This had important symbolic value—the home to the federal government would now be ruled in part in the manner of enclaves. Its inhabitants already effectively disenfranchised, they were now subject to Jim Crow–style regulation of transportation, schools, and so on.[75] More important, Wilson approved the establishment of an effectively white-only central state apparatus through his control over the United States Employment Service, which determined the staffing of federal agencies inside and outside Washington.[76] For enclave opponents seeking to reach past their rulers and make connections with allies in the federal government, a difficult task became even harder. While allies did emerge, the massive fact of a white-only federal administrative apparatus was now hiding in plain sight.[77]

Third, southern Democrats exploited their position in the national party to protect enclave rule. As the mass Democratic party developed in the 1830s, party leader Martin Van Buren secured commitments from state parties to deliver electoral votes in exchange for substantial autonomy over the conduct of their own affairs. In the twentieth century, this bargain continued to hold—the national Democratic party remained confederally structured. As a distinct institution whose actors possessed resources at least partially independent of state parties, the national party barely existed. State parties were free to oversee their primaries, conventions, and selection of delegates to national conventions.[78] Additionally, from the late nineteenth century until the New Deal, southern states contributed a large share of the party's Electoral College support (figure 2.2). Just eight years before Roosevelt's election, a majority of Democratic National Convention delegates refused to condemn the Ku Klux Klan. The national party did not seem threatening to southern enclaves.[79] The party's longstanding "two-thirds" rule—requiring

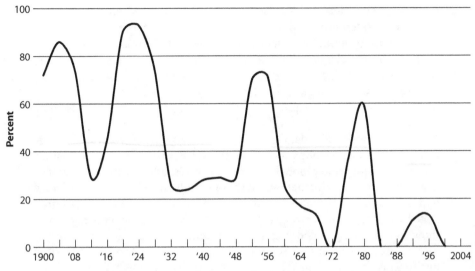

Figure 2.2. Southern contribution to Democratic
Electoral College vote, 1900–2004

a supermajority of the National Convention floor to approve the presidential ticket—amounted to a southern veto over presidential nominations.
It provided further insulation from pressures to alter racially exclusionary
and corrupt practices of southern state parties. In sum, southern influence
within the central state and national party helped fend off unwanted interference in enclave affairs.

Internal Supports of Enclave Rule

Walls may have blocked and deterred outside interference, but enclave rulers also defended themselves from domestic insurgencies and dangerous
intraelite conflict with six institutions and practices. Some of these supports
are at the same time defining attributes of enclave rule; this paradox is resolved by noting that, once enacted, some attributes, such as suffrage restriction and restrictions on civil society, were self-reinforcing.

First, *legislative malapportionment* provided Black Belt whites and their
clients with a commanding presence in state legislatures, which controlled
many more political resources than did governors. New or existing constitutions provided for malapportionment, but even at enclaves' founding
moments, few politicians imagined that existing disparities in representation would lock in Black Belt power for decades. However, by 1940, malapportionment was the most important element in Black Belt counties' continued domination of most Democratic parties. Even as urban business

interests grew in importance and occasionally embarked on political and economic modernization projects that impinged on the interests of rural elites, malapportionment provided a veto against them as well as against efforts to undo malapportionment itself.[80] Additionally, malapportionment seemed safe from federal assault. The same "political questions doctrine" that rendered the Guarantee Clause merely "aspirational" meant that malapportionment was a question to which the judiciary refused to fashion an answer.[81]

Malapportionment's damage to urban political influence can be exaggerated. Urban delegations often retained substantial power in legislators (in part through greater lobbying resources), especially in setting the legislative agenda. As was true nationally, though, bills introduced by legislators representing southern cities failed at much higher rates than those introduced by their small-town counterparts. And as the state-level narratives show, southern cities failed to carry the day when advocating major reforms, such as centralizing authority up to the state level, modernizing political institutions, rationalizing state agencies, establishing merit personnel arrangements, and so on. As H. L. Mencken writes, with malapportionment "the yokels hang on."[82]

Second, *Jim Crow*—the formal and informal regulation of interracial contact in bedrooms, schools, public accommodations, the workplace, and other spaces—greatly facilitated enclave rule. Emerging in fits and starts from Emancipation until the early 1900s, Jim Crow demarcated territories and jurisdictions over which rulers exercised authority, codified racial distinctions, and ordered much of the daily contact between the races. In doing so, it legitimated the continued disfranchisement of blacks as well as racial and regional disparities in public spending.[83] It also greatly reduced the prospects for organized, biracial dissent.

States forbade the desegregation of workplaces in some sectors, such as textiles. However, much more significant was firms' voluntary segregation of workplaces and exclusion of blacks from all but the lowest-paying jobs and good prospects for promotion. As Gavin Wright and others have shown, firms did so regardless of whether they were indigenous or externally owned, unionized, or located in areas with differing levels of white supremacy. Firms' decisions regarding black employees resulted *not* from pressure from their communities but because of managers' own views of the races' relative capacities to perform various tasks.[84] Other dimensions of Jim Crow constituted severe restraints on trade that ranged from home sales to commercial transport.

Exclusion of blacks from certain institutions and social contexts was not new, but segregation, codified by municipal ordinances and state laws, was a modern innovation. Some components of Jim Crow seem to give the lie to claims that Jim Crow amounted to a set of "folkways" impervious to "stateways." For instance, by criminalizing the publication of arguments in favor of social equality among the races, public authorities suggested both that stateways mattered for social outcomes, and that—at least early on—popular backing for segregation may have been weaker than assumed.[85] Later, the net of Jim Crow regulation was cast even wider, even proscribing interracial competition in checkers or dominoes, amateur baseball, and billiards. More important, the regulation of interracial sexual intimacy and marriage restricted white as well as black freedoms.[86]

Separation of the races, whether linked to a doctrine of "separate-but-equal" or not, was bound up in the ideology of white supremacy. White supremacy helped spread and perpetuate Jim Crow segregation, and vice versa, and was assiduously transmitted to children and enforced with social norms that required, among other things, blacks' deference toward whites.[87] Authoritarian regimes' symbolic power helps sustain them, and Jim Crow should be interpreted partly as instrumental. As historian David Brion Davis writes of antebellum racism, "[R]acial doctrine . . . became the primary instrument for justifying the persistence of slavery, for rallying the support of nonslaveholding whites, for underscoring the dangers of freeing a people allegedly 'unprepared' for freedom, and for defining the limits of dissent."[88] Certainly, Jim Crow and white supremacy were strongly supported by the region's white citizens. However, it is likely that, as C. Vann Woodward argues, Jim Crow was a contingent political outcome that resulted at least in part from the establishment of enclave rule, not a "natural" outcome rising inevitably out of southern soil. As will be noted in part 3 of this study, mass white support for Jim Crow could be overstated, especially when its defense was in tension with other valued goods.

Third, as discussed previously, *suffrage restriction* of blacks and poorer whites was both the essence of enclave rule and subsequently central to its stability. Suffrage restriction came in many shapes and sizes. The poll tax required that a seemingly small amount ($1 in 1900) be paid in order to cast a vote. When the tax was made cumulative, it could be prohibitively expensive. In 1945 when Alabama NAACP member Rosa Parks registered to vote, she owed the state $16.50 (more than $214 in 2013 dollars). By requiring individuals to pay the tax, save and bring to the polls a receipt to this effect, and often pay it three to nine months before an election, the poll tax was effective in disfranchising the poorest voters. And its effects were more extensive than merely lowering turnout, since this weakened the motivation of anti-Democrats to run for office. Fewer contested seats meant even lower turnout. When combined with other devices, the poll tax was very important in the early period of enclave rule.[89]

Additionally, by serving as a de facto literacy requirement for voting, the Australian ballot reduced turnout largely among anti-Democrats. By 1900 seven southern states joined the national trend and adopted it. Others

instituted tougher residency requirements for registration. When Democrats sought to prevent the defection of poorer white Democrats and Populists, they deployed "escape clauses" such as the "Understanding Clause" (in
which applicants for registration were required to read and comment on
some document) and the "Grandfather Clause" to "enfranchise otherwise
unqualified whites." Here, the discretion granted to local officials in implementing registration and voting rules was critical. In Louisiana, a white
applicant for registration passed a test to interpret the state constitution
by writing, "FRDUM FOOF SPETGH."[90] By raising the costs for regime
opponents or unsuccessful party candidates of mobilizing the politically
extruded, the party remained hegemonic. And as long as electoral appeals
were directed only at white voters, candidates never seriously contemplated
calling for Jim Crow's demise.

Fourth, and perhaps least appreciated, enclaves depended upon *restrictions on free and fair political contestation.* It could be argued that white
voter preferences, not institutional barriers or harassment of opposition
movements, rendered Republican and third-party candidacies futile. On
this view, "yellow-dog" Democrats were simply the products of custom. Of
course, this "custom" was consolidated only after hard-won repression of
anti-Democrats. Still, while party loyalty, whatever its origins, advantaged
Democrats, party-state institutions helped render opposition parties nearly
unthinkable. Democrats controlled all election laws and election administration, and they took care to keep barriers to entry of potential opponents
prohibitively high. Several states, by party rule or statute, barred previously
disloyal candidates, or those who failed to pledge themselves to the values
of the Democratic party, from running for office—even as independents.
In seven states, statutes forced parties to nominate statewide candidates by
primary, thus making Republican party-building very expensive. Even when
Democrats were not in danger of losing elections, like electoral authoritarians elsewhere, they recognized that "running up the score" helped convince potential officeseekers that to plan political careers outside the party
was pointless. By the 1930s four states in the Union did not provide for
public financing of primaries; all were southern. Another three paid only
for the Democratic primary. In traditionally Republican upland areas of
North Carolina, Tennessee, and Virginia, Democrats used other techniques
to defeat opponents, such as ballot-stuffing, ballot-stealing, and mysterious
poll closings. As in other electoral authoritarian polities, southern primary
and general elections were neither free nor fair.[91]

Fifth, like authoritarian polities everywhere, enclave rulers benefited from
a *highly constricted civil society.* Public authorities conducted propaganda
campaigns, surveilled the mail and movements of suspected dissidents,
and launched legislative investigations and legal attacks on the activities of
scores of groups such as the NAACP, biracial discussion clubs, and liberal

and popular front associations. Authorities prevented public facilities from hosting racially integrated meetings. Local law enforcement arrested and forcibly expelled labor organizers—and even the workers who met with them—from communities and even states. Birmingham authorities in 1940 responded to the appearance of white labor organizers by suspending habeas corpus. The threat of such harassment deterred countless other efforts.[92] Officials limited the freedom of the press, too. Worried about the departure of too many farmworkers, planters convinced Delta politicians to ban the dissemination of various publications, such as the (black) *Chicago Defender*, which encouraged emigration, as well as the NAACP's *The Crisis* and the United Negro Improvement Association's *The Negro World*. Macon, Georgia, banned the distribution of any printed writing of any kind other than newspapers or mail. Such instances proliferated.[93]

Sixth, rulers supplemented restrictions on civil liberties by directing, endorsing, or acquiescing in the physical coercion of their subjects. In the South, coercion took many forms, from imprisonment, expulsion, and destruction of property to torture, murder, and state execution.[94] All modern regimes construct and rely upon coercive institutions to maintain order, including democracies (which are less likely to repress their citizens when electoral competition is thriving).[95] But authoritarians are especially dependent on an effective—if rarely employed—coercive apparatus. Partisan violence had played a critical role in "redeeming" the South; indeed, it is difficult to imagine the demise of opposition parties and the founding of enclave rule in the absence of such violence. Violence and fear played a similarly important role in defending enclaves. Rulers relied on them to blunt challenges to Jim Crow, one-party rule, and a white-only politics. This meant deterring and repressing opposition movements, black protest and political mobilization, and unions and others opposed to the party project.[96] While authorities undertook many of these coercive tasks, private actors committed a great deal of violence. At times this amounted to a skillful coordination with community leaders to repress striking workers, union organizers, or the tacit delegation of unsavory tasks from authorities to "parties unknown."[97] In other cases, officials acquiesced to undesired violence, or actively opposed it by mobilizing state law enforcement. In doing so, they faced the added difficulties of broadcasting their power across highly rural and sparsely populated polities. Topography, weak law enforcement capacity, and popular sentiments frustrated the broadcast of coercive power by authorities—local, county, state, *and* federal.[98]

To maintain their conditional autonomy, enclaves had to ward off federal interference in southern law enforcement, which could range from federal prosecution of southern police, to the federalization of the National Guard, to occupation. Given the resonance of Reconstruction for southern whites, such interference might spark a backlash in the form of additional disorder and violence. Thus, rulers needed to relieve presidents and Congress of any pressures to intervene. This meant credibly signaling their ability to maintain order. Over time, rulers proved quite ambivalent about the presence of disorder. Partisan and later "establishment" violence stabilized enclave rule at key moments, and some violence—especially public lynchings—could serve civic-educative functions for both black and white audiences.[99] But elites were also concerned about the negative regional and national (and later international) reputations that (publicized) violence might foster, and also worried that lynch mobs might spark social disorder among whites.[100] Prodded by Congress, civic associations, and others, southern authorities mobilized public opinion and law enforcement personnel and fashioned legal and technological changes that effected a rapid decline in lynching in the 1930s.[101] Elected and appointed officials, law enforcement, and organized white supremacists threatened white-on-black violence in many ways, from whispers and threats, to signs posted in cotton fields and tacked onto black churches, to campaign rhetoric.[102] In doing so, they substantially altered the calculus of dissent for blacks and whites.[103] Also, various modes of coerced labor continued for more than seven decades after Emancipation. Local and county law enforcement, state legislators, and large landowners drew on vagrancy laws, corrupt "fee" systems, and the manipulation of tenant and sharecropper indebtedness to press black men into service. Individuals and firms leased convicts, mostly black men, to perform often-dangerous work under horrific conditions.[104]

Finally, enclave rulers supplemented largely institutional regime supports with cultural ones. Just after their founding, public authorities and supportive civic associations coordinated on a particular narrative of southern history and disseminated it via textbooks, state-sponsored art, and monuments in the public sphere. They successfully kept "vividly alive the memories of" Reconstruction as a humiliating period of black domination and foreign occupation. Such memories and their transmission to future generations constituted a powerful political resource. As Woodward writes, Democrats would "invoke the past to avert the future."[105]

But is it fair to claim that there really was no representative democracy in the South? After all, while many elections were fraudulent, election administration was often honest. Certainly, enclave rulers sought and won the consent of millions of their subjects, and direct primaries that chose Democratic nominees were essential in winning it. Indeed, new research has expertly revealed the frequent concordance of opinion among white southern constituents and their representatives in Congress. Some responsiveness, however, is not sufficient. All polities must be responsive to maintain rule; and the costs and efficiency losses of relying solely on coercion are too great. As discussed in chapter 1, most authoritarian regimes today regularly hold elections. All told, the restrictions on civil society and freedoms of association (white and public) detailed earlier, in combination with the treatment of opposition voters, movements, and parties, suffice to overwhelm the herrenvolk view.[106]

Black Politics under Enclave Rule

As enclave rule began, black resistance in what had become the United States had already entered its fourth century. It began even before arrival in the form of shipboard revolts, which ultimately reduced the size of the Atlantic slave trade. For years after the Revolution, self-styled "King of England" soldiers fought a guerilla war against Georgia and South Carolina planters. Many mass revolts and escapes from plantations preceded Emancipation, and almost 200,000 blacks joined Union forces to battle the Confederacy.[107] After working to reconstruct the South and resisting efforts to institute highly unfree labor arrangements and drive them out of politics during the chaotic Redemption period, blacks fought the founding of enclave rule as well. From speeches in constitutional conventions to protesting disenfranchisement to boycotts of newly segregated bus and trolley lines to lawsuits challenging suffrage restriction and Jim Crow statutes to armed self-defense in the face of white attackers, subnational authoritarianism did not emerge without a struggle.[108]

But in the face of enclave rule, how did southern blacks engage their polities? Often, they voted with their feet. Besides the small number who caught "Liberia fever" and actually left for Africa, some three million departed the region between 1920 and 1950.[109] The "push" of enclave rule was followed by the "pull" of wartime industrial jobs in the late 1910s. In the 1920s the devastating boll weevil infestation pushed rural blacks northward.[110]

Soon the pace of the "Great Migration" quickened. Northern factories paid labor agents to scan the Black Belt for black workers willing to leave. Alarmed planters and southern authorities reacted at times with conciliatory gestures, but also with police harassment and beatings and anti-enticement laws that criminalized the activities of the labor agents.[111] The Great Migration would have contradictory effects on southern enclaves. On the one hand, it worked as a "safety valve" that relieved pressure on authorities since those blacks who left were disproportionately better educated, less willing to accept unjust labor conditions, and more likely to become involved in protest activities.[112] On the other hand, this mass departure would come to threaten these authorities. It greatly expanded the size of black communities—and electorates—in northern cities, many of them, by the 1940s, in swing states. There, they pressured Democratic politicians to abandon their traditional guarantees of noninterference in enclave rule and instead begin to attack it (see chapter 5).[113]

Many blacks who remained were busy. First, a minuscule number of blacks voted, usually for Republican presidential candidates, but also in scattered nonpartisan municipal elections. Blacks involved in the leadership of state Republican parties looked outside their enclaves and garnered patronage for their support of nominees at Republican presidential conventions. Capitalizing on nonpartisan municipal races and bond referenda—for which the white primary was not used—blacks won substantial policy benefits, especially regarding school funding, public sanitation, and so on. In the 1930s, still unable to vote, many blacks, urban and rural, began expressing strong support for Roosevelt and for the national Democratic party. This was true even of many in the thin stratum involved in Republican party politics.[114]

Second, an even smaller number won status as brokers between black communities and various resource-holders, such as white northern philanthropists, foundations, universities, and local officials. Booker T. Washington's famed "Tuskegee Machine" won out over its competitors in securing access to patronage. Washington's successful appeals to these resource-holders were predicated on an understanding that black disenfranchisement and Jim Crow would continue long into the future.[115] These appeals were also underpinned by the new concept of "race relations," which helped elites sidestep demands articulated in terms of justice and reformulate them as calls for comity among groups.[116] A coalition of northern philanthropists, enclave authorities, and some black educators framed southern black schooling as industrial education, a vision which was based on, and itself perpetuated, black educational and economic disadvantage.[117]

The influence of Washington's machine can be overstated. Jim Crow spurred the development of a fairly independent black civic associational life—particularly churches, fraternal and sororal lodges, and small businesses. Many of these organizations' leaders and members established networks of black elites and themselves fashioned ongoing relationships with public authorities at all levels of government. Some networks were informal; others, like Mississippi's statewide Committee of One Hundred (see chapter 3), were formally structured. In any case, brokerage relationships hinged on the credibility of these elites' claims that they legitimately stood in for "their" communities. Outcomes ranged from the receipt of rents by the more cynical to real "race work" that resulted in not insubstantial social welfare benefits for localities.[118] Often reflecting their parishioners, black ministers were usually very risk averse concerning politics. Moreover, their churches were financially dependent on others—often white planters.[119]

Third, a surprising number of black southerners participated in oppositional and radical movements. Civic associations and issue-oriented lobbies attracted many so-called "middle class" blacks, tapping many women's clubs for members. Unions and more radical organizations went on strike, organized demonstrations and boycotts, and experimented with modes of what came to be called "nonviolent direct action."[120] But beyond tactical concerns, often these actions "encompassed but transcended racial goals," particularly when they followed a discussion of the often-conflicting material interests within black communities.[121] And sometimes these actors momentarily overcame, in Edward Gibson's terms, the party-state's monopoly on linkages with the national polity. For example, Ida B. Wells's formidable publicity campaigns against racist southern law enforcement and lynching reached over the heads of southern authorities to influential nonsoutherners. Besides joining some existing unions, blacks also crafted their own, such as those bringing together black and white sharecroppers and tenant farmers in Arkansas and Mississippi.[122]

Most important, NAACP national staff began organizing local branches in the South. By 1919, thirty were in operation. In that year, the organization's annual convention was entitled, "Making America Safe for Americans." The NAACP won some early victories, including the successful electoral punishment of opponents of antilynching legislation, and later helped block a U.S. Supreme Court nominee (mobilized black voters punished his nonsouthern backers, too). In the South, the organization's growing reputation as militant and successful helped convince local authorities to launch a "merciless backlash" against its new (and financially shaky) branches.[123] This was especially effective in rural areas, and by 1923, only five branches remained. Even where local authorities and others did not attempt to repress members, the collapse of cotton prices and then the Great Depression soon wiped out the extra income necessary for membership dues. At the same time, however, Marcus Garvey's short-lived United Negro Improvement Association (UNIA) fanned out across the region, scoring massive gains across the rural South (with more than four hundred branches by 1926).[124]

The political consequences of some modes of black civic engagement and the "infrapolitics" of everyday resistance are hard to apprehend and can be exaggerated.[125] However, in each of these three modes of engagement—electoral, elite brokerage, and civic and political associationalism—southern blacks won some measure of material benefits for their communities and themselves. In doing so, they kept alive memories of freer black engagement during Reconstruction and Redemption and pointed both to the contingency, and, they hoped, the mortality of enclave rule.

The South's Democratization, 1944–72

Like enclaves elsewhere, those in the South were secure enough, and productive enough for their main clients, that elite-driven reform or domestic insurgencies were highly unlikely to upend them. Rather, a combination of external interventions and insurgencies would be needed to dismantle authoritarian states and racially exclusionary state parties, and build democratic polities. In the periodization advanced here, the South's democratic transition began with the removal of one of the face cards in the stacked deck of one-party politics: the white-only Democratic primary.[126] The Supreme Court's abolition of the white primary occurred amid other important changes, to be sure, including a shift in the early part of the decade by Congress's nonsouthern Democrats, who for the first time began supporting some race reforms more strongly than their Republican counterparts.[127] But while there would be important payoffs two decades later in this shift, it posed no immediate threat. As chapter 4 shows, the Supreme Court's 1944 ruling did.

The transition ended as it began—with important restrictions on the activities of southern ruling parties. This time, however, the restrictions, which reversed the one-and-a-half-century-long tradition of autonomous state parties, emanated not from the central state but from the national party itself. After several blows to enclave state and local policies in the 1960s, the McGovern-Fraser reforms mandated the full incorporation of non-white Democrats into the national party and thus destroyed one of the last vestiges of enclave rule.

Each periodization strategy comes with its own analytic strengths and weaknesses. One weakness here is that enclaves were challenged by more than just sharp, discontinuous change triggered by external actors. For instance, gradual, secular changes, such as urbanization and the mechanization of agriculture, altered the relative influence of different interests allied with the regime. Despite this, I believe that the chief advantage to this periodization—that its focus on external challenges facilitates direct comparison of enclaves and their responses—makes it worth pursuing.[128]

The following five interventions posed highly similar and basically simultaneous challenges to all southern enclaves:

1. In 1944, the U.S. Supreme Court in *Smith v. Allwright* invalidated the white-only primary, thus providing new openings for black mobilization and incorporation into ruling parties.
2. In 1948 President Truman led the national Democratic party's embrace of racial equality. This shocking turnabout raised immediate doubts among rulers about the wisdom of pursuing policy and career goals as Democrats.
3. In 1954–55, *Brown v. Board of Education* and subsequent rulings invalidated "separate but equal" in education and other domains. Striking at the heart of Jim Crow, *Brown* required enclaves to decide whether and how to defend themselves. It soon triggered crises in the Deep South over the desegregation of college campuses.

4. The 1964 Civil Rights Act and the 1965 Voting Rights Act battered southern enclaves. Occurring amid increasingly emboldened domestic insurgencies, the legislation promised to sweep away Jim Crow and suffrage restriction.

5. In the coup de grâce for enclave rule, the national Democratic party in 1968–72 codified a new balance of power between the national and state parties. These reforms seemed to secure black (and Hispanic) incorporation into southern state parties.

While focusing on these democratization challenges, the narratives below feature analyses of the effects of others as well. For instance, in 1962 and 1964 federal courts required reapportionment on the principle of one person, one vote, and thus seemed to dismantle the Black Belt veto over economic and political reforms promoted by urban and suburban white business "moderates." These rulings had especially important and immediate consequences for some enclaves, including Georgia, and chapter 10 discusses them.[129]

Although democratization pressures eventually proved decisive in defeating southern enclaves, their half-century of stable governance was an impressive accomplishment. The next chapter assesses whether and how the characteristics of Deep South enclaves at the onset of the transition help explain their different responses to these challenges.

CHAPTER THREE

Deep South Enclaves
on the Eve of the Transition

THIS CHAPTER COMPARES four important features of Deep South enclaves on the eve of the transition: their political geography, centralization of political authority, party factionalism, and latent strength of their indigenous opponents. A review of these and other characteristics of these polities suggests that the modernization account discussed in chapter 1 cannot fully explain the variation in Deep South democratization experiences. Besides making room for a causal account emphasizing the importance of regime defenders, opponents, and the institutional topography on which they battled one another, the chapter also provides background information for the narratives to follow. As will be shown later, many more characteristics united than divided these polities. However, they did differ importantly in the degree to which they centralized political authority and in their intraparty factionalism. By 1940 differences also emerged in their degree of urbanization and somewhat in their organizational readiness for black insurgency.

Political Geographies

Over the first half of the twentieth century, Deep South enclaves shared similar political geographies. Ranging from about two to three million residents, each state was predominantly rural and agrarian. At the time of their foundings in the 1890s, the enclaves of Mississippi and South Carolina were majority-black (and remained so at least through 1925). In 1910 Georgia's black population share surpassed 45 percent.[1] By 1940 the three states were home to about one-quarter of the nation's blacks.[2] Each contained a majority-black Black Belt region featuring labor-intensive agriculture, the poorest blacks, and the wealthiest and politically most influential white landowners. Over the prewar period, Black Belt counties declined in population relative to those with a greater percentage of whites, as their inhabitants left for cities in the state and beyond.

South Carolina, the Deep South's smallest state, featured two broad areas. The rolling hills of the Piedmont comprised the "upcountry." South of the fall line stretched the coastal plain, or "lowcountry," comprising two-thirds of the state and part of or all of twenty-six of the state's forty-six counties.[3] Alone among British colonies in mainland North America, South Carolina was intended from the start to be a slave society. Early plans for the colony of Carolina, drafted largely by John Locke, called for a carefully delineated landed aristocracy, with different classes of nobles as well as freemen, serfs, and slaves. However, this vision had much less influence on Carolina's evolution than what was effectively its parent colony, Barbados. Sugar, cultivated by slaves in factories in the fields, for a while made Barbados's planters the richest in British North America. Its society had "a tiny white oligarchy and small white layers of petty bourgeois, impoverished freedmen, and bondsmen all resting upon a huge black base." The island eventually became overcrowded by fortune-seekers, and many of its white inhabitants headed to Carolina.[4] There, they immediately adopted Barbados' slave code and helped inculcate a very conservative political culture, especially in the lowcountry.[5] Economically and politically, majority-black Charleston dominated the colony, which was divided into counties and subdivided into parishes. The colony, and especially its lowcountry settlement, constituted "the most heavily slave-based, class-structured, gentry-dominated society in North America." Thanks to the cultivation and export of rice and indigo, soon it was the wealthiest.[6] This wealth amplified South Carolina's voice in national politics, where its elites led the defense of slaveholders' interests at the Constitutional Convention in 1789, incubated southern nationalist and "radical proslavery" thought in its colleges, and later developed the doctrine of nullification.[7] By the time of the ratification of the U.S. Constitution, more than three-quarters of white South Carolinians lived in the upcountry, where yeoman farmers worked land of poorer quality.[8]

By 1900 the lowcountry's longstanding dependence on international commodity markets, the collapse of its rice industry, and its isolation from the rest of the state combined to make it one of the nation's poorest areas.[9] The state's agricultural sector remained troubled. While cotton soon accounted for more than two-thirds of the state's total production, only one-half of the state's farmland was cultivated. Meanwhile, the upcountry grew with the turn-of-the-century textile boom; by World War I, one-fifth of the state's whites lived in its white-only mill villages, and textile production dominated the state's nonagricultural earnings. Still, on the eve of the transition, the state was not poised for a takeoff in economic development. The textile industry employed just 11 percent of the state's labor force and did not transfer skills to its workers. Prospects for developing an indigenous manufacturing base in the state seemed dim.[10]

As Jim Crow, the promise of industrial jobs, and the destructive boll weevil convinced some 200,000 blacks (one-quarter of the state's black population) to emigrate, the state became in 1927 majority-white. This fact did not escape the notice of officials, who proclaimed, "This means a new freedom in South Carolina [because of] the removal of a vague but always present shadow."[11] In 1940 one-quarter of the state's 1.9 million residents lived in cities, only two of which—Columbia and Charleston—reached a population of 50,000 (figure 3.1).[12]

Carved out of land ceded to the United States by Spain in 1795, Mississippi was sparsely populated by European settlers and riven by land controversies and conflicts with Indian tribes for its first few decades. Attaining statehood in 1817, Mississippi attracted white settlers from the southeast, who streamed into the state with their slaves, and in two decades it was majority-black.[13] Mississippi was divided into three broad regions: the Yazoo-Mississippi Delta; the Hills counties of the central, northern, and eastern areas of the state; and the Piney Woods and Gulf Coast areas to the south.

The Delta, stretching for two hundred miles but less than seventy miles wide, was famous for its incredibly rich soil. It covered all or part of nineteen of the state's eighty-two counties—all majority-black (see figure 3.2). Dominated by cotton, soybean, and rice production, the Delta has long held mythic status as the *ur*-South, but—economically, at least—was a post–Civil War phenomenon.[14]

South Mississippi's Piney Woods and Gulf Coast were predominantly white and featured lumber, textile, and other light industries (and, with the onset of World War II, shipbuilding), and generally voted with the Delta. Most of the state's whites resided in Hills counties, which were generally rural and featured less arable soil and, consequently, more subsistence farming. Because they lacked sufficient water power, industrial development was slow to arrive in these counties. In both South Carolina and Mississippi, whites in the upcountry and Hills counties, respectively, differed in class and cultural terms from better-off whites in the lowcountry and Delta. Upcountry and Hills whites more strongly favored prohibition and more generous social provisions, and produced the states' neopopulist candidates.[15] In Mississippi, the most rural and least industrialized of the Deep South states, about one-fifth of its 2.2 million citizens lived in urban areas. By 1940 only Jackson—about two-fifths black—had a population of at least 50,000.[16]

Georgia, the thirteenth colony, was founded in the 1730s as "an asylum for poor whites, orphans, and debtors" that would serve as a buffer between South Carolina and Spanish Florida. Because slavery might have deterred the arrival of white workers and even assisted the Spanish in inciting an insurrection, it was banned. This ban made it the "only free-soil region in the Western Hemisphere," but unraveled almost immediately.[17] In the twentieth century, political splits within Georgia often occurred along urban and rural lines. However, there was also substantial sectional conflict that did not map onto an urban/rural cleavage. While Georgia can be divided into several different regions, for my purposes Georgia's political geography

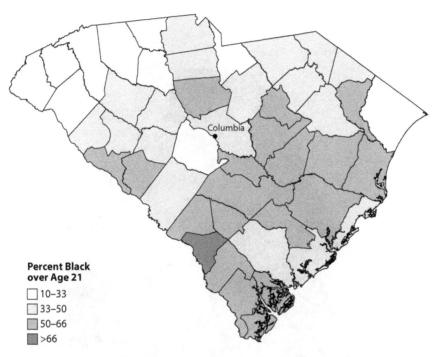

**Percent Black
over Age 21**

☐ 10–33
☐ 33–50
▨ 50–66
■ >66

Figure 3.1. South Carolina counties by race of voting-age population, 1940

during the period of enclave rule featured two broad sections. North Georgia comprised all or most of about fifty counties stretching from Atlanta northward, a mountainous area that was predominantly white and home to small farming and light manufacturing, particularly in the state's northwest corner. Over the course of the transition, north Georgia grew in population. Below the Piedmont was south Georgia, which comprised two regions: the Black Belt and the coastal plain. The Black Belt was a broad crescent of about sixty-five counties running from southwest to east across the middle of the state, and was home to a majority of the state's blacks, its largest farms, and the heart of its cotton production. South of the Black Belt lay the predominantly agricultural coastal plain; its approximately forty-five counties featured smaller farms and relatively more whites than in the Black Belt. By the early twentieth century, the state had been divided into 159 counties, most of them very small. In 1940 the most sparsely populated 121 counties were home to about 40 percent of the state's whites, as compared to 34 percent in the largest eight counties (figure 3.3).[18]

By 1940 Georgia was the Deep South's most urbanized state. Almost one-half of its three million residents lived in cities, compared to one-quarter and one-fifth of those in South Carolina and Mississippi, respectively.

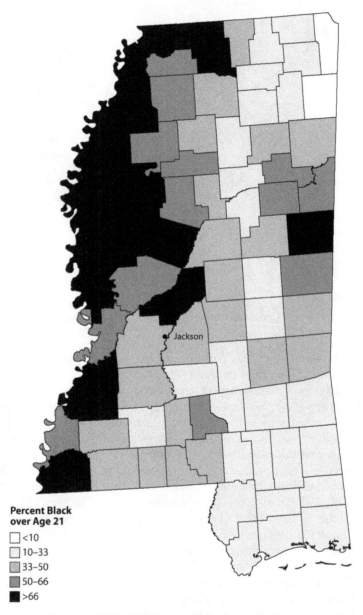

Percent Black over Age 21

☐ <10
☐ 10–33
▨ 33–50
▨ 50–66
■ >66

Jackson

Figure 3.2. Mississippi counties by race of voting-age population, 1940

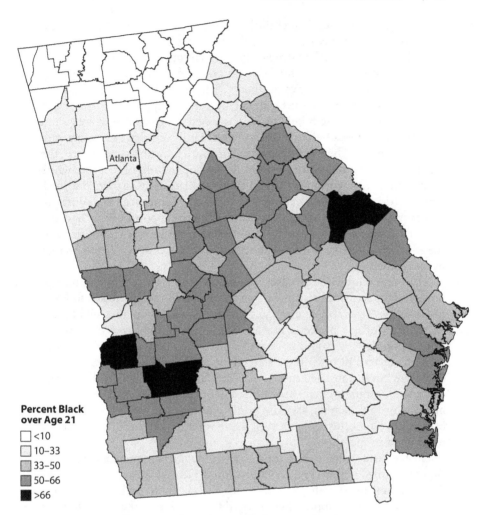

Figure 3.3. Georgia counties by race of voting-age
population, 1940

Atlanta, just north of the fall line, was the region's only city with a population greater than 100,000; four others reached 50,000.[19] By 1940 about
40 percent of Georgia workers were employed by manufacturing and service sectors. Georgia's industrial sector outpaced those in Mississippi and
South Carolina. Mississippi, lacking a concentrated industry such as South
Carolina's upcountry textile sector, lagged behind both states.[20]

The predominance of majority-black counties in the Deep South had
important political implications. As discussed later, enclaves often apportioned representation in senates and other institutions by county. This

meant that when Black Belt counties held a substantial share of these jurisdictions, their representatives would have greater influence. In all three states, led by South Carolina, majority-black counties were numerous.[21]

Deep South legislatures further disrupted the conversion of economic and social power into political influence. The three most politically powerful legislative chambers—the Georgia House, Mississippi House, and South Carolina Senate—were highly malapportioned in favor of rural areas, and usually favored Black Belt over upcountry or Hills counties. This meant outsized influence for the Black Belt whites of South Carolina's lowcountry, the Mississippi Delta, and south Georgia. As the populations of majority-white areas soared after World War II and those of Black Belt districts declined, malapportionment's political impact increased.[22] Moreover, malapportionment reverberated throughout the polity, since the apportionment of other sites of decision-making—such as the state party's executive committee and the allocation of delegates to the state party convention—was based on that of the legislature.

The Loosemore-Hanby index is a common tool for comparing malapportionment across legislatures (table 3.1). It can be interpreted as follows: in Georgia's General Assembly, 26.5 percent of seats were allocated to districts that, under a perfectly fair apportionment of white votes to white district populations, would not have received them. Put another way, more than one-quarter of votes in the state's House elections were wasted; that is, they were never translated into seats. The Dauer-Kelsay score indicates the theoretical minimum percentage of the white population needed to win a majority of the chamber, assuming only whites voted. For example, in the Mississippi House, just 21 percent of white voters could theoretically elect a majority of its members.

On the cusp of their long transitions to democracy, then, all three enclaves remained highly rural and agricultural. Georgia was the most urbanized and most industrialized Deep South enclave, followed by South Carolina and then Mississippi. Where they differed, however, the magnitude of these differences was modest. In all three states, majority-black and substantially black counties clustered together in Black Belt regions distinct from majority-white regions, and the former retained significant representational advantages over the latter.

The Centralization of Political Authority

Political authority was distributed horizontally and vertically across Deep South polities. Determined by state constitutions, statutes, regulations, and party rules, this authority helped determine which enclave actors were empowered (as well as required) to carry out various governance tasks. Political

TABLE 3.1
Malapportionment in Deep South Legislatures, 1940

	Loosemore-Hanby Index	Dauer-Kelsay Score
Georgia (House)	26.5	27.5
Mississippi (House)	23.1	21.3
South Carolina (Senate)	32.3	34.9

Sources: White population data per district are computed from the U.S. Historical Census Browser, accessed online (http://fisher.lib.virginia.edu/collections/stats/histcensus/). Mississippi legislative data appear in William N. Ethridge, *Modernizing Mississippi's Constitution* (Oxford, Miss.: Bureau of Public Administration, 1950).

Note: Because legislative elections were basically all white, and because Black Belt areas sought to exploit white voting power, both measures are for white populations. The formula for the Loosemore-Hanby Index—probably the most common metric for comparing malapportionment across legislatures—is

$$MAL = (1/2)\sum | S_i - v_i |,$$

where s_i is the percentage of seats allocated to district i and v_i is the percentage of the population living in district i. David Samuels and Richard Snyder, "The Value of a Vote: Malapportionment in Comparative Perspective," *British Journal of Political Science* 31 (2001), 651. To calculate the Dauer-Kelsay score, "The various legislative districts ... are placed in rank order from smallest population per member to largest, and the count proceeds from the smallest population end of the scale for a sufficient distance to accumulate that portion of the population that has the power to elect a majority" of the chamber. Paul T. David and Ralph Eisenberg, *Devaluation of the Urban and Suburban Vote*, vol. 1 (Charlottesville, Va.: Bureau of Public Administration, 1961), 3; Burt L. Monroe, "Disproportionality and Malapportionment: Measuring Electoral Inequity," *Electoral Studies* 13 (1994), 132–49. The author is very grateful to David Smith for help with this analysis.

authority also varied in how easily it could be altered. When enshrined in founding constitutions, it was less vulnerable to change. This would be important, as it would affect enclaves' prospects for improving their capacities to manage challenges once the transition commenced.[23]

In the early twentieth century, Deep South polities had much in common. First, the jurisdiction of the county remained more central to southern political life than it did in other regions of the United States, and it performed the traditional tasks of roadwork, schooling, law enforcement, and poor relief.[24] Second, southern states faced similar public finance challenges, including severe constitutional limitations on public borrowing, small tax bases, and meager fiscal capacities. Third, they generally featured weak executives who lacked significant budgetary and appointment powers and who oversaw inept, disorganized state agencies with weak planning capacities. Governors—usually prohibited from serving consecutive terms—had few patronage opportunities useful for enhancing their influence. Fourth, Black

Belt–dominated legislatures (themselves often poorly equipped to "puzzle" and plan) were more powerful than executives and poorly insulated state judiciaries. Legislatures usually produced particularistic statutes that distributed (or withheld) favors to particular districts, rather than pursuing broader public policies. They rarely made any significant investments in human capital. Here, loose and often ephemeral factions within the state Democratic party lacked both the incentives of typical parties to promote statewide party brands through broader policy initiatives as well as the capacity to do so. In this respect, one-party southern legislatures resembled their northern Republican counterparts.[25]

Despite public officials' generally low levels of autonomy from social groups and economic sectors and the weak capacity of state institutions, political authority in these states was not highly decentralized. Southern constitutions generally lacked "home rule" provisions for municipalities and counties. Legislatures often dominated county and local authorities, themselves hamstrung by highly limited fiscal powers.[26] The development of state highways furthered the relative power of state governments over local and county governments. During the nation's road-building craze of the 1910s and 1920s, the federal government encouraged states to develop state highways but failed to provide promised financial assistance. However, it did compel them to build competent state highway departments. With local governments unable to fulfill their traditional role as keepers of roads, state governments financed millions of miles of new highways. New sales and gas taxes augmented their administrative capacities, and road building soon dwarfed all other types of state expenditures. Highway departments became the most important sites of political patronage, and governors warred with legislatures to control them.[27] Mississippi developed the country's first state sales tax, and launched its most aggressive push to encourage local efforts to lure outside firms through subsidies and tax expenditures.[28]

Within this general pattern, Deep South enclaves differed in the degree to which authority was centralized. The dominance of South Carolina's Senate over the rest of the enclave—particularly over county government—meant that political authority was centralized in a small, Black Belt–dominated institution. In Mississippi, authority diffused to county governments, in part because of the unique office of sheriff. Georgia, shaped by an extremely malapportioned electoral system, large number of counties, and strong executive, mixed centralizing and decentralizing features. I discuss these features below in the context of these enclaves' founding constitutions.

South Carolina's Senate Dominance

Major elements of the state's suffrage restriction occurred before the Constitution of 1895. Chief among them was the 1882 eight-box law, which presented voters with a confusing array of ballot boxes so that illiterates would have little chance of having their votes counted. The law had a partisan intent, and, in combination with electoral fraud and violence, wrecked the state's Republican party. Tens of thousands of whites were disenfranchised as well as blacks.[29]

Still, conservative Democrats worried that only a "flimsy statute" stood between stable politics and black rule. Four years later, factional conflict between the lowcountry "Bourbons" and Benjamin "Pitchfork Ben" Tillman's movement of small farmers in the upcountry threatened the political status quo. The dispute was not ideological in nature. Capturing the governor's office, Tillman, a wealthy farmer, differed from lowcountry aristocrats (at the time the party's establishment) more in matters of style than policy. After Tillman served as governor, a fellow Tillmanite won the office in 1894, but only after defeating a challenger who did surprisingly well by mobilizing blacks and espousing their voting rights. In response, Tillman called for a constitutional convention to solidify white, Democratic rule. The popular referendum required for initiating a convention barely passed, and did so thanks to existing suffrage restriction. As Georgia's Populist leader, Thomas Edward "Tom" Watson, observed, "[T]he whole scheme of the Democrats in South Carolina [to rewrite the constitution] is to perpetuate the rule of their party."[30] The Constitution (which was never popularly ratified, but proclaimed the state's supreme law) expanded and protected the state's suffrage restriction scheme. In 1898 South Carolina elites consolidated enclave rule as it faced its last threat in the form of a mobilization of black Republicans. Three hundred white vigilantes tortured and killed blacks in Greenwood.[31] Enclave rule had taken hold in South Carolina.

The Constitution of 1895 accomplished much more than suffrage restriction. It reversed several elements of the state's Reconstruction-era constitution to which conservative Democrats had long objected. Before Reconstruction, South Carolina's constitutions did not guarantee counties legal status as fixed jurisdictions. But with the highly progressive Constitution of 1868—drafted almost entirely by freedmen and white Republicans—the state endowed counties with real responsibilities and taxing and spending powers, and made them accountable to local electorates (many of them majority-black). Blacks in South Carolina gained more political power than anywhere in the South; at one point, they held a majority of seats in the General Assembly (the state legislature's lower chamber). Both elements—county spending and black/anti-Democrat power—were on the minds of rulers as they sought to safeguard their prerogatives through a new regime.[32]

The new constitution provided for counties' existence but not for how they were to be governed, leaving the details to the General Assembly to establish by statute. If legislators disapproved of the behavior of county of-ficials, they could merely oust them, as many positions had no constitutional protection.[33] Additionally, since statutory limits on county borrowing had failed to stem county spending, the constitution allowed counties to tax and issue bonds only for a narrow range of purposes. State judges, chosen—and dominated—by the General Assembly, complied with restrictive interpreta-tions of county powers.[34] Finally, the constitution continued South Caro-lina's long tradition of weak governors with few appointment, budgetary, or patronage powers. As Governor Ernest "Fritz" Hollings once complained, without the ability to appoint public service commissioners, "there is no way for the governor to get the big utilities in behind him."[35] Institutional design in part reflected sectional conflict. The more populous upcountry would always have a much better chance of electing a governor than capturing the legislature (heavily malapportioned to its disadvantage). Thus, its politicians often favored stronger gubernatorial powers.[36]

As was true of only three other American states, South Carolina's sena-torial districts corresponded exactly to county boundaries, thus providing one senator for each of the state's forty-six counties. Since counties were formally weak, the Senate effectively governed them. Legislative delegations from each county, dominated by its senator, controlled the mode of gover-nance, appointments, appropriations, and administrative decisions.

The result was a remarkable fusion of the state's executive and legislative functions. This administration-by-legislature often took extreme forms. One county's annual "supply bill" (which provided for a tax levy, appropriations for county functions, and so on) specified the hiring of the ladies' restroom custodian at the courthouse.[37] Patronage and other rent-seeking opportuni-ties abounded for senators, who were understandably content to remain in the Senate rather than pursue other offices. Senator Edgar Brown—long the state's most powerful politician—remarked that "[governors come and go, but] I go on forever."[38] For the entirety of the state's democratization (from 1941 until his death in 1972), he served both as President Pro Tem and chair of the all-powerful Finance Committee. Solomon "Sol" Blatt served as House speaker for almost all of the period from 1937 to 1973. Brown and Blatt both led what would be called the "Barnwell Ring," a group of incred-ibly powerful politicians from the same small lowcountry county.[39]

In sum, South Carolina featured a strange mix of a powerful legislature, a weak executive, and counties ruled as senators' personal fiefdoms. The state's domination by the upper chamber provided additional power for the lowcountry even as it declined over time in population and socioeco-nomic influence. Defeating attempts to modify the constitution by upcoun-try politicians and lowcountry reformers, the Black Belt–dominated Senate effectively centralized political authority.[40]

Mississippi's Sharp Decentralization of Authority

Mississippi's Constitution of 1890 established the framework for enclave rule in the state.[41] The constitution was written in a convention, but never popularly ratified, as constitutionally required. The convention was called for a few different reasons. A major reason was the continued partisan threat facing Democrats. In 1889 state Republicans had shocked Democrats by contesting all statewide races. Earlier, Independents had threatened to fuse with blacks and Republicans and had backed equal voting rights.[42] Additionally, less-well-off farmers in the majority-white Hills counties wanted to secure many reforms, including greater popular control over judges, tougher corporate regulation, reapportionment, and more effective educational finance. After they pushed calls for a convention through both chambers of the legislature, the governor vetoed the resolution; constitutional conventions were too unpredictable.

However, U. S. Senator James Z. George, a former leader of electoral violence during Reconstruction, worried greatly about the state's preparations in case Congress passed the Lodge Elections Bill.[43] (The Lodge Bill would require fair registration and voting practices; it could do nothing about an electorate that had already been heavily restricted.) He convinced Black Belt whites to back the call for a convention, and it passed. The popular election for convention delegates had an extremely low turnout; disfranchisement did not emerge from a grassroots following. Democrats dominated the convention, and the leading Farmers' Alliance and Greenback party politicians opposed suffrage restriction. Still, the convention passed a strong disenfranchisement article comprising a very stringent residency requirement, a highly onerous poll tax, as well as an "understanding clause" that would function, most expected, as a grandfather clause for whites. The state adopted a new apportionment system that seemed more favorable to Hills whites; however, Hills representatives had miscalculated, and the new system remained highly favorable to the Black Belt, especially in the House.[44] After ratification, black turnout collapsed immediately.[45]

In contrast to South Carolina, Mississippi's polity was highly decentralized. Although its 1890 Constitution did not feature "home rule" provisions, the state's eighty-two counties retained significant formal authority and informal power relative to state-level actors and institutions. A powerful, five-member board of supervisors governed each county.[46] The state also featured a unique sheriff's office. The sheriff, unable to serve consecutive terms, garnered significant power through the office's dual role as county tax collector. Paid a percentage of taxes collected, sheriffs often made small fortunes. Over time, the state's sheriff lobby grew increasingly powerful, and for decades prevented the decoupling of the office's taxation and policing functions. As chapter 6 discusses, this decoupling frustrated efforts by several governors to centralize the state's policing apparatus.[47]

Mississippi's governor, referred to as the state's "chief observer," was perhaps the nation's weakest. As in South Carolina and Georgia, governors could not serve consecutive terms. Since voters separately elected several agency administrators, gubernatorial control of the executive branch was weak. This compartmentalization also diminished the office's patronage powers. Finally, the constitution offered the governor a limited role in state budgeting.[48]

The legislature featured a powerful House dominated by the state's most influential politician, Deltan House Speaker Walter Sillers. In the late 1880s, legislators associated with the Farmers' Alliance briefly took power, but conservatives held sway over the 1890 Constitutional Convention and, after securing disfranchising provisions, maintained a Delta-friendly apportionment formula for the House.[49] For Black Belt interests, this was critical, since—unlike South Carolina—Delta counties did not outnumber Hills counties.[50] Deltan legislators benefited from seniority and legislative expertise and from their occupation of the speaker's office.[51]

Generally, advocates of government reorganization sought both a reduction in the crazy quilt of overlapping departments and a strengthened executive. State lobbies of sheriffs and other county officials, fearing a loss of autonomy over county affairs, fought these efforts. And Black Belt legislators worried that a constitutional convention could be seized by those from majority-white counties to reapportion the legislature. Others feared that constitutional revision might invite federal judicial attacks on the Constitution's disfranchisement provisions.[52]

Georgia's Mixture of Centralizing and Decentralizing Elements

Georgia's Democrats demobilized their state's electorate earlier than perhaps any other southern state. After the state's Reconstruction ended in 1871 after a chaotic, violent period, Redeemers planned for a new constitution to replace the Reconstruction Constitution just ratified in 1868. As Morgan Kousser notes, it developed effective suffrage restrictions, in particular a cumulative poll tax, in the 1870s, and its Democrats faced one of the weakest Republican parties in the region. In 1877 Georgia ratified a constitution that sufficed for the purposes of its conservative Democrats. Thus, the state was unusual among enclaves in not substantially modifying or writing a new constitution in the 1890s.[53]

The Constitution of 1877, dominated by unreconstructed Confederate elites and fiscally conservative farmers, constrained public borrowing as well as state-sponsored economic development, and established a highly malapportioned legislature and tough voting restrictions. Authority was highly decentralized, and placed in the hands largely of county commissioners and other county officials. Numerous attempts in ensuing years to draft a new constitution that provided for a stronger state apparatus, increased taxing and borrowing powers, and a more powerful governor all failed.[54] Georgia Democrats did face a threatening Populist movement in the 1890s, but succeeded in repressing and co-opting it. The state's planters and "New South" townsmen and professionals had cemented their alliance and political hegemony.[55] They sponsored additional suffrage restrictions by constitutional amendment in 1907. This was the result both of desires to ensure that no "discord" in the "white ranks" could endanger the polity, and of a spiral of racist out-bidding in the 1906 gubernatorial campaign. These measures seem to have been effective. Black voter registration fell from 28 percent to 4 percent in just six years. White voter turnout also plummeted and did not recover for decades.[56]

In Georgia, county governance remained fairly autonomous from the state legislature. While special legislation established the size and shape of the Board of County Commissioners, given weak oversight of its implementation, state control over county affairs was quite limited. Decentralized governance in Georgia was problematic. One hundred and fourteen of the state's 159 counties had fewer than 20,000 residents, and were thus too small and poor to be effective, especially as new demands emerged in public health, welfare, and education.[57]

In many of the state's rural counties, courthouse "rings," composed of economically influential individuals, officials, and their networks of families and friends, dominated politics. Poorer whites—beholden to these "key men" for loans, mortgages, fertilizer, and so on—either were taken to the polls to vote as instructed or else remained home. County leaders could thus credibly commit their county's vote in gubernatorial elections and thus improve their returns on rent seeking. The state's electoral laws facilitated this control. South Georgia legislative delegations fended off the adoption of a statewide, mandatory secret ballot until 1949, and the state's punitive poll tax provided additional opportunities for controlling votes, as key men often paid this tax for "their" whites. Courthouse cliques marked ballots for voters outside polling booths and monitored their choices.[58]

Through both formal and informal powers, Georgia's governor was one of the South's strongest. The governor served as ex officio budget director, chose presiding officers and chairs of key committees in both legislative chambers, possessed relatively greater patronage powers, and so on.[59] While the legislature—highly malapportioned in favor of rural Georgia—served to block many political reforms advocated by urban politicians, the governor's legislative powers weakened the body somewhat.[60]

THE COUNTY-UNIT SYSTEM

By far the most important institution affecting the dispersion of authority in Georgia was its "county-unit system," a highly malapportioned electoral system used to nominate candidates in all party's primaries. It developed in the late nineteenth century during a period of ferocious conflict between often-radical small farmers and conservative "city" interests, and particularly in response to urban conservatives' reliance on electoral fraud to rob Populist leader Tom Watson and his white farmer base of a Democratic congressional nomination.[61]

In this system—enshrined as a party rule and later in statute—each county received twice its number of seats in the General Assembly. Thus, the eight largest counties each received six "unit votes," while the next thirty largest received four, and the smallest 121 counties received two. Gubernatorial candidates needed a majority of the 410 county-unit votes. As table 3.2 indicates, if rural counties united behind a gubernatorial candidate, he could win nomination without receiving a single vote in the state's fifty-six largest counties. Figure 3.4 labels the "six-unit" counties home to the state's largest cities, such as Fulton's and DeKalb's Atlanta and Richmond's Savannah. Since the legislature refused to reapportion itself from 1877 until ordered by federal courts to do so in 1963, the county-unit system reinforced in gubernatorial and other statewide elections the extremely strong rural bias of legislative politics. The result was, in V. O. Key's term, the "rule of the rustics."[62]

By the 1930s the county-unit system greatly enhanced the political power of rural conservatives. Since the system encouraged gubernatorial and other statewide candidates merely to seek county pluralities, it substantially lowered the costs of campaigning for the support of elites who "delivered" their counties, and heightened corruption.[63] "Moderate" politicians throughout the state privately opposed the system, but, needing to win "two-unit counties," supported it publicly. Once established, the county-unit system perpetuated itself. Legislators from two-unit counties had no reason to abolish it.[64]

Some urban politicians, progressives, and many newspaper editors and other "good government" advocates called for substantially revising or replacing the Constitution of 1877. They wanted a stronger executive, legislative reapportionment, greater state borrowing and taxation powers, county consolidation, and other reforms. As in Mississippi and South Carolina, numerous attempts to reform the Constitution by commission or convention failed. In Georgia, holding a constitutional convention would especially endanger the status quo, as its delegates would be apportioned by population, not by the county-unit system.

TABLE 3.2
Georgia's County-Unit System, 1940

County groups	Unit votes/county	% state population	% white VAP	% total unit votes
8 largest	6	30	34	12
Next 30 largest	4	26	26	29
121 remaining	2	44	40	59

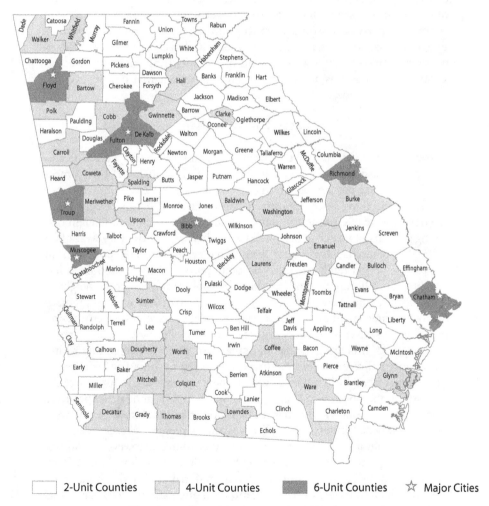

□ 2-Unit Counties   ▨ 4-Unit Counties   ■ 6-Unit Counties   ☆ Major Cities

Figure 3.4. Georgia's county-unit system, 1940

Because of the dominance of the lowcountry-controlled Senate over South Carolina's forty-six counties, political authority and resources in that state were substantially more centralized, and—if backed by state leaders—political reforms could be secured rapidly. On the other hand, Mississippi's counties and municipalities were vested with substantial formal authority and informal power, a fact that would facilitate a diversity of responses by rulers to democratization pressures but frustrate bids for developing new state-level governance capacities.

Finally, Georgia mixed a dispersion of political power across 159 counties with a strong executive, thus frustrating predictions about the implications of this distribution of political authority defending enclave rule. Because of the executive's strength and influence over state party machinery, a more centralized party-state would seem to promise coherent, unitary responses to democratization pressures framed quickly and decisively by powerful executives. However, the power of two-unit counties over the legislature and statewide nominations posed a counterweight to executive dominance.

Party Factionalism

Throughout the first half of the twentieth century, all public authorities in Georgia, Mississippi, and South Carolina were Democrats, and "The Democracy" dominated presidential voting (see figure 1.3).[65] Party nominations—effectively elections since opposition parties rarely contested Deep South elections—were often issueless affairs that turned on "friends and neighbors" voting patterns and colorful personalities.[66] When issues arose, they were often cultural in nature (such as liquor laws). What passed for Hills "populism" in the prewar period rarely extended beyond appeals for free textbooks, a less expensive auto license fee, and pensions for state employees. At the height of stable enclave rule in the 1920s and 1930s, appeals to defend white supremacy did not influence gubernatorial or state legislative elections, given the implausibility of effective black insurgency (see "Black Protest Capacity" later in this chapter).[67] Moreover, neither a popular insurgency rooted among whites nor an internal revolt within the party was on the horizon. For instance, organized labor had little influence within these state parties. In 1939, Georgia, Mississippi, and South Carolina ranked seventh, eighth, and last, respectively, among southern states in the share of their nonagricultural workers who were union members.[68] Intraparty conflict was always present, whether rooted in clashing ambitions, sectional tensions, or other sources. However, it did not often develop into conflict between cohesive, durable factions.[69] Still, Deep South Democratic parties featured different sectional, class, and cultural interests, and different modes of party organization often affected which interests would be able to guide enclave decision-making in key moments.

South Carolina

In the prewar period, South Carolina's intraparty strife climaxed in the 1930s. In the century's first three decades, traditional upcountry antipathies for the aristocratic and condescending airs of lowcountry politicians were manifest in battles over the regulation of child labor, prohibition laws, and other issues on which upcountry voters preferred cultural autonomy over a middle-class progressive ethos.[70] But in the 1930s upcountry/lowcountry conflict took on a sharper class cast. Fully 20 percent of Democratic primary voters in the 1920s and 1930s lived in mill villages, and in the late 1920s, one-fifth of mill-workers enrolled with the Union of Textile Workers. Former millhand (or "linthead") Governor Olin Johnston, whose political base lay in the upcountry, battled with increasingly cohesive cliques of lowcountry legislators over the control of the Highway Department, state budgets, constitutional reform, upcountry labor conflicts, electoral fraud, and much else.[71] Johnston sought labor-friendly social and employment policies, and backed striking textile workers in the bloody fights of the 1930s.[72]

The "Barnwell Ring" of lowcountry solons—led by Edgar Brown in the Senate and Sol Blatt in the House—effectively forced the upcountry to subsidize road-building in the lowcountry, then home to just one-quarter of the state's whites.[73] By the early 1930s, the Highway Department's annual budget outstripped all other state agencies combined.[74] After a comical if potentially violent standoff between the state militia and embattled highway officials beholden to the state Senate—replete with machine gun nests placed in the hallways of the Highway Commission building—lowcountry legislators eventually beat back Johnston's attempt to wrest control of state agencies and the Highway Department.[75] Lowcountry legislators had fashioned a political equilibrium well suited for pursuing their rent-seeking goals, and for protecting the interests of large landowners and, soon, larger textile firms. These forces increasingly embraced federal assistance and state-sponsored economic development.[76] When Johnston returned as governor in 1943, he no longer pushed his populist-labor program, nor challenged conservatives' hold on state administration. The governor's office had been weakened even further, and factionalism in the state was now dead.[77]

Finally, South Carolina's state party machinery reinforced the lowcountry's numerical advantages in the legislature. Delegate allocation to the state party convention was determined by the number of each county's members in the malapportioned General Assembly. Moreover, one member on the powerful state Democratic executive committee (SDEC) represented each county. Except for the election of the party chair by the floor of the convention, it was difficult for outside forces to overtake party machinery. Deep South SDECs would be important sites of enclave decision-making concerning national party relations, disfranchisement, and other matters. As the upcountry's share of the state's population increased over time, about one-half of South Carolina's SDEC remained in the hands of lowcountry representatives. Even when sectional tensions flared, the Senate's dominance weakened incentives to develop durable factions. As Key discusses, a good indicator of the state of factionalism is the number of gubernatorial candidates in Democratic primaries. In South Carolina in the 1930s and 1940s, this number reached eleven.

Mississippi

Like South Carolina, Mississippi politics featured a sectional divide on prohibition, public spending, and other matters, but no durable factions. In 1903, Hills legislators secured the passage of a law requiring the use of statewide primaries for party nominations. This helped Hills counties elect a string of farmer-friendly governors and secure some taxation and education policies that benefited these "white" counties. While the "Delta versus Hills" conflict described by Key characterized many statewide elections in the 1930s, sharp factional differences within the party or legislature were rare. Indeed, intraparty conflict on the eve of the transition had sunk to its lowest point in decades.[78]

As in the rest of the Deep South, Mississippi's Democratic party was a creation of the state. Statutes regulated virtually all aspects of the state's political parties. This extended to paying for the Democratic primary, as well as requiring a fairly apportioned SDEC committee (by congressional district, which were of roughly equal populations). Mississippi's SDEC determined the party's relationship with the national party, methods of nominating candidates and selecting delegates to the National Convention, and the state party's platform. Since a region of the state could not dominate the SDEC, state party machinery could not always serve in Mississippi as a site of strong authority over enclave affairs when elite preferences diverged. However, malapportionment did affect participation at state party conventions, as delegates were required by law to be allocated according to the apportionment of the (highly malapportioned) House of Representatives.[79] The party only rarely involved itself in nomination struggles, and avoided intervening in electoral disputes common in the more corrupt elections of Georgia and South Carolina. And the supply of numerous statewide elective offices reduced problems in regulating ambition within the party.[80]

Still, the party was dominated by a politically cohesive Delta that drew on malapportionment, legislative seniority, planters' unofficial control of legislative nominations, influential campaign donations in statewide elections, and the greater competence of its legislators.[81] Planters sought cheap farm labor, federal flood assistance and agricultural price supports, and a reduced tax burden for Delta counties. Well represented in the legislature, their interests were effectively articulated by the Delta Council, a partly state-funded pressure group that undertook research and planning, subtle lobbying, and the surveillance of unionization efforts among black share-croppers and, eventually, of black protest generally.[82]

Many Delta planters, south Mississippi industrialists and mill owners, and urban professionals began to coalesce on an agenda of state-facilitated, low-wage, industrial development. Whereas sectional and ideological cleav-ages once overlapped fairly neatly, by the late 1930s many Delta politicians helped Governor Hugh White pass the innovative Balancing Agriculture With Industry (BAWI) plan for enticing external capital into the state.[83]

As with South Carolina, Mississippi lacked an indigenous white liberal-ism organized by political or civic associations. The state's American Fed-eration of Labor (AFL) was very conservative, while the organizers of its Congress of Industrial Organizations (CIO) faced incessant hounding and red-baiting. Like South Carolina, the state lacked a discursive space for reconsidering the ruling party's project. The state's two dailies, the *Jack-son Daily News* and *Jackson Clarion-Ledger*, rhetorically safeguarded white supremacy.[84]

In sum, by 1944, Mississippi's rulers presided over a relatively issueless, demobilized polity.[85] As Martin Shefter argues, political elites mobilize pop-ular followings only when necessary. One indicator of the lack of such need in Mississippi by the 1930s was the state's turnout in the 1938 congressio-nal elections: 1.6 percent of the voting-age population. While cultural and class differences separated Hill and Delta politicians and citizens, and while political-economic interests varied with the state's topography, complicated alliances, personal feuds, and a Delta-dominated House reduced organized strife within the party.[86]

Georgia

Compared to other southern governors, Georgia's executive held greater power over state governance. Likewise, Georgia governors maintained tighter control of party machinery.[87] The party's victorious gubernatorial nominee named the state party chair and thereby controlled a majority of seats on the state's Democratic executive committee (SDEC) as well as del-egates to the national party's convention. However, the use of the county-unit system in nominating statewide candidates, combined with the fact that state party convention delegates were apportioned on the county-unit basis, meant that—regardless of the candidate—more rural south Georgia retained substantial influence within the party.[88]

On the eve of the transition, factional conflict within Georgia's ruling party was the Deep South's sharpest. Eugene Talmadge, a charismatic white supremacist demagogue, led a coalition of county courthouse rings and poorer white farmers against a much less cohesive "anti-Talmadge" faction of urban moderates and liberals across the state. Talmadge harkened back to his Populist hero, Tom Watson, in railing against the "moneyed interests" of the cities. The county-unit system allowed him to limit his rhetorical appeal to "two-unit" counties. Talmadge also relied heavily—if quietly—on a few large Atlanta firms to finance his campaigns.[89]

The Talmadge faction advocated and implemented policies that were much more conservative than those of the Populists. In 1934—during which almost 40,000 Georgia textile workers went on strike—Talmadge called out the National Guard and declared martial law. He ordered the detention of hundreds in what a journalist described as a "barbed-wire concentration camp" at Fort McPherson, near Atlanta. Talmadge would stroll up to the fence and read aloud to the strikers from the recent American bestseller, Adolf Hitler's *Mein Kampf.*[90]

His three terms as governor (1932–34, 1934–36, and 1940–42), during which Talmadgeites controlled the state legislature, lacked any substantial policy initiatives for his ostensible constituents. Instead, these years were marked by severe fiscal mismanagement, staunch opposition to the New Deal (discussed in chapter 5) and to governmental reforms, the use of the state apparatus to intimidate opponents, and the personal manipulation of state agencies.[91]

A shifting constellation of social groups, patronage and personalistic networks, and interest groups composed the looser anti-Talmadge faction. These included business leaders and professionals, "good government" whites represented by the League of Women Voters, most media outlets, and various county courthouse gangs co-opted by gubernatorial candidates who, for various reasons, remained outside the Talmadge faction.[92] Atlanta—the most important city of the Southeast—was home to many moderate and progressive civic groups and was the center of anti-Talmadge forces.

Although they supported governmental modernization projects and minor policy provisions for blacks, and decried the most visible abuses—especially those that attracted unwanted attention from the North, such as lynching and the state's infamous chain gangs—anti-Talmadge politicians did not challenge publicly the major pillars of white supremacy.[93] For decades, Talmadge opponents were bedeviled by their failure to coordinate consistently behind a single gubernatorial candidate. Without such coordination, and given how the county-unit system disadvantaged urban politicians and voters, the anti-Talmadge vote would be divided and Talmadgeites would win. Later, black voters, returning white war veterans, and many union members joined this constellation. However, on the eve of the transition to democracy, there was little reason to believe anti-Talmadge forces could overwhelm the "rule of the rustics."[94]

Given its size and future importance, Atlanta and its city politics deserve discussion. Before World War II, durable factions did not structure municipal elections. Rather, the city's sizable number of working-class whites backed different elite candidates. By the early 1940s owners of large firms and other elites began organizing more assertively on behalf of their own economic and civic goals, and sponsored a plan for governmental reform and economic development. After decades of municipal corruption, the city in 1936 elected William B. Hartsfield, a reform mayor backed by leading business figures. Hartsfield, who served as mayor for all but two years from 1937 to 1962, could not sustain a patronage-structured coalition even if he had wanted to; the Great Depression had battered the city's finances, and there was little opportunity for patronage.[95] Almost immediately, Hartsfield's political base became reform-minded elites. This meant that he could not expect to mobilize large numbers of working-class whites. Soon, middle- and upper-middle-class "good government" whites began to exit for the suburbs. Thus, until annexation efforts succeeded, Hartsfield had to reach out to Atlanta's black voters (who, before the abolution of the white primary, were less than 4 percent of the city's electorate).[96]

Compared to those of its neighbors, Georgia's ruling party was much more strife-ridden, and prone to crisis. Numerous times in the prewar period, governors and others deployed law enforcement personnel for partisan purposes, declared martial law, and even established a financial "dictatorship" over control of highway funds. Authorities were themselves arrested in standoffs over personal feuds, battles over sources of patronage, and schemes to empty state coffers. At a few moments in the narrative that follows, Georgia's ruling party—and with it, stable enclave rule—risked complete collapse.[97]

To sum up, party factionalism and intraelite conflict differed somewhat across Deep South enclaves. By World War II and the eve of the abolition of the white primary, factional conflict in South Carolina had subsided. While there were recurring tensions between politicians in the upcountry and lowcountry, sectional differences did not generate durable party factions. The situation in Mississippi was similar. Political economic differences among elites representing interests and voters in the Delta and the Hills counties generated some sources of conflict, but none was sharp enough to lead to durable factions. By contrast, in Georgia, a durable faction representing conservatives and many white farmers, headed by Gene Talmadge, faced off for decades against a looser grouping of white moderates, some white liberals, and—eventually—blacks. The anti-Talmadge faction was more diverse than its adversaries, but its members agreed that the Talmadgeites had to be defeated.

Finally, Deep South parties shared one key feature: they all sent representatives to Congress and to federal agencies who played key roles as bulwarks

against unwanted interventions and as procurers of federal monies and programs. Powerful federal officeholders included South Carolina's James F.
"Jimmy" Byrnes, who served as Roosevelt's "Assistant President," a Supreme
Court justice, and a powerful wartime administrator, who was almost picked
to serve as Roosevelt's final vice president; Mississippi Senator Pat Harrison,
chair of the powerful Finance Committee, who was instrumental in shep-
herding through the National Recovery and the Social Security Acts; and
Georgia senators Walter George and Richard B. Russell, who both com-
manded tremendous respect among their colleagues and who frequently
led southern forces in their chamber.[98] Notably, however, while southern
senators were, in the words of historian Keith Finley, the region's "principal
national spokesmen," they did not pay much attention or exert much influence over enclave governance. Indeed, they remained powerful in part by
generally remaining neutral in factional conflicts. Moreover, the politics of
congressional elections did not affect Democratic nominations down the
ticket, and failed to capture much voter interest.[99]

Black Protest Capacity on the Eve of the Transition

Black communities in Deep South enclaves did not differ greatly in their latent capacity to capitalize on federal challenges to enclave rule. While some
differences emerge when comparing antecedent conditions, the evidence
does not support the notion that these states' democratization experiences
are somehow attributable to different levels of black protest capacity. As this
study argues, it is difficult to imagine a historical explanation that moves
straightforwardly from antecedent levels of black insurgency to modes of
democratization. Still, the differences discussed here are likely to play some
part in any explanation.

It is worth noting that, in contrast to the era of agrarian populism before enclave rule, Deep South civil societies had atrophied considerably in
the ensuing four decades, at least with respect to reform movements and
liberal groups more common in the Outer South, such as the Southern
Conference on Human Welfare. In the 1930s these states lagged well behind the rest of the country in various types of civic mobilization. For
example, they ranked last in the number of Townsend clubs per congressional district.[100]

Once external challenges to enclave rule began in the mid-1940s, how
well positioned were black communities in the Deep South to exploit new
openings? Doug McAdam's work suggests that these communities' "organizational readiness" for the development of insurgency depended on their
existing associations, communication networks, and the presence of a "recognized leadership" to direct and coordinate black protest.[101]

Throughout the Deep South, black protest capacity was weaker in 1940 than at the turn of the century. The best available estimates suggest that 3 percent of voting-age blacks were registered to vote in Georgia, as compared to 0.4 percent in Mississippi and 0.8 percent in South Carolina (and 5 percent in the Outer South). Atlanta's approximately three thousand black registered voters composed about 4 percent of the city's electorate in 1940—or only one-half of their share in 1919.[102] Estimates of actual voting in these states' largest cities were much lower.[103]

The readiness to exploit new political openings can be captured by the number, size, and spatial dispersion of protest organizations. Most important among them is the NAACP, which began establishing local branches in the 1910s. National officials toured the South organizing branches, especially in cities. The number of southern branches increased from three to 131 from 1916 to 1920.[104]

As table 3.3 illustrates, other than the large number of members in a few urban branches in Georgia, there were not large differences across the states in the status of the NAACP in the late 1910s. This remained true on the eve of Pearl Harbor. Over the ensuing two decades, there would be a sharp decline in fortunes of the organization across the Deep South followed by some recovery. The 1920s and 1930s took their toll due to the combined effects of attacks by white supremacist organizations, the deleterious effects of the fall in cotton prices, and then the Depression. All else being equal, dues-paying was much more difficult for sharecroppers, who often had no cash on hand.[105] Changes had occurred, however. During the 1930s South Carolina blacks organized a state conference of branches, but, contrary to expectations that urban communities would spearhead organizing, rural areas sparked the creation of this network and its efforts to grow and spread the organization.[106] By 1940 there were no statewide networks of NAACP activists in Georgia.[107]

In 1947 wartime remittances and better-paying jobs at home, as well as a growing militant consciousness, produced sharp membership gains nationally as well as in the Deep South. By war's end, a divergence across the Deep South emerged. In Georgia and South Carolina, the organization benefited from the presence of thousands of blacks on military bases and from the work of the statewide conference, respectively. Moreover, in both states, college chapters and youth councils helped spark further growth. Mississippi lacked these features.[108] While Mississippi's lagging behind seems easy to explain, why South Carolina's NAACP organizers were so successful—and more successful than Georgia's, which possessed substantial advantages—is a mystery. Certainly the income and occupational differences between Mississippi and South Carolina were not great.[109] Black Mississippians developed some statewide organizations, such as the Committee of One Hundred. Its county affiliates negotiated with white elites to

TABLE 3.3
Estimates of NAACP Branches and Members, 1918–57

	1918	1940	1947	1950	1951	1954	1957
Georgia	6/427	7	50/13,000	42/3,400	39/4,400	48	35
Mississippi	2/36	4	15/1,000	24/850	20/1,500	40	28
S. Carolina	2/57	8	48/10,000	80/6,200	133/8,400	138	45

Sources: "Branches Authorized During Year of 1918," Part 1, Group 1, Series A, Box 23, Reel 13, 126–27, NAACP Papers; "Number of Voting Delegates to Which Each Branch Is Entitled—Houston Conference (1941)," Part 25, Series A, Supplement 1, Reel 10 (1941); "Number of Voting Delegates to Which Each Branch Is Entitled" (1947 Conference), Part 26, Series A, Reel 11; "Membership Status of Georgia Branches," (Dec. 3, 1952), Part 26, Series A, Reel 11, 265, NAACP Papers; "Membership Status—Mississippi Branches" (May 20, 1952), Part 25, Series A, Reel 3; "Number of VOTING Delegates to which Branches Are Entitled on Basis of Paid-Up Membership" (June 11, 1957), Supplement 2, Reel 5, all in NAACP Papers. Data from 1938 for South Carolina in Heard interview with black protest group leader, Heard papers. Mississippi membership listed for 1947 are actually for 1949; see "Record of Memberships Sent In and 40th Anniversary Quotas Paid, January 1 to November 25, 1949 (Mississippi Branches)," Part 26, Series A, Reel 15, 527.

reduce indiscriminate racial violence, to improve educational funding and social welfare provisions for blacks, and generally to structure interracial elite bargaining. However, it did not attempt to confront segregation or white supremacy in the political sphere.[110]

By 1950, after the national office had increased each individual's annual membership fee from one dollar to two dollars, national membership fell from 540,000 to 150,000.[111] In Georgia, for instance (table 3.3.), the number of paid members declined by almost 75 percent. South Carolina's branch in rural Clarendon County, soon to generate the lead case in what became *Brown v. Board of Education*, alone had more than five hundred members. (As part 3 discusses, the effects of enclave attacks on the NAACP and other black protest organizations were clearly evident by 1957, especially in South Carolina.)

McAdam and others suggest that blacks should have been better able to exploit new political opportunities as rates of black urbanization increased. By 1930 almost 30 percent of Georgia's blacks lived in urban areas, compared to 13 percent and 17 percent for Mississippi and South Carolina, respectively. Georgia's cities—particularly Atlanta and Savannah—were prewar regional centers of black civic associationalism and capital formation (table 3.4).

Was it true, as Mississippi Senator Theodore "The Man" Bilbo charged, that Atlanta, stocked with "quislings of the white race, and other racial minorities," was the hotbed of "southern Negro intelligentsia, Communists, pinks, Reds, and other off-brands of American citizenship in the South"?[112] Together, Atlanta and Savannah were home to more than one thousand

TABLE 3.4
Percentage of Blacks Living in Urban Areas, 1900–30

	1910	1920	1930
Georgia	19	23	30
Mississippi	9	11	13
South Carolina	12	14	17
Outer South	23	28	36

Source: U.S. Census, *Statistical Abstract of the United States*, various years.

black-owned businesses by 1940. Atlanta's six black colleges enrolled almost three thousand students. By 1933 black Atlanta supported the South's only black-owned daily newspaper and, by 1949, the country's first black-owned radio station. This infrastructure sometimes bore fruit.[113] Atlanta blacks exploited electoral rules for bond referenda to defeat proposed bond issues in the 1920s and 1930s, and also engaged in episodes of contentious politics.[114] Still, historian John Dittmer considers the period from Atlanta's 1906 race "riot" until World War II the nadir of black city politics.[115] With its economic, political, social, and educational network of black institutions, Atlanta was both the clearest "source of African American strength in the modern South" and also "the site of sustained segregationist resistance." The Klan influenced city politics in the 1920s, and it maintained a sizable presence in the police force for decades thereafter.[116]

McAdam and other analysts also emphasize the importance of a critical mass of economically independent actors—those less vulnerable to economic coercion—who are likely to organize protest. During Jim Crow, such persons included black landowners, federal employees, and professionals serving black communities. As of 1930, they did not much differ across the Deep South.[117]

Given the mode of most democratization pressures until the 1960s—federal judicial rulings requiring implementation through local lawsuits—the number of black attorneys would be especially important. The evident shortage in all enclaves was compounded by the fact that few agreed to support black protest. For instance, from 1900 to 1950, twenty black attorneys passed the South Carolina bar; not all embarked on legal careers in the state, and only one accepted civil rights cases. Such a shortage contributed to the continuing reluctance of the NAACP's national office to allocate resources to Mississippi for legal attacks on Jim Crow.[118]

Larger differences emerge when considering the share of rural blacks most vulnerable to economic coercion. Relative to tenants and independent black landowners, sharecroppers had the least leverage in bargaining with white landowners.[119] In 1945 the share of black sharecroppers among all black farm operators ranged from 40 percent in South Carolina to 58 percent in Mississippi.[120]

Finally, scholars have pointed to education and exposure to communication networks as important resources for black protest. But blacks did not differ markedly across the Deep South in their educational attainment or literacy rates. In 1930 South Carolina had the highest rate of illiteracy among blacks ten years or older.[121] However, in Georgia and South Carolina, there were larger gains in years of educational attainment from 1900 to 1940 than in Mississippi.[122] Some black churches nurtured black protest before the transition began; most did not. While data on cross-state differences here are elusive, historians seem to agree that—largely because of the greater financial support provided them—Mississippi's churches were less likely to take leadership roles in encouraging and sustaining protest than those in Georgia and South Carolina.[123]

In sum, by 1940 no Deep South rulers faced daunting black insurgencies. Levels of black political mobilization, urbanization, economic independence, and education were generally very low in all three states. Because of the critical mass of blacks in Atlanta, Savannah, and other cities, Georgia seemed better prepared to capitalize on external challenges to enclave rule. On the eve of World War II, by dint of the share of its black male labor force mired in sharecropping and the state's low levels of urbanization, Mississippi's black protest capacity was the lowest of the three states. South Carolina's black protest capacity lay in the middle. It should be stressed, however, that cross-state differences were not overwhelming. And—as mentioned in the discussion on black attorneys—different types of democratization pressures would require certain characteristics of a protest infrastructure that, on the eve of the transition, could not be fully anticipated by insurgents or their opponents.

Conclusion

South Carolina entered the transition with the most centralized state governance. Its party-state seemed firmly in the hands of the economically and socially isolated lowcountry, despite the increasing industrialization of the state's upcountry. Highly conservative lowcountry senators defeated the only major challenge to their rule in the 1930s, and black protest in the state did not seem especially promising.

In 1940, Mississippi was the most agricultural, least urbanized, and poorest of the three enclaves. Its highly decentralized polity featured important sectional differences that did not translate into sharp factional conflict within the ruling party, which faced the region's least-developed infrastructure for black insurgency.

Georgia entered the transition as the most populous, most industrialized, and most urbanized of the three enclaves. It combined a powerful executive and state party with decentralized county governance and a malapportioned electoral system and legislature that benefited rural Georgia. Featuring the sharpest factional conflict in the Deep South, it also seemed to offer the best prospects for black insurgency.

These Deep South enclaves did not differ dramatically from one another when it came to those antecedent conditions—including their political economies and black protest capacities—that might generate predictions about these states' democratization experiences. Of course, even if this variation cannot be predicted in advance with reference to antecedent conditions, it is possible that secular change in these structural features during the transition—say, a takeoff in industrialization and urbanization—might greatly outweigh the agency of key actors. The narratives that follow consider these possibilities. Still, this chapter provides suggestive evidence that the shape of institutions of party and state, as well as intraelite conflict, are critical components of explanations of these enclaves' different democratizations.

Finally, this chapter has revealed interesting differences in the degree to which political authority and resources were distributed within these enclaves. The explanation of modes of democratization offered by this study emphasizes this dimension of enclave rule. However, during the long transition, the degree of centralization was itself subject to change by political reformers. Thus, it will be argued, this factor is important less as an antecedent condition than as a key dimension shaping rulers' prospects to devise new institutional defenses of enclave rule.

PART TWO

The Transition Begins, 1944–48

CHAPTER FOUR

Suffrage Restriction under Attack, 1944–47

When democracy fails for one group in the United States, it fails for the nation.... A disfranchised group compels the disfranchisement of other groups. The white primary system in the South ... compels the white man to disenfranchise himself in order to take the vote away from the Negro.... The decent white South is deprived not only of decent government but of all real voice in both local and national government.... Today, ... politicians have every incentive to cut down the number of voters, black and white.... This is the only modern nation in the world that dares not control its own elections.

    —*W.E.B. Du Bois* (1930)

Those of us engaged in this racial struggle in America are like knights on horseback—the Negroes on a white horse and the white folks on a black. Sometimes the race is terrific. But the feel of the wind in your hair as you ride toward democracy is really something!

    —*Langston Hughes* (1943)

When the negroes have an opportunity of voting they will naturally vote against any of us who run. However I hope this will be in the distant future.

    —*Senator Burnet Maybank* (D-SC) (1945)

I tried to be a Democrat, but they wouldn't let me.

    —*Black activist Reverend William A. Bender, after trying to vote in Mississippi's U.S. Senate primary* (1946)

ON THE EVE OF WORLD WAR II, America's authoritarian enclaves appeared as stable as ever in the eyes of inhabitants and outside observers.[1] But in just a few years, two external challenges would batter enclave rule. First, the Supreme Court's 1944 invalidation of the all-white Democratic primary in a critical but almost-forgotten decision—*Smith v. Allwright*—struck at the heart of southern politics—one-party rule based on white supremacy.[2] Second, the national Democratic party's turn toward racial equality in 1948 threatened enclave rulers' conditional autonomy from both the federal government and the national party. Truman called for the central state apparatus to dismantle key aspects of enclave labor relations, regulation of interracial social contact, law enforcement, and so on. In doing so, he not only threatened enclave rulers, but also called into question, for the first time since the late nineteenth century, the viability of the national Democratic party as the most appropriate vehicle as they pursued their policy goals and career objectives.

Viewing federal interference in enclave rule as eminently reversible, Deep South enclaves sought to defy these challenges. This chapter finds that the modernization account discussed in chapter 1 seems to hold when comparing the differences between Outer South and Deep South responses to *Smith*. Moreover, the two Deep South states with greater black protest capacity, Georgia and South Carolina, did feature more impressive black mobilizations than Mississippi. However, the consequences of these episodes were not driven solely by such forces as economic development or black protest infrastructure. Rather, given different configurations of intraparty conflict, party-state institutions, and levels of black insurgency, *Smith* and the responses it invoked had different consequences for each enclave. Some repositioned the enclave on the eve of Truman's external challenge in 1948. Other consequences would continue to reverberate throughout the transition period. In the pages that follow, the Court's challenge to the white primary is reviewed to situate broadly rulers' dilemmas, opportunities, and options. Next, the chapter provides narratives of enclave experiences with the white primary challenge in South Carolina, Mississippi, and Georgia, respectively.[3]

The White Primary and *Smith v. Allwright*

Having emerged usually at the local level in the 1870s, by the early 1900s the white primary appeared throughout the South, mostly enshrined in state party rules. From a herrenvolk perspective, the appearance of the white-only direct primary was a democratizing reform since it allowed those opposed to the establishment to appeal directly to the (white) electorate and bypass the exclusive county and state-level executive committees that had long determined party nominations.[4] By the 1930s the white-only primary was Dixie's most powerful legal tool of suffrage restriction. In the Deep South, politicians revered the institution and considered it the cornerstone of one-party rule. In the absence of black participation, party factions had no incentive to court black votes and thereby endanger white supremacy.

There was never full compliance with white primary rules.[5] Some politicians among county courthouse rings allowed "their" blacks to vote occasionally, sometimes purchasing their votes. These leaders made such allowances when this very small black vote posed no threat to outcomes, or when an election was thought to be particularly close. Given the fact that black voter registration remained below 5 percent of the voting-age population across the entire South, and below 2 percent in the Deep South, actual black *voting* in Democratic primaries was effectively nonexistent.[6]

Perhaps reflecting the seeming impregnability of the white primary, white southern moderates, national leftist groups, and national black protest organizations did not prioritize its abolition. However, southern black organizations resisted the white primary from its inception. Texas NAACP activists led the way. Texas law allowed county party organizations to determine whether to require qualifications for primary voting in addition to those required by statute for general elections. In 1923, in an attempt to weaken San Antonio's machine, the state's Klan-dominated legislature passed a law forbidding blacks from voting in the state's Democratic party primaries.[7] The El Paso NAACP branch quickly filed suit. The national office of the NAACP placed many of its scarce resources, including top legal talent, into the case while announcing "the opening of a great attack on disfranchisement." In 1927 the Supreme Court in *Nixon v. Herndon* struck down the statute, which, in the words of historian Manfred Berg, was "almost a textbook violation of the equal protection clause" of the Fourteenth Amendment. But because the case dealt with Texas's statute, rather than the state party's regulations, the Court did not have to consider a much more vexing issue: whether a state in which a political party that, by its own private rules, restricted its membership on a racial basis violated the Constitution. The state's white primary had not been invalidated, but its enforcement by the state of Texas had.[8]

The Texas legislature quickly responded with a statute allowing executive committees of political parties to determine their own membership qualifications. The state party's executive committee then forbade blacks from participating in party affairs. Texas NAACP activists filed suit challenging this arrangement, and in 1932, the Supreme Court in *Nixon v. Condon* invalidated Texas' white primary on the grounds that the state improperly involved itself in parties' internal affairs. In reality, however, the ruling was a setback for opponents of the all-white primary. By limiting the constitutional issue to one of "state action"—rather than whether, under the Fifteenth Amendment, participation in primaries was a right held by eligible voters—the Court was sticking to its usual cynical formalism and signaling to southern enclaves that those white-only primaries established solely by parties themselves were permissible. The federal judiciary would continue to think of political parties as private, voluntary associations with unfettered control over their own membership and rules. Meanwhile, in response to the ruling, delegates at the state convention of Texas Democrats excluded blacks from party affairs.[9]

Tension mounted between black attorneys in Texas and the national NAACP, which, from a local perspective, seemed neglectful. Against the advice of the national office, which viewed *Condon* as a "defeat in disguise," attorneys in Texas filed another case to force the Court to rule on the white primary's constitutionality. In 1935 the Supreme Court handed down its ruling, *Grovey v. Townsend*. For black challengers, it was a "disaster." The unanimous Court found that the reassertion of a white-only primary by the state party's convention did not constitute "state action," and thus did not implicate the Fourteenth or Fifteenth amendments. Even though Texas regulated its political parties, this regulation did not transform them from private clubs into public utilities. The fact that Democratic primaries in Texas and the rest of the South were de facto general elections was constitutionally irrelevant. Almost twenty years after the "assault" on the white primary had begun, the only meaningful change was that the Court had now effectively strengthened its constitutional protection.[10] By the onset of the war, as Berg writes, "[W]ith the exception of the grandfather clause [in 1939], none of the legal instruments for racial disenfranchisement had been eliminated. . . . As a general rule, the southern states were unimpressed by the threat of being sued. The state courts were solid pillars of white supremacy in the first place, and individual registrars did not worry about being convicted by all-white juries."[11]

Soon, however, a new opening emerged. In 1921 the U.S. Supreme Court had limited Congress's power to regulate its own elections on the view that the results of party primaries did not themselves constitute "elections."[12] But in 1941, the Court reversed itself. Without confronting *Grovey*, it ruled in *U.S. v. Classic* that primaries implicated Fourteenth and Fifteenth Amendment rights if state law had made the primary "an integral part of the procedure of choice," or if "the primary effectively controls the choice."[13] Given that southern white primaries satisfied both criteria, many commentators concluded that *Grovey*, and with it the white primary, would soon be overturned and invalidated.[14] After an election official denied a Houston NAACP activist a ballot in the 1940 congressional primary, the national organization—prodded by its state branches—lent its support in a new suit brought by an NAACP member from Houston that capitalized on *Classic*.[15]

In June 1943 the U.S. Supreme Court granted certiorari, thus alerting southern enclaves to a new challenge to the white primary.[16] In oral argument, attorneys for the NAACP's Legal Defense and Educational Fund (LDF), William H. Hastie and Thurgood Marshall, claimed that the results of the Texas primary effectively determined the outcome of the general election, that election officials operated under color of state law, and that the Court's earlier conception of a political party had been misguided. The Texas Democratic party was not a voluntary political association but a "loose-jointed organization" with no clear membership; "the state election laws provided the only rules that governed the party and its elections."[17]

On April 3, 1944, the Court announced its eight-to-one ruling in *Smith v. Allwright*. It announced,

> The United States is a constitutional democracy. Its organic law grants to all citizens a right to participate in the choice of elected officials without restriction by any state because of race. This grant to the people of the opportunity for choice is not to be nullified by a state through casting its electoral process in a form which permits a private organization to practice racial discrimination in the election. The privilege of membership in a party may be, as this Court said in *Grovey v. Townsend*, no concern of a state. But when, as here, that privilege is also the essential qualification for voting in a primary to select nominees for a general election, the state makes the action.[18]

By excluding losing primary candidates from general elections, and by requiring election officials to withhold ballots from those not qualified by party conventions, Texas had designated the party primary an integral feature of its elections, and by explicitly excluding individuals on the basis of race it had violated the Fifteenth Amendment. The Court also warned that new versions of the white primary would be struck down.[19]

What had changed the Court's mind? It is important to note the Court's composition: only two justices from *Grovey* remained; Roosevelt had appointed seven new justices after 1937.[20] Perhaps Roosevelt had appointed justices devoted to racial equality or stronger voting rights (or both). Or perhaps America's entry in World War II, alone or in combination with blacks' service in it, helped sway the Court. Historians have recently advanced both views, yet both are difficult to demonstrate. Suffrage expansions often occur during wartime, as states commonly recruit from the disenfranchised and mobilize popular support among politically unincorporated social groups. Still, the Court did not need to undertake these tasks and did not leave behind much of a paper trail suggesting it underwent a collective ideological transformation in support of voting rights. Meanwhile, Roosevelt, who was responsible for wartime mobilization policies, never called for black reenfranchisement. In fact, when discussing the poll tax, he made clear that he was not referring to blacks; theirs was a problem to be "handled separately."

Finally, the LDF's request that the DOJ submit a supportive brief on behalf of the plaintiffs in *Smith* fell on deaf ears, reportedly because of the Roosevelt administration's fears of the reaction of southern politicians.[21]

Whatever brought about the Court's decision, national and southern responses were immediate and similar—all thought it had enormous implications. The *New York Times* declared that the ruling brought the United States "a little nearer to a more perfect democracy." In the eyes of *Time* magazine, the decision activated a "ticking time bomb" for the South.[22] The *New York Times*'s Arthur Krock noted that southern congressional leaders were pessimistic about the prospects for evading *Smith* legally.[23] The Roosevelt administration had little reaction, but black protest and opinion leaders hailed the ruling.[24] LDF co-counsel Hastie wrote that Americans would soon realize that the "Supreme Court released and galvanized democratic forces which in turn gave the South the momentum it needed toward ultimate leadership in American liberalism." After reporting on the reactions to the decision by black GIs in combat on New Guinea, the *Chicago Defender* editorialized that the decision was a "milestone in the battle to fully integrate Negroes into the mainstream of American life." W.E.B. Du Bois considered it "an extraordinary victory, not only for black America but also for white democracy in the United States and in the world."[25]

Several white newspapers in the Outer South supported the decision. White observers in the Deep South were anxious, and politicians' reactions ranged from mild concern to outrage and declarations of defiance.[26] Some suggested that parties return to the nomination of candidates by convention (which, presumably, could remain white-only). Generally, Deep South party leaders announced their opposition to judicial interference, their skepticism that the ruling applied to their state, and their determination to maintain the status quo. Alabama governor Chauncey Sparks suggested that instead of openly defying the court's ruling, states could "adapt" by determining voter qualifications.[27]

The Smith *Shock and Enclave Options*

Initial responses by officials varied considerably. Differences in reactions to the ruling helped nonsoutherners sort the so-called "solid" South into Deep South and Outer South. In Texas, the South's nominal defender of the white primary, party officials decided that they were out of legal options.[28] Some Outer South states chose to acquiesce to the ruling.[29] The urban South, which overlapped considerably with the Outer South, offered many advantages to blacks seeking to capitalize on the ruling, including larger NAACP branches with which to finance legal efforts to nullify the ruling; greater probability of DOJ prosecutions of intransigent registrars; and generally a less alarmed white political elite. After the decision, the white primary remained in only one Outer South state (Florida), and all five Deep South states.[30]

Smith v. Allwright had three immediate implications. First, there was the possibility that parties would have to allow blacks to vote in the summer's primaries. Second, depending upon candidates' preferences, backgrounds, and campaign styles, *Smith v. Allwright* posed problems for some office-seekers and opportunities for others. Some could easily outflank opponents on white supremacy; others would need to articulate immediate policy responses to the ruling. Last, and most important, black activists would likely seek to exploit the ruling through voter registration and turnout campaigns, and might be met by white supremacist countermobilizations and violence.

The ruling challenged Deep South politicians in their capacities both as party leaders and as public authorities. As would be true of their responses to most democratization challenges, their options ranged from acquiescence to overt defiance. Between these poles lay delaying compliance through the courts or bureaucratic processes; intimidating rhetoric and other behaviors that might raise the perceived costs for insurgents and federal officials of securing compliance; and relying on their federal officeholders somehow to mitigate the problems posed by these interventions.

For instance, Alabama amended its constitution to require potential registrants to "understand and explain" the state constitution to the satisfaction of county boards of registrars. Before a federal court struck it down, the Boswell Amendment—and disfranchisement devices more generally—split Alabama's ruling party along sectional and class lines. Although those seeking to secure its ratification framed the plan to voters as a means of limiting black voting, enclave leaders actually sought to provide a backup disfranchising device in case the repeal of the poll tax produced too many poor white voters in the state's northern counties. The Boswell Amendment would, in the words of one Democratic politician, "keep the white electorate small and more easily within control."[31]

South Carolina

On the eve of *Smith v. Allwright*, factional conflict within South Carolina's legislature and party was only latent, and the party remained highly regulated by the state. Party politicians were united in their pragmatic and principled commitment to maintain the white primary. Observing increasingly emboldened black political mobilization and restive white supremacist groups in a wartime atmosphere of rising racial tensions, rulers anticipated numerous immediate problems if the white primary were abolished. These included black penetration of county-level party councils and a concomitant disruption of rent-seeking arrangements and racial violence. Most importantly, they feared the demise of one-party rule in South Carolina.

Capitalizing on the state's lack of factional conflict and pliant state party officials, enclave rulers quickly fastened upon a radical solution. By repealing all statutes and state regulations pertaining to party primaries, South Carolina Democrats would continue their all-white primary in a state party they viewed as a private club able to determine its own membership. They thus effectively privatized the state's only real mode of political competition. Through this deregulation, rulers blocked a plausible black incorporation, reactivated sectional conflict, delayed political reforms in a way that made the emergence of the Dixiecrats (or States' Rights Party) more likely, and sparked black organizing outside of the party. Thus, in the short term, this response both prevented the rapid entry of black politicians and voters into the party (as occurred in Texas) and short-circuited the rise of a white supremacist "Southern Democratic Party" opposed to the national party. Taking advantage of the "new" white primary system, black activists made massive strides in political organization and voter mobilization. Ultimately, federal courts struck down the deregulation response. By the time they had done so, however, the other political reforms delayed by deregulation helped position the party to take a leadership role in the Dixiecrat revolt.

Black Party Participation before Smith v. Allwright

By the time of the ruling, South Carolina's ruling party had maintained a half-century of black disfranchisement through a combination of the direct, white-only primary, constitutionally mandated literacy and residential requirements, the nonsecret ballot, and credible—if latent—threats of extralegal violence and coercion. After black disfranchisement had been secured in the century's first decade, the state's poll tax was limited only to the noncompetitive general elections (thus still deterring the formation of other parties that would rely on the mobilization of poorer whites, including textile workers in the upcountry). Politicians and resource-holders of both races viewed the white primary as by far the most significant barrier to black voting, and the most formidable institutional bulwark of one-party rule.[32]

Officeholders, civic organizations, and opinion leaders agreed on the importance of preserving it.[33] A few saw biracial discussions about black voting as a useful way to gather information about black elite preferences.[34] Others thought highly constricted black suffrage—limited to the well educated—might effectively co-opt black elites and legitimate the status quo. In any case, black registration and voting were minuscule.[35]

In 1935, following the *Grovey* decision, powerbrokers in the state Senate introduced legislation to repeal all state regulation of political parties.[36] According to their logic, if the state code were scrubbed of all references to party activity, the primary would be unassociated with "state action" and thus rendered safe from federal judicial challenge.[37] This was a truly radical step; the lines between the ruling party and state apparatus were often blurry. Indeed, when the party ran deficits conducting its primaries, the state legislature occasionally stepped in with contributions to erase them.[38]

Deregulation would mean that primary elections administered solely by the party itself would no longer be subject to criminal laws regarding fraud and corruption. Even by southern standards, South Carolina's elections during and after Reconstruction produced high levels of violence, disorder, and corruption. Governors had relied on the National Guard to deter or halt primary election violence in Charleston more than once in the 1930s. Thus, party chair Ben T. Leppard worried that the deregulation solution could lead to elections over which "the state would be without authority."[39] These early deliberations would reflect some dilemmas involved in coping with *Smith*.

In 1938, at the end of upcountry "millhand" Governor Olin Johnston's first term as governor, the General Assembly empowered "the state convention of any political party, organization, or association to add to or limit the qualifications for membership therein for voting in any state, county, or municipal primary election." After this law's passage, the party eliminated the Hampton Rule, which had allowed into the primary a very small number of black men who had long backed the Democrats.[40] Governor Johnston welcomed this move while gearing up for his campaign to capture the U.S. Senate seat held by the state's preeminent white supremacist demagogue, Ellison D. "Cotton Ed" Smith. Like most whites, and all white politicians in South Carolina, Johnston was committed to white supremacy. However, he was not a racial demagogue. Preparing for his race against Smith, he worried about appearing insufficiently committed to white supremacy. Thus, during the campaign he took credit for eliminating the Hampton Rule, declared the possibility of black suffrage dead, and tried to dismiss the issue.[41]

In 1943, Johnston, once again serving as governor, planned to challenge Smith in the 1944 Democratic senatorial primary.[42] In the interim, factional conflict had subsided (see chapter 3). However, elites grew more concerned about the ruling party's ability to safeguard its historic project. World War II disrupted agricultural labor markets and sparked divisive mill strikes, and the national party appeared increasingly unreliable in sorting out these matters (see chapter 5). On a more serious level, white supremacy seemed everywhere under threat. War production sparked rapid growth in several cities and small towns, particularly as blacks left rural areas for more lucrative manufacturing positions, often to compete with whites for jobs. This was, for South Carolina's whites, a new phenomenon, given the state's segregation of nonagricultural workplaces and firm owners' exclusion of blacks for all but the most menial positions.[43] The newly established federal Fair Employment Practices Committee (FEPC) exacerbated matters. In the 1942 elections, "work or fight" legislation—which threatened black men with military service if they did not work reliably as farmworkers—took center stage. Interracial tensions in cities, especially Charleston, often boiled over into racial violence. The membership and activities of white supremacist groups such as the Klan increased, while the specter of a more assertive black population loomed.

Throughout the South, whites worried about black rebellion fomented by "outsiders" and bemoaned the declining social deference of many blacks. In response, enclave rulers publicly warned blacks (and, occasionally, organized white supremacists to reinforce the message) that the state possessed tools to deter and repress racial disorder.[44] Finally, increasingly assertive black political mobilization worried many of the state's rulers, and provided electoral opportunities for white supremacists. Black groups had already demanded entry into the Democratic primaries. And in 1943 the state's NAACP announced the equalization of black and white teachers' salaries as its main goal and initiated a federal lawsuit in Charleston. The state's most virulent white supremacist politicians exploded in rage upon hearing this demand, and began covert organizational efforts in late 1943.[45] This group combined the rougher progeny of the wild-eyed populist demagoguery of "Pitchfork Ben" Tillman with lowcountry aristocrats increasingly troubled by the national party's alleged embrace of blacks. They sought to fashion a "Southern Democratic Party" (SDP) that would capture the state party's machinery and lead a regionwide revolt against Roosevelt. If blacks were successful in breaching the state party, the SDP would be ready to step in and serve as the state's hegemonic all-white party.[46]

In the 1940s, fueled by better-paying war jobs and army service, South Carolina's NAACP grew rapidly. By 1946 paid membership exceeded 10,000 and the number of branches increased from fifteen to forty-eight (see table 3.3). The state Republican party remained fractured into three groupings, none of which sought to win elections, and was thus an unattractive vehicle for blacks seeking to force their way into state electoral politics.[47] In January 1944 the South Carolina NAACP conference scheduled a black voter registration drive and initiated a call for the formation of "Fourth Term for Roosevelt Clubs" (first known as "Colored Democratic Clubs" and financed by black publisher John McCray's *Lighthouse and Informer*) throughout the state. Black leaders endorsed the idea, and McCray became the spokesman for the movement. McCray then called for the creation of a South Carolina Negro Democratic Party (later, the Progressive Democratic Party [PDP]) to parallel the official state party until blacks were fully incorporated into the latter, when the PDP would disband.[48] Just two weeks before *Smith*, activists began to plan this auxiliary party.[49]

Anticipating Smith v. Allwright

Worried by the 1941 *U.S. v. Classic* ruling, the state party soon began considering how to protect the white primary. As he left office in January 1943, Governor Jefferies voiced the preference of much of the state's political establishment that the white primary had to be saved, even if it meant risking greater election fraud likely in the absence of the deregulation of election administration. Olin Johnston's inaugural address echoed the recommendation.[50]

Party officials—most of whom were also legislators—proposed legislation to repeal the state's primary laws and provide that each political party "shall be the sole judge of the qualification of its members." Signed into law by Johnston in April 1943, the statutes would go into effect in June 1944. However, statutes criminalizing primary election fraud and regulating primaries in local elections remained, and some worried that their presence would lead to the invalidation of the "private" white primary that *Grovey* reversed.[51] This legislation provided a ready-made solution to *Smith v. Allwright*, and had the effect of limiting discussion of alternative responses.[52]

U.S. Senator "Cotton Ed" Smith, Johnston's opponent once again in the upcoming senatorial primary, called the ruling "the greatest crisis in the history of the South, far worse than even Reconstruction since the Democratic party had now betrayed the South." Media responses varied from apocalyptic predictions to the calm embrace of a multiparty system. The *Charleston News and Courier* immediately called for a return to the favored method of aristocrats—the use of party nominating conventions, the apportionment of which would greatly advantage lowcountry elites. Johnston denounced this as a ploy against the common white people of the state.[53]

Johnston convened a special session eleven days after the ruling so that the state could effect a complete deregulation of its political parties. In his speech to the state legislature, he declared that "White supremacy will be maintained in our primaries. Let the chips fall where they may."[54] The speech launched Johnston's Senate campaign, and black activists responded angrily to his muscular defense of political white supremacy.[55]

South Carolina politicians interested in winning statewide or federal office worried about the short-term implications of *Smith* and the possibility of black influence over Democratic nominations. But state legislators, and especially lowcountry and Barnwell Ring senators and House leaders, were concerned mainly about *Smith*'s longer-term implications for the party and its project. The decision did not threaten them personally in the short term, since all had seniority and regularly ran unopposed. Moreover, none had progressive political ambitions. Almost all of the large public spending projects from which legislators could benefit financially were situated in the lowcountry. Legislators in majority-black counties seemed electorally secure, as black mobilization efforts to date had occurred mainly in Charleston, Columbia, and upcountry towns.[56]

However, even electorally secure lowcountry legislators feared that in the long run black voting would disrupt the rent-seeking that sustained their domination of their home counties. Like Delta planters in Mississippi, they had good reason to worry. County party organizations in the Black Belt were so demobilized that the development of even a small black voting bloc might translate into significant black influence over county executive committees, platforms, and possibly delegations to the state party convention. Thus, there was a consensus on the need for a strong response to the ruling, even if authorities differed in their reasons for concern.

The range of available options open to legislators seemed quite narrow. The preemptive passage of some deregulation constrained their imaginations. Some legislators suggested tighter educational requirements for voter registration. Such proponents, including the state's most powerful politician, Senator Edgar Brown, were from the lowcountry, and preferred fewer upcountry white millworkers in statewide elections. Thus, they hoped that educational requirements would eliminate some white voters. The entire legislative leadership, however, backed Johnston's call for complete deregulation.[57] A recurring criticism of deregulation echoed that raised in 1935—a largely private party meant that there could be no criminalization of electoral fraud. Given the state's record of fraud and even occasional electoral violence, some worried that deregulation would result in a party riven by conflict and disorder.

However, support for deregulation trumped such concerns. Almost unanimously, the legislature repealed more than 150 bills relating to party primaries in the six-day session.[58] South Carolina's Democratic party was now a private organization. A few liberal white South Carolinians dissented, but generally a broad consensus favored the move. The state party's executive committee, with equal representation by county, heavily favored the lowcountry.[59]

The Black Party Challenge

South Carolina's black leadership was a small and relatively cohesive set of leaders of such groups as the NAACP, the Negro Citizens' Committee (NCC) (created by NAACP leaders to embark on partisan work the NAACP was forbidden to engage in), the brand-new Progressive Democratic Party (PDP), and the black wing of the Republican party.[60] In the 1930s the NCC formed as a statewide organization with numerous local affiliates to help blacks register and to raise funds for challenging the state's white primary. These groups pursued distinct but overlapping goals, and many leaders were active in several (or even all) of these organizations. Following party deregulation, Columbia blacks sought unsuccessfully to register in the primary in order to establish a fact pattern for a test case against the partly privatized party.[61]

The PDP demanded that state Democrats award it eight of its eighteen delegates to the 1944 National Convention; when denied, it announced it would send its own delegation to Chicago.[62] The PDP then held its own state convention (with 150 delegates from thirty-eight of forty-six counties), and voted to back the national ticket as well as its own slate of statewide candidates.[63] The creation of a black political party was a remarkable, unprecedented development in the twentieth-century South, and was the result in part of the NAACP's impressive statewide organizing during the late 1930s and early 1940s.

To boost morale and build more local-level club organizations, charismatic black activist Osceola McKaine announced his PDP candidacy for the U.S. Senate—South Carolina's first black senatorial candidate since 1872. Racial tensions in the lowcountry, especially Florence County, continued to simmer. Two companies of the state's Home Guard were placed on alert for riotous black voters.[64] Ultimately, McKaine officially received about 3,200 votes, most of which came from Charleston, Sumter, and Florence counties. On the campaign trail, McKaine called for the state to adopt a secret ballot in order to reduce the intimidation of black voters.[65] Although McKaine lost, his candidacy, and the challenge to win delegates at the national convention, initiated a frequent black challenge to the ruling party. From 1940 to 1947, black voter registration increased from 0.8 to 13 percent (table 9.4). Enclave rulers now had to wrestle with the prospect of growing black political mobilization supported by resurgent protest organizations, as the startling growth of the NAACP in South Carolina demonstrated (table 3.3).[66]

Back to the Courts

The 1944 South Carolina senatorial election launched a complex legal fight over the constitutionality of the state's privatized primary and the exclusion of blacks from voting and participation in party affairs. This long battle activated latent sectional splits between upcountry and lowcountry county parties, and within the party's executive committee. Upcountry county parties agreed to comply with court rulings to allow blacks to vote and participate in party decision-making institutions, while the party's executive committee, still controlled by lowcountry representatives, ordered all county parties to defy court orders.[67]

In 1947 black groups filed an injunction in federal court to nullify the Democratic party's white primary. Party attorneys, arguing that the case should be dismissed, "termed the party primary 'a private nominating venture.'" U.S. Federal District Court Judge Waties Waring—a Charleston aristocrat and recent convert to racial equality—struck down the white primary. For Waring, the claim that "there is any material difference in the governance of the Democratic party in this state prior to, or subsequent to, 1944, is pure sophistry.... It is time for South Carolina to rejoin the Union. It is time to fall in step with the other states and to adopt the American way of conducting elections." The Fourth Circuit Court of Appeals affirmed Waring's ruling, and the Supreme Court refused to review the decision.[68]

While Governor Strom Thurmond professed to be "shocked" by the decision, and predicted that all Americans would rue the day it was made, editors of the (white) *Columbia Record* actually welcomed it as an accelerator of the state's transition to a two-party system.[69] Party leaders, however, still fought to maintain a white party. Prominent political journalist and adviser to the ruling party, William D. Workman, condemned Waring for his "usurpation of party prerogatives," but rejected the wisdom of legal challenges given Waring's threat to jail noncompliant party officials. Workman also rejected the call by some simply to surrender the Democratic party to "blacks and scalawags." Rather, he advocated "rigid educational or property qualifications" for all voters. Given abysmally low absolute levels of—and massive racial inequalities in—literacy and per capita elementary school expenditures (see chapter 3), such an "objective" standard could be highly effective in allowing for only the most gradual extension of suffrage to blacks and poorer whites. However, the sectional splits mentioned above frustrated efforts of party officials to restrict black voting through new educational requirements.[70]

The state party interpreted court rulings as allowing only "qualified" blacks—those registered to vote in the general election—to vote in the primary. It claimed compliance with this decision, but denied blacks "party membership."[71] This meant that blacks could vote only by presenting registration certificates demonstrating that they were qualified voters. It also meant that blacks could not participate in party decision-making, such as precinct meetings or county or state conventions. But Democrats in (upcountry) Greenville County permitted blacks to vote in primaries, and dropped a loyalty oath that the state party had recently instituted to weed out black voters.[72] As the state's most populous county, Greenville posed a real challenge to the state party's executive committee, as did Democrats in five other upcountry counties that defied the state party and complied with federal law. Observers noted that upcountry whites were capitalizing on black votes in statewide elections.[73]

Judge Waring's new preliminary injunction ordered the Democratic party to open enrollment of party membership rolls to blacks. Waring also struck down the party's loyalty oath. In 1948 blacks contested party posts in Columbia; five lowcountry gubernatorial candidates withdrew in disgust from the 1948 primary. According to one estimate, 35,000 blacks voted in the primary.[74] Higher courts affirmed his rulings and invalidated the "Alabama Plan" (requiring voters to interpret the state's constitution). In 1950 the General Assembly began restoring laws regulating primaries. Soon, four blacks won seats on the Columbia Democratic party executive committee. Thus ended the period of *formal* legal guarantees of white supremacy in statutes and party rules.[75]

Implications for the Future

South Carolina's ruling politicians shared a consensus to block the incorporation of blacks into their ruling party. Having anticipated the abolition of the white primary, they came to agree on a single, state-level policy response: the complete deregulation of the party. However, other options existed, including an abandonment of nominations by primary and a return to nomination by convention, or stiffer educational and property qualifications for voter registration. But both would have heightened factional conflict within the ruling party by disadvantaging poorer whites in the state's upcountry. In the short term, deregulation prevented the beginning of an incorporation of ambitious black politicians and resource-holders into the ruling party, as occurred in Texas. In blocking this incorporation, South Carolina Democrats avoided a much more volatile scenario as proposed by the virulently white supremacist Southern Democratic Party.[76]

As Hanes Walton suggests, South Carolina's rulers could have foregone the deregulation route and instead moved to "curtail"—formally or informally, legally or extralegally—the PDP's activities. After all, the Supreme Court had not declared its opposition to the range of legal and extralegal tools of repression employed throughout the region—and would refrain from doing so for two decades. But by choosing the deregulation path, "the way was open for the PDP."[77] And, starting in 1944 and continuing for more than a decade, the PDP set a major regional precedent by challenging the seating of the "regular" state party's delegates at the national party's convention.

The adoption of the deregulation plan was in direct tension with efforts to modernize the state's electoral administration by introducing the secret ballot and repealing the use of the poll tax in general elections. Both reforms would have aided minor-party movements. However, as long as state leaders sought to lobby for the constitutionality of deregulation, they could not afford to draft legislation securing these reforms without reasserting the role of the state in the administration of primary elections.[78] The reforms were not achieved until 1949 and 1950; thus, the state party would be able to consider abandoning the national party in 1948 without being too concerned about jeopardizing its hegemonic status vis-à-vis other political movements (see chapter 5)—a luxury that rulers in Georgia could not afford.

Mississippi

Mississippi's rulers responded defiantly to *Smith v. Allwright*. The effective use of threatened white-on-black violence helped deter a very large black mobilization to exploit *Smith*. Thus, the ruling had little immediate impact on black registration or voting. While the state's Democrats agreed on the need to preserve the white primary, sectional differences and the relatively decentralized nature of party-state authority resulted in few innovations by the party or the state to weaken black mobilization.

Black Party Participation before Smith v. Allwright

As war clouds appeared on the horizon, the state's white rulers foresaw no real threats to the white primary or one-party rule. They sincerely believed that "their" blacks had no desire to participate in electoral politics. In the event that the white primary or other barriers to black suffrage weakened, these rulers believed that low educational levels, apathy, and intimidation would prevent blacks from capitalizing on such changes.

However, there was some difference of opinion. Generally, politicians from majority-black counties in the Delta and elsewhere were more concerned about lowering barriers to suffrage. While coordinating to secure better black schooling, Delta elites actively opposed educational reforms that might awaken black political aspirations. For example, in 1940 they unsuccessfully sought to amend legislation providing free textbooks in order to prevent the distribution to black schools of civics textbooks that mentioned democratic rights and duties.[79] And they defeated attempts from 1935 to 1940 by Senator Theodore Bilbo and Governor Paul B. Johnson—Hills populists—to repeal the state's poll tax. True, there were nonracial incentives for Delta politicians to seek to maintain the poll tax—by the 1930s it dampened white Hills turnout much more than black turnout. But the fact that Delta legislators could strategically invoke the repeal's implications for black voting testified to the greater political salience for them of these dangers.[80]

War somewhat disrupted the state's racialized political economy. First, the substantial share of the state's black population inducted into the armed forces—some 78,000—merged with growing consciousness-raising among blacks to change black elite goals. Rather than seeking marginal policy improvements, groups such as the black teachers' organization began to call for the equalization of teachers' salaries, and to consult with Thurgood Marshall and the NAACP concerning the pursuit of lawsuits on behalf of black teachers. In 1942 even the typically cautious statewide network of black leaders, the Committee of One Hundred, vowed to pursue more aggressive demands, including voting rights. Second, service in the armed forces and black female participation in better-paying industrial jobs in factories along the booming Gulf Coast and in Memphis raised incomes for locals. This fueled, as elsewhere, a rise in the number and size of NAACP branches statewide (table 3.3), despite the fact that the national office did precious little to build the organization in Mississippi compared to its investments in other states. As Thurgood Marshall would remark in 1950 to a high-ranking member of the national office, "We have never done a good job in Mississippi." The branches also organized a state conference in 1946.[81]

Third, throughout the Black Belt, tighter labor markets for black agricultural laborers and domestic servants, and growing concerns about a decline in black deference toward whites and adherence to Jim Crow norms—especially among younger blacks—made a return to the prewar status quo less likely. Interviewers from the federal Bureau of Agricultural Economics found that many white Deltans sincerely believed popular rumors of regionwide and coordinated black rebellions fomented by outsiders, including Eleanor Roosevelt.[82]

Fourth, friction between off-duty black servicemen and whites in small towns near military training bases, as well as between blacks and whites on these bases, fueled deadly skirmishes at Camp Shelby, Camp McCain, and Camp Van Dorn.[83] Fifth, in 1944 and 1945 returning black servicemen transformed local protest patterns. Their very presence in some towns and cities sparked white assaults, as in Jackson, by uniformed white policemen. Such incidents led Percy Greene, editor and publisher of the *Jackson Advocate*, and the Committee of One Hundred and other organizations to demand the hiring of black police.[84] In general, the war produced social and economic dislocation, white fears of an unreliable black labor supply, emboldened returning veterans, and larger and more ambitious black protest organizations.

Meanwhile, on the eve of *Smith*, the means by which rulers maintained white supremacy in the political sphere remained effective. Other than a few exceptions, the white primary, the recently strengthened poll tax, and literacy and residency requirements secured an all-white Democratic electorate.[85]

Responding to Smith

Rulers' responses to *Smith v. Allwright* were predictable. Conservative former governor Mike Conner remarked that the decision was "in accord with the policies and purposes of the New Deal," which had "repudiated the principles of the Democratic party." Governor Tom Bailey, while also conservative, was more closely aligned with the Roosevelt administration and remained fairly quiet. Firebrand U.S. Representative John Rankin, whose

Tupelo district had few blacks, declared, "One of my greatest fears has been realized." The state's white press was outraged.[86]

Other party elites were more subdued. Because statewide and legislative elections were held in odd-numbered years, Mississippi politicians faced little pressure to develop a quick response to the ruling. Other than a few municipal elections, the state's blacks could not seek to capitalize on the ruling in 1944.[87] Because of this, rulers lacked urgency in staking out potentially difficult positions on the issue, as occurred in South Carolina. This fact, combined with the absence of pressure on the ruling party by white supremacist groups, encouraged the party to delay its response. Relative to its counterparts in other Deep South states, the Klan remained dormant.[88] Like other Deep South state parties, Mississippi's party took the position that *Smith* applied only to Texas and changed none of its own practices.

Inspired by the decision, younger black activists inside and outside Mississippi's NAACP considered a legal challenge to the state's white primary. Some worried that the NAACP was too far ahead of black public opinion. Blacks had no access to the polls in the July municipal elections in Jackson. Eventually, they decided to accede to Thurgood Marshall's advice and wait for a federal election to challenge the state party's dismissal of *Smith*.[89]

In December 1944, Percy Greene's black newspaper, the *Jackson Advocate*, began publishing a series of editorials that cited discrimination by registrars and other practices—not the poll tax—as the main barriers to black voting. Throughout 1945 more black veterans returned to Mississippi, and many enrolled at Jackson State, Tougaloo, and other schools. They founded a Mississippi branch of the regional Progressive Voters League (PVL) and chose T. B. Wilson as its president. Because it was an indigenous and nonpartisan educational organization, white politicians considered the PVL less threatening than the NAACP. Better able to secure support from black church and lodge leaders, its membership grew quickly.[90] As was the case throughout the South, Mississippi's PVL shared leadership, members, strategy, and tactics with the state's NAACP.

Black activists in early 1946 delivered a public statement to Governor Bailey and the legislature that seemed to wake up lawmakers to the need to act. In it, they threatened federal lawsuits if the state did not improve black schools or enhance black access to the ballot.[91] The PVL board asked the state Democratic executive committee (SDEC) to clarify party rules regarding black voting in the upcoming primary. The SDEC comprised three representatives from each of five fairly apportioned congressional districts. Unlike other Deep South party institutions, Mississippi's SDEC was thus less vulnerable to capture by a particular sectional interest.

Although the SDEC met, it did not answer the PVL demand or announce a change in policy. Privately, it concluded that blacks were legally permitted to participate in the party's primary, and considered means of deterring activists. However, it failed to issue instructions to county parties or election commissioners.[92] Black veterans in Jackson led efforts to help others read and interpret Mississippi's Constitution, and inform other veterans about their voting rights. Because of the understandable fears many blacks had about traveling to county courthouses to register to vote and pay their poll taxes, veterans organized large groups to travel together. None, however, traveled to the Delta, which they considered too dangerous.[93]

Legislators clearly differed over the urgency of crafting a state-level response to the ruling. Deltan Fielding Wright, an influential member of the Senate and future Dixiecrat leader, sought the passage of a statute along the lines of the South Carolina plan that would privatize state regulations of the primary.[94] Wright had already planned to run for governor in 1947, and he hoped to demonstrate his leadership to the Delta. However, most legislators bypassed deregulation because they did not fear black suffrage.[95] Indeed, the legislature exempted veterans from paying poll taxes for one year. In signing the law, Governor Bailey claimed that other devices would prevent black primary voting. Legislators allied with U.S. Senator Bilbo had long sought a full repeal of the poll tax, and the veterans' exemption served as a useful way to advance the cause. Thus, sectional interests led to differing perceptions of the threat of black voting. However, these differences did not extend into electoral politics. At the end of the session, the entire Senate issued a proclamation endorsing Wright's gubernatorial bid. Given the traditional election of a non-Delta governor, this proclamation underscored the degree to which sectional conflict in the legislature had subsided.[96]

The 1946 Senatorial Election

In 1946, Senator Bilbo's reelection campaign proved the state's most important political event. Long the Senate's most infamous racial demagogue and one of the South's most reliable New Deal supporters, he had never campaigned primarily on white supremacy. But Bilbo's rhetoric, and the reactions it sparked, marked the turning point in the party's response to *Smith v. Allwright*. From town to town, Bilbo stoked white fears of black insurgency at home and federal intrusion from "abroad." As the primary drew nearer, he also warned blacks not to vote.[97] The DOJ refused to protect black voters despite a wealth of evidence of both past violence and possible future violence. The lack of federal protection for black activists and voters was not a problem of just the 1960s, of course, but of prior decades as well.[98] Bilbo rejected the NAACP's call for federal marshals to observe the election, committed his own legal assistance to any whites facing legal proceedings for protecting white supremacy by guarding the polls, and scoffed at the possibility of federal prosecutors' securing convictions in Mississippi.[99]

The headline of the *Jackson Daily News* warned blacks, "DON'T TRY IT!" The paper's editor, Fred Sullens, also reminded potential black primary voters, as well as the state party (which had not publicized the rule), that state law required that participants in party primaries must vow to support the party's nominee in the general election and have been in accord with the party over the prior two years.[100] Many leading politicians and journalists viewed Bilbo's rhetoric as counterproductive, for it might hasten federal interference in state elections.[101] One of Bilbo's opponents charged that, were it not for Bilbo's race-baiting rhetoric, "there would be no registered Negroes and no attempt by them to vote on July 2." This was wrong, of course; efforts to mobilize black voting preceded the campaign. But this view summed up ruling politicians' ignorance of black activists' preferences and behaviors.[102] Ultimately, about 2,500 blacks voted in the primary, about one-third of the total number registered. Abuses of blacks and their ballots varied considerably.[103] In some areas, whites allowed black voting. In others, including the all-black community of Mound Bayou, county sheriffs attempted to void black votes on the grounds that the voters were not actually loyal party members. Black voters faced threats of violence and beatings before and after voting by law enforcement officials and private actors.[104]

Bilbo won a huge victory, including a majority of the Delta, the traditional base of his opposition. Confidential elite interviews and newspaper reports agreed that Bilbo's opposition to the Fair Employment Practice Committee (FEPC) and to black voting convinced thousands of Delta whites, including planters and other economic elites, to support him for the first time.[105] The 1946 senatorial primary was the first federal election in Mississippi since 1944, and black activists used witness reports to file complaints of voting rights violations with the Justice Department. They sent thirty-odd affidavits, but U.S. Assistant Attorney General Thomas Caudle announced that no investigation would occur because of "insufficient evidence." Blacks and two white voters, soon joined by national black protest groups, then filed a formal complaint with the U.S. Senate Special Committee to Investigate Senatorial Campaign Expenditures, charging that Bilbo's rhetoric created a climate of violence and intimidation.[106]

The committee, motivated primarily by partisan (Republican) motives to embarrass national Democrats, held an extraordinary set of hearings in Jackson. This public examination of black suffrage restriction had been unprecedented at either the state or national level since the late nineteenth century, and it initiated a long period of at least intermittent federal government and national media attention on the state. Almost two hundred blacks, most of them veterans, registered to testify, and almost seventy did so.[107] In his defense, Bilbo claimed that party rules forbade black voters, but a party official refuted this claim, revealing that the SDEC had privately ruled to permit black voting.[108]

The hearings were significant in other ways. First, they informed rulers of black organizing efforts, and especially of the critical role of veterans in exploiting the temporary poll tax exemption.[109] Many county-level politicians knew of black mobilization efforts, but state leaders often did not. This knowledge helped build support among party politicians for a state legislative response to the white primary's abolition—along the lines of Wright's deregulation proposal. Second, they revealed a split within the party on membership and voting requirements. Third, the hearings sparked much larger voter registration efforts by black veterans.

If rulers had been complacent since *Smith*, they now snapped to attention. In December 1946, Mississippi's Democrats began to deliberate seriously about their response to *Smith v. Allwright*. At this early stage of the assault on enclaves, it may seem obvious that rulers were united in preferring the continued exclusion of blacks from party affairs. For Georgia, this assumption is incorrect. But in Mississippi, as in South Carolina, rulers were indeed unified in preferring an all-white party.[110]

Party rulers differed in their views on the magnitude of the threat of black insurgency. Estimates of the number of black voters in the 1946 primaries hovered between 2,500 and 4,000. But because of the failure to collect and maintain centralized registration statistics, politicians differed widely in their estimates of how many blacks attempted to register and vote (the highest estimate was 40,000). This led to very different expectations about the effectiveness of different suffrage restriction devices, including registrars' use of the "understanding" clause; interracial elite negotiation; intimidation of, and violence against, voters; and vote-counting chicanery.

As blacks mobilized to pay poll taxes before the February 1, 1947, deadline, it was unclear how many blacks would register in time for that year's gubernatorial primary. There was also uncertainty over the possibility of defying *Smith* through party deregulation, as in South Carolina. Litigation over South Carolina's party deregulation had begun, and Mississippi politicians were uncertain about its outcome. Some even despaired of finding any effective method of suffrage restriction and called for a countermobilization of white voters. Finally, state officials, and particularly Acting Governor Fielding Wright, did not know what restrictions a legislative majority might accept; he traveled throughout the state to sound out legislators on a possible special session, and on deregulation.[111]

Possible strategies varied by level of governance (county or state), by their bluntness (that is, the likelihood of restricting suffrage among poor whites), and by their subsequent impact on party-state capacities to fend off further threats to enclave rule. Before the special session, viable options included doing nothing (on the view that county officials would manage local challenges); a South Carolina–style deregulation; the enforcement or tightening of state constitutional requirements of literacy and education;

and even the abandonment of the primary and a return to nomination by convention. The latter was a nonstarter, however, given white farmers' embrace of the direct primary as their signal political achievement after the Populist revolt.[112]

Mirroring debates at the constitutional convention of 1890, state-level solutions could produce widely different consequences for different regions of the state. For instance, the liberalization of primary voting rules would likely increase voting by both blacks and poorer whites—both likely to weaken the political power of Delta planters. The converse was also plausible—tightened suffrage requirements applied equally to both races might well advantage Delta elites. Although white elites and most voters throughout the state backed white supremacy, the electoral consequences of the white primary's abolition worried white politicians in Delta counties—then more than 70 percent black—much more than those in other parts of the state.

Regardless of strategy, most party politicians sought to avoid a choice that necessitated a constitutional convention. As discussed in chapter 3, governors frequently made such calls, and always were rejected.[113] Usually, county-level interests feared reversing the state's relatively sharp decentralization of power. Finally, for those gubernatorial candidates who sought to avoid—for whatever reason—a race-baiting campaign, there was a temporal constraint—black primary voting needed to be halted or weakened before the August 1947 primary.

Finding significant support for his deregulation plan, Governor Wright convened a special session. In his opening address, Wright surveyed the high stakes. He lambasted *Smith v. Allwright* and criticized unwanted interference in the state's politics. He declared that Mississippi "shall ever vigorously defend [its] right" to provide for voting qualifications and that the state would "preserve and maintain the dignity and integrity of the Democratic party in this State." On policy options, though, he deferred to constitutional experts.[114] With an eye to avoiding the potential damage caused by overheated rhetoric in lawsuits defending enclave practices, Wright carefully avoided defending white supremacy by name.

Legislators considered several options. First, deregulation would be more difficult in Mississippi than in South Carolina, for the state's constitution required that the legislature regulate primaries; thus, deregulation could not go into effect without a constitutional amendment, and this could not occur until November at the earliest, after the gubernatorial election. This delay, combined with its uncertain constitutional validity, rendered deregulation unpopular. Some legislators favored waiting to allow time for federal courts to rule on the South Carolina plan. Delta legislators, as well as Governor Wright, rejected this option. Others sought better implementation of educational restrictions; this meant restricting voter registration, not party participation. Other options included empowering county commissioners to develop difficult qualifications on their own that would not be subject to appeal; adopting Arkansas's device of requiring that voters swear their fealty (punishable by perjury) to a party's stated principles; and allowing county committees to conduct annual registrations of voters during which their qualifications might be challenged.

The House quickly passed a bill allowing parties to administer an oath to party at polling places. Senate opposition focused on the possibility that a party faction seizing a county's party executive committee could use re-registration to disfranchise the opposing faction. Two senators criticized black disfranchisement, and one even denounced segregation—dissent not present in South Carolina's deliberations at its special session.[115] The party principles bill passed, as did legislation granting county executive committees greater discretion over voter registration as well as the authority to challenge applicants on their loyalty to party principles.[116] National media mocked the arrangement.[117]

Party chair Judge Hubert Holmes, addressing the SDEC, declared that "there are those who have participated in our primaries who were of a different political faith.... Let us tighten up the belt of democracy and exclude from our party those who are not in accord with the principles as enunciated by Thomas Jefferson and Woodrow Wilson." A Delta-dominated party subcommittee then enumerated the party's principles.[118] House Speaker Walter Sillers hoped that the party's actions would serve "to exclude, if possible, [its] infiltration [by] those who would destroy it." After the unwelcome intrusion of the Bilbo hearings, state politicians avoided discussions of white supremacy in deliberations over party principles.[119] The state and state party behaved as one. But the state party, as one leading member of the State Democratic Executive Committee admitted, lacked administrative capacity to enforce county- and local-level compliance with the party loyalty requirement. Generally, and in contrast to Key's view that enclave decisions resulted from intemperate Bilboites, evidence suggests that rulers' choices were determined by estimates of threat levels facing the party, the administrative or legal difficulty of implementing options, and temporal constraints. Leading actors were economic elites who encountered institutional and factional constraints and had good reason to be cautious about the long-term efficacy of the deregulation option.[120]

Black groups, already featuring overlapping memberships, now began coordinating their activities. In an extraordinary meeting in Jackson, their leaders decided to ask black voters to affirm the SDEC's party principles.[121] Uncomfortably for Mississippi's Progressive Voters League (PVL), the national PVL approved a platform that clashed directly with them. Wilson, PVL's president, urged blacks to vote in the Democratic primaries but also acknowledged that some preferred Republican candidates, despite the fact that black activists in Mississippi did not consider using the Republican party as a political vehicle (the state Republican party remained until 1952 nothing more than a patronage operation).[122] As they confided to Alexander Heard, black Republicans blocked voter registration efforts in their two strongholds, Vicksburg and Natchez. Meanwhile, veterans in Jackson trained voters on registration regulations and publicized Truman's address to the NAACP convention in Washington.[123] Despite these efforts, black voter registration rose only to about 1 percent of the state's black voting-age population in 1947 (see table 9.4). Primarily because of voter intimidation, black insurgency in Mississippi remained extremely weak.

On the eve of the August 1947 gubernatorial primary, about twelve thousand blacks were registered, and about half voted.[124] The PVL recommended that blacks report themselves to be in accordance with party principles, and added, "We believe that such things as the FEPC, poll tax, and lynching laws should be left to the states." It also noted that "our members are being advised to create no disturbance if their vote is challenged and they are turned away." Rejecting the view that the principles were chosen to depress black turnout, SDEC chair Herbert Holmes noted that the loyalty oath would be required of all voters, and that he expected that some whites would be challenged. Reports suggested that election officials generally did not administer the oath requirement to black voters.[125] Moreover, blacks generally faced less opposition than they had in 1946.[126]

During the special election to replace the now-deceased Bilbo, however, black turnout was lower. In a close race, John Stennis defeated William Colmer (and others) by about five thousand votes. Mississippi's white liberals and black voters preferred the more rhetorically moderate Stennis.[127] Significantly, there was no "party" decision or behavior regarding black voting— only some counties "tightened their belts."

In 1948, during the burgeoning Dixiecrat revolt, U.S. Senator Jim Eastland (D-MS) prodded legislators to push through a proposed state constitutional amendment that would require voters to be of "good moral character." As a device to restrict suffrage, this would be a very powerful county-level tool to be used at the discretion of registrars. Eastland worried about the prospects of black voting, especially in the Delta, if federal anti-poll tax legislation were passed. After the amendment passed, however, opposition grew among many county-level politicians, who worried that factions would be able to punish one another with such a flexible instrument. Party leaders, including House Speaker Sillers, decided not to campaign for its passage, and observers agreed that this doomed the amendment's popular ratification (which failed by more than a three-to-one margin). The goal of turning back democratization challenges—or at least certain means of doing so—could sometimes be in tension with intraparty factional politics.[128]

Implications for the Future

Mississippi Democrats were not pressured by their electoral calendar to act in 1944. Moreover, the state's relatively weaker black protest capacity meant that black Mississippians were less ready to capitalize on the ruling. Thus, severe threats to white supremacy—while attractive to some Democrats as a campaign issue—did not loom on the horizon for many Mississippi politicians. By the time most politicians determined they had to act, the deregulation plan seemed riskier. As the South Carolina case revealed, the stakes were about more than merely black voting. Balancing sectional differences in threat assessments and in preferred strategies, the state's officeholders chose to empower county-level party actors to allow or disallow black voting. The *Smith* shock would not have major short-term effects on the Magnolia state, in stark contrast to Georgia.

Georgia

In the Deep South, the abolition of the white primary had the greatest impact on Georgia. In the context of sharp factional conflict, the ruling sparked impressive black mobilization across the state. Soon, the enclave response to the ruling dominated the gubernatorial election of 1946 and contributed to the triumph of the white supremacist Talmadge faction. Subsequent efforts by white moderates to build alternative political movements almost fractured the ruling party. For Georgia, *Smith v. Allwright* induced such chaos within the ruling party that its leaders would opt to keep the party on the sidelines of the Dixiecrat revolt. In the longer run, the outcome of the 1946 gubernatorial election helped to weaken anti-Talmadge forces for almost two decades, thus ensuring that the Talmadgeites would be at the helm during the critical 1950s.

Black Political Participation before Smith v. Allwright

In 1900 in an effort to attract Populist voters back to their party, conservative Georgia Democrats codified an all-white primary in party rules.[129] Observing state politics from his position at Atlanta University, W.E.B. Du Bois declared that the white primary's real victims were not blacks—who by then were already disfranchised by other devices and practices—but poor whites.[130] By the 1920s state law regulated party primaries, primary voter qualifications, and registration requirements. However, state law did not require county parties to use a secret ballot for primary elections, unlike general elections; few did so.[131]

As discussed in chapter 3, by 1940 Georgia's black population was the nation's largest. It comprised more than one-third of the state's voting-age population, and about one-third of its 159 counties were majority-black (see figure 3.3). White supremacy in the political sphere relied on the white primary and county-unit system, as well as the county-level implementation of the poll tax and other constitutionally established requirements.[132]

Blacks voted only, and sparingly, in general elections for Republican candidates, and in municipal elections in Atlanta and a few other cities.[133] Black registration and voting in fact declined over the first four decades of the century. By 1940 it stood at 3 percent of the state's black voting-age population (table 9.4). As occurred elsewhere, black protest organizations diffused throughout the state (table 3.3). Black soldiers based at Fort Benning and in Atlanta organized NAACP membership and voter registration drives, and better-paying industrial jobs drew blacks to cities and supported membership dues.

Factional Conflict on the Eve of Smith

In 1942, two years before *Smith*, the anti-Talmadge faction successfully coordinated behind a single candidate—Attorney General Ellis Arnall. Capitalizing on several scandals and miscues that occurred in his opponent's camp, Arnall upset incumbent governor Gene Talmadge.[134] In 1942 Talmadge, long benefiting from his domination of enough "two-unit" counties to win the gubernatorial nomination administered under the county-unit system, was seeking the state's first four-year gubernatorial term in his ninth statewide campaign.[135] His defeat, declared *Time* magazine, "ended the reign of the most high-handed, low-browed local dictator that U.S. politics has known since the days of the late Huey Long."[136]

Arnall benefited from Talmadge's reputation as an "imitation Hitler," and on certain occasions countered Talmadge's central message of defending white supremacy with racist rhetoric of his own.[137] Nevertheless, Arnall had a reputation among Georgia's black protest leaders and those elsewhere as racially progressive, and the *Pittsburgh Courier* and *Chicago Defender* interpreted his victory as proving that the "Race Issue Is Dead in Dixie" and signaling a democratic awakening.[138]

White anti-Talmadge officeseekers, activists, and others did not come together in a cohesive, durable faction. They disagreed among themselves on important issues, but all agreed that Talmadge and his supporters harmed their interests. Their agendas highlighted state-sponsored economic development and political reforms. The political reforms—most importantly reapportionment, as well as the reduction of political corruption—were in a sense most urgent, since reapportioning the state legislature would be necessary to secure economic development policies seen to benefit north

Georgia. Democratizing reforms, such as the easing or elimination of suffrage restriction and the destruction of state-mandated segregation, were not priorities. Indeed, most did not support these moves. Most mainstream anti-Talmadgeites were "good-government" moderates interested in ending political corruption. A much smaller group of liberals were critical of white supremacy but more active as economic liberals (supporting unions, critiquing corporate dominance of taxation and other policies, and so forth).[139]

As governor from 1943 to 1947, the nationally ambitious Arnall won one stunning legislative success after another. He repaired the state's higher education and penal systems, secured numerous state governmental administrative and budgetary reforms, restored (with the benefit of the war) the state's fiscal health, and repealed the state's poll tax. Others credited him also for lowering the state's voting age to eighteen, and implementing the federal Soldiers' Voting Act.

In general, on the eve of *Smith*, key members of both party factions did not believe that blacks or others threatened white supremacy in the political or social spheres. Politicians could observe that precious few blacks paid their poll tax. Party leaders did not substantially alter party regulations in the years before *Smith*.[140] Arnall's election and vast popularity among voters and legislators also support the view that Georgia's ruling class did not perceive clouds of racial threat looming on the horizon. Factional conflict in the early 1940s persisted, but Arnall's skillful leadership seemed to have weakened the Talmadge faction. Events would soon alter this assessment. Even so, anti-Talmadgeites evinced no desire to depart from the consensus on white supremacy.

Immediately after the ruling, Arnall remained silent, while Talmadge decried both the U.S. Supreme Court's decision and Arnall's inaction. Meanwhile, the ongoing Constitutional Revision Commission—chaired by Arnall—examined existing provisions pertaining to primary elections; its private deliberations suggest that leading politicians, including Arnall, endorsed South Carolina's deregulation plan.[141] By early May 1944 several thousand blacks had registered in an orchestrated campaign, but party chair J. Lon Duckworth announced that the July primary would remain white-only.[142] Black groups around the state criticized the resolution and reaffirmed their intent to participate; however, few county committees or precincts allowed them to do so. Meanwhile Arnall, after his initial silence, called *Smith* "a blow to liberalism" and claimed that attempts to incorporate blacks and federal (as opposed to state-level) anti–poll tax legislation would weaken his reform agenda.[143]

The NAACP branch in Columbus financed a test suit against county officials to apply *Smith v. Allwright* in Georgia. Black activist Primus King filed in federal court against the Muscogee County (Columbus) Democratic party committee, seeking $5,000 in damages for his being barred from voting in the party primary.[144] The party demurred, concluding that Georgia Democrats were not party to *Smith v. Allwright*.

Rulers' Beliefs and Preferences

Georgia's rulers imagined several options before them. The first, which would be the de facto choice if a new constitution were not ratified, was to do nothing. This would place the issue directly in the hands of federal courts, which would decide whether Primus King's suit would invalidate party rules. Second, the deregulation option, endorsed by Arnall and the commission, was a live option. Third, as proposed by some black groups, the legislature could acquiesce to a desegregated party primary but adopt new qualifications for voter registration. Fourth, the party could adopt new ostensibly nonracial qualifications for party "membership." Fifth, the party could delegate to county parties the authority to restrict black turnout.

A few institutional features of Georgia's party-state structured the debate. First, given the governor's relatively greater influence within the legislature (see chapter 3), it would be somewhat more difficult than in other enclaves for a rural-dominated legislature to overwhelm Arnall's preferences. Second, the county-unit system effectively insulated gubernatorial elections from the possible harms of black voting. Although blacks had voting-age majorities in approximately forty-seven counties, the vast majority of registered black voters then inhabited the largest cities, which were in the electorally irrelevant six-unit counties. Thus, there was less urgency than there would have been in the absence of the county-unit system. Third, Talmadgeite concerns about the maintenance of the county-unit system were in tension with a deregulation response. This tension played a critical role in the state's deliberations, and deserves a closer look.

As discussed in chapter 3, the state code protected the county-unit system. More than two decades after legislators from small counties safeguarded the system by changing it from a party rule to state law, the Talmadge faction feared that party regulations barring electoral fraud and establishing rules for settling contested legislative elections—then quite common—were vulnerable to attack by its opponents, who might someday control state party machinery. Thus, after a resounding victory in 1940, the Talmadge-dominated party, in response to the heavily corrupt administration of former Governor Eurith "E. D." Rivers, quickly secured recount and other antifraud rules via statute.[145] Deregulation would thus mean transferring the county-unit system and antifraud statutes governing primaries from state law to party regulation, and thus place them at risk. While some Talmadgeite forces would, in the period 1945–1948, support deregulation, many remained concerned about the corruption of the electoral administration.

Regarding *Smith v. Allwright*, Arnall's decision seemed to have been to take no action. He chose not to call a special session to respond to the decision. Even in his January 1945 State of the State address, he failed to mention the white primary.[146] In calling for a repeal of the poll tax, he saw "no danger" that, in its absence, black voting would harm the party given the presence of the white primary; however, he refused to articulate a plan for defending the white primary.[147]

The next month, when Georgia scrapped its poll tax, seven states remained in the land that President Roosevelt called "Polltaxia."[148] The poll tax was under attack in both Congress and in the states. A coalition that would become increasingly frequent over the coming decades—black activists, leftist organizations, unions, and assorted liberals—worked both in Washington and in state capitals from 1938 through 1950. By this era, the tax was thought to disfranchise about six million whites and four million blacks. These efforts helped repeal the poll tax in Arkansas, Florida, Tennessee, as well as Georgia (Louisiana and North Carolina had already done so). The U.S. House passed legislation five times during the 1940s that repealed the poll tax in federal elections, but southerners in the Senate stood firm, employing the filibuster to block passage.[149]

Arnall's ambivalence regarding the white primary—seeming to back a South Carolina–style deregulation, but publicly doing very little to defend it—intersected with his personal political ambitions. He hoped to secure a vice-presidential nomination, and knew that defending political white supremacy would dash these hopes. On the other hand, winning reelection would likely require holding on to many two-unit counties where the white primary remained more popular. In early 1945 he attempted to convince the legislature to amend the constitution so that governors could serve consecutive terms. He almost succeeded; if he had, his enormous incumbency advantages and great popularity would have assured him reelection. Spurred on by his national ambitions—with ties to the progressive wing of the national party—and aided by the state's anti-Talmadge faction, he might have crafted a very different, and much earlier, incorporation of blacks into the party, with massive implications for the state's subsequent political development.

As the 1946 gubernatorial primary approached, the anti-Talmadge faction failed to work out a stable leadership succession. The state's most powerful political operative, House Speaker and kingmaker Roy Harris, had been instrumental in Arnall's election and in the passage of his legislative program. He expected to be anointed the faction's gubernatorial candidate for the 1946 election and thus felt betrayed when Arnall attempted to seek reelection by amending the constitution. He also disagreed with Arnall's failure to safeguard political white supremacy. Harris exited the faction, helped defeat the constitutional amendment providing for successive gubernatorial terms, and became one of the top strategists for white supremacy among the Talmadgeites.[150] Meanwhile, Arnall attempted to burnish his national image—primarily through staking out more liberal positions on black voting and by repressing the newly resurgent Klan. More important, he sought to help elect an anti-Talmadge candidate in the 1946 gubernatorial election; otherwise, his political future would be in jeopardy.

In late 1945 a federal judge ruled in *Chapman v. King* that blacks could vote in the white primary.[151] Several prominent Georgia newspapers backed the decision. However, Arnall warned blacks not to vote, and the state appealed the ruling, both to the disappointment of black group leaders. Still, the SDEC—controlled by Arnall—announced that blacks could vote in the gubernatorial primary.[152] The U.S. Fifth Circuit Court of Appeals soon upheld *King*, but the majority opinion suggested a way out—complete deregulation of the party. Roy Harris called for a special session to repeal the state's primary laws, à la South Carolina. Gene Talmadge, preparing for another run for governor, agreed. Senate president Frank Gross spoke out against such a special session, partly because he claimed that the county-unit system might be endangered if not fixed in statute.[153]

Arnall's own political dilemma now came quickly into focus. His national political prospects would be damaged by failing to comply with the ruling; however, embrace of the decision and a public stand in favor of black incorporation into the party would likely help Talmadge and thereby possibly destroy Arnall's future in state politics. Eventually, Arnall took a strong stand and announced his opposition to any scheme to evade the courts and, further, that deregulation would risk both the county-unit system and free and fair elections. He also vowed to block a special session called by the legislature. Arnall informed the SDEC that the white primary was dead, and the committee altered party rules to permit black voting in the upcoming primary.[154]

Black Georgia's Response to Smith

In 1942 there occurred a "decisive shift in the organizational structure and scale of activities" among Georgia's black activists. In that year Reverend Mark Gilbert revitalized the Savannah NAACP, setting in motion a revitalization of the statewide NAACP network. Very supportive of the branch's Youth Council, it soon would boast the country's largest (which would nurture a future statewide NAACP leader, W. W. "Wesley" Law).[155] In early 1946 black Georgia—in concert with white progressive groups—achieved astonishing results. As in other states, a small black protest leadership populated several overlapping groups, including the state's Republican party, the NAACP, and other statewide networks (table 3.3).[156] A. T. Walden, state secretary of the Georgia NAACP conference of branches, was also president of the Georgia Association of Citizen Democratic Clubs (CDCs).[157] Soon, there were about seventy-five such clubs statewide totaling some 15,000–20,000 members. The CDC endorsed statewide candidates, while local clubs backed their local candidates as they chose. In 1946, the organization employed twenty-five full-time organizers.

In Atlanta, a large voter registration drive brought together several black political and civic organizations. Black registered voters in 1946 increased from about 3,000 to about 21,000 (from about 4 to 27 percent of the city's electorate).[158] Existing black Democratic Clubs, such as the Atlanta Civic and Political League, and the Georgia Veterans League and other black organizations participated in the drive. Across the state, about 125,000 blacks registered—more than 100,000 of them outside Atlanta—in a remarkable mobilization that propelled black voters overnight from a negligible presence to about 20 percent of the state's electorate.[159]

A Turning Point: The 1946 Gubernatorial Election

Georgia's 1946 gubernatorial election amounted to a key moment in the state's political development. A victory of whites and blacks allied against the Talmadge faction would have begun a statewide incorporation of blacks into the ruling party, and perhaps transformed—and even ended—enclave rule in Georgia. However, the faction was hampered by its dispute over leadership in 1945 and its difficulty in coordinating candidates in the 1946 primary. Because of the Talmadge faction's impressive suppression of black voting, Gene Talmadge won the 1946 primary with a minority of the popular vote but a narrow victory in the county-unit vote. Exploiting the bizarre Three Governors Controversy (discussed later), the Talmadge faction expanded its control over party machinery and reigned supreme through the 1950s and early 1960s.

Talmadge made clear that "the One Issue in This Race is White Supremacy."[160] In declaring his candidacy, Talmadge promised to restore the white primary and invoked South Carolina's deregulation plan as a model.[161] Arnall endorsed James V. ("Jimmy") Carmichael, general manager of metro Atlanta's giant Bell Aircraft plant, as his successor; Carmichael agreed that the white primary was dead and opposed efforts to repeal statutes regulating primaries. Talmadge attacked Carmichael indirectly by campaigning against Ellis "Benedict" Arnall. Political kingmaker Roy Harris condemned Arnall and announced he would either run for governor himself or help elect a candidate devoted to saving the white primary. Arnall, meanwhile, assisted reformers in attacking Harris's "Cracker Party" machine in Augusta. In a stunning result, black voters and a large voter registration drive organized by white reformers (many of them war veterans) defeated Speaker Harris in the state legislative primaries that preceded the gubernatorial primary.[162]

Given Harris's defeat, the field of gubernatorial candidates narrowed. Many thought that if Carmichael prevailed, Arnall could control Georgia's delegation to the 1948 National Democratic Convention.[163] Famously corrupt former governor Rivers jumped into the race and asserted that "the Negroes will vote," but campaigned against Arnall. Apparently paid by Talmadge forces to enter the race (a not uncommon practice), he split the anti-Talmadge vote. Another remarkable feature of the primary was that plans to suppress black voting circulated to such a degree that black organizations contacted federal attorneys in Georgia. The Department of Justice ordered the FBI to investigate days before the primary for evidence of a conspiracy. A U.S. District Attorney in Macon also investigated allegations of blacks being purged from the registration rolls in Black Belt counties.[164] They were there, in effect, to monitor the election—the first such southern election monitored since Reconstruction.[165]

Soon after announcing his candidacy, Talmadge's newspaper, *The Statesman*, offered a blueprint for restricting black suffrage. It cited three rarely invoked sections of the state code that held that any Georgia citizen could challenge the registration of any registrant by claiming that the registrant was, for reasons specified in the challenge, unqualified to vote. Talmadge's campaign mailed thousands of challenge forms to Talmadge men in every county, including supportive superior court judges.[166]

However, federal law enforcement officials did not investigate registration or voting processes. Challenged voters could request a hearing to restore their registration. While there was a wide diversity in procedures across counties, in many, the burden of proof lay with the challenged voter. Failure to appear at hearings often resulted in disqualification.[167] Talmadge campaign officials traveled across the state to interrogate witnesses at these purge hearings. According to historian Joseph Bernd, factional loyalties determined the decisions of relevant officials—usually tax collectors, who served as registrars. All told, more than 16,000 registered black votes were purged.[168]

Elsewhere, especially in Georgia's Black Belt, night riders, cross-burnings, physical intimidation, and murder all took their toll on black turnout.[169] In a particularly tense town, a supporter asked Talmadge how to prevent blacks from voting; he responded by scrawling across a piece of paper the word "Pistols."[170] Carmichael accused Talmadge of promoting crowd violence against blacks on the eve of the primary.[171] Indeed, the summer of 1946 featured a wave of racial violence throughout the South, much of it targeting returning black veterans in uniform. Georgia accounted for most of this violence, and it was partly due to reports of it that Truman established his Committee on Civil Rights (see chapter 5).

Talmadge owed his highly contingent victory to his forces' suppression of black voters and to the failure of the anti-Talmadge forces to coordinate behind a single candidate.[172] Especially in light of the fact that Carmichael lost despite winning a plurality of the popular vote, state and national media castigated the state and Talmadge forces.[173] Governor-elect Talmadge soon announced that the party's upcoming convention would arrange for a "white man's primary" under the county-unit system, and called on the legislature to repeal primary statutes in order to comply with federal courts.[174]

The Three Governors Controversy

Just before the mere formality of the general election, Talmadge died. Thence began a complex and comic conflict during which, over the course of more than two months, three governors presided—or attempted to preside—over Georgia: Talmadge's son Herman; Arnall; and the duly elected lieutenant governor, Melvin Thompson. Vague rules of gubernatorial succession eventually led to the Talmadge-dominated legislature's corrupt selection of Herman Talmadge as governor.[175]

The House quickly passed the (Gene) Talmadge white primary bill. This legislation combined South Carolina's deregulation plan—complete repeal of primary-related statutes—with stricter enforcement of registration laws and new, periodic registration of voters. All laws relating to primaries were now repealed. In signing the law, Governor Talmadge voiced concern that political white supremacy was not yet safe, since blacks could vote in general elections, for which the winner needed a simple plurality of the vote, as the county-unit system applied only to Democratic primaries (thus, black voting power in cities could help elect an anti-Talmadgeite candidate).[176]

Soon white moderates and a few white liberals outraged by the legislature's actions formed the "Aroused Citizens of Georgia." The group sought "to maintain a true Democratic party" under the name "the Democratic Party of Georgia." It declared that the party's leadership had forfeited the right to use the party name by their "efforts . . . to perpetuate their rule by a series of unlawful, unconstitutional and undemocratic actions" culminating in the white primary bill.[177] The possibility that white supremacists could be defeated in a general election by a party of white moderates and liberals as well as blacks was, for Talmadgeites, all too real. This made the extension of the county-unit system to general elections even more urgent. A constitutional amendment, to be approved by popular vote, to extend the county-unit system to general elections was defeated by House moderates. Backers justified the proposal by pointing to the threat that a rival (Democratic) party might form, as well as the threat of black voting. Supporters of Lieutenant Governor Melvin Thompson opposed the amendment on the same grounds as those articulated by the Aroused Citizens movement.

In March 1947 Georgia's Supreme Court named Thompson governor until a special election could be held in November 1948. Sixty-three days after the crisis began, Herman Talmadge left the governor's office, and Harris immediately announced Talmadge's candidacy for the special election. Georgia once again had a single governor. Thompson addressed a joint session of the General Assembly, and declared that Talmadge and his forces "now have no right to speak for the Democratic party," and that "today, again, law and order prevails in Georgia." He vowed to veto Talmadge's white primary legislation.[178]

Now Thompson—and other white moderates opposed to the Talmadge faction—faced a real dilemma. If Thompson vetoed the legislation, he would deliver a ready-made issue to Herman Talmadge, who maintained control of the party machinery. If he signed it, he could remove the issue, run as a candidate for a *separate* Democratic party, and defeat Talmadge with the help of black voters in a general election. Thompson sought to establish his bona fides on white supremacy, and promised to carry out the party's platform without disturbing it.[179] But he opposed the white primary law as written, and instead called for the legislature to pass two bills recently introduced by his supporters. The first required racially segregated ballot boxes (well suited for suffrage restriction), and the second restored state regulation of primaries and established educational requirements for voter registration applicants.[180]

Talmadge forces were intent on blocking the passage of any legislation that might allow Thompson to claim credit for protecting white supremacy. Theirs was a risky strategy—to accept potential gains in black suffrage in order to improve the probability of Talmadge's return to office and pass more satisfactory legislation. Both chambers were gridlocked by factional division and adjourned without passing any bills involving party primaries.[181]

The anti-Talmadgeite and moderate "Democratic Party of Georgia" scheduled a state convention to name its own Democratic state executive committee. Control over the powerful executive committee would have a large bearing on the 1948 gubernatorial election. Talmadge-picked House Speaker Fred Hand demanded that Thompson call a special session to pass Thompson's proposal for educational requirements on voter registration.[182] Thompson argued that the legislature had already rejected the bill. Meanwhile, Peters announced that "his" (Talmadgeite) party would continue planning a separate primary to be held if Thompson rejected Speaker Hand's appeal. In the meantime, the Democratic National Committee recognized Governor Thompson as the titular head of the party.

Both Democratic parties set dates for meetings to arrange for the 1948 primaries. State courts would have to decide which faction controlled the party.[183] In late 1947, a Richmond Superior Court judge declared Talmadgeite James Peters as the rightful legal chair of the Democratic executive committee.[184] Anti-Talmadgeites' efforts to take over the state party machinery had failed. But other options to challenge the ruling party, and steer the enclave in another direction, remained available.

Anticipating the 1948 Gubernatorial Election

Understandably, politicians perceived a great deal of uncertainty about the stability of the ruling party and one-party rule.[185] Whether a second party would be led by a faction of blacks, moderate urban whites, and white liberals loyal to the national party, or by a rural- and white supremacist-dominated faction opposed to the national party, would depend on the outcome of the 1948 gubernatorial primary. It was also unclear whether Talmadge could win a general election. White supremacists did not (merely) fear black suffrage. In the words of House Speaker Fred Hand, "What we don't want 'em to do is to get in a position in our party so they can be manipulated. [L]et 'em have their own party, a black Democratic party if they want."[186]

Other Talmadgeites did not expect the development of a second party and deplored black incorporation attempts.[187] Noteworthy here is the rhetorical abandonment of white supremacists' dedication to one-party rule. This speaks to the degree to which the state party had been imperiled since *Smith*. Roy Harris thought a second party in Georgia would be a Republican party,

> unless you want to go along with the Henry Wallace pinks . . . I don't know whether the niggers will go Republican or not. I do know we're going to have a white man's party in Georgia. . . . It won't make any difference what the Supreme Court decides on the South Carolina primary. The Negro is going to motivate Georgia politics for years to come. Under a two-party system the Negro would be the balance of power. . . . We can't let the niggers run Georgia. They'll do it, though, if Thompson gets elected next year.[188]

Georgia's ruling party teetered on the precipice of collapse and barely righted itself. A second "Democrat" party that incorporated blacks might battle the white supremacist rump party in general elections—and thus outside the confines of the county-unit system. Given the statewide nature of Georgia's black insurgency, such a party would be highly competitive and would likely transform enclave rule and hasten the state's democratization. But electoral violence and repression of black voters in 1946 suggested that the Talmadge faction would not concede enclave rule without a fight.

Implications for the Future

In contrast to those in South Carolina and Mississippi, Georgia's rulers divided sharply along factional lines. Black Georgia's impressive mobilization and their involvement with the anti-Talmadge faction helped prevent the state from reaching a consensus on responses to *Smith*. These factors, in conjunction with the enormously important county-unit system and the progressive political ambitions of key individuals, produced acquiescence to, and then defiance of, *Smith*. From 1944 to 1946, acquiescence facilitated the impressive rise in black registration and voting. Thereafter, the repression of black voters and the aftermath of the pivotal 1946 gubernatorial election threatened to split the party.

On the eve of Truman's challenge to southern enclaves, the ruling party remained unstable. Legal disputes over who controlled party machinery would help keep Georgia out of the Dixiecrat movement in 1948. As chapters 5 and 8 make clear, conflict over the white primary ultimately weakened the anti-Talmadgeite faction, which did not recover for two decades. In sum, the ruling produced in Georgia the region's most complex and profound effects, which reverberated throughout its transition to democracy.

Conclusion

Smith v. Allwright provided the first major jolt to the southern body politic.[189] Itself indebted to a long struggle by the Texas branch of the NAACP, the ruling offered black activists across the Deep South further motivation to convert existing protest networks into attempts to enter ruling parties or to fashion satellite parties. In South Carolina and Mississippi, there was a general consensus on defiance, evasion, and then adjustment, as rulers considered new ways to minimize the effects of the ruling. In Georgia, the ruling struck the state during a period of severe factional conflict, and almost destroyed one-party rule. Intraparty conflict, political institutions, and black mobilizations combined to produce these states' different experiences. The white primary's demise did not, of course, dismantle disfranchisement, but it did mean that rulers would need to sharpen new tools to reduce the impact of blacks on Democratic primaries and electoral politics more generally. The next shock—Truman's transformation of the national party into a vehicle at least rhetorically committed to racial equality—followed almost immediately.

CHAPTER FIVE

Driven from the House of Their Fathers

Southern Enclaves and the National Party, 1947–48

Because of the rotten boroughs of the South, real democratic government is impossible in the North. The Democratic party cannot become a liberal body, because the bulk of its support depends upon disfranchisement, caste, and race hate in the South. It depends on minimizing participation in politics by all people, black and white, and [the] stifling of discussion. . . . How are we going to restore normal democracy in the United States?

  —*W.E.B. Du Bois* (1930)

It will be a great tragedy if we are driven from the house of our fathers by a bunch of Johnny-come-lately pink-tinted radicals who . . . now have control of our party. To supinely submit to the President's program would be a greater tragedy.

  —*Senator Richard B. Russell* (D-GA) (1948)

The South and Southern Democracy as we know it is in the hands of a foreign element.

  —*Governor Ben Laney of Arkansas on the national party platform* (1948)

WEEKS BEFORE PRESIDENT HARRY S. TRUMAN shocked the southern enclaves by announcing a threatening policy agenda, another federal intervention crossed the Mason-Dixon line and rumbled through the South: the Freedom Train.[1] Sponsored by the nonprofit American Heritage Foundation, it brought, for all to see, priceless documents such as the Declaration of Independence, the Constitution, the Emancipation Proclamation, the recently inked United Nations Charter, and the Gettysburg Address. Public reverence for these items was bad enough. (Recall that state legislators from the Mississippi Delta opposed references to democracy in civics textbooks for black schools.) But to make matters worse, the Foundation bowed to pressure from black activists by deciding that local authorities had to guarantee nonsegregated viewing of these artifacts of American democracy. Some southern cities refused, and so the Train skipped them. The message seemed clear—American freedom was coming, and it would not compromise itself for anyone.[2]

For decades, of course, the federal government and the national Democratic party had been far from uncompromising in their dealings with southern enclaves. In 1928, four years before Franklin Roosevelt's election, the party "demand[ed] that the constitutional rights and powers of the states shall be preserved in their full vigor and virtue. These constitute a bulwark against centralization and the destructive tendencies of the Republican Party."[3] Moreover, the Roosevelt era promised southern politicians renewed influence over national policymaking. However, the national party's massive electoral successes during the 1930s meant an influx of nonsouthern voters, activists, and members of Congress, and this weakened southerners' influence within it. Enclaves swore at the national party sporadically throughout the 1930s, but southern white voters and most party politicians swore by the Roosevelt administration until the early 1940s. Anger at the administration, and at increasingly emboldened unions and black protest organizations and their northern supporters in Congress, mounted over the war years. After a brief honeymoon with Truman, enclave rulers quickly soured on him, and their anger boiled over in 1947 and 1948 as he pledged to use the central state to interfere with enclave rule in the spheres of labor relations, interracial social contact, and law enforcement. For the first time since Redemption, southern authorities seriously doubted whether the national Democratic party was the most effective vehicle for advancing their political careers and policy goals.

The year 1948 marked the South's first serious interstate coordination outside Congress since the inception of enclave rule in the 1890s.[4] After much deliberation about how to respond to Truman, a plan was hatched. Four Deep South Democratic parties—those in South Carolina, Mississippi, Alabama, and Louisiana, but not Georgia—placed the "Democratic" party label on general election ballots above lists of electors pledged to a "States' Rights Party" (SRP) ticket of South Carolina Governor Strom Thurmond and his running mate, Mississippi Governor Fielding Wright. By contrast, the "Democratic Party" label did not appear above a list of presidential electors pledged to back the national Democratic ticket of President Truman and his running mate, U.S. Senator Alben Barkley (D-KY).[5] The SRP (nicknamed the "Dixiecrats" by a newspaper editor short of column inches) carried only these four states and garnered about 17 percent of the southern vote. In part because of southern white voters' party loyalty, the national ticket held the rest of the South, where ballots provided Truman and Barkley with the Democratic party label. Despite the loss of four southern states, Truman edged past Republican New York Governor Thomas Dewey. He did so with the critical support of black voters, who helped him deliver razor-thin victories in California, Illinois, and Ohio.[6]

The SRP had three main goals. First, it sought to cost Truman the election in order to make painfully clear to the national party the consequences of threatening enclave interests. Second, its leaders hoped to unify the entire region in a collective defense of enclave prerogatives. Third, they wanted to establish a vehicle that, if necessary, could be used in future dealings with the national party. All the while, politicians taking part in the SRP hoped their efforts did not harm their political careers; most important, they wanted to avoid punishment by voters back home or by angry party leaders in Washington, who might take away their seniority privileges in Congress or their access to federal patronage.

Traditional interpretations of the Dixiecrat movement view it as an abject failure since its participants failed to meet their immediate goal of defeating Truman. However, as will be discussed later, the Dixiecrats did accomplish other goals. Revisionist accounts claim that the movement launched two-party competition in the South. It is true that in 1948 many southern whites refused to back the national Democratic ticket for the first time in decades. But revisionists do not explain exactly how this accelerated the growth of two-party politics, either in the region as a whole or in individual states.[7]

The Dixiecrat revolt mattered greatly, but not in the ways commonly claimed by historians. Regionally, the shock of the national party's abandonment of its traditional support of enclaves began a tumultuous period between state and national levels of the party. Although Truman was reelected, national Democratic leaders, in an effort to avoid another revolt, quickly backtracked on the party's commitment to racial equality and its promises to interfere in enclave rule. Over the longer term, the Dixiecrat revolt sparked a fundamental dispute about the relationship between the national party and its state parties. By the early 1970s, this dispute (discussed at the end of this chapter) would be resolved largely in favor of the national party—no longer would state parties have substantial autonomy over their internal affairs. And for the Deep South enclaves under study, the Truman shock engendered responses, by both rulers and black (and some white) insurgents alike, that altered the balance of power within state Democratic parties and affected the prospects for Republican growth. These changes would affect how enclaves responded to attacks on Jim Crow and suffrage restriction in the 1950s and 1960s.

This chapter charts the causes and consequences of the Dixiecrat revolt. It describes and explains southern enclaves' growing unease with the national party through the 1930s and 1940s, and then offers narratives of the experiences of South Carolina, Mississippi, and Georgia. As with other external interventions, the Truman shock and responses to it varied within the Deep South depending on different configurations of intraparty conflict and party-state institutions.

The Central State, National Party, and Southern Enclaves, 1932–46

Since their inception around the turn of the twentieth century, southern enclaves used their influence within the Democratic party to establish, and then maintain, their conditional autonomy from the central state and national party. Southern Democrats controlled a growing fraction of the party's congressional delegation, and, significantly, committee chairmanships. Through these positions, they conspired to block noxious legislation, as well as objectionable appointments to federal agencies and the federal bench during the Woodrow Wilson years. In return, the region delivered almost unanimous Electoral College support for the Democratic ticket.[8] Its share of National Convention delegates, coupled with the two-thirds rule, amounted to a southern veto over presidential nominations and party platforms. The Democratic party was the only conceivable national vehicle for the region's rulers. Most southern whites could scarcely imagine voting for the Republican party, responsible as it was for Sherman's March and the horrors of Reconstruction.

Southern enclaves celebrated their party's capture of the White House in 1933. When Wall Street crashed in 1929, the South—and especially the Deep South—was already in serious trouble. The destruction of cotton harvests by the boll weevil, subsequent overproduction by farmers and a collapse in cotton prices, and then a wave of farm foreclosures and bank failures had brought the region to an economic precipice.[9] As the Great Depression deepened, southern politicians sought both federal relief *and* noninterference in enclave affairs.

During Roosevelt's first term (1933–37), southern representatives in Washington protected their enclaves by exploiting their pivotal positions in congressional leadership posts and in committees to shape the design and implementation of New Deal relief and recovery measures. The traditional outflow of the region's resources quickly reversed.[10] Farmers, workers, and the teeming ranks of the unemployed received critical financial transfers and jobs through programs such as the Civilian Conservation Corps, the Works Progress Administration, and many others. The administration's rural electrification program had a profound effect on rural southern life and millions of southerners felt indebted to Roosevelt. Federal relief kept southern cities solvent, too, and urban southerners and city officials benefited hugely from large infrastructure projects, some of which, such as the Atlanta sewer system, had lasting effects on public health in the region. The New Deal had other longer-term effects, such as the public works and transportation projects that helped transform the South's economic infrastructure.[11]

Whether by defeating legislative proposals, substantially modifying them, or controlling their implementation at local levels, southern politicians fended off unwanted intrusions in enclave governance. These included antilynching legislation (which had majority support among southern whites and the region's white newspapers), the regulation of southern wages and working conditions, and limits on the use of the poll tax. Even more important, the Social Security Act and the Fair Labor and Standards Act excluded farmworkers and domestics from pension benefits, a minimum wage, and oversight of their working conditions. Here and in many other cases, including local authorities' control over unemployment insurance and Aid to Dependent Children, New Deal policies did not disrupt planters' access to farm labor.[12]

While Louisiana Governor Huey Long and Georgia Governor Gene Talmadge attempted to challenge Roosevelt's renomination in 1936, their movements gained little traction and reflected the president's great popularity in the region (to be fair, Long's seemed threatening but was cut short by his assassination in 1935).[13] At the 1936 National Convention, as Roosevelt prepared for his reelection campaign, some of his closest northern supporters won a battle begun at the previous convention—the repeal of the two-thirds rule. As the Democrats developed a mass party in the 1830s, it required that any presidential nominee secure the backing of a two-thirds supermajority of convention delegates. This two-thirds rule effectively gave southern Democrats a veto over the nomination of candidates who might be "unfriendly" to the region. One hundred years later, the two-thirds rule remained for southern Democrats a highly valued means of influence over the presidential nominations and a symbol of the party's commitment to its most loyal region. But many outside the region blamed the rule for often-lengthy convention balloting—and even the nomination of undistinguished candidates during the party's lean years of the 1910s and 1920s.[14]

During Roosevelt's first term, party boss Jim Farley quietly organized support for the rule's repeal at the 1936 convention. Roosevelt first backed the repeal only privately for fear of angering southern politicians. As the convention opened, most southern delegations strenuously objected to repeal. Without the rule, they claimed, the national party, the cause of states' rights, and the South would all suffer. Others demanded compensation in the form of increased delegate representation for the South.[15] The vote to repeal—which meant requiring a simple majority of convention delegates to nominate a national ticket—passed easily. Of the eleven delegations from the ex-Confederacy, only three favored repeal. Georgia, Mississippi, and South Carolina all strongly opposed the rule change.[16]

This change, while seemingly weakening the South's hold on the party's presidential nominations, did not constitute a frontal assault on southern prerogatives. Rather, the loss of the two-thirds rule seemed to codify the new reality: the declining importance of the region's share of the party's Electoral College totals. In fact, Roosevelt would have won reelection in 1936 without winning any southern states.[17] The rule's repeal would gain significance only when combined with nonsouthern delegates' hostility to the pillars of enclave rule. The convention did feature some troubling portents—for the first time in the party's history, the convention floor included black delegates with full voting privileges, as well as the first black Democratic member of Congress, Chicago's Arthur Mitchell.[18] Upon seeing a black minister deliver an invocation, Senator "Cotton Ed" Smith (D-SC) muttered, "I'm sick and tired of the whole damn thing. That ain't my kind of democracy."[19]

Each of Roosevelt's three reelection bids gave national Democrats reasons to worry. Even the 1936 race was for a while expected to be close.[20] From his first term, the national party began serious efforts to mobilize black voters in cities outside the South. In 1936 blacks doubled their support for Roosevelt over 1932 levels to nearly 65 percent.[21] Still, party officials did not assume that this support was now guaranteed. Changes at the Democratic National Committee (DNC), including the formation of a "Colored Division" and party sponsorship of black canvassing efforts, reflected the new attempt to incorporate nonsouthern blacks into the national party.

Through 1937 southerners on Capitol Hill backed the administration on most issues, including Roosevelt's controversial court-packing plan. Deep South representatives were especially effective in crafting federal policies that benefited their primary clients, Black Belt planters. The Agricultural Adjustment Act (AAA) provided them with parity payments in exchange for reductions in production, thus shielding them from market risk. Many took their farmworkers' share of these payments and then expelled them from their land. From the 1930s on, this and similar federal agricultural price supports tempered planters' worries about maintaining the status quo in farm labor markets. These policies also accelerated black—and white—outmigration from the rural South, which in turn led planters and manufacturers to move more quickly to mechanize southern agriculture.[22]

Gradually, however, various conservatives intensified their opposition to particular New Deal policies such as the Fair Labor Standards Act of 1938. A manifesto, drafted by the well-respected Senator Josiah Bailey (D-NC), rallied conservatives on both sides of the aisle.[23] Roosevelt's halfhearted effort in 1938 to campaign in Democratic primaries against a few of Congress's more conservative members both reflected and encouraged the development of a more cohesive conservative bloc. While this "purge" was directed mainly at nonsouthern incumbents, the region's politicians perceived it as an unprecedented interference by the national party into state party nominations; many new Roosevelt opponents and strong supporters were furious.[24]

The purge followed on the heels of the publication of the *Report on Economic Conditions in the South*, written by southern New Dealers with ties to the administration.[25] The report charged that the South was the country's "number one economic problem," and catalogued dire problems such as poverty, the state of southern public health, and economic mismanagement, among many others—but did not mention Jim Crow, suffrage restriction, or other antidemocratic practices. It galvanized many white southern moderates and liberals, some of whom soon joined reform organizations; and it also heightened the fears of many southern rulers that the administration's sights were now trained on key elements of the "southern way of life."[26]

Moreover, there began to coalesce in Washington a group of officials in the central state who could foster links directly with enclave challengers—in Edward Gibson's terminology, they could break the "monopoly" of linkages that rulers maintained between enclaves and the federal government. In addition to the white liberals just mentioned, across several cabinet departments a group of about forty-five blacks formed the Federal Council on Negro Affairs, known as the "black cabinet."[27] This grouping was perhaps more important for what it portended about the future than for its immediate policy implications. Still, for southern authorities who remembered that the last Democrat occupying the White House had brought Jim Crow to the civil service, the black cabinet provided another worrying sign.

While southern disaffection mounted, especially among Democrats in Congress, by the 1940 National Convention (which included thirty black delegates, all from the non-South) those Democrats opposing an unprecedented third term for Roosevelt did not coalesce as a sectional movement. Indeed, only Virginia sent delegates to the National Convention without instruction as to which candidate to support.[28] While politicians grumbled about the takeover of the party by the CIO's Political Action Committee and the NAACP, white southern voters backed Roosevelt by typically huge margins.

The onset of war exacerbated rulers' anger and fear of further federal interference—especially in the region's labor markets—even as economic and social changes sparked by the war challenged enclaves from within. The Fair Employment Practices Committee (FEPC)—the result of the March on Washington Movement and its potential to bring chaos to the streets of the capital—posed a twin threat. The federal government, for the first time since Reconstruction, committed itself (albeit unevenly) to monitor "fairness" in employment.[29] And the committee symbolized, and further encouraged, the policy influence of national black protest organizations within the executive branch and the national party.[30]

On another track, race liberals pressed for antilynching and anti–poll tax legislation. In 1942 the House passed legislation to ban the use of the poll tax in federal general elections. Representative Eugene Cox (D-GA) attacked it as a "sorry bid for the Negro vote." On this issue, as on a host of others, southern politicians argued that the burgeoning intraparty coalition of blacks and labor endangered the region. Southern senators successfully filibustered the legislation, although their opposition to it had little to do with its merits. Several southern states, including Georgia, had already abolished the poll tax, and others planned to do so. The poll tax by that time was of declining importance as a barrier to black suffrage. Rather, southern members rejected the bill as auguring further interventions in states' electoral administration.[31]

Also in 1942, Congress passed the Soldiers' Voting Act, which would help armed services personnel—of any race—vote back home in federal and state elections. Again concerned with precedent, southerners designed highly cumbersome procedures by which soldiers could apply for, receive, and file ballots. The act resulted in so little voting that an embarrassed Roosevelt sought additional action. In late 1943, Congress returned to the issue, and planned to establish a War Ballot Commission, which would distribute federal ballots for soldiers and then forward them to state election officials. Southern Democrats gutted the legislation, which posed few problems since it applied only to general elections. Still, Senator Jim Eastland (D-MS) decried sending "carpetbaggers into the South to control elections." According to historian Robert Garson, this proposal "aroused more sectional bitterness than any other item of legislation during the war." The tense debate prompted Senator Josiah Bailey (D-NC) to suggest a radical strategy:

> We can form a Southern Democratic party and vote as we please in the electoral college, and we will hold the balance of power in this country.... [I]f we must be in a party in which we are scorned as southern Democrats, we will find a party which honors us.

Five years before the Dixiecrat movement, leaders had begun to ruminate about forming an alternative to the national party.[32]

After the 1942 midterm elections, Democrats retained a mere six-seat majority in the House. Southerners, now composing a greater share of congressional Democrats, seemed better able to waylay federal interference. They flexed this muscle the following summer by defunding several New Deal programs backed by labor and black organizations. Southern

Democrats also investigated war spending, executive overreach, and other alleged abuses.[33]

Tellingly, though, a confidential postelection survey of state party leaders by the DNC revealed that while southern party chairs were twice as likely to oppose the administration's labor policies, they voiced little concern about the administration's possible impact on white supremacy. While southern rulers and their main clients faced substantial wartime dislocation in the form of new migration waves, farm labor shortages, increasingly militant blacks, and troubling labor policies—they did not anticipate an attack on the South's brand of white supremacy.[34]

Minor disputes occurred when southern parties withheld financial contributions to the DNC because of their displeasure over Roosevelt's management of patronage in the South, his turn toward labor, and other matters.[35] The South contributed the greatest share of the party's funds. Since southern congressional candidates ran uncontested, national party leaders could use contributions from the region to help elect much more liberal nonsouthern congressional candidates.[36] In a sense, southern legislative, electoral, *and* financial contributions underwrote both the expansion of the modern U.S. state and helped bring about the national party's seeming dominance. Roosevelt well understood the risks of attacking southern political-economic prerogatives.[37]

The summer of 1943 produced the peak of wartime social unrest, much of it involving white crowd violence against blacks. Black crowds also confronted civilian and military police, especially on southern military training grounds and in surrounding communities.[38] Many southern officials blamed this disorder on the meddling of outsiders.[39] In response to these tensions, the administration formed a "White Cabinet" to improve federal efforts to prevent racial disorder. By mid-1943, party observers assumed that Roosevelt would stand for a fourth term, and expected southern delegations to bargain for a vice-presidential nominee to replace the too-liberal Henry Wallace, and for greater representation at the convention to compensate for the loss of the two-thirds rule.[40]

Southern rulers' disaffection with the national party outpaced that of white southern voters. However, a November 1943 survey of Democratic county chairs revealed mounting anger over federal race policies.[41] Anti–New Dealers in Mississippi interpreted its August gubernatorial primary, won by arch-conservative Mike Conner, as auguring a southern movement opposing a fourth term.[42] Such movements were scattered across the country, but the most concerted occurred in the South, where manufacturing, banking, and oil interests funded them. Some politicians planned to try to block his renomination, whether by threatening to walk out of the convention or, if the national party's platform did not sufficiently reflect southern demands, to select uninstructed presidential electors who would be free to vote for others besides the national Democratic ticket. Their demands included a restoration of the two-thirds rule, a reaffirmation of the doctrine of states' rights, opposition to federal poll tax legislation, and the removal of any call for social equality among the races. The group sought enough allies so that the South, by controlling from sixty to one hundred electoral votes, could throw the election to the U.S. House.[43]

In June, just two months after the *Smith* ruling, a Gallup poll revealed that more than 60 percent of southern whites favored a two-party system in the South. But a survey of eight southern states also showed that support for Roosevelt ranged from 68 percent (Texas) to 89 percent (South Carolina). At the National Convention, the party adopted a platform, over southern delegates' objections, which included a plank supporting racial equality but avoiding strong support for related policies. The "race" plank, as the NAACP's Walter White remarked, was a mere "splinter." The Republican platform, on the other hand, denounced the poll tax, opposed lynching, backed a permanent FEPC, and promised to investigate the desegregation of the military.[44] Still, three southern delegations—Louisiana, Mississippi, and Virginia—backed Senator Harry Byrd (D-VA) rather than the Roosevelt-Truman ticket. In all, only ninety of 1,176 delegates opposed Roosevelt.[45] Thus, some tactics of 1948 were already available—and chosen by some Texas Democrats—by 1944.[46] Just four years before Truman committed the national party to back democratization challenges, the 1944 Democratic platform evaded mention of race reforms.

The National Party's Embrace of Racial Equality in 1947–48

Upon Truman's ascension to the presidency in 1945, southern politicians were, in the main, optimistic about resolving tensions with the national party. The native Missourian pleased the South by choosing South Carolina stalwart James Byrnes to serve as secretary of state and Texan Tom Clark as attorney general. Earlier, Truman had told the *Charleston News and Courier* that he did not believe in the "social equality" of the races. However, southern politicians denounced his support for a permanent FEPC and a full employment plan, wage increases, the federal takeover of tidelands oil deposits offshore southern states, and so on. Southerners on Capitol Hill howled at Truman's veto of the antilabor Case bill in 1946 and of Taft-Hartley in 1947. Despite Truman's cultural ties to the Outer South and some hopeful signs, his wavering on key issues worried southern politicians.[47]

Nonsouthern Democrats in Congress also began to threaten enclave prerogatives in the 1940s. In contrast to the conventional wisdom that dates the realignment of America's major parties on race to the 1960s, new research shows that Democratic senators and representatives outside of the South had begun outpacing their Republican counterparts in their support for race reforms by the early-to-mid 1940s.[48] This support was manifest when these Democrats spoke on behalf of racial equality, cosponsored "race" legislation, and urged that such legislation bypass southern-controlled committees and be voted on by the full chamber. A bit later nonsouthern Democrats' stronger support for race legislation (compared to that of Republicans) emerged in voting patterns.[49] The gradual shift over this period occurred not because of the whims of individual legislators but because of the organization of a black-labor-liberal coalition on Capitol Hill. Not surprisingly, these locally rooted national lawmakers faced this pressure back home as well from increasingly liberal, and assertive, party activists. Nonsouthern Democratic state parties overtook the "Party of Lincoln" in publicly backing policy responses to a range of racial injustices by the mid-1940s.[50]

The central state and clients of the national party challenged rulers further.[51] A lawsuit filed by the NAACP's Legal Defense Fund to desegregate the University of Texas law school influenced 1946 gubernatorial elections, and the Supreme Court's invalidation of mandatory segregated interstate bus travel helped Gene Talmadge eke out a pivotal victory in Georgia.[52] And in the CIO's Operation Dixie, field organizers began in 1946 to sweep through the South in a quixotic effort to score huge unionization gains, particularly among textile workers. Southern authorities, almost all of them hostile to unions, took this assault very seriously. Over the past decade, the influence of unions in the "house of their fathers" had grown quickly, and labor clearly opposed many of the pillars of enclave rule. Operation Dixie was launched as the country was undergoing the largest strike wave in its history. It was no surprise that southern newspapers and business lobbies mounted a propaganda campaign against it, or that southern authorities intimidated and coerced both organizers and workers very effectively. The Operation failed badly.[53]

Election violence stemming from black voting efforts in the Black Belt greatly affected Truman's own thinking. The wave of violence against black would-be voters—especially those still in uniform—was a wakeup call to many moderates and liberals.[54] In September, a report by the National Emergency Committee Against Mob Violence stunned Truman, who vowed to back "imperative" federal legislation.[55] But in the 1946 midterms, Democrats lost control of both chambers. Southerners now composed a majority of the party's House caucus, and were one shy of a majority of Senate Democrats (figure 2.1).

Truman quickly established a Presidential Committee on Civil Rights. Before it released its analysis and recommendations, in a growing effort to reach northern black voters in swing states outside the South, the president addressed ten thousand NAACP members from the Lincoln Memorial in 1947:

> We have reached a turning point in the long history of this country's efforts to guarantee freedom and equality to all citizens. . . . There is much that state and local governments can do in providing positive safeguards for civil rights. But we cannot, any longer, await the growth of a will to action in the slowest state or the most backward community.[56]

Despite the speech, South Carolina governor Strom Thurmond publicly praised the president's "seasoned experience, demonstrated ability, and tact in international affairs," and called for his renomination. In the fall of 1947 Truman's campaign advisers concluded that the South's support could be taken for granted, and thus that his reelection strategy should focus on the North and West. The Republican candidate was expected to make strong appeals to black voters, and Truman must respond in kind. Truman agreed.[57] Challenging Truman's left flank, Henry Wallace announced his candidacy representing the Progressive Party and called for a host of intrusive policies targeting the South.[58] An even more serious threat—a "Draft Eisenhower" movement—would continue until just five days before the Democrats' 1948 National Convention.[59]

In October 1947 the NAACP published *An Appeal to the World*, which sought the United Nations' help in internationalizing the attack on southern enclaves and stamping out racial injustice nationwide.[60] The U.N. would soon approve the nonbinding Universal Declaration of Human Rights, which urged all nations to eliminate racial discrimination within their borders. Enclave defenders worried that emerging human rights law could soon be used to target their political practices. In the 1950s their representatives in Congress backed the proposed Bricker Amendment to the U.S. Constitution, which would have severely restricted the federal government's authority to take part in international treaties.[61]

The NAACP's *Appeal* was effectively upstaged by the simultaneous release of *To Secure These Rights*, the report of Truman's Committee. The boldness of its recommendations surprised the president. Among others, it called for the creation of a new FEPC; anti–poll tax and antilynching legislation; legislation guaranteeing voting rights in primaries; a permanent civil rights commission within the Executive Office of the President; the desegregation of the military and of interstate transport; and the destruction of Jim Crow in the District of Columbia. Truman's report was perhaps the first-ever attack on segregation that could be linked to the White House: "There is no adequate defense of segregation," it read, and called for the "elimination of segregation . . . from American life." Echoing the citizenship schools of Reconstruction and the 1930s and foreshadowing those of the

1950s and 1960s, it called for public education that would "inform the people of the civil rights to which they are entitled and which they owe one another." Truman, the humble ex-haberdasher, expected the committee's work to be "an American charter of human freedom in our time."[62]

On February 2, 1948, Truman addressed a joint session of Congress. While he dropped several of the committee's recommendations, he urged legislators to strengthen the DOJ's Civil Rights Section, repeal the use of the poll tax in federal elections, criminalize the failure of public officials to prevent lynchings, establish a permanent FEPC, and desegregate interstate transport. After the convention, he issued executive orders that chipped away at Woodrow Wilson's Jim Crow civil service and began to desegregate the military.[63] Many southern politicians likened the president's agenda to a new Reconstruction. In the words of Senator James O. Eastland (D-MS), the "South we know is being swept to its destruction. . . . It is . . . in imminent danger." A Gallup poll reported Truman's disapproval rating among southern voters was 57 percent. Earnest consultations among enclave rulers began across the South.[64]

President Truman had done more than back individual pieces of legislation; he had signaled their high priority as well as his intention as the party's standard bearer to commit it to racial equality. These actions had the gravest implications for southern rulers. First, they pledged the central state to disrupt low-wage, racialized labor markets; a white-only political sphere; and racially segregated civic spheres. Second, they pointed to the heightened contradictions within the national party's congressional delegation. Despite some institutional advantages in facing off against liberal nonsouthern Democrats in Congress, southern politicians now faced a seemingly intractable problem in the White House. (And while southern politicians, like most observers, expected Truman to lose his reelection bid, his likely Republican opponent, New York Governor Thomas Dewey, was a racial progressive.) Third, the reliability of the national party as a guarantor of enclave rule was disappearing. Were enclave rulers best able to secure their career and policy goals by remaining within it? What was to be done?

New Dilemmas for Southern Democrats

As of February 1948, southern politicians faced different challenges and opportunities depending on how they were situated in the party. Those in Congress—many of whom had begun to vote with conservative Republicans on many issues—could openly oppose their president, but at the risk of party reprisals that might mean the loss of hard-earned committee positions and patronage. Southern governors—the nominal heads of state parties— were forced to decide whether to attempt to manipulate party machinery in order to send uninstructed delegations to the National Convention. While the national party could by party rules (usually through its Credentials Committee) expel delegations—whose help was needed in electing the national ticket—it did so at its own peril. And state party officials had to decide whether to accede to their governor's preferences or pressure him to take another course of action. As political scientist Allan Sindler writes, "Capture of the state party organization would bring with it the ability to instruct the state delegation as to its participation in the national convention, and, most crucially, to decide what presidential electors were to go under what party label. In this sense, the 1948 presidential contest in the South was fought out within the governing bodies of the state Democratic parties."[65]

Of course, southern Democrats also differed in their adherence to the project of southern "Democracy," their officeholding ambitions, and their time horizons. As with their responses to *Smith v. Allwright*, Outer South and Deep South state parties diverged in their responses to the Truman shock. Several states, including Arkansas, Florida, Louisiana, North Carolina, Tennessee, and Texas, adopted a "no-bolting view," in some cases for subtle, electoral reasons.[66] Abandoning the national ticket was more than just personally risky—the Republican platform differed little from Truman's, and a Republican victory might endanger enclave rule, too. Worse, with a Republican in the White House, southern Democrats would have even less influence.[67] Finally, how would southern white voters respond to what could seem like an act of disloyalty? After all, from 1920 to 1948, the Republican share of the southern vote in gubernatorial and congressional elections declined in a majority of southern states. There were thus no secular trends for the Dixiecrats to capitalize upon.[68]

Eventually, all Deep South parties but Georgia's supported the States' Rights Party (SRP). The SRP relied on grassroots support by whites in Black Belt counties, and on the financial support of southern—and northern—corporate industrial interests—the same forces that promoted gathering southern opposition to the New Deal in the 1930s and labor regulation in the 1940s.[69] Despite the name, the movement was *not* a party—or at least not yet. It fielded no other candidates, nor attempted to do so. Few of its activists—or voters—expected the ticket to win. Rather, they sought either to throw the election to the House, where southern members could exercise great influence over the winner, or at least to contribute to Truman's defeat and help the national party return to its senses. As detailed in the following narratives, in the Deep South, choices concerning whether and how to respond to Truman's "shock" were influenced by factional conflict, political ambition, and the ways in which state party machinery advantaged certain actors over others. And these choices would have important consequences on how southern rulers responded to *Brown v. Board*, and whether—and how—they and other ambitious politicians considered joining the Republican Party.[70]

South Carolina

The national party's embrace of racial equality disturbed most of South Carolina's rulers. Governor Strom Thurmond—eyeing a Senate race against a national party loyalist—seized the party machinery and used it to sponsor the States' Rights movement. Most important, the state's participation in the movement encouraged one of South Carolina's most powerful politicians, James Byrnes, to consider exiting the national party and embracing the Republicans—in contrast to most authorities elsewhere in the Deep South.

Relations with the National Party, 1936–48

From the nullification debates of the 1830s to secession and the Dixiecrat revolt, South Carolina's rulers often assumed a leadership position in defending the South. In the first half of the twentieth century, the state delivered the region's strongest support for the national party ticket (see figure 1.3).[71] And Roosevelt delivered for South Carolina. For instance, even before securing nomination in 1932, the state's leading politicians had lobbied him about federal help in revitalizing the lowcountry. The ensuing federally supported Santee Cooper River project connected the state's most important river system with its chief port (Charleston Harbor), thus ending the lowcountry's long isolation from the rest of the state. Just as important, it brought inexpensive electricity to the region.[72] But over the course of the New Deal, leading South Carolina rulers began to part company over their support for the national party.

Longtime U.S. Senator "Cotton Ed" Smith became a leading opponent of the White House. His opposition to Fair Labor Standards legislation in 1937 prompted Roosevelt's unsuccessful attempt in 1938 to "purge" Smith.[73] In stark contrast to Smith, the state's other U.S. senator, James F. "Jimmy" Byrnes, remained closely linked to the national party and the administration. Despite his position on the right edge of the New Deal, he was a confidant of the president, and may have been Roosevelt's preferred vice-presidential running mate in 1944. Later he served as Truman's Secretary of State.[74]

Meeting in convention every four years, party leaders in 1938 reaffirmed their devotion to white supremacy and voiced increasing concern about the national party's electoral appeals to black voters.[75] Delegates voted overwhelmingly to abolish a party rule that required Democratic voters to back the party's presidential nominee.[76] In 1944, as occurred in Texas, Mississippi (as discussed later in this chapter), and other southern states, South Carolina Democrats began to split on the question of a fourth term for Roosevelt— and, more generally, on the national party itself. The party's convention followed closely on the adoption of the deregulation response to the abolition of the white primary. Its most devoted white supremacists almost succeeded in overtaking the convention and instructing the party's delegation to oppose Roosevelt's renomination. They did convince the party to adopt a white supremacy resolution.[77] As mentioned in chapter 4, the white supremacists had already begun to organize a Southern Democratic Party (SDP) by capitalizing on the appearance of the black Progressive Democratic Party (PDP). They hoped that by pushing Roosevelt's electors onto a PDP ballot, the Democratic Party would merge with the radically white supremacist SDP, and thus they would preserve an all-white state party.[78] The dissenters also pushed through what would be an important innovation in state party rules. By forcing the convention to recess rather than adjourn, and then reconvene after the National Convention, the party could wait to decide whether to back the national ticket until after the candidates and platform became known.[79]

Ruler Preferences and Responses to the Truman Shock

On the eve of Truman's challenge to the South, South Carolina party politicians remained unified in their defense of Jim Crow, but—as detailed in chapter 4—minor cracks had begun to emerge on the question of black incorporation into the state party. Several upcountry counties supported sporadic black participation in party affairs. And while the all-important state legislature remained in the hands of lowcountry politicians united in their defense of enclave rule, rulers differed in their time-horizons and views on the national party. Barnwell elites, such as Senate leader Edgar Brown and House Speaker Sol Blatt, were older, highly invested in the national party, and electorally invulnerable. As shown in chapter 4, they were tactically cautious as well.

Governor Strom Thurmond, elected in 1946 as a moderate, anti-Barnwell Ring force for political and economic modernization, planned to challenge New Dealer Olin Johnston in the U.S. Senate race in 1950.[80] Thurmond had won solid upcountry support but fared less well in the lowcountry. Thurmond was friendly to organized labor, and advocated for a state-level minimum wage law, better working conditions in industry, and workers' compensation. As historian Joseph Crespino notes, he embarked on this pro-labor agenda even as Congress beat back Truman's veto of the Taft-Hartley Act. Regarding the poll tax, Thurmond seems to have feared the very real possibility of a federal statute banning the practice, which would provide proponents of the state's democratization with a precedent to do much more damage to the pillars of enclave rule. Thus, he called for a popular referendum to remove the tax—which applied only to general elections, not to Democratic primaries—from the constitution. After some opposition by those who worried about increases in black voting, the General Assembly relented, and the public approved it in 1949.[81]

Thurmond won national praise in 1947 for his quick denunciation of a stunning lynching in Greenville, and for maintaining order. As late as October 1947, Thurmond praised Truman and backed his reelection.[82] In a Senate run against Johnston, Thurmond would be at a disadvantage, since Johnston had a secure base of support in the mill villages of the upcountry. Thus, he would have to maximize support from Black Belt whites. Given that Thurmond was titular head of the state party, and the state's representative in regional discussions on national party relations, his motives were of great importance in the enclave's response to Truman's endorsement of racial equality. Finally, considering that Barnwell leaders were devoted party loyalists—Edgar Brown was known as "Mr. Democrat"—the "revolt" in South Carolina was a revolt from not just the national party but also the state's leading politicians.

Bolting the Party

In early February 1948, after Truman's address to Congress, southern governors met at their regularly scheduled conference. There, Mississippi governor Fielding Wright convened a separate meeting to discuss the region's options, but only representatives from Alabama, Arkansas, Georgia, Mississippi, and South Carolina attended. Most governors refused to support a bolt. Thurmond, also opposed to abandoning the national party, called for a forty-day cooling-off period so that southern leaders could wrest concessions from Truman and the DNC. Most important, he wanted assurances that Truman would reverse course on his civil rights agenda in Congress and help craft a South-friendly platform. In doing so, Thurmond sought to appear suitably tough for his electorate. The governors backed Thurmond's motion.[83]

Southern politicians had a disappointing meeting with DNC chair Howard McGrath, who made clear his inability to offer any concessions. Rather, he could only promise his own support of a weak civil rights platform. An angry Thurmond joined Wright, Virginia governor William M. Tuck, and Arkansas governor Ben Laney in backing "some as yet undefined independent political action." By the end of April, only state parties in Mississippi, South Carolina, and Alabama backed such action.[84] Most southern parties planned to recess their conventions until after the National Convention in the hopes that the national party could be convinced to "come home"; if not, readjourned conventions would name—and instruct—their state's presidential electors. Senator Richard B. Russell of Georgia—later the South's leading strategist of massive resistance—gave Thurmond the idea that governors could control state party machinery and freely instruct electors without endangering their standing in the national party. If only three or four states did so, the party might reverse its position on civil rights.[85]

Among South Carolina Democrats, support began to build for Thurmond's call for an independent southern ticket that might win sufficient electoral votes in the South to send the election to the U.S. House of Representatives. Thurmond never voiced privately any expectation of the ticket's victory, or that it might develop a national appeal. Of all the States' Rights activists, Thurmond's rhetoric mostly concerned constitutional doctrine and federalism, not rallying cries of white supremacy. In preparation for the summer's convention, precincts and county conventions in the lowcountry opposed Truman's renomination.

As mentioned earlier, given white voters' steady loyalty to the Democratic party, *any* successful rebuke of the national party rested on the transfer of the party label on the presidential ballot to a different presidential ticket. Thus, even after the DNC failed in its legal challenges to secure the party label for its nominees, a successful bolting strategy would require control of the state party organization. This effort would be aided—at least informally—by support from federal officeholders. Senator Olin Johnston had a particularly difficult decision to make. Strongly opposed to Taft-Hartley and long identified with the New Deal, Johnston did not want to bolt the party. However, he, too, valued the maintenance of white supremacy. Seeking to maintain his strong ties to the national party, he thought that southern Democrats should try to prevent Truman's renomination from within. As he wrote Mississippi's Wright, "Most of us would prefer to fumigate the Democratic Party than abandon it to those who have temporarily gained control."[86]

Compared to statewide officials and federal officeholders, local and county-level party officials, Robert Garson writes, were "unencumbered by the fear of political punishment and had fewer ideological ties to the administration." They sought to secure county delegations committed to independent political action. In February, several lowcountry county parties announced that they had severed their ties with the national party. These moves greatly influenced state party chair William Baskin, viewed by most as possessing little ability or inclination to lead.[87] Here, the party's delayed compliance with the abolition of its white primary affected its response to the challenge from the national party. If not for its prevention of black participation in party affairs, blacks would have participated in county conventions, and there would have been significantly less "grassroots" support for the Dixiecrats.

Baskin and the party's executive committee voted to oppose any presidential nominee who supported "civil rights," and they instructed the party to name electors committed to "states' rights." In doing so, the party moved ahead of Thurmond and limited his options. In May, the party convention—as usual, malapportioned in favor of the lowcountry—instructed delegates to the National Convention to back Thurmond for president.

Politicians loyal to the national party angrily organized the "Citizens Democratic Party" (CDP). Supported by the small group of indigenous white liberals associated with the Southern Regional Council and other moderate and progressive groups, it strongly opposed the party oath intended to block black participation. Given strong white public opposition to Truman, it did not publicly back him. However, it did pledge itself to the national ticket. The CDP demanded that the state party only instruct delegates to the National Convention not to walk out. Otherwise, it would name its own delegates and challenge the seating of the state party's delegation. Rebuked by Baskin, the CDP appointed twenty delegates.[88] Moreover, six upcountry county parties allowed blacks to sign enrollment books, become members, and avoid a party oath.

The CDP was not alone in challenging the seating of the state party's delegation at the National Convention—the black Progressive Democratic Party (PDP) engineered its own challenge that drew on evidence used in the white primary court ruling it had just won (see chapter 4). At the meeting of the national Credentials Committee, PDP leader John McCray promised that the "party" would dissolve as soon as the state party incorporated blacks. Thurmond defended the state party, but walked out after refusing to answer questions by a black committee member from Missouri. Eventually, the committee agreed to seat South Carolina's regular delegation.[89] Meanwhile, at the States' Rights meeting in Jackson in May, Thurmond shocked his closest advisers by signaling his willingness to accept the States' Righters' presidential nomination.

By late July, under threat of criminal prosecution, Baskin ordered all county committees to enroll all qualified voters. Prior to the August party convention, he received pledges from executive committee members to back Thurmond's nomination. Those backing Truman sought to convince the state to print a "Democratic" ballot with two slates of electors—the state still lacked a secret ballot—but Thurmond instructed the party not to allow pro-Truman electors to appear as Democratic electors.[90] Given this opposition, and the great reluctance expressed by many of the state's members of Congress, the executive committee sought to develop a "moderate" course by which it would maintain ties to the national party and support Thurmond as the SRP's nominee. It named eight electors committed to the SRP only after defeating radicals and loyalists.[91]

Members from upcountry counties were furious with the state party's pledge to the Dixiecrats. They attempted in vain to pledge the party to Truman and to convince the legislature to decide the issue. On severing ties with national Democrats, Baskin claimed that only the convention could legally do so—thus, a legislative solution remained unavailable. Rumors spread that upcountry parties would exit the state party, and its newspapers rebuked the Dixiecrats as elitist reactionaries.[92]

DNC chair Howard McGrath announced that by endorsing Thurmond, the South Carolina party had now severed ties with the national party.[93] Candidates "will be automatically leaving the party by not supporting Truman." But the costs of defection were ambiguous. McGrath took pains to make clear that the national party was not "throwing out" any office seekers, but that they were exiting on their own—their support for the SRP was equivalent to their backing the Republican or Progressive Party. He acknowledged that the party lacked authority to expel individuals but could reject them as DNC members.

Meanwhile, party loyalists organized a "Citizens Committee" in Columbia in order to secure a place on the ballot for Truman and Barkley. The national party was establishing similar groups of what McGrath called "loyal Democrats" in the South, and began providing the CDP with financial and organizational assistance. The PDP remained committed to the national party, and urged blacks not to support the Wallace campaign. After its failure to secure seating at the National Convention in 1944, the PDP's position was delicate—leaders thought that their coordination with the CDP would further damage the possibilities of reconciliation with the "regular" party. On their view, any biracial cooperation would aid the Dixiecrat movement.

At this time, U.S. Representative Mendel Rivers was the state delegation's *only* member to back the States' Rights ticket.[94] Byrnes remained noncommittal. By early August, Johnston announced that he would back the national party despite his opposition to Truman's support for racial equality. Expecting a 1950 challenge by Thurmond, he planned to run as a party loyalist. Senator Burnet Maybank—whose political base remained in the lowcountry—announced his nominal support for the States' Rights movement. Very late in the game, the rest of the state's members of Congress reluctantly climbed aboard the Dixiecrat bandwagon. As expected, the States' Rights ticket won a large majority in South Carolina, but lost Anderson and Spartanburg counties, and generally did much more poorly in the upcountry.[95]

Aftermath

The DNC soon implicitly recognized the regular, and Dixiecrat-dominated, state party as the state's "real" Democratic party. Loyalist Democratic organizations abandoned plans for party-building and separate primaries. Immediately after the election, Thurmond's advisers warned of the costs of remaining linked to the SRP. First, they worried that voters would think that they would not be able to vote in the 1950 senatorial primary if they participated in States' Rights local committees. Second, rabid white supremacists increasingly dominated the States' Rights movement, and links with them could damage Thurmond's standing.[96]

At the state party's 1950 convention, Dixiecrat delegates overwhelmed their opponents, and secured the state party's compliance with new electoral laws that established literacy qualifications for all voters. In that year, Byrnes officially reentered state politics with a sweeping gubernatorial victory following his break with Truman over foreign and domestic policy.[97] Also in 1950, Senator Johnston narrowly defeated Thurmond in his reelection bid. On the defensive for his support of the national party in 1948, Johnston relied on labor unions, working-class whites, and black voters in the upcountry. Despite Johnston's denunciations of civil rights, South Carolina blacks strongly backed Johnston as the candidate more loyal to the national party; in doing so, they exerted influence over a statewide election for the first time in the twentieth century.[98]

Governor Byrnes, while rejecting bids to lead a reconfigured SRP, gradually loosened his ties to the national party by calling on voters to choose the next president without reference to party labels. The SRP was very poorly organized, and several governors in late 1951 denounced it, as well as Byrnes's hint that the South could prosper under a Republican president. In 1952 southern governors supported Stevenson, but Byrnes and Mississippi's Fielding Wright reserved the right to change their minds. Mainly, they sought to measure Eisenhower's popularity in the South.[99]

In 1952 South Carolina's state party declared itself independent of the national party. At the National Convention, delegations from South Carolina, Virginia, and Louisiana refused to pledge their loyalty to the national party, and liberal Democrats tried to unseat them. This bid failed, but the convention ruled that only those delegations pledged as loyal would be seated in 1956 and thereafter.[100]

South Carolina politicians again faced complex choices in their readjourned state convention in August. They could back the national Democratic ticket, Eisenhower, or an independent slate to be instructed later. Some recommended that the convention present two slates of electors on the November ballot, one pledged to Democrats, one to Republicans, thus providing an option for voters who wanted to support Eisenhower without having to vote Republican.[101] Eventually, the state party voted overwhelmingly to support the national ticket, but advised party members that they would not risk their standing in the party if they voted for another presidential candidate.[102] At the convention, there was a great deal of enthusiasm for Eisenhower and criticism of Truman and the Democratic ticket of Adlai Stevenson and John Sparkman. Byrnes eventually endorsed Eisenhower.[103]

A survey of party elites revealed that the "South Carolinians for Eisenhower" movement, organized largely by Democrats to place a separate (non-Republican) slate of electors on the ballot, sprang forth from two motives. Some organizers sought a more reliable vehicle for defending white supremacy than the increasingly rickety "house of our fathers." Others were drawn to a traditional Republican small-government message. Precinct-level analysis bore this out at the mass level, too: Eisenhower was strongest among lowcountry whites in majority-black areas and among better-off whites in emerging metropolitan areas. Eisenhower narrowly lost, receiving 49 percent of the vote. Upcountry working-class whites, the base of support for Senator Olin Johnston's strongly backed Stevenson. In a sign that the state Republican party machinery was still too hapless and uninterested in growing or winning elections, almost all of Eisenhower's supporters backed the slate of electors representing "South Carolinians for Eisenhower," not that of the Republican party.[104] As chapter 7 shows, the experimentation of a growing number of white elites and voters opposed to the national Democratic party would grow more complicated throughout the 1950s and early 1960s.

In a complex process generated by the vagaries of factional conflict, party rules, and personal ambition, South Carolina took part in the Dixiecrat revolt. Its leadership in the revolt is attributable to the ambitions of Thurmond, who planned an upcoming campaign against Olin Johnston, a party loyalist. As will be made clear by the experiences of Mississippi and Georgia, the decision concerning how to respond to Truman's shock cannot be read off of the state's political economy, political culture, or the strength of black insurgency.

More so than with the state's deregulation response to *Smith v. Allwright*, the state's participation in the Dixiecrat revolt activated sectional differences within the ruling party. These would largely be overwhelmed by *Brown* and the state's "massive resistance" to racial desegregation. Although not apparent immediately, Byrnes's behavior during the revolt and after would inspire other white supremacist officials as they began to inch toward using the Republican label to pursue careers and policy goals. However, as chapters 7 and 10 show, the South Carolina Republican Party's growth was limited and delayed in ways traceable to Democrats' temporary embrace of the SRP. This would prove to be the period's most important legacy for the state's subsequent democratization.

Mississippi

In Mississippi, leading politicians, less reliant on the national party for patronage and other benefits and still strongly committed to the project of enclave rule, mobilized white civil society in a triumphant revolt. As chapter 6 details, Mississippi's experience in the States' Rights movement made it less likely that politicians would begin considering the Republican party as a suitable vehicle for pursuing policy and career goals.

Relations with the National Party, 1936–48

Along with South Carolinians, Mississippi voters boasted the country's strongest support for Roosevelt. From 1932 through 1944, Roosevelt's vote totals ranged from 94 to 97 percent.[105] And, following Deep South patterns, almost seventy-five thousand Mississippians (out of a total population of about two million) worked for a New Deal agency between 1935 and 1940, and tens of thousands of rural whites benefited from rural electrification and several relief programs.[106] The state's elites followed their voters. In 1937 Theodore Bilbo backed Roosevelt's Court-packing plan—the first U.S. senator to do so—and a Mississippi Bar Association resolution voiced its approval. Bilbo also made headlines by calling for FDR to serve a third term. Unlike other southerners, Bilbo did not abandon New Deal legislation even when northern Democrats introduced antilynching and anti–poll tax legislation.[107] In 1939, the state's support for the New Deal reached its high-water mark with the election of Paul B. Johnson as governor on a "little New Deal" platform.

The state's most influential national politician, Senator Pat Harrison, strongly backed the national ticket. Serving from 1919 until his death in 1941, Harrison chaired the powerful Senate Finance Committee throughout the 1930s. He had backed the politically risky choice of Catholic Al Smith in 1928, and endorsed Governor Roosevelt in 1931. Harrison had a national reputation as a party speaker, given his service in the Democratic Speaker's Bureau. In the judgment of one historian, he "exerted more national power and influence than any Mississippian since Jefferson Davis." A protégé of Bernard Baruch, Harrison harbored ideological objections to the New Deal but for partisanship and patronage motives remained loyal to Roosevelt.[108]

Harrison's death in 1941 facilitated the growth of anti–New Deal forces in the state party.[109] In 1943 these forces won two key elections viewed by many as referenda on the New Deal. First, James O. "Cotton Seed Jim" Eastland, decrying the "communistic" influences of the New Deal, captured Harrison's seat despite strong opposition from the administration. And in the first gubernatorial primary, 64 percent of voters supported anti-Roosevelt (and anti-fourth term) candidates who denounced federal interference in the state's racial order.[110] The eventual winner, Thomas Bailey, quietly received money from New Dealers in Washington, who viewed him as less conservative than his opponent.

1944: A Mini-Revolt Fails

By 1944, however, Acting Governor Dennis Murphee warned Roosevelt that his "enemies had captured control of the Mississippi Democratic party." Although the vast majority of the state's voters continued to back Roosevelt, several Deltan party elites took control of moribund county conventions in order to dominate the state convention.[111] Pro-Roosevelt Bilbo had reason to be worried. Unlike in Texas, Mississippi Democrats remained sufficiently united such that there would not be enough dissenters to hold a "rump" convention. The state party convention confirmed administration fears by sending a delegation uninstructed on which nominee to support, but instructed to resist social equality planks and to demand the restoration of the two-thirds rule and specific planks on states' rights, white supremacy, and labor relations. It also named an uninstructed slate of nine presidential electors. In a measure of the governor's weak influence over the state party, the convention triumphed over the pro-administration preferences of Governor Bailey.[112]

By late June, the region's bolters lost momentum, and Bailey and other governors worked to block any southern delegations from instead endorsing Virginia Senator Harry Byrd.[113] But on the eve of the election, three of the state's nine electors announced that they would vote for Byrd. They noted that the party's convention in June freed them to vote as they wished if the Chicago convention failed to restore the two-thirds rule or if it backed racial equality planks, and that the party's nominees no longer represented "the Democratic party as Mississippians have known it for fifty years." Voters were outraged. Under the governor's orders, the Highway Patrol distributed new ballots across the state that omitted the names of the three "mavericks." Bilbo, Eastland, and Bailey urged voters over statewide radio to vote for the loyalist slate. Roosevelt won 93 percent of the vote. None of the congressional primary candidates openly opposed Roosevelt, and all incumbents won reelection.[114]

Ruler Preferences and Responses to the Truman Shock

Mississippi rulers were relieved when Truman won the vice-presidential nomination. But by mid-1947—after the tumultuous summer of 1946, Truman's abandonment of the South on several policy issues, and his shocking address to the NAACP's annual conference—Mississippi politicians, like those in other states, strongly opposed his renomination.[115] By year's end, Truman's Civil Rights Committee released its report, and Mississippi politicians believed that extreme steps must be taken to alter the national party's course. House Speaker Walter Sillers confided to friends that southern Democrats must guard against those who would accept national party patronage and thereby crucify "the South on a cross of racial equality and non-segregation . . . and destroy everything we southerners . . . hold most dearly." He vowed to introduce legislation that would—somehow—effect a divorce between the state and national Democratic parties.[116]

Mississippi's rulers imagined a broad set of responses to Truman's move. First, they could simply send a delegation to the National Convention to write a South-friendly platform and back the national ticket. Second, they could repeat their 1944 gambit of deferring their choice of presidential nominee until after the convention. Third, they could begin seriously to explore the formation of a regional ticket that could throw the election to the U.S. House, where the South might again exercise something like a veto over presidential selection. An even more radical choice—a leadership role in regional coordination in constructing an alternative regional ticket—had not yet emerged as a possibility.

Mississippi's rulers were highly unified in seeking to reverse interference by the national party and central state apparatus. But as in South Carolina, rulers' preferences about strategies varied with their institutional positions. Unlike governors in South Carolina and Georgia, Mississippi's governor, Fielding Wright, did not harbor desires for higher elective office. Taking office in January 1948, he won because of his efforts to maintain the white primary. Radicalized Deltan politicians greatly influenced Wright, who before was relatively nonideological. Compared to governors of other states, Wright possessed less control over his state's federal patronage; thus, he calculated relatively lower costs in taking steps that might trigger punishments by federal actors (see chapter 3).

The state legislature, whose most influential members dominated the SDEC, was in some ways one of the most progressive in decades. Young war veterans made their presence felt, and the 1948 session featured several progressive legislative achievements. However, the state's most powerful politician remained House Speaker Walter Sillers.[117] Like members of South Carolina's Barnwell Ring, he had no progressive political ambitions. Unlike members of the Ring, however, Sillers did not hope to remake the Delta through federally sponsored economic development initiatives. Thus, he was unconcerned about the consequences of a bolt for the Delta. In January, before his inauguration, Wright announced that if Truman backed the recommendations of his Civil Rights Committee, he would help engineer Mississippi's exit.

Most of the state's federal officeholders were fiercely reactionary, and opposed the national party and Truman administration largely on labor issues.[118] Mississippi had relatively little access to federal patronage, especially after Harrison's death; these officeholders were thus more emboldened to exit the party. Both senators were very new to the chamber and had little seniority. Eastland was fiercely white supremacist, while former judge John Stennis, cautious by nature, privately advocated party loyalty. Judge Herbert Holmes, a key advocate of revolt, still chaired the SDEC, which was stacked with Wright supporters. Finally, white Democrats loyal to the national party—including liberals, labor leaders, federal government employees, and some pro-segregationists still backing the New Deal—offered little resistance within the state party to the growing move to reject the national party's nominees.[119] In sum, influential politicians united in their opposition to the national party and its nominees.

Because of its propitious timing—days after Truman's Joint Address had been leaked in the press—Wright's inaugural address served as the state party's first response to what seemed to be the national party's abandonment of its loyal southern enclaves. In it, he hinted that the state would "break" with the party to defend "vital principles."[120] More important as an indication of the preferences of the state party, Mississippi's legislature praised the speech and warned others not to interfere in the South. The SDEC also backed Wright.[121]

The Reaction: Mississippi Walks Out

After Truman's address to Congress on February 2, 1948, Wright called for an open statewide meeting that same month and for the party convention in June to refuse to endorse the president; he then asked all southern parties to follow suit. Jackson's Jaycees and its Junior Bar Association praised the governor. SDEC chair Herbert Holmes agreed partly with Sillers' call for a southern presidential candidate.[122] Wright soon became the impatient but determined leader of the southern resistance. The open meeting attracted almost five thousand from all eighty-two counties, and roundly condemned the president and the national party and called for a regionwide meeting of "True Jeffersonian Democrats." With "a minimum of confusion, the Democratic party of Mississippi was converted into a vehicle for anti-Truman sentiment."[123]

Black groups quickly endorsed Truman in a mass meeting and asked the governor and state legislature to establish a biracial commission on race relations. There was no response. Later that fall, a black group committed to Truman collaborated with white pro-administration Democrats.[124] After the southern governors' disappointing meeting with DNC chair Howard McGrath, Mississippi's SDEC instructed delegates to oppose any "civil rights" candidate, and to walk out of the convention if a civil rights plank were approved. The state's electors "must be States Righters." By March, Wright had headquartered the regional States' Rights movement in Jackson, begun campaigning across the South, and addressed Mississippi's whites in a stirring radio address.[125]

The People's Committee of Loyal States' Rights Democrats soon suggested that all of the state's estimated 400,000 (white) Democrats help capture county party conventions for the cause by each contributing a dollar to the campaign and wearing a States' Rights Democrat button. The impressive mobilization resulted in some strange excesses; for instance, the legislature "considered a bill which would have required all radio stations within the state to play 'Dixie' at the end of each day's programs."[126]

In a subsequent radio address, Governor Wright took the unprecedented step of speaking directly to black Mississippi. He sought to explain the aims of the States' Rights Party (SRP), allay black fears about it, and asked them to "place their trust in the innate, uncoerced sense of justice of the white people with whom they live." "Your individual rights and liberties shall be respected and safeguarded, not by the Federal Government, but by your duly constituted local and state authorities. You have the opportunity of assisting in the preservation of peace and decorum in our midst." He then issued an ultimatum—if blacks supported such outsiders, the state would no longer be a happy place for them.

Afterward, black newspaperman Percy Greene threatened a black exodus from the Delta. The NAACP considered Wright's speech a "clear invitation to mob violence." L. O. Crosby, a white businessman and patron of black education leaders, feared such an exodus and vowed to help secure better policies on a range of issues if black leaders publicly backed segregation and worked to calm their followers. One such leader, now constrained by a more assertive black counterpublic, refused to do so despite the financial costs to his school.[127]

In March, Mississippi's Young Democrats announced their support of Governor Wright's efforts. The state's few loyalists included backers of Bilbo, labor officials, federal employees, and some liberals. Before the state party reconvened in early August, the press mentioned "reports of 'organized resistance'" to the States' Rights movement on some college campuses.[128]

In June, Mississippi Democrats came together and instructed their delegates to the Democratic National Convention that if they bolted or were denied credentials, they were to proceed directly to a States' Rights rally in Birmingham.[129] The new practice of recessing, rather than adjourning, the state Democratic party's convention worked to the bolters' advantage. It would make it impossible by party rules for loyal Democrats to meet in a "rump" convention, since recess meant the convention would remain in session.[130]

At Philadelphia, the unified States' Rights delegation narrowly avoided expulsion and replacement by a loyalist delegation that included blacks.[131] Sillers, a member of the Platform Committee, presented a minority report that he claimed was not a "sectional plank." Ultimately, southern resistance to the proposed platform backfired, as delegates adopted a significantly more antisouthern platform. Almost all of the remaining southern delegates cast their ballots for the South's favorite son, Senator Richard B. Russell. The Mississippi delegation then walked out and headed for Birmingham.[132]

Eighty-seven percent of Mississippi voters supported the States' Rights ticket (the same percentage as would vote for Goldwater in 1964).[133] About 2,500 blacks voted for Dewey. Percy Greene coordinated the Truman campaign among blacks, and from this emerged a new black protest organization, the Mississippi State Democratic Association. It worked with the PVL and NAACP to register blacks. Another 4,500 blacks split their votes between Wallace and Truman.

Aftermath

The party's revolt led to a three-year conflict over the control of federal patronage that divided the party and led to legal and political battles over which faction possessed the "Democrat" brand name. Since the 1948 party convention selected SDEC members, the small band of national party loyalists had no legal authority to dispense federal jobs. County committees passed resolutions backing the party's denunciation of the loyalists, who attempted to organize pro-Truman Democrats at precinct and county levels, but on an anti–civil rights platform. In 1949 Wright called for a special session to determine the "true" party in an effort to influence the DNC's deliberations, but the Credentials Committee ultimately removed States' Rights members of the DNC from all four Dixiecrat states (Alabama, Louisiana, Mississippi, and South Carolina). Truman loyalists sought to organize an official Democratic party, declared the SRP dead, and suggested that it ask for forgiveness. But they were roundly denounced by Governor Wright and much of the party establishment.[134]

Meanwhile, States' Rights activists attempted several times to jump-start the "party" both in Mississippi and regionally, but these efforts failed. In 1952 the state party backed the South's favorite-son candidate, Russell, and sent uninstructed delegates to the National Convention; if the nominees and platform were not acceptable, the convention would reconvene. The party then declared itself a "free and independent political party." Upon reconvening, however, party regulars bowed to the inevitable and forced the state party to back the national ticket of Stevenson and Sparkman. The state party did not follow South Carolina's lead in attempting to treat Eisenhower supporters well, and lacked any strong pro-Eisenhower leadership of the type offered by South Carolina governor James Byrnes. Party chair Tom Tubb even called for legislation—not party regulations—to oust Eisenhower backers from the party.[135] Some SRP activists attempted, like those in South Carolina, to organize an "Independents for Eisenhower" movement that included House Speaker Walter Sillers, but it was a smaller affair. As in South Carolina, nominal state Republicans were so riven by factional disputes that they did not manage even to place a slate of official Republican electors on the November ballot. Still, Eisenhower received 40 percent of the state's vote (with an "Independents-for-Eisenhower" slate of electors). His support was greatest in the Delta, not in urban areas; Eisenhower won large majorities in eighteen of twenty counties that were more than 60 percent black. Planters and larger firm owners there provided financial support.[136] As chapter 6 shows, Republican party building would not emerge in earnest until the late 1950s.[137]

The Dixiecrat revolt briefly caused chaos in the party but, as detailed in chapter 6, served over the medium term to facilitate the party's unified anticipation of, and response to, *Brown*. As in South Carolina, it also ushered in a period in which the party regularly flirted with endorsing Republican presidential candidates. Mississippi rulers sought to confine all such movements within, or alongside, the Democratic party. Lacking a well-respected figure like Byrnes to galvanize its forces, Mississippi Republicanism would emerge more slowly than in South Carolina.

Georgia

As with the abolition of the white primary, the national party's embrace of racial equality had significant consequences for Georgia's transition from authoritarian rule. On the eve of Truman's shock, chaos reigned within Georgia's ruling party. Black Georgia had just developed the most impressive statewide insurgency in the Deep South. Facing a united front of white moderates and liberals and more than 100,000 registered blacks, the right-wing, white supremacist Talmadge faction responded with repression and violence. In the aftermath of the 1946 gubernatorial election and the Three Governors Controversy, anti-Talmadgeites considered developing a separate, biracial party loyal to the national party. Legal control over the "Democrat" label remained unclear, and both Talmadgeites and their opponents were unsure that one-party rule—and with it stable enclave rule—would continue.

Capitalizing on their repression of black voters and the disarray among their foes, Talmadgeites won another important election and controlled party machinery in 1948. The progressive ambitions of key faction members, coupled with the uncertainties surrounding "ownership" of the party, caused factional leaders to avoid the Dixiecrat revolt. This decision helped ensure Talmadgeite domination until the early 1960s, and meant that Georgia's leading white supremacists would guide the party-state's responses to *Brown* and ultimately help produce the state's bifurcated democratization.

Relations with the National Party, 1936–48

As in the rest of the Deep South, Georgia's white electorate overwhelmingly supported Roosevelt and the New Deal. However, the state's reactionary Talmadgeite leadership through much of the 1930s and 1940s disrupted relations between the state and national parties. In 1935, as South Carolina and Mississippi competed with one another to secure Roosevelt's largest margin of victory in the upcoming election, Governor Talmadge considered challenging Roosevelt for the nomination.[138] After a complicated series of illegal strong-arm tactics and other shenanigans by Talmadge, the DNC organized pro-Roosevelt forces within the state, and Talmadge relented and backed Roosevelt's renomination.[139] In opposition to Talmadge—and setting a precedent for similar efforts in the 1940s—a small group of moderates organized the "Free Democrats" and railed against Talmadge's disloyalty and "bossism" in Georgia.

In 1938—as in South Carolina and Maryland—Roosevelt targeted the state's venerable senior senator, Walter George, for defeat.[140] Despite great opposition to this (ultimately unsuccessful) interference in state elections, Roosevelt remained extremely popular. As Roosevelt prepared for his unprecedented third nomination in 1940, Talmadge again won the party's gubernatorial nomination. The party remained divided into two broad factions: a group of liberals and others valuing party "regularity" backed his renomination, and a faction uniting those who supported Talmadge and George that opposed Roosevelt and the New Deal.[141]

As described in chapter 4, Ellis Arnall hitched his star to the liberal wing of the national party and won the governorship as a strong supporter of the New Deal and director of the state's Roosevelt-Wallace clubs. In 1943, however, regional opposition to Roosevelt and the national party swelled.[142] Still, at the 1944 National Convention, Arnall managed the convention floor for Henry Wallace, and praised him in his seconding speech for the vice-presidential nomination. Significantly, unlike delegations from other southern states, Arnall held Georgia's delegation united in favor of both Roosevelt *and* Wallace.[143] Georgia's congressional delegation—featuring a pair of respected senators in Walter George and Richard Russell—was both highly conservative and loyal to the national party.

Until the late 1940s, Georgia's relations with the national party mirrored in some respects those of other Deep South enclaves. But, because of the governor's relatively greater powers over state party machinery, and the fact that Georgia in this period featured a quite liberal and then a right-wing governor, the state party oscillated a good deal. In the aftermath of the Three Governors Controversy, the state party, once factionalized, now lay fractured. As detailed in chapter 4, many anti-Talmadge elites made strides toward the construction of an alternative—and biracial—Democratic party loyal to the national party.[144] The 1946 party convention, dominated by Talmadgeites after the elder Talmadge's corrupt victory over Carmichael, selected a new executive committee (SDEC) that would serve until the 1948 convention. But it also transferred the power to appoint sixty at-large SDEC members from the governor to the party chair.

Thus, when the anti-Talmadge Thompson became governor and concluded the Three Governors Controversy, the Talmadge faction retained control of state party machinery. After losing the governor's office, Herman Talmadge commented, "I don't give a damn what Washington thinks, I'm running the Democratic party in Georgia." Governor Thompson won the DNC's official imprimatur and rallied anti-Talmadge forces to convene the party. Litigation in state court ensued over which faction controlled the Democrat brand name. Complicating matters, in 1948—alone among Deep South enclaves—Georgia would hold a gubernatorial election.[145] Here, Herman Talmadge would likely face Thompson. However, Democrats in six-unit counties pursued lawsuits seeking to invalidate the county-unit system. If successful, party primaries would be chosen by popular vote. Urban and black votes would likely carry the day for Arnall, still leader of the party's progressive wing, and enclave rule in Georgia would be transformed. Additionally, if anti-Talmadge forces succeeded in building a political movement outside the party, their gubernatorial nominee would battle Talmadge in the general election that, critically, was governed by popular vote, not the county-unit system. The statewide mobilization of blacks could thus provide a second path toward the reform—or even end—of enclave rule.

Voters absorbed Truman's shock amid this litigation. Meanwhile, Governor Thompson stood with other southern governors against Truman's civil rights program as "unnecessary" and "unwise," but backed the national ticket. Regardless of his true preferences—he seemed to want to remain a loyal Democrat—the fact that the DNC supported his position in his litigation over the party label made his loyalty mandatory. Later, he backed Thurmond's call for a cooling-off period. At this time, the state's white supremacists still favored remaining within the national party, given the evils of the Republican party.[146]

In late February 1948, in what Joseph Bernd termed "a brilliant victory" for the Talmadge faction, the Georgia Supreme Court ruled unanimously that the faction legally controlled state party machinery.[147] This meant, among other things, that a Talmadgeite SDEC would select National

Convention delegates instructed to oppose Truman's renomination. The naming of presidential electors and control of the general election ballot would rest with the winner of the September 1948 gubernatorial primary, whose forces would control the SDEC.[148]

Ruler Preferences and Responses to the Truman Shock

A variety of motives—and institutional arrangements—shaped the preferences of key actors regarding Georgia's relations with the national party. The preferences of the Talmadge faction, the anti-Talmadge faction, and the state's leading federal officeholder, Senator Richard Russell, are described later. The most important factor in the state party's response was its divided nature. Before a primary, the split between the governor's office and the state party machinery meant that the party could not act decisively. This was important because gubernatorial leadership was paramount in the shaping of enclave relations with the national party. Gubernatorial pronouncements, together with governors' participation in meetings with national party elites and regional coordination efforts, were politically the most decisive elements of the ruling party's management of the crisis over the national party's embrace of racial equality.

Members of the Talmadge faction immediately denounced Truman's civil rights program. With control of the party-state at stake in the 1948 gubernatorial election, immediate electoral concerns guided the faction's decision-making. Differing ideological positions within the faction would emerge more sharply after the election. Concerning the state's participation in the Dixiecrat revolt, Roy Harris recommended a wait-and-see approach to party chair Peters, Talmadge, and like-minded strategists around the South. In deciding not to join Mississippi and South Carolina in the growing revolt, the faction was, according to Harris, influenced by "very little sentiment in Georgia favorable for bolting the National Organization."[149]

Thus, Peters attended the Jackson rally in May and announced the Georgia delegation's support for a resolution urging the selection of anti-Truman delegates to the National Convention. But he also announced that the Georgians did "not favor, nor would we commit the Democrats of Georgia to bolt the Democratic party, nor do anything which could aid in the establishment of a third party." Over the spring, Peters perceived growing grassroots opposition to Truman, but sentiment remained fairly well split.[150] Critically, Talmadge faction leaders expected that the gubernatorial election would be a referendum on which faction more strongly opposed the national party's platform. They expected to win the election, but imagined Talmadge could lose if anti-Talmadge forces successfully branded them as disloyal. Thus, their pronouncements on the Dixiecrat party remained vague.

In July, before the September election, the 1946 party convention reconvened to denounce Truman but selected uninstructed delegates to the National Convention. It also endorsed Eisenhower for president and Russell for vice president, but the latter refused to have his name introduced. At the National Convention, the Georgia delegation remained after losing platform battles. In addressing the convention, Charles Bloch—soon a leading strategist of massive resistance—exclaimed, "You shall not crucify the South on this cross of civil rights."[151] As it planned Herman Talmadge's gubernatorial campaign, the Talmadge-controlled party privately supported bolters in Alabama and elsewhere and publicly denounced Truman, but did not back the SRP.[152]

A minor flare-up during the campaign illustrates the mixed motives guiding the Talmadge faction. SDEC chair Jim Peters caused a stir when he was quoted as saying that the 1948 state party convention would "avoid . . . the negro issue." The fate of the faction remained bound up in the issue of white supremacy. Although young Herman Talmadge was less devoted to white supremacy than his father—or the senior members of the faction—the situation narrowed the faction's choices on race policies and its attitudes toward the national party. If the faction were to triumph, it would need to suppress black votes and mobilize white supremacists.

Politicians long loyal to the national party—and to Truman himself—composed the anti-Talmadge faction. However, the faction was divided internally; its failure to converge on a single candidate had contributed greatly to its 1946 defeat. Many viewed Governor Thompson, campaigning to finish Gene Talmadge's term, as unintelligent and the dupe of former governor Eurith "E. D." Rivers.[153] Thompson's ambivalence over white primary legislation found echoes in his response to Truman's challenge. While denouncing the national party and joining Thurmond's call for a cooling-off period during which governors might negotiate with national officials, he also publicly backed Truman's renomination.

The faction came together, but weakly. Stronger candidates Carmichael and Arnall decided not to run. Arnall campaigned for Thompson, and denounced Talmadge's race-baiting and his significant role in "disgracing" the state. Anti-Talmadge politicians had long staked their careers on endorsements and patronage from national party actors and their support of the New Deal. Their disgust over the 1946 campaign, the shame brought on the state in the wake of the Three Governors Controversy, and the continuing "tyranny" of the county-unit system pushed others—especially urban reformers—closer to the national party despite opposition to Truman's civil rights proposals.[154]

In 1948 all of Georgia's federal officeholders had the good fortune of running unopposed. For sincere and strategic reasons, though, they still strongly denounced Truman's proposals. Among them, the most influential in state party affairs was Senator Richard Russell. By 1945 he had come to lead the chamber's southerners, but backed most of Truman's non–civil rights domestic and foreign policies. The national party's turn against the South horrified him, and he worried about interference in southern law enforcement.[155] However, he remained devoted to "party regularity," and opposed his own nomination as a favorite-son candidate in Philadelphia, or consideration of his nomination as a States' Rights presidential candidate at the Birmingham convention.[156] He did suggest to Thurmond that if a few southern governors could take hold of party machinery and name electors opposed to the national ticket, the South might help throw the election to the House. Russell ultimately announced—along with several of the state's members of Congress—that he would vote for Truman.[157]

Throughout the transition period, it could be expected that federal officeholders would play key roles in fashioning enclave defenses and actions. Russell's role in Georgia party affairs is instructive here. As the undisputed leader of the South's congressional resistance, Russell was a likely candidate to manage Georgia's handling of the crisis. However, the extensive correspondence detailing the strategizing of the party elite rarely mentions him; rather, it points to his consistent deference to the views of young Herman Talmadge.

The 1948 Gubernatorial Election

Thompson and Talmadge—the two factions' "nominees"—both strongly opposed Truman's civil rights program while promising new social policies and state administrative reforms. White supremacy, of course, was the main issue, and Talmadge ran mostly against Arnall and Rivers. He also attacked Truman's civil rights program as "the most dangerous threat to Georgia's way of life since Reconstruction," and linked Thompson—via Arnall—to the incredibly unpopular Progressive Party candidate Henry Wallace (who polled 0.1 percent in the state), and to Atlanta opponents of the county-unit system.[158]

Benefiting from some grassroots revulsion against the national party and the White House, talented stump speaker Talmadge won 130 of 159 counties, but won the popular vote by only 7 percent. Talmadge forces admitted their surprise that black voter registration and turnout were lower than in 1946. But this surprise was disingenuous—once again, black voters confronted various electoral barriers, slowdowns in black precincts, and Klan cross-burnings and other attacks in a handful of counties. And Talmadge men, such as House floor leader Bob Elliott, embarked on white voter registration drives to blunt the impact of the "Negro bloc vote."[159] Importantly, however, after the disappointing results following the amazing statewide black mobilization in 1946—and the fear engendered by that campaign's electoral violence—black and biracial efforts to mobilize against Talmadge declined substantially. Indeed, the defeat of 1946 left a profound mark on statewide black protest. From 1947 to 1949, state membership in the NAACP declined sharply; almost all of this decline occurred in south Georgia (the Black Belt and coastal areas) (table 3.3).[160]

Party Choices after the Gubernatorial Election

The size of Talmadge's September 8 victory suggested to many that there was strong support for the Dixiecrat movement in Georgia and in the South generally. Some saw the results themselves as a referendum on national Democrats and a clear mandate for Governor-elect Talmadge to lead Georgia out of the national party. SDEC chair Jim Peters—himself highly trusted by white supremacist forces—warned Talmadge that, indeed, he had no other choice.[161] Moreover, the Talmadge forces now had even greater control over state party machinery owing to their ability to clear out remaining pro-Thompson members. The pressure from outside continued, especially from elites in Alabama and from Thurmond himself, who delivered well-attended speeches in the state. However, because of institutional constraints and the time-horizons of key Talmadge actors, dominant forces within the state party kept it on the sidelines.

Talmadge forces considered selecting presidential electors pledged to Truman, Thurmond, or leaving them unpledged. Peters perceived that Georgia's white public opinion was "about evenly split" between those backing Truman and those backing Thurmond.[162] Faction hardliners, led by Roy Harris and Charles Bloch, called for "the naming of Democratic electors in Georgia opposed to any candidate supporting a civil rights program." Bloch's position was shaped largely by his deeply principled constitutional and white supremacist opposition to Truman's turn toward what Thurmond called "a police state." Harris, now the state's key white supremacist organizer and pamphleteer, thought the faction would benefit from a principled stand; Peters generally supported this position.[163]

Talmadge, however, was just beginning what he hoped would be a long political career. Since governors could not seek consecutive terms, he eyed a 1950 U.S. Senate race against the aging Walter George. And Talmadgeite Bob Elliott preferred staying with the national party for strategic reasons:

> The decision...should be made in the light of circumstances in 1950, not 1948. We have already won in 1948; we want to win again in 1950.... By September

1950, Dewey will have been in office almost two years, and his popularity and that of the Republican party will have waned. Many of our own people who support [Dewey] will be turning back to the traditional party of the South. The question of party regularity will then arise to haunt those who may have deprived the people of the State of the opportunity to vote the regular party ticket in 1948.... Let the names of the candidates appear.... This is the only sure way to maintain party regularity. This will eliminate ghosts in 1950.

Since the fate of the faction may rest with Talmadge's next campaign, he urged, this consideration above all must guide the faction.[164]

Institutional constraints also militated against a bolt from the national party. First, unlike governors elsewhere—who had the time and resources to mobilize voters and develop organizations devoted to states' rights—Talmadge had to devote his attention to winning the gubernatorial election. Second, Thompson, still governor until January, used his influence in the legislature and party to pressure the party to name pro-Truman electors. After the demise of the white primary, the party remained tangled up in the state. Thus, the General Assembly blocked his efforts and then freed electors to vote as they liked.[165]

The situation grew increasingly confused, as the state of the law regarding ballot regulation and the positions of the Talmadge faction both remained unclear. In October, Ed Willingham, a Talmadge supporter from Augusta and the chair of Georgia's States' Rights organization, claimed "the Talmadge organization is behind us 100 per cent." However, the SDEC on October 2 appointed twelve electors verbally pledged to Truman if he won a majority of Georgia's votes. This greatly dimmed Dixiecrat prospects in the state. With the "Democratic" party label affixed above a list of electors (conditionally) pledged to Truman, States' Rights nominees could win the state's electoral votes only if a plurality of Georgia voters abandoned their traditional party loyalty and instead embraced the States' Rights Party (SRP).

For the remaining month, Talmadge himself avoided a straightforward endorsement of any ticket, remarking only that he endorsed "Talmadge as a candidate for governor." Unable to develop an SRP infrastructure, followers of Thurmond and Wright won only 20 percent of the state's vote and only ten counties—most of which bordered Thurmond's own home county of Edgefield, South Carolina. This compared to 61 percent for Truman and 18 percent for Dewey. Regional differences between north Georgia and south Georgia played out as expected. Moreover, they were actually regional differences, not urban/rural splits. Thurmond reached 30 percent in the Black Belt, and even did as well in metro as in south Georgia, but garnered less than 11 percent of the vote in north Georgia (and 12 percent in Atlanta's Fulton County).[166] A majority of black voters—unlike those in other Deep South states—voted Republican for president. In December, all twelve electors—including Charles Bloch—complied with the SDEC and backed Truman.[167]

Aftermath

After its 1948 defeat—in which it had successfully united behind a single, but weak, candidate—the anti-Talmadge faction collapsed again in 1950, as Thompson lost to Talmadge.[168] By 1950 Russell publicly wished for a stronger southern Republican party so that the South, taken for granted by Democrats, could return to being influential within the party. But he rejected a suggestion for institutionalized cooperation among southern Democrats and Republicans in the Senate.[169] Russell's position as Capitol Hill's leader of southern resistance and his influence in the Democratic caucus maintained his attractiveness as a favorite-son candidate. Russell sought to use the 1952 presidential election to increase the South's leverage within the party. Southern elites eventually convinced him to embark on a quixotic bid for the Democratic nomination.[170] After this bid failed, Russell remained loyal to the "house of his fathers." Unlike South Carolina's governor, James Byrnes, Russell would not try to lead Georgia politicians to embrace the Republican party.

As chapter 8 shows, the Talmadge faction continued to dominate statewide elections throughout the 1950s and early 1960s. Georgia's relations with the national party remained troubled, as the party continued to reconvene after National Conventions to consider its fealty to the national ticket and platform. Given their tenuous control of party machinery, Talmadge leaders worried that abandoning the national party would risk the faction's dominance in the future. By remaining on the sidelines of the Dixiecrat revolt, the faction safeguarded Talmadge rule in the 1950s. Under these conditions, Georgia rulers responded to *Brown* with a "massive resistance" that fractured statewide networks of black protest, paving the way for Georgia's eventual bifurcated democratization.

Conclusion

Truman won about 53 percent of the popular vote in the South despite not appearing below the "Democratic Party" label in three SRP states and appearing not at all on Alabama's ballot. Focused on a possible reelection bid in 1952, Truman's instinct as a "party regular" was to minimize punishment of States' Righters in Congress, and not to attempt to "purge" them by backing their primary opponents. Thus, the seniority of wayward southern members of Congress was not curtailed, and federal patronage continued to flow to Dixiecrat supporters—much to the consternation of many southern Democratic loyalists. Ten of fifteen Senate committees remained chaired by senators from the South and Border South. But the DNC did expel five rebellious Deep South members.[171] Truman's race reforms agenda quickly faded. His reelection posed no new short-term dangers to enclave rule, as the filibuster dispensed with legislation establishing a permanent FEPC and abolishing the poll tax.[172]

For all of southern Democrats' rage at Truman's rhetorical commitment to racial equality, it is worth noting that during the New and Fair Deals—from 1933 to 1952—the United States created III new federal agencies. As historian Thomas Sugrue points out, only one of them, the FEPC, focused centrally on race reforms, and it quickly dissolved. The Civil Rights Division of the DOJ, which was quite small, emerged as the only component of the rapidly expanding central state apparatus focused in part on attacking the pillars of enclave rule. The abolition of the white primary, the Truman "shock," and the next democratization challenge—*Brown v. Board of Education*—demonstrated that federal courts and black challengers remained for the moment the true adversaries of enclave rule.[173]

Partly because of the manner in which the *Smith* ruling affected them, Deep South enclaves diverged somewhat in their responses to Truman's shock. While they took different tacks in dealing with the abolition of the white primary, ruling parties in South Carolina and Mississippi remained relatively cohesive. As elite outrage at the national party intensified, these parties also cohered around a strategy to abandon—at least temporarily— the house of their fathers. Their participation in the Dixiecrat movement began a complicated period of experimenting with different modes of partisan influence in national politics. In Georgia, however, the ruling party, riven by existing factional conflict that *Smith* only exacerbated, remained on the sidelines of the Dixiecrat revolt. This occurred in large measure because the governing faction—the white supremacist Talmadgeites—worried about the effects of disloyalty on their future power prospects. Factional conflict, the shape of party institutions, and the recent experiences with the loss of the white primary all shaped these responses.

The Truman shock does not seem to have had a transformative effect on the region. But, besides its particular effects on Deep South enclaves' management of subsequent democratization pressures and the complex ways it shaped Republican party growth in these states (see part 3), it did begin more than two decades of contentious and often turbulent controversy— legal and political—over the relationship between the national and state parties. Whereas the litigation and aftermath of *Smith* saw southern state Democratic parties go to battle with federal jurists in defense of a particular understanding of parties as private clubs, during the Dixiecrat moment many Deep South Democrats picked a different fight, this time with national party leaders. In undertaking their revolt, Dixiecrats reasserted a version of a states' rights argument.

For them, the national Democratic party was confederally organized. There was no "national party" independent of and above its constituent parts, the state parties. Thus, state parties were under no obligation to affix the "Democratic Party" label on the ballot above the national ticket or attend the National Convention—or even support the national party's campaign. Ballots were under the control of the state, which by law delegated much of this authority to state parties. The national party could not order the state parties to provide the "Democratic" party label to the national ticket. And delegations to the National Convention could not be forced by it to back certain candidates—in effect, there was no "loyalty" to the national party that state parties could fall short of, because the constituent units, the state parties, came first. Members of state parties should therefore be treated as remaining in good standing—and not viewed as deserters or defectors—if the national party was out of step with their interests. On this states' rights view of parties in a federal polity, state parties could, if they liked, take on the role of "regional patriots."[174] On the basis of the party's long history of granting autonomy to its state parties (discussed in chapter 2), this was a compelling argument.[175]

In 1952 state parties in six enclaves—including Georgia, Mississippi, and South Carolina—once again planned to meet after the National Convention. After learning of the national ticket and its platform, they would decide whether to back the national ticket, and where to place the Democratic party label—above a list of electors pledged to the national party nominees or to someone else. At a DNC meeting before the convention, national Democrats—including those supporting Senator Estes Kefauver (D-TN)—devised a "loyalty pledge" that it would require of all delegates. This would obligate them both to place the national ticket on ballots and to campaign on its behalf. Southern Democrats found it insulting (as well as, in some cases, in conflict with state law back home), but it passed. At the convention, the floor almost expelled delegations from Louisiana, South Carolina, and Virginia for refusing to take the loyalty pledge. South Carolina's delegation was voted back in after Governor Byrnes reassured officials that state law would require that the national ticket appear on the ballot, but that state party rules prevented delegates from pledging their support for the ticket. Eventually, a desperate Illinois delegation, wanting to keep its former governor atop the national ticket, brokered a compromise such that delegations would not have to make the pledge—at least not that year.[176] Four-fifths of southern delegates voted for Georgia Senator Richard B. Russell.

The platform approved at the national convention represented a sharp reversal from Truman's. Serious calls for race reforms were watered down. Alabama Senator John Sparkman, who had backed the Dixiecrat revolt, helped draft its "civil rights" plank. This time, fifty-five *black* delegates walked out in protest. The party then nominated him to serve as Adlai Stevenson's running mate.[177] After the convention, the controversies petered out. The Stevenson-Sparkman ticket appeared on ballots in every state, and received the emblem as the ticket of the "Democratic Party." Many southern politicians, including former SRP'ers, campaigned for the national ticket. Three southern governors, including James Byrnes, would campaign for Eisenhower, but outside of the official confines of their state party.

Stevenson won only nine states, seven of them in the South. Stevenson's popular vote in the South was a narrow majority, about the same as Truman's. However, this time there was no SRP candidate on the ballot; the Republican share of the southern vote had increased from about 30 to about 49 percent. But this result did not suggest a direct effect of the Dixiecrat movement; a majority of congressional districts in the region that had supported Thurmond backed Stevenson. The 1952 voters for Eisenhower were not Thurmond voters. Even if an emerging metro Sunbelt was voting for Eisenhower on anti-statist grounds, the 1952 gains were not evidence that the Dixiecrat movement was producing a two-party region.

The dispute at the heart of these controversies about the relative power of state parties vis-à-vis the national party—who "owned" the very valuable party label, to whom was loyalty owed, and so on—would continue until the momentous McGovern-Fraser party reforms. By empowering the national party to interfere in the most important practices of its state parties, these reforms seemed to decisively reject the "confederal" view of the national party. They are discussed in chapters 9 and 10. But while the democratization pressures of the 1940s challenged enclaves' ruling parties, those of the 1950s would strike them at the heart of their state and local governance.

PART THREE

The Clouds Darken, 1950–63

"No Solution Offers Except Coercion"

Brown, Massive Resistance, and Campus Crises, 1950–63

There is no one way, but many.... The South proposes to use all of
them that make for resistance. [*Brown*] tortured the Constitution—the
South will torture the decision.

    —*John Temple Graves*, strategist of massive resistance (1955)

Must South Carolina indulge bluster and vituperation in place
of summoning candor and courage? Have ignorance, poverty, and
prejudice fed on each other until the white community has sunk to
second-rate capacity? ... Some will say that the conscience of the state
is dead.... If that is true, no solution offers except coercion, while we
entertain the hope that prudent acquiescence will substitute for more
valorous self-correction. If the white people of South Carolina furnish
no worthy response in the crisis, then humiliation and rehabilitation
by other hands is their portion.

    —*Broadus Mitchell*, historian (1958)

In sum, the Southern resistance movement is a foredoomed effort.
The question is, how long can it be sustained and at what cost in
human suffering and degradation?

    —*Harold Fleming*, Southern Regional Council (1956)

FOR MORE THAN HALF A CENTURY, the Supreme Court underwrote the
creation and maintenance of white supremacist public spheres.[1] But on
May 17, 1954, southern enclaves faced their most important challenge when
the Supreme Court struck down state-mandated segregation in public education. Now, amid the unwillingness or inability of other national political
institutions to reorder the South, the Court took aim squarely at them.[2]
By overturning the "separate but equal" doctrine, judicial actors—inspired

by and inspiring black protest—now threatened the racial segregation of a variety of public spaces, from libraries to parks to beaches.[3] In so doing, *Brown* ushered in a broad federal challenge to the ability of enclave rulers to regulate their civil societies as they chose.

Brown and subsequent rulings affected southern enclaves in a number of ways. They altered education policy, reshaped intraparty conflict, encouraged rulers to develop new institutional capacities to fend off desegregation, and inspired both black insurgencies and white supremacist countermobilizations. Generally, desegregation was less fervently opposed by politicians in the Outer South and proved less traumatic. Likewise, in these states, black electoral influence increased throughout the 1950s. Black voter registration doubled to 39 percent from 1947 to 1960 (table 9.4). But across the Deep South, the *Brown* ruling and rulers' responses to it led both to a surge in white supremacist civic and political mobilization and to concomitant setbacks for black protest and indigenous white liberals. By the end of the 1960–61 academic year, all of the 457 school districts in Georgia, Mississippi, and South Carolina maintained completely segregated primary and secondary schools. Their public universities also remained off-limits to anyone of African descent.[4] By the early 1960s these enclaves faced crises over the court-ordered desegregation of these universities.

The narratives in part 3 demonstrate similarities in the ways in which enclave rulers hoped to counter federal courts, domestic insurgents, and their allies "abroad." Politicians in the three Deep South enclaves under study pursued strategies of "massive resistance," by which they sought to decry, deter, and then defer the racial desegregation of their schools.[5] But while they shared similar preferences, differences in factional conflict and rulers' coercive capacities resulted in different handlings of the college desegregation crises (occurring from January 1961 to January 1963). These crises ranged from the relatively quiet desegregation of Clemson in South Carolina to the violent chaos of the University of Mississippi in Oxford.[6]

The college crises were not the biggest single moment in the battle over the implementation of *Brown*; that honor must be reserved for the 1969–70 school year, when hundreds of southern districts were ordered to desegregate at once, setting up a potentially calamitous, regionwide crisis (see chapter 10). However, the earlier timing of the college crises meant that their handling would ultimately be more important for these enclaves' modes of democratization.

This prologue sets the stage for the narratives in chapters 6–8 by noting the region's changing political economy, describing enclave efforts to preempt *Brown*, and outlining the ruling and its implementation by federal courts and an ambivalent central state. It then maps the contours of the South's "massive resistance," discusses how the deployment of the U.S. military at Little Rock became the South's "crucible for racial politics," and closes with a brief discussion of the emergence of presidential Republicanism in the metro South.[7]

The Changing Southern Political Economy

In the two decades after Pearl Harbor, the South's political economy had undergone substantial change, much of it spurred by external forces. World War II and then the Cold War brought military installations, defense contracting, and more higher-wage manufacturing jobs.[8] Federal transportation initiatives such as the Interstate Highway Act of 1956 connected once-isolated regions with one another and spurred economic development. The infrastructural developments during the New Deal and after were absolutely critical. After all, southern wages had been extremely low relative to national wages for many decades, but they had not spurred substantial external capital investment or the relocation of firms from "abroad," in large measure because southern or federal authorities had not yet lowered transportation, energy, and other infrastructural costs for these investors.

By 1960, after a surprisingly stagnant decade of southern economic growth, the effects of New Deal and of mobilizing for wars, hot and cold, began to pay off with external investment.[9] Additionally, the relocation of nonsouthern firms to the region accelerated. Many were attracted by all eleven southern states' rapid passage of "right-to-work" statutes, which signaled to unions and firms alike a growing resolve by state authorities to improve the region's attractiveness to external investors.[10]

All of these forces spurred the region's urbanization. The share of southerners living in cities doubled from 1930 to 1960 to more than one-half.[11] Suburbs began to emerge in the larger cities of the Outer South and in some Deep South cities, notably Atlanta. Urbanization and suburbanization, the share of higher-wage jobs, and defense contracting were all more pronounced in the Outer South than in the Deep South.[12] And within the Deep South, Georgia and South Carolina continued to pull ahead of Mississippi.[13]

Whereas 90 percent of African Americans called the South home in 1900, that share declined to 50 percent by 1960. Economic and political conditions continued to spur black and white emigration. Indeed, from 1920 to 1960, nearly eight million southerners left the farm (many to southern cities as well as to the non-South). Accompanying this trend was the consolidation of land by fewer and fewer commercial landowners.[14] The number of black and white sharecroppers fell by one-half from 1940 to 1960 (to about 160,000 and 100,000, respectively).

This fact was cause and consequence of the growing mechanization of agriculture.[15] By 1955, the number of person hours required to "cultivate and harvest a bale of cotton fell from 160 under hand cultivation and harvest to less than 20 under complete mechanization." As mechanization continued, planters' preoccupation with preserving the political and economic conditions necessary for labor-intensive agriculture diminished somewhat— although they still remained high in the three states under study.[16]

In sum, these changes diversified the types of economic interests making claims on the region's politicians. These interests increasingly demanded state-sponsored development necessary for securing their preferred brand of economic growth, such as larger state fiscal capacities required for producing better-educated workforces. And among these interests there emerged larger numbers of so-called white "business moderates." These men, while preferring Jim Crow segregation, began to perceive the costs of defending the status quo through the defiance of federal authority as mounting higher and higher. As events demonstrated, violence and disorder discouraged both external capital investment and firm relocation.[17] All this said, the rural and Black Belt bias in institutions of party and state meant that Deep South politicians continued to cater to the interests of planters and other large landowners.

Assaults on Jim Crow, 1940–54

Jim Crow—extending from racially segregated maternity wards to parks to cemeteries—was a cradle-to-grave system of racial separation and white supremacy. As discussed in chapter 2, Jim Crow lent legitimacy to suffrage restriction and one-party rule. Beginning in the 1940s, the federal bench began threatening several elements of this system. It nipped at the margins of segregated transportation with rulings on interstate bus travel; other decisions dealt with public accommodations, juries, and other settings. But Jim Crow's cornerstone was public education.[18]

Education remained states' most important policy provision, dominating state and local governments' expenditures and administrative responsibilities. Education issues—from the redistribution of education finance across states, to the provision of free textbooks, to political oversight of university teaching—often dominated otherwise-issueless elections. In social terms, public schools served as the front lines of the most sensitive battleground of segregation: white anxieties about interracial sexual intimacy.[19] For black parents, of course, better schooling, whatever the racial composition of the classroom, promised improvements in the life chances of their children—even after taking into account how racially restricted southern labor markets might blunt the impact of increased educational attainment on incomes.[20] Comprising both a political and a cultural threat to white supremacy and a complete disruption of financial and administrative arrangements, *Brown* shook southern enclaves to their core.

Moreover, unlike attacks on state parties such as those against the white primary and Truman's shock, *Brown* challenged rulers—and especially governors—directly in their capacity as policymakers, not merely as party leaders. As the Great Depression throttled the public finances of local and county jurisdictions, states began assuming a greater and greater share of education expenditures. With state funding, growing state influence over education administration followed.[21] By the 1940s states across the country began centralizing educational policymaking. And through their appointment of, and influence over, university regents, governors played a critical role in higher education policymaking. Thus, battling federal interference with education would involve legislatures and, increasingly, executives, as well as local and county officials.

In the late 1930s federal courts began considering a line of cases concerning the desegregation of graduate school education, but these narrow rulings did not threaten *Plessy v. Ferguson*.[22] One decade later, the successful desegregation of the armed forces astonished southern politicians. Even so, they generally viewed "separate but equal"—and by extension, their continued, if limited, federal authorization to mandate racial segregation in many spheres—as safe from external assault.

Meanwhile, legal and political campaigns for educational reform emerged from within enclaves in the 1940s. Led by NAACP branches, and backed by newly aggressive black teachers' associations, black activists sued to equalize black and white teachers' salaries. These campaigns—which broadened to include schooling infrastructure and transportation—often bore fruit, as the following narratives demonstrate. Across the South, black teachers earned just one-half of what white teachers earned in 1938, but by 1950 this share increased to 80 percent.[23]

In 1950 three Supreme Court rulings altered rulers' expectations of the longevity of "separate but equal." In the most important of these, the Court held that the operation of racially segregated law schools was *inherently* unequal; black-only schools could not provide black students with, among other things, access to important economic and social networks existing at flagship law schools. In these cases, the Court ordered the admission of black applicants to the all-white law schools.[24] As southern politicians understood, while not explicitly invalidating the "separate but equal" doctrine, these cases left the constitutional protection of Jim Crow in tatters. Georgia politician Roy Harris, for instance, predicted that the Court would "go all the way" and strike down *Plessy*. But while some rulers thought that racially mixed schools were inevitable, others had faith that various options—such as the privatization of public education—could delay this outcome for decades. Still others hoped that by drastically reducing racial inequalities in educational outcomes, they could convince jurists to preserve "separate but equal"—at least in education.[25]

Racial disparities in school infrastructure and teachers' pay were often massive, and were quite higher in majority-black areas, where local officials were least interested in disrupting the supply of unskilled black labor by providing skills through public education. Several states embarked on large campaigns to reduce these disparities, but doing so placed substantial pressure on their fiscal capacities, and also required the development of new administrative agencies. While historian C. Vann Woodward suggests that rulers must have been irrational to expect that rendering public education separate *and* equal would have prevented the ruling in *Brown*, evidence presented in part 3 suggests that elites had good reason to believe that *Brown* could indeed be averted.[26]

Efforts to improve black schooling stemmed from other sources as well. First, those white elites most concerned with attracting external capital investment and the relocation of nonsouthern firms sought to improve schooling for all in order to develop better-skilled labor forces. Benefiting from larger postwar coffers, several states embarked on ambitious "minimum foundation programs" designed to improve the quality of schooling in the poorest areas, black *and* white.[27] Second, the paternalism of many Black Belt elites motivated calls for correcting the worst abuses of "separate but equal." On the eve of *Brown*, other alterations to Jim Crow occurred on a voluntary basis, but usually in the Outer South. There, several cities voluntarily desegregated public facilities such as libraries and parks, while some civic associations racially integrated. And some forty private colleges and universities admitted small numbers of blacks voluntarily, a few even in the Deep South. Generally, however, the Deep South's white-only and black-only schools remained so.[28]

Brown I and *Brown* II

As the Court heard argument and reargument on *Brown* and its companion cases, the Eisenhower administration expressed ambivalence about the Court's possible invalidation of *Plessy*. Eisenhower himself seemed to disapprove of judicial intervention on the issue, and—warned by his "great friend," South Carolina Governor James Byrnes—worried that a ruling striking down *Plessy* could result in riots, violence, and even the immediate privatization of southern schools.[29] But the Court ultimately agreed with the petitioners: "In the field of public education the doctrine of 'separate but equal' has no place. Separate educational facilities are inherently unequal."[30] However, citing the diversity of local conditions—and carefully weighing the implications of various options for the South *and* for the Court's legitimacy—the Court chose not to issue an implementation decree, and instead ordered counsel to help it devise one.[31]

White southern reactions to the decision first had "an air of unreality" about its importance. Many politicians and opinion leaders in the Deep South reacted with splenetic pronouncements, but most Outer South and some Deep South media outlets were muted. Many state-level politicians and members of Congress exhibited a surprising calm. Woodward even notes that northern whites congratulated their southern counterparts for their "restrained tone." The region's leading white sociologist, Howard Odum, predicted that the South would "likely . . . do an excellent job of readjustment."[32] Another white moderate, Arkansas journalist Harry Ashmore, preached to white audiences a "Doctrine of Inevitability" in order to build support for compliance.[33] Both the most committed segregationists and white moderates marked time as they waited to learn the shape of the Court's implementation decree. The region's black protest groups hailed the ruling, as did many teachers' associations and white liberals. Leading white supremacists called it illegal and vowed to defend segregation at all costs.

The Court, meanwhile, took the temperature of key actors, considered legal and practical barriers to speedy desegregation, and dealt with its own institutional changes.[34] Uncertainty over whether the Republicans should appeal to the South's black or white voters contributed to the administration's ambivalence. Justice Department officials backed a stronger implementation decree than the White House, but Eisenhower himself added a crucial paragraph to the government's brief. It directed the Court to consider how "psychological and emotional factors" differed across white communities and suggested that these factors would be critical in successfully implementing desegregation.[35]

The Court did not announce *Brown*'s implementation decree until May 31, 1955—more than one year after "Black Monday." In the ruling, the Court directed district courts only "to admit to public schools on a racially nondiscriminatory basis with all deliberate speed the parties to these cases." These courts would require school officials to make "a prompt and reasonable start toward full compliance," after which district courts could consider why more time might be needed.[36] Critically, school desegregation could not be implemented through class action suits. A state's schools would be desegregated one by one across thousands of districts—if at all. This severely strained NAACP financial and personnel resources, since few black parents, even if willing and able to enlist as plaintiffs, could themselves pay for litigation or find attorneys who would take such cases.[37]

Many enclave rulers thought that, because of its language and its delegation of authority to federal district judges, the Court had blinked. Of the fifty-eight federal district judges not based in circuit courts, all were white and but five were native southerners; almost all had previously held elective or appointive office. Further encouraging southern politicians, Judge John J. Parker's ruling in *Briggs* (South Carolina's companion case to *Brown*) set the tone for lower courts' interpretation of *Brown* II. Parker held that as long as officials did not block students from attending any public schools on racial grounds, it was lawful under the Constitution if parents voluntarily sorted their children by race into different schools: "The Constitution . . . does not require integration," but "merely forbids the use of governmental power to enforce segregation." Summing up the view of many politicians, Lieutenant Governor Ernest Vandiver of Georgia remarked that *Brown* II's mention of "reasonable" time could mean "one year or two hundred."[38]

Generally, southern politicians thought the ruling was as favorable as could be expected, while black litigators applauded the decision as politically astute. This was a reasonable inference. The Court had dragged its feet, and had done so in large measure because of its fear that the federal judiciary's legitimacy would be greatly damaged by issuing enforcement orders that were met with defiance. From the Court's perspective, the silence of the White House and Congress was deafening. Eisenhower never spoke out strongly in favor of *Brown*, and over the coming years, Congress' liberals could not convince their colleagues to issue symbolic resolutions affirming the decision as the law of the land, much less provide "carrots" and "sticks" to induce southern compliance with school desegregation.[39]

From Marking Time to Massive Resistance, 1955–58

Immediately after *Brown* II, the national NAACP office immediately called on local branch members to petition their school boards to develop de-segregation plans, to educate and mobilize parents to join suits against intransigent school boards, and to reach out to whites via civic associations and social networks.[40] Black families and their attorneys braved threats and reprisals of many kinds and filed sixty such petitions in the summer following the ruling. As black groups mobilized, concern mounted among southern authorities. In December 1955, partly inspired by the *Brown* rulings, and eventually moving from a demand for a fairer implementation of separate-but-equal to a demand that it end, a well-trained cadre of mostly women activists, as well as unionists, those involved in the local NAACP branch, and a young Martin Luther King, Jr., launched a bus boycott in Montgomery that they would sustain for 381 days.[41] The prospect of other indigenous protests (allegedly fomented by outsiders) was worrisome. In February 1956, in response to a campus riot, state police deployed to enforce the court-ordered desegregation of the University of Alabama by Autherine

Lucy instead withdrew her from the school, allegedly for her own safety. The school remained segregated. By early 1956 rulers were in a near "panic."[42]

Southern elites began excited deliberation about employing the legal doctrine of "interposition," first championed by *Richmond News Leader* editor James J. Kilpatrick. Harkening back to the antebellum period, on this dubious constitutional interpretation a state could "interpose" its sovereignty between its inhabitants and what the state took to be an illegal federal statute or judicial decision. Advocates thought that collective action by state legislatures announcing their rejection of *Brown* could enable the South to demonstrate that compliance was impossible, and force the courts to beat a hasty retreat. By mid-1957, eight southern legislatures had endorsed interposition.[43] Even though it was soon rejected by federal courts, interposition was "of enormous consequence" because it "afforded a conceptual basis for total *state* opposition" to *Brown*'s enforcement.[44]

In March, most of the southern congressional delegation signed a "Declaration of Constitutional Principles" that denounced *Brown* but, because of cross-state disagreements, avoided calling the decision "illegal" or endorsing interposition.[45] This so-called "Southern Manifesto" represented the difficulties faced by those politicians seeking to unify the region to resist federal interventions. Efforts to stage a revolt from the national party in 1948 had already pointed to these challenges.[46] As historian Tony Badger shows, the audience of the "Southern Manifesto" was less nonsoutherners who were estimating enclaves' resolve, but rather "wavering southern politicians." And the goal—coercing these fence-sitting "moderates" into "supporting a united regional campaign of defiance" of *Brown*—succeeded. About two-thirds of southern federal officeholders "succumb[ed] to what they perceive[d] to be mass popular segregationist sentiment" and signed the Manifesto.[47]

In 1956, working through southern governors' conferences and national party conventions, "bitter-end" segregationists such as South Carolina governor George Bell Timmerman sought to improve interstate policy discussions, pressure the national party to back the southern cause, and search for a means by which southern congressional influence could parry judicial attacks on segregation. However, the battle to maintain segregation was fought at and below the state level, and this limited prospects for coordination at the federal level.[48] Whether enclaves could unite behind more than defiant rhetoric remained unclear.

During this period, tens of thousands of whites, many of them returning veterans today acclaimed as members of the "Greatest Generation," sparked an efflorescence of white supremacist civil society. In the summer of 1954, White Citizens' Councils (WCCs)—later described as combining "the agenda of the Ku Klux Klan with the demeanor of the Rotary"—hatched in Mississippi and spread quickly across the South, but remained largest in the Deep South.[49] These were community-level groups of primarily middle- and upper-class white professionals, landowners, and civic leaders who were outraged and worried by federal judicial assaults on Jim Crow. They employed economic and sometimes physical coercion to deter blacks from filing desegregation petitions.[50] WCCs and others also sought to educate nonsoutherners on the "realities" of race relations and of the calamitous effects of school integration.[51] Other whites launched boycotts against white firms thought to be insufficiently committed to Jim Crow.[52]

The Klan was resurgent, too, by the late 1940s. Most of this resurgence was based in Georgia and "slosh[ed] over like an overfull cesspool from its Georgia stronghold ... to adjacent areas in Alabama, Tennessee, South Carolina, and Florida." In addition to blacks, these new and larger Klans targeted whites for being out of step with "public morals," especially alcohol consumption. Departing from the experience of the second Klan of the 1920s, which many politicians then joined, in the late 1940s, southern white publics, civic organizations, and public authorities responded with anger, derision, and state repression. There was now a clear perception that the failure of the South to repress these organizations might trigger unwanted federal interventions.[53]

Federal Bureau of Investigation (FBI) Director J. Edgar Hoover, whose white supremacist views infused his agency, looked favorably on members of the White Citizens' Councils as "leading citizens of the South," and contrasted them with the "racial hatred" of black protest organizations. But while he thought the WCCs could help control racial tensions, he also worried about the role of southern elites in fomenting white crowd violence, acknowledging that the Councils could "become the medium through which tensions might manifest themselves."[54]

Subtle policy debates occurred amid a hegemonic discourse of defiance, but white moderates and liberals—perhaps the primary target of the WCCs—lost influence in them.[55] As historian Numan Bartley concludes, "The South simply lacked an adequate institutional foundation for a viable liberalism."[56] This absence was not an accident, but an outcome of enclaves' response to *Brown*. And it was also in keeping with the intolerance in authoritarian regimes everywhere toward autonomous civic organizations that generated challenges to incumbents.[57] White moderates called for a slow, token desegregation beginning in the Outer South, and preached patience to black activists. Here, tiny numbers of blacks would enter previously all-white schools.[58] Still, their opponents were dispirited, too. In a reversal of the typical enclave monopolization of linkages to the national polity and influence over national political discourse, by the mid-1950s white southern elites began complaining that a "paper curtain" blocked out principled defenses of segregation from national media outlets.[59]

Most important, the white supremacist countermobilization, in concert with a rash of state legislation and local ordinances targeting black organizations, depressed black protest capacity throughout the South.[60] By 1949 the infrastructure for black protest in the South had expanded enormously, as the combined benefits of the movement of blacks to southern cities, higher incomes, and other advantages produced large increases in the number of NAACP branches and their memberships (table 3.3). The region had more than seven hundred branches, with about 175,000 dues-paying members. This growth spurred similar gains in black voter registration, as NAACP branches sponsored many such drives, especially in cities.[61]

State attacks on the organization (described in chapters 6–8) would reverse much of this progress. By one estimate, the region lost 250 NAACP branches and almost fifty thousand members in a three-year period.[62] The most concerted state-level assaults on the organization occurred in Alabama, Louisiana, and Texas, as well as Georgia and others. In the Deep South, formal and informal attacks on black protest and the social and economic intimidation of white moderates and white liberals were more intense.[63] These attacks took on greater importance as southern authorities, encouraged by Hoover's FBI, linked black protest to communism and then exploited anticommunism as an additional frame with which to delegitimize black demands and justify further surveillance and repression.[64]

Scholars argue that these attacks altered somewhat the trajectory of black protest in the South. Effectively shut down by authorities in Alabama from 1956 to 1964, and in Louisiana and Texas for shorter periods, the hobbled NAACP made way for other actors in black communities—including students and religious leaders—to develop new organizations in the late 1950s and—more so—in the early 1960s.[65] From the Southern Christian Leadership Conference to the growth of southern branches of the Congress on Racial Equality to the Student Nonviolent Coordinating Committee and scores of more local and less well-known groups, these new organizations were thought—sometimes incorrectly—to be much more oriented tactically to nonviolent direct action than southern NAACP branches. Thus, the argument goes, not just the range of southern blacks engaged in black protest widened, but so did the goals and tactics of this protest. Historians and sociologists view this diversity as largely salutary for the domestic insurgencies facing off against enclave rulers, in that it made the modes of protest less predictable and its repression and cooptation by southern authorities more difficult. (Chapters 6–8 evaluate this perspective in the Deep South enclaves under study.)

But black protest continued throughout this period of enclave massive resistance to *Brown*. There was fairly steady growth of black voter registration throughout the Outer South, which was the product of unheralded pushes by regional NAACP staffers (table 9.4). Still, at the height of massive resistance in 1956, about three-quarters of southern blacks remained unregistered. Among those who were registered, voting rates were quite low.

According to one well-regarded study, the dropoff from voter registration to primary voting across the region ranged from 20 to 89 percent.[66] But by the end of the decade, the NAACP took on an even larger registration campaign, in which it claimed to register some one-half million black southerners, mostly in the Outer South. Many of these voters helped Kennedy in his narrow win in 1960.[67]

Enclave Responses to *Brown*

Given the nature of the legal remedies that *Brown* set in motion, each state—in negotiation with federal judges and, by the mid-1960s, federal administrators—fashioned its own pace in desegregating schools and other racialized spaces. Southern politicians and white publics—if not regional religious organizations—maintained a consensus preference for segregation. But politicians disagreed about the best methods of maintaining it.[68] White elites and nonelites also differed in the intensity with which they valued Jim Crow, especially relative to other valued goods which might be in tension with the defense of white supremacy. Ultimately, the intensity of enclave resistance to desegregation did divide along expected lines, as several Outer South states allowed token desegregation of some schools. Of course, token desegregation amounted to an accommodation, not capitulation.[69]

Regime responses to *Brown* varied on three key dimensions: the lengths to which rulers would go in preventing desegregation; the virulence of their position-taking on desegregation and white supremacy generally; and the degree to which they bolstered state institutional defenses against black insurgency and other threats to order. On the first dimension, some were willing to tie their (or their successors') hands by committing to the "Doomsday option"—the automatic abolition of the public school system should schools be ordered desegregated, usually preceded by the removal of state constitutional guarantees of public education and promises of tuition credits for white parents to send their children to white-only private schools.[70] As the narratives demonstrate, the high-risk nature of such signals to courts and local electorates could restrict states' abilities to adjust to democratization pressures.[71]

As was true with other transition challenges, rulers differed in their beliefs, policy preferences, time horizons, and available options. Some perceived high stakes for intraparty conflict in enacting "massive resistance." In the words of an official in the dominant Byrd faction in Virginia's ruling party, the strategy was designed to "keep us in power another twenty-five years." Enclave rulers differed in their beliefs about black elite and mass preferences, black protest capacity, and the likely success of legal defenses of segregation.[72] Politicians also disagreed on the likely success of defiance in defeating federal courts. Some remarked—publicly *and* privately—that sufficiently unified and cunning opposition could force the federal government to reverse itself. Others were much more pessimistic. Finally, many thought they could, through legal resistance, buy time for what might be a slower and more orderly desegregation. As usual, views on what constituted "enough" time varied with career ambitions and policy goals.[73]

The Crisis at Little Rock

Across the South, Little Rock helped reshape rulers' expectations about Jim Crow's longevity. The Arkansas capital had initially been a success story of interracial elite bargaining and planned desegregation. But in September 1957, Governor Orval Faubus called out the state's National Guard to block the entrance of nine black students into Central High School, citing safety concerns. A federal district court forbade him from interfering in the school district's implementation plan, and in response, Faubus withdrew the Guard. A white crowd then met the nine and blocked their entrance. If this was "massive resistance," it is important to remember that this phenomenon was not limited to the South. Two weeks before the Little Rock crisis began, a mob of four hundred whites harassed a black family that had just moved into Levittown, Pennsylvania. State troopers needed a week to quell the disorder.[74]

Constrained by a traditionally narrow range of options for maintaining order, and after having bungled the crisis in many ways, the Eisenhower administration finally federalized the Arkansas National Guard. It also deployed the U.S. Army's famed 101st Airborne Division in Little Rock for two months.[75] In doing so, the central state had intervened to protect southern black citizens for the first time in seventy years.[76] Two years after the Southern Manifesto, the Supreme Court in *Cooper v. Aaron* not only forced the city's beleaguered school board to keep Central High School open, but also explicitly repudiated interposition and nullification.[77]

Arkansas' white moderates demonstrated to their counterparts elsewhere the futility of current strategies. Hardliners had asked white parents to be prepared to close all public schools. With Little Rock, the central state called their bluff; would parents elsewhere support hardline stances that now seemed futile? Temporarily, the intervention boosted WCCs, sparked a new wave of defiant rhetoric from the region's officeholders, and occasioned outrage against the administration by some southern whites. But southern metro elites feared playing host to "another Little Rock." Little Rock officials spoke to white civic and business leaders throughout the South. Presenting financial evidence of the impact of (publicized) disorder on external investment, they urged, "Keep your schools open. You will never regret it."[78]

With respect to actual desegregation of southern schools, Little Rock did not bear immediate fruit. As of the 1958–59 school year, the distinction between the Deep South and the Outer South was hardly apparent, beyond token (but, for many whites, psychologically bracing) change. Significant increases in the share of black students no longer attending all-black schools occurred in areas bordering the South (Washington, D.C., Delaware, Missouri, Maryland, West Virginia, and Oklahoma). However, for five Outer South states—Arkansas, North Carolina, Tennessee, Texas, and Virginia—this share remained below 1.5 percent. For the five Deep South states and Florida, it remained zero. By the 1959–60 school year, about 0.2 percent of the South's black students attended school with whites.[79]

But many rulers drew longer-term lessons from the episode. Before Little Rock, enclave rulers were unsure of what was in store for their regimes. Some sincerely believed that there was nothing inevitable about the collapse of Jim Crow. Moreover, it was unclear what the pace of any such change might be, who might preside over these changes, and how these changes might restructure partisan politics in the South. After Little Rock, uncertainty about transition outcomes decreased. The central state had both demonstrated its resolve and committed itself to desegregation; a full reversal of national interference in southern social and political practices now seemed impossible. There was not unanimity on this matter, of course.[80]

Little Rock also had important effects on southern challengers to enclave rule. For those outside the region, it greatly accelerated the growth of what became a consistent "race beat" held by journalists at national white newspapers. National elites and nonsoutherners would now be inundated with information about enclave rule and publicity of potentially damaging practices. Even more important, challengers within enclaves became more convinced that well-publicized violence by white crowds and law enforcement might induce massive federal intervention.[81]

The Growth of Republicanism in the Metro South

Little Rock had another important effect—it interrupted Republican growth in the metropolitan South. Since Eisenhower's galvanizing run for the White House in 1952, Republicans had made significant headway among better-off whites in urban (and, increasingly, suburban) areas, especially in the Outer South. Even more surprising, large majorities of better-off whites in Deep South metro precincts backed Eisenhower. As southern white incomes increased, class stratification among them increased as well. Its electoral consequences seemed to emerge quickly; traditional differences between the Outer and Deep Souths now seemed to be replicated within the Deep South itself.[82] Both the general dynamic in the Outer South and the stratified dynamic within the Deep South seem to lend support to the modernization approach discussed in chapter 1.

After winning four Outer South states in 1952, Eisenhower sought to spread his (rather bland) message of "Modern Republicanism" throughout the region. While welcoming the growing numbers of white young professionals to the party, this message, which was focused on federalism and fiscal conservatism, was insufficiently conservative for many of the Democratic activists involved in movements like "South Carolinians for Eisenhower." Still, national Republicans, for the first time in decades, began sincere efforts to build party infrastructure in the South. The Republican National Committee (RNC)'s "Operation Dixie" centered first on encouraging living room discussions about the party. It moved on to replacing nonexistent party operations, often run by aging patronage-seekers, with offices at the state and local levels that were run by whites and actually devoted themselves to winning elections.[83]

This work paid off. By the mid-1950s southern Republicans contested local, state, and federal elections at a growing rate, and—just as importantly—with candidates of improving quality.[84] Some state Democratic parties responded with additional barriers to party competition. For instance, targeting party switchers, a Florida statute barred candidates from running for office unless they had been registered in their party for at least two years.

The 1956 election occurred at the height of many whites' anger over *Brown*. Once again the Democratic nominee, Adlai Stevenson, stated that racial equality could not be legislated and criticized his party's loyalty pledge. Regarding *Brown*, he said that "we don't need reforms or groping experiments." Doing so helped him retain the support of key southern members of Congress and others, including Mississippi's Fielding Wright and Strom Thurmond. The tamping down of a southern revolt did little to improve the national ticket's overall results. Stevenson carried only seven states nationally, six of them southern (including all Deep South states).[85] Conversely, the Republicans' national party platform showed that endorsing both *Brown* rulings was not inconsistent with appeals to many better-off metro southerners. Eisenhower won five Outer South states, as well as a majority of all southern votes. On one estimate, fully 39 percent of southern blacks backed him. Southern Democrats were scared. Moreover, this development suggested that opposition party development could be a democratizing force in the South—in Gibson's terms, that the South's democratization could be a "party-led" process. Chapters 9–11 discuss this possibility.[86]

Soon, however, as Eisenhower feared, Little Rock—as well as Republican support for the Civil Rights Acts of 1957 and 1960—took their toll on both Republican party-building efforts and "bottom-up" activism in the region.[87] Many white southern Republicans blamed Eisenhower. Southern party officials resigned, and financial donations plummeted. In 1958 the party contested only twenty-three U.S. House seats (only one took place in the Deep South), barely half of that of the previous cycle. Whether southern white opposition to Little Rock was a permanent change or a temporary disruption in Republican party-building was unknown. By the end of the 1950s, the partisan sorting of whites *and* blacks across the South still remained up in the air.[88]

Campus Crises: *Brown* and the Desegregation of Higher Education

Throughout the 1950s, the central battlefield created by *Brown* covered primary and secondary education. By 1956 fifty state-supported colleges and universities—along with sixty private institutions—had desegregated in the region, but none in the Deep South.[89] But in the early 1960s crises over court-ordered desegregation of public universities became important moments in the dismantling of Deep South enclaves. Public universities—often sources of great pride for whites—had great cultural resonance in these states. Throughout the twentieth century, their management was often a major issue in state politics.[90] Moreover, in part because of the key role of governor-appointed regents, college desegregation episodes placed governors on center stage. In states adopting the "doomsday" option, governors would be responsible for implementing the closing of universities ordered by courts to desegregate. And because of concerns about violence in these most intransigent states, they occasioned a great deal of media coverage. National perceptions of southern politics had long tracked high-profile politicians—especially the most photogenic demagogues—and violence. Enclaves were on trial in these crises, and the verdicts would affect these states' reputations.

Besides directly invoking executive authority and involving significant media attention, college desegregation episodes differed from the desegregation of primary and secondary education in another respect. While the strength of statewide black insurgency shaped the latter—since black communities had to proceed district by district in demanding desegregation—black insurgency was *not* directly relevant to the pace of college desegregation, which required a single, if persistent, lawsuit. And given the overall state of black education, higher education desegregation was not a high priority among black activists. Many southern school districts still lacked high schools for black students. For young men, the educational gap between whites and blacks in 1950 was, for the most part, the difference between a high school and elementary school education.[91]

In approaching court-ordered desegregations of college campuses, governors could choose from a few options. They could honor rhetorical (and sometimes legal) commitments to close schools rather than allow them to desegregate, try to ensure their peaceful desegregation, or take steps to raise the costs of federal oversight of state compliance so high that federal authorities—or black students—gave up (as happened with the University of Alabama in 1956). Regardless of their choice, rulers had good reason to avoid mass bloodshed and disorder. Maintaining order in these episodes meant restricting possibly violent white crowds from accessing campus spaces. Over the course of the 1950s, in crafting responses to *Brown*, rulers developed different state capacities that would be of varying utility in managing threats to order, on campuses and elsewhere. As the rest of this book demonstrates, the manner in which the decade of massive resistance was navigated would shape these states' diverse democratization experiences.

CHAPTER SIX

"No Task for the Amateur or Hothead"

Mississippi and the Battle of Oxford

HAVING SUCCESSFULLY BLUNTED a significant black mobilization after the abolition of the white primary, Mississippi's rulers co-led the Dixiecrat revolt in 1948, and hardline white supremacists remained within the ruling party. With the *Brown* shock, the state's rulers faced their first major black insurgency in decades. Over the course of the 1950s, surprising black defiance toward the state's politicians strengthened the hand of organized white supremacists within the ruling party. At the same time, Mississippi featured the Deep South's most "moderate" gubernatorial leadership of the decade. A standoff between its governors and the increasingly emboldened White Citizens' Council (WCC) forces led to a stalemate over the development of an effective coercive apparatus, with negative consequences for managing the desegregation crisis at the University of Mississippi. This chapter reviews the state of black education before *Brown*, describes the state's massive resistance to the ruling, and demonstrates how a combination of intraelite dissensus and weak party-state capacities help explain the enclave's navigation of the desegregation crisis at the University of Mississippi.

Public Education and Black Protest before *Brown*

On the eve of World War II, Mississippi's Jim Crow system seemed impervious to attack from within or without, and racial disparities in social policy provision had worsened over previous decades. Spending for black education remained especially woeful.[1] In 1950, 70 percent of black Mississippians aged twenty-five or over had attained less than a seventh-grade education, and fewer than 1 percent had graduated high school. At that time, the spending ratio per capita was about four to one in favor of whites, and white teachers received more than two and one-half times the salary that their black counterparts received. Ninety-five percent of the state's one-room, one-teacher schools were used by black students.[2]

A black teachers' salary equalization movement developed in late 1941 at the instigation of the Mississippi Association of Teachers in Colored Schools (MATCS).[3] The MATCS consulted with Thurgood Marshall about its legal strategy for winning "separate but equal" teachers' pay, but disruptions caused by the war and the difficulties in finding attorneys willing to take such cases (see chapter 3) delayed matters for several years. In calling for better black teachers' pay and enhanced outlays on black education, the organization found allies in the Delta Council (the quasi-official pressure group of Delta agriculture) and the state's Manufacturers Association. These organizations viewed improvements in educational infrastructure as critical for developing a base of better-off black consumers in the majority-black Delta and, more importantly, for preventing a larger exodus of black labor. Before the 1950s planters did not anticipate the mechanization of Delta agriculture.[4]

Signaling their resolve, the two organizations formed the Mississippi Citizens Council on Education (MCCE) to advocate a massive state commitment to black and white schooling well beyond equalization. Occupying the broad ideological middle of the ruling party, the MCCE's plan would require $34 million annually, and more than $100 million for school construction.[5] By calling for greater black educational spending, the MCCE expected that black leaders would respond by voicing their support for segregation.

One important element of all enclaves' political modernization during and after the war was improved collection of policy-relevant data, especially regarding education. Upon the publication of such information, politicians and opinion leaders often expressed genuine surprise at the extent of existing racial disparities.[6] In Mississippi, a Delta-dominated state legislative committee collected such data and called for a program of black school construction and improved teacher pay in 1945. Soon after the war, both the MATCS and the state's NAACP called for lawsuits demanding equal teacher pay. The legislature then approved more than $3 million for school construction and improvements—a paltry sum, given existing inequities. However, as historian Andrew Workman rightly notes, this call for educational improvements marked a departure in post-1890 Mississippi; now black citizens were organizing to make direct demands of state institutions, rather than working through white patrons.[7]

But the drive for improving black education is attributable mainly to black protest. In 1948, the state's NAACP filed a salary equalization suit against Jackson's public schools with the assistance of the MATCS and the NAACP's Legal Defense Fund. Although dismissing the case on technical grounds, the judge did back the petitioners' substantive claims. In response, Governor Fielding Wright quickly secured funding from the legislature to begin salary equalization.[8] The case coincided with the Dixiecrat revolt, and after Governor Wright spoke directly to the state's blacks with his radio address (see chapter 5), black newspaperman Percy Greene threatened a black exodus. Delta planters took the problem seriously and once again sought public commitments to segregation by black education leaders. Most demurred, even after Governor Wright agreed to form an interracial council. But after more militant black leaders publicly refused to endorse segregation as a "permanent state," he declined to appoint the council.[9]

While the salary equalization suit was in the legal pipeline, the legislature, at Wright's urging, met in special session to craft an equalization plan. The *Jackson Daily News* criticized massive racial inequalities in education policy, and pointed to a Virginia county that, working with black leaders, ended a legal suit by improving black schooling. As elsewhere, rulers' motives for improving black education were plural—economic, paternalistic, and political.[10] After the Supreme Court's 1950 rulings, the NAACP increased its attack on segregation laws.

At the time, the state's NAACP represented a mixed bag. In late 1950, its first paid staff member planned voter registration drives and a push for teachers' salary equalization. But its membership and branch dispersion still lagged behind its neighbors (table 3.3). Although the NAACP state conference did not yet represent the majority of black educational and community leaders—who criticized equalization programs but not segregation—elite bargaining between the races changed in 1951. Feeling burned by the failures of the 1950 equalization plan, particularly regarding teachers' pay, the state's black teachers' organization took more militant positions. As other black organizations joined the teachers in adopting more militant stances, there was increasing conflict among the black leadership, as reflected and heightened by the formation of the new Regional Council for Negro Leadership (RCNL) and the NAACP's open rejection of segregated education. The RCNL, though more cautious than the NAACP, eventually turned away from its Delta Council patrons and won some gains.[11]

By the late 1940s rulers' opinions on the means of preserving segregation varied more widely than those concerning a white-only electoral politics. Those supporting an equalization program cited the need to preempt a judicial destruction of "separate but equal," the possibility of a loss of black agricultural labor to outmigration, and traditional noblesse oblige. Others—particularly Hills county legislators and county officials—viewed equalization as a costly gambit, and were reluctant to impose greater property taxes in order to finance the program, especially since the Delta would receive most of the new spending.[12] Similarly structured conflict had stymied state modernization and other reform efforts since the 1930s (see chapter 3).

In 1951, three years after the Dixiecrat revolt, the party nominated Hugh L. White for governor. White, well known for championing the South's first major state-sponsored industrialization program in the 1930s, drew on planters and business interests in his runoff against the more populist Hills candidate, Paul B. Johnson, Jr. The race featured a relative absence of white supremacist discourse, but fewer than six thousand blacks voted in the runoff, mostly for Johnson. White won with 51 percent of the vote, which followed a Delta/Hills cleavage.[13] Stylistically more of a racial paternalist than his Dixiecrat predecessor, White sought to secure black elite support for a significantly more ambitious equalization plan. Instead of Wright-style bullying, he delivered several speeches to black audiences, particularly at black colleges such as Alcorn and Jackson State, whom he called on to prepare to assume the mantle of "full" citizenship. In 1953, on Lincoln's birthday, he became the first governor to address an audience in the all-black town of Mound Bayou. In this speech, he described what he termed "voluntary segregation"—the continued existence of segregated schools and the equalization of facilities.

Even after the Supreme Court agreed to hear the school segregation cases, Mississippi's rulers had good reason to regard voluntary segregation as tenable. Many conservative black educational leaders publicly opposed desegregation, and claimed that a majority of the state's blacks agreed with them.[14] The black Mississippi Teachers Association's leadership disagreed, and assisted the state NAACP.[15]

Given the heterogeneity of black elite preferences about both segregation and strategies for attacking it, it is understandable that leading politicians would soon misconstrue black organizations' responses to *Brown*. But an ideologically diverse black public was not the only reason for this misunderstanding. As in other enclaves, most of the state's politicians shared a sense of denial about the true preferences of black elites and masses that reinforced their lax attitude about procuring better intelligence about black organized protest. It was not until after *Brown* II (see later in this chapter) that state actors began concerted efforts toward improving intelligence-gathering.

From the beginning of his term, White devoted much of his energy to securing an equalization plan.[16] As the Supreme Court planned to hear additional argument in the segregation cases, White called a special session to craft policies intended both to signal a sincere commitment to "separate but equal" and, if the doctrine were overruled, to convince blacks to back voluntary segregation.[17] White urged the legislature to pass the program recommended by the eighteen-member Legislative Recess Educational Committee, which had castigated the state for its long-tolerated racial disparities in spending. It called for a large program of school district consolidation, the construction of additional black schools, the provision of transportation for black students, and the equalization of teachers' pay. Many legislators continued to express their opposition to a belated attempt at equalization;

the late hour convinced many that such an attempt would fail to convince courts of their sincerity in effecting "separate but equal."[18]

The equalization plan constituted the carrot of voluntary segregation, but other legislators searched for a stick. Likely the state's most powerful politician, House Speaker Walter Sillers backed a proposed constitutional amendment authorizing the legislature to abolish the school system if courts ordered desegregation. Though it passed the House, the Senate defeated it, along with the equalization plan. A wait-and-see attitude, combined with Hills' opposition to the subsidy of Delta education, led to the passage of the equalization plan but a failure to finance it.[19]

The legislature also established the Legislative Education Advisory Committee (LEAC). Similar to South Carolina's Gressette Committee (see chapter 7), its mandate extended well beyond devising education policy. The LEAC could devise means of prohibiting common-law marriages and—as in South Carolina—strategizing about state responses to likely federal court rulings on segregation. The state's Delta-heavy political elite dominated the committee.[20] Later, Sillers secured the vesting of the LEAC with subpoena power; on his reading of the situation, subpoena power would allow the committee to secure statements from county law enforcement officers regarding the severity of the challenge to order created by any public controversy over schooling. This in turn would provide the state with legal cover to invoke its police powers to maintain order.[21] Although the state's infamous State Sovereignty Commission (see later in this chapter and chapter 10) would develop separately from the LEAC, it was in the creation of the latter that the state's politicians began to think more carefully about segregation strategy and the need to bolster the state's policing apparatus.

On the eve of *Brown*, state preparations for the possible invalidation of *Plessy* lagged behind those of other states. While other state legislatures featured opposition to equalization programs, Mississippi's unwillingness to commit financially to equalization reflected its less cohesive legislature, less influential gubernatorial leadership (in comparison to South Carolina and Georgia), and the fact that the state's first genuine consideration of equalization seemed to occur perhaps too late to influence the Court. Meanwhile, many black educational administrators and teachers expressed ambivalence about withholding support for equalization plans that would be of great material gain to them. But private preferences regarding segregation and material gains under equalization were not the only motivating factors of some conservatives' position. Black educational administrators ultimately answered to white school boards, and had no tenure.[22] But the state's NAACP now committed itself solidly to the view that segregated schools were inherently unjust. Indeed, months before *Brown*, the NAACP filed a suit to desegregate the University of Mississippi's law school. Meanwhile, only some of the worst racial disparities in education funding had been attenuated.[23]

Black Monday and State Response

Mississippi politicians professed surprise, but not shock, at the ruling. The state's most prominent white supremacist writer, Fred Sullens, voiced an apocalyptic view that differed from the "Delta's calm acceptance of the decision."[24] Officeholders and school officials anticipated that any substantial changes to the state's Jim Crow system would be long in coming.[25] Despite this consensus, differences in levels of devotion to segregation and in electoral pressures resulted in different rhetorical responses and policy preferences. Frank Smith, the lone moderate in the state's congressional delegation, backed compliance.[26] U.S. Senator Jim Eastland, then seeking reelection, spoke of defiance of the ruling as an obligation for all whites. He also quietly facilitated the organization of the WCCs, and reportedly told groups privately that the "only way we can stop this is by force and violence." In his reelection campaign, he touted the state's invocation of its police powers to halt any court-ordered segregation.[27] In contrast, the state's other U.S. senator, John Stennis, backed equalization and expected school desegregation to take decades. He sought to develop a network of practical segregationists more adept at conflict management than those politicians aligned with Eastland.[28]

The day after Black Monday, Governor White convened the LEAC to examine the state's options. Reflecting the continuing opposition of many county-level officials, the association of county supervisors—weighted, because of the distribution of Hills and Delta counties, toward the former—opposed the LEAC and doubted the feasibility of an equalization plan. In June 1954 the LEAC met in closed session, and discussed several stopgap measures should equalization fail to deter blacks from suing for desegregation.[29]

The Failure of Interracial Bargaining

The summer of 1954 marked a turning point in the enclave's management of race relations. Mississippi's rulers had embraced interracial elite bargaining to educate themselves about black elite preferences and to legitimate policymaking. After *Brown*, Governor White sought to build support for voluntary segregation through an unprecedented public meeting with black leaders. The meeting ended the reliance on interracial bargaining and reflected rulers' poor understanding of their black subjects. It also stiffened the backs of both black militants and white supremacists.

The ruling energized black protest concerning school desegregation and voting rights, both in its aggressiveness and in its diffusion across the state. The national NAACP dispatched national and regional staff to help the state organize new branches and devise a post-*Brown* political strategy. In the early 1950s the number of NAACP branches had doubled from twenty to forty (table 3.3). As in other states, Mississippi's NAACP conference vowed to encourage local citizens to petition for desegregated schools immediately and to request a hearing; if officials refused, the NAACP would file a lawsuit.[30] Rough estimates suggest that in 1954 about 4 percent of the state's voting-age blacks had registered to vote, and that they were twice as likely to be registered in majority-white as majority-black counties, but the levels were very low: 5.8 percent and 2.4 percent, respectively.[31]

Rulers' expectations before the meeting accorded with White's—black leaders would not risk the abolition of publicly supported schooling, and would support voluntary segregation. On the advice of a small and supportive group of prominent black conservatives, White decided to meet with about one hundred black leaders in order to build support for the plan.[32] Prior to the meeting, the LEAC announced a two-pronged approach to safeguarding segregation. First, equalization of school facilities would continue on a district-by-district basis; if blacks agreed to voluntary segregation, funds would be extended. Second, the state constitution would be amended to allow the legislature to abolish the public school system. The amendment would allow for the complete abolition of state-supported black schooling, but also permit public subsidies for white-only private schools. It served as a talking point to pressure blacks to back voluntary segregation.[33]

Meanwhile, on the eve of the meeting, NAACP leaders reiterated their support for *Brown* and declared that the organization would begin to file petitions at the district level. While black conservatives argued for at least waiting for *Brown*'s implementation decree before backing desegregation, a large majority backed a plan—to be presented to Governor White—in which biracial district-level councils would fashion implementation plans.[34] Conservative elites realized that they had miscalculated the sentiment of other black leaders. Ultimately, the group selected speakers who would announce black Mississippi's expectation that the governor would enforce the *Brown* ruling. Even so, some thought petitioning local school boards was premature in the absence of Supreme Court guidelines, and might well be counterproductive given white opposition.[35]

On July 30, Governor White opened the meeting by lauding the state's positive race relations, and then turned the meeting over to Speaker Sillers. In the presence of eighty-eight blacks and a number of white officials, the RCNL's T.R.M. Howard then read a statement declaring that the black participants had "not come to help work out any trick plan to circumvent the decision of the Supreme Court outlawing segregation in the public schools.

We believe the decision is a just and humane decision." Black citizens, he maintained, favored "strict observance of the Supreme Court's integration order," black participation on school boards at all levels, and a plan for school consolidation.[36] Sillers desperately called on an avowedly pro-segregation black leader, who remarked that "the real trouble is that for too long you have given us schools in which we could study the earth through the floor and the stars through the roof." With that bombshell, White adjourned the meeting. He later remarked, "I am stunned ... I have believed that the vast majority of Negroes would go along. Now I am definitely of the opinion you can't put faith in any of them on this proposition."[37]

After the meeting, White assembled the LEAC, which unanimously supported his call for a special session. After substantial debate, a group of white school officials also backed the repeal of the state's school system as a "last resort," but called for another special session to appropriate monies for new school construction. And—after White reassured them that the state would enact a real equalization program—a group of black educators announced a change of heart and backed voluntary segregation.[38]

The legislature—still dominated by the "Sillers Caucus"—eventually agreed to submit the deregulation amendment for popular ratification.[39] Some legislators from Hills counties worried that poorer counties—then subsidized by the Delta—would suffer from deregulation. Indeed, sixty-one of the state's eighty-two counties received extra financial support. But Sillers opposed the equalization plan and supported the amendment. Legislators also disagreed across this cleavage on the proper mode of taxation to finance equalization.[40]

In an effort to calm white voters concerned about an imminent closing of schools, the LEAC published a question-and-answer brochure that noted several other means by which segregation could be maintained. These might suffice for "10 to 20 years, or probably longer," according to the brochure. Ambitious politicians likewise assured whites that the amendment would be triggered only in extreme cases, whereby the state would provide alternative means of guaranteeing segregated education.[41] The ratification movement—backed by the newly formed White Citizens' Councils (see later in this chapter)—faced opposition from the NAACP, some labor organizations, and a band of white newspaper editors who for the next decade would call for restraint in managing racial conflict.[42]

In the lead-up to the referendum, Deltan legislators threatened school officials in the Hills counties with a withdrawal of their support for school construction financing unless they backed the amendment; LEAC and Governor White sent similar signals. Although winning by a two-to-one margin, the amendment reflected this Hills/Delta conflict. County-level returns showed that majority-white Hills counties often strongly rejected the amendment, while the twenty-six counties that already featured chapters of the White Citizens' Councils (WCCs)—mostly in the Delta—gave the amendment huge majorities. During the 1954 legislative primaries, the state party's accusation that black voters were national—not "Mississippi"—Democrats, together with the intimidation brought on by the WCCs, dampened black turnout.[43]

The governor and lawmakers pushed through, with white voters' help, another device meant to stymie black assaults on segregation and black protest more generally. In 1952 state legislators debated proposals to modify Section 244 of the state constitution in order to tighten literacy requirements for voter registration. Proponents of this reform publicly declared that the purpose of the change was to slow black voting, and the legislature passed it, but popular ratification failed.[44] Two years later, the amendment—receiving strong backing from the newly organized WCCs—passed with almost 60 percent approval. All registrants would be required to read a section of the state constitution *and* offer a "reasonable interpretation." Before, applicants had to complete one of these two tasks. In 1960 the state added a "good moral character" clause sufficiently flexible for racist implementation.[45] This new suffrage restriction tool worked quickly. Others did, too, including county registrars' expanded use of their discretionary authority to require that voters reregister.[46] The office of Attorney General (and next governor) James P. Coleman estimated that the state's qualified voters numbered about 500,000, of whom about 22,000 were black; the state disqualified some 10,000 blacks, it estimated, for failure to pay the poll tax and for other reasons. By 1955 the NAACP claimed that black voter registration had declined from 20,000 to 8,000.[47]

After the passage of the two constitutional amendments, Governor White and other politicians set out to fund adequately an equalization plan to make voluntary segregation a reality. The state's small tax base meant that current fiscal capacities were insufficient to embark on a large spending program. After significant gridlock over a variety of proposed solutions, White grew concerned about the increasingly restive conservative black educators, themselves impatient about the possibility of a sham equalization plan and increasingly constrained by assertive black activists. After much wrangling, the legislature passed a $60 million bond issue, as well as a 14 percent surtax on eight industries and several smaller taxes. For White, equalization was a "gamble" hinging on blacks' near-unanimous preference for segregation.[48]

Responding to talk of abolishing public schools, a dissenting legislator joked, "Mississippi, having been in the forty-eighth position all these years in the field of education, now proposes to get out of it altogether."[49] Still, while the state had installed a doomsday device, it demonstrated less willingness to begin preparing for a Mississippi after public education.[50] Thus, before *Brown* II—as leaders continued sincerely to believe that a voluntarily segregated Mississippi was still possible—authorities devised a combination of inducements and threats. In doing so, the Delta's legislative dominance, combined with consonant gubernatorial preferences, helped the state develop new revenue streams and improve public education for whites and blacks. These developments are inconceivable—at least in the 1950s—without *Brown*.

Brown *II and State Response*

Brown II's absence of a deadline for initiating desegregation plans and its reliance on federal district courts relieved Mississippi's politicians. Meanwhile, the NAACP registered its disappointment, while white moderate Deltan Hodding Carter expected only "token integration . . . for the foreseeable future."[51] In 1955 another gubernatorial campaign began. One year before, state parties in Georgia and South Carolina nominated those candidates best known as arch white supremacists. In contrast, Mississippi's party selected the most "moderate" segregationist, Attorney General James P. Coleman, who promised that he would "not keep our schools in a constant uproar while winning this fight." Throughout the campaign, which occurred amid national and international outrage over the murder of Emmitt Till, Coleman staked out ground as the candidate most skillful in providing a cool-headed and orderly defense of Jim Crow. In a record turnout for a gubernatorial runoff, Coleman comfortably defeated Paul B. Johnson, Jr.—widely viewed as the "better" white supremacist. Capitalizing on their bias against the stylistically more populist Johnson, Coleman received backing from Delta and urban financial donors.[52] Alone among five candidates, Coleman did not stand with the WCCs during his campaign.[53] Many leading politicians remained optimistic about voluntary segregation, despite the fact that weeks after *Brown* II, black parents—aided by local NAACP branches—had filed desegregation petitions with school boards in Jackson and four other towns.[54]

The Greatest Generation Mobilizes for White Supremacy

Mississippi spearheaded the South's white supremacist civic mobilization. Beginning in the Delta, the state's WCC movement became the region's largest. In 1953, Robert "Tut" Patterson, a thirty-two-year-old decorated former paratrooper and plantation manager in the Delta's Sunflower County, worried a great deal about a federal assault on Jim Crow. He articulated his concerns in neo-Nazi publications, and in the fall attended a strategy meeting at the home of Senator Jim Eastland, who owned one of the county's largest plantations. In the summer of 1954, Patterson called together a small group of men in Indianola to discuss it. Community leaders, including the town's mayor and attorney, considered ways by which communities could ward off threats posed by courts and race agitators. After a public rally, the first White Citizens' Council was born, and spread quickly throughout the state.[55]

The membership of the first council resembled that of later ones—all men, many of them returning veterans, most of them professionals or better-heeled landowners. Council members viewed those who would join the Klan as coming from a rowdy and lawless lower class, and throughout their history were at pains to distinguish themselves from the Klan, despite their own endorsements of coercion. Indeed, in the mid-1950s, Mississippi Klan strength paled in comparison to that in other enclaves. However, historians suggest that the effective presence of violence in repressing black protest and the successful intimidation of white moderates and liberals deterred the Klan's growth. As events began to spiral out of control in the early 1960s, the WCCs would be unable to argue to angry working-class whites that they had deterred incursions into sovereign Mississippi, and Klan growth ensued.[56]

Initially the Councils spread quietly. A cofounder noted that the "Negroes know that we are organizing, but he . . . does not know what we plan to do. The best thing . . . is to put him where he has stayed for 40 years and keep him guessing." By mid-October, the group claimed 25,000 dues-paying members across the state.[57] The WCCs received early support from elites, including Senator Eastland, state legislators, local officials, and the Hederman family, which controlled the state's most important daily papers, the *Jackson Daily News* and *Jackson Clarion-Ledger*. However—in contrast to the organization's embrace in Georgia and South Carolina—men with aspirations to hold statewide office did *not* join.[58] But though they may not have joined, by March 1955, no office seekers had spoken out against the WCCs.

The establishment of new Councils and membership growth were unsteady, and tracked closely along perceived threat, such as counties in which black parents filed suits with school boards. By 1956 they claimed about 80,000 members in three hundred Councils spread across sixty-five of the state's eighty-two counties. Unsurprisingly, they were strongest in the Delta and river counties, and weakest on the Gulf Coast and in the northeastern Hills counties. Belatedly, Gulf Coast whites organized Councils in response to black efforts to desegregate beaches.[59]

The WCCs exerted influence over party nominations to ensure that black voters were not targeted for electoral appeals, and considered moving to private prenominations if black registration—which the Councils vowed to "discourage"—grew too much. Meanwhile, they would "anticipate . . . moves by agitators and devise legal means for handling any problems that may arise," as well as apply "economic pressure to troublemakers."[60] Troublemakers were those black parents bold enough to file desegregation petitions in their local school districts.[61] The "pressure" took many forms. For instance, in Yazoo County, the local White Citizens' Council placed an ad in the local paper that listed the names and addresses of those who had signed desegregation petitions. Of the fifty-three signers, all but two suffered economically. One member of the Yazoo City WCC attributed the economic coercion to spontaneous behavior, not coordinated WCC efforts. In some cases, signers' names appeared on placards posted in town stores or in cotton fields.[62]

The group also boycotted white businesses and newspapers thought to be "soft" on segregation, including a much-publicized affair involving the Falstaff Brewing Company. In social scientist Joseph Luders's language, the Councils "raised the costs of capitulation," and this tactic worried many business leaders.[63] Besides maintaining white supremacy, some Council members found motivation for the suppression of black activism in a Chamber of Commerce–style drive to attract capital investment. Journalist David Halberstam observed that "every little town has its industrial development group seeking outside (usually northern) support, and this is the single most telling factor in the community's attitude toward the future." As one Council member remarked, "We know that no industrialist is going to move here to escape labor unrest if there's racial unrest."[64]

Although the WCCs did not develop a realistic plan for preserving segregation, it met other needs for its members. Future Sovereignty Commission official Erle Johnston joined the group, but claimed that it served only as an "emotional purgative" for anxious white men. By chilling public discourse they deemed insufficiently white supremacist, the Councils "suspend[ed] freedom of speech in many areas."[65] While its effect has sometimes been overstated, the institution did—as elsewhere—restrict civic and political discourse. For instance, the Mississippi Human Relations Council was dormant from 1957 to 1961, in part because presiding officers were pressured not to serve.[66] WCCs advertised their views in newspapers and then on television across the South. Later, in 1958, in an act of intimidation that suggested a waning confidence in mass white preferences for segregation at (almost) all costs, the Jackson branch, like those in Alabama and Louisiana, conducted a "survey" of white attitudes on education and housing segregation: 99 percent answered in accord with the WCCs' position on segregation. Councils in other states did likewise in an effort to silence white moderates and liberals.[67]

Additionally, WCCs' social and electoral pressure on white politicians fostered a chilling atmosphere. Unnamed assailants threatened the life of liberal House member Joe Wroten, who was also obliquely threatened by fellow legislators. As occurred in other enclaves, already-tenuous academic freedom declined. In one episode, several Mississippi university faculty resigned in protest at the "screening" of campus speakers; legislators applauded their exit.[68]

Still, the state featured a group of "moderate" newspaper editors. Often castigated by the WCCs—and in one case burned in effigy—these journalists criticized the state's massive resistance policies, and often the WCCs themselves. Generally, they preached patience, compliance with federal law, and genuine communication between the races at the local level. They also usually supported voluntary segregation, criticized the NAACP as the mirror image of white extremists, expected a long and protracted desegregation, and shared authorities' estimates about black mass preferences.[69]

The WCCs were most important in stifling black protest and black desegregation demands. At first, black leaders voiced optimism about the prospects of successful reform. The RCNL's T.R.M. Howard confidently reported in 1955 that "we are definitely whipping the economic freeze" of the WCCs. Soon, though, political violence spiked to its highest levels in decades. Early in the year, white assailants killed two black activists; one was shot in full view of a sheriff on the lawn of the county courthouse.[70] By the end of the summer, young Emmett Till's body had been found, and national and international coverage and condemnation soon followed. By the end of the year—after Howard and other RCNL and NAACP activists absorbed death threats, economic reprisals, and other harassment—the renowned activist had fled the state. The countermobilization by white supremacists left black activists reeling.[71]

But they battled back. Before leaving Mississippi, Howard, along with the NAACP, had sought during that same year to raise $250,000 to be held in a black-owned Memphis bank to relieve black farmers and others subject to economic reprisals. In March 1957 almost every student at the all-black Alcorn College struck to protest the anti-NAACP writings of one of their faculty.[72] But these defenses failed, and ultimately existing desegregation petitions stalled or were dropped.

The state's NAACP was stymied in both its growth and activism by the national office, which considered Mississippi a lost cause, and did not devise a serious plan for the state's desegregation. The national office's behavior, then (to local NAACP activists) and now, seems in large part self-fulfilling. To the extent that the national organization featured Mississippi in its programming, it used the state—especially after the infamous murder of Emmett Till—to increase membership not in the state but nationally. A nationwide fundraising campaign in 1957 declared, with a nod to Hitchcock's latest film, "M is for Mississippi and Murder." Frustrating local activists further, the national office, as chapter 9 shows, intervened mainly to secure its hegemony in a state to which it offered little help by, for example, ordering its staff not to cooperate with activists working with CORE. The organization filed no school suits until 1963, and only then did so due to constant badgering by field officer Medgar Evers.[73] Although written off by the national office, state-level NAACP activists continued community-organizing efforts, even in some of the most resistant locales. Networks developed during the mid-1950s proved crucial in the mobilizations of the 1960s.[74]

Outside of school desegregation and voter registration, black activists fought for the desegregation of public spaces. Dismissing the concerns of the state's risk-averse NAACP president, C. R. Darden, NAACP youth chapters boycotted stores in Jackson. On the Gulf Coast, where NAACP branches chafed against Darden's fears of damaging his organization, adult members launched a "wade-in" of segregated beaches. After both blacks and white supremacists had been injured in a melee, black activists successfully pressured the Kennedy administration to sue Biloxi to force the opening of the beaches to all. Perhaps more important, though, these events helped topple Darden, and Aaron Henry became the NAACP's state president. In less than a year, black Mississippians, led first by students, attacked segregation and unequal treatment in libraries, parks, pools, train stations, movie theaters, and elsewhere across the state.[75]

The Coleman Administration and "Practical Segregationism"

Like almost all state politicians, Governor James P. Coleman supported the maintenance of Jim Crow. However, arguing that guarding the state's traditions was "no task for the amateur or hothead," he consistently backed less confrontational strategies to desegregation in his mounting conflicts with the WCCs.[76] Coleman usually succeeded in blocking both legislative "red meat" and white supremacist efforts to insinuate themselves within the state apparatus. However, the legislature's Investigating Committee geared up to examine the civic activities of school teachers.[77] Opposing Senator Jim Eastland and others, Coleman mocked interposition as "foolish, ruinous and legal poppycock" and considered such tactics counterproductive.[78] More important, he successfully opposed the abolition of the public school system. Instead, Coleman asked "loyal Negroes" to work with white civic leaders to achieve voluntary segregation.

Finally, he beat back opponents of the construction of a racially integrated Veterans Administration hospital in Jackson in a move that the *Jackson Daily News* likened to the Munich appeasement. In doing so, Coleman cited his main rationale for covert rather than overt resistance—the costs to the state's reputation, both in terms of inciting further federal encroachments of state sovereignty, and in depressed external capital investment.[79] He also broke publicly with the WCCs.[80] Although the White Citizens' Councils achieved impressive gains, the organization and its allies failed to dominate the party-state in the 1950s.

Relations with the National Party

In the mid-1950s, Mississippi Democrats maintained *better* relations with the national party than did those in Georgia or South Carolina. As elsewhere, party officials disagreed on whether to back the national party's ticket and platform. After *Brown*, with local-level white supremacist forces mobilized, States' Rights forces seemed better positioned to overtake the party machinery. Before the 1956 presidential convention, this dispute continued previous battles between loyalists and States' Righters.

By 1956, any independents who had backed Eisenhower in 1952 remained blocked from using the state's official party. Four years earlier, inspired by Eisenhower's candidacy, a group of young white Mississippians led by Wirt Yerger began to battle with the reigning faction of the state's Republican party, the Black-and-Tan group led by Perry Howard, to rehabilitate the party back into an actual vote- and office-seeking organization. In 1956 the national party agreed to grant Yerger full control over the party by 1960. It would continue to organize at the county level, and in 1962, a month after Oxford, it contested twenty-one state legislative races, an impressive feat (it lost all of them). Meanwhile, though, many of the most prominent "Independents for Eisenhower" in the Delta were sufficiently troubled by the White House's support for *Brown* that they continued to invest in third-party efforts of the kind that South Carolina's governor, George Bell Timmerman, would champion.[81]

White Citizens' Council (WCC) forces sought to overtake county conventions and thereby win out at the state convention and instruct Mississippi's delegates to back a national ticket only if it supported interposition. SDEC chair Tom Tubb responded angrily at this intervention by the WCCs into party politics. Coleman, backed by Tubb and U.S. Senator John Stennis, defeated WCC forces by ensuring an unpledged delegation and by allowing the state convention to reconvene. And before the National Convention, Coleman took a leadership role in subverting South Carolina governor George Bell Timmerman's summer conference of southern parties.[82]

After the state party formally backed Adlai Stevenson, U.S. Representative John Bell Williams—who one decade later would, as governor, engineer the party's divorce from the national party—declared that he would bolt, attend a States' Rights convention, and back its electors, unpledged to either national party. Coleman declared that States' Righters "should be read out of the Democratic party." Adlai Stevenson carried the state comfortably.[83] Given the contrast between national party relations during Coleman's term and that of Governors Barnett and Williams in the 1960s, Coleman's party leadership points to yet another discontinuity in Mississippi's transition between the 1950s and the 1960s. Coleman's most consequential clash with WCC forces occurred in creating the State Sovereignty Commission (SSC).[84]

Enhancing State Capacities

State authorities already drew on the LEAC, the mission of which was first to provide a defense for *Plessy*, and then to preserve voluntary segregation through an equalization program. It drafted legislation aimed at weakening black legal protest and the NAACP. The legislature also provided local authorities with a significant new tool: a "breach of the peace" law that criminalized the advocacy of civil disobedience or even the call to violate "the established traditions, customs, and usages of the State of Mississippi."[85] But, in creating the SSC, many rulers envisioned something quite different.

Walter Sillers and other Deltans sought an executive agency under the direction of a small committee that would improve the state's intelligence-gathering, and then devise and implement strategies to weaken insurgents, and improve the state's reputation through an aggressive public relations campaign.[86] More casual monitoring of black protest had occurred in the past, of course. In the late 1940s, the Delta Council spied on meetings of a sharecroppers' union. But the state had never institutionalized its efforts to make reliable inferences about black insurgency.[87]

During legislative debate over establishing the agency, however, proponents framed it as akin to Virginia's Commission on Constitutional Government, which circulated historical documents in an effort to promote states' rights. After learning that pro–WCC legislators backed the proposal, the legislature's few progressive members opposed it.[88] Others feared what might occur were it staffed by WCC activists. Still, the legislature quickly approved it, and Coleman—knowing that a veto would fail—relented, assuming he would be able to appoint "moderates" as overseers who would prevent major missteps.[89]

The well-funded agency featured a small staff of professional criminal investigators and public relations staff, and was overseen by an advisory committee appointed by the governor. Before *Brown*, governors sought to estimate support for voluntary segregation among black elites; by 1955 governors and other officeholders wanted to anticipate and undercut the growth of NAACP branches and other sites of black protest. The SSC gathered information about black insurgency primarily through paid black informants, usually prominent conservatives and school administrators.[90] Sometimes the informants did not remain secret; the NAACP publicly criticized Reverend Henry H. Humes, editor of the black weekly *Delta Leader*, for receiving money from the SSC.[91]

Other than some propaganda films targeted at white northern audiences, the SSC remained sluggish for a few years.[92] Coleman used it to halt quietly several attempts to desegregate the state's white universities, but generally preferred a relatively ineffective SSC to an active agency dominated by hard-liners.[93] Angry WCC officials called it Mississippi's "State Surrender Commission," and legislators slashed its appropriations.[94]

Coleman's real agenda of institutional reform concerned constitutional revision and the development of a more professional and centralized coercive apparatus. In a standoff with WCC forces and with local and county officials jealously guarding their authority, Coleman failed to secure these reforms by the end of his term in 1960—which in turn had implications for the state's democratization.

Southern Enclaves and Policing Institutions

Across southern enclaves, coercive institutions reflected traditional American norms of localism in the area of law enforcement. Just as the central state lacked much authority, capacity, or willingness to intervene in the regulation of law enforcement at the state level, states themselves devolved law enforcement tasks and authority to counties and municipalities. State officials would often chafe against their lack of authority and informal influence over local and county law enforcement authorities. These jurisdictions—especially in rural areas—featured weak law enforcement institutions. Local police and sheriffs' departments were poorly staffed, trained, and equipped. Crowds involved in lynchings had little trouble in overwhelming small, poorly defended jails. Of course, in a roundabout way, this situation supported paternalist arrangements, as planters—presiding over a politics producing a weak law enforcement apparatus—often shielded their workers from assaults in what resembled Mafia "protection" rackets.

Thus, as in most states before World War II, coercion in southern enclaves remained in the hands of local police and elected county sheriffs, who held "ultimate responsibility" for maintaining order. Until 1960 almost all such personnel in the Deep South were white. At the state level, enclaves possessed militias and, by the 1930s, highway patrols.[95] However, most enclaves lacked state police forces. Highway patrols were authorized mainly to manage traffic safety, lacked jurisdiction to pursue suspects off major highways and roads, and suffered from poor training and equipment. Thus, they were ill suited to control spaces where crowds that were likely to challenge "law and order" might gather.[96] In contrast, state police had wide-ranging—and statewide—police powers, answered to governors, could enter jurisdictions without first being requested by local or county authorities, and possessed investigative and deployment branches. In the absence of state police, governors could not compel local and county law enforcement to enforce unpopular state laws.[97]

Bootleggers, Sheriffs, and the Failure of Constitutional Reform

Previous governors made sustained attempts to reorganize and centralize the state government. In the 1930s, seeking to implement some of the centralizing recommendations of a massive, state-commissioned Brookings study of Mississippi government, Governor Mike Conner attempted three times to call a constitutional convention. Each time, a diverse coalition of interests defeated him. Influential "drys" feared a repeal of the state's new prohibition law.[98] Deltans feared reapportionment, and commissioners of the Highway Department—which then employed more than fifty legislators—assumed that Conner would use the opportunity to rob them of their power. Finally, the powerful sheriffs' lobby feared that the state would make the office appointive, thereby migrating authority and power horizontally to other county officials, and upward to state agencies.[99]

During World War II, in an effort to develop new revenue, Delta legislators convinced their counterparts from the Hills counties to implement a "black-market tax" on illicit commodities or property. State personnel stationed on the state's borders collected a tax from bootleggers on their way to Mississippi. Bootleggers then bribed sheriffs—particularly those in Delta and Gulf Coast counties—to allow safe passage and safe operation of brothels and gambling establishments.[100] Given the precious revenue provided by liquor sales to the state's General Fund, counties—and particularly sheriffs—now exercised even greater leverage over the cash-strapped state.[101] Governors hesitated to deploy the National Guard to handle disturbances unless requested by the sheriff.[102] The power of sheriffs limited the prospects for enhancing Mississippi law enforcement, *and* for reforming state government more generally.

The power of sheriffs frustrated state prosecution of Gulf Coast gambling and other mafia operations during the late 1940s and early 1950s. Governor Fielding Wright would deploy the National Guard only if the relevant county sheriff requested its deployment. For Coleman, this "made the sheriff the king and he could be just as corrupt as he wanted to be—or just as weak as he wanted to be—and feel no fear of the state in Mississippi moving in on him[,] although his job was to enforce" state laws. While the National Guard was too blunt a force, "the legislature had been careful not to give us anything else, so we used that."[103]

The state Supreme Court held that the Guard could be deployed only if the Governor first fulfilled certain grounds in declaring an emergency. When this was not possible, governors tried to intimidate sheriffs into restricting criminal activities themselves. When establishing the Patrol, legislators limited it to enforcing traffic laws. For Coleman, "[T]he Mississippi Delta . . . was a fiefdom of its own. . . . [Its] leaders in the legislature . . . just wouldn't permit any . . . state police." As Attorney General, Coleman "did not attempt to enforce the prohibition laws on the Mississippi Gulf Coast—or in Adams County—or in Warren County—to any great extent because it was an utter impossibility."[104]

By the late 1950s, when Coleman attempted to centralize state policing and secure other reforms through constitutional revision, the job was even more difficult.[105] The state's highly decentralized law enforcement apparatus consisted of three major elements: an 11,000-man National Guard; a 225-man Highway Patrol; eighty-two county sheriffs' offices; and local police. While some towns hired black police to patrol black neighborhoods, all other officers were white.[106] The governor controlled only the National Guard and the Highway Patrol.

As in South Carolina and Georgia, Mississippi executives preferred a state police to the Highway Patrol, and preferred that the latter have greater, rather than less, jurisdictional authority. Their least preferred arrangement was the status quo, which consisted of a lightly armed and poorly trained Highway Patrol authorized only to deal with traffic-related crimes and equipped with weak police powers. Delta legislators, however, blocked any attempts to create a state police force, or bolster the authority of the Highway Patrol.[107]

Coleman hoped that through a constitutional convention he could empower advocates for economic development through a long-overdue reapportionment. Additionally, he hoped to protect the enclave by improving state law enforcement and removing constitutional provisions regarding education and disfranchisement that might draw closer scrutiny of state practices by federal jurists. As he would later recall, constitutional reform "could have really forestalled a lot of the troubles that caused Mississippi a lot of grief."[108] But highly conservative rural legislators, as well as Speaker Sillers, narrowly defeated his bid for a convention. The strong opposition of groups of county officials, especially the sheriffs' lobby, shaped the thinking of Sillers and other legislators. In addition, Deltan legislators feared reapportionment and an alteration of state liquor laws.[109] This conflict pitted Black Belt conservatives against business moderates and urban forces. As mentioned in chapter 3, conflicts over constitutional reform and state-building flared up intermittently for decades. But, unlike earlier battles, this one occurred in the midst of federal challenges to enclave rule. While Coleman hoped to improve the state's defenses as he championed the cause of economic development, these efforts now lay in tension with the electoral and economic motives of rural conservatives beholden to county officials. In the process, rulers reached a stalemate—a weak surveillance agency controlled by WCC hardliners, and the defeat of efforts to improve a poorly organized and decentralized coercive capacity.

The Oxford Fiasco

The University of Mississippi had long been one of the state's most revered white institutions. This was perhaps most true in the 1950s, when the school could boast a nationally ranked football team, multiple Miss America pageant winners, and several Rhodes scholarship recipients.[110] Moreover, the governance of the university often served as a hot-button issue in political campaigns. During massive resistance, White Citizens' Council (WCC) leaders warned faculty that their views were being monitored.[111] The university's desegregation quickly captured white Mississippi's attention. The crisis began in the fall of 1962, when, after an improbable, sixteen-month battle, federal courts ordered the immediate matriculation of the mercurial James Meredith, a young air force veteran whose suit to matriculate had been financed in part by the NAACP.[112]

Factional Conflict and Rulers' Preferences

At the time of the crisis, Democrats maintained a complete monopoly over Mississippi's offices. Over the course of the Barnett administration (1959–63), the WCCs secured substantial influence within party-state institutions. Ross Barnett, a folksy personal injury attorney, had reached the governor's mansion in 1959 on his third try. Like South Carolina's Timmerman and Georgia's Marvin Griffin, Barnett exhibited a fondness for rhetorical brinksmanship, once vowing to "rot in jail before [letting] one Negro even darken the sacred threshold of our white schools."[113] His biggest priority in office was recruiting external capital investment. Taking office in 1960, his administration was soon bedeviled by profligate spending and unrealistic commitments of patronage for his supporters; his popularity was very low.[114]

Barnett himself obviously preferred the status quo in the university's racial policies. And while he was thought to be a hardline white supremacist, he was not opposed to all modes of the "practical segregationism" more reminiscent of the Coleman administration. For instance, he had continued to support State Sovereignty Commission staffer Erle Johnston after Johnston spoke out against the WCCs.[115] And Barnett showed a strong desire to maintain "law and order" in his deployment of the Highway Patrol to escort Freedom Riders through the state in 1961. Mississippi officials, writes historian John Dittmer, "had learned the lessons of Birmingham and Montgomery" (where Alabama officials allowed white crowds to attack the riders).[116] Still, Barnett's election elevated the reach of the WCCs in the state apparatus. According to historian Neil McMillen, the Councils became "a kind of cabinet extraordinary for racial affairs," led by spokesman William J. Simmons, who served as a close adviser.[117]

Eighteen months before the crisis, black direct action in Mississippi began in earnest, as black college students launched a sit-in campaign in Jackson institutions, and the Student Non-Violent Coordinating Committee (SNCC) began a voter registration project. By 1962 the Congress of Racial Equality (CORE) had deployed in the Delta. In a familiar pattern, WCC president William Simmons and other hardliners would convince Barnett to take strong stances on racial matters, but then Jackson's business moderates would "cool the governor down."[118]

The most rural of the Deep South enclaves, Mississippi began to urbanize quickly after World War II. Over the 1950s, the share of residents living in urban areas increased by more than one-third. In the 1940s and 1950s, the state continued to experience net outflows of both blacks and whites (almost two-thirds of a million, and more than two hundred thousand, respectively). Of those remaining behind, a larger and larger share began moving into Mississippi's cities in the 1950s.[119] By 1960 metro Jackson's population reached 250,000. While the state's dominant economic lobby had long been the Delta Council, in 1948 business leaders organized the Mississippi Economic Council. As with so-called business moderates elsewhere, professionals and firm-owners in Jackson and throughout the state worried that the state's handling of external challenges and domestic insurgencies would negatively impact the state's economic development. As a Jackson bank executive noted, "Two things can hurt us, violence or closing the schools." State officials working to attract industries concurred. Indeed, the state had just cut corporate and personal income tax rates to help with these efforts.[120]

The moderates, however, were more timid than WCC hardliners in participating in politics. First, the severely malapportioned legislature reduced their influence in both chambers. Second, cooperation on economic planning between Mississippi moderates and Delta planters had not developed as much as that of their counterparts in South Carolina. Third, as the WCCs remained powerful in the early 1960s, and many moderates felt pressure to join, they faced a difficult problem in publicly identifying and cooperating with one another. Their numbers seemed fewer than was in fact the case. As the likelihood of a court-ordered desegregation of the University of Mississippi became clear, *Delta Democrat-Times* publisher Hodding Carter argued, white Mississippians were under no illusion that federal authority could be defied. While usually backing segregation, none of the state's nineteen dailies advocated violence.[121] As in all Deep South enclaves, authorities would fight the desegregation as far as courts permitted, and then relent.

Managing the Crisis

But on September 13, 1962, in a televised address penned by the WCCs' William Simmons, Barnett "interposed" Mississippi's sovereignty between the state and federal courts, thus rejecting the court-ordered desegregation.[122] Barnett privately admitted to school officials that he understood the untenability of interposition, but thought he could bluff the Department of Justice "into backing down."[123] Besides interposing his authority, Barnett announced that state universities would close before they desegregated. Ole Miss student leaders quickly contradicted him, voicing their desire to keep the school open.

Thence began a long two weeks of telephone discussions between Barnett and the Kennedys, which the latter secretly taped. In these discussions, Barnett negotiated for the administration to allow him face-saving arrangements by which federal authorities would force him to submit to the school's desegregation only at gunpoint. Four times, he broke agreements, vacillated, and hoped that by invoking his police powers he could send the case back to court and delay Meredith's matriculation for "about a year."[124] As the standoff dragged on, business leaders began privately urging the governor not to close the university.

But Oxford, Mississippi, had begun to attract curious onlookers and white supremacists from across the South and the nation. U.S. Army Major General Edwin Walker, commander of U.S. forces at Little Rock, who was later relieved of duty in Europe by President Kennedy for his rabidly right-wing indoctrination of U.S. troops, issued a "public battle cry" for white supremacists to converge upon the university to defend it from desegregation. Klansmen and others from the South heeded the call.[125]

Before a fifth and final set-piece in which Meredith would enroll in the university's Jackson office while Barnett "waited" for him in Oxford, Barnett attended a Saturday UM-Kentucky football game in Jackson. Walking onto the field at halftime, he worked the crowd into a frenzy, after which he told his advisers, "I can't do it. Did you see that crowd?" Afterward, still enthralled, he called off the plan and convinced the White House to bring Meredith to Oxford on Monday. President Kennedy, no longer believing Barnett to be credible, federalized Mississippi's National Guard.[126]

In attempting to compel compliance through policing, the U.S. central state lacked many options. The FBI dealt only with investigations, not enforcement. Other armed federal agents, in agencies such as the Border Patrol and the Bureau of Prisons, lacked training or experience. The U.S. Marshals service, maintained by the DOJ, seemed to be one of the only options for escorting Meredith to the registrar's office. But the service, numbering about eight hundred officers, had a reputation as a landing ground for lucky winners of political patronage, and its officers were not trained for crowd policing.[127]

On Sunday, as outsiders converged on Oxford, the town grew increasingly tense, and Barnett began to fear the outbreak of violence. Mostly, though, he feared his own public humiliation if the Kennedys leaked tapes of the phone calls, as the attorney general threatened. He then agreed that the marshals would bring Meredith to Oxford on Sunday, one day ahead of schedule, in order to preempt the arrival of additional angry white supremacists. After a brief, staged "confrontation" with the state's Highway Patrol, Meredith would then be allowed to register.[128]

Meanwhile, Barnett dispatched to Oxford four confidants—all prominent politicians—and armed them with an executive proclamation that authorized them to "do all things necessary" to protect the state. However, he did not arm them with the truth of his stage-managing with the Kennedys. They thought that the Highway Patrol, and various county sheriffs and others, were being dispatched actually to "defend" the campus from the marshals. Only the head of the Highway Patrol, T. B. Birdsong, knew of the governor's arrangements with the White House. Even the governor's WCC advisers remained unaware of the plans. Seventy business leaders met to issue a resolution supporting "law and order," but could not agree on its wording.[129]

By federalizing the National Guard, Kennedy had "removed from Governor Barnett control of the only adequate instrumentality capable of preserving law and order should an emergency arise."[130] As white supremacists and curious onlookers streamed into the state, the state lacked the capacity to halt them from entering Oxford. Barnett attempted desperately to amass sufficient forces to block off the town and the campus, but the state's Highway Patrol was not up to the task. It had established a presence on campus, but was completely disorganized; these problems worsened as the patrol attempted to coordinate the spontaneous arrival of various sheriffs and their deputies. Of course, there was no precedent, and certainly no training, or even basic communications infrastructure, for mobilizing such a group.[131] Birdsong grew exasperated and confused by contradictory orders from Barnett and others.

That afternoon, marshals arrived on campus and encircled the main administration building—they planned to stay there until it opened the next day, when Meredith would be escorted to the registrar's office.[132] Attorney General Robert F. Kennedy, placed in command of military forces assembling around the state, failed to alert the military of the marshals' presence on campus. Curious, joking students stretched out on beach towels as they watched the marshals assemble. As the day went on, true "outside agitators" swept into town.

Eventually, a crowd of about 2,500 developed, and—under the leadership of General Walker—grew increasingly angry and began to pelt the marshals with rocks. By this time, most students had returned to their dormitories. As the marshals responded with tear gas, Walker issued a "battle cry" and called on a crowd of about eight hundred to move in formation on the marshals. A full-scale riot had broken out; the marshals soon were under fire from rifles, pistols, and shotguns. Highway patrolmen circulated rumors that marshals had killed some of their colleagues, and Lieutenant Governor Johnson had to persuade them not to respond in kind.[133]

By 10:00 p.m., federal troops, led by a military police battalion, moved in. Within one day, twenty thousand troops, plus the eleven thousand National Guardsmen, had swept into the Oxford area and detained almost three hundred civilians. Many Oxford whites were relieved at their arrival and blamed the disorder on out-of-state whites. Soon, army intelligence and FBI agents swarmed the area.[134]

The Immediate Aftermath

Meredith somehow slept through the night's events in a campus dormitory. Despite numerous death threats and other inconveniences, Meredith decided to remain on campus—under guard by U.S. deputy marshals and 300 army troops—and was graduated the following fall. The school's newspaper charged that the riot brought "shame and dishonor." Indeed, undergraduate applications decreased by 30 percent, and top administrators and faculty resigned.[135]

Statewide, many whites were alternately angered and embarrassed by the debacle. White resistance to black organizing in the Delta and elsewhere ratcheted upward (see chapter 10).[136] The state's business moderates were angry and ashamed, but for different reasons.[137] Hours after chaos descended upon the campus, more than one hundred white business leaders met and issued a call for law and order, and pleaded with Barnett to keep the university open. But they remained quiet as shriller voices denounced the federal government's "illegal invasion" of the state. Jackson's Junior Chamber of Commerce made this case, as did a report by the state legislature.[138]

National and international media lambasted Barnett and the entire state. The White House considered cutting defense spending in the state, which had been growing considerably over the 1950s. From late 1962 on, the Kennedy administration collected data on federal financial assistance to the state in a file headed, "Stick It to Mississippi." Almost immediately, Mississippi lost out on a bid to lure Westinghouse Air Brake Company, which instead chose South Carolina. In the words of a prominent segregationist in Alabama, "Mississippi will be a long time living Oxford down. . . . Violence only hurts the segregation cause."[139]

Chapter 10 situates Oxford as a turning point in the state's democratization. But this argument holds only if the outcome was contingent, rather than determined by antecedent conditions, as some have argued.[140] Barnett's reckless attempts to situate himself as a brave defender of the state's "traditions" certainly created conditions for disorder and violence to take hold. However, much of this disorder involved white supremacists from outside the state. Lacking a well-trained, well-equipped, and well-organized state police force, even a less reckless governor would have had a difficult time deterring or repressing white supremacist disorder. Factional conflict within the party frustrated the development of a robust coercive capacity. Thus, a combination of rulers' preferences and institutions, poor federal planning, and bad luck produced this crisis outcome. It would unleash processes that shaped the state's democratization.

CHAPTER SEVEN

"Integration with Dignity"

South Carolina Navigates the Clemson Crisis

BEFORE *BROWN*, South Carolina's rulers sought to preempt the invalidation of state-mandated segregation by improving black education and thus make "separate but equal" more palatable to jurists. After the ruling, they quickly converged on a strategy of massive resistance: decrying, deterring, and deferring threats to white supremacy in the public sphere. By fall 1962, South Carolina was the only state in the nation with completely segregated public schools. However, as 1963 dawned, a crisis over the court-ordered desegregation of Clemson College was brewing. Fearing—with good reason—another Little Rock, rulers skillfully secured a nonviolent, orderly desegregation that earned them national praise. Drawing on this success and the processes it accelerated, South Carolina authorities successfully limited interference by the federal government and civil rights forces, safeguarded their careers, and advanced the evolving goals of their political-economic clients. After a vicious defense of Jim Crow, South Carolina's rulers went on to navigate the remainder of the 1960s and achieve a harnessed democratization.

The relative calm of South Carolina's transition period has often been attributed to the state's political culture, and especially that of its elites. This chapter casts doubt on that account. First, it reviews the state of black education before *Brown* and South Carolina's attempts to preempt the decision. Second, it details the state's responses to *Brown* in the 1950s and early 1960s. It demonstrates that South Carolina's leaders were second to none in their attacks on white civil society as well as black protest organizations. Third, it describes how the state bolstered its institutional resources to manage democratization pressures. Fourth, because of the state's early development of conservatives opposed to the ruling party, I discuss their emergence through the 1950s and early 1960s. Finally, the chapter explains how politicians capitalized on ruling party cohesion and an improved coercive apparatus to navigate the Clemson crisis.

Segregation and Education on the Eve of *Brown*

South Carolina's state-financed public education did not begin until Reconstruction. As elsewhere, racial disparities in teachers' salaries, quality and number of facilities, and per capita expenditures grew over time, especially after the founding of enclave rule. By 1921 the state spent almost ten times as much per capita on white schooling, and this was reflected in racial gaps in the length of the academic year, years of schooling attained, and literacy rates.[1]

In 1945, in response to NAACP suits in Charleston (then almost one-half black), authorities began to reduce racial disparities in teachers' salaries. Unlike subsequent changes in education policy, this move was not motivated by a desire to forestall challenges to *Plessy*; rather, expanding revenues, the racial paternalism of lowcountry politicians, and rising black demands drove this effort.[2] Soon black activists used courts to attack not just violations of "separate but equal," but "separate but equal" itself.

Anticipating *Brown*

Inspired by a speech by state NAACP president James Hinton, clergyman Joseph A. DeLaine in Clarendon County filed a lawsuit in federal district court in 1947 demanding equalization in school transportation in the form of the equal provision of school buses.[3] At the time, the county led the state in the share of its workforce claimed by agriculture. Thus, on the modernization approach to predicting black insurgency, this was a highly improbable site of the state's organized resistance to enclave rule. After a federal judge dismissed the case, blacks in the county continued until December 1950, when, with NAACP assistance, litigants dropped existing suits and attacked segregation itself as an equal protection violation. In May 1951 the federal district court convened a special three-judge panel. Robert Figg, one of the state's ablest attorneys and an aide to former governor Strom Thurmond, admitted that "separate" was not "equal," and asked for "reasonable time" for the state's equalization efforts to bear fruit. He also argued that the dismantling of segregated institutions would lead to "dangerous tensions and unrest." However, the panel rejected the suit, leaving Judge Waring—of white primary fame—to pen an angry dissent.[4] The federal bench had, however, served notice to the state's rulers. As with politicians elsewhere across the South, after the June 1950 U.S. Supreme Court decisions, South Carolina authorities thought state-mandated segregation was in real danger, and that attaining separate but actually equal school systems might secure it.[5]

Formerly "Assistant President" to Roosevelt, Governor James Byrnes (1951–55) had also served briefly as a Supreme Court justice and, under Truman, as secretary of state. Byrnes was by 1950 the most renowned southerner in national affairs, and the region's most respected politician. His opposition to desegregation brought it an additional modicum of respectability in national policy discourse. In 1950, South Carolina elected Byrnes governor practically by acclamation. In his 1951 inaugural address, which drew a crowd of nearly one hundred thousand, he announced his plan for rectifying racial inequality in public schooling. He remarked, "It is our duty to provide for the races substantial equality in school facilities. We should do it because it is right." And, he added, "It is wise."[6] Observers viewed Byrnes's leadership as pivotal in securing such a rapid change in state policy. Moreover, his example had a regionwide impact. The fact that South Carolina was "home" to one of the five suits that would soon comprise *Brown* may have given the state added impetus to attempt to equalize educational spending.

Byrnes vowed that the races would not be mixed in schools "for some years to come." If ordered to desegregate, the state would "reluctantly" abandon public schools, which were 43 percent black. He blamed the problem on "the politicians in Washington and the Negro agitators in South Carolina," and claimed that—even in the absence of litigation—he "would have urged this school program to help the [state's] white and colored children."[7]

Byrnes called for a massive school-building program, about two-thirds of which would be devoted to black schools. Moreover, the state would complete its efforts to equalize black teachers' salaries and promotion procedures. The program would be financed by a 3 percent sales tax, as well as a $75 million bond issue. Traditionally, the state had the country's lowest levels of per capita state and local taxation, principally due to its reliance on extremely low assessed valuations of real estate.[8] Byrnes's sales tax was the first step toward a much more robust (and regressive) fiscal capacity for the state. The General Assembly swiftly passed these measures.[9]

South Carolina also established by concurrent resolution the South Carolina School Committee, which came to be known as the Gressette Committee, after its chair, L. Marion Gressette, a prominent lowcountry senator known as "Mr. Segregation."[10] The committee, which remained in operation until 1966, was the South's first official body dedicated to strategizing about the maintenance of segregation. It brought together in closed hearings five members of each chamber, and five members selected at large. The legislature's most skilled parliamentarians led the committee, and Charleston's most respected attorneys staffed it.[11]

The General Assembly—on the Gressette Committee's recommendation—established "preparedness measures" that would come into effect were *Plessy* overturned. First, it authorized local officials to lease or sell school property under the assumption that churches or other nonprofit organizations would step in to manage schools. Second, each student transfer would have to be authorized by each principal.[12]

Most important, the General Assembly followed Byrnes's call to repeal the state constitution's provision requiring the state to provide public education.[13] In November—in the midst of a Byrnes-organized campaign of "South Carolinians for Eisenhower"—voters approved the repeal by a margin of more than two to one. The pro-repeal vote tracked closely along voting for the States' Rights Party in 1948—support was strongest in the Black Belt, and weakest in the upcountry, where five counties rejected it. The NAACP and other black groups opposed it, but they were joined by very few white liberals or others concerned with the state's promise to abolish public education rather than accept even token desegregation.[14]

On the eve of *Brown*, rulers were unsure of the likely success of the equalization strategy. Even if they thought the overturning of *Plessy* was inevitable, they could still hope that equalization might facilitate continued segregation. Certainly, many whites believed that Byrnes could do more than delay segregation's demise.[15] But elites considered few alternatives to equalization, and the support of the highly popular Byrnes guaranteed its rapid passage. The use of a sales tax to finance the plan—rather than increasing property taxes for middle- and upper-class whites—made equalization easier to swallow.

"Black Monday" in South Carolina: Rulers Respond

Responses to *Brown v. Board* among South Carolina's elite varied from outrage to muted disappointment. Byrnes professed to being "shocked" by the ruling, but called for all "to exercise restraint and preserve order." And he temporarily halted further allocation of monies for school construction. Black elite responses varied. NAACP president James Hinton called for a biracial committee of leaders to develop implementation plans. He announced that groups of black parents were in the process of filing nine desegregation petitions with school boards, but then called for a wait-and-see approach until the implementation decree. Rulers rejected Hinton's call for biracial dialogue, partly because the NAACP opposed the equalization program.[16] A minority of black educational administrators—who were expected to lose many jobs as black and white schools were consolidated—continued to support a dual system, while white teachers' associations continued to support the status quo. A small minority of white church groups celebrated the decision.[17]

Quickly, William Workman—the state's most prominent political journalist and an adviser to white supremacist politicians—outlined for his readers five possible responses to *Brown*. These ranged from acquiescence to nullification; in between, options included the abolition of public schools, "evasive action" (such as state provision of tuition grants for private schools), and "passive resistance" (a quieter noncompliance).[18] In fashioning responses, politicians featured a narrow distribution of beliefs and preferences concerning segregation. Regarding the influence of various institutions, as with most public policy issues, the General Assembly—and particularly the Senate—dominated deliberation and decision-making. Federal officeholders exercised little policy influence; nor had political reforms sufficiently empowered the executive to challenge legislative dominance.

Moreover, the legislature itself remained dominated by the rural lowcountry. Its senators chaired twenty-five of the chamber's thirty-three standing committees. Three of the state's five most populous upcountry counties, in addition to those representing Charleston and Columbia, could claim no committee chairs.[19] The composition of the Gressette Committee mirrored this distortion. These lowcountry senators voiced the most concern about—and the most defiance toward—*Brown*. In the 1954 constitutional amendment vote, upcountry representatives, while reliably segregationist, were less likely to back more extreme positions. However, lowcountry dominance, coupled with Byrnes's leadership, meant that pivotal legislators united behind the Gressette Committee. Byrnes tried to convince blacks— and those judges soon to issue an implementation decree—that only "voluntary segregation" would keep the peace.[20]

All South Carolina officeholders publicly backed segregation, as did most media.[21] These officials disagreed over two matters. One concerned the costs that rulers were willing to let the state absorb in order to maintain segregation. The backing of the doomsday option required a belief in the viability—financial, administrative, and otherwise—of privatized school systems. Second, the decision to invoke this option depended largely on one's beliefs about the likelihood of court-ordered desegregation. This belief in turn depended on the likely efficacy of southern defiance of courts, and on blacks' commitment to desegregation and their ability—district by district—to secure it.[22]

Politicians' public utterings could differ greatly from privately held preferences. A gap could emerge for a number of reasons: perceptions regarding the views of their white constituents (often incorrect); issues of timing, primarily due to the relationship between one's ambitions and the electoral calendar; and factional alliances that might constrain room for maneuver. Thus, even assuming consensus on the desirability of segregation, preferences about strategies for preserving it could diverge because of beliefs about mass opinion, black preferences and protest capacity, the efficacy of federal courts, and the efficacy of various substitute policies if the repeal of the public school system were triggered.

After *Brown* II in mid-1955, the costs and benefits of these choices would become clearer. In 1954, however, elites shared a few important beliefs. The vast majority of South Carolina politicians sincerely believed that the state's blacks—including black education professionals—favored continued segregation. Gradually, it dawned on some public officials and their confidants that black South Carolinians—not merely "northern agitators"—preferred integrated schools.[23] Politicians disagreed on the likely success of defiance in defeating federal courts. Some remarked—publicly and privately—that sufficiently unified and cunning opposition could win the day. Others expressed skepticism, noting that "there wasn't a lawyer in South Carolina that didn't know what the outcome was going to be." And some legal experts doubted the long-term viability of evasion, but thought they could stall for a slower desegregation, at least long enough that it did not occur on their watch.[24]

In 1954, the state held two important elections: first, a U.S. Senate election to replace Burnet Maybank, who had died while in office; second, a gubernatorial race that chose the governor for the remainder of the pre–Little Rock period. In the Senate election, the party's executive committee bungled its preferred nomination of Edgar Brown, leader of the Barnwell Ring. Along with Senator Olin Johnston, Brown co-led the faction more loyal to the national party.[25] Former moderate Governor Strom Thurmond, now closely linked to hardline white supremacists, had lost a 1950 Senate race to Johnston, and his political future was perhaps in doubt. In that race, the black weekly paper *Lighthouse & Informer* called on its readers to defeat "Dixiecratism" by backing Johnston; it claimed that about sixty thousand black voters led to Johnston's victory.[26]

Four years later, the state party itself, defying Governor Byrnes, voted to nominate state senator Edgar Brown and avoid a primary. The decision caused an uproar, and Thurmond won a fluke victory as a write-in candidate. The dispute reflected and exacerbated conflict between the loyalist and States' Rights factions, and also worsened a personal feud between Thurmond and Brown dating back to Thurmond's 1946 gubernatorial race.[27] The States' Rights/loyalist cleavage mapped loosely onto a lowcountry/upcountry sectional split. Loyalists were less ideologically cohesive and backed segregation, but for a variety of reasons tied their political futures to the national party.[28]

In the gubernatorial election, moderate Lester Bates, a national party loyalist, faced off against States' Righter George Bell Timmerman. As with most southern elections in 1954, candidates competed over which of them had a reliably white supremacist background and a plausible answer to *Brown*. Timmerman was clearly superior on these grounds. He offered a "three-school" plan in which the state would provide two racially segregated school systems, plus a racially mixed system for those parents preferring integrated schools.[29] Timmerman won a large victory that would heighten considerably the state's commitment to massive resistance.[30] Despite the abolition of the white primary and some gains in black voter registration, the black vote was irrelevant in both elections.

Brown II and the Timmerman Administration

In his 1955 inaugural address, Timmerman announced his opposition to any solution to the segregation problem that smacked of "the cowardly approach of gradualism, which seeks to minimize opposition by careful selection of a few victims at a time." He stated—and perhaps even believed—that 98 percent of the state's blacks preferred segregation. Many politicians did not take Timmerman seriously, and he deferred greatly to the General Assembly. Still, his position-taking shaped the parameters of policy discourse.[31] As governor, Timmerman continued his defiant rhetoric. On NBC's *Meet the Press* he claimed that segregation would continue for another "thousand years."[32]

After *Brown* II's announcement, state politicians expressed relief, but Clarendon County officials remained on alert, and expected that schools would be closed if courts ordered their desegregation. Black South Carolinians responded to the ruling with desegregation petitions across the state, many sponsored by local NAACP branches.[33] Serious consideration of the abolition of public schools was not limited to politicians. Charleston-area desegregation petitions by black parents sparked mass meetings of several hundred white citizens each, who—with little if any dissension—approved resolutions declaring their preference to close area schools rather than operate them on a desegregated basis. Senate micromanagement of county affairs (described in chapter 3) allowed flexible responses to desegregation efforts. Through "supply bills," some lowcountry counties planned to halt the funding of only those schools in which race mixing might occur.[34]

The General Assembly responded to *Brown* II with policies meant both to facilitate the state's withdrawal from the provision of public schooling *and* to raise the expected costs of court-ordered compliance in the eyes of both federal actors and black activists. The Gressette Committee championed most of these statutes, including the broadly supported repeal of the state's compulsory school attendance law.[35] Additionally, the state denied funds to schools involved in court-ordered student transfers, including any institution of higher learning. Were any white college or university shut down, a key center of black organization and protest—the all-black South Carolina State College in Orangeburg—would also be shuttered.[36]

In 1955 the Gressette Committee, after consultations with Byrnes and Timmerman, backed the "interposition" of South Carolina's sovereignty between the federal bench and school officials. Joining Virginia and the rest of the Deep South states, South Carolina's General Assembly unanimously passed an interposition resolution. Legislators disagreed on what exactly it was that they had done. Some thought it to be merely a form of protest; others considered the state's endorsement of the doctrine to constitute a declaration of nullification. While it had little practical importance, as elsewhere, the resolution further narrowed the options of segregationists.[37] At the same time, many politicians worried privately that blustery rhetoric could backfire by heightening outside observation of the state and its policies. Such worries mounted with Senator Thurmond's record-breaking filibuster of the 1957 Civil Rights Act, which embarrassed state leaders.[38]

In this period, the General Assembly centralized segregation policies that had once been set by local ordinances, such as those governing bus and railway waiting rooms and restrooms. But inspired by the *Brown* ruling, black activists attacked other state-mandated segregation at both local and state levels, and launched lawsuits to desegregate state-operated parks and beaches.[39] Anticipating their defeat in federal court, state legislators ordered the popular Edisto Beach state park closed, declaring it a "monument" to the "vindictiveness of race agitators."[40]

Drawing on the *Brown* rulings, the NAACP backed a black Columbian's suit demanding the invalidation of municipal ordinances regulating bus seating. Although the Supreme Court struck down the laws, the governor's father, Judge George B. Timmerman, dismissed the case upon its being remanded to federal district court. Ultimately, black students at Allen University—with the belated support of the state's NAACP—successfully performed a "direct action" test of the Supreme Court's ruling without incident.[41]

Repressing Domestic Insurgency

Important responses to *Brown* extended well beyond the actions of public authorities. Their behavior helped fuel a mobilization of white supremacist civil society that itself further encouraged state defiance. The spread of the White Citizens' Councils (WCCs), the resurgence of the Klan and similar organizations, and the everyday actions of many white civic groups and individuals significantly weakened black protest capacity, and restricted white liberals' participation in civic and political discourse. Importantly, state and county officials supported and expanded upon this tightening of the public sphere. South Carolina's flowering of white supremacist civil society was tightly integrated in, and nurtured by, party officials and economic elites.

The WWC movement in South Carolina reached its peak from mid-1955 to summer 1956. At that point the WCCs boasted about 30,000–40,000 members and some fifty-five local branches in almost one-half of the state's forty-six counties, almost all of them in the lowcountry.[42] Branch location and sequence of founding generally followed the location and timing of the filing of desegregation petitions or lawsuits; branches tapered off as these were withdrawn or unsuccessful. Characteristic of a state elite long suspicious of the political participation of the citizenry, WCC leaders did not seek to maximize membership or number of branches. Also influenced by the fact that state officials were then engaged in efforts to weaken a resurgent Klan (see later in this chapter), they preferred to screen applicants to produce a more "respectable" membership. The White Citizens' Councils—officially endorsed in a General Assembly resolution—attracted white-collar professionals, landowners, local politicians, and community leaders.[43]

WCC members intimidated—economically and physically—signers of school desegregation petitions. Most commonly, WCCs advertised these signers' names in local newspapers, after which many of them either withdrew their names or lost their jobs. Leaders of the organization, as well as black activists, deemed this strategy successful in reducing the number of petitions—only thirteen of which had been filed by late 1955—and lawsuits against districts that ignored these petitions. By spring 1956, blacks had filed no desegregation suits beyond Clarendon County. After boasting about its economic tactics, WCC leaders subsequently denied using them. Some Councils held meetings with blacks they identified as community leaders, where they preached against the NAACP in order to foster better "race relations."[44]

The most protracted conflict with black school desegregation petitioners occurred in Orangeburg, home to the all-black South Carolina State College and one of the state's critical sites of black protest.[45] In response to a desegregation petition, the local WCC publicized the names of its signers; more than one-half withdrew their names. But State College students led a "reprisal boycott" of twenty-three white firms owned by WCC supporters who had withdrawn credit for black merchants backing the petition. Meanwhile, black-owned banks loaned money to those dismissed from their jobs or otherwise coerced economically, the NAACP coordinated other monies, and a biracial group from New York shipped food and clothing. State Law Enforcement Division (SLED) agents were authorized by the General Assembly to investigate the local NAACP branch as well as other potentially disruptive activists.[46]

The White Citizens' Councils in South Carolina were closely tied to officeholders and political-economic elites. The General Assembly saluted the WCCs in a joint resolution in 1956, and attracted Thurmond, Senator Olin Johnston, former governor Byrnes, and other party leaders who heaped praise upon the organizational network and jointly attended one of its rallies. Lieutenant Governor Ernest "Fritz" Hollings stated his "belief that the Citizens' Councils, by mobilizing the best leadership at the community level, can help to restore decency in government and maintain peace and security for all people, both white and Negro." Politically active groups such as the Farm Bureau forged connections with the Councils.[47] Additionally, the state's leading newspaper, Charleston's *News and Courier*, became their "unofficial organ."[48]

Most tellingly, WCCs' leadership overlapped significantly with the "Committee of 52," a statewide group of right-wing elites.[49] Committee members such as Emory Rogers (formerly lead attorney for the Clarendon County school board) and Micah Jenkins nurtured a small network of Eisenhower activists; unlike others, however, these lowcountry activists rejected offers to join the state Republican party for several years.[50] Interestingly, Barnwell Ring leaders such as state Senator Edgar Brown maintained their distance from the Councils.

Few white supremacist groups—other than various Klan outfits—persisted after the WCCs developed a statewide organization in 1955. The Klan, meanwhile, drew large rallies—perhaps the largest in the entire South—and was most active among blue-collar workers in the upcountry, where the WCCs were weakest (pointing to the class differences between the WCCs and Klans). An October 1956 Klan rally in Spartanburg numbered between 6,000 and 10,000 persons. Thence followed sustained membership drives, including the distribution of food, clothing, and other goods to needy (white) families, as well as arson attacks on black churches in Kershaw County.[51]

Formal and Informal Restrictions on Civil Society

Besides backing efforts to convince blacks of the virtues of "voluntary segregation," South Carolina's rulers also sought formally and informally to suppress civic and political discourse opposing massive resistance to segregation—and this meant restricting the influence of the state's few white moderates and liberals. South Carolina's responses to *Brown* did not crush a burgeoning racially moderate public sphere; prior to *Brown*, none existed. Thus, the state's experience departs from historian Michael Klarman's "backlash" thesis, in which *Brown* and resistance to it disrupted a growing indigenous southern liberalism in the early 1950s.

The state featured few of the usual suspects of southern dissent, such as unions, moderate and liberal civic organizations and churches, or prominent liberals in the media. Critically, state repression of union organizing efforts in the 1930s, combined with the vagaries of the textile industry, helped eventually convince most millhands that labor organization was futile.[52] Few organizations or even networks of white moderates existed. Some, such as the YMCA in Greenville, remained on the defensive for sponsoring interracial programs.[53] Unlike those elsewhere, union affiliates did not express their support for *Brown* and had to fend off accusations that they funded the NAACP.[54]

Partly encouraged by *Brown*, some white moderates and liberals began organizing in the mid-1950s. However, the state's branches of the Council on Human Relations—often involved in fostering interracial dialogue and preaching compliance on *Brown*—remained only weakly tied to the liberal, Atlanta-based Southern Regional Council (SRC). By 1958 fewer than six SRC branches existed.[55] The state Federation of Women's Clubs also backed compliance, as did various conferences of Methodists, Presbyterians, and Episcopalians.[56]

In 1957, in the period's most important intervention by moderates and liberals, upcountry Episcopalian clergy organized the "Concerned South Carolinians." The group quietly attempted to mobilize like-minded religious and community influentials on behalf of a vague moderate stance on segregation and more generally to foster constructive dialogue. However, before the group could offer its thoughts, Governor Timmerman publicized and mocked it. In a pamphlet the group published during the Little Rock crisis, *South Carolina Speaks*, several writers offered a wide range of views on the issue; most attempted to steer a course between the NAACP and the WCCs. Later, unknown assailants twice firebombed the home of one of the contributors; the volume noted that one contributor left the state "to assume the Pastorate of the Union Church, Santiago, Chile."[57]

Dissent from official policies could meet with a mixture of official rhetoric and civic disapproval and coercion. But in other cases, state policymaking directly constricted freedoms of speech and association. With the prodding of Governor Timmerman and Senator Gressette, University of South Carolina Regents dismissed education school dean Chester Travelstead after he voiced support for school integration; faculty at USC and other schools were forced out. Howard Quint, USC professor and author of the most comprehensive study of state politics, felt compelled to leave the region.[58] And the General Assembly (the legislature's lower chamber) called on the State Library Board to remove those texts "antagonistic and inimical" to the state's traditions. These actions, some of them never publicized, cannot be reduced merely to acts of position-taking for consumption by rabid white constituents.[59] In several lowcountry communities, individuals and groups prevented biracial public meetings—even one facilitated by the mayor.[60] Such episodes are emblematic of elite efforts to restrict, or at least discourage, conciliatory civic and political discourse.

Racially moderate whites reported dozens of cases of intimidation and economic reprisals.[61] Legislation, resolutions, and rhetoric of state elites did more than chill discourse about desegregation in the public sphere; they deterred many school officials, in the upcountry and elsewhere, from proceeding with desegregation plans. That they might have chosen to implement them is evident in discussions of the 1955 annual meeting of the South Carolina School Boards Association. A statement signed by more than one hundred officials, hailing from thirty of the state's forty-six counties, ostensibly rejected massive resistance. Of all enclaves, South Carolina waited the longest to appoint an advisory committee to the U.S. Commission on Civil Rights. Countering the view later offered by self-serving elites and sympathetic commentators that state leadership moved past massive resistance in the late 1950s, a privately circulated report concluded that "if any state abandons its entire system of public education to evade compliance with the Constitution, that state may be South Carolina."[62]

Attacks on Black Protest Organizations

Suppression of white civil society paled in comparison to the assaults launched on the NAACP and other black protest organizations. However, the attack on the biracial NAACP related, of course, to restrictions on white civil society. Advocates of the interpretation of the South as a herrenvolk democracy (discussed in chapter 2) implicitly interpret attacks on black organizations as racist, but not authoritarian. However, many of these groups called for biracial discussions and action. Assault on them must be interpreted as an authoritarian assault on all civil liberties, black and white.

Public officials even more forcefully restricted black civil society—and especially freedoms of speech and association on which black protest organizations relied. At the state level, public officials attacked the NAACP's legal status, tactics, and membership through statutes, regulatory activity, and rhetoric; these actions also legitimized unofficial attacks on black protest groups and activists. First, the state sued the NAACP for its failure to register as a "foreign corporation." If successful, the suit would have meant stiff penalties for the cash-strapped organization. Politicians called for banning the organization through other means. For instance, Lieutenant Governor Ernest Hollings suggested that the state could classify the NAACP as "subversive" and thereby declare it "illegal" in a constitutionally valid way. This classification would also ease the legality of state surveillance of the organization.[63]

Attacks on NAACP membership proved more effective. Again, officials sought to develop means of weakening the organization that could survive litigation in federal courts. The state enacted a law that proscribed membership in the organization by any current or future public employees—including teachers. Those officials who did not fire present members themselves could face fines or jail time.[64] By targeting public employees—especially black teachers—rulers struck at the heart of the NAACP's current and potential membership, since public employees were more economically independent from whites than were agricultural workers. NAACP membership records reveal that teachers formed the backbone of many of the more active branches.[65]

Faced with a federal suit by fired black teachers in 1957, the state replaced the statute with one requiring all state employees to list all of their membership affiliations. The NAACP and labor organizations indicated that they would pursue legal battles against this law as well if passed; the U.S. Supreme Court refused to overturn it.[66] A handful of dailies mocked this wave of repression. For instance, the *Greenville Piedmont* asked, "Who Next, If NAACP Banned?" But the largest and most influential newspapers backed it.[67]

At the Elloree Training School for black teachers, officials required teachers to complete a questionnaire that asked whether one or one's family belonged to or provided support to the NAACP, or favored school integration. Twenty-four of thirty-one teachers refused to complete the questionnaires; in response, officials refused to renew their employment contracts. Most filed suit in federal court, seeking an injunction from distributing the questionnaire and from firing the teachers on First and Fourteenth Amendment grounds. The panel required that plaintiffs pursue all administrative remedies at the state level before it would accept the case back in federal court.[68]

After efforts to ban the organization failed, state officials turned their attention to its tactics. Like other states, South Carolina enacted a punitive antibarratry statute.[69] Eventually, the law was struck down. As with other attempts to stymie the NAACP, the law's passage reflected uncertainty concerning the chances that any single tactic could survive federal scrutiny, and rulers' position-taking efforts.[70]

The state adopted additional strategies. After the Committee of 52 called for a criminal investigation of the procurement of signatures for desegregation petitions, Governor Timmerman announced that law enforcement officials would investigate, and that his own constabulary force would compile a list of all names on the petitions. More importantly, the state sought to weaken the status of black colleges as incubators of protest. The state's only publicly financed black college, South Carolina State College, was subject to a legislative investigation of campus activities by the local NAACP branch in order to ascertain which faculty members and students were "sympathizers." The state then purged antisegregation administrators and faculty there and at the private Allen College in Columbia, where the governor himself fired faculty.[71]

Often, the state legislature managed interracial contact and black protest through its remarkable oversight of county governance (see chapter 3). Senators used supply bills and other county-specific legislation to weaken black protest organizations. For instance, laws were passed in seven counties that required those engaging in NAACP membership drives to obtain a permit first from county officials. These laws had other benefits for local elites; some counties used this "permit system" to weaken union membership drives. And a 1959 law required the NAACP to submit lists of members and financial contributors to judges.[72]

Perhaps most important, the anti-NAACP rhetoric of state officials served to legitimize a range of coercion of black protest groups and individuals by the White Citizens' Councils and other ostensibly private actors. Throughout the 1950s, South Carolina maintained relatively low levels of physical violence, as compared to the intensity of crowd violence and assassinations of activists in Alabama, Georgia, and Mississippi, and riots in Arkansas, Tennessee, Virginia, Delaware, and elsewhere. Threats of coercion proved effective in deterring desegregation petitions outside the Charleston area.[73]

The development of CORE in South Carolina gets at the paradoxical nature of black protest in the state in the 1950s. Its development there was the product of the work of the organization's regional field organizer, James T. McCain. His arrival in CORE's national office in 1957 pointed both to the surprising strength of black protest in South Carolina—especially in rural areas—as well as the less surprising strength of state authorities' repression of the NAACP during the 1950s. McCain, a former school principal in Clarendon County, head of the state's black teachers' association, and president of a local NAACP branch, lost his job as a result of his political engagement. Like Rev. Joseph DeLaine, leader of the county's school protest that found its way as a companion case in *Brown*, he then left the state. McCain capitalized on his networks in South Carolina and quickly set up several (all-black) affiliates, many of whose members were longtime NAACP members. Focusing on voter registration drives rather than the heart of CORE's mission—the more dangerous direct-action protest—his work would bear fruit during the Voter Education Project (discussed later).[74]

The Progressive Democratic Party (PDP) had by the late 1950s become relatively inactive, partly in response to official and unofficial harassment, including red-baiting. And black efforts to participate in Democratic primary voting and party meetings continued to be the subject of official and unofficial opposition. The national Democratic party was not very helpful either; in response to its challenge of the regular party's delegation before the 1956 National Convention, the DNC promised PDP leaders some representation at the 1960 Convention in Los Angeles, but the promise went unfulfilled.[75] Echoing Byrnes's earlier remarks about the dangers brought by those whites who would enter into "secret political trades" for black votes, Governor Timmerman in 1956 claimed that multiparty politics would cause "nothing but permanent strife and damage," and that he was "not prepared to turn the . . . party over to any radical element or other irresponsible group."[76]

Black political mobilization did bring some material gains. For instance, Charleston blacks, coordinated by the local NAACP chapter, defeated a school bond issue because it took as its premise the legitimacy of an equalization program and voluntary segregation. And blacks in the upcountry mill town of Rock Hill fought back against a local WCC and white supremacist "labor" groups and organized a successful bus boycott in 1957. In the end, however, rulers' massive resistance succeeded in crushing the NAACP. While the organization had eighty "paid-up" branches in 1950, and an amazing 138 in 1954, just three years later their number was reduced to 45 (table 3.3).[77] The unprecedented mobilizations of the 1940s were over, and they had left behind few obvious resources and infrastructure to be exploited in the 1960s (see chapter 10). After being red-baited by the NAACP's national office, legendary activist (and Republican) Modjeska Simkins lost her position as the state organization's field secretary and was replaced by Rev. Isaiah DeQuincey "Deke" Newman. The state seemed to be open to interventions by national black protest organizations, but for a number of reasons they never arrived (see chapter 9).[78]

Enhancing State Capacities

South Carolina politicians developed three important new state capacities during the 1950s. First, the Gressette Committee facilitated elite deliberation and policy planning related to defending white supremacy. In addition, contemporaries and historians credit the committee with preventing the passage of even more embarrassing and potentially counterproductive legislation (such as the racial segregation of plasma), and in delaying desegregation long enough such that by the time the state "ran out of courts," white attitudes had adjusted sufficiently that the state was spared large-scale violence.[79] Other enclaves developed similar institutions; given the Senate's dominance of South Carolina politics, however, the Gressette Committee was especially influential.

Second, in the late 1950s, the legislature strengthened one of the nation's weakest executives by granting the governor new warrants of authority to manage threats to order. A 1957 law authorized the governor to shut down, or place under state operation, any "transportation or other public facilities," and allowed any public official to enforce the provisions of the governor's declaration of a state of emergency when persons or property were threatened.[80] State officials considered the expansion of the state's police powers as a means of sidestepping compliance with court-ordered desegregation, *not* to prevent racial violence. The *Columbia State* called the governor's new powers "virtually dictatorial."[81] Faced with few desegregation petitions, even fewer lawsuits, and little overt white supremacist or black violence, the state's governors did not rely on these powers, but they would soon prove useful. Third, and most important, rulers bolstered the centralization, professionalization, and effectiveness of the state's policing apparatus. These steps improved rulers' ability to monitor, deter, and repress white supremacist organizations, black insurgents, and other crowd disturbances.

Before the massive resistance period, South Carolina's coercive capacities reflected American norms of localism in the area of law enforcement. By tradition its slaveholders and planters preferred to exercise "informal authority" over "their" blacks.[82] Its cities had weak but highly corrupt police departments. In the 1930s the Klan infiltrated local law enforcement in Columbia and Greenville.[83] At the county level, sheriffs exercised significant authority and responsibility in keeping the peace. At the state level, governors used the militia, or National Guard, at great political cost in preventing electoral fraud in Charleston and alternating between supporting and repressing striking textile workers in the 1930s.[84]

In the mid-1930s, the state reestablished a constabulary force.[85] In effect, these fifty-odd armed officers, dispersed throughout the state, constituted the governor's personal police force. Governors used them for a number of purposes, from illegal service as campaign workers to the investigation of rumored arms caches in black communities during World War II.[86] In the 1930s legislators defeated previous attempts to combine the Highway Patrol and the constabulary into a stronger, centralized state police force. Reforming the Highway Patrol activated interbranch conflict over control of the highly valuable Highway Department, and the development of a state police force with extensive police powers would weaken the power of county sheriffs. Thus, the Highway Patrol, to governors' disappointment, remained under the "indirect control of the state legislature."[87]

However, after lowcountry senators emerged triumphant from their battles over the Highway Department, the legislature ceded to Governor Thurmond's wishes during the late 1940s to reorganize the constabulary force into the State Law Enforcement Division (SLED). In contrast to Mississippi and Georgia, where local law enforcement authorities drew on their economic influence and institutional advantages to form powerful lobbies to defend their power, South Carolina's sheriffs could not block the establishment of the SLED, a professional independent law enforcement agency with broad powers. With the appointment of J. P. "Pete" Strom in 1957, the SLED grew in scope and importance.[88] Strom was more than merely the chief of the SLED. Although SLED's purpose was primarily investigative and despite the fact that Strom was technically a civilian, Governor Hollings (1959–63) empowered him to coordinate local and state law enforcement, including the Highway Patrol and National Guard.[89]

In the 1950s the SLED's value to rulers relative to the Highway Patrol became clear. South Carolina's rulers in the 1950s viewed the Klan as a potential source of disorder and embarrassment. But it was not always so; in 1949 the state's General Assembly warmly received the Grand Dragon of the state's largest Klan organization. Soon, Klan activities expanded, and Governor Byrnes pushed through an anti-masking statute in 1951. Byrnes criticized the performance of the State Highway Patrol during a "riotous

[Klan] meeting" in Anderson County. An investigation revealed that high-way patrolmen had assisted Klansmen during their rally and participated in beatings.[90] For governors, the Highway Patrol was less useful, given its narrow jurisdictional authority, and because—under the aegis of the Highway Department—it remained independent of their control.[91]

In contrast, governors relied on the SLED to perform a wide range of tasks. During the 1950s, it foiled a Klan plot to assassinate powerbroker Bernard Baruch; infiltrated the Klan, which led to arrests, convictions, and a decline in Klan membership; and monitored black signers of desegregation petitions.[92] But despite efforts by Byrnes to weaken them, various Klan organizations grew emboldened, holding public meetings, especially in the Piedmont. Hollings estimated Klan membership at sixteen thousand in 1959—twice the Klan's strength in Mississippi in the chaotic 1960s.[93]

Besides challenging the state's Klans, the SLED answered governors' calls to maintain order during black protest. When sit-ins swept through the state in 1960, Hollings promised to detain both black protesters and white bystanders. The SLED supervised local authorities, organized mass arrests, and facilitated dialogue among demonstrators and local officials.[94] The centralization and efficacy of South Carolina's coercive apparatus should not be overemphasized. Traditional norms of localism still exerted influence over the practices of state and local actors. Local police and sheriffs, in particular, retained a significant amount of official and unofficial power. On the eve of the Clemson crisis, the capacity and willingness of state police to repress white crowds were largely untested.

The Clemson Crisis

Clemson College, a land-grant school and one of the state's largest higher educational institutions, was located in the upcountry and attracted rural whites interested in scientific agriculture and engineering. It was the alma mater of much of the political elite, and its desegregation would be the state's first of any public school. Black students had made several forays to desegregate the University of South Carolina, but with no luck. By the end of 1962, the desegregation lawsuits of Charleston native Harvey Gantt had wended their way through federal courts. Significantly, the "Battle of Oxford" (chapter 6) occurred in late September. Then-governor Ernest Hollings sought to halt and then delay breaches of enclave rule, such as court-ordered desegregation. By the autumn of 1962, it became clear that the state would lose its final appeals and Gantt would soon be escorted onto campus by federal officials. As white supremacists announced plans to block Gantt's matriculation, South Carolina's rulers considered their options. As an editorialist wrote, "The walls of Jericho, our citadel of . . .

segregation, are going to come tumbling down. Not all at once. Brick by brick. How shall we react?"[95]

As will be discussed in chapters 10 and 11, South Carolina experienced rapid economic takeoff in the 1960s. This fact could lead some to conclude that the state's politicians cohered around a dedicated strategy to secure external capital investment, and thus that a consensus around the state's economic development makes explaining the state's fortunate handling of the Clemson crisis an easy task. This would be misguided. By the late 1950s, South Carolina's economy was in transition, but to what was unclear. In 1950, the Atomic Energy Commission broke ground on the Savannah River Plant, soon a critical component in the construction of America's hydrogen bombs. A two-billion-dollar project on par financially with the construction of the Panama Canal, for a time it employed more than eight thousand workers and seemed to augur rapid economic modernization. Meanwhile, the share of agricultural production in the state had declined sharply. Despite mechanization, in 1958 the state produced less than half as much cotton as it had in the 1930s. Farm acreage had declined by about 40 percent since 1940. Governors such as James F. Byrnes and George Bell Timmerman were not particularly aggressive as industrial recruiters.

Moreover, efforts by governors and others to enhance the state's taxation structure in order to make the types of infrastructure investments sought by potential investors continued to die in the lowcountry-dominated legislature.[96] And while South Carolina remained much more industrialized than Mississippi, textiles still accounted for more than one-half of the state's industry. This lack of diversity in industrial employment, as well as the continued prevalence of low-wage, low-skilled jobs, worried officials. In the late 1950s, two-thirds of the state's workforce was, according to a state Senate report, "functionally illiterate."[97] Finally, while during the 1940s and 1950s the city's metro counties—Greenville, Richland (home to Columbia), Charleston, and others—experienced rapid growth, they did not fit the "Sunbelt" story. The "overwhelming majority" of those moving into these counties, and into South Carolina more generally, were not Yankee transplants but rather southerners from elsewhere—principally North Carolina and Georgia.[98]

The Emergence of Anti-Democrats in South Carolina

As political scientist Gregory Sampson demonstrates, the state's "modern" Republican party began in 1952, when a group of white upcountry activists attempted to wrest control of the party from the highly cynical, patronage-seeking operation of Bates Gerald.[99] By 1954–56, they had accomplished this takeover with the help of the RNC. From the middle 1950s until the early-to-mid 1960s, the party grew steadily, but remained centered in the upcountry. Many of its activists and voters had first pulled the lever for "South Carolinians for Eisenhower" (SCFE) in 1952. In this sense, the Dixiecrat revolt, which itself fed into the SCFE, might be seen as helping to further South Carolina Republicanism. However, after *Brown*, other SCFE supporters—those more focused on defending white supremacy than embracing Eisenhower's "modern Republicanism"—either floated back to the ruling party (then under the stewardship of reliable white supremacist George Bell Timmerman), or attempted to fashion yet another independent movement. In 1957 U.S. Senator Strom Thurmond rejected the state Republican party as a useful political vehicle and called on independents to seize the ruling party machinery from loyalists such as Sen. Edgar Brown.[100]

Once South Carolina's Democrats endorsed Stevenson in 1956, these lowcountry activists established their own slate of electors pledged to Senator Harry Byrd (VA), a classic enclave defender. While the state's voters backed Stevenson, Eisenhower and Byrd each garnered about 25 percent and 30 percent of the vote, respectively.

The 1956 presidential election was important in a few ways. First, a majority of the state's voters were now anti-Democrat. Indeed, besides the razor-thin victory by John F. Kennedy in 1960 (which he won in large part because of a large turnout by black South Carolinians), a majority of the state's voters have opposed the Democratic presidential nominee since 1956.[101] Second, South Carolina whites were now comfortable voting Republican; unlike in 1952, when Eisenhower supporters chose an independent slate of electors, in 1956 the one-quarter of the electorate backing Eisenhower actually voted for the "Republican" label. Third, Eisenhower's base of support changed radically. Winning a very small share of the black vote in Columbia and Charleston in 1952, he won large shares in 1956. Conversely, ecological regression analysis of upper-class precincts in Columbia and Charleston shows that these whites left Eisenhower for Byrd, probably because of the administration's siding with the plaintiffs in *Brown*. In this way they departed from the pattern of metro whites in the Outer South.[102] Moreover, the independent slate for Byrd received endorsements from Sen. Strom Thurmond and former governor James Byrnes. This fact frustrates the conclusion that the Dixiecrat revolt helped grow southern Republicanism in a straightforward way. Byrnes, the key player in the movement backing Eisenhower in 1952, backed a protest candidate four years later.

Finally, from 1948 to 1956, the state's presidential electorate had doubled. While there had been some increase in black voter registration (table 9.4), this rapid expansion instead was caused primarily by the abolition of the poll tax, the introduction of the secret ballot in 1950, and much greater interest on the part of white South Carolinians in multiparty presidential politics.[103] A doubling of the electorate is clearly a democratizing moment. (Whether whites' mobilizing on behalf of, say, Senator Harry F. Byrd in order to defend other pillars of enclave rule is to be viewed as democratizers greatly complicates the labeling of actors during this long transition to democracy.

As elsewhere in the South, Little Rock hurt the Republican cause in South Carolina. The state's richest person, Yankee transplant and textile magnet Roger Milliken, had become a key fundraiser for the Republicans. He professed his shock at Eisenhower's actions. From this moment on, South Carolina's Republican party took a hard right turn. Theirs was neither the ideology of Black Belt whites defending Jim Crow, nor the sunnier modern Republicanism of white professionals in the suburbs of the Outer South. Rather, these Republicans remained centered in the upcountry, and rather than prioritizing white supremacy, they instead remained devoted to the tenets of the John Birch Society. Textile firm owners' extreme hostility to unions found an ally in Senator Barry Goldwater (R-AZ), who in 1958 became the hero of the antiunion right.[104] At its 1958 state party convention, NAACP field secretary "Deke" Newman attempted to prevent what a party official admitted was the "dissolution of biracial Republicanism" in South Carolina by attending the convention and securing approval of a pro–civil rights plank in the state party platform. He failed.[105] By 1960 they formed the most conservative delegation at the Republican national convention, fought hard to dilute the pro–civil rights plank in the national platform, and immediately became leaders in the "Draft Goldwater" movement.[106]

Also in 1958 the white supremacist Independents clustered in the low-country tried and failed to take over the Democrats' state party convention. They also rejected overtures by state Republican officials to join forces. These independents, several of them holding leadership positions in the White Citizens' Councils—and one of whom, U.S. House member Albert Watson, would run one of the Deep South's most racist campaign in decades in 1970 (see chapter 10)—still could not commit themselves to the Republican party. Instead they formed another independent movement, centered in Columbia and the lowcountry, in support of Nixon and Lodge in 1960. This is important, because it helps support chapter 10's claim that the Clemson crisis unleashed dynamics that spurred Republican growth in the state. Had these white supremacists been incorporated into the state Republican party before Clemson, this interpretation would be harder to sustain.

Finally, by 1964, these hardline segregationists had joined the state's Republican party. More, they had wrested control of its leadership positions from the upcountry founders of the party. Besides the fact that they perceived Goldwater as holding similar views, these lowcountry activists had another, more pragmatic reason to retire from independent movements— the Republican party presented opportunities to pursue elective office. South Carolina Democrats, especially in the lowcountry, had a very long queue of ambitious officeseekers; many young professional men were too impatient to remain in the state party. They also liked the idea of not having to finance an expensive primary election; the state Republican party did not yet select nominees by direct primary.[107]

Factional Conflict and Rulers' Preferences

Three key features of South Carolina's party-state shaped the state's handling of Clemson's desegregation. First, the governor, because of the nature of the issue, possessed substantial authority, visibility, and leadership opportunities. Second, lowcountry senators controlled many elements of higher education policy. Third, influential politicians and groups with strong bases of popular support—such as former governor James Byrnes, leading segregationists, and large firm owners—were capable of influencing the behavior of white publics in responding to the Clemson situation.

Hollings's preferred outcome was not obvious.[108] A young but highly experienced politician, he had recently served as lieutenant governor in the Timmerman administration. His tenure as governor (1959–63) avoided the harsh rhetoric of his predecessor.[109] However, a public dispute with the state's most influential businessman, and his ordering of mass arrests and criticism of sit-in participants and other civil rights protesters, placed him on the "right" when it came to racial and political reforms. At first it was unclear if he could be counted among the state's meager number of "business moderates."[110] Hollings had won office in 1958 by "out-segging" his opponent, and had done the same in a failed bid for Olin Johnston's Senate seat.[111]

However, his national ambitions directed him toward a strategic accommodation with court-ordered desegregation. Hollings sought to maintain good relations with the national party that would be useful for another try. Thus, he and other loyalists directed the party's support for Kennedy, who relied on black voters in narrowly beating Nixon. Like virtually all Deep South Democrats, he preferred that desegregation be delayed until he left office; however, Hollings remained cautious about taking actions as governor that would make life difficult for the Kennedy administration.[112] Moreover, he was extremely dedicated as an industrial recruiter. During his term, the state attracted more than $800 million in capital investment. Additionally, in a move that would pay serious dividends in the 1960s, he shepherded through the legislature a program to develop a series of vocational education centers throughout the state in order to improve the state's workforce.[113]

Lowcountry legislators might have been expected to call for noncompliance with federal judicial rulings. White voters in the lowcountry since 1948 had abandoned the Democratic national ticket for failing to defend white supremacy. Located in the upcountry, Clemson was highly influenced by nearby textile and other manufacturing interests. The lowcountry seemed to have little stake in Clemson.[114] However, their senators, led by the venerable Senator Edgar Brown (a Clemson trustee), proved critical in assisting Hollings in with its desegregation. From 1940 to 1960, twenty-one counties, mostly in the lowcountry, declined in population. Their representatives—including House Speaker Sol Blatt, long a foe of efforts to pursue infrastructural investment in the upcountry—hoping to attract external capital and to develop new sources of economic growth, had very recently become increasingly allied with upcountry manufacturing interests. They were thus more amenable to working with the concerns of these upcountry economic elites—even if it meant raising taxes—to underwrite infrastructural improvements that could help attract external capital.[115]

These men, well positioned as influential firm owners, lobbyists, and spokesmen for South Carolina business, preferred an orderly desegregation for several reasons. First, many of them had strong attachments to the school and preferred that it remain open. Second, they were focused on fostering a positive reputation for the state and for the upcountry, home to most of the state's foreign direct investment. Hollings worked hard to help them attract such investment.[116] Third, many of these owners sought to develop a more highly skilled labor force among whites and blacks, and the regional university would likely play a positive role in this process.[117]

Other influentials disagreed. Among them, former Governor Byrnes had recently drawn a hard line against any school desegregation and, as a Clemson trustee, hinted that he might speak out against state compliance. He remained very popular among the state's whites, and Hollings and others worried that the former governor's pronouncements on Clemson might spell disaster. Governor-elect Donald Russell praised Mississippi governor Ross Barnett's "courage and resolution," and hinted that Oxford might discourage South Carolina's compliance with the outcome of Gantt's suit. State Representative A. W. "Red" Bethea, a Clemson alumnus and the most outspoken segregationist legislator, vowed to lead a march on the campus. The public statements of "Mr. Segregation," Senator Marion Gressette, were thought to be critical in shaping the responses of legislators and dedicated segregationists.[118]

Finally, WCC leaders, already flirting in earnest with exiting the party, contemplated disturbing the school's desegregation. They provided substantial support to William Workman's losing bid, as a Republican, for Olin Johnston's U.S. Senate seat. Workman had recently authored a vigorous white supremacist defense of the South. Campaigning just after the imbroglio in Mississippi, Workman spoke for a large share of the state's elites when he interpreted recent events as "a cold-blooded, premeditated effort to crush the sovereign state of Mississippi into submission." Comparing Kennedy to Hitler, he hoped that when "South Carolina's turn comes, she'll defend her rights."[119]

Managing the Crisis

In the fall of 1962, Hollings, his political allies, and university officials were quite uncertain about what would transpire at Clemson, and with good reason. While they had several months' warning before the state's legal appeals were exhausted, rulers worried greatly about a violent conflagration. They had just witnessed the influx of white supremacists from all over the country into Oxford, Mississippi; avoiding white crowd violence might be more complicated than infiltrating the klaverns of the oft-hapless Klan. They also witnessed the immediate damage done to Mississippi's national reputation, ability to attract external capital, and the school itself. State Senator Edgar Brown, still one of the state's most powerful politicians, confided to a friend, "We think Little Rock can't happen here, but it can."[120]

Hollings sought, above all else, to ensure that Clemson would remain peaceful and orderly, and that the state's reputation would not be damaged. To avoid violence meant preventing the assembly of white crowds on campus. To prevent crowds, Hollings set out to avoid the deployment of federal marshals, manage state media, and deter white supremacists from disrupting Gantt's arrival. By symbolizing a federal breach of state "sovereignty," the presence of federal marshals might spark greater white supremacist anger, as well as call into question Hollings's competence in navigating the crisis.[121] Thus, a marshal-free desegregation meant persuading the Kennedys that they were not necessary.[122]

To do so, state authorities took advantage of the timing of Gantt's arrival at Clemson and of their well-organized state law enforcement. Hollings dispatched the SLED's Chief Strom and his legal counsel, Harry Walker, to still-smoldering Oxford to draw lessons from the fiasco.[123] The eventual plan called for highway checkpoints regulating access to campus, SLED aircraft, the presence of 150 SLED personnel nearby, and a media blackout on campus until Gantt arrived. Moreover, Clemson officials threatened to expel students who took part in disorder and violence meant to halt the desegregation. State planning helped persuade Burke Marshall, head of the DOJ's Civil Rights Division, as well as the Kennedys that federal personnel would not be necessary.[124]

Through private briefings, Hollings also succeeded in persuading the state's editors and journalists to "prepare" their (white) readers with Clemson's imminent desegregation.[125] Days before Gantt was to arrive, university officials, Senator Brown, and other trustees held a televised press conference, and the state Chamber of Commerce, a group of textile industry leaders, and other business elites issued a press release: "Not only must we insure law and order at Clemson College, but we must preserve and protect the good name of South Carolina."[126]

The administration remained concerned by the threatened mobilization of white crowds by Bethea and WCC leaders, and by Senator Gressette's efforts to rally a group of state legislators to take steps to block the desegregation. Several state elites embarked on a quiet campaign to persuade fellow politicians and others to eschew defiance and call for a peaceful desegregation, or at least remain quiet (as Byrnes would do).[127] Critically, Senator Brown worked with House Speaker Sol Blatt to convince and cajole state legislators to avoid speaking out against the planned desegregation. Clemson president Robert Edwards, a textile magnet, allegedly threatened Gressette: were Gressette to use his influence with white supremacists to oppose Hollings's plan, the relocation of an Eastman-Kodak plant to Gressette's Calhoun County might not proceed as planned. Calhoun County had just experienced a decade of markedly slower economic growth compared to its neighbors. Gressette complied, and issued a statement that the state had "lost this battle," and that the "war cannot be won by violence or by inflammatory speeches."[128] Representative "Red" Bethea began an angry, tearful speech on the floor of the General Assembly, but Speaker Blatt adjourned the chamber to prevent press coverage. The most important speech was far from inflammatory. In his farewell address to the General Assembly, outgoing Governor Hollings declared that "South Carolina is running out of courts. If and when every legal remedy is exhausted, this General Assembly must make clear South Carolina's choice.... We ... must ... move on for the good of South Carolina and the United States. This should be done with dignity. It must be done with law and order."[129]

January 28, 1963, was anticlimactic. Only media and curious students and other onlookers watched as Gantt arrived, registered, and moved into his dormitory. With no armed federal personnel on campus, a large show of force, and restricted access to campus, no angry crowds emerged. Later, two officers of the WCC alleged that SLED personnel detained its field secretary before he could reach the campus.[130]

The Immediate Aftermath

South Carolina earned kudos from national media, as editorialists in papers small and large contrasted Clemson with the University of Mississippi. Weeks later, the *Saturday Evening Post* cover story, "Integration With Dignity," offered a breathless account of "how South Carolina kept the peace."[131] In April, President Kennedy met with a delegation of about twenty South Carolina (white) journalists, and applauded the state—and its media—for helping to make Clemson's desegregation so smooth, "particularly with the dramatic contrast with Oxford so evident to all." He then noted that the state's defense contracts had more than doubled from 1960 to 1962, from $31 million to some $65 million. Attorney General Robert F. Kennedy, in a speech at the University of South Carolina's law school, called the Clemson episode "states' rights at its best" and lauded state leaders. Congratulations also appeared in the black press. Morehouse College president Benjamin Mays attributed the state's exceptional handling of the crisis to its quality of leadership.[132] As chapter 10 shows, subsequent desegregation moments in South Carolina schools would prove to be more difficult, and at times violent—but the state's image in the non-southern mind had already been established. Just a few years after "massive resistance," the state's harnessed democratization had begun.

Observers of South Carolina have often repeated Harvey Gantt's culturalist account of the orderliness of Clemson's desegregation: "If you can't appeal to the morals of a South Carolinian, you can appeal to his manners."[133] This chapter has shown that, in contrast, rulers themselves viewed a peaceful desegregation as anything but determined by the state's political culture. Similarly, "Integration with Dignity" is an oft-repeated trope that shapes white South Carolina's self-understanding; it is also quite misleading.[134] A culturalist explanation is tripped up by the viciousness of the state's massive resistance. Many aspects of rulers' factional conflict in the 1930s and responses to black insurgency and federal judicial attacks on Jim Crow undermine claims that the state's leaders traditionally preferred dignified acceptance to undesirable change.

Certainly—as they themselves recognized—state politicians were fortunate to be confronted with the Clemson crisis only after Oxford and its lessons. And they were even more fortunate not to have faced the crisis when Timmerman occupied the governor's mansion.[135] As in other enclaves, and in other moments in their own state, South Carolina's authorities did not offer a single, coherent response to the crisis. However, Hollings benefited from the relatively centralized nature of the enclave's policymaking institutions, the preferences of lowcountry politicians, and a robust coercive apparatus. He effectively built a coalition of elites, negotiated with federal officials, and repressed white supremacist forces, thus securing a peaceful, if token, desegregation. As chapter 10 will demonstrate, this crisis management enhanced the state's image among investors and federal authorities, and accelerated the growth of the Republican party in the state in ways that reinforced rulers' commitment to strategic accommodation.

CHAPTER EIGHT

"No, Not One"

Georgia's Massive Resistance and the Crisis at Athens

ON THE EVE OF *Brown*, Georgia's ruling party remained controlled by the rural elites and white supremacist politicians composing the Talmadge faction (now led by Governor Herman Talmadge). Having barely defeated a nascent biracial faction of white moderates and liberals and blacks in the 1940s, and still holding only tenuous legal control of party machinery, the Talmadge faction kept the party on the sidelines of the Dixiecrat revolt. In doing so, the faction helped ensure that it would be at the helm throughout the 1950s.

Through their massive resistance, enclave rulers successfully avoided the desegregation of state-supported schools for more than six years. Additionally, during the 1950s, Talmadgeites made progress on one of the faction's main goals of *Smith v. Allwright*—the repression of the statewide infrastructure of black protest. However, Georgia's policy responses to *Brown* combined to tie the hands of its governor. The Talmadge faction's clumsy handling of the desegregation of the University of Georgia (UGA) in 1961 heightened the sectional dimension of intraelite conflict, with important consequences for the state's eventual democratization. This chapter reviews the state of black education before *Brown* and Georgia's attempts to preempt the ruling, describes how factional conflict affected rulers' development of new institutional defenses to ward off democratization pressures, details the Talmadgeites' attacks on black protest throughout the 1950s, and then offers an explanation of how Georgia's rulers mishandled the UGA crisis. Chapter 10 demonstrates the importance of Georgia's responses to *Brown* and its progeny for the state's eventual bifurcated democratization.

Prelude to *Brown*

As was true throughout the Deep South, Georgia's schools remained securely segregated on the eve of *Brown*. By 1940, as black protest swelled in the state, racial disparities in spending had changed little since the onset of authoritarian rule. In that year, black student per capita spending was 31 percent of that for white students.[1] Although applauded as a progressive and racially moderate governor, Ellis Arnall did not address educational spending for blacks. In 1950 the state stood next to last in the nation in per capita years of schooling attained, and forty-third in per capita spending on primary and secondary education.[2]

Immediately after the war, officials expressed concern about this state of affairs.[3] Before the U.S. Supreme Court's 1950 school desegregation cases, Georgia's rulers—as elsewhere—sought to raise education levels generally in order to stimulate economic growth. As the legislature investigated educational policy, it also began a more concerted effort to find new ways to raise revenues. Georgia lacked a state sales tax and placed a very minimal tax burden on better-off individuals as well as on corporations. In 1949 the state launched the Minimum Foundation for Public Education, which within a decade had revamped education in the state for blacks and whites through a massive consolidation of school districts and large investments in school construction and teachers' salaries.[4]

Governor Herman Talmadge made clear in 1949 that he would continue to prioritize the defense of white supremacy as he prepared to run for re-election in 1950. The anti-Talmadge faction was already in tatters and failed to converge behind a single candidate.[5] Now, Talmadge, Roy Harris, and other hardline white supremacists raised—for the first time—the specter of school desegregation. Black lawsuits provided evidence that the threat was real. Talmadge won a whopping 71 percent of the county-unit vote, though he barely scraped by in the popular vote. Melvin Thompson, the leading anti-Talmadgeite candidate, later accused Roy Harris, still the state's most effective operator of the county-unit system, of stealing fifty small "two-unit" counties from him; Harris put the number closer to thirty-five.[6] Observers concluded that the June 1950 Supreme Court decisions (discussed in the Prologue to part 3) helped seal Talmadge's win.[7]

In 1951 Talmadge secured a state sales tax, which transformed the state's fiscal capacity. One year later it accounted for almost one-third of the state's total revenue. By 1964, the ratio of black to white per pupil spending increased from 31 percent to 68 percent. These fiscal choices reflected Talmadge's personal ambition as well as the importance of Atlanta corporations in statewide elections. Talmadge's embrace of the regressive sales tax—and lowered taxes on business and the elimination of the state property tax—jibed well with his planned Senate bid.[8]

Black Protest and Politics before Brown

In Georgia, black mobilization on education policy preceded that in other states. In Atlanta, the development of black protest capacity—particularly the growth of the city's NAACP branch—was long intertwined with education issues, since black voting on municipal bond issues was often pivotal in determining outcomes. In the 1930s blacks began legal challenges to racial disparities in education. In 1949, the (black) Georgia Teachers and Education Association began a statewide campaign for the equalization of teachers' salaries and of school facilities, which was interpreted as a warning shot before filing suits in federal courts. At the time, approximately 70 percent of black schools had only one or two teachers.[9]

Longtime Atlanta NAACP leader A. T. Walden helped sponsor such suits in Atlanta in the late 1940s. In 1949 federal courts ordered the Atlanta school board to reduce racial disparities. In part because of their investments in a biracial accommodation with Mayor Hartsfield, much of the city's black establishment opposed frontal assaults on segregation.[10] In 1952 the Atlanta NAACP converted demands for equalization into calls for overturning *Plessy's* separate-but-equal doctrine. By then, regional NAACP leaders were criticizing Walden—and black Atlanta leaders generally—for being slow to challenge segregated education itself.[11]

Factional Conflict and the State on the Eve of Brown

Before the *Brown* ruling, Talmadge forces mounted two major efforts to solidify their factional dominance within the party and provide institutional safeguards for the party's historic project. Both efforts failed, but the faction maintained its hold over both the governor's office and the state legislature for the entire massive resistance period. The failures are instructive for understanding the dilemmas facing Georgia's rulers in the 1950s.

Although the 1940s ended with the defeat of liberals' and moderates' efforts to form an alternative political vehicle linked to the national party, Talmadge forces could not discount the possibility that its opponents might mount a general election challenge. As discussed in chapter 4, challenging the Talmadgeites in a general election—decided by popular vote, not the county-unit system—could be successful. Given this possibility, Talmadge called for extending the county-unit system to general elections. Since the specter of black "bloc voting" might emanate from outside the ruling party, *intra*party devices to restrict suffrage would not work. Thus, the faction's second project to consolidate its power was an attempt to suppress black voter registration.[12]

Casting about for alternatives to weaken black voting, faction leaders alighted on neighboring Alabama's approach: a state constitutional provision supplying local officials with new—and nominally nonracial—discretion in judging whether potential registrants could "understand and explain" portions of the state constitution. However, before the General Assembly's 1949 session convened, a U.S. federal district court invalidated the provision. Alabama's Boswell Amendment had disfranchised thousands of blacks but few whites (see chapter 4).[13] With this avenue blocked, Georgia lawmakers quickly considered other options before the next elections.

Talmadge persuaded the legislature to pass a Re-Registration Act, which required the reregistration of *all* voters by May 1950, thus striking from the rolls the names of more than 1,250,000 voters. Those applicants who could not demonstrate their ability to read and write would have to answer correctly at least ten of thirty questions about state government. These would be "framed in such a manner that a person with fair average intellect and attainments can understand them." Individuals who failed to vote at least every two years would have to register again; each time would mean an additional registration fee. Thus, through a back door the state had reimposed a poll tax (which had been repealed in 1945). Legislators and party officials made clear that they sought to reduce "Negro bloc voting," although poorer whites would suffer the same consequences. However, for Talmadge faction leaders, lowering primary turnout by poorer whites in two-unit counties critical to the faction's success did not pose a real problem, since elites in those counties could produce favorable election results in any case.[14]

A large uproar ensued from several quarters. Black groups opposed the legislation for obvious reasons. Many whites resented the test, and poorer counties refused to finance its implementation. The state's dailies, the powerful state Association of County Commissioners, and other groups criticized the statute. Only a few of the state's 159 counties fully implemented the law. Officials in many counties did not understand it, while others targeted only black registrants. In more than thirty counties, registered white voters even outnumbered the white voting-age population.[15] In January 1950 journalists estimated that the state's qualified electorate for the upcoming gubernatorial election would be about one-half of the 1.25 million registered before the law's passage; however, what seemed to be a postponement in the law's implementation soon became permanent.[16]

In addition to attempting the reregistration of voters, Talmadge and his advisers continued their efforts to extend the use of the county-unit system to general elections, making attempts in 1950 and 1952. The General Assembly approved a constitutional amendment to be sent to the voters in November 1950.[17] Campaigning for the amendment in "two-unit" counties was facilitated by the opposition of the "evil" city groups—such as the Southern Regional Council—that had been fighting the county-unit system for years in state and, later, in federal courts. In addition, proponents for the county-unit system's expansion argued that constitutional protection for the system would be more durable than its continued regulation by statute. Fresh from his gubernatorial triumph, Talmadge worked extremely hard to secure popular ratification. However, affluent urban opponents—led by a committee of Thompson backers—defeated the amendment. Crucially, appearing on a general election ballot, the proposal was itself decided by popular vote, not by the county-unit system. Talmadge blamed the loss on, among other things, public misunderstanding and insufficient campaign funding, and vowed to try again.[18] The 1952 amendment would require all general election candidates to have been nominated by a party primary. This would mean an expensive *and* rural-dominated primary, since the county-unit system applied to *all* parties' primaries. Thus, the amendment would make the development of a state Republican party or of splinter parties loyal to the national Democrats extremely difficult.[19]

To campaign once again for ratification, the Talmadge administration managed to draw on revenues generated by the state sales tax. It amassed a five-to-one spending advantage over the amendment's opponents. Once again, the administration received the backing of all faction leaders, including 1954 gubernatorial hopeful Marvin Griffin. Additionally, given the steady growth in Georgia's cities, U.S. Senator Richard Russell favored "modifications" to the system. "If we do not make some mild concessions,... we will lose the entire Unit System and give the cities complete control of the politics of our state." In a speech to the Boston Kiwanis, Talmadge suggested that the amendment's failure would produce a dystopic future in which "the people have to see [Atlanta NAACP leader A. T.] Walden first before some glassy-eyed politician can do something for them."[20]

The amendment failed once more. While the amendment won majorities in 121 counties, it was defeated in all chiefly urban counties. Urban voters opposed both attempts to extend the county-unit system (by more than 70 and 60 percent, respectively). Overall, a majority of north Georgians—including, notably, majorities in rural areas in north Georgia—opposed the amendment both times, while working-class white precincts in Atlanta supported it much more than better-off white Atlantans.[21] These results provide further evidence that Georgia's factional conflict was sectional in nature, and was not reducible to an urban/rural split. Turnout in this presidential election year was much higher than in 1950, but the proposal went down by a similar margin.[22]

These failed reforms draw attention to two key barriers rulers faced in effectively "castling" factional hegemony and political white supremacy in Georgia: the growing power in general elections of urban (and, soon, suburban) voters, and the strangely mixed distribution of political authority across levels of the polity. The failure to secure compliance of local and county jurisdictions with the Re-Registration Act pointed to a key paradox of Georgia's enclave, which paired the Deep South's most powerful executive with relatively powerful county-level political authorities.[23] The influence of Georgia's county commissioners and "courthouse rings" fell in between their South Carolina counterparts (dominated by the state legislature) and those in Mississippi (blessed with de facto home rule).

In each attempt, the governor—as leader of the state party, wielder of great influence over the General Assembly, and leader of the ruling faction—developed a blunt tool. When combined with the state's decentralized election administration and the state's still-weak fiscal capacity, the device failed. That it failed is not to suggest that black voting increased greatly; on the contrary, less formal devices and socioeconomic conditions continued to suppress black suffrage until the implementation of the Voting Rights Act.[24] Rather, this episode suggests again that different configurations of political authority frustrated southern rulers' efforts to design new capacities to ward off challenges to enclave rule. The conclusion of this chapter amplifies this point.

Anticipating Brown

Well before *Brown*, Georgia's rulers expressed pessimism about judicial trends. After the June 1950 school decisions, Roy Harris anticipated that the Court would "go all the way" and strike down *Plessy*.[25] Georgia's efforts mirrored those of other enclaves and will only be sketched here. First, the state created a new agency, the Georgia Commission on Education (GCE), in order to develop new strategies for defending segregation. Talmadge chaired the commission, and in swearing in its members in January 1954 he proclaimed his willingness to use the state militia to maintain segregated schools. As elsewhere, the GCE planned ahead by calling for laws that would prepare the state for the abolition of its public school system, as well as possibly moving to a tuition grant arrangement. Funds would be withheld from those public institutions that desegregated, whether voluntarily or ordered to do so by courts.[26]

After the Ruling

After Black Monday, Talmadge announced, "We shall insist upon segregation regardless of consequences," and declared that the state would "not comply with the decision. Even if troops were sent down ... they wouldn't be able to enforce it." Meanwhile, Roy Harris declared his hopes for defusing the ruling through equalization efforts.[27] The president of the Georgia Education Association—the white teachers' union—backed a resolution revoking "forever" the teacher's license of any who approved of or submitted to teaching integrated classes, or who belonged to the NAACP.[28] A new regulation required teachers to submit to an oath to "uphold, support, and defend" the state's constitution and laws.[29]

In the aftermath of the ruling, Lieutenant Governor Marvin Griffin—a loyal Talmadgeite running as the "white man's candidate"—won the 1954 gubernatorial primary. Bifactionalism in Georgia was now dead, as national party loyalist (and anti-Talmadgeite) Melvin Thompson received less than 25 percent of the popular vote and only 14 percent of county-unit vote. Further underscoring the demise of the anti-Talmadge faction, Thompson backed the county-unit system, and refused to oppose Talmadge's proposed Private School amendment to the state constitution. This provision (called the "segregation amendment" by its backers) authorized the state legislature to provide tuition grants to parents for private schools were the state to abolish its public school system. Despite benefiting from an all-out blitz of support from party leaders and the state apparatus, it barely passed in the face of strong opposition from the "Atlanta crowd," most newspapers, and those white supremacists who considered it unworkable. While passing overwhelmingly in south Georgia, voters in the small towns and countryside of north Georgia split almost evenly on the proposal. Paralleling the grow-ing political stratification of Atlanta's municipal elections, white working-class voters in Atlanta resembled the Black Belt whites of south Georgia in their strong support for the amendment, in stark contrast to the whites of the city's northside suburbs. The next year, the state legislature empow-ered the governor to close any public schools ordered by courts to deseg-regate, and in 1956 the state installed a doomsday option by mandating the defunding of any unit of its public universities faced with racial integration.[30]

In 1955, preparing for his upcoming candidacy, Talmadge published *You and Segregation;* he then won a U.S. Senate seat and held it until 1981. The now-dominant Talmadge faction featured more contested leadership battles and its cohesiveness declined, but it still faced no concerted opposition.[31]

In the 1954 gubernatorial primary, candidates' proposals reached absurd heights. At GCE-sponsored hearings during the campaign, Tom Linder, an old lieutenant of Gene Talmadge and prominent white supremacist, called for a mandatory oath-swearing for every parent. Those choosing integration might be assigned to a sanitarium for the mentally ill. Marvin Griffin, the winning candidate and clumsy white supremacist, as governor later visited Little Rock during its crisis, prompting one critic to call him "a roving am-bassador of turmoil." By 1959 the Griffin administration earned a "reputa-tion as one of the most corrupt, amoral, mismanaged, and inefficient ad-ministrations in Georgia history."[32]

Repressing White Civil Society and Black Protest

Like elsewhere, Georgia's rulers set out quickly to restrict both white and black public spheres. Griffin even attacked the press through major changes in libel laws to spur suits against Atlanta's newspapers. Already by late 1955 the president of Georgia's Council of Churches had told his organization's members that he was "deeply concerned" by the "atmosphere . . . which denies freedom of speech on the segregation question. . . . [F]ree discussion is curbed by fear of . . . social and economic reprisals." As in the Gene Talmadge years, academic freedoms were again endangered.[33]

But in the rest of the Deep South, state repression and civic white supremacist mobilization fueled one another. Georgia differed in this regard. There, the White Citizens' Councils (WCCs) never developed into a potent political force. Rather than a sign that white Georgia lacked a critical mass of devoted and practical white supremacists, this difference seemed to have resulted from state politicians' clumsy attempts to transform the Councils into a top-down organization, rather than remaining a "bottom-up" showing of white supremacist civic spirit by community pillars.[34] In keeping with Griffin's leadership and political traditions, officeholders coerced state employees to join. By mid-1956, fewer than twelve Councils existed in the entire state.[35] The independent power bases of county courthouse cliques likely dampened the Councils' potential influence, and their growth and dispersion, across the state's 159 counties.[36]

Unlike other Deep South legal authorities, Georgia's Talmadgeite attorney general, Eugene Cook, refused to repress resurgent Klan organizations. Similarly, the state's General Assembly in 1949 refused to join the region-wide trend of attempting to weaken the Klan by criminalizing masked appearances in public.[37] But Cook did spearhead the Deep South's attack on the NAACP. This attack consisted of numerous investigations, statutes governing nonprofit organizations, and oaths for state employees—including black teachers. An Atlanta NAACP leader was sentenced to one year in prison for refusing to turn over membership records. Later, the state tried to defund the organization by levying a huge tax bill on it.[38] And, less formally than in other enclaves, local notables threatened black parents with economic reprisals if they dared support desegregation petitions and lawsuits.

Although Georgia did not develop a state surveillance agency as Mississippi did, and although it lacked the professional state law enforcement agencies of South Carolina, it did enhance existing coercive capacities, especially its Bureau of Investigation (GBI). The GBI went to work surveilling black activists and investigating the biracial Koinonia Farm, a utopian Christian community.[39] In addition, authorities empowered the GCE to conduct hearings and investigations of suspected dissidents; it soon infiltrated the Highlander Folk School (in Tennessee), the famed social justice leadership training school, as well as campus groups.[40] Unlike Mississippi's Sovereignty Commission, the GCE owned wiretapping and other surveillance equipment.[41] Moreover, the governor won broader emergency powers to deploy the National Guard.[42] Finally, additional statutes required local authorities to request help from the governor in case of a threat to law and order, and authorized law enforcement personnel to enter any jurisdiction with full police powers to enforce segregation laws.[43]

Consequences for Statewide Networks of Black Protest

A national NAACP strategy meeting held in Atlanta after *Brown* II had little effect on the hesitation to litigate on behalf of school desegregation expressed by recognized black leaders. The state conference asked its approximately fifty-eight branches to file petitions, but only eight did so. By 1956 the black voter registration rate in Georgia surpassed only that in Alabama and Mississippi, despite the fact that a large share of the state's blacks lived in Atlanta and other cities and had recently been mobilized after *Smith*. From 1956 to 1957, the number of NAACP branches declined by 40 percent (from fifty-eight to thirty-five branches) (see table 3.3 for 1957 data).[44] Black observers blamed apathy in the cities and fear in rural areas (especially in the Black Belt, where economic reprisals against registrants remained likely).[45]

In retrospect, what was termed "apathy" appears to be an understandable response to black elite accommodation with white business interests.[46] In Atlanta, from the late 1940s through the mid-1960s, a coalition of middle- and upper-class whites and blacks held together against working-class whites to elect "business moderates" William Hartsfield and Ivan Allen. Failing to annex more moderate whites in middle-class suburbs, Hartsfield had to turn to black voters in 1945 and 1949. Indeed, for two decades, more than half of the city's whites opposed this dominant coalition.[47] Endorsements by the bipartisan Atlanta Negro Voters League (ANVL) effectively determined black voter choice. The critical black vote in mayoral elections netted minor gains, such as the appointment of black police officers, the repression of white supremacist groups, and the desegregation of city buses and golf courses.[48]

One reason why this accommodation meant a lack of militancy on the issue of desegregation was that leaders such as the NAACP's Walden worried that staking out tough policy demands might place their "business moderate" partners in a difficult situation, and thereby endanger the coalition. Coalition maintenance came first. In the early 1950s business elites allied with Hartsfield, in addition to the ANVL, helped Hartsfield win passage of the Plan of Improvement, which tripled Atlanta's size and brought into the city's electorate some one hundred thousand mostly middle-class and better-off whites from the northern suburbs. In the process, the share of the black electorate declined from 41 to 33 percent. When Walden met with Hartsfield in 1955, the topic of school desegregation never arose.[49]

Atlanta's black elites did little either to mobilize against the Talmadgeites or to assist blacks elsewhere in the state in organizing local protest capacity. The combination of formal assaults on black organizations and informal physical and economic coercion in the state's urban *and* rural areas wreaked

havoc on Citizens Democratic Clubs, NAACP branches, and their membership figures statewide. The 1956 assassination of NAACP leader Dr. Thomas
H. Brewer—who had been instrumental in exploiting *Smith*—effectively
halted the vibrant black organization and activism in Columbus.

By 1956—a decade after *Smith* and the pivotal 1946 gubernatorial race,
and after a period of increasing black incomes and education—black voter
registration in Atlanta had increased from 21,244 to 23,440. But given the
substantial increase in the size of the black population over that decade, this
constituted a decline in the voter registration rate.[50] The number of black
registrants in Macon actually declined by almost 60 percent from 1948 to
1956.[51] On one estimate, the share of voting-age blacks registered to vote in
south Georgia trailed behind that of blacks in Alabama and Mississippi.[52]

The repression of the 1946 election and of massive resistance greatly
weakened continuities between the mobilization of the 1940s and the protests to come in the 1960s.[53] By the 1960s—in contrast to those in Alabama,
Louisiana, Mississippi, and South Carolina—Georgia's local protest movements were not linked by statewide organizations. It is no coincidence that
by the end of 1957, Georgia—from almost any perspective the Deep South
state with the greatest advantages in black insurgency—had no ongoing
lawsuit calling for the enforcement of *Brown*.[54]

Factional Conflict and the Battle over Atlanta's Schools

Georgia's next governor, Ernest Vandiver (1959–63), was a more respectable,
upstanding Talmadgeite compared to Griffin, but they did not differ much
on key issues. In 1957 Vandiver declared that if Eisenhower federalized the
Arkansas National Guard, "the sovereign states [would] be mere puppets of
a central dictatorship."[55] He faced little opposition in the 1958 gubernatorial
primary, which lacked a viable anti-Talmadge candidate. But when a rabidly
white supremacist fringe candidate attacked him as weak on the "race issue,"
his campaign staff advised him either to promise that schools would not be
desegregated on his watch, or simply vow to fight for the status quo to the
fullest extent of the law.[56]

Vandiver chose the former, maximalist, position: "We will not bow our
heads in submission to naked force. We have no thought of surrender . . . I
make this solemn pledge . . . When I am your governor, neither my three
children, nor any child of yours, will ever attend a racially mixed school in
the state of Georgia. No, not one."[57] Soon, the state's leading segregationist
politicians endorsed him. Less than one year after Little Rock, Vandiver
promised to employ the State Highway Patrol and the National Guard to
preserve segregation. He won 156 of 159 counties, but his position-taking
tied his hands in ways that frustrated the state's handling of the crisis over
the University of Georgia's desegregation.[58]

In his inaugural address, Vandiver denounced moderation, and declared that "there is no such thing as token integration." Over the next two years, he proposed six new segregation bills, renewed his commitment to defund desegregated schools, and continued to attack "advocates of surrender." Those who would support even token desegregation were "fomenters of division and discord." For good measure, he added, "We have not yet begun to fight."[59]

In 1958 blacks in Atlanta had filed suit against the city's school board in federal district court; a ruling was expected by the 1959–60 school year. After his victory, Vandiver announced his opposition to Mayor William Hartsfield's call for pupil placement legislation, and vowed to maintain complete segregation.[60] Federal courts required Atlanta to submit a desegregation plan by December 1, 1959. Mayor Hartsfield claimed that the closing of Atlanta's schools would be "a catastrophe of world-wide magnitude." But in a 1960 address, Vandiver again committed to withdrawing funds from desegregated schools; the legislature backed him. He also promised a gathering of two thousand members of the Georgia States' Rights Council that he would never accept the "complete abdication" that token desegregation represented. Vandiver guessed that 95 percent of Georgians backed closing the schools, and claimed a mandate to do so.[61]

The threat of a successful school desegregation suit in Georgia was a real one; Talmadgeites worried in particular about the forbearance of Atlanta's school board if faced with a decision either to comply or close: as Atlanta went, the state might go, too. Thus, the Talmadge faction had to centralize education policy, and in doing so violated the longstanding norm of localism in public education. Moreover, given the state's doomsday option (the automatic defunding of any desegregated schools), the Talmadge faction understood the high stakes for the future of the faction in how it handled court-ordered desegregation.

James Peters, longtime Talmadgeite and now chair of the State Board of Education, privately informed Roy Harris that Ellis Arnall and others would encourage federal courts to order the integration of the state's schools and thus force Vandiver to fulfill his promise to close them. This would allow Arnall to run for governor in 1962 on the promise of reopening them, as he had vowed to do. Lawmakers representing north Georgia had already begun expressing anger at the prospect that their region's schools would be sacrificed to preserve segregation in Atlanta's schools. Were the schools to close, then, Peters expected whites in north Georgia to reprise their role as pivotal voters in statewide elections by coalescing with better-off whites and blacks and opposing south Georgia. The Talmadgeites would then "lose control of the government and entrench Ellis Arnall and the integrationists . . . for decades to come." Peters stated the matter slightly differently in public, but the point was the same: at stake, now that massive resistance was a lost cause, was whether compliance with democratization challenges would be "under control of the friends of segregation or the proponents of integration."[62]

But Vandiver assembled a group of state elites, the Sibley Commission, and then benefited from its call to defuse Georgia's doomsday device. The commission held public hearings throughout the state about whether the state should accept the "local option" (whereby individual school districts could decide for themselves whether to accept any desegregation) or continue to resist massively to federal courts. White sentiment ran in favor of closing schools to avoid desegregation, but differed along sectional—but not urban versus rural—lines. For instance, whites in rural areas of north Georgia opposed school closures much more than their counterparts in the state's Black Belt, even those in south Georgia's largest cities, such as Macon. Eventually, John Sibley, the state's preeminent corporate attorney and a credible segregationist, built on the nascent mobilization of middle-class urban and suburban whites to accommodate strategically to external democratization pressures. The commission recommended a number of face-saving measures to reduce desegregation to token numbers but save public schooling. However, it still supported a state constitutional amendment that no students in the state could ever be compelled to attend an integrated school.[63]

The mobilization of white parents, corporate leaders, and civic groups behind this strategy—particularly those involved with "Help Our Public Education" (HOPE), a coalition of middle- and upper-middle-class white parents centered in Atlanta—began to reap benefits. They did so in part by refuting Vandiver's claim that white Georgia was unified on the issue. Still, there remained no effective organized *electoral* opposition to the Talmadgeite faction.[64]

The Atlanta Chamber of Commerce, later framed in Atlanta mythology as a leading force in the city's relatively peaceful navigation of the 1960s, continued to resist for a full four years *after* Little Rock despite several pleas by Hartsfield, HOPE, and others that the Chamber stand against massive resistance. It is worth noting as well that, against the predictions of a modernization approach to southern democratizations, large (and often international) corporations based in Atlanta—those most expected to denounce massive resistance—refused to heed several calls by Hartsfield to do so as late as 1960.[65]

After the release of the Sibley Commission's report, federal district Judge Frank A. Hooper—who before had threatened to close all schools in the state if the General Assembly and Vandiver did not repeal the state's doomsday option—granted Atlanta's school board another year's delay (until September 1961) in desegregating its schools. The NAACP protested the judge's seeming deference to state officials. In the fall of 1960, televisions broadcasted images of mob violence in New Orleans during its school crisis.[66]

Additionally, black students from Morehouse and Spellman colleges re-commenced with demonstrations in front of Rich's, the city's most famous downtown department store, after months of unproductive negotiations about the store's treatment of black customers and employees and of op-position from the city's black elite.[67]

The UGA Crisis

More than those of other enclaves, Georgia's higher educational system had long featured prominently in state politics, from the accreditation crisis in the 1942 gubernatorial race (discussed in chapter 4), to controversies over freedom of expression and the participation of Georgia Tech in the 1955 Sugar Bowl against a racially integrated opponent. Moreover, the University of Georgia at Athens had a special resonance for much of white Georgia and most politicians. Governor Vandiver later noted that by 1960 "there was a feeling of impending doom. . . . The University of Georgia is just part of the fabric of Georgia. . . . The university would have been more difficult to close down than any other school."[68]

In 1957, after a seven-year struggle, thirty-year old Atlanta resident Horace Ward dropped his suit to desegregate UGA's law school. As the university awaited the ruling, the student newspaper, *The Red and Black*, worried about violence, still hearing on campus the "echo of a disgusting spectacle that took place at the University of Alabama [in 1956]. It must not happen here." By then, state law required that the law school be closed if courts ordered its desegregation. The law school and other units at UGA did not formally bar students' applications on the basis of race; rather, new nonracial crite-ria were developed to help school officials reject black students. In 1959, Hamilton Holmes and Charlayne Hunter applied for admission to UGA's undergraduate college. They were denied admission on the grounds that rooms in dormitories were not available. After a few other fruitless applica-tions, a team of attorneys filed suit on their behalf in federal district court. The state's politicians expected a long series of delays before a ruling was handed down.[69]

Rulers' Preferences

Leaders of the loosely grouped Talmadgeite faction all preferred that UGA remain segregated, and almost all agreed that it should be closed rather than desegregated. Vandiver himself later claimed that all but two of about fifty of his advisers called for him to close UGA. Vandiver was caught be-tween his faction, his rhetorical commitments, his own preferences for seg-regation, and his political ambitions. In 1960, just months before the crisis, he had helped deliver Georgia to John F. Kennedy after traveling to Washington to secure a promise that the then-senator would as president never send troops to Georgia. As Kennedy's inauguration drew near, Vandiver continued to lobby for appointment as secretary of the army; he also contemplated a run for the U.S. Senate. In the increasingly racially liberal national party, an extreme defense of segregation might be costly.[70]

Yet he remained the champion of south Georgia. While considered less venal than Griffin, his predecessor, and presumably interested in "efficiency in government," Vandiver remained devoted to the county-unit system, even as he realized that the system in a number of respects held back the state's political modernization.[71]

His position-taking illustrated the growing divisions within the ruling party on responses to desegregation pressures. For instance, when black students involved in Atlanta's sit-ins issued "An Appeal for Human Rights," mayor Hartsfield argued that it expressed "the legitimate aspirations of young people throughout the nation and the entire world" (in doing so he echoed the 1960 national Democratic party platform, the party's strongest yet on race reforms).[72] Vandiver, in contrast, termed it a "left-wing statement" meant "to breed dissatisfaction, discontent, and evil."

Hartsfield and other urban civic and business leaders remained constantly fixated on the state's national reputation. Earlier authorities had been similarly fixated in the 1930s (regarding lynching) and the 1940s (regarding the state's shameful penal system). Now, as opportunities for economic expansion beckoned, they worried about reckless defenses of segregation, and agreed with the president of Atlanta's Federal Reserve: "If we behave like a banana republic, we shall get and deserve the economic rewards characteristic of a banana republic."[73]

Managing the Crisis

Throughout 1960, the lawsuit filed on behalf of Holmes and Hunter worked its way through federal district court, and a court-ordered desegregation drew near. On January 6, 1961, Judge William A. Bootle ruled that the University of Georgia at Athens maintained a "tacit policy" against blacks, and he ordered the students' immediate admission.[74] State lawmakers—including the governor himself—had tied their own hands, placing the governor in an untenable position. Bootle's ruling provided Vandiver only a few days to respond. And the state's response truly was Vandiver's: as head of the Budget Bureau, only the governor could, as required by law, defund all racially desegregated units within public universities.

Just two days before Hunter and Holmes were scheduled to appear on campus, Vandiver, in a speech to the state legislature, lamented the ineffectiveness of the state's segregation defenses, lambasted federal judges, and requested that the legislature pass the Sibley Commission's "child protection" amendment. Later that night, performing the "saddest duty of [his] life," he announced that he would defund the university and thereby close it. As he did so, he requested that the legislature repeal this "albatross" of a provision (which he had supported) and wished aloud for "a new plate of armor" to protect segregation.[75] Two hundred UGA students responded that night with demonstrations; some hanged Holmes in "blackface effigy" and chanted, "Two, four, six, eight, we don't want to integrate." But two thousand students petitioned that the school remain open.

A riot had been scheduled for the night of January 11, after the first day of classes for Hunter and Holmes. The law students who planned it (and who invited onto campus local Klansmen) meant to replicate the successful defense of segregation mounted by whites at the University of Alabama in 1956.[76] The university lacked its own police force, and had not prepared for campus security problems related to desegregation. Town and gown coexisted uneasily, as much of Athens's white population consisted of poor, white textile workers.[77] While state action concerning the school's fate rested mainly in the hands of Governor Vandiver, there were other important sources of enclave policy. For instance, Lieutenant Governor Garland Byrd secretly promised students that they would avoid any criminal or disciplinary sanctions for their involvement in a planned disturbance.[78] As the crisis brewed, would Vandiver maintain order on campus?

Stationed nearby, Georgia Highway Patrol (GHP) officers ignored several calls by Athens's small (thirty-nine-man) police force to save them. Troopers arrived one hour after it ended. Athens mayor Ralph Snow complained, and the FBI later corroborated, that campus authorities and those at the state capitol knew in advance about the riot. GHP officials claimed they could not deploy troopers without the governor's authorization. As in South Carolina (chapter 7), the most hardline politicians retained great influence in the patrol.[79]

The Immediate Aftermath and the "Second Battle of Atlanta"

Afterward, Vandiver denied any advance knowledge of a planned riot, but many observers presented convincing evidence to the contrary. Even after it became evident that Judge Bootle intended to require that the students return to campus, Vandiver continued to resist carving out a responsible role for the state by ordering state troopers to watch over them. He claimed to be worried about setting a precedent of dispatching state police without a request by local authorities. For instance, he vowed not to use the Highway Patrol or National Guard to implement the desegregation of Atlanta's schools. But he also acknowledged that a continued frontal assault on desegregation could invite disastrous federal intervention. South Georgia party officials, such as Albany newspaper publisher and state party chair James Gray, criticized this view.[80]

Other defenders of south Georgia within the ruling party stuck to their guns. Vandiver's executive secretary, Peter Zach Geer—the state's next lieutenant governor—saluted the rioters for having the "character and courage not to submit to dictatorship and tyranny." Both chambers of the General Assembly—given urban growth, now even more highly malapportioned in favor of south Georgia—comfortably passed resolutions defending the rioters as well as those faculty who did not denounce them.[81]

Meanwhile, north Georgia papers blasted the governor's handling of the crisis and disputed his self-serving account. In the words of the *Atlanta Journal*, "The preservation of honor and dignity of the state collapsed Wednesday evening in cynical and shameful fashion. . . . Good faith and common sense could have prevented it." National media reported the riot extensively, and splashed photos of Hunter's exit from campus. HOPE thought this coverage and the state's actions had brought "irreparable harm" to the state's image. A federal judge ordered the students' return, and at Vandiver's urging the General Assembly finally repealed the "doomsday option" and replaced it with a plan to secure token desegregation, a "local option" that allowed school districts to close their schools by popular referendum, and private school tuition grants for parents who objected to desegregated schooling for their children.[82]

In the absence of a federal "occupation," the Athens riot would not be as costly as events in Oxford. Still, while Vandiver was somewhat less boorish than Barnett, the two acted in a similar fashion. Knowing that tens of thousands of white Georgians and a large majority of Atlantans wanted to end massive resistance, Vandiver, historian Matthew Lassiter writes, "chose instead for a period of several years to appeal to the most bitter and reactionary elements of the political spectrum under pretense of speaking for a unified white population." And the state's business leadership seemed quite craven, especially given the expectations of a modernization perspective. Atlanta's Chamber of Commerce publicly opposed school closings because of their economic consequences, but did so some two weeks *after* the embarrassment at UGA, and after Vandiver's own call to repeal massive resistance statutes. The city's media, mayor, cautious, older black leadership, and better-off white campaigners for open schools soon built Atlanta's mythological exceptionalism; the city's business leadership helped not at all.[83]

That fall, Atlanta moderates and the anti-Talmadge forces in the ruling party emerged victorious in what some residents called the "Second Battle of Atlanta": token school desegregation. The city's school board had approved for transfer of just ten of 123 black applicants, to the consternation of Georgia's Council on Human Relations (the state affiliate of the liberal Southern Regional Council). The national NAACP rejected the snail's pace of the board's plan and called on black Atlanta's parents to generate a wave of transfer requests. Parents' groups that supported and opposed the changes provided contradictory "assistance" to parents at the four high schools involved. The Atlanta Police Department deterred potentially disruptive and violent segregationist demonstrators with a "large show of force." Still, as just nine students changed schools, plaudits rained down on Mayor Hartsfield and the city, starting with a long salute by President Kennedy. A decade of favorable, and often glowing, coverage from the *New York Times* commenced with its characterization of Atlanta as "an island of moderation in a sea of militantly segregationist sentiment."[84]

The modernization approach retains its allure. Imagine a counterfactual in which malapportionment and the county-unit system were invalidated before *Brown*. In this scenario, Georgia—or at least Atlanta and the state's other cities—would likely have avoided massive resistance and proceeded with limited desegregation, as occurred in North Carolina. Here, by removing malapportionment—the obstacle blocking the translation of demographic and economic power into political influence—the modernization approach would be vindicated.

Vandiver's management of the UGA crisis, occurring in the context of the brewing battle over the limited desegregation of Atlanta, exacerbated sectional conflict within the ruling party. North Georgia elites, black or white, could not rely on even the most responsible Talmadgeite leaders to serve their interests. The outcome of the crisis, and the negative attention it garnered outside of the state, would galvanize anti-Talmadge politicians in the smaller towns and larger cities of north Georgia. The contrast between elite responses to court-ordered desegregation became even clearer as Atlanta politicians prepared for token school desegregation. After the UGA crisis, the "two Georgias" divided both the state apparatus and the state party machinery.

Moreover, by the early 1960s, as nonviolent direct action continued to sweep the South, little effective statewide capacity remained to guide this protest. This was all the more surprising given black Atlanta's numerous advantages in developing such a network. The city's conservative black elites had made it difficult for more militant Atlanta blacks to mobilize a statewide black insurgency. As chapter 10 demonstrates, this combination—a divided party-state and the failure of black Atlanta to help mobilize south Georgia—brought about a bifurcated democratization.[85]

PART FOUR

Modes of Democratization and Their Legacies since 1964

CHAPTER NINE

The Deathblows to Authoritarian Rule

The Civil and Voting Rights Acts and National Party Reform, 1964–72

The question is no longer of white against black.... [I]t is whether or not white people shall remain free.... We speak now against the day when our Southern people who will resist to the last these inevitable changes in social relations, will, when they have been forced to accept what they at one time might have accepted with dignity and goodwill, will say, "Why didn't someone tell us this before? Tell us this in time."

—*William Faulkner* (1955)

If we don't do our job, others will do it for us. Our failure to build a strong state government will create a too strong federal one.

—*Governor Ernest "Fritz" Hollings of South Carolina* (1961)

We will march through the South, through the heart of Dixie, the way Sherman did. We shall pursue our own scorched earth policy and burn Jim Crow to the ground—nonviolently. We shall fragment the South into a thousand pieces and put them back together in the image of democracy.

—*SNCC Activist John Lewis* (1963)

By God, the white Mississippian is free. That's the hardest thing for me to remember now—how tiny a thing you could do ten years ago and be in desperate difficulty. You know, what dissenting remarks could destroy you politically or make you fear for your job, or get you run the hell out of the state. That just doesn't happen anymore.

—*Mississippi journalist and Democratic activist Hodding Carter III* (1975)

THE ABOLITION OF THE WHITE PRIMARY, the national party's grudging yet growing commitment to oppose enclave rule, federal judicial attacks on the Jim Crow system, and the actions of indigenous challengers who compelled and then exploited these democratization pressures all buffeted enclaves in different ways.[1] The remainder of the 1960s brought on the death blows to enclave rule: the Civil and Voting Rights Acts. These massive assertions of federal authority initiated the swift dismantling of southern authoritarian polities. The Voting Rights Act helped establish free and fair elections and elect authorities, white and black, opposed to the ruling party's project, while the Civil Rights Act demolished racially exclusionary civic and economic spheres and desegregated the southern public sector. These statutes—in concert with federal judicial decrees—opened up floodgates of federal oversight and efforts by black protest groups to test compliance across several policy areas. At the end of the decade, national party reforms greatly reduced the independence of ruling parties to nominate candidates, select presidential convention delegates, and maintain other practices by which they excluded blacks. By 1972, insurgents and their allies abroad successfully democratized the eleven southern enclaves.

Across the Deep South, rulers generally attempted to minimize the interference of meddlesome federal bureaucrats and "outside agitators" even as they dismantled authoritarian states and parties. As one put it, "[We tried to] get the best deal we could—or at least get the [feds] off our back."[2] In order to harness the revolution—to minimize the costs of democratization absorbed by rulers and their clients while making visible, if superficial, concessions—enclaves generally hoped to limit such interventions. But their ability to do so was constrained by processes set into motion by their handling of prior democratization pressures, such as the college desegregation crises. Thus, enclaves faced different levels of interference from federal troops, black demonstrators, voter registration officials, election observers, Department of Health, Education, and Welfare (DHEW) bureaucrats, Internal Revenue Service (IRS) auditors "persecuting" segregated Christian academies, and so on.

This chapter first describes state authorities' consensus preference for effecting a "harnessed revolution." Second, it describes in more detail the challenges posed by the Civil and Voting Rights Acts, and then documents the surprising variation in the degree to which outsiders interfered in enclaves' responses to these landmark statutes. These differences are illustrated in several ways, including federal oversight of the Voting Rights Act and deployments by black protest organizations. Third, it briefly outlines the coup de grâce of the transition—the McGovern-Fraser national Democratic party reforms of 1968–72.

Mississippi experienced by far the greatest levels of intervention, followed by Georgia (predominantly south Georgia). South Carolina faced very little. This chapter provides evidence that these patterns do not reflect objective criteria of need. Rather, some enclave rulers—those in South Carolina, in particular—were able to exploit their state's reputation in the early 1960s as relatively more peaceful and orderly and convince federal authorities and protest organizations to bypass their state. Chapter 10 argues that different levels of oversight and intervention had their own significant—and often surprising—effects on the modes of democratization these states underwent. Chapter 11 then argues that these different modes had important legacies for partisan change and economic development that still reverberate today.

Rulers' Preferred Outcome: A "Harnessed Revolution"

On the eve of the civil and voting rights legislation, almost all Deep South politicians remained publicly opposed to such interventions. One member of the U.S. House backed the Civil Rights Act, while no senators and four house members voted for the Voting Rights Act (VRA). Both laws had been preceded by prolonged and well-publicized demonstrations, repression, and disorder in the South. In 1963 the Southern Christian Leadership Conference's (SCLC) Birmingham campaign and authorities' reactions to it stunned the nation. That summer, some one thousand demonstrations were held in 115 southern communities, leading to some twenty thousand arrests. Two years later, the passage of the Voting Rights Act, already existing in draft form, was sped along in large measure due to the televised repression and violence in Selma, Alabama.[3]

Together, these statutes would force enclave authorities—local and county officials, party officers, state legislators, administrators, and executives—to decide whether, when, and to what degree to comply. Facing different governance challenges, and possessing different electoral concerns and ideological dispositions, Deep South authorities would sometimes differ in their preferences regarding the speed and quality of compliance with federal directives. However, they *all* sought to minimize federal oversight, as well as the use of nonviolent direct action by black insurgents (especially those from outside the state). Both policy and electoral concerns reinforced this position.

By the early 1960s enclave rulers shared a basic commitment to building national—and international—reputations for their communities or states as orderly, business-friendly locales ripe for external capital investment and firm relocation. In doing so, they competed with one another, sometimes mocking their neighbors' relatively greater racial strife and political instability. Of course, efforts to instill positive perceptions in the minds of potential investors, opinion leaders, and politicians outside the region began much earlier. But by the early 1960s there appeared both new opportunities to attract "foreign" direct investment as well as new pressures to do so, as the mechanization of agriculture reordered Deep South economies, and as national news outlets began covering the South much more closely.[4] After the college crises, national legislation presented Deep South enclaves with further tests to burnish—or repair—the reputations of their cities and states as stable, law-abiding communities.

Enclave politicians, from local and county authorities to governors, over time increasingly aligned with the "Chamber of Commerce" crowd. These business leaders shared a remarkable consensus in favor of the racial status quo. They would exert their considerable influence on behalf of a peaceful, gradual, and controlled pace of change. But they would usually do so only when convinced that the losses they would bear through boycotts, or the effects of disorder on their community's economic climate, would outweigh those that they (often incorrectly) assumed would accompany desegregation of their retail outlets or firms.[5] This investment in the status quo did not depend on the identity of firm owners. As Gavin Wright finds, throughout the South, "none of the national chains took active steps to change the policy in their southern franchises, even when they came under pressure beginning in 1960."[6]

Alignment with business leadership was not uniform. There was substantially more pressure on governors than, say, county officials or state legislators, to coalesce with business interests, in part because it fell to governors to travel outside the state in search of external capital investment.

To maintain "law and order" and avoid white crowd disturbances and interracial clashes, political elites had to avoid federal interventions that might incense many Deep South whites, and deter direct-action campaigns by insurgents, which likewise might spur tense and possibly violent confrontations. Almost all Deep South authorities shared with white publics a distaste for desegregation, especially if secured through a "second Reconstruction." These motives reinforced their preference for ordered polities.

Besides preferring to limit visible interference from the federal government and black protest organizations, most Deep South authorities wanted to avoid *either* overt defiance to federal directives, *or* a sudden acquiescence to them. Such resistance might involve authorities' refusal to cooperate, the intimidation of federal officials from implementing laws, or the encouragement of disorder. From the perspective of Deep South rulers in 1964, overt defiance could bring at least three negative consequences: increased federal intervention; bolstered insurgents' efforts to challenge this defiance; and a damaged reputation among potential investors in search of stable communities.[7] Defiance also had electoral costs. Promising and then failing a successful enclave defense could damage one's reputation. During a failed 1967 bid to return to the governor's mansion, Mississippi's Ross Barnett was roundly criticized for his role in bringing about a massive federal intervention that was counterproductive from the perspective of hardline segregationists. Conversely, defiance would alienate the rising number of black voters, who could punish Democrats not just by staying home in November but through their growing influence in Democratic primaries. Thus, the electoral incentives facing Deep South authorities depended greatly on the timing of the emergence of black party incorporation and the Republican threat.[8]

On the other hand, a sudden acquiescence to orders to dismantle Jim Crow segregation was also problematic. It could incite a backlash in the form of white supremacist mobilizations among some elements long prepared for anything but "surrender." South Carolina governor Ernest Hollings recalled that, before the Clemson crisis, it seemed like "high time that we started sobering people up, before it turned out to be too late." This "sobering up" meant a gradual preparation of white publics for change, not a sudden capitulation.[9] The policy costs of acquiescence were accompanied by electoral dangers. Even when Democrats facing Republican challengers began to craft appeals to black voters, they proceeded cautiously. If they were seen as allowing their state's "sovereignty" to be breached, minimizing white defections from the party might be even more difficult. Indeed, over the course of the 1960s, white politicians came to realize the power of electoral appeals to whites angry about the interventions—particularly in school administration—of "meddlesome bureaucrats," as George Wallace and many other officeseekers articulated to great effect over the next decade.[10]

Therefore, in addition to an overall preference for retaining autonomy over the dismantling of the enclave institutions they had built and maintained, most regime incumbents preferred to steer a middle course—a strategic accommodation of individual interventions of central state and the national party. This would involve delaying change where possible (particularly through litigation) before calling for "lawful compliance," drawing on the power of their federal representatives to limit interference from federal agencies, and other tactics. They would "harness the revolution," and thus control the pace of what they now perceived to be inevitable change, convince outside audiences to overestimate the actual compliance occurring, and limit the degree to which democratizing reforms threatened their careers and the interests of their clients. As described in chapter 1, having induced external interventions through their "massive resistance," Deep South enclaves could no longer effect an acquiescent democratization, which would have required an earlier dismantling of enclave rule.

Expanding Federal Oversight of
Southern Democratizations

The 1964 Civil Rights Act transformed the circumstances in which enclave politicians attempted to govern, pursue careers, meet the needs of important clients, and honor their own ideological commitments. It met stiff resistance in Congress, and only a single Deep South officeholder, U.S. House member Charles Weltner from Atlanta, voted for the Act.[11]

First, Title II prohibited racial discrimination in public accommodations engaged (very broadly speaking) in interstate commerce, and Title III prohibited state and local governments from restricting the use of public facilities by race. Although Title II occasioned both great controversy and concern about southern states' likely compliance with it, the desegregation of public accommodations, in the words of President Johnson, "spread faster and more effectively than its most optimistic supporters thought possible." While the Outer South adhered to the law sooner, compliance came fairly easily and without nearly as much cajoling as one would have expected if one took seriously politicians' estimates of whites' devotion to Jim Crow. Likewise, firm owners were "surprised by the relative lack of adverse reaction on the part of white customers" to the desegregation of southern retail outlets.[12] As legendary activist Bayard Rustin wrote, Title II revealed Jim Crow's longstanding civic and commercial spheres to have been "an imposing but hollow structure."[13]

Second, the Act empowered the attorney general to sue intransigent school districts. The pace of compliance with judicial desegregation decrees could speed up significantly. This lifted a significant burden from black parents and their allies, since desegregation would not depend so much on black parents' willingness to engage in difficult, expensive, and often dangerous suits.[14]

Third, the Act enhanced the capacity of the U.S. Commission on Civil Rights to gather information—commonly from domestic insurgents on the ground—and publicize enclave practices. The commission had often fought presidents *and* adversaries in Congress in its efforts to draft and publish reports detailing problems in law enforcement, the implementation of federal laws, and so on. This publicity function is, as Edward Gibson suggests, critical in subnational democratizations, since it allows internal challengers to forge more effective alliances with powerful allies "abroad." In the wake of the 1964 Act, the commission began producing scores of reports that influenced local actors, members of Congress, and the media in their perceptions of enclave rule and shaped decisions about further interventions needed to secure southern compliance.[15]

Fourth, the Act's Title VII effected a surprisingly rapid increase in black wages by prohibiting racial discrimination on the part of larger employers in hiring and promotion. The desegregation of the textile sector, the region's largest industry, was "the single largest contributor" to the sudden closing of the racial wage gap in South Carolina from the mid-1960s to the mid-1970s.[16] Successful implementation of Title VII varied with local black protest capacity. In particular, NAACP branches played a critical role in collecting complaints and passing them on to the often-beleaguered Equal Employment Opportunity Commission and to attorneys.[17]

Fifth, in 1972 insurgents and their allies in Congress expanded greatly the reach of Title VII in order to dismantle the "state" half of the South's authoritarian "party-states": racially discriminatory and white-only public sectors.[18] By allowing individuals as well as the DOJ to sue state and local governments in their capacity as employers, and by extending antidiscrimination protections to some ten million employees nationwide, the Equal Opportunity Act of 1972 both increased the hiring of blacks and Hispanics and—in doing so—reduced their unfair treatment by law enforcement personnel and others.[19]

Sixth, the Act established the little-known Community Relations Service, which quietly helped secure community (or at least elite) consensus on compliance issues around the country, and especially in the South. Bound by confidentiality, staffers defused tensions and violence through visits to more than two hundred communities in the Act's first eighteen months alone.[20]

Finally, and perhaps most important, Title VI of the Civil Rights Act of 1964 greatly expanded the Act's reach by prohibiting racial discrimination by those institutions receiving federal financial assistance. Discovery of such discrimination put federal monies at risk, and thus the likelihood of southern compliance with various directives increased instantly. State and local governments had grown steadily more dependent on federal money since World War II, and these grants-in-aid shot up in the 1960s until they composed almost one-fifth of state and local revenues.[21]

Paramount here was the Elementary and Secondary Education Act of 1965 (ESEA). In combination with Title VI, ESEA's funding of hundreds of southern school districts finally began to secure *Brown*'s promise. As Gary Orfield observes, "the *Brown* decision had been totally irrelevant in the great majority of southern districts because no one had ever filed a suit against them and there was virtually no voluntary compliance."[22]

In its first year, ESEA funding in seventeen southern and border states amounted to almost $600 million (over $4 billion in 2013 dollars). In some areas, school districts voluntarily desegregated without much fuss. Early on, however, the Department of Health, Education, and Welfare's (DHEW)

Office of Education announced "freedom of choice" guidelines that school districts had little trouble complying with. Here, districts had to try to honor requests by individual parents that their children enroll in a particular school. Practically, this meant that black parents would each have to petition to have their children attend an until-then all-white school. Little desegregation occurred. Later, however, guidelines toughened and federal courts demanded evidence of actual progress in complying with *Brown*. The termination of funding was not an empty threat; by 1966 the DHEW cut off or delayed funds for more than 20 percent of districts in the region.[23] In this way, ESEA funding helped swiftly desegregate southern schools (see chapter 10).[24] Title VI also teamed up with Medicare and federal assistance for hospital construction to desegregate southern hospitals. This had tremendous long-term effects on southern public health. In the short term, racial gaps in infant mortality collapsed almost immediately.[25]

Of course, for Title VI to be effective substantial federal oversight was needed. Early on, the oversight capacity of federal agencies and cabinet departments lagged well behind. In 1965 just twelve DHEW staff members were charged with implementing Title VI; a single staffer was assigned the task of inducing the desegregation of America's hospitals. By 1970 twenty-two federal departments and agencies had issued regulations spelling out Title VI compliance requirements.[26] New spending programs also held out promise of accelerating democratization reforms and empowering local challengers to enclave rule. The Office of Economic Opportunity (OEO) exploited a brief, two-year window of opportunity in national politics and distributed hundreds of millions of dollars around the country through Johnson's War on Poverty.[27] Imbued with an ethos of "maximum feasible participation," OEO programming encouraged members of communities receiving funding to plan and implement it. Much of this money reached black and white liberal activists through Community Action agencies (CAAs), where they converted these funds into patronage opportunities and budding political careers.[28]

Many OEO projects engendered enormous controversy, perhaps none more so than the Child Development Group of Mississippi, an ambitious statewide Head Start program. Competing factions of Democrats loyal to the national party (see chapter 10) fought for control over the operation of its eighty-four centers, which—employing more than 1,100 workers— amounted to valuable patronage and party-building resources. But the most important cause of War on Poverty–related battles in the South was the traditional unwillingness of elites and employers to allow federal resources to flow directly to recipients and possibly disrupt the status quo. Soon, Congress allowed governors and local authorities to exert much more control over antipoverty programs.[29] Deep South enclaves often differed sharply in the amount of OEO spending that occurred in their communities. From

November 1964 through mid-1969, this amount varied from $143 million in Georgia to $280 million in (much smaller) Mississippi to only $91 million in South Carolina.[30]

Federal food assistance followed a similar pattern. According to a Department of Agriculture survey of households conducted in the late 1960s, the share of those with poor diets ranged from 23 percent in Georgia to 24 percent in South Carolina to 26 percent in Mississippi. However, the share of state inhabitants receiving food assistance ranged from 5 percent in Georgia and South Carolina to 14 percent in Mississippi.[31] Need seems not to explain different levels of assistance. Similar patterns emerged with respect to the enforcement of the Voting Rights Act, again even accounting for various objective measures of need (see later in this chapter).

To sum up, federal statutes ordered the destruction of key pillars of enclave rule: Jim Crow civic spheres, white-only public sectors, and suffrage restriction. And democratizers and their allies in Washington exploited carrots as well as sticks in quickening the pace of compliance with these statutes. In particular, the Civil Rights Act's Title VI greatly expanded the central state's opportunities to exert influence over enclave governance. Given initially weak federal administrative capacity to ensure this compliance, in a sense the South's democratization would continue to evolve into the 1970s and 1980s.

Federal Oversight of Voting Rights in the Deep South

The Civil Rights Acts of 1957 and 1960 attempted to remove barriers to voting by encouraging federal litigation against local officials, but for a variety of reasons this county-by-county approach did not work.[32] The 1964 congressional elections produced the largest Democratic majorities in both chambers since 1938, and President Johnson instructed his advisers to begin drafting a radical attack on southern suffrage restriction. Many of them were hesitant, fearing both a massive southern backlash and the law's invalidation by the Court.[33] As a draft neared completion in March 1965, the nation's reaction to Selma accelerated matters.[34] Despite the fact that a majority of southern whites expressed support for a voting rights bill, on final passage no Deep South senators and just 32 of 106 southern House members—just three of them from the Deep South—backed the legislation.[35]

The Voting Rights Act breathed life back into the Fifteenth Amendment by proscribing any voting practice or qualification made on the basis of race. The Act defined voting broadly to include local, state, and federal elections, as well as party caucuses, primaries, and so on, and applied nationwide.[36] Other provisions were temporary and applied only to certain jurisdictions.[37] The Act automatically suspended the use of a literacy requirement in any jurisdiction in which, as of November 1, 1964, the share of registered voters fell below one-half of the voting-age population and in which there existed a "test or device" that limited registration or voting. All five Deep South states, Virginia, and about one-quarter of North Carolina's counties were thus "covered" by the law.[38]

The act authorized the DOJ, at its discretion, to intervene in other significant ways in these covered jurisdictions. It could deploy examiners to oversee voter registration, as well as dispatch election observers to report on election practices. Most radically, all covered jurisdictions were obligated to submit any proposed changes in their election rules to the attorney general or federal courts for approval (or to be "pre-cleared"). Section 5 was an unprecedented mode of federal lawmaking; its working assumption was that states and localities were out of compliance with national law, not honoring it. "Preclearance" amounted to placing much of the South into a "form of federal receivership."[39] However, Section 5 was barely used before 1971. Because the DOJ was granted authority to decide whether, and where, to deploy federal examiners, this issue quickly became the most controversial.[40]

Deploying Federal Examiners

For a host of reasons, the Johnson White House and the attorney general were very hesitant about deploying federal examiners. First, they feared a backlash from southern whites, and perhaps widespread crowd violence. As they had for decades, southern politicians' expressions of concern that federal interventions would cause mass bloodshed influenced the decisions of federal authorities. Second, they wanted to avoid angering southern Democrats whose help they continued to need on Capitol Hill and within the national party.[41] Third, they feared that these officeholders—or Johnson himself—would pay dearly at the ballot box if "armies" of examiners headed South. The possibility of sending examiners to many of the counties in covered states was further limited by the federal government's lack of existing capacity. The administration had not spent much time planning the law's implementation, and had trained no one to oversee local clerks as they registered voters, or do the job themselves.[42] As Attorney General Nicholas Katzenbach wrote privately to Johnson, he planned to send as few examiners as possible without offending black protest groups.[43] Instead, he hoped for voluntary compliance and continued voter registration drives by nonprofit organizations.[44] Anger at the policy emerged quickly, and black leaders charged the administration with having in effect "repeal[ed]" the Voting Rights Act.[45]

Within two years of the Act's passage, examiners had been sent to twenty-eight of Mississippi's eighty-two counties, two of South Carolina's forty-six counties, and one of Georgia's 159 counties. Neither of the two designated counties in South Carolina was among the twelve in which by 1968 fewer than one-half of eligible blacks had registered and in which the black registration rate was less than two-thirds of the white rate.[46] By mid-1966 examiners were active in just forty of the more than five hundred eligible covered counties, and by 1968, the number had grown to sixty-four mostly majority-black counties in five states.[47] Black voter registration in examiner counties was 72 percent, compared to 51 percent in nonexaminer counties.[48] Over time, Mississippi received more than the combined total of those sent to all other states. Table 9.1 shows the share of blacks in each state who lived in "designated" counties. This large difference continued (table 9.2).[49]

The DOJ's paltry coverage in Georgia and South Carolina (no examiners were ever sent to North Carolina or Virginia) did *not* result from a lack of complaints by black protest organizations and individuals. While there is no extensive documentary record of the DOJ's decision-making regarding the dispatch of examiners, the Act's historian, Steven Lawson, writes that in "deciding where and when to send federal examiners, Justice Department policymakers took political factors into account." As chapter 10 suggests, the reputations of Deep South enclaves in the eyes of the federal government

TABLE 9.1

Percentage of State's Black Voting-Age Population Residing in Counties Featuring Federal Examiners, 1965–67

Georgia	2
Mississippi	32
South Carolina	4

Source: U.S. Commission on Civil Rights, *Political Participation* (Washington, D.C.: Government Printing Office, 1968), 222–56. Voting-age population data are for 1960. A county is classified as featuring an examiner if any examiner appeared in it between August 1965 (date of the Act's inception) and September 1967.

TABLE 9.2

Counties Designated for Federal Examiners 1965–80

	No. of Counties Designated	% All Counties Designated
Georgia	19	12
Mississippi	42	51
South Carolina	4	9

Source: U.S. Commission on Civil Rights, *The Voting Rights Act: Unfulfilled Goals*, 103–4.

and others that emerged over the course of the transition may have played a key role here.[50]

State and county officials opposed the presence of registrars, and with good reason. Counties in which registrars were present had higher levels of black voter registration. Additionally, not all deployments of examiners were equal. Some counties received more personnel than others; in some counties, examiners fanned out into the countryside to enroll new voters rather than remaining in the county seat. In others, local organizing drives occurred jointly. In such counties, the impact of examiners was largest. The largest gains in Mississippi occurred in counties that had a prior history of black political mobilization.[51]

Observing Local and County Elections

Similar differences occurred in the deployment of election observers from 1965 until 1980 (see table 9.3). A total of fifteen hundred federal observers monitored primary and general elections across the South during 1966 and 1967. However, the DOJ sent the brunt of them to Mississippi, despite scores of complaints by blacks elsewhere of harrassment, intimidation, violence, systematic discrimination in the selection of polling officials, and other problems. As with the deployment of examiners, election observers headed to south Georgia, largely bypassing communities north of the fall line.[52] Overall, from 1966 to 1974, the DOJ observed elections in all five Deep South states. Of the more than seven thousand observers, more than three-quarters were deployed to Alabama and Mississippi.[53]

The Takeoff in Voter Registration and Black Elected Officials

Black election triumphs spurred black incorporation into state Democratic parties. But it also helped break down racially exclusionary party-states in two ways: directly, through these officials' own service, and indirectly,

TABLE 9.3
Department of Justice Observation of Local and County Elections, 1966–80

	No. Counties Observed	% Counties	No. Observers
Georgia	15	9	466
Mississippi	38	46	6,462
South Carolina	4	9	443

Sources: U.S. Commission on Civil Rights, *The Voting Rights Act: Ten Years After*, 398–401; U.S. Commission on Civil Rights, *The Voting Rights Act: Unfulfilled Goals*, 101–2.

through the positive impact they had on increasing black public sector employment (see chapter 11). This was not an overnight process, of course. In 1965, there were about thirty-six thousand local, state, and national elected officials in the entire former Confederacy. Fewer than seventy-five, or about two-tenths of 1 percent, were black.[54]

Blacks in several southern states made major gains in voter registration before the Voting Rights Act. In a panic after the tumultuous freedom rides, the Kennedy administration, in what would be a futile effort to discourage nonviolent direct action, persuaded black protest organizations to direct their energies to voter registration through a nonprofit organization funded by those close to the White House. The Voter Education Project secured substantial gains in some areas, but more than four-fifths of the gains were outside the Deep South. As of April 1964, black registration reached about 1.94 million, or 39 percent of the black voting-age population. Thus, more than three million blacks remained unregistered.[55]

Primarily through its use of examiners, the federal government intervened to a much greater degree in Mississippi than in South Carolina or Georgia, and this intervention seems to have had significant consequences. Two such consequences—rates of voter registration and the election of black officials—are reviewed here. In 1960—just after the height of massive resistance—black voter registration in Mississippi stood at only 5 percent. This compared with Georgia's 29 percent and South Carolina's 16 percent. By 1970, Mississippi blacks registered to vote at higher levels than those in South Carolina or Georgia (table 9.4), and by 1976 led all southern states.[56]

County-level black voter registration totals are a better indicator of blacks' ability to secure electoral influence and win offices at local and county levels. At 80 percent, Mississippi quickly led these enclaves in its share of counties with at least one-half of eligible blacks registered (compared to 46 percent in South Carolina and 52 percent in Georgia). Mississippi also led in absolute and relative terms in the election of black officials (table 9.5).[57]

Estimates in 1968 of the degree of black political power in Deep South majority-black counties suggest that of Georgia's twenty-three majority-black counties, two had "some" power; for Mississippi's twenty-five majority-black counties, twelve ranked as having "some" or "substantial" power; and of South Carolina's twelve majority-black counties, two were considered to have "some" black power.[58]

These differences cannot be explained by the relative influence of these states' federal officeholders. By the early 1960s Congress's liberal Democrats had begun to mobilize effectively against southern Democrats.[59] However, all southern states—including those in the Deep South—continued to exert huge influence within the national party, Congress, federal agencies, and the White House. In particular, Mississippi members exercised substantial

TABLE 9.4
Percentage of Black Voting-Age Population Registered to Vote, 1940–70

	1940	1947	1952	1956	1960	1964	1968	1970
Georgia	3	19	23	27	29	44	56	64
Mississippi	0.4	1	4	5	5	7	59	68
South Carolina	0.8	13	20	27	16	39	51	57
Outer South	5	18	25	30	39	56	67	69

Sources: David J. Garrow, *Protest at Selma: Martin Luther King, Jr., and the Voting Rights Act of 1965* (New Haven: Yale University Press, 1978), 7, 11, 19, 189, 200; Harold Stanley, *Voter Mobilization and the Politics of Race* (New York: Praeger, 1987), 97; U.S. Commission on Civil Rights, *The Voting Rights Act: Unfulfilled Goals*, 19.

TABLE 9.5
Total Number of Black Elected Officials, 1968–80

	1968	1974	1980
Georgia	21	137	249
Mississippi	29	191	387
South Carolina	11	116	238

Sources: Joint Center for Political Studies, *National Roster of Black Elected Officials*, vols. 4 and 10 (Washington, D.C.: Government Printing Office, 1974, 1981). Data for 1968 are from U.S. Commission on Civil Rights, *Political Participation*, appendix 1.

Note: Almost all of these were local and county offices.

power from the chairs of the House Rules Committee and Agriculture Appropriations Subcommittee, and in the Senate, where John Stennis and Jim Eastland chaired the Senate Armed Services and Judiciary committees, respectively.[60] Thus, the surprising differences in oversight of the implementation of the Voting Rights Act remain.

What explains them? Some of the magnitude of these differences is understandable. Particularly because of Mississippi's very low level of black voter registration in the early 1960s (table 9.4), attorneys in the DOJ's Civil Rights Division prioritized deploying examiners to Mississippi, Alabama (next lowest in 1960, at 14 percent), and Louisiana.[61] However, the size of the differences in deployments of examiners and election observers, given articulations of the need for oversight in Georgia and South Carolina, is puzzling.

From 1964 to 1972, about 1.5 million southern blacks registered to vote, as did about 3.5 million whites. This increase among whites stunned observers. Of course, southern—and especially Deep South—enclaves had long de-mobilized their electorates, black and white. In a 1958 nationwide ranking, Mississippi, South Carolina, and Georgia ranked fiftieth, forty-eighth, and forty-seventh, respectively, in their voter turnout as a share of the voting-age population (ranging from 5 to 7 percent of the voting-age population).[62]

By early 1968 white voter registration in the seven covered states had shot up greatly, reaching almost 80 percent. In Mississippi and Alabama, the share of whites who were registered reached 92 and 83 percent, respec-tively.[63] The head of the U.S. Civil Service Commission, who oversaw the examiners, informed President Johnson that immediately after the Act's passage, Klans in Alabama and Mississippi held rallies that doubled as voter registration drives.[64] James Alt corroborates this view, finding that a sharp increase in white voter registration, particularly in areas with relatively large black populations, constituted a countermobilization to black gains. Other evidence suggests that much of the region's increase in white voter reg-istration is attributable to rising incomes, lowered barriers to registration (literacy and residential requirements in particular), the demise of the poll tax in four southern states, and rising interest in two-party politics and the increased mobilization of voters that accompanied it.[65]

Across the Deep South, black voters and politicians soon dealt with a second stage of efforts meant to weaken black political power.[66] Whereas examiners addressed direct efforts to disfranchise black voters, southern au-thorities next moved on to efforts to dilute the impact of black voting and minimize the prospects for successful black candidacies. These sprang from a number of motivations, including partisan goals (desire to stem white exit from the party by preventing black officeholders), political-economic inter-ests (elites in majority-black areas fearing undesirable policy changes were blacks to win office), incumbency, and simple racism. Fraud and chicanery continued, and candidate qualifications were increased to deter black third-party candidates. More important were gerrymandering, sharp increases in candidate filing fees, the conversion of elective offices to appointed ones, ma-jority vote requirements, the annexation and incorporation of mostly white areas to substantially black areas, and other formal and informal practices that disrupted the translation of black votes into black seats in office. Of these, the most common and effective vote dilution strategy was the conver-sion of hundreds of southern electoral jurisdictions from single-member to at-large districts. Affecting municipal and state legislative elections, the use of multi-member districts meant that each voter in a jurisdiction would vote for the entire number of seats to be filled rather than a single member. In jurisdictions that switched from single-member to multimember districts, minority officeholders immediately lost their seats.[67]

Almost five years after the Voting Rights Act's passage, Section 5 was basically inoperative. Over that time, the vast majority of covered jurisdictions did not submit any electoral changes for pre-clearance; of those that did, fewer than 5 percent were denied.[68] Section 5's potential to halt voter dilution efforts emerged only with the help of the Supreme Court in 1969, which offered an expansive interpretation of the Act that suggested that pre-clearance applied not merely to disfranchising devices but also those meant to dilute the impact of votes. Then, following the Voting Rights Act's reauthorization in 1970, the strengthening of administrative capacity in the DOJ's Civil Rights Division led to a sharp rise in the use of pre-clearance as well as a sharp decline in voter dilution tactics (see chapter 11).[69]

Finally, it is worth noting that these voter dilution efforts were not limited to public offices. In Alabama, for instance, the State Democratic Executive Committee changed the mode of election to the body to at-large voting. In 1968, of the approximately seventeen hundred SDEC slots in ten southern states, blacks held ten of them.[70]

Deployments by Black Protest Organizations

In 1960 the stunning spread of "sit-ins" by thousands of black college students accelerated the collapse of Jim Crow practices of downtown businesses in the Outer South, but retailers were largely successful in protecting the status quo in the Deep South.[71] Still, by energizing a relatively untapped group of activists and drawing on a pioneering mode of protest, the movement "broke decisively the NAACP's hegemony" over black insurgency. Thus commenced a period of competition and coordination among black protest organizations, all of which employed confrontational and provocative tactics of nonviolent direct action, from "pray-ins" to "wade-ins" to jail-ins to picketing, marches, and boycotts.[72]

Levels of black protest in southern states were never solely a matter of the local conditions thought to determine them, such as urbanization (see chapter 2). The influx of resources from elsewhere—money, volunteers, in-kind assistance, and so forth—often significantly shaped the pressures facing enclave rulers, both directly, in terms of protesters' attacks on the pillars of enclave rule, and indirectly, through their pressure on the federal government to intervene more aggressively. Decisions by national offices concerning where and how to allocate scarce resources were thus very important, and were often driven by considerations unrelated to these organizations' perceptions about a locale's structural readiness for black insurgency. These included competition and cooperation with other groups, enclave rulers' responses to their presence, and federal responses (and nonresponses) to enclave repression of black protest.

In their allocation of personnel and resources across the Deep South, national and regional black protest organizations generally resembled the interventions of the federal government. Out of all proportion to the actual needs of indigenous challengers to enclave rule, these organizations moved heavily into Mississippi, ignored South Carolina for the entire decade, and deployed in a sporadic and uneven fashion in Georgia.

The Student Non-Violent Coordinating Committee (SNCC) sustained projects of community organizing, voter registration, and nonviolent direct action throughout the region.[73] At its peak in 1964–65, SNCC deployed some two hundred field staff (plus more than two hundred full-time volunteers) predominantly in Mississippi, as well as in southwest Georgia, Alabama, and Arkansas. SNCC had little presence in South Carolina, in part because of successful efforts by the state's NAACP to prevent SNCC's involvement in voter registration work, and in part because of effective repression of SNCC activists (as in Rock Hill in 1961).[74] Fierce resistance encountered in the Deep South convinced many of its field staff to attempt to induce well-publicized violence and disorder by public authorities in order to force the hand of federal officials to protect protesters and launch a second Reconstruction. While the organization was headquarted in Atlanta, it did not effectively exploit this location by embarking on substantial projects in the city or to provide support to other sites of black protest outside of the four counties of its southwest Georgia project (SNCC's Atlanta project is discussed in chapter 10).[75]

The Congress on Racial Equality (CORE) was the oldest of the challengers to the NAACP, having pioneered the modern use of nonviolent direct action in the urban North. CORE was not a mass membership organization but a "federation of local groups, with a relatively weak national board and staff providing a moderate degree of coordination." CORE rose to prominence in the South by assisting the sit-ins of 1960 and especially by sponsoring the 1961 freedom rides. Seeking a "showcase" in the South, most of its energies were absorbed by VEP drives in Mississippi and Louisiana and by its participation in Mississippi's Council of Federated Organizations (COFO) (see chapter 10).[76] While CORE began the decade with a presence in South Carolina (discussed in chapter 7), and succeeded in a few local movements (as in Sumter County), the state's NAACP field secretary, "Deke" Newman, blocked CORE from capitalizing on its early presence. Its Atlanta operation disappointed national officials.[77]

The Southern Christian Leadership Conference (SCLC) emerged out of the Montgomery bus boycott. Like SNCC and CORE, the SCLC was not a mass membership organization. Rather, it was an indigenous alliance of affiliates managed in a fairly top-down manner from Atlanta by Martin Luther King, Jr., and his aides. SCLC did not deploy widely throughout the South. Instead it launched a smaller number of "major, sustained community-wide projects."[78] Most famous were its long, protracted efforts in Birmingham, Selma, and Albany (the most important town in the Black Belt of south Georgia). These did not often succeed in desegregating retail outlets and local labor markets, and at times they actually weakened local protest capacity (as in Albany).[79] However, SCLC campaigns had major effects on national politics, especially by increasing pressure to pass the Civil Rights Act and Voting Rights Act.

SCLC emerged very late on the Mississippi scene, in large measure because of the state's severe shortage of black ministers willing to assume leadership roles in fostering and sustaining nonviolent direct action. John Dittmer attributes this shortage to a structural feature of the enclave: Mississippi had "few urban centers capable of sustaining a strong, socially responsible ministerial alliance."[80] The SCLC was also little involved in South Carolina. By the time it sought VEP funding to engage in voter registration drives there, the state's voter registration was already high relative to that of the rest of the Deep South, and this may have deterred its deployment. Finally, despite being based in Martin Luther King's hometown of Atlanta, SCLC had few initiatives in Atlanta or—besides Savannah and Albany—in Georgia (see chapter 10).[81]

The NAACP's local affiliates remained critical players in Deep South black protest. The NAACP in fact continued to dominate protests in South Carolina despite the state repression it faced during the 1950s. The organization's regional and national offices were also important for their investments in local capacity, whether substantial (as in Atlanta), or meager (as in Mississippi).[82] And the national office influenced other groups' deployments, as suggested earlier, by pressuring local officers to block competitors—particularly SNCC and CORE.[83]

In the 1960s deployments by these organizations were shaped not merely by factors such as competition and local protest infrastructure, but by rulers' responses to these groups, and especially their nonviolent direct action. The country's traditional norms of local control over law enforcement (see chapter 6)—coupled with the reluctance of federal executives to exercise their authority and the FBI's "hands-off reputation" regarding the protection of insurgents—meant that the burden of keeping the peace, and deterring additional civil rights deployments, fell on state and local authorities. As chapter 10 shows, the conscious effort to trigger overreactions by public authorities and white crowds at times succeeded, but often did not. Just as important in encouraging or deterring further investments by these resource-strapped organizations were rulers' attempts to repress them through the legal means of arrests, court injunctions of protests, fines, bail policies, and so on. As SNCC's Bob Moses reported from Mississippi, "All direct action campaigns for integration have had their backs broken by sentencing prisoners to long jail terms and requiring excessive bail." SNCC's southwest Georgia staff likewise reported that "a great deal of time is spent just getting people out of jail, documenting stories of threats and losses of jobs on the part of [voter registration] applicants, and dealing with [other problems]."[84]

To sum up, SNCC and CORE converged on Mississippi as the site of much of their community organizing and nonviolent direct action. Neither organization mustered a sustained presence in South Carolina. As chapter 10 suggests, the fact that South Carolina effectively remained on the sidelines during the 1960s can be attributed not just to these organizations' conclusion that the state offered few opportunities for dramatizing white lawlessness, but also because of the NAACP's effectiveness in exploiting its links with state authorities to pressure SNCC and CORE from entering the Palmetto state in significant numbers. After SNCC and CORE withdrew from the region and began to disintegrate, greater movement dependence on the federal government effectively blunted the importance of external investments in indigenous insurgencies. But by then, these interventions' impact on the democratization of Deep South enclaves was already evident, as the next chapter demonstrates.

National Party Relations and the McGovern-Fraser Reforms

As insurgencies grew in power over the 1960s, southern state parties' relations with the national party became increasingly contentious. Enclave rulers constantly revisited the question of whether associating with the national Democratic party advanced their careers and policy goals, as chapter 5 discusses. In particular, every four years they had to decide whether to back the ticket and how to respond to the national platform, and determine to what extent their own enclave's party "label" was linked to the national party. Often they refused to endorse or campaign for the national presidential nominee. Occasionally they went further and endorsed other party's nominees, or used their control of electoral administration to complicate the national party's ballot access. Besides these collective decisions, usually made at state party conventions, federal officeholders from southern enclaves fashioned their own stances toward the national party.

Much of the important politics of national party relations occurred at National Conventions. Beginning in earnest in 1944, when South Carolina's Progressive Democratic Party challenged the credentials of the state's ruling party in Chicago, for three decades, black insurgents challenged the privilege of racist state parties to monopolize the use of the party label within enclaves. As nonsouthern state parties liberalized on race reforms, their delegations became more amenable to rejecting delegations from parties that refused to incorporate black elites and voters fairly and fully. As long as ruling parties were allowed to maintain policies keeping their parties effectively all-white, and blacks at the state level challenged their respective state's delegation to the Democratic National Convention, this incorporation remained incomplete.

Thus, by the early 1960s a critical question in national party relations became whether to incorporate blacks into the party, and on what terms. As with other elements of the transition, ruling party politicians disagreed. For some politicians, a quick reconciliation with the national party on the issue of black incorporation was useful for their own careers. Some of them were younger politicians whose lofty political ambitions would benefit from a good reputation in national party circles; others preferring a quick reconciliation did so because, facing Republican challengers in general elections, they feared that independent black parties would withhold from them badly needed votes.[85] Still other politicians were either fully committed to the ruling party project or believed that their constituents or clients were; for them, reconciliation with the national party ranged from unimportant to highly objectionable.

For others, troubled relations with the national party were useful in crafting appeals to resentful white voters. Many older enclave politicians had retained deep emotional attachments to the "house of their fathers," and so would contemplate black incorporation in order to remain loyal Democrats. Finally, federal officeholders, often active at National Conventions, worried about losing seniority status in Congress, control of federal patronage, and so on.

National party actors had decisions to make, too. Refusing to recognize a delegation of southern "regulars" could risk angering other southern parties and voters, while recognizing them could anger blacks, labor, and delegations from nonsouthern states. Besides refusing to seat delegations, party leaders contemplated attempts to "purge" certain officeholders, withhold federal patronage and contracts to the state, revoke the legal right to use the "Democrat" label, and so on.[86]

In 1960 and 1964, respectively, the Democratic and Republican national parties took strong steps to reposition themselves with respect to racial equality. In 1960 the Republican platform featured a vigorous defense of civil rights and praised sit-in protesters. Four years later, at the Cow Palace in San Francisco, Goldwater insurgents laughed and booed at a salute to the party's traditional support of civil rights.[87] This followed the defeat of a proposal that would prohibit racial discrimination in delegate selection, and a crushing defeat of a platform amendment backing the Civil Rights Act. In a reverse-Dixiecrat moment, fourteen black Republican delegates stormed out in protest. Goldwater received a majority of white votes in all southern states but Texas.[88] Four years later, more than one-quarter of all national Republican delegates were southern—up by one-half since 1952.[89]

At the 1964 Democratic convention in Atlantic City, President Johnson greatly feared that the recently passed Civil Rights Act would bring a "white backlash" against his candidacy, and the party generally. Challenging the credentials of several southern delegations posed further risks. After the Mississippi Freedom challenge (discussed in chapter 10), the Mississippi delegation and one-half of Alabama's delegates left the convention. The party then ruled that delegations would be seated at the 1968 convention only if their parties fostered widespread participation for all. Otherwise, the convention would recognize a diverse delegation of loyalists.[90] These rules, forged by the DNC's Special Equal Rights Committee (SERC), would serve as precedent for the revolutionary McGovern-Fraser party reforms of the early 1970s. It called on state party chairs to publicize all of its meetings, scrap any loyalty oaths meant to exclude blacks, and develop and then publicize clear qualifications and procedures for filling all party offices. These requirements quickly became criteria to help settle credentials challenges four years later.[91]

In 1968 the Credentials Committee heard challenges to six southern delegations. It rejected those from Alabama and Mississippi, and half of Georgia's delegation; three other black and biracial challenges to the parties of North Carolina, Tennessee, and Texas failed.[92]

Over the next two years, the national party deliberated on and drafted further requirements that state parties had to meet in order to be recognized as their states' official Democrats. Beyond those established by SERC, these included taking "affirmative steps to overcome past discrimination, including minority presence in the state delegation in reasonable relationship to group presence in the state as a whole."[93] Sparked both by controversies over southern delegations and the anger of "new left" activists over their treatment throughout the country, these reforms "revolutionized the presidential nomination system by introducing previously unheard-of due process guarantees backed by the authority of national party law and attempting to force an equitable representation of minority groups in party affairs." State parties interpreted guidelines on representativeness as establishing de facto quotas.[94]

In the South, South Carolina and Mississippi were among the first to comply with the "guidelines," while Georgia Democrats did so later. However, Mississippi's situation was complex: the "party" recognized by national Democrats and by the McGovern-Fraser reformers was not in fact the entire state party, but a smaller, unstable biracial grouping of those loyal to the national party; the larger group of segregationist "regulars" remained absent from national conventions and thus outside the halls of the national party from 1964 to 1976. As discussed in chapter 10, compliance with national party reforms both reflected and further shaped the timing and degree of black incorporation into state parties. South Carolina's rapid reconciliation with the national party, the sectional split in Georgia's relations with national Democrats, and Mississippi's twelve-year "divorce" would have important implications for these enclaves' democratizations and the legacies they would come to shape.[95]

Finally, in a sign of how even southern Democrats had surrendered on their "states' rights" vision of national-state party relations (discussed in chapter 5), four southern governors resisted the McGovern-Fraser reforms in part by taking the national party to federal court. There, they made an equal protection challenge to new rules about the allocation of delegates to state party conventions. These politicians were now too weak to secure their preferred policy within the party itself. Even worse, the effort to secure it in federal courts meant that they had to surrender their long-held view that state parties could not be regulated in this way.[96]

Despite their preferences for minimal oversight of state compliance with democratization reforms, Deep South enclaves differed markedly in these breaches of their "sovereignty." For in terms of both the Voting Rights Act and national black protest organizations, interventions fell heavily upon Mississippi, barely touched South Carolina, and—with the exception of significant civil rights deployments in the southern part of the state—largely spared Georgia. The next chapters argue that these differences cannot be explained without reference to these enclaves' management of college desegregation crises; moreover, these differing degrees of outside intervention, coupled with ruling party responses to national party reforms, helped shaped these enclaves' diverging paths out of Dixie.

CHAPTER TEN

Harnessing the Revolution?

Three Paths Out of Dixie

THIS CHAPTER TRACES HOW THE LONG TRANSITION, begun in the 1940s, culminated in different modes of democratization. As enclave rulers came to believe that change was inevitable, most sought to harness the revolution, striking a fine balance between resisting federal intervention without appearing too defiant, and accepting some change without appearing too quiescent. Harnessing the revolution meant influencing the pace of seemingly inevitable change; it served the overarching goals of protecting the political careers of enclave rulers and the interests of many of their political-economic clients. But by this point, Deep South states differed in the external pressures they faced, the degree of cohesion in their ruling parties, their institutional capacities to manage democratization pressures, and their external reputations, and thus were variably constrained in their ability to accommodate strategically. They would differ, sometimes dramatically, in the degree to which they maintained order, the manner in which they incorporated black officeseekers and voters, and how they reconciled with the national party.

The narratives that follow do not cover the entirety of the tumultuous 1960s. Rather, they illuminate how prior responses to democratization pressures, factional conflict, and party-state institutions shaped modes of democratization. In particular, they show how these forces account for differences in the degree of compliance with federal directives, as well as the timing and nature of black incorporation and reconciliation with the national party across the Deep South. Along the way, the narratives suggest how Republican growth in this region was to varying degrees both consequence and cause of rulers' responses to democratization pressures.

Mississippi

After the *Brown* shock, black mobilizations in Mississippi helped organized white supremacists secure a key role in the party-state, despite opposition by Governor James Coleman. Conflict between Coleman and the White Citizens' Councils (WCCs), in the context of the state's relative decentralization of authority, resulted in stalemated efforts to centralize the state's law enforcement capacity. This in turn contributed to the Oxford debacle, which exerted its own influence on the state' democratization.

By the early 1960s most state-level authorities in Mississippi were determined to avoid defiance and instead strategically accommodate to democratization challenges. But their substantial efforts to exit "the doghouse [they] found themselves in" came to naught.[1] By the end of the decade, the state had instead stumbled through a protracted democratization of delayed and disorderly compliance, resistance to black incorporation, and a delayed reconciliation with the national party. This resulted in large measure from two related processes accelerated by the disastrous events at Oxford.

First, the humiliating Oxford episode sparked a white supremacist mobilization that, given the state's feeble law enforcement capacity, resulted in substantial disorder and violence. This violence set off a spiral of interventions by the central state, more violence, and an impressive black insurgency that combined "local people" with a number of black protest organizations determined to leave their mark on the state.

Second, Oxford's encouragement of white supremacist mobilization in the state complicated efforts by state-level politicians to accommodate democratization pressures strategically. This problem was exacerbated by the fact that Mississippi's relatively decentralized enclave limited state officials' control of local and county authorities and party officers. The national party punished Mississippi Democrats for their failure to dismantle their racist state party. The ruling party then fissured into a rump white supremacist wing, a center-left biracial wing, and a more radical, mostly black faction. Chaos reigned among incumbents of the dying regime, but with surprising consequences.

By the early 1970s these processes thus produced massive, unwanted violations of state sovereignty, a terrible reputation among potential economic investors as a disorderly polity, and a delayed reconciliation with the national party. Over the long run, this protracted democratization ironically accelerated black political mobilization, stalled Republican growth, and slowed the state's economic development.

Scholars generally claim that Mississippi's democratization must have been produced by rulers with different motives, different white publics, and so on.[2] In contrast, this narrative suggests that while the state's mode of democratization differed from other Deep South enclaves, this outcome was not preordained by antecedent conditions or determined by secular changes since the transition began, such as a relatively slower rate of urbanization. Nor do Mississippi's ruling politicians seem to have sharply different preferences than those elsewhere. Rather, Mississippi's protracted democratization was significantly determined by the interactions of ruling politicians' behaviors and the party-state institutions that constrained and enabled them.[3] First, I review leading politicians' preferred responses to democratization pressures. Second, I describe the processes unleashed by the "Battle of Oxford."

Rulers' Preferred Strategies

As discussed in chapter 6, after the fall 1962 debacle at Oxford, leading politicians and resource-holders within the state's ruling party diverged somewhat in their preferred strategies toward external challenges. Increasingly, business leaders preached for calm, lawful compliance with federal directives. Meanwhile, WCCs grew simultaneously more defiant in their rhetoric and less influential within both the state legislature and the governor's mansion. After their promises to block desegregation and federal intervention were shown to be empty, their effectiveness in chilling white public discourse concerning desegregation faded. In 1963, Barnett—whose star steadily sank among white Mississippians—took steps suggesting that, despite his rhetoric, he favored a strategic accommodation to inevitable change.[4]

One year after he "stood tall" at Oxford, Lieutenant Governor Paul Johnson, Jr., won the governorship. Reliably white supremacist in tone, he received the support of aging House Speaker Walter Sillers and other important Deltans, who feared that the return of James Coleman to the governor's mansion would lead to a new, and for them a very unfavorable, constitution.[5] On taking office, Johnson changed his tune. In his January 1964 inaugural address, aimed at both domestic and national audiences, Johnson surprised most everyone by acknowledging the state's "transition," rejecting defiance and white supremacy, and warning all that the state would maintain order.[6] His speech signaled his—and business moderates'—desire for strategic accommodation to change, and hinted at plans for expanding and centralizing state law enforcement.[7]

Johnson's call for lawful compliance and adjustment to imminent civil rights legislation was not shared by all key officials. Leaders of the WCCs preached school closings and defiance of the public accommodations provisions of the Civil Rights Act. However, the growing group of business moderates populating state agencies, advising the governor, and making inroads in the legislature would help secure peaceful court-ordered desegregations of public schools in cities across the state.[8]

After blacks sued several school boards in 1963 and won court decrees mandating their desegregation by fall 1964, emerging groups of white parents helped, too. As in Georgia, where white middle-class parents campaigned against school closures, Mississippians for Public Education responded to WCCs' calls to close these schools with its own public campaign. While credible public opinion polling in this period is elusive, a confidential survey commissioned by the state Republican party is perhaps instructive. In February 1963, 60 percent of Mississippians favored closing its schools rather than desegregate them. In September 1964, after the state's most tumultuous summer in a century, the share of respondents holding this view had fallen to 32 percent. This was an incredibly rapid change in an eighteen-month period, especially given that this preceded the passage of the ESEA, and the carrot of federal aid had not yet been dangled to Mississippi's financially strapped school districts.[9] Nonviolent direct action, often on a large scale, also won concessions from local authorities. The 1965 campaign in Natchez, the state's Klan stronghold, was incredibly impressive in this regard.[10]

In the small towns of the Delta—which still dominated the malapportioned lower chamber of the state legislature, and would receive the brunt of "outside agitators"—this business moderation was less prevalent. Unlike South Carolina's lowcountry, agribusiness in the Mississippi Delta continued to thrive, especially given the generous price supports these landowners received from the American taxpayer.[11] Perhaps more important, the state would feature a growing split between state-level officials—those most involved in negotiating with federal authorities—and local and county officials, over whom Mississippi's state-level officials had less control than their counterparts in South Carolina. Here, the relative decentralization of Mississippi's polity would complicate efforts to accommodate strategically both to federal and national party directives to incorporate black elites and voters.

The Spiral of Intervention and Disorder

As will be argued here, the debacle at Oxford unleashed important processes that helped produce a protracted democratization. But it is important to acknowledge that while black protest organizations made large interventions in the state after Oxford—particularly, but not only, in the form of the Mississippi Summer Project of 1964 (or Freedom Summer)—many of these forces were on the ground before Oxford, including SNCC and CORE, which both arrived via the freedom rides of 1961 and the Voter Education Project that followed. In the absence of a disastrous desegregation of the University of Mississippi, would the state have experienced no violence or disorder? As the following evidence will suggest, that is not a sustainable counterfactual. Moreover, there were impressive indigenous insurgencies that both preceded the arrival of "outside agitators" and were catalyzed by them. Still, the argument offered here is that in the absense of Oxford one can imagine without too much difficulty a less tumultous, violent, and protracted end to Mississippi's authoritarian regime.

While most of the state's elites—led by Governor Johnson—sought to accommodate present and future interventions strategically, a significant white supremacist mobilization occurred at the local level in the Delta and the state's southwest counties. A combination of humiliation, anger, panic, and fear spread across white communities. Mississippi's Klans had been dormant in the years leading up to Oxford, and had been among the Deep South's weakest in the 1950s. Their growth had been forestalled in part by the emergence of the WCCs. However, the combination of the massive intervention of the U.S. military at Oxford and of "outside agitators" fueled the rise of these organizations. From the summer of 1963 until the conclusion of 1964's Freedom Summer, statewide Klan membership rose from fewer than four hundred members to some seven thousand. They were centered in the southwest part of the state, the base of the Council of Federated Organizations (COFO), the umbrella civil rights group, and where most Freedom Summer volunteers worked (see later in this chapter).[12] Indeed, the period's leading historian, John Dittmer, credits the Oxford fiasco with heightening resistance to COFO activity throughout the state.[13]

Most troubling for the state's leaders, these Klans worked assiduously to recruit local law enforcement officers—or at least render them sympathetic to the cause. Eventually, some local police officers, a few sheriffs and their deputies, and even about five members of the state's weak Highway Patrol (MHP) joined Klan organizations. As became clear to South Carolina officials in the 1950s, successful investigations required reliable intelligence from local actors, and MHP and FBI personnel discovered that many peace officers could not be trusted.[14] This frustrated efforts to prevent violence during the Freedom Summer.

To the extent that Oxford heightened white resistance, it also helped embolden black Mississippians. In the summer of 1963, white violence "seemed to anger Delta blacks more than it frightened them." Joining a regionwide wave of black protest, "local people who had suffered quietly for generations gathered new strength and resolve, inspired by and inspiring the grassroots leaders" then emerging.[15] Supporting the view that independent black landownership produced more favorable conditions for black insurgency, Mississippi's most impressive local movement emerged not in a large city but in rural Holmes County, a small, majority-black county adjoining the Delta and Hills regions of the state. There, the New Deal–era Resettlement Administration purchased land, divided it into more than one hundred farms, and sold it on favorable terms to black farmers. Twenty-five years later, the county had a thriving local movement and would soon elect Mississippi's first black state legislator in seven decades.[16]

Alerted early in 1964 to the upcoming Freedom Summer, Governor Johnson framed the intervention as a challenge to the maintenance of order, and immediately attempted to centralize and professionalize the state's law enforcement. However, as discussed in chapter 6, the sheriffs' lobby remained strong, and Johnson failed to reduce their power quickly—a necessary condition for the development of effective state policing.[17] Offered to trade their roles as county tax collectors in exchange for the opportunity to serve consecutive terms, sheriffs chose to continue with their highly lucrative tax farming. Even with the passage of a constitutional amendment decoupling the offices of sheriff and tax collector, the sheriffs' lobby succeeded in blocking its implementation.[18] But while Johnson promised not to violate local and county law enforcement prerogatives unless disorder occurred, he did substantially upgrade the state's Highway Patrol. In addition to doubling the number of patrolmen, Johnson convinced the legislature to grant "general police powers" to the MHP's investigators, who—acting on Johnson's authority—soon infiltrated Klans and cleared out law enforcement personnel sympathetic to them. In a sudden turnabout in state politics, in 1965 the MHP began monitoring WCC meetings![19]

Still, the dominance of local law enforcement by police and sheriffs forced the state to intervene, angering local authorities in the process. For instance, in the Delta's Adams County, a one-month curfew meant a lockdown on liquor sales, which outraged the local sheriff as a violation of norms of localism.[20] Some legislators representing these interests even called for the repeal of the MHP's police powers. Eventually, the failure of local law enforcement to maintain order required Johnson to dispatch six hundred and fifty National Guardsmen, who conducted armed patrols and staved off the racial disorders so familiar to northern cities.[21]

As shown in chapter 6, Governor Coleman succeeded in keeping Mississippi's State Sovereignty Commission weak. During the early and mid-1960s, it still remained small—employing only three full-time investigators—but was important as a "racial troubleshooting" agency. The SSC often worked to undermine black protest, and supplied county and local law enforcement officials with sensitive intelligence—most infamously by giving Neshoba County authorities the license plate number of the car driven by Michael Schwerner, Andrew Goodman, and James Chaney, three civil rights workers murdered during 1964's Freedom Summer.[22] The other side of the "troubleshooting" coin involved attempting to mediate local racial conflicts quickly and quietly, as well as weaken the forces that might imperil a harnessed revolution. In its role as conflict mediator, it embarked on, as historian Joseph Crespino notes, "subtle efforts to deter white racial extremism, attempts to resolve local racial disputes as quickly and quietly as possible, [and] new conciliatory public relations efforts that emphasized positive changes in the state's peace relations," among others.[23] In particular this meant targeting white supremacist organizations such as the Americans for the Preservation of the White Race.[24]

The state's "black-market tax" on illegal liquor embarrassed the "dry" Governor Johnson, as did the corruption it engendered. In 1964 he won its repeal. Partly motivated by his desire to professionalize the state's law enforcement, he then set out to reform the state's liquor laws.[25] With Sillers's help, he won passage of legislation allowing counties to legalize liquor (the "local option"). Meanwhile, the MHP and State Tax Commission would oversee liquor tax revenue and enforce liquor laws. Eventually, the tax collection function was decoupled from the office of sheriff, and sheriffs' dominance of county politics weakened and their stranglehold on law enforcement reform finally ended.[26] MHP quickly became a professional force.[27] By then, however, it was too late. In part because of the white supremacist mobilization in response to Oxford, the state's traditional decentralization, and the failure of Coleman and others in the 1950s to centralize the state's coercive apparatus, Mississippi rulers after Oxford could not deter interventions and disorder and thus salvage the state's reputation.[28]

The Invasion of "Outside Agitators"

Representatives of national black protest organizations began working in Mississippi in 1961. Linking up with long-established networks of black resistance, activists associated with SNCC, CORE, and the state's NAACP created an umbrella group, the Council of Federated Organizations (COFO), to foster community organizing, boycotts, sit-ins, civic education, and voter registration drives in the Delta.[29] The privately funded Voter Education Project also worked in the region, but failed to score substantial gains in registration and withdrew.[30] Both full-time civil rights workers and indigenous blacks supporting them faced significant physical and economic coercion by actors public and private. As historian John Dittmer has argued, two insurgency strategies lay in tension. Some activists wanted to conduct quiet, gradual grassroots organizing. Here, activists would, in the words of legendary activist Ella Baker, take "uninitiated people and work with them to the point that they began to understand where their interest really was and the relationship to their own capacity to do something about it."[31] Others hoped for dramatic, well-publicized revelations of white "lawlessness" to stimulate nationwide demands for the federal protection of workers and for national civil rights legislation. After the white supremacist mobilization in 1963 and the concomitant corrosion of local law enforcement and heightened coercion of civil rights workers, the balance shifted toward the latter strategy.[32]

During this summer and after, black protest organizations intervened in Mississippi at sharply higher levels than in other states. In the Freedom

Summer of 1964, somewhere between 450 and 650 young, mostly white volunteers from outside the South converged on the state. Following in tow was a large contingent of journalists, whose coverage of Mississippi dwarfed that of the rest of the South. Volunteers would register voters, teach in "freedom schools," and engage in various other community organizing projects. Their mere presence, it was expected, would induce violence and national media attention. Oxford, having encouraged both the state's white supremacist mobilization and the corrosion of law enforcement, thus encouraged black protest strategists to launch this intervention. Its media coverage and symbolic value greatly outweighed the number of voters registered (only about 1,600).[33] As shown earlier, the relative decentralization of the polity frustrated rulers' efforts to improve state policing before the fateful summer.

During the summer, a wave of Klan violence swept over the state's heavily black counties. "Unknown assailants" burned thirty-five black churches; in the course of investigating one of these arson attacks, three civil rights workers disappeared outside Philadelphia, Mississippi. As gun sales surged across the state's southwest counties, there were at least eighty beatings, thirty-five shootings, and six murders.[34] These well-publicized events ratcheted up pressure on the White House to intervene to protect civil rights workers. President Johnson dispatched former CIA director Alan Dulles and FBI chief J. Edgar Hoover to Jackson to help monitor white supremacist penetration of Mississippi law enforcement, investigate the disappearance of the Philadelphia Three, and suggest, not so gently, that the state's failure to maintain order would lead to a much larger federal intervention. Governor Johnson welcomed a large (and temporary) federal investigative presence. For a time, the FBI office in Jackson was the country's largest outside Washington.[35] Eventually, the bodies of the three activists were found; they had been murdered by a group of Klansmen that included members of local law enforcement. The size of the hunt for their bodies confirmed for many Mississippi activists that the movement would benefit from white victims.[36]

In cross-national perspective, the killing of six insurgents in the course of wrenching social, political, and economic change is shockingly low. Of course, other killings had occurred in the past and more would occur in the future, but the degree of "lawlessness" observers claimed to have existed in Mississippi, relative to other Deep South enclaves, is much exaggerated. While the summer of 1964 occasioned about one thousand arrests in the state, thirteen hundred blacks were arrested by South Carolina's state police in a single day in 1963. None of Mississippi's towns or cities experienced major rioting, in stark contrast to events in northern cities during the summer of "white backlash."[37]

However, the damage had been done, as national and international media seared the construction of "Mississippi," the national pariah, into the American mind. After Oxford, the *New York Times* saluted the Kennedy administration for "pursu[ing] relentlessly the task of democratizing backward corners of our own country." After the Freedom Summer, Reinhold Niebuhr wrote that "Mississippi standards can sink so low that only the legal and moral pressure of the larger community can redeem them—just as only the pressure of the British Commonwealth can save Northern Rhodesia from becoming another South Africa. Not all the states of the Southern Confederacy have sunk to the standard of inhumanity."[38]

By the end of the year, the NAACP's national office, Martin Luther King, Jr., and others announced a nationwide boycott of products sold by Mississippi firms. In 1964 new plant construction fell by 28 percent, and at least one dozen firms already in the state decided to move elsewhere; one moved from Mississippi to Louisiana to avoid an "MS" mailing address. The state estimated that tourism revenues dropped by some $60 million. The worst dreams of Mississippi's business moderates were coming true.[39]

Federal Oversight of Mississippi's Democratization

Efforts by the state's insurgents to induce a heavy federal intervention in some respects paid off. Indeed, connections forged between these activists and central state actors helped foster a larger intervention. For instance, communications between President Johnson and Mississippi activist Charles Evers (brother of slain NAACP field secretary Medgar Evers) concerning both state-sponsored violence and voting examiners helped persuade the president to lean more heavily on Governor Johnson.[40]

As illustrated in chapter 9, the brunt of federal oversight of the Voting Rights Act occurred in Mississippi. Before its passage, the state attempted to preempt the legislation—"a federal assumption of jurisdiction and 'takeover' for twenty years or more"—by amending constitutional provisions for literacy and understanding tests.[41] After the law's passage, counties varied substantially in their responses. Some, such as U.S. Senator Jim Eastland's home county of Sunflower refused to comply; other county registrars immediately suspended literacy tests and allowed all to register. Others engaged in petty practices to delay black voter registration.

Eastland, chair of the Judiciary Committee, used his formidable influence within the Johnson administration to keep Sunflower County free from federal examiners for two years.[42] But even Eastland's influence could not overcome the state's reputation. About two years after the Act's passage, twenty-eight of the most intransigent of Mississippi's eighty-two counties "received" examiners.[43] In concert with community organizing by indigenous groups and out-of-state activists, the (threatened) presence of these examiners was enormously effective, as black voter registration increased from 7 percent of the black voting-age population to 59 percent between 1964 and 1968 (table 9.4). Suddenly, the black share of the entire electorate rose from almost nothing to 25 percent. There followed a remarkable change in the rhetoric of white office-seekers. In one of a number of such spectacles, the mayor of Canton in 1966 joined NAACP president Roy Wilkins and a mainly black crowd in singing "We Shall Overcome." By 1968 the state's blacks led the Deep South in voter registration; in 1976 and 1986 they led all southern states. From 1965 to 1966, state NAACP membership doubled to ten thousand. [44]

But, as in the rest of the Deep South, the absolute number of new white registrants vastly exceeded that of blacks. From 1960 to 1970, white voter registration increased from about 40 percent of the white voting-age population to 70 percent. As discussed in chapter 9, this increase had a number of sources. The federal abolition in the 1960s of the poll tax for all elections, via constitutional amendment and Supreme Court jurisprudence, helps explain some of this increase, as Mississippi's poll tax had been one of the most onerous in the South. Additionally, as occurred elsewhere, the emergence of Republican contestation of statewide offices increased voter interest and turnout. Rising incomes also likely mattered. The degree to which politicians mobilized whites in an express attempt to answer black voter registration remains unclear. However, it is safer to argue that in Mississippi this increase was the result not of increased interest in politics but to a countermobilization in response to the emergence of black Mississippians in electoral politics. The increases in the state preceded the emergence of real two-party competition, and also occurred before the Wallace campaigns.

Disproportionate interventions in Mississippi also occurred with regard to federal oversight of elections. More than six hundred observers and DOJ staff fanned out through the state for its 1971 elections, considered the fairest in state history. They were joined by northern elected officials and celebrities.[45] As shown in chapter 9, these trends continued throughout the 1970s. Like South Carolina and most other southern states, Mississippi prevented more successful black candidacies by targeting not only voter registration and turnout but also by diluting the black vote. Gerrymandering state legislative and congressional districts was common. Mississippi allowed counties to use at-large districting to fill the seats of their powerful boards of supervisors. Freedom Democrats successfully overturned the state's legislative reapportionment plan in federal courts. These courts acted much more quickly in forcing Mississippi, relative to other states, to return to single-member districts, allowing the growth of black elected officials in Mississippi to surge ahead of other Deep South states.[46]

The massive increase in potential black political power did not translate quickly into powerful electoral influence. Especially in the Delta, planters and business owners successfully protected their prerogatives. Rapid black outmigration in the wake of mechanization weakened black voting; black candidates often needed their jurisdictions to be about two-thirds black in order to win. Fear of economic and physical coercion, or the withholding of federal commodity disbursements by planters controlling them, continued to frustrate the translation of numbers into political power.[47]

Meanwhile, interventions by the federal government and black protest organizations complicated the state's compliance with the Civil Rights Act. After taking an intransigent approach to sit-ins and other local protests for the desegregation of public accommodations, Jackson's Chamber of Commerce and mayor called for a lawful acceptance of the Civil Rights Act, and local businesses swiftly complied as soon as the law was passed. However, the House, as well as state leaders of the White Citizens' Councils (WCCs), denounced the Chamber of Commerce for doing so. The WCCs called for defiance, the privatization of public institutions, and school closings; its Jackson branch threatened boycotts against compliant white businesses.[48]

The House remained in the hands of representatives of Delta planters and pro–WCC legislators from the state's small towns. Delta business interests lagged behind those of the state's cities and other regions in their support for compliance with federal directives. Although the WCCs had lost their influence in the governor's office—as well as in the State Sovereignty Commission—after Oxford and the Freedom Summer, their calls for renewed resistance remained influential in the state legislature. By then, however, the legislature had a minor role to play in compliance with democratization pressures when compared to executive leadership and local and county authorities.[49]

However, after the economically disastrous 1964, the state's chamber of commerce—the Mississippi Economic Council—issued a statement calling on school officials, businesses, and individuals to comply quickly with the Act. The Mississippi Manufacturers Association and more than fifty other state and local business organizations signed on to it, as did state associations of sheriffs, county supervisors, circuit clerks, and voting registrars. Underscoring politicians' concerns about the state's image, U.S. Senator John Stennis read the statement into the *Congressional Record*.[50] At the local level, mediators from the federal Community Relations Service persuaded business elites to make similar public declarations. An elite consensus had taken hold; however, it had been delayed by the state's inability to deter white supremacist violence.

This inability, of course, continued to exact significant reputational costs. In Jackson, in 1970, highway patrolmen and Jackson police responded to a crowd disturbance at the black Jackson State College. Thinking they were being fired upon, they let loose a "28-second fusillade." Two black students were killed and twelve were injured. In stark contrast to South Carolina's "Orangeburg Massacre" (see later in this chapter), the event sparked great amounts of media coverage, national outrage, and intense FBI investigation. Also in contrast to Orangeburg, local authorities acknowledged the fault of the patrolmen.[51]

Meanwhile, by 1968, the political economy of the Delta had undergone unbelievably rapid change, with contradictory effects on the state's democratization. The mechanization of agriculture in the Delta had increased very quickly over the course of just a few years. This was both consequence and cause of other demographic and political changes. Mississippi underwent a net black emigration from the state in every decade during the transition, losing about 300,000 blacks in the 1940s, 1950s, and 1960s each.[52] As this outmigration from the Delta proceeded, planters increasingly took advantage of existing technologies by investing in mechanization. This further sparked an exit of blacks from the Delta.

The number of sharecroppers in the region collapsed from about twenty thousand in 1959 to about zero in 1967. In that year, only 5 percent of the Delta's cotton was hand-picked. Farm employment was now reduced to seasonal jobs and day laborer slots, but these dried up as well. Federal policy, not mechanization, explains this rapid change. Jamie Whitten, chair of the U.S. House Appropriations Subcommittee on Agriculture, helped push through Congress the 1965 Food and Fiber Act, which made even more profitable the decision by landowners to accept parity payments rather than continue cotton production on all of their land. The size of the payouts were massive. Stunningly, Dittmer writes, the "demand for plantation seasonal labor fell by more than 75 percent between 1965 and 1967."[53]

Making matters worse, black Mississippi's allies in Congress were persuaded by a labor movement in the Delta to modify the Fair Labor Standards Act of 1938—the source of so much anger and fear among planters during the New Deal. The law's minimum wage would now cover farmworkers. Benefiting from the new cotton payment scheme as well as mechanization, Delta planters did not panic this time as the hourly wage was tripled. Instead, they stopped hiring and invested in chemical weed killers. Only a few months would pass before U.S. senators were conducting a "hunger tour" in the Delta. At the country's first federally funded community health center, doctors wrote prescriptions for food, insisting to troubled bureaucrats that food was the medically indicated treatment for hunger. Senator Robert F. Kennedy, in a remark that could have applied to enclave rule more generally, said, "This was a condemnation of all of us."[54] These changes reduced the stakes for planters in opposing the state's democratization; for democratizers, they probably also reduced the stakes in securing it.

The Fracturing of the State Party and National Party Relations

As discussed in chapter 9, national party relations constituted a key battleground in blacks' efforts to win incorporation in southern Democratic parties. While South Carolina incorporated blacks and reconciled with the national party quite quickly, in Mississippi, owing to the state's tumultuous democratization, the process was much slower and more contentious.

From 1948 to 1968, Mississippi backed losing presidential candidates. However, enclave rulers retained significant influence within the federal government. In the mid-1950s, Governor Coleman kept the state party loyal to the national ticket. In 1960, Governor Barnett refused to support the Kennedy-Johnson ticket. Coleman strongly backed Kennedy in 1960, which damaged his prospects for reelection in 1963. While South Carolina's white supremacists began working within Republican channels for Nixon in 1960, Mississippi's Barnett led a strong independent electors bid—the state's eight electoral votes went to Virginia Senator Harry Byrd. Nor did Barnett speak for all prominent Democrats, as both Coleman and Senator John Stennis publicly campaigned for Kennedy.[55] By the Freedom Summer of 1964, the combination of the intervention at Oxford, the national party's support of civil rights, and a new mobilization of black Mississippi transformed relations with national Democrats.

In fall 1963 black Mississippians organized an amazing protest and display of their potential political power through the "Freedom Vote." This mock election, in which more than eighty thousand blacks participated (about 16 percent of the state's black voting-age population), featured a campaign of stump speeches by candidates. Over a three-day period, blacks and some whites voted in churches, grocery stores, pool halls, and beauty parlors. In doing so, they refuted many white politicians' claims that Mississippi blacks were uninterested in political participation, as well as meeting organizers' goal of using the campaign to coordinate local protest in service of a statewide movement.[56]

Building on this demonstration, black activists developed the Mississippi Freedom Democratic Party (MFDP). Composed of COFO-affiliated activists, Freedom Democrats attempted to participate in the regular party's precinct meetings, county conventions, and state convention. Barred from most party precinct meetings and thus from all district conventions and the state convention, the MFDP developed a parallel structure. It organized county conventions in thirty-five of eighty-two counties, a state convention with some three hundred delegates, and then challenged the seating of the regular party's delegation at the National Convention in Atlantic City.[57]

The Freedom Democrats—a biracial movement—claimed to be Mississippi's "true" state party of Democrats. The state's "regulars," they argued, lost claim to this mantle by blocking black participation in party primaries and meetings, rejecting the national party platform, and remaining devoted to white supremacy. The regular party responded with a court injunction blocking the use of the name "Democrats" in the Freedom Democrats' activities. Mississippi's regulars sent an uncommitted and unpledged slate of delegates to Atlantic City. It was likely that the white supremacist regulars would then approve a slate of electors backing the Republican nominee, Senator Barry Goldwater.[58]

The Johnson White House wanted above all to avoid a floor flight over credentials challenges that might trigger the exit of several southern delegations and divide the party. However, accepting the racist southern delegations might risk mutinies by northern delegations. On the night of riveting televised testimony by Sunflower County sharecropper and Freedom Democrat leader Fannie Lou Hamer, a momentarily distraught President Johnson drafted a speech announcing his decision not to accept his party's nomination.[59]

Mississippi's DNC committeeman, E. K. Collins, denied there were any racial barriers to party participation, denounced Freedom Democrats as "these power-hungry soreheads," and pleaded, "You will kill our party if you do not seat the lawful delegation from Mississippi." National leaders fashioned a compromise that called for Mississippi regulars to be seated if they promised to back the national party ticket. The sixty-six Freedom Democrats would then "be welcomed as honored guests" at the convention, and two of their leaders would serve as "delegates-at-large" (and would therefore be barred from speaking or voting). Convention delegates backed the compromise, as did King, Bayard Rustin, and others. However, SNCC and CORE leaders, such as Robert Moses, John Lewis, and James Forman, opposed it; the MFDP rejected it as unjust and condescending. The Freedom Democrats were deeply angered and disappointed, and many retired from activism. Others would soon swear off any further efforts to seek incorporation into the regular state party; instead they would go it alone. But for now, the organization campaigned for Johnson, and would continue to challenge others for possession of the party label.

The state's regulars also rejected the proposed settlement, and all but three returned home.[60] Governor Johnson announced from Jackson that "Mississippi's debt to the national Democratic party is now paid in full," and that the state party could endorse whomever it liked.[61] Johnson eventually endorsed George Wallace. After the election, House Democrats stripped U.S. House member John Bell Williams of his seniority on the Commerce Committee for backing Goldwater. But the rest of the congressional delegation stuck with President Johnson.[62]

After the state backed Goldwater by huge margins (87 percent, the identical share of the vote received by the Dixiecrat ticket in 1948), the fissuring of the ruling party continued. In the summer of 1965 liberal and moderate whites, and blacks associated with the NAACP, joined with state AFL-CIO officials to form the Mississippi Democratic Conference (MDC).[63] The MDC, these activists hoped, would serve as the state's loyalist Democratic party, distinct from both the white supremacist "rump" party of regulars and the more radical—and almost all-black—Freedom Democrats. As state AFL-CIO president Claude Ramsay noted, the "MDC is not in competition with the Democratic party. None exists. The Conference will fill the void."[64] Soon the MDC folded, however, having failed to win enough White House backing given Johnson's concern about angering the state's senators, and also after the financially strapped AFL-CIO could no longer help fund it. More importantly, almost three-quarters white, the MDC failed to secure sufficient support from blacks.

A coalition of white liberals and moderates and some NAACP leaders then battled the Freedom Democrats over possession of the official charter of the Young Democrats, which communicated the imprimatur of the national party. The former eventually won it, and then received some assistance from the DNC and the White House and seemed to secure "veto power" over federal patronage. Joining with older national liberal organizations that sought to isolate SNCC, COFO, and the Freedom Democrats, the White House helped transfer a large patronage source—most of the network of Head Start centers around the state—out of the hands of the MFDP to the Young Democrats.[65]

For the White House, if the MFDP became the "official" Democratic party, the state—and its powerful federal officeholders—would be lost forever.[66] While recognition by the DNC as the state's official "Young Democrats" hardly constituted control of the ruling party, it did give its activists "both visibility and an organizational base from which to operate" in the longer battle to become the state's official Democratic party.[67]

Chaos began to reign. Multiple slates of candidates vied for office; some ran as traditional Democrats. Others—usually Delta blacks—ran as independents affiliated with the Freedom Democrats in general elections against "regular" Democrats. Still others competed in local and state legislative primaries as "loyalist" Democrats.[68] Eventually reaching something akin to a noncompetition agreement, the MFDP focused on the Delta, while the loyalists focused on the River counties to the southwest.

Although the white supremacist rump party did not receive the DNC's convention invitation or select DNC members, it elected all statewide and federal candidates using the "Democratic" label, and thus controlled most federal patronage. Stunned by the treatment they received at the hands of the national party, and appalled by the "communistic" stances taken by the Freedom Democrats, most local and county officials rejected the incorporation of blacks into the state party. Mississippi's "Democratic Party" was no longer a coherent entity, but a set of ambitious politicians, activists, and voters divided by race, ideology, and geography.[69]

At the end of his term (1963–67), Governor Johnson stood with those regulars who remained loyal to the national party. However, hardline segregationist and former U.S. House member John Bell Williams captured the governor's mansion. He, like Johnson before him, surprised observers by calling for a rapprochement with Washington: "Whether we like it or not, federal aid and . . . programs have become a way of life in America." He also denounced white supremacist violence and sought a Mississippi that had seen "its last rebellion against lawful authority."[70]

Securing token representation at the state party convention in 1968, national party loyalists sought to induce Williams's noncompliance with the national party's Special Equal Rights Committee (SERC). He in effect agreed, refusing to name any blacks among the at-large delegates to the convention in Chicago. Instead, he named whites loyal to George Wallace or a favorite-son candidate. That summer, the "Loyal Democrats of Mississippi" formed, as the NAACP-Young Democrats grouping reconciled with remnants of the Freedom Democrats and AFL-CIO. The Loyal Democrats held conventions in seventy-two of the state's eighty-two counties, and won recognition in Chicago as the official Democratic party of Mississippi; more than one-half of its delegates were black. At the National Convention, the party kept its promise from 1964 and sent home the regular delegation, as well as one-half of Georgia's delegation. Governor Williams refused to attend, announcing that "Mississippi, as far as I am concerned, is no longer associated with the national Democratic party. . . . I don't think we can continue to call ourselves Democrats . . . at least not in the sense that we are part of the national Democratic party."[71] Thus, Williams backed compliance with the Civil Rights Act and other federal directives, but—heavily influenced by local politicians and his own experiences—chose estrangement over reconciliation.

After returning from Chicago, the regular Democrats announced their full support for George Wallace's candidacy. For these regulars, three options remained open: they could switch parties, reconcile with the national party by incorporating blacks, or continue to muddle through "as an independent state Democratic party of white people, tolerating [blacks] only when [necessary]." Most regulars took the third path, as the regular party secured the nomination of every candidate for statewide office—all of them successful—and controlled most federal patronage.[72] Most important, as a group clearly distinct from national party liberals, regular Democrats could continue to win the support of racially resentful white voters. Meanwhile, from 1968 to 1972, the loyalists, led by the NAACP's Aaron Henry, won national party recognition as the only official Democratic party organization.[73]

In 1971, Mississippi elected a fairly moderate governor, William Waller, who won out over the loyalist-nominated Charles Evers. There was no Republican challenger. Waller, like Johnson before him, hailed from the group of regulars who remained loyal to the national party. Calling for a reunification of the state party and thus a reconciliation with the national party, Waller called himself "a national Democrat" and called for granting leadership positions in the rump party to blacks. The rump party could not agree on terms of a merger, however.

While the party remained fractured, the loyalists drafted a new party constitution in 1970 with the help of the national party. In doing so, they were one of the first state Democratic parties to be ruled in full compliance with party reforms.[74] At the same time, state officials refused to recognize this grouping as the state's official party. But the regulars had under Waller's leadership begun substantial reforms, including beginning the desegregation of state government and attracting large numbers of blacks to the regulars' precinct meetings. Waller also won agreement from the then-all-white SDEC to enlarge it and reserve new spots for blacks. The segregationist party chair was replaced with a more moderate white.

In their negotiations with the regulars to rebuild the state party, the loyalists demanded that the state begin a rapid desegregation of its public sector by hiring blacks "at a 2-to-1 ratio in state employment until equity" was achieved.[75] At the time, only about 6 percent of state employees were black, while the state remained more than one-third black. Title VII's extension to state and local governments was welcome, but its weak enforcement mechanisms meant that this vestige of enclave rule would be slow to reform in the absence of electoral motivations for conservative white Democrats (see the discussion of South Carolina later in this chapter).

Negotiations still failed to unite the party. In a lawsuit over the party label, southern politics provided yet another irony. Loyalists—the descendants of black activists who exploited *Smith v. Allwright*—argued in court that federal courts had no jurisdiction over party affairs, and the regulars—now on the outs with the national party for eight years—pleaded in federal court for formal recognition as the state party of Mississippi. At the 1972 National Convention in Miami, the Credentials Committee again recognized a delegation of biracial loyalists led by Aaron Henry. In a sign that, while reconciliation with the national party remained ongoing, Mississippi's democratic transition was wrapping up, Governor Waller disavowed the party's past.[76] Finally, in 1975, loyalists and regulars hammered out a settlement. Envisioning a tough reelection fight, Senator Eastland welcomed the changes. In 1976 the national party credentialed Mississippi "regulars" for the first time since 1960. After twelve long years of disarray, Mississippi Democrats finally pieced themselves back together.[77]

Black Candidacies Inside and Outside the Party

As Mississippi's Democratic party split into three groupings, black activists ran for local, county, statewide, and federal offices through affiliations with both the Freedom Democrats and the MDC/loyalists. Freedom Democrat Party (FDP) candidates usually ran in general elections as independent candidates, while loyalists ran in Democratic primaries. Often, black candidates finished first in a Democratic primary, only to lose in a runoff against a white candidate. In 1967 Robert Clark, an FDP candidate from Holmes County, won a seat in the lower chamber of the state legislature, becoming the state's first modern-era black legislator, and soon Mississippi's unofficial "black governor."[78]

Charles Evers garnered great influence through extensive voter registration campaigns in southwest Mississippi. In 1971 he mounted an impressive if unsuccessful campaign for governor representing not the Freedom Democrats but the loyalists. His candidacy galvanized blacks throughout the state, and black voter registration surged again. Three hundred and nine black candidates ran for office, 191 of them outside the Democratic party, and fifty-one won their races, though these were usually minor, local positions. Legendary activist John Lewis remarked that Mississippi had "the most politically aware black people in the nation."[79]

Shut out of the "regular" wing of the party, blacks faced serious obstacles as independents. In 1966 the legislature passed an open primary law that would have placed all candidates into a single "primary" with a majority-vote requirement. In this way, an independent black candidate could not exploit a split between white candidates in the two major parties and win office. Given that many loyalist candidates ran as independents because regulars dominated Democratic primaries, "the open primary law would virtually assure their defeat by forcing them into a large primary field, and if victorious there, into a runoff election which would most probably materialize into a solid bloc vote." However, Johnson vetoed it. Williams signed the law four years later. By this time, the state had fifty black elected officials, the third most in the South, and Evers had recently scared the regulars with a strong bid for a U.S. House seat. Loyalists quickly filed suit and a federal judicial panel struck down the open primary law. The law signaled two important (and related) phenomena. First, it illustrated the regulars' serious efforts to weaken candidacies from outside their grouping. Second, it pointed to the weakness of the state's Republican party. As discussed later, South Carolina Democrats, facing a very different electoral landscape, were attempting at this same time to more tightly *close* party primaries.[80]

Over time, these barriers receded. In 1975 Evers endorsed white populist Cliff Finch, a Democratic regular, in the party's primary. In a sign of the unification of the party, Finch won twenty-three of twenty-five majority-black counties, despite the appearance of an independent black candidacy in the general election. As table 9.5 shows, Mississippi led the Deep South in black officeholding.[81]

Delayed Black Incorporation, Delayed Republican Growth

As left-wing black candidates challenged white Democrats in primary and general elections, and as Democratic regulars continued to remain outside the national party, it became well-nigh impossible for Mississippi Republicans to liken white Democrats to the party, and politics, of Hubert Humphrey and George McGovern. The delayed reunification of Mississippi Democrats substantially slowed the development of Mississippi Republicanism.

In 1963 state Republicans challenged the Democrats in the state's first semicompetitive, two-party gubernatorial race of the twentieth century. Republican nominee Rubel Phillips garnered 38 percent of the vote by running as a white supremacist. The election galvanized the state's voters; turnout in the general election increased 600 percent over the uncontested 1959 race. In 1964 the party captured its first congressional seat since Reconstruction. The state's top Republicans disagreed on the nature of its appeals and electoral strategies. In the summer of 1965, as Congress put the finishing touches on the Voting Rights Act, Governor Johnson called a special session to remove constitutional provisions restricting suffrage on the hope that doing so might help the state avoid the deployment of federal examiners. The state's Republican chair, Wirt Yerger, opposed the removal of these provisions in the upcoming constitutional referendum. However, Rubel Phillips backed their removal in a joint appeal with Johnson on statewide television. Voters agreed with Phillips and Johnson by a three-to-one margin.[82]

By 1966—as black incorporation failed to occur, and the regular Democratic party nominated highly conservative candidates—it was increasingly evident that Republicans had nowhere to run. A new Republican party chair began criticizing regular Democrats from the racial left.[83] In the 1967 gubernatorial race, black votes became important for the first time. Phillips ran again for governor, but now did so as a racial moderate well to the left of the Democrats' John Bell Williams. He stumped for black votes and attacked white Democrats for their obsession with safeguarding the state's "sovereignty." The Freedom Democrats endorsed him. As one observer noted, Mississippi Republicans were now "much closer to the national Democrats than the Mississippi Democrats." Phillips also backed more educational spending, compliance with Department of Health, Education, and Welfare desegregation directives, as well as political reforms, including a merit system for state employees and the abolition of the fee system for sheriffs.

Phillips's campaign netted just 30 percent of the vote, and performed best in urban precincts. Republican party identification among the state's whites stood at 6 percent.[84] Such floundering would continue. For instance, in 1972, the Nixon administration campaigned strenuously for the reelection of embattled Democratic senator Jim Eastland against Gil Carmichael, a racially moderate Republican whom the Committee to Re-elect the President blocked from the platform when Vice President Spiro Agnew visited the state.[85]

A Protracted Democratization

Mississippi, despite the best intentions of many of its state officials, failed to escape the doghouse it had built for itself. By unwittingly inducing a set of massive federal and civil rights interventions, ruling politicians were unable to prevent black political power from accelerating well past what Delta rulers had any reason to expect. By the time state institutions could be reformed and a more effective policing apparatus put into place, it was too late. Once regular Democrats relented to incorporating blacks into the party, African American political organization had developed such that rulers could not meet their price. Black activists could demand such a price because of their movement, a blend of indigenous and externally supported black insurgency. The movement in Mississippi, John Dittmer writes, "became the strongest and most far-reaching in the South. . . . [I]n no other southern state was mass protest as extensive and as enduring."[86] These dynamics left the regular Democrats as the repository of white racial resentment, and left them also with a party label unblemished by the increasingly liberal national party of Humphrey and McGovern. Republican party-builders, comprising both racist reactionaries and moderate businessmen, had precious few options when it came to position-taking. Processes accelerated by Oxford, in concert with the ways in which the party-state's decentralization frustrated rulers intent on quickly refashioning state capacities, account for the state's protracted democratization.

This argument contrasts with scholarship on Mississippi, which—implicitly or explicitly—endorses a "Mississippi exceptionalist" outlook. Here, the state's protracted democratization is attributed to its status as the worst, or most racist, or most violent state. Chapter 6 offered ample evidence that a series of contingent events—not structural features of the state, such as its political culture or economy—helped produce the fiasco of military intervention. Some may argue, however, that while Oxford was contingent, it was not important in explaining the state's protracted democratization. For example, it could be argued that the events at Oxford did not spark the white supremacist violence in its wake, and that this violence would have occurred in any case. Similarly, it could be argued that the degree of federal oversight in Mississippi was merely an objective response to the state's needs. This is plausible; evidence of the actual decision-making processes of officials at the DOJ and elsewhere regarding oversight of enclave compliance with federal directives is spotty. Still, it is difficult to square this interpretation with the magnitude of the differences among Deep South enclaves discussed in chapter 9.

South Carolina

As historian William C. Hine has remarked, "South Carolina never has been closely associated with the civil rights movement." Indeed, scholars and participants rarely mention the state and its relatively tranquil transition. Many South Carolinians and sympathetic observers credit this outcome to the "dignity" of its leadership, who some consider to have been imbued with "aristocratic ideals and principles." In contrast to such accounts, this study argues that South Carolina's harnessed democratization resulted from a fortuitous set of circumstances propelled in part by the Clemson crisis.[87]

South Carolina's triumphant management of this crisis contributed to two emerging processes. First, the outcome encouraged rulers to continue to accommodate strategically to black insurgency and the Civil and Voting Rights Acts. By doing so, they demobilized organized white supremacists and generally maintained order. Second, the Clemson episode rapidly accelerated the exit of white supremacists from the ruling party into the Republican party, and the incorporation of blacks into the Democratic party.

These processes reinforced one another. Strategic accommodation to black insurgency and federal directives encouraged black politicians to pursue political careers and policy goals within the state Democratic party, thereby speeding the exit of organized white supremacist activists. This exit relieved pressure on the party to defy democratization pressures. Conversely, the departure of these activists and white voters into the Republican party meant that incorporating black elites and voters was an even more urgent task.

As a result of both processes, the state deterred interventions by national black protest organizations, minimized federal oversight, and helped ambitious politicians reconcile with the national party. By the early 1970s, South Carolina's rulers had secured the best deal they could—a harnessed democratization. This was a boon to white Democrats at the time, who both minimized outsiders' oversight of the state's democratization and safeguarded their own careers. In doing so, they fostered their own preferred brand of economic growth while contributing to their party's long-term demise.

The Implementation of Strategic Accommodation

The successful handling of Clemson initiated a self-reinforcing process by which strategic accommodation became the only feasible strategy for state rulers. First, the demonstrated success of rulers' efforts to secure an orderly, if token, desegregation helped legitimate the strategy. And, as chapter 7 described, its effective implementation immediately paid off, as the state received the president's public congratulations and signals of a rapid increase in Department of Defense contracts awarded to South Carolina firms.[88]

Of course, state authorities faced other challenges. In the fall of 1963, the imminent court-ordered desegregation of the state's flagship school, the University of South Carolina (USC), worried state officials. Larger than Clemson and located in Columbia, the state's capital, USC resonated more deeply with the state's whites.[89] In the prelude to its desegregation, students demonstrated, lynching in effigy one of the two entering black students; moreover, unknown assailants bombed the home of one of the students. Signaling the state's determination to deter and repress violence, the National Guard conducted highly public antiriot training in fields near campus. As always, elites privately and publicly justified these efforts as necessary for protecting the state's good name. Eventually, the day in question was one of "orchestrated calm."[90]

After the successful repression of white supremacist disorder at Clemson, governors continued to depend heavily on the State Law Enforcement Division (SLED) to defuse potential problems. The SLED cajoled local authorities to conduct peaceful mass arrests and enforce antidemonstration ordinances. Its deployment of black police officers helped limit violence and deter black direct action protests in Rock Hill, and frustrated Martin Luther King, Jr., and others who expected to induce a violent response by authorities.[91] In such deployments, the SLED drew on its authority to intervene in local jurisdictions, and benefited from the fact that local law enforcement officers were weaker than those elsewhere in the South. As shown in chapter 7, having developed in 1950s to a much greater degree in South Carolina than in Georgia or Mississippi, South Carolina Klans had been weakened by SLED infiltrations and investigations during that decade. The outcome at Clemson further discouraged the Klan's growth, and these organizations never again posed serious threats to law and order.[92]

The maintenance of order in South Carolina was generally successful. As Joseph Luders has found, the state finished the 1960s with the fewest violent clashes in the Deep South. Some observers have used this fact to explain the state's relatively peaceful democratization as stemming from an unusually accommodationist black leadership.[93] The state's remarkable black mobilization in the 1940s casts doubt on this interpretation (see chapter 4). Moreover, the relative lack of violence does not indicate black hesitation to protest. Chapter 7 demonstrates that the state's blacks were as aggressive as those anywhere in trying to exploit opportunities presented by *Brown*. Indeed, a March 1960 demonstration in Orangeburg was at the time the largest southern protest event of the century, and the regionwide Freedom Rides of 1961 grew out of discussions in the state's CORE affiliate.[94]

The limited federal oversight of South Carolina's transition and the low levels of investment by black protest organizations in the state were both consequence and cause of this maintenance of order. As discussed earlier, the presence in the South of federal officials—especially those involved with law enforcement and voting—often sparked great resentment among many whites. However, in part because of the state's well-tended reputation among journalists, federal authorities, and others, South Carolina remained virtually free of them. Only four of the state's forty-six counties ever "hosted" federal examiners, and only two of them did so before 1970—lowcountry Clarendon and Dorchester counties—despite substantial criticism inside and outside the Johnson administration and assaults on indigenous black protest leaders (table 9.3). Actual attempts to disfranchise voters were of course outnumbered by voter dilution efforts, and examples of these in the state proliferate. To take just one example, eleven counties that used single-member districts switched to at-large districting to deter successful black candidacies. However, the DOJ did not subject these changes to pre-clearance, and thus they went into effect.[95] Later, federal judges criticized Attorney General Richard Kleindienst for coddling the state in the reapportionment of its powerful Senate. The Senate did not have to conduct a racially less-discriminatory apportionment until 1983–84, and thus remained all-white until then.[96]

Likewise, as discussed in chapter 9, except for CORE, national black protest organizations largely bypassed the state. As historians of these groups have shown, state officials' effective repression of nonviolent direct action, in addition to substantial pressure from the local NAACP to leave the state, caused these groups to go elsewhere. NAACP field director Rev. "Deke" Newman, former head of the Spartanburg CORE branch during the days of the state repression of the NAACP, told reporters in the early 1960s that there was "no place for CORE" in South Carolina.[97] The state's black protest remained largely in the hands of NAACP activists. Lacking either large, episodic "invasions" such as Mississippi's Freedom Summer, or sustained community organizing campaigns such as SNCC's southwest Georgia project, the slums of Columbia and Charleston and the hunger-wracked stretches of the lowcountry were left basically untouched by outsiders. As with the absence of large numbers of federal authorities, this pattern meant that white supremacist organizations had a more difficult time recruiting members than did those in Mississippi and Georgia. Unsullied by violence and disorder, state leaders could more easily burnish the state's reputation among federal authorities and black protest organizations as having achieved "integration with dignity."[98]

The successful implementation of strategic accommodation allowed South Carolina politicians, in the words of historian Marcia Synnott, to use "their record of compliance to justify tokenism and to limit black gains." The SLED helped enforce municipal antipicketing ordinances, and also discouraged local officials from conducting structured negotiations with demonstrators. In so doing, the state—despite its reputation—did not desegregate its lunch counters, public spaces, restaurants, and hotels much more quickly than more disordered enclaves.[99] And the virtual absence of sustained campaigns by black protest organizations in South Carolina communities slowed the pace of compliance with the Civil Rights Act even further. Like many of the state's cities, Greenville, the center of the fast-growing upcountry, refused several opportunities to accede to protests and court orders, instead choosing to close city pools rather than desegregate them.[100] Similar outcomes occurred in school desegregation, as Charleston's experience demonstrated.[101] The state's reputation would be difficult to change. For the state's most influential black protest leader, the NAACP's "Deke" Newman, remarked that "despite all that might be considered progress in terms of interracial cooperation, beneath the surface South Carolina is just about in the same boat as Alabama and Mississippi."[102]

Partisan Sorting of Elites and Voters

In a second and related process, Clemson rapidly accelerated the entry of black elites and voters into the state Democratic party, as well as the exit of white supremacist organizers into the Republican party. This process, a sequence of intertwined moves and countermoves among important resource-holders, had three important effects on the transition: it increased ruling party cohesion and thus facilitated the use of strategic accommodation; it helped ambitious Democrats reconcile with the national party; and it forced the ruling party to incorporate black elites and voters, further helping minimize outside interference.

Republican growth was an important element of the state's harnessed revolution in that it spurred along black incorporation into the Democratic party as well as reinforced rulers' incentives to accommodate strategically to black insurgents and the central state. Conversely, Republican growth and position-taking were shaped enormously by enclave rulers' choices, as well as those of national Republicans. Goldwater, for instance, undermined the credibility of those (increasingly few) state Republicans, such as Charleston Republican Arthur Ravenel, who crafted appeals to black voters.

Certainly, much of this sorting seems inevitable in retrospect. Eventually, blacks everywhere backed Democratic presidential candidates, and then state Democratic candidates. Additionally, as two-party politics took hold, some number of important white resource-holders within ruling parties would exit for other pastures. However, several key issues remained unknown: *which* Democratic officeseekers, activists, and voters would leave? Would they be those critical in helping the party maintain its hegemonic position in state governance, or—more happily for Democrats sold on strategic accommodation—would it be those who might stymie their ability deftly to manage democratization pressures? Would this exodus occur before decisions critical to navigating the transition had been made, or after? Such matters would prove important in all Deep South transitions.

State governance remained securely in Democratic hands throughout the 1960s. As discussed in chapter 7, Republican activists began resuscitating the moribund state party in the mid-1950s, when voters' support for Republican presidential candidates began. Before Clemson, a confusing mix of anti-Democrats experimented with various party vehicles. As the state Republican party remained centered in the upcountry and turned hard-right for Goldwater in the late 1950s, their overtures to the electorally and organizationally valuable network of well-known White Citizens' Council (WCC) activists were rejected. These lowcountry anti-Democrats preferred to continue to attempt to forge an independent movement.

However, in late 1962, on the eve of the Clemson crisis, the possible marriage of business-focused right-wingers and hardline segregationists within the Republican party became more likely with the U.S. Senate campaign of William D. Workman. Hollings's refusal to stand alongside Mississippi governor Ross Barnett in Oxford greatly angered these activists, and Workman's rock-ribbed defense of white supremacy attracted them.[103] They would later be among those detained on the road to Clemson by SLED personnel. In assisting Workman in his Senate campaign, these activists hedged their bets about the future utility of pursuing their goals within the ruling Democratic party. Soon after Clemson, they switched their party affiliations and began planning their own bids for state and federal office.[104]

This happened for a few reasons. First, their attempts at forming a third party were made more difficult by state laws meant to block new parties. Second, their timing in developing an independent movement unconnected to a national party was unfortunate—they sought to focus on state and local affairs just as voters were increasingly turning toward national politics. By the early 1960s, they led the lowcountry charge in wresting control of the Republican party apparatus from upcountry hard-right businessmen. They were also able to offer the state party their impressive networks of white supremacists and other lowcountry activists, which the Greenville-based party leaders lacked.[105]

As small numbers of prominent white supremacists exited the Democratic party, there commenced an early, if quiet, incorporation of black elites and voters into the state Democratic party. In 1960, after several years of attacks on the NAACP and other black organizations, black voter registration stood at just 16 percent of the state's black voting-age population, and turnout was a good deal lower. This registration level was lower than it had been before *Brown*, and barely surpassed the level reached during the black party mobilization of the 1940s (table 9.4).[106] Soon, however, an impressive series of voter registration drives associated with the Voter Education Project and the NAACP produced large gains. From 1958 to 1962, the number of black registrants in South Carolina increased by almost one-quarter, and grew further still by 1966.[107] Later, it would emerge that state Democrats had made secret cash payments to black religious leaders and also secretly helped fund the state NAACP's voter registration drives.[108] Before the Voting Rights Act, the black share of the electorate had reached 17 percent. Just one year later, additional drives netted another forty-five thousand black registrants, and the black share of the electorate reached 21 percent—and as a share of the Democratic primary electorate it was a good deal larger.[109]

Taking note of these trends, white supremacist Democrats began worrying about surviving Democratic primaries. Leading the pack was U.S. Senator Strom Thurmond. Speaking privately with his confidant and sounding board William Workman, he feared a much more difficult 1966 Democratic renomination because of the "trashy element" now in the primary electorate and mulled over different options. According to Workman's telephone transcript,

> Strom concurs that if the sound people don't vote in Democratic primaries, those primaries will come to reflect the will only of [the] trashy element [and] he fears cannot win nomination if only trashy Democrats vote. [Thurmond] feels that he may have to run by petition in 1966 if this trend continues. [He] suggests [the] desirability of retaining the conservatives in the Democratic party of South Carolina and taking over that party as an entity separate and independent from the national Democratic party. Hints that he possibly would vote with Rep[ublican]s to organize the Senate if conditions warranted. . . . Feels trend will be for Democrats to be put under pressure to be Democrats nationally as well as in State.[110]

Soon thereafter, Thurmond announced his switch to what he called the "Goldwater Republican party" at the height of the 1964 presidential race. However, he was not a party-builder. He maintained a separate campaign organization and finance operation, and in order to avoid alienating voters who wanted to split their tickets, he would not promise to vote for other Republicans.[111] While Thurmond did not transform the state's Republican party—it had already sorted out its ideological and sectional identity by the time he switched—he did encourage other white supremacist Democrats to switch parties, including a member of Congress, Albert Watson (discussed later). By 1967, confounding the usual Outer South/Deep South expectations, the state's Republican party was known nationally as the most effective Republican organization in the region.[112]

If Thurmond was not yet a very loyal South Carolina Republican, he quickly became southern Republicans' most important leader. As Richard Nixon sought the 1968 Republican presidential convention, he faced several challengers, including southern Republican favorite Ronald Reagan. Even if Nixon won the nomination, he also expected to face George Wallace in the general election. In short, he needed help. At a private meeting with Thurmond and a few other Republicans, Nixon apparently offered to fight for several southern Republican policy items in exchange for help with the nomination. These included pressuring DHEW to ease up on southern school districts (noting Columbia's school district in particular), the nomination of pro-southerners for the Supreme Court, regular consultations with southern Republicans, and even help with the state's textile sector. Thurmond did his part, working the phones to ensure that southern delegations stuck with Nixon. He also worked hard to persuade pro-Wallace activists in enough southern states (including his own) to avoid the Wallace temptation and instead back Nixon. Eventually, just four southern states went with Wallace (Alabama, Georgia, Louisiana, and Mississippi).

After Nixon's inauguration, Thurmond's top aide, Harry Dent, became the president's southern adviser. Soon, the White House was referred to by some as "Uncle Strom's Cabin."[113] Dent, speaking before a group of southern Republican party officials, told them, "This Administration has no southern strategy but rather a national strategy which, for the first time in modern times, *includes* the South, rather than *excludes* the South from full and equal participation in national affairs.... The Democrats seem to have written the South out of the Union, but the Republican party is writing the South into the Union on an equal basis."[114]

Nixon was looking ahead, not back—he expected another challenge by Wallace in 1972. Nixon ordered his DHEW secretary, Robert Finch, to personally ensure that any action on school desegregation was "inoffensive to the people of South Carolina."[115] True to his word, for the first time ever, the DOJ began siding with southern school districts.[116] And in another first during the long transition, there were now major divisions between federal agencies and the White House concerning how much compliance the South's democratization actually required, especially with respect to school desegregation and voting rights. Enclave defenders were again exerting influence on the central state, but now were doing so as Republicans.[117]

In 1966, as blacks increasingly participated in Democratic primaries and the suddenly relevant general elections, Democratic gubernatorial candidate Robert McNair reportedly won 99 percent of the black vote.[118] As the most vocal white supremacists began switching parties, the ruling party grew more cohesive, and more and more committed to accommodating democratization pressures. White Democrats remaining in the party were less likely to be ideologically committed to the most virulent white supremacist politics. And as relatively moderate gubernatorial administrations since 1959 routinized interracial elite dialogue and bargaining, and employed similar tactics in responding to external challenges and maintaining order, it became increasingly implausible for the moderating ruling party to change course and return to "massive resistance."

Relations with the National Democratic Party

After the Dixiecrat revolt, South Carolina Democrats continued to have troubled relations with the national party. Governors from 1948 through 1956 attempted to force the state party to endorse different presidential candidates, while loyalists, such as the state's "prime minister," Senator Edgar Brown, worked to block such moves. In 1964 the Mississippi Freedom Democrats challenged that state's delegation to the National Convention in Atlantic City, and, until 1976, blacks and white liberals succeeded in convincing the national party to send home part or all of several southern delegations for failing to incorporate blacks into their parties.

But in South Carolina, the early sorting of white supremacists and blacks out of and into the ruling party helped it reconcile with national Democrats. In 1968, South Carolina's was the only Deep South delegation in Chicago to *avoid* a credentials challenge on the basis of racial discrimination.[119] In both a sign of the state party's reconciliation with the national party, as well as a further incentive to comply quickly and easily, Governor McNair—like Georgia's Ellis Arnall twenty-four years before him—was entertaining hopes of securing a vice-presidential nomination. Instances of gross racial discrimination in party primaries were rare and poorly publicized. Meanwhile, an aging Edgar Brown served on the DNC's Special Equal Rights Committee as it drafted directives later used to unseat southern delegations. South Carolina Democrats were among the first in the South to comply with the McGovern-Fraser reforms.[120]

Meanwhile, Democrats with larger political ambitions both benefited from and advanced a closer relationship with the national party. For instance, in 1970, lowcountry native Senator Ernest Hollings announced, in the fashion of *Casablanca*'s Captain Renault, that "there is substantial hunger in South Carolina. I have seen it with my own eyes." Hollings conducted a highly publicized tour of the most abject areas of the lowcountry, and published a call for a national hunger policy. Here, the democratizing Deep South—discovering and seeking to stamp out extreme hunger, malnutrition, and material deprivation in the stubborn pockets of the South Carolina lowcountry and the Mississippi Delta—seemed to bear out economist

Amartya Sen's claim that famines and democracies are mutually exclusive.[121] Hollings secured enough black votes to serve seven terms in the Senate.[122] Given the greater share of blacks identifying themselves as Democrats, white Democrats had an increasingly difficult time convincing whites resentful of racial equality or federal interventions (or both) that they remained ideologically distinct from "national" Democrats (as discussed later).

South Carolina's Final Crises: Orangeburg, Charleston, and Lamar

Toward the completion of the state's dismantling of Jim Crow and suffrage restriction, South Carolina experienced three crises while Robert McNair served as governor. None knocked the state off its trajectory. However, each illuminates the contingency of the state's strategic accommodation to democratization pressures, as well as the material benefits South Carolina blacks did—and did not—secure through this harnessed democratization.

Robert McNair was governor during six critical years (1965–71). His tenure as governor was preceded by two years as Lieutenant Governor and several terms in the state House. In the House, he was mentored by the long-serving lowcountry Speaker Solomon Blatt. A "moderate" focused on maintaining order and burnishing the state's reputation, McNair was backed by a broad coalition that included lowcountry and upcountry politicians, the state's corporate leaders, and—with the help of the state's top black civil rights attorney, Matthew J. Perry—black voters.[123] Although he garnered a minority of the white vote in his 1966 election, by this point, Republicans needed fully two-thirds of the white vote in order to win statewide elections.[124]

McNair responded to pressure from among the state's black protest leaders—nearly all associated with the NAACP—to secure policy benefits. He attempted to make black appointments to state agencies, but was able to appoint, as he said, only two "tokens" without raising the ire of state legislative leaders. Black leaders were more successful in pressuring him to eliminate racist county-level administration of Aid to Families with Dependent Children. Black enrollment shot up dramatically over the span of just one year. Similarly, they secured from McNair the country's first statewide food stamp program. Starting with twenty thousand recipients in 1967, within seven years it serviced 360,000 South Carolinians.[125] Despite the emergence by the mid-1960s of a fairly solid consensus around strategic accommodation, the state's legislature—still dominated by smaller, rural counties—made some policy changes difficult, such as the reinstatement of the state's compulsory school attendance law.[126]

By 1968, when South Carolina failed to avoid what became known as the "Orangeburg Massacre," black activists had a difficult time getting anyone outside the state to notice.[127] Orangeburg, located in the state's Black

Belt and just one hour from Columbia, was both the "fountainhead of [the state's] white ultraconservativism" and, as home to the black South Carolina State College, the center of black student activism.[128] Politically dominated in the 1950s by a White Citizens' Council (WCC), black protest had been simmering for fifteen years. Now four years after the passage of the Civil Rights Act, many commercial firms and public spaces remained segregated, despite mass demonstrations (one of which led to the arrest of 1,300). Anger at the treatment of black activists by the president of the college sparked a boycott of classes and a march on Columbia. However, nights of street protests ratcheted up student anger. A demonstration calling for the desegregation of All-Star Bowling Lanes culminated in the shooting deaths of three black students by highway patrolmen, as well as many injuries. Governor Robert McNair quickly blamed "black power advocates"—a frame the *New York Times* accepted—and the only person arrested (and later convicted, at McNair's urging) was the SNCC's Cleveland Sellers. McNair had possessed executive authority to force the bowling alley's compliance with Title II of the Civil Rights Act, but had refused to use it.[129] After Martin Luther King, Jr., was murdered, the ensuing nationwide riots left the Orangeburg killings lost in the shuffle of a very chaotic year.[130]

By this time, a larger, protracted, and more serious crisis had already begun. Low-income hospital workers at the state's Medical College and Charleston County Hospitals would eventually bring the city to a halt in one of the most tense labor confrontations in the South since the 1930s.

The state's commitment to oppose the unionization of its workers had long been a chief selling point in its industrial recruitment efforts. Anti-unionism also served as glue uniting upcountry industrialists and textile mill owners with their counterparts in the lowcountry. After the sluggish 1950s, the state was now on a roll. While the mid-1960s were years of sharp economic growth nationally, South Carolina's growth was even more impressive. Capital investment almost doubled from 1964 to 1966 to $911 million ($6.5 billion in 2013 dollars). Sparked by Michelin, Hoechst, and several other German firms, annual foreign direct investment entering into the Palmetto state almost quadrupled from 1963 (the year of Clemson's desegregation) to 1966. Per capita income increased 40 percent from 1960 to 1965.[131] These successes made developing an elite political consensus much easier. As a member of the General Assembly, McNair had sponsored the state's 1954 right-to-work legislation. He saw no reason to change course now and make concessions to workers.

At stake in the Charleston crisis was whether public sector workers could organize and strike. An even larger, unspoken issue was whether a major city could be left at the mercy of black protesters.[132] The city's largest employer, the Medical College and Charleston County Hospitals, were completely segregated, poorly run institutions (by whites only) that offered quite subpar care to their black patients and below minimum-wage pay to their unskilled, predominantly black workers. Trouble brewed for more than a year after workers and sympathizers began holding weekly meetings to discuss calls to reinstate a group of fired employees. Soon the meetings grew to more than four hundred participants who now called for higher wages and union recognition. The killings at Orangeburg further fueled activists' anger.

The workers faced off against a hostile city, including an unsupportive stratum of better-off blacks who had a long-established accommodation with the city's white leadership. Governor McNair's ham-fisted efforts to negotiate a settlement failed. McNair declared—falsely—that public sector unions were prohibited by state law.[133] In 1969, some thirteen months after workers first began agitating for better treatment, the hospital fired twelve key workers, including the group's emerging leader, veteran activist Mary Moultrie. The next day, the workers struck, demanding union recognition and the reinstatement of the twelve fired workers.

The confrontation grew much larger in scope, and the stakes grew higher as well, as a New York City hospital workers' union helped organize the strike. Even more important, the Southern Christian Leadership Conference, then floundering in the wake of King's assassination and the unsuccessful Poor People's Campaign, decided to intervene and expand the confrontation. Soon, the SCLC organized a boycott of Charleston, a strike by schoolchildren, and several other efforts intended, in the words of Andrew Young, to keep "the city on edge." The city and state responded to mass marches with the state's first dusk-to-dawn curfew since World War II, and with the deployment of more than one thousand National Guardsmen with fixed bayonets.

Eventually, DHEW brokered a compromise that was intended to halt the strike and reinstate the fired workers. At the eleventh hour, however, South Carolina Republicans successfully pressured the Nixon administration to rescind the proposal. Two more increasingly tense weeks followed. More than one thousand marchers were arrested, and firebombs lit up Charleston's night sky. South Carolina's ruling politicians, including Governor McNair, believed that there was a good chance that the city would "burn." Finally, Nixon officials forged another agreement, and the crisis ended. The administration and the state had achieved their two shared goals; in Harry Dent's words, these were blocking unionization and ridding the state of the SCLC.[134]

Charleston's black community experienced a sudden rise in voter registration and soon elected the state's first black state legislator in seven decades. Not unlike other earlier citywide campaigns throughout the South, however, protesters did not win their main demands. Besides illustrating to a national audience the hollowness of the state's strategic accommodation, the episode also highlighted the limits of the state's vaunted capacity for crisis management and for understanding black insurgency.

Throughout the crisis, McNair's reliance on existing channels with older members of black Charleston stymied productive communication. As in the case of Orangeburg, by limiting dialogue to NAACP staffers, he misread the situation. Finally, the episode pointed to a strange dynamic toward the end of the region's democratization, especially after Nixon's ascension to the White House in 1969: South Carolina's ruling party no longer had a monopoly on what counted as "responses" to pressures from within and without the state. While Governor McNair and other Democrats issued statements, organized talks, secured court injunctions against strikers, and deployed troops, state Republican officials were now in the position of winning—even if temporarily—reprieves from co-partisans in a friendly administration.

Still, Orangeburg and Charleston did not much alter the trajectory of South Carolina's democratization. One can imagine that they would have been of greater importance if they had occurred earlier, before the self-reinforcing processes of partisan sorting and rulers' cohesion around strategic accommodation had advanced. Of course, the fact that they occurred in the late 1960s was itself in large measure the product of rulers' behavior. After all, there had been years of foot-dragging at local and state levels such that much of commercial Orangeburg remained out of compliance with public accommodations laws; resistance to higher education reforms (affecting both South Carolina State College in Orangeburg and the Charleston Medical College); and resistance to the desegregation of all-white public sectors in Charleston and beyond. These episodes occurred several years after the Clemson crisis, and the state's harnessed revolution was basically accomplished by 1968 with state Democrats' acceptance of a racially inclusionary state party. Still, if these events—especially those in Charleston—had produced mass bloodshed, it is possible to imagine that the self-reinforcing process by which rulers became increasingly committed to strategic accommodation might have been short-circuited in ways that would have affected the final key moment in the state's transition: the conflicts over school desegregation of 1970.

In February 1970, federal courts forced hundreds of southern school districts to implement immediately desegregation plans "in the largest single transition of the *Brown* era."[135] Two were in South Carolina: the upcountry booming city of Greenville, and the declining lowcountry county of Darlington. Greenville, under the leadership of a moderate Republican mayor and with the backing of a broad coalition of civic and business leaders, seemed to possess many of the advantages of a metro area in the Sunbelt Outer South. Still, white opponents to peaceful desegregation organized. A future two-term Republican governor, evangelical Christian Carroll A. Campbell, petitioned Governor McNair to nullify the court order. For good measure, he led a motorcade "of several thousand parents" to Columbia for a rally. More than 100,000 whites signed Campbell's petition for the cause. However, in Greenville "the center held." National media covered the first day of school and applauded the city as it peacefully reassigned twelve thousand students and five hundred teachers.[136]

But days later in Darlington County, likely Republican gubernatorial nominee, U.S. House member Albert Watson, delivered a scorching speech in which he demanded that the assembled segregationists "stand up and use every means at your disposal" to block the desegregation of the county's schools. The next day, a white crowd of about two hundred in Darlington's county seat of Lamar gathered under the watchful eye of a cordon of fifty highway patrolmen in riot gear. As three buses of black teenagers approached the school, the crowd attacked the patrolmen and the buses with ax handles, mace, and homemade clubs. Responding with tear gas, the patrolmen rescued the children just before two buses were turned on their side. Authorities closed the schools, another group of angry whites continued its boycott of public schools, and Nixon, McNair, and most of the state's political establishment denounced the incident.[137]

Tensions concerning court-ordered school desegregation continued throughout 1970 amid the state's first seriously contested, two-party gubernatorial election of the twentieth century. The race gave voters a clear choice, not an echo, as it pitted Albert Watson against Democrat John West. West had already developed a reputation as a racial moderate after becoming Lieutenant Governor in 1967.[138]

By 1970, Democrats made public appeals to now more-mobilized black voters, who composed one-quarter of the state's electorate.[139] However, black incorporation in the ruling party remained incomplete. Younger black activists organized the United Citizens Party (UCP) in 1969 in response to Democrats' resistance to nominating black candidates for local, county, or state legislative seats. Democrats thought that Republicans quietly funded the 1970 gubernatorial campaign of a UCP candidate.[140] Given that the influential NAACP and black church leadership was tightly linked to the Democratic party, UCP activists could not convince sufficient numbers of black voters to withhold their support from the Democrats. Thus, unlike other southern black parties, the UCP had little chance to grow.[141]

In an effort to avoid electorally costly movements such as the UCP, state Democrats at their 1970 convention took several steps to cement black incorporation into the party. Blacks comprised about two hundred of the convention's nine hundred delegates, and helped elect a black vice chair. Along with a few white liberals, they also helped defeat a plank of the platform that praised the token compliance of "freedom-of-choice" school desegregation. Most significantly, later that year, eight black candidates for the General Assembly were "sponsored" by party leaders, and three won seats.[142] Eventually, West drew the support of about 90 percent of black voters, who black groups effectively mobilized. Watson received almost 60 percent of white votes, but West triumphed.[143]

The West Administration and South Carolina's Democratization

During the West administration (1971–75), South Carolina completed its democratization. Beginning with his inaugural address, West committed the state rhetorically and substantively to dismantle racist state institutions and pushed the state party further in incorporating black elites and voters. For Senator Hollings, West "really talked like a Governor leading his people rather than like the head of a militia defending them against Washington."[144] A former state senator, West was well placed to exploit the cohesiveness of party-state institutions to secure meaningful democratic and racial reforms.

These included the desegregation of state agencies, crafting affirmative action programs, appointing black judges, and enhancing poverty programs. West also spearheaded efforts to reorganize the Senate and secure home rule for counties.[145] Perhaps his most important legacy was the Human Affairs Commission, which, when vested with subpoena powers, soon became one of the country's most powerful antidiscrimination agencies. Although compliance was often spotty, by the end of West's term, black employees made up more than one-quarter of the state administration (compared to 6 percent in Mississippi). Among the Deep South states, because of state Democrats' incorporation of black elites and voters, South Carolina advanced the furthest in dismantling white-only public sectors. West also continued to foster informal channels for interracial elite bargaining. Importantly, he expanded the range of black voices to be considered when engaging in "interracial dialogue." The Commission included Bill Saunders, a black power activist in Charleston who was centrally involved in the hospital strike. These and other accomplishments earned him national praise, and soon his name crossed the lips of national party leaders in discussions of possible 1972 vice-presidential nominees.[146]

A Harnessed Revolution

Among the southern democratizations, the gap between reputation (securing "integration with dignity") and reality was perhaps largest in South Carolina.[147] Through the interaction of the two processes described, the Clemson crisis facilitated the state's smooth democratization experience. In limiting outside intervention, peacefully repressing indigenous black protest, slowing the pace of desegregation, generally maintaining order, and taking short-term steps that benefited their own careers, South Carolina Democrats harnessed the revolution. The performance of compliance brought many returns to white Democratic officeholders. They could take credit for maximizing state autonomy from the worst of federal and black protest groups' interference, and effectively position themselves as worthy of the continued support of conservative whites as well as blacks.

State Democrats worked hard to limit the political damage done by their early and relatively smooth incorporation of blacks. In order to convince white voters that the state party had not surrendered to the national party's racial liberalism, they took several effective formal and informal steps to deter large black participation in primaries (which would have resulted in more liberal nominees), maximize this participation in general elections, and deter black candidacies. Statewide Democratic candidates attracted a minority of white voters from 1966 on, but almost always compensated with sufficient black support.

As a sop to black leaders frustrated by the state's lack of black officeholding (see table 9.5), the party appointed a black vice-chair, and named famed black civil rights attorney Matthew Perry as the state's Democratic National Committeeman. While three blacks won seats in the General Assembly (the state legislature's lower chamber) in 1970, only when federal courts required the use of single-member districts in 1974 did black representation in the General Assembly begin in earnest. The more powerful Senate divided itself into fifteen multimember senatorial districts, all with white majorities. The chamber was the South's last to move to single-member districting, and (thus) the last to desegregate—almost two decades after the Supreme Court's reapportionment decisions.[148]

Some Democratic party leaders were aware that the state's democratization experience might advantage Republicans over the long term. Party chair Don Fowler observed, "Some in the party saw what was happening," but, as former lieutenant governor Earle Morris noted, there was virtually no discussion about the party's longer-term future.[149] Instead, concern about the impact of black candidacies on the party's reputation occurred only in the context of incumbents' worrying about their own careers. For the entire decade, politicians in decision-making bodies acted on their own individual interests. They did so effectively, but established harmful legacies for future users of the "Democrat" label, as chapter 11 argues.[150]

Chapter 7 already considered the argument that Clemson was not a contingent outcome but was determined instead by an antecedent condition: the state's political culture. It could be argued instead that, while Clemson was a contingent outcome, it was irrelevant for the state's transition, which had other causes. Possible here is the argument that rulers' strategic accommodation was motivated by the need to incorporate blacks into the party quickly because of growing competition with state Republicans. However, at the time of planning for Clemson's desegregation, blacks had no significant role in the party, and lowcountry white supremacist activists had not yet abandoned the ruling party for the Republicans. Instead, motivations for an orderly desegregation were articulated privately among politicians and pointed to a combination of state elites' economic priorities as well as their own career goals. An alternative argument, sometimes advanced by historians, holds that the state's relatively placid transition is best attributed to the moderate nature of the state's black protest leadership. This chapter has considered counterarguments to the view that black protest in the state was timid. But if this position were accurate, it would be necessary to explain how the state's protest leadership moved from bold and provocative in the 1940s to cautious in the 1960s. Doing so would ultimately mean identifying causal forces during the transition, and returning our attention to the dynamics of regime change offered in this study.

Georgia

On duty when the shock of *Brown v. Board of Education* occurred, Georgia's Talmadgeite faction pursued a massive resistance policy that undermined black insurgency and limited the executive's range of options in education policy. Meanwhile, older, tactically cautious black elites had cemented an early accommodation with the city's business establishment and white middle class. The state's vacillating governor allowed UGA's desegregation to become an embarrassment for north Georgia. The aftermath of the crisis, in concert with federal courts' abolition of the county-unit system in 1962, sharpened sectional conflict within the party.

On the eve of the Civil Rights and Voting Rights Acts, Georgia's bifurcated democratization had begun to take shape. Georgia rulers north of the fall line avoided massive federal oversight of their compliance with landmark legislation, quickly incorporated black elites, and reconciled with the national party. Leading Democrats in south Georgia's Black Belt defied federal directives, presided over a disorderly and violent period, and advocated abandoning the national party. While they encountered some interventions by national black protest organizations, south Georgia rulers did not face the sustained challenges facilitated by north Georgia's black activists that they might have expected.

This bifurcated democratization generated legacies that continue to shape the state's politics and economics. Today the state faces a "two Georgias" problem, as the socioeconomic development of north and south Georgia has continued to diverge. Chapter 11 suggests that this divergence grows in part out of the state's navigation of its turbulent transition, not merely from socioeconomic differences unrelated to the politics of regime change.

Ruling Party Factions on the Eve of
Landmark National Legislation

From 1940 to 1960 the urban share of the state's population rose from 34 to 55 percent, as the state's largest cities grew and—as occurred everywhere in the South—its Black Belt declined in population. By 1960, fully one-third of the state's population resided in metro Atlanta.[151] The eight largest counties comprised 41 percent of the state's population, but only 12 percent of its county-unit votes, while the 121 least populous counties had 32 percent of the population but 59 percent of the unit vote. Under the system, while the state remained an effectively one-party regime, metro voters—including the growing number of black voters—had little influence in statewide elections and little impact on state legislative elections.[152] Even Georgia's congressional representation was shaped by the county-unit system, as primaries for several of them used the system.[153]

At the dawn of the 1960s the Talmadge faction lumbered along, bringing together rural politicians and county courthouse cliques benefiting from the status quo, those who placed a higher premium on maintaining white supremacy, and those involved in economic sectors less sensitive to the perceptions of audiences "abroad." It drew electoral support from poorer white farmers and white working-class voters in the cities.[154]

The state's fastest-growing manufacturing areas lay in north Georgia. By 1960 the urban-rural divide in Georgia's politics remained sharp, and the malapportionment structuring Georgia's legislature and statewide elections was even more pronounced, as nonnative Georgians (at this date most of whom were southerners from other states) poured into cities and suburbs, and the population of the countryside began a steep decline. However, the political split in Georgia was sectional as well as urban/rural. For instance, as chapter 8 demonstrated, rural and small-town whites in north Georgia frequently opposed the Talmadge faction, especially when it seemed to overstep in its massive resistance to democratization pressures.[155]

As described in chapter 8, the ruling party's anti-Talmadge faction failed to recover from the elections of the late 1940s and remained disorganized throughout the 1950s. However, as metro Atlanta and its growing middle and upper-middle classes and business firms more tightly bound themselves to the national and international economies, anti-Talmadgeites began to confront seriously the possibility of the closing of the state's schools. Mobilizing for collective action through the Sibley Commission, HOPE, the Southern Regional Council, and other groups, Atlanta's Mayor Hartsfield and other officials successfully campaigned statewide to convince state legislators and community elites of the virtues of orderly compliance with token levels of court-ordered desegregation. In doing so they finally dragged along the city's surprisingly laggard "business moderates" (see chapter 8).[156]

In 1960 the city's white leaders prepared for the imminent court-ordered desegregation of its primary and secondary schools. Moreover, Governor Vandiver's handling of the January 1961 UGA crisis clarified the growing differences in how leading politicians in north and south Georgia assessed the costs of massive resistance; north Georgia politicians grew increasingly restive about the continued leadership by the Talmadge faction—even with the "respectable" Vandiver at the helm.[157]

The Death of Malapportionment and the County-Unit System

As the state's cities and suburbs grew in population, the importance of the county-unit system as the bulwark of white, rural power grew along with it.[158] Still, metro politicians with dreams of winning the governorship or other statewide offices had to continue to defend the system publicly, even as they privately supported lawsuits against it.[159] Throughout the 1940s and 1950s, constitutional challenges to the county-unit system were defeated by the Court's diffidence about entering the "political thicket" of questions it considered best left to other branches of government.[160] In 1962, soon after *Baker v. Carr* sounded the death knell of legislative malapportionment, a federal judicial panel outlawed the county-unit system (which, as shown in chapter 3, was keyed to the apportionment of the state's General Assembly). Georgia had entered a "new political age."[161]

The abolition of the county-unit system had several major consequences. First, since the state's powerful governor would be nominated by popular vote, the governor could now avoid being encumbered by the state's rural counties—most of which were below the fall line. Second, just before *Baker v. Carr* was announced, Deep South malapportionment remained extreme, and Georgia led the way. Just 23 percent of the state's population would be needed to secure a majority in the House, compared to 29 percent for Mississippi's House, and 46 percent for South Carolina's (see chapter 3).[162] With reapportionment, the center of gravity in both chambers would swing toward metro Georgia and its suburbs—this meant the first appearance in real numbers of black Democratic and white Republican contestation of state legislative elections.[163] Third, this combination meant that the balance of power within the ruling party would also shift toward metro Georgia. Rulers now could rely on an executive and legislature both more willing and more able to accommodate strategically to democratization challenges. Several institutional reforms that would have been impossible during the "rule of the rustics"—particularly those that weakened county officials, such as the centralization of the state's coercive apparatus—were now within the realm of possibility. The lobby of county commissioners, and the strength of individual courthouse cliques, had been permanently weakened.[164]

In 1962, for the first time since 1908, statewide officials would be nominated by popular vote, and black voters would influence the proceedings. At this time about 30 percent of black voters were registered, and they comprised about 14 percent of registered voters. The differences between the two major candidates in the Democratic primary made clear the importance of the timing of the abolition of the county-unit system, arriving as it did before the state had to confront questions of compliance with landmark federal legislation.[165]

The Talmadge wing of the party put forward former governor Marvin Griffin, the buffoonish white supremacist who had presided over four unusually corrupt years of massive resistance in the mid-1950s. That the faction cohered around Griffin suggested that it was nearing exhaustion after the twin blows of the UGA crisis and the death of its crown jewel, the county-unit system.[166] The second major candidate was Carl Sanders, a young Augusta attorney who had served as Vandiver's floor leader in the Senate. Sanders was a "practical segregationist" of the kind who led Mississippi in the late 1950s (Coleman) and South Carolina in the early 1960s (Hollings).[167] As Sanders described himself, "In my case 'moderate' means that I am a segregationist but I am not a damned fool." One of only two Vandiver aides who had favored keeping UGA open, Sanders campaigned on the need for reforming state agencies, attracting industrial development, improving public education, and forging a positive, investment-friendly reputation for the state.[168]

In a sign that even Talmadgeites in north Georgia had been chastened by the UGA crisis, former governor Vandiver backed Sanders as well. Even after a year of sit-ins and other nonviolent direct action, Sanders won handily, doing much better in north Georgia than south Georgia. Sanders drew critical support from most of corporate Atlanta and other cities' business leaders, and many two-unit county elites backed him as well. He would have won even if the county-unit system had structured the election.[169]

The successful Sanders administration secured a host of reforms in education, criminal justice, and other areas. More important, much of Georgia remained on track to accommodate strategically to democratization pressures. If the county-unit system had been invalidated just a few years later, it is not difficult to imagine how differently a Griffin administration and a "rustics"-dominated legislature would have governed while at the helm during the early compliance tests of the Civil Rights and Voting Rights Acts. Instead, by 1964, Georgia's two democratization processes were under way.

While reapportionment and the death of the county-unit system benefited white Democratic moderates loyal to the national party, it did render state politics more complex. The return of nomination to statewide office by popular vote and a fairly reapportioned legislature suggested that blacks in Atlanta and elsewhere would both exert much more influence in state gubernatorial primaries and also capture state legislative seats in central cities. Similarly, the growing numbers of Republican voters in the suburbs emerging around Atlanta and other cities could now begin to make rapid gains in the state legislature, beginning with the favorable reapportionment of the Senate in 1962. Thus, loyalists needed both to consider whether and how to incorporate black activists and voters into the state Democratic party, as well as convert state party machinery useful for governing enclave affairs into an organization actually adept at mobilizing voters and winning competitive elections.[170]

As in South Carolina, black voter registration in Georgia experienced its largest increase before the Voting Rights Act. After holding steady from 1962 to 1964, the share of eligible black Georgians who were registered to vote increased from 29 percent to 44 percent, or by more than one-half. By 1968, it had increased to 56 percent. These gains are attributable to the Voter Education Project's efforts and to the separate registration drives by the NAACP. Also, black interest in supporting Johnson and opposing Goldwater helped matters.[171]

But while the number of black registrants over the 1960s increased by more than 160,000 votes, the number of white registrants exceeded one-half million, and white voter registration increased from 57 to 85 percent. This increase occurred too quickly to be explained by secular changes such as urbanization and rising incomes. Indeed, most of the new registrants were poorer Black Belt whites, many of whom now perceived the possibility of a black takeover of offices in majority-black counties. Thus, a countermobilization story seems closer to the truth. The campaigns of George Wallace mobilized working-class whites during this period. Additionally, evidence also points to their mobilization by segregationist candidates in statewide races, who now needed to turn out rural whites, and not merely do well enough to capture the two- and four-unit counties in which many resided.[172]

North Georgia's Harnessed Democratization

Like those elsewhere, Democratic politicians in North Georgia preferred to comply with federal legislation at their own pace and with as much autonomy as possible.[173] As with Sanders—and the anti-Talmadgeite faction historically—Atlanta's business and political leadership did not call for accommodating federal directives and indigenous black protest on principled grounds. Above all, this leadership wanted to forge a reputation for the city, and the state, as modern, enlightened, orderly, compliant, and ripe for investment.[174]

They partly succeeded. By convincing the outside world that they were responsive to black protest and had desegregated the city themselves in an orderly fashion, Atlanta quickly developed a national and international reputation as an "example" to the rest of the South for its "good sense and dignity." The city consolidated its place as the commercial powerhouse of the Southeast; however, the reputation of Atlanta and the rest of north Georgia did not extend below the fall line dividing north Georgia from south Georgia.[175]

Despite an elite consensus for accommodating strategically to racial reforms, the city, and north Georgia generally, did not vote as one in municipal or statewide elections. As described in chapter 8, from the late 1940s, Atlanta's white supremacists squared off—usually unsuccessfully—against a coalition of white business moderates, white middle-class voters, and virtually all of the city's black voters. Through his mayoral bids against this coalition, Atlanta restaurant owner Lester Maddox steadily built a following among working-class whites in the city and beyond who appreciated his own defense of segregation. Thus, in both municipal and statewide elections, the "big city" vote often divided.[176]

Sit-ins swept through downtown Atlanta in 1960. Unlike hundreds of other southern cities, Atlanta's leadership refused to forge a citywide agreement on white firms' desegregation of lunch counters and other spaces. Sit-in demonstrators were furious at NAACP leader A. T. Walden for what they saw as his too-accommodationist negotiations with city officials and firm owners.[177] However, many firms made well-publicized commitments to desegregate when school desegregation was to begin. In the months after the ambivalent results of the UGA crisis, attention switched to Atlanta's fall 1961 court-ordered school desegregation. Both Atlanta's leadership and the state's organized white supremacists viewed the stakes as extraordinarily high in determining the shape of the state's democratization. The episode was peaceful, and kudos flowed in. However, this desegregation involved only nine students. The city was perfecting the performance of compliance with federal directives.[178]

Even those Atlanta downtown shopping establishments which by 1961 demanded that the city's schools remain open refused to desegregate their own lunch counters.[179] By 1963 more than one-half of restaurants and hotels that had promised to desegregate had reneged on these agreements. At the end of the year, Martin Luther King, Jr., concluded that the city lagged "behind almost every major southern city in its progress toward desegregation." By the time of the Civil Rights Act in June 1964—after a major joint project by SNCC and the SCLC demanding desegregation—Atlanta still lacked a public accommodations ordinance. Continued anger over the performance of the city's black establishment in negotiating on behalf of demonstrators led to Walden's resignation from the Summit Leadership Conference, the fragile coalition of protesters and older elites. Historian Adam Fairclough writes that King, on the verge of accepting the Nobel

Peace Prize, had "realized that he carried little weight with the city's famous 'power structure.'"[180]

However, the city's reputation as progressive and compliant was by then well established. Indeed, in 1963 Mayor Ivan Allen, Jr. (1962–69)—alone among southern officeholders—testified in Congress in support of the public accommodations provisions of draft civil rights legislation (and did so at the request of President Kennedy). In 1967, seven years after the first wave of sit-ins, new, less-publicized sit-ins occurred at the office of the city's school superintendent to protest the slow pace of desegregation.

In 1961, in the first election to succeed the twenty-five-year reign of Mayor Hartsfield, Allen, a key player in Atlanta's downtown establishment, faced off against white supremacist activist Lester Maddox. Allen's platform revolved around "Forward Atlanta," the Chamber of Commerce's new agenda for metropolitan development, while Maddox denounced this "Peachtree Peacock" for encouraging the NAACP to take over municipal government. Allen won in an election that mirrored those of the past. Maddox dominated the precincts of white working-class voters, but Allen, like Hartsfield before him, won a majority of the vote by combining virtually unanimous black support with the middle- and upper-class whites on the city's north side.[181]

Atlanta's business leadership secured the city's reputation by relying on its longstanding alliance with the city's older, more risk-averse black elites. In the late 1950s only a small share of these leaders supported desegregation suits for Atlanta's schools or those elsewhere in the state, and soon, during the sit-ins and other protests, they undercut students' negotiations with city officials on a citywide desegregation agreement. Younger black activist Whitney Young—echoing the national NAACP office—complained that even the city's blacks had begun to believe the "press clippings" about Atlanta.[182]

Besides stoking the city's economic growth, these "press clippings" had two other important consequences. First, after state authorities successfully diluted the impact of minority voting (described later), the city's reputation helped the state's federal officeholders convince the Johnson administration to minimize oversight of the state's implementation with the Voting Rights Act. Only three of Georgia's 159 counties hosted federal examiners, and Johnson's former mentor, Georgia Senator Richard Russell, persuaded the president that the state had earned the opportunity to oversee its own implementation.[183] Second, the apparently successful and well-publicized accommodation helped demobilize the area's white supremacists; this assisted municipal authorities in maintaining order through the rest of the decade. Atlanta escaped the deadly armed clashes occurring in Augusta and elsewhere.[184]

Atlanta's Role in Georgia's Democratization

The generational, ideological, and tactical disagreements within Atlanta's black community had important implications not only for Atlanta's democratization experience but also for the rest of the state. As discussed previously, the work of Doug McAdam and other scholars would suggest that Atlanta's black community—with its critical mass of universities, economic power, communications networks, battle-hardened activists, and civic and political institutions—would assume a leadership role for black politics throughout the state.

Surprisingly, however, this did not occur. In contrast to other Deep South states, black insurgencies across Georgia were not united by statewide networks. Partly because of the effectiveness of the state's 1950s repression of black protest capacity, there was little continuity from the mobilizations of the 1940s to those in the 1960s. Moreover, while the SCLC and SNCC had an administrative presence in Atlanta, they did not play substantial roles in the city's black protest.

By the time SNCC did focus on the city in its Atlanta Project in 1966, it had been isolated by the Summit Leadership Conference, blamed for a riot in the Atlanta neighborhood of Summerhill, and had substantial difficulty securing the participation of black neighborhoods. Indeed, this project abandoned the organization's commitment to community organizing in favor of a "top-down" approach, and it was unsuccessful in radicalizing residents of Summerhill and the Vine City neighborhood in the name of "community control."[185]

As discussed in chapter 9, many analysts consider the southern assault on the NAACP as counterproductive, since, the argument goes, the organization's repression in the 1950s cleared the way for other organizations, including those adept at nonviolent direct action and a range of tactics that southern authorities often had difficulty countering. This argument may be useful in understanding democratizations of other southern enclaves, but this discussion suggests that Georgia's attack on the NAACP was quite effective—and quite damaging. In the absence of the NAACP's statewide network, other black protest groups did emerge to work in the state, but none catalyzed Atlanta's advantages into a statewide insurgency.

Thus, the massive resistance against the NAACP may help explain why, as historian Stephen Tuck concludes, "Atlanta protest did not act as the vanguard for urban protest in the state." The fact that it did not do so contributed to the differences in the democratization experiences of the "two Georgias." If black Atlanta had been used as a beachhead from which to fan out across the state, the stark differences across the state might have narrowed considerably—as suggested by the statewide mobilization of 1946 (discussed in chapter 4).[186]

Black Party Incorporation in North Georgia

The relationship between Atlanta's older black elite and militant younger protesters was complex. Many of the former, including the NAACP's A. T. Walden and leading religious figures such as Rev. Martin Luther King, Sr., often provided students with much-needed support, including legal aid after sit-in arrests and financial help to make bail. They also argued constantly over tactics, particularly when students wanted to continue demonstrations and boycotts that upset the older black elite's coalition partners in the city's business establishment. The South's only daily black paper, the *Atlanta Daily World*, worked at cross-purposes with student leaders and regularly criticized them. For the many white moderate Democratic politicians loyal to the national party but hardly opposed to enclave rule, this intra-black conflict was a salutary development. By aligning themselves with older black leaders and criticizing nonviolent direct action, these politicians could continue to forge appeals to a broad array of white voters without earning the ire of black voters—particularly since the choices of the latter were substantially influenced by the endorsement slates of organizations controlled by the older black elite. Finally, in helping themselves in this manner, loyalists delegitimized more militant black protest.[187]

In north Georgia, there were three main elements of black incorporation: black support for the national presidential ticket, black participation in party affairs, and black officeholding. In all respects, blacks in north Georgia were incorporated earlier and more thoroughly than those in south Georgia. Well incorporated into Atlanta's dominant coalition from the late 1940s, many black elites remained hesitant about the national party until the early 1960s. The Eisenhower administration's support for *Brown* delayed the move to the national Democratic ticket. Even in 1960, close to 60 percent of the city's black voters backed Richard Nixon.[188]

Still, blacks in metro Atlanta provided critical support to the more moderate Democratic congressional candidates, as well as the state's two liberal members of Congress, Charles Weltner and James Mackay. Atlanta's biracial municipal coalition resulted in the inclusion of a few black leaders in party institutions, such as the city's Democratic Executive Committee in the 1950s. By 1962, Walden won a seat on Georgia's SDEC, a rarity in the South. As with many features of Atlanta politics, this "incorporation" was more illusory than real in that it did not translate into reliable black support for Democratic presidential candidates until 1964. And some metro Atlanta blacks vied for state Senate seats as Republicans into the early 1960s; however, those who won did so as Democrats.[189]

In another sign that this incorporation was hollow, white Democrats continued to resist black suffrage and black candidacies. As the threat of black influence emerged, vote dilution devices were used. As early as 1953,

Augusta switched to at-large elections in order to keep its city council white. One decade later, Sanders—then president pro tem of the state Senate, called for the chamber to move to at-large elections in order to block the election of a black senator from Fulton County.[190] And before the Voting Rights Act, Sanders as governor convinced the legislature to tighten the state's "understanding" test for potential voter registrants, as well as establish a majority-vote requirement for local, state, and federal elections designed to stymie black candidacies. Sanders did not succeed in convincing President Johnson that the Voting Rights Act should leave literacy requirements undisturbed, but the majority-vote law survived judicial scrutiny.[191]

By the late 1960s, Atlanta's biracial coalition began to show signs of stress. Substantial conflict between younger activists and elder black leaders, combined with the disappointing results of nonviolent direct action in the city, increased younger activists' impatience with the coalition. Moreover, as the black share of the city electorate surpassed 40 percent, many whites themselves grew less comfortable with it. Meanwhile, the city's school desegregation proceeded unevenly, and school enrollments were moving from two-thirds white to two-thirds black.

In 1969, Sam Massell, a fairly progressive white resident of one of the city's tonier neighborhoods, won the mayor's race despite facing the business establishment's preferred candidate. The older black elites also backed the establishment candidate. For the first time, however, most of the city's black voters rejected their endorsement and instead backed Massell. Despite failing to win the support of 40 percent of whites at any income level, Massell won with substantial black support. Black activist Maynard Jackson, who had emerged from outside the more conservative black leadership, served as vice-mayor.

Four years later, Massell faced off against Jackson. Massell framed the election as a referendum on the city's survival. With the campaign slogan "Atlanta's Too Young to Die," Massell and his supporters warned white voters that Jackson's election would mean the city's takeover by its black residents and a collapse in property values. Jackson dominated in black precincts and won about one-fifth of the white vote to become the South's first black mayor of a large city. Jackson's election advanced north Georgia's democratization. In particular, his administration desegregated the city's public sector. He quickly improved black hiring by city agencies, as well as dispensing city contracts to black firms.[192]

Still, the policy benefits secured by black officeholding in Atlanta were often meager. Sometimes this was due to their inability to guide federal policy, as when urban renewal displaced seventy-five thousand residents, most of them black, from downtown Atlanta. At other moments, the nature of the biracial accommodation itself produced meager benefits, such as when a deal was struck whereby blacks retained substantial control over school

administrative jobs in exchange for an acceptance of increasingly high levels of school segregation. Just as it had done in the early 1950s, the national
NAACP castigated the local NAACP's leadership for, in this case, "trading
the dream of integration for a separate and unequal school system."[193] As
discussed later, the politics of gubernatorial elections in 1966 and 1970 revealed the incomplete, bifurcated nature of black party incorporation.

In sum, the small towns and cities of north Georgia experienced a harnessed revolution. Authorities in these areas accommodated strategically to
federal directives regarding desegregation and civil and voting rights. They
oversaw minimal amounts of disorder and violence, absorbed surprisingly
little in the way of investments by national black protest organizations, and
avoided a massive federal intervention that would have been costly in the
ways described in chapter 9.[194] Burnishing the reputation of Atlanta and
the rest of north Georgia, the region's rulers—whether in local, county, or
state government or in chambers of commerce, successfully navigated the
turbulent decade.

South Georgia's Protracted Democratization

South Georgia—particularly in the state's Black Belt—experienced a protracted democratization. In many areas, local and county authorities met
federal legislation and black protest with defiance and state-sponsored
violence. State-level law enforcement, such as the state's Highway Patrol,
fomented disorder and bloodshed, both in small towns and the region's
larger cities, such as Augusta.[195] Indigenous black activists, cut off from
statewide networks of organizational assistance developed in the 1940s (see
chapter 4), sometimes failed to ensure nonviolence on the part of black
protesters. The result was additional disorder and delayed compliance with
federal legislation, including a protracted dismantling of racist local law
enforcement. Cities were not immune to such violence, as demonstrated by
the bloody disturbances in Augusta in 1970.[196] In addition, south Georgia
featured a much-delayed black incorporation into Democratic county parties and a longer estrangement from the national party.

On the eve of the Civil Rights and Voting Rights Acts, the Black Belt of
south Georgia remained predominantly rural, and—perhaps just as important with respect to federal compliance efforts—divided into about sixty-
five counties (see chapter 3). Decisions concerning compliance with federal directives and responses to black protest lay in the hands of local and
county officials in rural nonfarm areas and small towns. While the demise
of the county-unit system had weakened the power of county courthouse
"rings," most counties remained dominated by local notables. Many of these
notables were still loosely affiliated with former Talmadge faction leaders
such as former governor Marvin Griffin and state party chair James Gray

(based in Albany, the "capital" of Georgia's Black Belt). As in Mississippi, local and county authorities retained greater autonomy over responses to democratization pressures than did their counterparts in South Carolina.

In 1965 south Georgia still contained twenty-four majority-black counties. As in the Mississippi Delta and the South Carolina lowcountry, the influence of business moderates was much weaker in these Black Belt counties than elsewhere in the state. Large landowners, merchants, and local and county authorities in south Georgia were less concerned with attracting external capital. The region's politicians were usually less interested in winning statewide office and thus had no need to accommodate to growing black power in larger cities. Finally, powerful mobilizations of blacks in these areas posed realistic challenges of a black political takeover. For all of these reasons, authorities were much more likely to embrace defiance in the face of external democratization challenges and indigenous insurgencies. Of course, there was a good deal of diversity in rulers' interests and their responses to such pressures. Many counties south of the fall line—especially in coastal Georgia—were predominantly white and navigated the decade much more smoothly. However, the reputation of the region would be shaped by widely reported instances of disorder and violence in the Black Belt. While the racial politics of Georgia's Black Belt resembled that of the Mississippi Delta, patterns of external intervention differed. South Georgia was subject to much lighter federal oversight of its compliance with the Civil Rights and Voting Rights Acts, as well as lower levels of interventions by national black protest organizations.

Voting rights enforcement was largely a matter of securing the compliance of officials county by county, since election administration was, in Georgia as elsewhere, performed by counties. The Justice Department's leading race relations troubleshooter, John Doar, admitted that in the deployment of examiners to Georgia, the state had been "neglected." Doar blamed this on the practical problems introduced by the combination of the decentralization of voter and election administration to the county level, and the large number of counties in the state (159). As Doar put it, "It takes a lot of shoe leather to cross and re-cross the state."[197] In 1965, in twenty-one of twenty-four majority-black counties, average registration rates for blacks and whites were 15 and 91 percent, respectively. While the three Black Belt counties receiving examiners experienced sharp gains, the rest of the Black Belt remained relatively free of federal oversight, in part due to the influence of U.S. Senator Richard B. Russell in the Johnson administration.[198] By the early 1970s, Georgia's Black Belt lagged substantially behind the Delta and South Carolina's lowcountry in black political mobilization. Additionally, as of 1969, Georgia submitted only one electoral law change for preclearance, even though hundreds of others had been implemented, mostly in south Georgia, and were often meant to dilute black voting power. Rates of successful black candidacies partly attest to the effectiveness of these laws.[199]

Following the demise of the state's massive resistance and its repression of black protest organizations, and following the flowering of nonviolent direct action across the South, north Georgia's activists failed to revive statewide networks of black protest. They also failed to intervene in south Georgia, where massive resistance had eviscerated infrastructure for black protest. As of the mid-1960s, Albany's C. B. King was the only black attorney south of Atlanta taking civil and criminal cases.[200]

National black protest organizations did invest sporadically in the region. First, in 1961, the Southern Christian Leadership Conference joined ongoing protest in Albany and helped form a coalition of groups (including the NAACP and SNCC) called the Albany Movement. A city of about 50,000, Albany was almost one-half black and the center of Georgia's Black Belt. For several months, black residents gathered in weekly mass meetings and demanded a full desegregation of the city's public spaces. The city's white establishment was highly cohesive, and the city was home to state party chair James Gray, a hardline white supremacist who owned the local media outlets. This establishment delegated substantial police powers to Police Chief Laurie Pritchett, who successfully blunted nonviolent tactics and convinced the SCLC to withdraw. Pritchett was soon famous for his tactical acumen—both in training his personnel not to resort to the type of violence that might induce federal intervention (or the intervention of other black protest organizations), and in defusing black protest through mass arrests, fines, and bail policies. As one SNCC worker remarked, "We ran out of people before [Pritchett] ran out of jails." However, authorities' tactical success was not enough; critical here, as elsewhere, was elite cohesion. As historian J. Mills Thornton has shown, it was a lack of elite cohesion, not bad tactics, that was at the root of failures to avoid violent repression of black protesters in Selma.[201]

It is worth noting here that after its reemergence in the late 1950s, Georgia's statewide conference of the NAACP took no steps to resuscitate Albany's NAACP branch, which had fallen dormant during the massive resistance of the 1950s. Moreover, the NAACP often refused to assist movements initiated by SNCC. This was quite a departure from the cooperation illustrated by the COFO in Mississippi. Since SNCC took a leadership role in much of south Georgia, this unstated policy had large ramifications.[202]

The SCLC did help blacks in Savannah secure some policy demands in its summer 1963 project. But the main external investment in south Georgia's democratization was SNCC's Southwest Georgia Project. From 1961 to 1967, SNCC personnel led by Charles Sherrod fanned out into twenty-three counties in the Black Belt. As with SNCC efforts in Mississippi, organizers attempted to register voters and provide civic education in the most brutal counties. In some areas these efforts succeeded. In others, local blacks rejected nonviolence and responded in kind to gangs of armed whites, who local police and highway patrolmen had let loose on peaceful marchers. In Sumter County's Americus, the great hope of the region, Klan marches—one of which was led by Lester Maddox—attracted close to one thousand participants, and gun sales skyrocketed after black gangs attacked whites in deadly clashes. Still, assistance from black protest forces in Savannah pointed to benefits that could have been generated by help from other protest centers in Georgia, as their help with demonstrations and boycotts resulted in the appointment of black polling clerks, followed by sizable gains in black voter registration.[203] Eventually, SNCC personnel withdrew to Mississippi.[204]

Unlike Mississippi, south Georgia's violence did not result in new waves of black protesters and federal law enforcement officials, despite the well-publicized acquiescence—and, often, participation—of local law enforcement in violent repression of black activists.[205] The Highway Patrol had ties to many south Georgia legislators, still influential in the politics of the Highway Department, and its performance south of the fall line often violated the wishes of state-level authorities such as Governor Sanders. Advocates of a more centralized policing apparatus were not able to secure reforms until the early 1970s. Moreover, in scores of south Georgia counties, authorities successfully delayed desegregating public spaces and dismantling racist law enforcement institutions until the 1970s.

Thus, while north Georgia's democratization paralleled that of South Carolina, south Georgia's protracted democratization did differ from Mississippi's. Like Mississippi, there was significant violence, disorder, resistance to lawful compliance with federal directives, and resistance to incorporating blacks into local and county party organizations. But unlike Mississippi, state actors and federal officeholders, exploiting north Georgia's reputation for the sake of the state as a whole, helped the region avoid a large deployment of federal officials to enforce the Voting Rights Act (tables 9.2 and 9.3). The split nature of Georgia's democratization had important consequences for the state's overall pace of black incorporation, reconciliation with the national party, and implementation of democratizing reforms.

A Divided Ruling Party

By 1966, as the political networks of county elites across the highly depopulated two-unit counties had become irrelevant in a post–county-unit system world, the state's factional divide between Talmadge and anti-Talmadge forces had subsided. The Democratic gubernatorial primary spanned a wide ideological spectrum, from the racially liberal former governor Ellis Arnall (see chapter 4) to populist Jimmy Carter to a number of white supremacists, including Lester Maddox, the famed Atlanta restaurant owner and leader of working-class white Atlantans' opposition to the city's biracial coalition. For the first time in the century, Democrats faced a credible Republican challenger, Howard "Bo" Callaway, a textile heir and former Talmadgeite. Callaway emerged from the state party's first direct primary.[206]

In the primary, blacks favored Arnall, the most racially liberal candidate. Arnall won a plurality of the primary vote, but Carter's success, coupled with the new majority-vote requirement, forced Arnall into a runoff against Maddox. Maddox won in an upset, thus pitting Maddox against Callaway. Callaway warned voters that Maddox's election would mean "four years of martial law and an end to industry coming to Georgia," and better-off whites across the state agreed with him. Blacks and white liberals, facing a choice between two right-wing segregationist candidates, conducted a write-in campaign for Arnall, who won 7 percent—almost all from black voters.[207] Sweeping the cities, Callaway finished first, but was denied a majority of the vote, and so the election was sent to the Democrat-dominated General Assembly, which elected Maddox. Afterward, Martin Luther King, Jr., called Georgia "a sick state produced by the disease of a sick nation."[208]

Candidates did not divide strictly on sectional lines. Indeed, the future leader of the loyalist party faction, Jimmy Carter, hailed from the Black Belt's Sumter County, while Lester Maddox—the favorite of many newly registered and poorer, rural whites—was from Atlanta. Still, the election demonstrated the state party's increasingly bifurcated nature, as whites in the working-class precincts of Georgia's cities joined up with whites in south Georgia to delay the incorporation of blacks into the state party.[209] Given the governor's ability to dominate delegate selection to the National Convention, the election of Maddox would stall this incorporation, and thereby complicate the party's reconciliation with the national party. As historian Timothy Boyd writes, the 1966 election "virtually guaranteed a showdown between Maddox and Loyalists over control of the state party."[210]

Relative to the governor's rhetoric, the Maddox administration was surprisingly progressive.[211] Throughout his term, Maddox maintained a job approval rating of 62 percent, as well as 58 percent support on his management of racial issues. He outpaced the legislature in his progressive stances on education, welfare, and labor policies. However, he refused to make headway on the desegregation of the state's public sector, and appointed just a few blacks.[212] The different democratization experiences of the "two Georgias" were clearly apparent in state Democrats' reconciliation with the national party.

Georgia Democrats and the National Party

Among Georgia's leading officeholders, only Governor Carl Sanders campaigned for President Johnson in 1964. Georgia's bifurcated party was visible in Atlantic City. Inside the convention hall, Governor Sanders chaired the Rules Committee that expelled Deep South delegations for their racial discrimination, and Georgia's delegation included two black politicians from Atlanta. Outside the convention hall, Lester Maddox—the state's next governor—paced the boardwalk to protest President Johnson and the Civil Rights Act. South Georgia politicians backed Goldwater.[213]

In 1968, Governor Maddox and the state party chair, Albany's James Gray, controlled a delegation to Chicago that was not committed in advance to the national ticket; only 2 percent of the delegation was black.[214] In order to protest the national party's positions on racial matters, "law and order," and Vietnam, Maddox declared his candidacy for the Democratic nomination and then seemed to back George Wallace.

Ellis Arnall's independent write-in campaign for governor in 1966 generated a biracial, loyalist organization, the Georgia Democratic Party Forum. It challenged the Maddox delegation under the new SERC guidelines (see chapter 9), and dispatched to Chicago its own delegation—led by black politician Julian Bond—split evenly by race. A full rejection of the segregationist regulars would hurt Vice President Hubert Humphrey's prospects in the South, but their seating would anger northern liberals. Thus, the Humphrey-dominated Credentials Committee crafted a compromise that would split Georgia's delegation between the Forum's loyalists and the regulars. The Forum delegation agreed to the compromise, but Maddox and Gray opposed it. About twenty of the regulars defied the governor and remained in Chicago.[215] The National Convention experience seemed to have damaged the state party. Across the state, whites abandoned the Democratic presidential ticket for George Wallace; in Atlanta, fewer than 30 percent of whites of any income level backed Humphrey. Ninety-eight percent of blacks voted for Humphrey, and most of his canvassing efforts were limited to urban black neighborhoods.[216]

State party chair James Gray spoke for most south Georgia party officials by concluding that "We feel . . . sore and baffled. The white conservative vote in the South is not wanted by the present leaders of the Democratic party. . . . [We] . . . have to go home and make some other arrangements, Georgia has a score to settle."[217] Meanwhile, a range of Democrats loyal to the national party welcomed the McGovern-Fraser commission when it held hearings in Georgia in 1969.[218]

Generally, Georgia's approach to reconciliation with the national party lay in between the early accommodation of South Carolina Democrats and the longer estrangement of Mississippi. By 1976, Georgia produced two presidential nominees: Jimmy Carter, and Maddox as the nominee of Wallace's American Independent Party. The potential costs of these divisions were minimal. Five of the most powerful state Democratic politicians abandoned the party after the 1968 National Convention. The five switchers had all failed to win office as Republicans by 1971, and observers argue that this slowed down substantially the influx of ambitious politicians into the state Republican party.[219]

Georgia's Bifurcated Democratization

Over the course of the 1960s, north and south Georgia experienced different patterns of peaceful compliance with federal directives, black party incorporation, external reputations, and stances toward the national party. Of course, Georgia remained a single polity, with a single state apparatus. But the bifurcated nature of its transition had *statewide* implications for its future governance.

In 1969 the Negro Voters League endorsed famed south Georgia activist C. B. King for governor. Running in the 1970 Democratic primary against racial moderate Carl Sanders and white populist Jimmy Carter, King won seventy thousand votes.[220] Carter was now the unofficial spokesman for racially resentful white men, especially followers of George Wallace. As Carter reached out to Wallace, and even longtime white supremacist politicians Roy Harris and Marvin Griffin, black voters deserted him. However, he later won in a runoff against former governor Carl Sanders, and then defeated Hal Suit, a racially moderate Republican candidate, who had trounced a hardline segregationist. Carter's coalition pieced together a coalition of poorer whites as well as blacks that surpassed Suit's advantages in the suburbs.[221]

Carter would eventually make his name as a racially moderate, "New South" governor with his inaugural address. As the *New York Times* editorialized, "Yes, That Was a Georgia Governor Speaking." In the address, Carter called for an end to racial discrimination, a strengthened state law enforcement apparatus, and repairing sectional splits among Georgians. Bathed in positive national publicity, Carter parlayed this fame into active participation in presidential politics (first by helping organize a movement to block George McGovern's nomination).[222]

The technocratic Carter's main goal during his tenure was a reorganization of the state apparatus, the state's first significant overhaul since 1931.[223] More significantly, and parallel to the West administration in South Carolina, the Carter administration (1971–75) oversaw the final stages of the state's democratization. During this period, the state embraced peaceful, lawful compliance with federal directives, committed itself rhetorically to racial equality, and began desegregating the state apparatus and addressing socioeconomic inequalities.

Carter's racial reforms took three main forms. First, he increased black gubernatorial appointments from three to fifty-three, and encouraged increasing black public-sector employment more generally. Second, he developed institutions meant to reduce racial tensions and legitimize state efforts to reduce racial injustice. These included the Civil Disorder Unit, a biracial group under the direction of the governor that would arrive on the scene of racial conflicts and facilitate negotiation and bargaining (somewhat analogous to the federal government's Community Relations Service). In developing the unit, Carter maneuvered around the Highway Patrol, over which he had less influence and which remained segregated until midway through his term (longer than in Mississippi). In addition, he created the governor's Council on Human Relations, a biracial group similar to that developed by Governor West in South Carolina.[224] Third, he took important symbolic steps, such as removing white supremacist Roy Harris from the state university system's Board of Regents, and installing in the state capitol portraits of three blacks—including, most controversially, Martin Luther King, Jr.[225]

Carter seemed personally to embody an overcoming of the "Two Georgias." A populist, culturally conservative Baptist, Carter was comfortable with south Georgia audiences, Atlanta blacks, and the white corporate establishment.[226] However—further demonstrating the bifurcated nature of the state's politics—much of Carter's agenda of political modernization was blocked by former governor Lester Maddox. After an easy election as lieutenant governor, Maddox's star rose as he presided over the Senate, led a large, powerful coalition of senators, and appointed members of committees. Many observers assumed in 1971 that Maddox would be reelected governor in 1974.[227] This uneasy power-sharing stymied several statewide reforms, among them a badly needed constitution (the current one, drafted in 1877, had been amended more than three hundred times). A new constitution was drafted and passed the House; however, the Maddox-influenced Senate defeated it in 1970.[228]

As this chapter has demonstrated, Georgia's sectional divide was not reducible to urban versus rural conflict or to political-economic differences. The combination of factional conflict, patterns of black mobilization, and institutions of party and state throughout the 1940s, 1950s, and 1960s actually widened the state's existing sectional split. Soon Georgia would produce the Deep South's first-ever president. Jimmy Carter's presidency affirmed the region's democratization. However, his state's own transition culminated in the early 1970s with an uneasy, sectionally bifurcated democratization.

Conclusion

By 1972 the South had been democratized. The three Deep South enclaves under study had been dismantled. Jim Crow regulations, suffrage restriction, and the political extrusion of blacks and the poorest whites had all been overturned. Over the previous few years, the region's schools had been transformed from the country's least racially integrated to their most integrated.[229]

Moreover, the practices of these enclaves' ruling parties were now regulated by an empowered national Democratic party. The destruction of white-only governance—including both black elected officials and a desegregated state apparatus—occurred more slowly than did the destruction of other pillars of enclave rule, but in all three states this process was well under way, and material benefits of democratization had begun to trickle into the neighborhoods of blacks and the poorest whites. And in all three enclaves, multiparty competition had produced by 1972 fairly moderate "New South" governors. Perhaps most important, the democratization of these enclaves had consolidated quickly. All major political actors in these states shared an expectation that democratic governance was here to stay, and all accepted the reality of a permanent oversight of southern politics by the central state and national party.

The year 1972 serves as an appropriate ending point for the transition in a few other ways. First, southern Democrats' opposition to the national party climaxed in that year and quickly collapsed thereafter. The Ninety-second Session of Congress (1971–72) produced the century's lowest level of southern Democrats' support for legislation backed by a majority of House Democrats. Only 14 percent of southern Democrats classified as party loyalists and 62 percent as party opponents. From 1972 on, these trends reversed sharply until, by 1988, some 70 percent of southern Democrats were party loyalists and just 5 percent typically opposed legislation supported by the House Democratic caucus.[230]

Second, Strom Thurmond won reelection in 1972, and would continue to do so until he won his final campaign in 1996 (at the age of ninety-four). While blacks did not support him, he had by this year hired a black staffer and begun to bring home federal spending to his black constituents, even as he served as a pioneer of the New Right in U.S. politics.[231] Thurmond's career is emblematic of the successful adjustment of enclave rulers to democratization pressures, and to what many see as the rather meager fruits of the installation of democratic rule in the region (discussed in the chapter 11). Third, in 1972 busing exploded as a national controversy, and the Nixon administration moved "beyond nonenforcement and attempted to override the Supreme Court's urban desegregation requirement by simple legislation."[232] Although this effort (barely) failed, the tumultuous politics of busing led many to agree with Alabama governor George Wallace that "the whole United States is southern!"[233] Whether true or not, in 1972 a growing national perception of declining regional differences had taken hold; this was another sign—as with Thurmond, an uneasy one—that enclaves had been destroyed. Some legacies of the ways in which they had been destroyed are discussed in the next chapter.

CHAPTER ELEVEN

Legacies and Lessons of the Democratized South

MORE THAN HALF A CENTURY AGO, V. O. Key declared that politics was the South's main problem, while the South remained America's main problem. This book has suggested that the central feature of southern politics we have overlooked since Key—the self-interested choices of political elites constrained by institutions of state and party—blocked, then stalled, and finally shaped the aftermath of a stunning achievement: the region's democratization. This achievement offers many lessons about regime change, political parties, the American past, and, perhaps, the American future.

Interpreting South Carolina, Mississippi, and Georgia as subnational enclaves of authoritarian rule, this book has provided a new way of apprehending the American South. This concluding chapter pushes the boundaries of this analytical framework a bit further—and farther. After briefly summarizing my findings, I offer a way to supplement existing approaches to the study of contemporary electoral and economic change, focusing in particular on how the framework of authoritarian enclaves might enhance our understanding of the rise of southern Republicans and the South's uneven economic development. In closing, I draw some implications of the research for the study of the South, American political development, and regime change.

Three Paths Out of Dixie

From the abolition of the white primary in 1944 until the McGovern-Fraser party reforms of the early 1970s, democratizers assaulted the authoritarian enclaves of the Deep South. Each of their challenges—and the responses that these tests engendered—influenced the balance of power among ruling party factions and the party-state capacities used by politicians to defend enclave rule. As recently as the late 1950s, Deep South rulers were working off the same template of massive resistance. But by the early 1970s, their enclaves had exited authoritarian rule along different paths. Their experiences differed in terms of the orderliness of compliance with federal directives, the timing and nature of black incorporation into the ruling party, and the timing and nature of its reconciliation with the national party.

After some two decades of forthright resistance to any racial reforms, as well as attacks on white civil society and black protest, South Carolina's rulers exploited cohesive elite networks and an effective coercive apparatus to navigate safely the desegregation crisis at Clemson. This outcome provided increasing returns to rulers' strategic accommodation to democratization pressures. They capitalized on the state's external reputation to maintain order, deter interventions by national civil rights organizations, and limit federal oversight of party-state compliance with federal directives. By doing so, rulers accelerated the exit of white supremacist activists from the state's main party, and sped the party's incorporation of blacks and its reconciliation with the national party. Limiting the disruptive effects of democratization in the short term, South Carolina successfully harnessed the revolution.

Mississippi also resisted early democratization pressures. However, during the 1950s the state's decentralization of authority stymied reformers' attempts to overhaul the state's policing apparatus and pursue other institutional reforms. The party faction's dominance by White Citizens' Council (WCC) forces, coupled with the state's disorganized law enforcement, resulted in the debacle at Oxford. The massive military intervention induced a white supremacist backlash that further corroded law enforcement and accelerated a massive intervention from national civil rights organizations. The ensuing spiral of interventions and disorder resulted in substantial federal oversight of Mississippi's compliance with federal directives. An incredibly quick mobilization of black Mississippi occurred, but it did so partly outside of the confines of the ruling party. In the chaos of a fissured state Democratic party, rulers' relations with the national party became estranged—and remained so into the mid-1970s. In sum, Mississippi's rulers stumbled through the 1960s. By failing to deter white supremacist violence, they unwittingly induced the violations of Mississippi's "sovereignty" against which they had long railed.

Finally, Georgia's white supremacist rulers narrowly escaped a collapse of the state Democratic Party in the late 1940s. Securing the dominance of the Talmadge faction, they pursued a "massive resistance" to democratization pressures through the 1950s. In doing so, they decimated statewide networks of black protest. By the time black direct-action movements swept the state, the likely engine of statewide black insurgency—black Atlanta—had accommodated to corporate interests by trading critical support in mayoral elections for meager policy benefits. This accommodation effectively neutralized the development of statewide insurgency networks. Instead, Georgia's Black Belt activists were left largely on their own to deal with powerful county interests and state-sponsored violence. Atlanta's carefully developed reputation as a "dignified," compliant city reaped benefits for the cities and smaller towns of north Georgia, and helped deter the more substantial interventions by civil rights organizations and the federal government that occurred in south Georgia. The "two Georgias" quickly diverged, as north Georgia experienced a harnessed revolution and south Georgia, a protracted democratization.

The narratives offered here all point to the contingency and complexity of rulers' efforts to manage threats to their power. Outcomes could not be predicted with reference to structural features of the polity; instead, they were products of the political ambitions of some rulers, as well as conflict and cooperation across sectional and factional divides. Political institutions, often with sharp sectional biases, refracted how socioeconomic power would be converted into rulers' responses, thus constraining and enabling different authorities as they managed democratization challenges. And the mobilizations of black insurgents, within and outside these enclaves, shaped all of these dynamics in helping produce different modes of democratization.

Two other features of these narratives deserve mention. First, the bluntness of policy instruments aimed at black political participation complicated enclave defenses. Some policy options were opposed because they would repress poorer whites; other lawmakers favored such options for this very reason. Thus, policy discussions could both raise factional tensions and alter the balance of power among factions. Second, while it may be too strong a claim to argue that the seeds of the enclaves' demise were sown in their founding, the constitutions of the late nineteenth century limited enclaves' fiscal and administrative capacities and the legal authority of actors, especially governors. When developing new capacities required constitutional revision, it posed a double threat to many: it could disrupt balances of power among section and faction by altering sectional biases in institutional arrangements, and it might expose the enclave to further federal judicial oversight.

Legacies of Paths Out of Dixie

Recent trends in partisan competition and economic development are shaped partly by the different modes of democratization experienced by Deep South enclaves. Through what Arthur Stinchcombe termed "historical causation," the past continues to "work" on the present despite the fact that many of the conditions of the past no longer hold.[1] Collective reputations—widely dispersed perceptions, well earned or not, that are shared by persons situated within organizations and locales—illustrate this dynamic. Even after the conditions that produce a reputation are no longer present, the reputation may continue to affect outcomes. And, as discussed later, even after the reputation is finally overcome, its effects continue to reverberate. In helping shape both contemporary partisan change and patterns of economic growth, legacies of different democratizations have worked on the present through reputations—both the "brand names" of political parties, and the reputations of communities, counties, and states polities as peaceful and orderly.[2]

Different paths out of Dixie generated consequential reputations that still shape the present. In terms of partisan change, I suggest that a relatively smooth reconciliation with the national Democratic party damaged state Democratic parties; reconciliation branded the state party as too accommodating of intervention against white supremacy. South Carolina's rulers managed to incorporate blacks and reconcile smoothly with the national party, but they were therefore unable to maintain a state party "brand name" that differed sufficiently from that of the national party. They thus doomed state Democrats over the long run. In Mississippi, by failing to accommodate strategically to democratization pressures, rulers positioned the rump state party such that Republicans had nowhere to run. In doing so they unintentionally benefited state Democrats for more than two decades. In South Carolina and north Georgia, accommodation of democratization pressures garnered greater success in capital accumulation and accelerated economic growth. Conversely, Mississippi and south Georgia, where accommodation failed, suffered greatly on this score.

Partisan Change in the Deep South

When political scientists study "southern politics," they almost always focus on the region's rise in Republican officeholding (figure 11.1).[3] This is understandable, given the importance of this phenomenon in national politics (see chapter 1). Political scientists have tackled several related puzzles, including the pace of Republican growth, variations in Republican success across levels of offices, and cross-state variation in Republican advancement. This variation exists in the Deep South (figure 11.2) in terms of partisan control of statehouses.

Before 1960, Democratic parties did not differ in their officeholding patterns. But by the 1980s, they had diverged sharply in their control of state- and national-level offices. The largest divergence has occurred between the two states long considered most ripe for Republican takeover, Mississippi and South Carolina. In 1986, Republicans held only 7 percent of lower House seats in Mississippi, and 26 percent in South Carolina. By 1998 that share in South Carolina had reached 56 percent, and the state Democratic Party had been declared dead—fewer than 10 percent of white men then identified as Democrats.[4] But in Mississippi, the Democratic state party remained strong for much longer.[5]

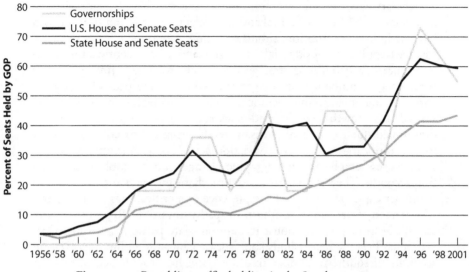

Figure 11.1. Republican officeholding in the South, 1956–2001

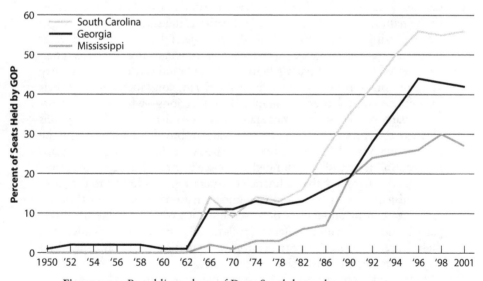

Figure 11.2. Republican share of Deep South lower houses, 1950–2001

Scholars have identified several mechanisms that have both accelerated and delayed the Republican takeover. Accelerators of Republican growth have included urbanization, suburbanization, economic development, attractive Republican presidential candidates, and, most recently, a top-down Republican party-building strategy. Conversely, Watergate, Jimmy Carter's presidency, incumbency advantages, the typically slow pace of change in partisan attachments, and Democratic control of legislative redistricting slowed this growth.[6] By the mid-1990s some of the cross-state variation diminished due to national partisan trends, racial redistricting, and other forces.[7] Most arguments about variation across space in southern Republican success emphasize demographic change, and resemble modernization accounts. They enumerate several mechanisms, such as the growth in white per capita income, and the presence of a critical mass of nonnative whites freed of traditional southern antipathy toward the Republican party and likely to help build robust Republican state parties.[8] This line of research has become increasingly sophisticated, but—as with modernization accounts of southern democratizations—still has trouble accounting for cross-state variation in the Deep South.

Party Labels as Collective Reputations

One approach that can supplement these demographic arguments emphasizes party labels, as well as state party autonomy over "its" label relative to the national party. The party brand name is the single most important electioneering resource. In the United States, given the distribution of voter preferences, a state party may seek to narrow or widen any perceived difference between the state party's brand and the brand of the national party. The party brand is thus double-edged. Politicians constantly confront their incomplete control over the brand. Others' actions—whether in the national party or within one's own state party—can shape voters' perceptions of where the party stands on particular issues or broader matters, whom the party represents, and what its likely prospects are. In securing the "means of election," teams of like-minded office-seekers require assistance from, among others, party activists, financiers, interest groups linked to the party, national party institutions, and well-known national figures. But these actors exert considerable, even decisive, influence over the value of a state party brand. Politicians at different levels of the party remain vigilant about their degree of control over the collective reputation they draw upon, and how they might adapt if such problems emerge.[9]

In the contemporary South, given racial demographics and the distribution of voters' preferences, the Democratic candidate must convince sufficient numbers of white voters that he or she bears a suitably conservative brand. Independent of ideological preferences, racial antagonism continues to influence white southern partisanship more strongly than in other regions of the country. In fact, racial polarization in presidential voting has increased even more during the Obama era.[10] Democratic candidates can assume that they will not win a majority of white votes. When the brand fails to convince, they are in deep trouble.[11]

Ideally, conservative white Democrats prefer an incomplete incorporation of blacks in their state parties. Black votes are needed in the general election, but their presence in primaries is likely to result either in more-liberal white candidates (bad) or black liberal candidates (worse). Since the early 1990s party switching has been rampant, almost always involving electorally insecure white incumbents who switch from the Democratic to Republican party. Additionally, the quality of Republican candidates has increased steadily.[12]

The contemporary value of party labels in Deep South states has been shaped by these states' various democratizations. In particular, the timing and nature of the incorporation of blacks into state Democratic parties later constrains the ability of these parties to craft racially conservative electoral appeals. These legacies, in concert with the socioeconomic mechanisms advanced by modernization accounts, help explain Democrats' abilities to hold on to state legislatures. Below, this argument is illustrated with reference to South Carolina and Mississippi.[13]

South Carolina

As of the early 1970s, Democrats remained the hegemonic party. Despite Thurmond's move to the Republican party, Thurmond did little to help fellow Republicans, as they regularly complained.[14] However, beginning with John West's defeat of white supremacist Albert Watson in the 1970 gubernatorial race, a majority of whites have voted for the Republican candidate in every statewide election.

Obviously, Democrats in South Carolina for a time successfully diluted black voting and black candidacies.[15] But the damage had been done, primarily as a result of two factors. The first is the timing of the incorporation of blacks into the party. This occurred much earlier in South Carolina than in Mississippi, and gave Republicans a head start in crafting racially conservative campaign appeals. Second, the nature of the state party's relations with the national party—in this case, a national Democratic Party to the left of the median white voter—is critical. As chapter 10 illustrates, the state party's embrace of the national party was quite close; its leaders have remained active in national party councils and generally have done a poor job of running from the party.[16] In linking themselves to the national party, leaders affected the "South Carolina Democrat" label back home.

Conversely, Republican growth in the state has been based on a combination of suburban growth and "racially conservative" appeals. Republican activists have discussed the conscious use of white supremacy to build the party. Their statewide victories have relied on "harvest[ing] conservative white voters in South Carolina's rural areas and small towns. There and elsewhere, the Republican message of social and economic conservativism has resonated with the racial subtext of state politics."[17] Republicans also effectively used the ongoing controversy over state sponsorship of the Confederate battle flag. In 1990, Democrats nominated a black state senator for governor, a sign of the weak control of the party by conservative whites. Over the 1990s, white party identifiers never reached 20 percent.[18]

Mississippi

As in South Carolina, Mississippi Democrats were dominant in the early 1970s, but remained so for a much longer time. As chapter 10 demonstrates, Republicans got a much slower start in Mississippi's state politics. Their candidates in the 1960s wavered between making white supremacist and racially liberal appeals, because they were generally unable to represent themselves to white voters as racially more conservative than the party of Jim Eastland, one of the U.S. Senate's leading white supremacists. Conversely, Democratic office-seekers successfully convinced white voters that a "Mississippi Democrat" differed greatly from, say, a "McGovern Democrat." This slow start helped Democrats maintain their supply of higher-quality candidates. As late as 1975, the Republicans failed to field a gubernatorial candidate. The Democrats lacked a state headquarters, while the Republican party featured a full-time paid staff, headquarters, and a budget of $200,000. In that year, Republicans won one seat in the statehouse.[19]

Even Republican successes pointed to the structural advantage of the Democrats and the unwitting party chaos unleashed by the state's protracted democratization. In 1972, Republican Thad Cochran won a U.S. House seat by fewer than six thousand votes, while a black independent candidate tallied more than eleven thousand. Even after the state Democratic party re-unified, in 1978, Cochran won Eastland's open seat by fewer than eighty thousand votes, while black independent candidates secured more than 135,000. Such "failures" by state Democrats to remain unified reaffirmed the ability of white Democrats to credibly claim to white voters that they were not beholden to blacks.[20] Obviously, Mississippi voters have not hesitated to back Republican presidential candidates (figure 1.3). However, as late as 1990 the Democrats kept pace with Republicans in white party identification. The strength of the "Mississippi Democrat" party label is not reducible to incumbency advantage; Democratic candidates won open seats as well. In the late 1980s, Democrats still dominated the statehouse and controlled county offices.[21] The argument described here is only suggestive, but hints at how democratization legacies might help illuminate partisan change.[22]

Legacies of the Transition for Economic Development

A second important legacy of democratization experiences works through a state's reputation in the eyes of potential investors. As argued in chapter 9, most Deep South rulers shared a common strategy of seeking rapid economic growth through capital accumulation, and mobilized resources to secure it.[23] But, as with Deep South Democrats' ability to hold on to state legislatures, divergence has occurred in these states' manufacturing growth, attraction of foreign direct investment, and receipt of prime contracts from the Pentagon.

Figure 11.3 charts the takeoff in value-added manufacturing among Deep South enclaves. Table 11.1 illustrates contemporary levels of foreign direct investment in these states. Finally, figure 11.4 compares these states' personal income per capita with the national average. As these data indicate, Georgia's advantages over the other states have grown sharply since the early 1970s, while Mississippi has lagged behind.

Scholars usually attribute such differences not to variations in political processes or institutions, but to differences in human capital, proximity to markets, natural resources, and other endowments. More recently,

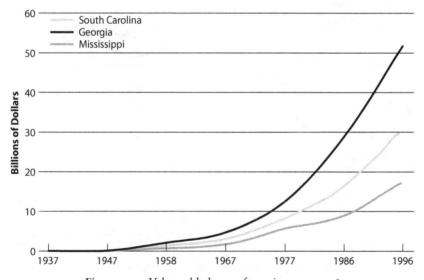

Figure 11.3. Value-added manufacturing, 1937–96

TABLE 11.1

Foreign-Owned Firms as Percentage of All Businesses, 2001

Georgia	7.1
Mississippi	3.0
South Carolina	8.8
U.S. average	5.6

Source: Statistical Abstract of the United States, 2004–2005 (Washington, D.C.: Government Printing Office, 2005), 804, table no. 1285.

Note: Firms are considered foreign-owned if a foreign owner "has a direct or indirect voting interest of 10 percent or more."

economists have argued that some locales are blessed by dynamics of increasing returns, as investment and growth beget more growth. There is substantial disagreement among economists concerning whether the South has (or will) fully converge with the non-South, and they still debate the causes of variation within the region, the importance of federal— and particularly military—spending, and so on.[24] It is worth considering how the politics of the recent past may affect contemporary economic patterns.[25]

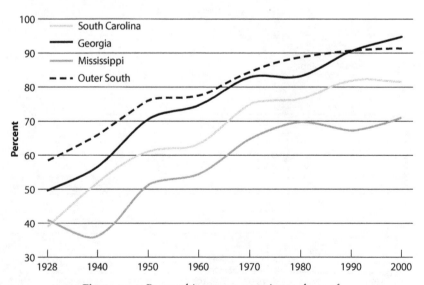

Figure 11.4. Personal income per capita as share of national average, 1928–2000

Here, I want only to point to the long-term economic consequences of the variations across polities in terms of their reputations for being stable and orderly. Generally, perceived political instability and disorder reduces (expected) profit rates because of labor stoppages, wage hikes, damage to persons and property, and uncertainty about the future.[26] Even when the objective conditions change, the effects of perceptions of instability can persist.

In the American South, communities, counties, and states seem to have been more successful over time in attracting external capital when they have garnered reputations as peaceful, orderly polities. Even when those with burdensome reputations have successfully attracted such capital, they usually have had to make additional concessions to investors in the form of tax breaks, antiunion policies, and other inducements. Such concessions help explain cross-state variation in rates of both domestic and foreign investment.[27] Southern political leaders have viewed their reputations as having economic consequences, and they may be right.

South Carolina succeeded in burnishing its reputation as a place of ideal, low-wage, orderly, and attractive communities.[28] The engine of the state's economic development has been the upcountry, formerly home to farming and textile mills. External capital has been crucial, as the state's textile industry collapsed during the early 1980s. Following BMW's investment, many other foreign firms, such as Fuji and Michelin, have sunk roots in the region. By 1982, South Carolina ranked third nationally in the share of its workforce engaged in manufacturing.[29]

As shown in chapter 10, during the 1960s, firms that had already invested in Mississippi actually pulled out of the state, fearing economic dislocations and social unrest. As late as the 1980s, Mississippi politicians were still working hard to overcome the state's reputation among investors, industrialists, and media leaders—in doing so, they were more than a decade behind other southern states.[30] The state's fiscal capacity now relies on riverboat casinos, and local black officials feel compelled to market their communities as dumping grounds for nuclear waste.[31]

Atlanta's reputation as the "city too busy to hate" eventually earned it several multinational corporations, professional sports teams, and the Olympics. South Georgia, however, remains underdeveloped. Of the state's 159 counties, ninety-six are ranked "persistently poor," and the region remains underfunded in human development, as evidenced by recent controversies over the low enrollment of south Georgia students at the University of Georgia.[32] In the 1970s, Governor George Busbee's extensive travels throughout North and Central America, Europe, and the Far East advertised Georgia and encouraged investment in the state. These efforts seem to have helped produce impressive results, as the number of international companies in the state increased from 150 in 1975 to 680 in 1982—the vast majority of them north of the fall line dividing north and south Georgia.[33]

Gavin Wright, the dean of southern economic historians, has recently called for a better understanding of the political sources of the southern political economy:

> In each of the southern states a new political equilibrium has been established in support of a particular brand of political economy. Of course this political leadership has historical links to the older, prewar South. *But its manifestation as the distinctive regional economic tendency is the outcome of a complex political selection process*, rather than a simple expression of exogenously defined regional economic interests.... *[T]he South now derives its economic interests from its politics, whereas formerly it was the other way around.*

These equilibria were produced partly by the legacies of their democratization experiences.[34]

The South: A New Research Agenda

As I have previously suggested, placed in the light of the democratization framework offered in this book, existing questions about the South may be usefully recast. Additionally, some new questions about southern politics—especially during and after the transitions to democracy—present themselves. All pose interesting opportunities to place southern political development in cross-national perspective.

Democratization

To render persuasive the interpretations of Deep South democratizations that I have offered in this study, their observable implications must be tested. In particular, given my emphasis on the importance of intraelite cohesion, any factional conflict within ruling parties during the long transition needs to be measured precisely through primary elections data. Additionally, claims about the pace, timing, and causes of the sorting of blacks and whites into state Democratic and Republican parties must be demonstrated through time-series analysis. And the relationship between federal oversight of compliance, civil rights organization deployments, and disorder must be measured precisely.

Second, it is important to understand how the democratization experiences of Alabama and Louisiana compare to those interpreted here. If similar dynamics of intraelite conflict, party-state capacities, and elite efforts to minimize external interference do not appear in these cases, why not, and with what implications for our understanding of Georgia, Mississippi, and

South Carolina? Does the ironic relationship between skillful management of the transition and long-run damage to the ruling party hold up in these cases?

Third, how does the experience of the Outer South compare to that of Deep South states? Unlike the Outer South, the Deep South did not feature any instances of *acquiescent* democratizations. How much do the transitions in the Outer South differ from one another? While intraelite cohesion and party-state capacities may be decisive in explaining paths out of the Outer South, it could be that states' coercive capacities may not be as central as they appear to have been in the Deep South. And opposition party development in the Outer South may have advanced enclave collapse in contrast to the Deep South. Would an evaluation of the Outer South lead to a modification of the interpretation of Deep South enclaves? Finally, throughout the South, the deepening of democratization gains during the 1970s and beyond is likely to have been shaped by the nature of black mobilizations in the 1960s in ways we do not yet understand.

Coercion and Violence

When ethnically diverse polities undergo wrenching social and political change, mass bloodshed often follows. Given the ferocity with which organized white supremacists valued the party's historic project, the region featured surprisingly little violence. Fewer than ninety individuals' deaths across the entire South have been attributed to political violence during the transition.[35] Why is this so, and what can scholars of the South—and of communal violence generally—learn from this outcome? Certainly, many political authorities were motivated to avoid interracial violence, but what of the "supply" side of the equation? It is worth investigating whether—as suggested earlier—white mass publics' devotion to white supremacy was as complete as enclave rulers (claimed to have) believed. As occurs in other authoritarian regimes, rulers *and* their subjects often overestimate the degree of popular support for the regime because those opposing it are fearful of communicating their preferences to others (see prologue to part 3). Perhaps this dynamic of "preference falsification" can help explain why most confrontations in the South fizzled out.

Political Modernization

Southern enclaves were born in a moment of constitution-writing, and died in similar fashion. After attempting, with varying degrees of success, to bolster their party-state capacities to resist democratization, all southern states embarked on significant constitutional reform and rewriting during the late 1960s and 1970s.[36] These institutional changes went far beyond the manipulations of electoral laws described in chapter 10 (typical of periods of suffrage expansion elsewhere).[37] Generally, leading politicians attempted to overcome decades-old institutional arrangements that now stymied their efforts to secure career and policy goals—especially making the state more effective for capital accumulation. In South Carolina, authorities succeeded in finally bringing "home rule" to counties, while politicians in Mississippi sought to centralize many features of their polity. Under what conditions did political modernizers succeed, and with what consequences for political and economic developments? The question of state-(re)building after democratization is an increasingly important one for scholars of comparative politics. Of particular importance is the ability of ambitious politicians to reform or design political institutions—apart from electoral laws—to build in advantages for themselves for the long run.[38] The South offers eleven new cases to this literature.

Transitional Justice

Newly democratized societies commonly grapple with several issues grouped under this heading. These include the official accounting of the crimes of the ancien régime, the prosecution of transgressors, truth and reconciliation commissions, apologies and reparations, and controversies over state-sponsored symbols. While all involve reckoning with the past, these embody a struggle to (re)define a polity's values, membership, and aspirations for the future, and they are particularly vexing in ethnically diverse societies.[39] In the South, the most divisive debates have involved state-sponsored symbols,[40] although other issues have also flared up.[41]

Since the 1960s black southerners have demanded changes in public art that, in many cases, had been altered in the 1950s to rally defiance. Over the past decade—prodded by increasingly influential black state legislators and threats of economic boycotts—reputation-minded governors in several states have attempted to modify state flags or remove the Confederate battle flag from state property. Prominent politicians and business leaders have backed the removal of part or all of such elements from these flags, while public opinion surveys reveal hard divisions along racial and class divides. Experiences of states have varied, both in the political processes used to deliberate about symbols and in their outcomes. Scholars are developing sophisticated understandings of the ways in which racial attitudes, ideology, and party identification shape mass opinion on these controversies. In addition, it is worth considering how different modes of democratization have shaped the way former enclaves debate these issues.[42]

Inequality and the Benefits of Democracy

As Lord Bryce noted, democratizers usually have materialist motivations—they seek to eradicate the "tangible evils" confronting them.[43] Given the dramatic shift in social policy provision and subsequent increases in inequality as rulers founded enclaves (chapter 2), there is good reason to expect that the fruits of democracy would be substantial. How successful were democratizers in reducing the inequalities experienced under the thumb of southern oligarchs?

Blacks have secured modest policy benefits as they have exerted electoral power.[44] Similarly, they have benefited from the dismantling of racist law enforcement, the desegregation of public- and private-sector labor markets,[45] and the end of white supremacist rhetoric.[46] The region also experienced the most thorough desegregation of public schools, and today its suburbs are less segregated than those in other areas of the country. But even the policy agendas of the region's celebrated "New South" governors of the early 1970s "rarely extended beyond racial moderation and reform of state governmental structures, prisons, mental health programs, and education." The stubborn poverty still experienced by many Deep South citizens is illustrated in table 11.2. This is especially pronounced in the rural South, although it persists in the urban South as well, as Hurricane Katrina brought to national light. Scholars have found that "outside investment seems to reproduce rather than disrupt local patterns of inequality and poverty." Generally, the region remains a set of low-wage economies favorable to capital; its boosters today proudly cite its top rankings in warm business climates and chilliest workers' climates. Black legislative caucuses, led by Mississippi's, have won important gains.[47]

Placed in a cross-national context, this outcome may not be too surprising. Scholars of regime change have offered several complementary explanations of the empirical regularity by which democratic transitions tend *not* to result in substantial redistribution. As many writers have argued, rulers

TABLE 11.2
Percentage of Persons below Poverty Level, 1969–95

	1969	1975	1980	1990	1995
Georgia	20.7	18	13.9	15.8	12.1
Mississippi	27.8	18.5	24.3	25.7	23.5
South Carolina	23.9	17.2	16.8	16.2	19.9

Sources: Statistical Abstract of the United States, 1980, 467, table 777; Statistical Abstract of the United States, 2000, 477, table 777.

are more likely to concede to democratization pressures when the expected costs of regime change are lower.[48]

In the conclusion to *Southern Politics*, V. O. Key notes that "an underlying liberal drive permeates Southern politics" that would be "mightily strengthened" once blacks secured enfranchisement. However, it could be argued that because enclave rulers held out long enough, by the time of the democratic transitions, many of the broader questions about the region's political economy had been settled. Southern authoritarians, defying Reinhard Bendix's famous claim about the sequencing of democratization and industrialization, may have triumphed after all.[49] This possibility suggests counterfactual analysis of the timing of the South's overall regime change and of different transition experiences to divine their impact on the fruits of democracy.

The New New South: The U.S. South in Hemispheric Perspective

Latin America's three most important countries—Argentina, Brazil, and Mexico—have all recently experienced regime change. Extrications from authoritarianism have been followed by often incomplete democratizations. Perhaps one-third of Mexico's thirty-two subnational jurisdictions could be classified as authoritarian enclaves.[50]

The southern enclaves of the past and Latin America's contemporary enclaves have some features in common. Probably most importantly, Latin America's enclaves are often relatively more agrarian and ruled by landed elites who carefully perpetuate clientelistic relations with their workers. There are, of course, dissimilarities as well. U.S. enclaves survived through a period of stable national politics, and the national polity had long been democratized, while today's enclaves persist in only very recently democratized polities. Additionally, ranked ascriptive identities structured southern enclaves, in contrast to those in Latin America. Still, many lines of common inquiry concerning the causes and consequences of enclave rule present themselves.

For instance, some comparativists suggest that enclaves imperil a polity's democratic consolidation, whether by providing a safe place for the development of an authoritarian comeback or through other mechanisms.[51] Short of imperiling a state's democratization, enclaves might disrupt or halt the state-level implementation of federal reforms. But the South's relationship to the formation of the modern American state during the New Deal and World War II suggests a disquieting hypothesis about Latin America's enclaves. Perhaps such enclaves *facilitate*—rather than frustrate—the completion of democratization processes at the federal level. Bargains between politicians situated at the federal and state levels can provide the glue necessary to begin important reform projects. Under certain conditions, authoritarian enclaves may for a time need to be nurtured, not attacked, in order to consolidate national-level democratization.[52] Generally, the existence of enclaves in these federal polities, in concert with some similarities in the political-economic features of these enclaves, suggests a remapping of the U.S. South in hemispheric perspective.

The South in American Political Development

The subfield of American political development (APD) currently suffers from a lack of coherent debates, missed opportunities to place the United States more squarely in cross-national perspective, and, generally, from the loss of the boldness that characterized much of its early work.[53] But in excellent recent research, scholars have proposed counterfactual Americas that pivot on the South. These proposals posit that the shape of the central state apparatus, the American welfare state, party system, and political economy would all look quite different had the twentieth-century South developed differently—in particular, if the national Democratic party had not been an uneasy combination of "Sweden meets South Africa," in the words of Ira Katznelson. By protecting southern prerogatives through their pivotal place in Congress, enclave rulers blocked the advent of social democracy in the United States.[54]

This bold line of careful research offers tremendous possibilities. But are these counterfactuals persuasive? Is the present shape of U.S. state and society the South's fault? Was the non-South (not to be confused with the urban North of New Deal yore) really "Sweden"? Recent historical scholarship casts some doubt on sharp distinctions between levels of racial conflict in the South and non-South.[55] It is far from obvious that—in the absence of enclave rule—American national institutions would have crafted a substantially different central state and a thoroughly altered political economy. Moreover, this study has demonstrated that the southern enclaves were irreducibly American. These enclaves' emergence, persistence, collapse, and aftermaths have been shaped profoundly by the indifference and timorousness of the rest of the country. This indifference raises doubts about the plausibility of the flowering of social democracy in the North, much less the rest of the country.

APD would benefit from releasing the South from the "Why no socialism?" interrogation room, and instead exploit the region to understand better the development of the American polity in cross-national perspective. I have suggested here how we might return to the study of macrohistorical processes such as democratization, state-building, and long-term economic change. Current developments in contemporary Latin America provide more reasons to do so.

With this research, I hope to contribute to an important new line of inquiry that disrupts traditional narratives of American democracy and suggests a different kind of American exceptionalism. Several scholars have been highly persuasive in arguing that we have long underestimated the degree to which American democracy has been contested. In particular, building on the work of southern historians, they show that suffrage—the lynchpin of democratic rule—has been contested throughout our history, that its expansion has been anything but linear, and retraction and expansions have been contingent throughout.[56] Triumphalist narratives of the inevitability of universal suffrage in America are left reeling. And suffrage remains contested—witness the current debate over felon disenfranchisement and the new wave of voter suppression tactics, which are likely to worsen after *Shelby v. Holder*'s weakening of the Voting Rights Act.[57] Others have raised important questions about the support for democracy in U.S. political and legal thought.[58]

My understanding of the South fits with this line of research. I also emphasize suffrage and suggest a different periodization of America's democratic development.[59] But my work is a departure as well, because it concerns not just suffrage but also democratic governance. On my view, not only universal suffrage but also a completely consolidated *democracy* is a recent arrival on U.S. shores. A whole host of requirements of democratic rule, including associational freedoms and the rule of law, have been consolidated only since the early 1970s. Richard Valelly argues that the United States is distinct among democracies for having enfranchised, disenfranchised, and *re*enfranchised groups of its citizens while remaining a democracy.[60] Similarly, Richard Bensel motivates his masterwork on the politics of American industrialization by wondering how the United States managed to undergo rapid industrialization while remaining democratic. My work suggests that the country *did* undergo a change in regime type—it transformed itself from a federal democracy at the turn of the twentieth century into one featuring stable enclaves of authoritarian rule.[61]

One implication of this perspective is that APD scholars might reorient their comparisons. Rather than looking solely to Europe—the preoccupation of scholars of the welfare state—we might benefit from looking South, where several other polities have wrestled simultaneously with questions of racial hierarchies, labor, and politics in a post-emancipation context. Latin America is now home to many authoritarian enclaves in the region's newly democratized federal polities. The United States differs, of course—it was a federal democracy before the abolition of slavery, and it tolerated pockets of authoritarianism for three-quarters of a century. Contemporary Argentina, Brazil, and Mexico are now grappling with enclaves just after the installation of democratic rule, and in a completely different historical moment.[62] But it should be at the very least an open question whether accounting for

America's status as a "late, late, democratizer" is best understood by focusing on Western Europe and not the polities with which the United States seems to share a good deal more.[63]

If the consolidation of democracy across the entire polity took so long to occur, was so complex and contingent, should we view it as permanent? Certainly we can imagine new restrictions on associational freedoms and on suffrage.[64] More broadly, this study reminds us of the importance of the partisan environment in safeguarding—or threatening—democracy well after it seems secured. Many other questions need answering if we are to understand the causes of America's belated democratization. How robust have been America's cultural commitments to democratic rule? What kinds of commitments about democracy in the non-South both sustained democratic rule there and sustained enclave rule elsewhere? How should we assess institutions such as federalism and confederally structured parties?[65]

Scholars must free the study of black politics from the confines of the "social movement" in which it has for too long been trapped. By focusing attention on the stars of Key's stage—southern Democratic politicians—the true achievement of southern blacks and their allies can be fully appreciated. This focus allows us to see clearly these actors not as movement activists, but as domestic insurgents fighting to tear down and rebuild political regimes; not as seekers of "rights," but as democratizers. It is perhaps a continuing victory of the region's authoritarian rulers that we refer to these democratizers almost exclusively as movement-specific activists; through their long adjustment to democratization pressures, these rulers narrowed our gaze from wide-ranging "tangible evils" to abstracted "rights."

As Faulkner famously wrote—and as all writers on the South seem determined to quote—the "past is never dead. It's not even past." Despite a half-century of overwhelming change, the legacies of slavery, Reconstruction, Redemption, enclave rule, and the long struggle to overcome it hang heavy over the region. These seem to be an albatross around the necks of those striving to fulfill the hopes of the region's democratizers. However, the legacies of the past are only that—they shape and constrain possible futures, but do not determine them. Delivering a eulogy over the graves of these enclaves in 1972, the Staples Singers offered to take us to a place freed of "smiling faces / lying to the races." True, three decades later, the anthem is best known as the soundtrack to a Ford commercial. While more of a rebuke than a portrait of reality, "I'll Take You There" remains a blueprint of a South still worth building.[66]

Notes

Abbreviations in the Notes

AC   *Atlanta Constitution*

AHR   *American Historical Review*

AJ   *Atlanta Journal*

AJPS   *American Journal of Political Science*

APSR   *American Political Science Review*

ARPS   *Annual Review of Political Science*

ASR   *American Sociological Review*

CNC   *Charleston News and Courier*

CR   *Columbia Record*

CRMDA   Civil Rights in Mississippi Digital Archive, University of Southern Mississippi

CS   *Columbia State*

CSM   *Christian Science Monitor*

GHQ   *Georgia Historical Quarterly*

Heard Papers   Alexander Heard Papers, Vanderbilt University

JAH   *Journal of American History*

JCL   *Jackson Clarion-Ledger*

JDN   *Jackson Daily News*

JEH   *Journal of Economic History*

JMH   *Journal of Mississippi History*

JNE   *Journal of Negro Education*

JNH   *Journal of Negro History*

JPH   *Journal of Policy History*

JOP   *Journal of Politics*

JSH   *Journal of Southern History*

LAT	*Los Angeles Times*
LBJL	Lyndon Baines Johnson Presidential Library, Austin, Texas
MCA	*Memphis Commercial-Appeal*
MDAH	Mississippi Department of Archives and History
MSSC	Files of the Mississippi State Sovereignty Commission
NAACP Papers	Papers of the National Association for the Advancement of Colored People
NYT	*New York Times*
RBRL	Richard B. Russell Library for Political Research and Studies, University of Georgia
Sampson	Gregory B. Sampson, "The Rise of the "New" Republican Party in South Carolina, 1948–1974: A Case Study of Political Change in a Deep South State," Ph.D. diss., University of North Carolina-Chapel Hill (1984)
SAPD	*Studies in American Political Development*
SCHM	*South Carolina Historical Magazine*
SCPC	South Carolina Political Collections, University of South Carolina
SDEC Papers	Papers of the Georgia State Democratic Executive Committee
SHC	Southern Historical Collection, University of North Carolina
SNCC	Papers of the Student Nonviolent Coordinating Committee
SOHP	Southern Oral History Program, University of North Carolina
SSN	*Southern School News*
TAPP	The American Presidency Project, University of California, Santa Barbara
TNR	*The New Republic*
WHCF	White House Central Files
Workman Papers	Papers of William D. Workman SCPC
WP	*Washington Post*
WSJ	*Wall Street Journal*

CHAPTER ONE:
Southern Political Development in Comparative Perspective

1. The epigraphs to this chapter are from J. Morgan Kousser, *The Shaping of Southern Politics: Suffrage Restriction and the Establishment of the One-Party South, 1880–1910* (New Haven: Yale University Press, 1974), 8; and V. O. Key, Jr., with Alexander Heard, *Southern Politics in State and Nation* (Knoxville: University of Tennessee Press, 1984 [1949]), 661. On the University of Georgia (UGA) crisis, Robert Cohen, "G-Men in Georgia: The FBI and the Segregationist Riot at the University of Georgia, 1961," *Georgia Historical Quarterly* 83 (1999), 524 and 528–32 (hereafter *GHQ*); *Atlanta Journal*, Jan. 15, 1961 (hereafter *AJ*).

2. William Doyle, *An American Insurrection: The Battle of Oxford, Mississippi, 1962* (New York: Doubleday, 2001), 257, 280–89.

3. Jerome V. Reel, Jr., "Clemson and Harvey Gantt," in Skip Eisiminger, ed., *Integration with Dignity* (Clemson, S.C.: Clemson University Digital Press, 2002), 44–52; *New York Times*, Jan. 31, Apr. 4, 1963 (hereafter *NYT*); *Charleston News and Courier*, Jan. 30, 1963 (hereafter *CNC*); George McMillan, "Integration with Dignity: The Inside Story of How South Carolina Kept the Peace," *Saturday Evening Post* 236 (Mar. 16, 1963), 16–21. "[S]tepping dapper" is taken from Don DeLillo, *Underworld* (New York: Scribner, 1997), 12.

4. The Outer South (also termed the "Peripheral South," "Rim South," and "Upper South") consists of Arkansas, Florida, North Carolina, Tennessee, Texas, and Virginia; the "Deep South" covers Alabama, Georgia, Louisiana, Mississippi, and South Carolina. I discuss conceptions of "the South" in chapter 2.

5. Just after the Civil War, Republican Mississippi governor James Alcorn counseled whites to respect blacks' civil and voting rights as part of an effort to render Reconstruction a "harnessed revolution." James C. Cobb, *The Most Southern Place on Earth: The Mississippi Delta and the Roots of Regional Identity* (New York: Oxford University Press, 1992), 61.

6. These concepts, as well as types of democratization processes, will be discussed later in this chapter.

7. By 2011, there were more than 10,500 black elected officials nationwide. Joint Center for Political and Economic Studies, "National Roster of Black Elected Officials: Fact Sheet" (November 2011). The 2010 Census reports that the eleven-state South is home to about 48 percent of the 42 million Americans who declare "Black" or "African American" as at least one of their races. Bureau of the Census, *The Black Population: 2010, 2010 Census Briefs* (Washington, D.C.: U.S. Department of Commerce, September 2011), table 5, p. 8; Bureau of the Census, *Age and Sex Composition: 2010, 2010 Census Briefs* (Washington, D.C.: U.S. Department of Commerce, May 2011), table 3, p. 7. By 2000 southerners had recently elected almost six thousand black officials, more than 60 percent of the nation's total. Joint Center for Political and Economic Studies, *Black Elected Officials: A Statistical Summary, 2001* (Washington, D.C.: Joint Center, May 2002). Due to penal disenfranchisement and other restrictions on the suffrage, the number of adults eligible to vote falls short of the region's voting-age population of 73 million. Becky Pettit, *Invisible Men: Mass Incarceration and the Myth of Black Progress* (New York: Russell Sage Foundation, 2012),

chap. 5. On the important distinction between voting-age population and voting-eligible population, see Michael P. McDonald and Samuel L. Popkin, "The Myth of the Vanishing Voter," *American Political Science Review* 95 (2001), 963–74 (hereafter *APSR*). On the role of southern partisan change in producing today's high levels of ideological and partisan polarization in Congress, see Nolan McCarty, Keith T. Poole, and Howard Rosenthal, *Polarized America: The Dance of Ideology and Unequal Riches* (Cambridge: MIT Press, 2006), 52–54.

8. Influential recent studies include Earl Black and Merle Black, *Politics and Society in the South* (Cambridge: Harvard University Press, 1987), and *The Rise of Southern Republicans* (Cambridge: Harvard University Press, 2002); Merle Black, "The Transformation of the Southern Democratic Party," *Journal of Politics* 66 (2004), 1001–17 (hereafter *JOP*); Byron E. Shafer and Richard Johnston, *The End of Southern Exceptionalism: Class, Race, and Partisan Change in the Postwar South* (Cambridge: Harvard University Press, 2006); David Lublin, *The Republican South: Democratization and Partisan Change* (Princeton: Princeton University Press, 2004); Joseph A. Aistrup, *The Southern Strategy Revisited: Republican Top-Down Advancement in the South* (Lexington: University Press of Kentucky, 1996); and Nelson W. Polsby, *How Congress Evolves: Social Bases of Institutional Change* (New York: Oxford University Press, 2005). See also John H. Aldrich, "Southern Parties in State and Nation," *JOP* 62 (2000), 643–70; J. Morgan Kousser, "The Immutability of Categories and the Reshaping of Southern Politics," *Annual Review of Political Science* 13 (2010), 365–83 (hereafter *ARPS*). I discuss this literature in chapter 11. I learned of a major new study too late to learn from and engage with it: M. V. Hood, Quentin Kidd, and Irwin L. Morris, *The Rational Southerner: Black Mobilization, Republican Growth, and the Partisan Transformation of the American South* (New York: Oxford University Press, 2013).

9. Howard Schuman, Charlotte Steeh, Lawrence Bobo, and Maria Krysan, *Racial Attitudes in America: Trends and Interpretations*, rev. ed. (Cambridge: Harvard University Press, 1997).

10. See Ronald Inglehart and Christian Welzel, *Modernization, Cultural Change, and Democracy: The Human Development Sequence* (New York: Cambridge University Press, 2005). See also David J. Elkins and Richard E. B. Simeon, "A Cause in Search of an Effect, or What Does Political Culture Explain?" *Comparative Politics* 11 (1979), 127–45.

11. On political elites, see, e.g., Robert D. Putnam, *The Comparative Study of Political Elites* (Upper Saddle River, N.J.: Prentice Hall, 1976); Mattei Dogan and John Higley, "Elites, Crises, and Regimes in Comparative Analysis," in Dogan and Higley, eds., *Elites, Crises, and the Origins of Regimes* (Lanham, Md.: Rowman and Littlefield, 1998), 3–28. On elite agency during regime transitions, Guillermo O'Donnell and Philippe C. Schmitter, *Transitions from Authoritarian Rule*, vol. 4: *Tentative Conclusions about Uncertain Democracies* (Baltimore: Johns Hopkins University Press, 1986).

12. For a modernization narrative by a leading historian, see Numan V. Bartley, *The New South, 1945–1980: The Story of the South's Modernization* (Baton Rouge: Louisiana State University Press, 1995).

13. On North Carolina, see Key, *Southern Politics*, chap. 10. David R. Mayhew characterizes this range as stretching from "pre-1960s Virginia (honesty, deference, low turnout, quiet nominating process) [to] Louisiana (the New Orleans machine tradition, populism, buffoonery, corruption, hypercompetitive nominating pro-

cesses)." Mayhew, *Placing Parties in American Politics: Organization, Electoral Settings, and Government Activity in the Twentieth Century* (Princeton: Princeton University Press, 1986), 236, fn. 88. Historians and contemporaneous observers interpreted Mississippi as a more populist state inhabited by rough-hewn whites with quick-trigger tempers and a high tolerance for violence and disorder. From this milieu of "rednecks," Mississippi drew its political leadership. Albert D. Kirwan, *The Revolt of the Rednecks: Mississippi Politics, 1876–1925* (Lexington: University Press of Kentucky, 1951). Meanwhile, South Carolina's historians have stressed its tradition of aristocratic social and political relations in attempting to explain the state's less turbulent and more decorous transition. See, for instance, the masterwork of Walter B. Edgar, one of the state's foremost historians, *South Carolina: A History* (Columbia: University of South Carolina Press, 1998), 541, 552; John G. Sproat, "'Firm Flexibility': Perspectives on Desegregation in South Carolina," in Robert H. Abzug and Stephen E. Maizlish, eds., *New Perspectives on Race and Slavery in America: Essays in Honor of Kenneth M. Stampp* (Lexington: University Press of Kentucky, 1986), 175; Marcia G. Synnott, "Federalism Vindicated: University Desegregation in South Carolina and Alabama, 1962–1963," *Journal of Policy History* 1 (1989), 292–318 (hereafter *JPH*). For an excellent critique of the actions of South Carolina leaders that upends their "self-exculpatory" account of the state's transition, see Tony Badger, "From Defiance to Moderation: South Carolina Governors and Racial Change," in Winfred B. Moore, Jr. and Orville Vernon Burton, eds., *Toward the Meeting of the Waters: Currents in the Civil Rights Movement of South Carolina during the Twentieth Century* (Columbia: University of South Carolina Press, 2008), 3–21.

14. To be fair, South Carolina's massive resistance experience does not necessarily cast doubt on the importance of elite political culture in explaining change; it could instead suggest that the characterization of that state's elites as aristocratic, dignified, and unusually image-conscious may require revision. While political skill, farsightedness, and intelligence are traits on which some Deep South leaders may have differed, the narratives will suggest that these attributes reflect other, more important causal factors, such as how enclaves managed factional conflict.

15. For arguments pointing to the middle and working classes, see Barrington Moore, Jr., *Social Origins of Democracy and Dictatorship* (Cambridge: Belknap Press, 1966), and Dietrich Rueschemeyer, Evelyne H. Stephens, and John D. Stephens, *Capitalist Development and Democracy* (Chicago: University of Chicago Press, 1992), respectively. Ruth Berins Collier's *Paths Toward Democracy: Working Class and Elites in Western Europe and South America* (New York: Cambridge University Press, 1999) shows that the importance of particular classes as drivers of democratization varies across region and era. Furthermore, she finds that more recently, democratization has emerged as a "joint project" in which the participation of working classes, in addition to self-interested actors situated in other classes or organizations, has been critical in securing suffrage (34, 55, 76, 172). Seymour Martin Lipset brings together cultural and economic modernization arguments in "Some Social Requisites of Democracy: Economic Development and Political Legitimacy," *APSR* 53 (1959), 69–85. These class-centered accounts have not always fared well. Moreover, income levels do not help explain subnational variation in democratic governance in a range of cases, including Argentina, Brazil, India, and Russia, where poorer provinces often outperform richer ones. James Mahoney, "Knowledge Accumulation in

Comparative Historical Research: The Case of Democracy and Authoritarianism," in Mahoney and Dietrich Rueschemeyer, eds., *Comparative Historical Analysis in the Social Sciences* (New York: Cambridge University Press, 2003), 131–74; Carlos Gervasoni, "A Rentier Theory of Subnational Regimes: Fiscal Federalism, Democracy, and Authoritarianism in the Argentine Provinces," *World Politics* 62 (2010), 331. For a recent study that focuses not on classes as actors but ascriptive groups, see Jeffrey S. Kopstein and Jason Wittenberg, "Beyond Dictatorship and Democracy: Rethinking National Minority Inclusion and Regime Type in Interwar Eastern Europe," *Comparative Political Studies* 43 (2010), 1089–118.

16. Jack M. Bloom, *Class, Race, and the Civil Rights Movement: The Changing Political Economy of Southern Racism* (Bloomington: University of Indiana Press, 1987). For an excellent account of mobilized white middle-class residents of metro Atlanta and Charlotte, see Matthew D. Lassiter, *The Silent Majority: Suburban Politics in the Sunbelt South* (Princeton: Princeton University Press, 2007).

17. Mahoney, "Knowledge Accumulation in Comparative Historical Research," 147–48; Rueschemeyer, Stephens, and Stephens, *Capitalist Development and Democracy*, 270–71. Moore, *Social Origins of Democracy and Dictatorship*, introduced the "labor-repressive agriculture" concept, which has been criticized for helping produce economically deterministic explanations of long-term political trajectories. Theda Skocpol, "A Critical Review of Barrington Moore's *Social Origins of Dictatorship and Democracy*," *Politics & Society* 4 (1973), 1–34; and Marcus J. Kurtz, "Understanding Peasant Revolution: From Concept to Theory and Case," *Theory and Society* 29 (2000), 93–124. Pointing to the cases of Mexico and Syria, David Waldner demonstrates that "the elimination of anti-democratic landed elites" is far from a sufficient condition for democratization. Waldner, "Democracy and Dictatorship in the Post-Colonial World" (unpublished manuscript in the author's possession, 2004), 33. For applications of Barrington Moore's approach to the post–Civil War South, see Jonathan M. Wiener, *Social Origins of the New South: Alabama, 1860–1885* (Baton Rouge: Louisiana State University Press, 1978); Wiener, "Class Structure and Economic Development in the American South, 1865–1955," *American Historical Review* (hereafter *AHR*) 84 (1979), 970–92; Dwight B. Billings, Jr., *Planters and the Making of a "New South": Class, Politics, and Development in North Carolina, 1865–1900* (Chapel Hill: University of North Carolina Press, 1979).

18. The rarity of democratic regimes in agrarian societies is well established, and scholars have offered many explanations of this regularity. Rueschemeyer, Stephens, and Stephens, *Capitalist Development and Democracy*, 2, 23, 60, 288–89; Robert A. Dahl, *Polyarchy: Participation and Opposition* (New Haven: Yale University Press, 1971), 54, 82–88. Elisabeth Jean Wood argues that in these situations, tools to repress agricultural workers "include restrictions on labor mobility, immigration controls, suffrage restrictions, and extralegal violence." Wood, *Forging Democracy from Below: Insurgent Transitions in South Africa and El Salvador* (New York: Cambridge University Press, 2000), 5. See also James A. Robinson, "Economic Development and Democracy," *ARPS* 9 (2006), 508–10, 515; Carles Boix, *Democracy and Redistribution* (New York: Cambridge University Press, 2003); Dahl, *Polyarchy*, 15, 54.

19. Marxist variants of this argument draw even starker comparisons among polities with different degrees of labor-dependent landed elites. On this view, southern state and local officials are likened to handmaidens of "local class structures," which

have "direct effect[s] on resistance to suffrage expansion." David R. James, "The Transformation of the Southern Racial State: Class and Race Determinants of Local-State Structures," *American Sociological Review* 53 (1988), 205 (hereafter *ASR*).

20. Elites controlling access to suffrage liberalize it only when they perceive a threatening mobilization by the disenfranchised—especially an unexpected one. These elites see themselves as better off than if they do not do so, but—and this is why the suffrage is "conquered," not "granted"—after liberalizing the suffrage they are still worse off than they were before facing this threat. Adam Przeworski, "Conquered or Granted? A History of Suffrage Extensions," *British Journal of Political Science* 39 (2008), 294, 307–38, and *passim*. Przeworski examines suffrage extensions pertaining mainly to class, not ascriptive identities such as race. Given the coincidence of racial and class cleavages in the South, his findings are relevant to its democratization.

21. Thus, for V. O. Key, Black Belt planters dominated the politics of their states (*Southern Politics*, chap. 1). Accommodations reached among planters and owners of low-wage, industrial, rural firms are discussed in James C. Cobb, "Beyond Planters and Industrialists: A New Perspective on the New South," *Journal of Southern History* 54 (1988), 56 (hereafter *JSH*).

22. C. Vann Woodward uses the phrase in "The Search for Southern Identity," in Woodward, *The Burden of Southern History* (Baton Rouge: Louisiana State University Press, 1993 [1958]), 10. Generally, see Gavin Wright, *Old South, New South: Revolutions in the Southern Economy Since the Civil War* (New York: Basic Books, 1986), and Gavin Wright, *Sharing the Prize: The Economics of the Civil Rights Revolution in the American South* (Cambridge: Harvard University Press, 2012). Also see Matthew D. Lassiter and Kevin M. Kruse, "Bulldozer Revolution: Suburbs and Southern History since World War II," *JSH* 75 (2009), 691–706. For a Marxian account that traces the evolving interests of officeholders and their economic clients, see Philip J. Wood, *Southern Capitalism: The Political Economy of North Carolina, 1880–1980* (Durham, N.C.: Duke University Press, 1986).

23. Elites' resistance to political liberalization is considered more likely in economically more unequal societies. Anticipating that their wealth will be taxed at higher rates, economic elites pressure authorities to repress, rather than concede to, democratizers. In highly unequal democracies, the "median voter" will be even poorer relative to the mean of the income distribution, and will prefer higher taxes to redistribute more income downward. Daron Acemoglu and James A. Robinson, *Economic Origins of Dictatorship and Democracy* (New York: Cambridge University Press, 2006); Stephan Haggard and Robert F. Kaufman, "Inequality and Regime Change: Democratic Transitions and the Stability of Democratic Rule," *APSR* 106 (2012), 495–516; Christian Houle, "Inequality and Democracy: Why Inequality Harms Consolidation but Does Not Affect Democratization," *World Politics* 61 (2009), 589–622. For an excellent treatment of the literature, see Barbara Geddes, "What Causes Democratization?" in Carles Boix and Susan C. Stokes, eds., *The Oxford Handbook of Comparative Politics* (New York: Oxford University Press, 2007), 317–39.

24. Joseph E. Luders, "The Politics of Exclusion: The Political Economy of Civil Rights in the American South, 1954–1965," Ph.D. diss., New School for Social Research (2000); Luders, *The Civil Rights Movement and the Logic of Social Change* (New York: Cambridge University Press, 2010).

25. Wright, *Sharing the Prize*. There is also good reason to expect liberalizing political reforms to lag behind economic modernization. Economic inequalities are usually exploited by those who can wield their political influence to lock in and perpetuate these inequalities over time. Stanley L. Engerman and Kenneth L. Sokoloff argue that long-term economic growth trajectories across U.S. states (and among post-Emancipation New World polities more generally) have been heavily shaped by the divergence in agricultural patterns. See Engerman and Sokoloff, "Factor Endowments, Institutions, and Differential Paths of Growth among New World Economies," in Stephen Haber, ed., *How Latin America Fell Behind: Essays on the Economic Histories of Brazil and Mexico, 1800–1914* (Stanford: Stanford University Press, 1997), 260–304.

26. Doug McAdam, *Political Process and the Development of Black Insurgency, 1930–1970* (Chicago: University of Chicago Press, 1982), 90–94. Also see Aldon D. Morris, *The Origins of the Civil Rights Movement: Black Communities Organizing for Change* (New York: Free Press, 1984). For some insights on the political preferences of southern blacks, see Donald R. Matthews and James W. Prothro, *Negroes and the New Southern Politics* (New York: Harcourt, Brace, and World, 1966). Kelly M. McMann makes a similar argument about the importance of economic independence for encouraging individuals to press claims for democratic governance—in this case, workers' low level of dependence on state employers—in McMann, *Economic Autonomy and Democracy: Hybrid Regimes in Russia and Kyrgyzstan* (New York: Cambridge University Press, 2006).

27. McAdam and others have also detailed differences among authorities in whether and how they adjusted their tactical responses to protest in order to avoid violence and disorder. In this way, they argue, rulers' actions are often important in explaining whether movements are more or less likely to secure concessions. McAdam, *Political Process*, 56–57, and "Tactical Innovation and the Pace of Insurgency," *ASR* 48 (1983), 744. He notes further that black insurgency could help authorities already committed to political change for economic reasons to justify such reforms. Also see Steven E. Barkan, "Legal Control of the Southern Civil Rights Movement," *ASR* 49 (1984), 552–65; Aldon D. Morris, "Birmingham Confrontation Reconsidered: An Analysis of the Dynamics and Tactics of Mobilization," *ASR* 58 (1993), 621–36. In focusing more attention on the ways in which rulers' interests, institutional settings, and capacities come together to shape their behavior, my analysis is more similar to J. Mills Thornton's *Dividing Lines: Municipal Politics and the Struggle for Civil Rights in Montgomery, Birmingham, and Selma* (Tuscaloosa: University of Alabama Press, 2002).

28. David Collier and Ruth Berins Collier, *Shaping the Political Arena: Critical Junctures, the Labor Movement, and Regime Dynamics in Latin America* (Princeton: Princeton University Press, 1991), 11.

29. Kousser, "The Immutability of Categories and the Reshaping of Southern Politics," 366.

30. By flattening the "civil rights movement" into a teleplay of divinely inspired direct action, the historiography of the South is often "more theatrical than instructive." Charles Payne, *I've Got the Light of Freedom: The Organizing Tradition and the Mississippi Freedom Struggle* (Berkeley: University of California Press, 1995), 418; Charles W. Eagles, "Toward New Histories of the Civil Rights Era," *JSH* 64 (2000), 815–48. Among a growing line of research on these politicians, see, e.g., Lassiter,

The Silent Majority; Joseph Crespino, *In Search of Another Country: Mississippi and the Conservative Counterrevolution* (Princeton: Princeton University Press, 2007); Keith M. Finley, *Delaying the Dream: Southern Senators and the Fight against Civil Rights, 1938–1965* (Baton Rouge: Louisiana State University Press, 2008).

31. On the normative status of elections and universal suffrage, see Przeworski, "Conquered or Granted?" 291; Dahl, *Polyarchy*, 55. More broadly, Ian Shapiro calls "the democratic idea" "close to nonnegotiable in today's world," observing that "authoritarian rulers seldom reject democracy outright." Shapiro, *The State of Democratic Theory* (Princeton: Princeton University Press, 2003), 1.

32. Regimes can be thought of as that set of procedures that "regulate access to state power." Gerardo L. Munck, "The Regime Question: Theory Building in Democracy Studies," *World Politics* 54 (2001), 123. The benefits to rulers of holding elections are discussed in Edmund Malesky and Paul Schuler, "The Single-Party Dictator's Dilemma: Information in Elections without Opposition," *Legislative Studies Quarterly* 36 (2011), 491–530; and Jennifer Gandhi and Ellen Lust-Okar, "Elections under Authoritarianism," *ARPS* 12 (2009), 403–22. On the relative durability of one-party regimes compared to those ruled by military juntas, personalist dictatorships, and other types, see Barbara Geddes, "What Do We Know about Democratization after Twenty Years?" *ARPS* 2 (1999), 132, 125, 124. Amid a quickly growing literature on electoral authoritarianism, see especially Steven Levitsky and Lucan A. Way, *Competitive Authoritarianism: Hybrid Regimes after the Cold War* (New York: Cambridge University Press, 2010). Also see Beatriz Magaloni and Ruth Kricheli, "Political Order and One-Party Rule," *ARPS* 13 (2010), 123–43; Yonatan L. Morse, "The Era of Electoral Authoritarianism," *World Politics* 64 (2012), 161–98.

33. For data on regime transitions since 1950, see Magaloni and Kricheli, "Political Order and One-Party Rule," 124–25, 128–29. On democratic consolidation, see Munck, "The Regime Question," 126–28. Here, the term refers to the stability of democratic governance, which requires stable expectations among political contestants concerning the uncertainty of electoral outcomes, and thus their shared beliefs that each views democratic rule as durable. Adam Przeworski, "Some Problems in the Study of the Transition to Democracy," in Guillermo O'Donnell, Philippe C. Schmitter, and Laurence Whitehead, eds., *Transitions from Authoritarian Rule*, vol. 3: *Comparative Perspectives* (Baltimore: The Johns Hopkins University Press, 1986), 47–63.

34. On Brazil, see Frances Hagopian, *Traditional Politics and Regime Change in Brazil* (New York: Cambridge University Press, 1996); Alfred P. Montero, "A Reversal of Political Fortune: The Transitional Dynamics of Conservative Rule in the Brazilian Northeast," *Latin American Politics and Society* 54 (2012), 1–36. On Russia, Kelly McMann and Nikolai Petrov, "A Survey of Democracy in Russia's Regions," *Post-Soviet Geography and Economics* 41 (2000), 155–82; McMann, *Economic Autonomy and Democracy*. On Argentina and Mexico, Edward L. Gibson, *Boundary Control: Subnational Authoritarianism in Federal Democracies* (New York: Cambridge University Press, 2013), chaps. 4 and 5, respectively. A recent study finds that one-fifth of Argentine provinces and almost one-third of Mexico's states warrant the label "authoritarian." Agustina Giraudy, "The Politics of Subnational Undemocratic Regime Reproduction in Argentina and Mexico," *Journal of Politics in Latin America* 2 (2010), 58–59. Carlos Gervasoni paints a different portrait in Gervasoni, *Conceptualizing and*

Measuring Subnational Democracy: An Expert Survey Approach, Working Paper 23, The Committee on Concepts and Methods (IPSA-CIDE, 2008). Also see Allyson Lucinda Benton, "Bottom-Up Challenges to National Democracy: Mexico's (Legal) Subnational Authoritarian Enclaves," *Comparative Politics* 44 (2012), 253–71. For a critique of the concept of subnational authoritarianism, see Jacqueline Behrend, "The Unevenness of Democracy at the Subnational Level: Provincial Closed Games in Argentina," *Latin American Research Review* 46 (2011), 150–76.

35. Gibson, *Boundary Control*. In this book I use "ruling party" and "hegemonic party" interchangeably. Reconstruction combined military occupation with subsidized party-building. Richard F. Bensel, *Yankee Leviathan: The Origins of Central State Authority in America, 1859–1877* (New York: Cambridge University Press, 1990). As Key writes, "The predominant consideration in the architecture of southern political institutions has been to assure locally a subordination of the negro population, and, externally, to block threatened interferences from the outside world with these arrangements" (*Southern Politics*, 665).

36. Gibson, *Boundary Control*, 25–26, 29. For a somewhat analogous discussion of outside leverage over *national* electoral authoritarian regimes, see Steven Levitsky and Lucan A. Way, "International Linkage and Democratization," *Journal of Democracy* 16 (2005), 20–35.

37. On the overstated benefits to rulers of juridical sovereignty, see Stephen D. Krasner, *Sovereignty: Organized Hypocrisy* (Princeton: Princeton University Press, 1999), 1–2. Guillermo O'Donnell discusses problems of law enforcement and rule of law in "On the State, Democratization and Some Conceptual Problems," *World Development* 21 (1993), 1357; also see Rebecca Bill Chavez, *The Rule of Law in Nascent Democracies: Judicial Politics in Argentina* (Stanford: Stanford University Press, 2004). The quotation appears in Edward L. Gibson, "Subnational Authoritarianism and Territorial Politics: Charting the Theoretical Landscape," paper presented at the Annual Meetings of the American Political Science Association, Boston (2008), 15.

38. Samuel P. Huntington, *The Third Wave: Democratization in the Late 20th Century* (Norman: University of Oklahoma Press, 1991); Edward L. Gibson, "Politics of the Periphery: An Introduction to Subnational Authoritarianism and Democratization in Latin America," *Journal of Politics in Latin America* 2 (2010), 3. On democratization amid decentralization, see Richard Snyder, "Scaling Down: The Subnational Comparative Method," *Studies in Comparative International Development* 36 (2001), 93–94; Richard Snyder, *Politics After Neoliberalism: Reregulation in Mexico* (New York: Cambridge University Press, 2001); and Tulia G. Falleti, *Decentralization and Subnational Politics in Latin America* (New York: Cambridge University Press, 2010). The quotation appears in Edward L. Gibson, "Subnational Authoritarianism: Territorial Strategies of Political Control in Democratic Regimes," paper presented at the Annual Meetings of the American Political Science Association, Chicago (2004), 20.

39. Gibson, *Boundary Control*, 5; Gibson, "Subnational Authoritarianism," 19 and 21. But Agustina Giraudy argues that under many conditions, this incentive does not dominate national-level politicians' decision-making here. Giraudy, "Varieties of Subnational Undemocratic Regimes: Evidence from Argentina and Mexico," *Studies in Comparative International Development* 48 (2013), 51–80.

40. Just one decade after the wave of regime change that began in 1989, the post-Soviet space—for decades all communist, one-party regimes and socialist

economies—was the world's most diverse region with respect to types of regimes. Herbert Kitschelt, "Accounting for Post-Communist Regime Diversity," in Grzegorz Ekiert and Stephen E. Hanson, eds., *Capitalism and Democracy in Central and Eastern Europe: Assessing the Legacy of Communist Rule* (New York: Cambridge University Press, 2003), 49, 54; Valerie Bunce, "Rethinking Recent Democratization: Lessons from the Postcommunist Experience," *World Politics* 55 (2003), 167–92; Michael Mc-Faul, "The Fourth Wave of Democracy and Dictatorship: Noncooperative Transitions in the Postcommunist World," *World Politics* 54 (2002), 212–44.

41. See, for example, Adam Przeworski, *Democracy and the Market: Political and Economic Reforms in Eastern Europe and Latin America* (New York: Cambridge University Press, 1991); Dankwart A. Rustow, "Transitions to Democracy: Toward a Dynamic Model," *Comparative Politics* 2 (1970), 337–63. The best analysis of the class composition of pro-democracy coalitions, Collier's *Paths Toward Democracy*, shows that the importance of the working classes varies across region and eras.

42. By limiting the range of reforms under consideration and attempting to exclude hardliners and radicals, pacted transitions are thought to smooth the way through the turbulent early years and make the country's democratic consolidation more likely. O'Donnell and Schmitter, *Transitions from Authoritarian Rule*, 4:37; McFaul, "The Fourth Wave of Democracy and Dictatorship," 217. Generally, see Terry Lynn Karl and Philippe C. Schmitter, "Modes of Transition in Latin America, Southern and Eastern Europe," *International Social Sciences Journal* 128 (1991), 269–84; Gerardo L. Munck and Carol Skalnik Leff, "Modes of Transition and Democratization: South America and Eastern Europe in Comparative Perspective," *Comparative Politics* 29 (1997), 343–62. For a more favorable view of the participation of radical opposition elements—even in pacted transitions—see Nancy Bermeo, "Myths of Moderation: Confrontation and Conflict during Democratic Transitions," *Comparative Politics* 29 (1997), 306, 314–16.

43. Different modes are thought to shape the prospects for consolidating stable democratic rule, the prospects for subsequent levels of disorder and violence, the likelihood of involvement in interstate conflict, the nature of transitional justice, and so on. Munck and Leff, "Modes of Transition and Democratization," 343, 345; Gerardo L. Munck, "Review Article: Democratic Transitions in Comparative Perspective," *Comparative Politics* 26 (1994), 361; Milan Svolik, "Authoritarian Reversals and Democratic Consolidation," *APSR* 102 (2008), 153–68; Lars-Erik Cederman, Simon Hug, and Andreas Wenger, "Democratization and War in Political Science," *Democratization* 15 (2008), 509–24.

44. In Mexico, subnational transitions have been party-led. There, "electoral laws in the states are nationally controlled, federal oversight of federal elections in the states is institutionalized, and local authoritarian rule relies heavily . . . on informal and illegal practices." Gibson, *Boundary Control*, 6, 25, 31–33.

45. Collier, *Paths Toward Democracy*, 24. I owe the term "party-state" to Richard F. Bensel, who used it to describe the Republican party's control of the central state apparatus during Reconstruction (*Yankee Leviathan*, 3).

46. Helpful discussions of incorporation include Collier and Collier, *Shaping the Political Arena*, chap. 1 (quotation at 3); Waldner, "Democracy and Dictatorship in the Post-Colonial World," 19; David Waldner, "Rural Incorporation and Regime Survival" (unpublished manuscript in the author's possession, Jun. 30, 2011); Martin

Shefter, *Political Parties and the State* (Princeton: Princeton University Press, 1995); and Robert C. Lieberman, *Shaping Race Policy: The United States in Comparative Perspective* (Princeton: Princeton University Press, 2005), chap. 1.

47. Quotation is from Shefter, *Political Parties and the State*, 10. For incumbents, incorporation of those they have previously excluded promises "certain costs but only uncertain benefits." Waldner, "Democracy and Dictatorship in the Post-Colonial World," 18–19.

48. Quotations appear in Karen Orren and Stephen Skowronek, "Regimes and Regime Building in American Government: A Review of Literature on the 1940s," *Political Science Quarterly* 113 (1998–99), 696, and Robert Kaufman, "Liberalization and Democratization in South America: Perspectives from the 1970s," in O'Donnell, Schmitter, and Whitehead, *Transitions from Authoritarian Rule*, 3:88, respectively. Generally, see Waldner, "Democracy and Dictatorship in the Post-Colonial World," 20–21.

49. The party might respond by making a clear collective choice, whether through established procedures or by granting authority to particular actors. Alternatively, its response might be the aggregation of many individuals' choices, such as an uncoordinated mass exodus from the party. Third, more autonomous state officials might act on their own initiative. Finally, the party's response may be a cacophony of conflicting behaviors by numerous individuals acting in the name of the party, and may send no clear signal of "the" party's behavior.

50. Waldner, "Rural Incorporation and Regime Survival"; Alfred P. Montero, "No Country for Leftists? Clientelist Continuity and the 2006 Vote in the Brazilian Northeast," *Journal of Politics in Latin America* 2 (2010), 113–53.

51. As Herbert Kitschelt rightly notes, elite cohesion must be invoked as a cause with great care, as it may be too proximate to the outcomes it is intended to explain. Rather, those factors that help account for a certain level of elite cohesion—for example, consensus among elites of different economic sectors—might warrant greater emphasis. The state-level narratives that follow take care to make these distinctions. Kitschelt, "Accounting for Post-Communist Regime Diversity," 72. On the importance of elites' miscalculations and misunderstandings during a transition, see Nancy Bermeo, "Interests, Inequality, and Illusion in the Choice for Fair Elections," *Comparative Political Studies* 43 (2010), 1119–147; Marek M. Kaminksi, "Do Parties Benefit from Electoral Manipulation? Electoral Laws and Heresthetics in Poland, 1989–93," *Journal of Theoretical Politics* 14 (2002), 325–58.

52. On the important distinction between the autonomy of state actors relative to social groups or classes and their capacity to implement preferred goals, see Theda Skocpol, "Bringing the State Back In: Strategies of Analysis in Current Research," in Peter R. Evans, Dietrich Rueschemeyer, and Theda Skocpol, eds., *Bringing the State Back In* (New York: Cambridge University Press, 1985), 17, 9.

53. Beatriz Magaloni, Alberto Diaz-Cayeros, and Federico Estevez, "The Erosion of Party Hegemony, Clientelism, and Portfolio Diversification: The Programa Nacional de Solidaridad (Pronasol) in Mexico," in Herbert Kitschelt and Steve Wilkinson, eds., *Patrons or Policies? Patterns of Democratic Accountability and Political Competition* (New York: Cambridge University Press, 2007), 182–205.

54. As "political institutions carry on through time under existing mandates, they will over time likely riddle the political world with obsolescent and incongruous controls." The quotations appear in Karen Orren and Stephen Skowronek, *The*

Search for American Political Development (Cambridge: Cambridge University Press, 2004), 21, 86. Similarly, as Michael Mann writes, "[S]tates institutionalize present social conflicts, but institutionalized historic conflicts then exert considerable power over new conflicts." *The Sources of Social Power*, vol. 2 (New York: Cambridge University Press, 1993), 52. Of course, institutions undergo change gradually as well, and not merely in response to exogenous shocks or responses to them. See Grzegorz Ekiert, *The State Against Society: Political Crises and Their Aftermath in East Central Europe* (Princeton: Princeton University Press, 1996). Also see James Mahoney and Kathleen Thelen, "A Theory of Gradual Institutional Change," in Mahoney and Thelen, eds., *Explaining Institutional Change: Ambiguity, Agency, and Power* (New York: Cambridge University Press, 2010), 2, 7–9, and *passim*; Michael Mann, "The Autonomous Power of the State: Its Origins, Mechanisms, and Results," *Archives Européenes de Sociologie* 25 (1984), 185–213; David Waldner, "Policy History: Regimes," in Neil J. Smelser and Paul B. Baltes, eds., *International Encyclopedia of the Social & Behavioral Sciences* (Oxford: Elsevier, 2001), 11,547–48.

55. See James Mahoney, Erin Kimball, and Kendra L. Koivu, "The Logic of Historical Explanation in the Social Sciences," *Comparative Political Studies* 42 (2009), 114–46. For a rare debate about the subfield, see John Gerring, "APD from a Methodological Point of View," *Studies in American Political Development* 17 (2003), 82–102 (hereafter *SAPD*), and responses by Richard Bensel, Stephen Skowronek, and Rogers M. Smith (103–15). A leading text advancing the study of American political development, Orren and Skowronek's *Search for American Political Development*, notes "an 'awkward silence' regarding the lack of a consensus—or even a debate—on the concept of 'political development'" (29). Their book has no sustained engagement with the study of political development as practiced by scholars of comparative politics and political sociology. Also see Alfred Stepan and Juan J. Linz, "Comparative Perspectives and the Quality of Democracy in the United States," *Perspectives on Politics* 9 (2011), 842.

56. James Mahoney and Dietrich Rueschemeyer, "Comparative Historical Analysis: Achievements and Agendas," in Mahoney and Rueschemeyer, *Comparative Historical Analysis*, 3–15. Also see James Mahoney, "Nominal, Ordinal, and Narrative Appraisal in Macrocausal Analysis," *American Journal of Sociology* 104 (1999), 1154–96; James Mahoney, "Strategies of Causal Analysis in Comparative Historical Analysis," in Mahoney and Rueschemeyer, *Comparative Historical Analysis*, 337–72; John Gerring, *Social Science Methodology: A Unified Framework*, 2nd ed. (New York: Cambridge University Press, 2012), chap. 12. This study also draws on historical institutionalism, a related research program that emphasizes the manner in which institutions "structure conflict so as to privilege some interests while demobilizing others," and sees them as "enduring legacies of political struggles." In doing so, this research often reveals how the "the various institutional arrangements that make up a polity emerge at different times and out of different historical configurations. For this reason, the various 'pieces' do not necessarily fit together into a coherent, self-reinforcing, let alone functional, whole." Kathleen Thelen, "Historical Institutionalism in Comparative Politics," *ARPS* 2 (1999), 388. For helpful descriptions, see Kathleen Thelen and Sven Steinmo, eds., *Structuring Politics: Historical Institutionalism in Comparative Analysis* (New York: Cambridge University Press, 1992); Peter A. Hall and Rosemary C. R. Taylor, "Political Science and the Three New Institutionalisms," *Political Studies* 44 (1996),

936–57; Ira Katznelson, "Structure and Configuration in Comparative Politics," in Mark I. Lichbach and Alan S. Zuckerman, eds., *Comparative Politics: Rationality, Culture, and Structure* (New York: Cambridge University Press, 1997), 81–112; Paul Pierson and Theda Skocpol, "Historical Institutionalism in Contemporary Political Science," in Ira Katznelson and Helen V. Milner, eds., *Political Science: The State of the Discipline* (New York: W. W. Norton, 2002), 693–721.

57. The structure of this study is inspired by several works in comparative politics, especially Collier and Collier's renowned work on labor incorporation in Latin America, *Shaping the Political Arena*; Peter Gourevitch, *Politics in Hard Times: Comparative Responses to International Economic Crises* (Ithaca: Cornell University Press, 1986); Snyder, *Politics After Neoliberalism*; Deborah Yashar, *Demanding Democracy: Reform and Reaction in Costa Rica and Guatemala, 1870s–1950s* (Stanford: Stanford University Press, 1997); and James Mahoney, *Legacies of Liberalism: Path Dependence and Political Regimes in Central America* (Baltimore: Johns Hopkins University Press, 2001).

58. James Mahoney offers quite positive and compelling evaluations of the potential contributions of case study research for hypothesis testing in Mahoney, "The Logic of Process Tracing Tests in the Social Sciences," *Sociological Methods & Research* 41 (2012), 570–97. For a less positive view, which I share, see John Gerring, *Case Study Research: Principles and Practices* (New York: Cambridge University Press, 2006), 39–43. In the discipline's mainstream, the pessimism is more complete, and also based on different arguments. See, e.g., Gary King, Robert O. Keohane, and Sidney Verba, *Designing Social Inquiry: Scientific Inference in Qualitative Research* (Princeton: Princeton University Press, 1994); and Jasjeet S. Sekhon, "Quality Meets Quantity: Case Studies, Conditional Probability, and Counterfactuals," *Perspectives on Politics* 2 (2004), 281–93.

59. Quotations appear in David Waldner, "Process Tracing and Causal Mechanisms," in Harold Kinkaid, ed., *The Oxford Handbook of Philosophy of Social Science* (New York: Oxford University Press, 2012), 67–71; David Collier, Henry E. Brady, and Jason Seawright, "Sources of Leverage in Causal Inference: Toward an Alternative View of Methodology," in Henry E. Brady and David Collier, eds., *Rethinking Social Inquiry: Diverse Tools, Shared Standards*, 2nd ed. (Lanham, Md.: Rowman and Littlefield, 2010), 161–99, 318, 324; and Gerring, *Case Study Research*, 178–80. A "causal-process observation" (CSO) is defined by Collier, Brady, and Seawright (318) as "an insight or piece of data that provides information about context, process, or mechanism," and is contrasted with "data-set observations," which appear in quantitative format and constitute comparable observations gathered systematically as part of an array of variables. Perhaps the key difference between them is that CSOs elude systematic comparison. On what process tracing can actually deliver, particularly with respect to the testing of causal explanations and the elimination of alternative hypotheses, see David Waldner, "Process Tracing and Comparative Politics," in Andrew Bennett and Jeffrey T. Checkel, eds., *Process Tracing in the Social Sciences: From Metaphor to Analytic Tool* (New York: Cambridge University Press, forthcoming).

60. Gervasoni, *Conceptualizing and Measuring Subnational Democracy*; Carlos Gervasoni, "Measuring Variance in Subnational Regimes: Results from an Expert-Based Operationalization of Democracy in the Argentine Provinces," *Journal of Poli-*

tics in Latin America 2 (2010), 13–52. For an alternative approach, see Giraudy, "Varieties of Subnational Undemocratic Regimes."

61. For helpful discussions, see "Roundtable on Periodization and American Politics," *Polity* 37 (2005), 511–57; Paul Pierson, *Politics in Time: History, Institutions, and Social Analysis* (Princeton: Princeton University Press, 2004); Ira Katznelson, "Periodization and Preferences: Reflections on Purposive Action in Comparative Historical Social Science," in Mahoney and Rueschemeyer, *Comparative Historical Analysis*, 270–302; Jeffrey Haydu, "Making Use of the Past: Time Periods as Cases to Compare and as Sequences of Problem Solving," *American Journal of Sociology* 104 (1998), 339–71; James Mahoney, "Path Dependence in Historical Sociology," *Theory and Society* 29 (2000), 507–48; Andrew Abbott, *Time Matters: On Theory and Method* (Chicago: University of Chicago Press, 2001 [1992]); and Anna Grzymała-Busse, "Time Will Tell? Temporality and the Analysis of Causal Mechanisms and Processes," *Comparative Political Studies* 20 (2011), 1267–97.

62. Historian Timothy Garton Ash told Václav Havel during the heady days of 1989, "In Poland it took ten years, in Hungary ten months, in East Germany ten weeks; perhaps in Czechoslovakia it will take ten days!" Garton Ash, *The Magic Lantern: The Revolution of '89 Witnessed in Warsaw, Budapest, Berlin, and Prague* (New York: Random House, 1990), 78. Whether and how the transition's duration matters independent of the forces that brought it about is an important but difficult issue. For a helpful discussion, see Grzymała-Busse, "Time Will Tell?"

63. Ruth Berins Collier, "Combining Alternative Perspectives: Internal Trajectories versus External Influences as Explanations of Latin American Politics in the 1940s," *Comparative Politics* 26 (1993), 1–29.

64. Waldner, "Process Tracing and Comparative Politics," 4. Compare James Mahoney and Daniel Schensul, "Historical Context and Path Dependence," in Robert E. Goodin and Charles Tilly, eds., *The Oxford Handbook of Contextual Political Analysis* (New York: Oxford University Press, 2006), 454–71, and Scott E. Page, "Path Dependence," *Quarterly Journal of Political Science* 1 (2006), 87–115.

65. James Mahoney and Richard Snyder, "Rethinking Agency and Structure in the Study of Regime Change," *Studies in Comparative International Development* 34 (1999), 18; Mahoney, *Legacies of Liberalism*, 7.

66. Mahoney would consider these "reactive sequences," which involve reaction and counterreaction mechanisms that "give an event chain an 'inherent logic' in which one event 'naturally' leads to another event." Mahoney, "Path Dependence in Historical Sociology," 511, 526–27, 530, 532; Abbott, *Time Matters*, 199. For a different terminology, see P. J. Lamberson and Scott E. Page, "Tipping Points," *Quarterly Journal of Political Science* 7 (2012), 175–208.

67. Wolfgang Streeck and Kathleen Thelen, "Introduction: Institutional Change in Advanced Political Economies," in Streeck and Thelen, eds., *Beyond Continuity: Institutional Change in Advanced Political Economies* (New York: Oxford University Press, 2005), 8–9.

68. Gerring, *Case Study Research*, 131.

69. Key, *Southern Politics*, chap. 1. Does it makes sense to "case" the South in terms of states, as opposed to subregions, counties, cities, and so on? Could there not be enclaves within enclaves? This is an important issue which I will not pursue here.

At this exploratory stage of research, it makes sense to begin with enclaves-as-states. For relevant discussions, see Philip J. Ethington and Jason A. McDaniel, "Political Places and Institutional Spaces: The Intersection of Political Science and Political Geography," *ARPS* 10 (2007), 127–42; Stephen Aron, "Frontiers, Borderlands, Wests," in Eric Foner and Lisa McGirr, eds., *American History Now* (Philadelphia: Temple University Press, 2011), 261–284; and Gibson, *Boundary Control.* Also see Charles C. Ragin, "'Casing' and the Process of Social Inquiry," in Charles C. Ragin and Howard S. Becker, eds., *What Is a Case? Explorations of the Foundations of Social Inquiry* (New York: Cambridge University Press, 1992), 217–26.

70. The Outer South itself is diverse, featuring both "traditional" states (Arkansas, North Carolina, Tennessee, and Virginia) and "megastates" (Florida and Texas). The latter have had very different racial and ethnic politics. Neal R. Peirce, *The Megastates of America* (New York: Norton, 1972).

71. William Ward Rogers, Robert David Ward, Leah Rawls Atkins, and Wayne Flynt, *Alabama: The History of a Deep South State* (Tuscaloosa: University of Alabama Press, 1994).

72. Historians have published superb state-level monographs of the period, and I am very indebted to them. Exemplary here is John Dittmer, *Local People: The Struggle for Civil Rights in Mississippi* (Urbana: University of Illinois Press, 1994).

73. The share of tenants among all farm operators in 1910 was the highest in the region, varying from 63 to 66 percent. Theodore Saloutos, *Farmer Movements in the South, 1865–1933* (Lincoln: University of Nebraska Press, 1960), table 2, 237. Rueschemeyer, Stephens, and Stephens employ the slightly modified concept of "labor-intensive agriculture" in response to critiques of "labor-repressive agriculture" (*Capitalist Development and Democracy*, 163–65).

74. Among other limitations, examining only the Deep South means omitting the role of Hispanics in shaping the founding, maintenance, and destruction of enclaves in Florida and Texas. See, e.g., Zaragosa Vargas, *Labor Rights Are Civil Rights: Mexican American Workers in Twentieth-Century America* (Princeton: Princeton University Press, 2004); Thomas A. Guglielmo, "Fighting for Caucasian Rights: Mexicans, Mexican Americans, and the Transnational Struggle for Civil Rights in World War II Texas," *Journal of American History* 92 (2006), 1212–37 (hereafter *JAH*).

75. Kurt Weyland, "The Diffusion of Regime Contention in European Democratization, 1830–1940," *Comparative Political Studies* 43 (2010), 1148–176; Valerie Bunce, Michael McFaul, and Kathryn Stoner-Weiss, eds., *Democracy and Authoritarianism in the Postcommunist World* (New York: Cambridge University Press, 2010).

76. Alexander Heard, "Interviewing Southern Politicians," *APSR* 44 (1950), 886–92; Alexander P. Lamis and Nathan C. Goldman, "V. O. Key's *Southern Politics*: The Writing of a Classic," *GHQ* 71 (1987), 261–85. The terms on which Heard's interviews were conducted prevent scholars from naming the interviewees or quoting them directly, so I paraphrase from the interview transcripts and note an individual's profession or political position. The only work of which I am aware that uses the Heard interviews is Dittmer, *Local People.* This study also draws on other extremely valuable contemporaneous interviews conducted throughout the transition period, such as those from the mid-1940s contained in Calvin Kytle and James A. Mackay's *Who Runs Georgia?* (Athens: University of Georgia Press, 1998 [1947]), as well as scores of oral histories conducted in the 1970s and 1980s. Of course, it is difficult to judge the

veracity and accuracy of retrospective remembrances by southern politicians, activists, and others. Many southern politicians have good reason to "white wash" their behavior. Thus, contemporaneous private interviews are given more weight than those conducted years or even decades after events. Even these may feature honest mistakes, of course. As the old Russian proverb goes, "He lies like an eyewitness." Quoted in Robert Conquest, *The Great Terror: A Reassessment*, rev. ed. (New York: Oxford University Press, 1990), 109.

77. Some of these sources are often unreliable. Archival collections can reflect poor record-keeping by southern states, and many "incriminating" documents are removed before collected papers are made available. Newspapers present their own challenges, especially regarding protest and dissent. White southern newspapers featured highly limited, partial, and inaccurate coverage of black politics and protest. Also see Daniel Myers and Beth Caniglia, "All the Rioting That's Fit to Print: Selection Effects in National Newspaper Coverage of Civil Disorders, 1968–1969," *ASR* 69 (2004), 519–43; Ian Lustick, "History, Historiography, and Political Science: Multiple Historical Records and the Problem of Selection Bias," *APSR* 90 (1996), 605–18.

78. Please see http://press.princeton.edu/titles/9469.html for links to this material.

79. Dan Slater and Erica Simmons, "Informative Regress: Critical Antecedents in Comparative Politics," *Comparative Political Studies* 43 (2010), 889; Collier and Collier, *Shaping the Political Arena*, 30.

80. Wilbur J. Cash, *The Mind of the South* (New York: Alfred A. Knopf, 1941), vii. Historian James C. Cobb writes that the non-South is not "simply another region . . . but an 'emotional idea' of the remainder of a triumphantly superior America," even "virtually synonymous with the idea of America itself." Cobb, *Away Down South: A History of Southern Identity* (New York: Oxford University Press, 2006), 2; Matthew D. Lassiter and Joseph Crespino, "Introduction: The End of Southern History," in Lassiter and Crespino, eds., *The Myth of Southern Exceptionalism* (New York: Oxford University Press, 2010), 3–20.

81. Keyssar, *The Right to Vote*, xv. The view that suffrage change has been monotonic and liberalizing is an old one; see Alexis de Tocqueville, *Democracy in America*, trans. Harvey C. Mansfield and Delba Winthrop (Chicago: University of Chicago Press, 2000), 1:55; E. E. Schattschneider, *The Semi-Sovereign People: A Realist's View of Democracy in America* (Hinsdale, Ill.: Holt, Rinehart, and Winston, 1960), 100–101.

82. Similarly, Edward Gibson observes that the "democratic national government of the United States held sway over the planet, but did not challenge authoritarian political systems within its own borders until the second half of the 20th century." Gibson, *Boundary Control*, 4.

CHAPTER TWO:

The Founding and Maintenance of Southern Enclaves, 1890–1940

1. The epigraphs in this chapter are from Henry W. Grady, "The New South," speech before the New England Society of New York, Dec. 22, 1886, in Joel Chandler

Harris, *Henry W. Grady: His Life, Writings, and Speeches* (New York: Cassell, 1890), 15–16; W.E.B. Du Bois, "Georgia: Invisible Empire State," *The Nation* 120 (Jan. 21, 1925), 63; Key, *Southern Politics*, 4; Saul Bellow, *The Adventures of Augie March* (New York: Viking, 1953), 1.

2. For rich discussions, see Cobb, *Away Down South*; Edward L. Ayers, "What We Talk about When We Talk about the South," in Edward L. Ayers, Patricia Nelson, Stephen Nissenbaum, and Peter S. Onuf, eds., *All Over the Map: Rethinking American Regions* (Baltimore: Johns Hopkins University Press, 1996), 62–82; and Howard W. Odum, *Southern Regions of the United States* (Chapel Hill: University of North Carolina Press, 1936). V. O. Key uses the eleven-state definition, and bases it in large part on loyalty to the Democratic party (*Southern Politics*, 10–11). The Katznelson definition adds Delaware, Kentucky, Maryland, Missouri, Oklahoma, and West Virginia, as well as Washington, D.C. Ira Katznelson and Quinn Mulroy, "Was the South Pivotal? Situated Partisanship and Partisan Coalitions during the New and Fair Deal," *JOP* 74 (2012), 606–7; Sean Farhang and Ira Katznelson, "The Southern Imposition: Congress and Labor in the New Deal and Fair Deal," *SAPD* 19 (2005), 1, fn. 1. This coincides with the definition used by the Bureau of the Census, which also groups states into three subregions: the South Atlantic, West South Central, and East South Central. On school segregation, see Charles T. Clotfelter, *After "Brown": The Rise and Retreat of School Desegregation* (Princeton: Princeton University Press, 2004), 2, 18–19, 22, and 217–18. Also see Davison M. Douglas, *Jim Crow Moves North: The Battle over Northern School Segregation, 1865–1954* (New York: Cambridge University Press, 2005). For discussion of other modes of state-mandated segregation outside of the sphere of education, see C. Vann Woodward, *The Strange Career of Jim Crow* (New York: Oxford University Press, 2000 [1955]); Arnold Hirsch, *Making the Second Ghetto: Race and Housing in Chicago, 1940–1960* (Chicago: University of Chicago Press, 1998 [1983]); and Thomas J. Sugrue, *Sweet Land of Liberty: The Forgotten Struggle for Civil Rights in the North* (New York: Random House, 2008).

3. Quotation appears in Evelyne Huber, Dietrich Rueschemeyer, and John D. Stephens, "The Paradoxes of Contemporary Democracy: Formal, Participatory, and Social Dimensions," *Comparative Politics* 29 (1997), 323. Here, states are seen as "organizations claiming control over territories and people [which] formulate and pursue goals that are not simply reflective of the demands or interests of social groups, classes, or society." State autonomy concerns goal formation, while state capacity concerns the capacity to implement "official goals." Skocpol, "Bringing the State Back In," 9. On conceptions of the autonomy of public officials vis-à-vis private interests, see Skocpol, "Bringing the State Back In," 3–37; and Eric A. Nordlinger, *On the Autonomy of the Democratic State* (Princeton: Princeton University Press, 1981). On violations of the requirement that political institutions be sufficiently autonomous, see J. Samuel Valenzuela, "Democratic Consolidation in Post-Transitional Settings: Notion, Process, and Facilitating Conditions," in Scott Mainwaring, Guillermo O'Donnell, and J. Samuel Valenzuela, eds., *Issues in Democratic Consolidation: The New South American Democracies in Comparative Perspective* (Notre Dame, Ind.: University of Notre Dame Press, 1992), 57–104. For Adcock and Collier, the violation of the autonomy requirement "does not merely make countries somewhat less democratic; it undermines the meaningfulness of the other defining attributes of

democracy." Robert Adcock and David Collier, "Measurement Validity: A Shared Standard for Qualitative and Quantitative Research," *APSR* 95 (2001), 559.

4. For a less demanding proceduralist view, see Joseph Schumpeter, *Capitalism, Socialism, and Democracy* (New York: Harper, 1975 [1942]); Adam Przeworski, "Minimalist Conception of Democracy: A Defense," in Ian Shapiro and Casiano Hacker-Cordón, eds., *Democracy's Value* (New York: Cambridge University Press, 1999), 23–55. On dichotomous conceptions, see Adam Przeworski, Michael E. Alvarez, José A. Cheibub, and Fernando Limongi, *Democracy and Development: Political Institutions and Well-Being in the World, 1950–1990* (New York: Cambridge University Press, 2000). For valuable critiques and discussions, see David Collier and Steven Levitsky, "Democracy with Adjectives: Conceptual Innovation in Comparative Research," *World Politics* 49 (1997), 430–51; Zachary Elkins, "Gradations of Democracy? Empirical Tests of Alternative Conceptualizations," *American Journal of Political Science* 44 (2000), 287–94 (hereafter *AJPS*); Gerardo Munck and Jay Verkuilen, "Conceptualizing and Measuring Democracy: Evaluating Alternative Indices," *Comparative Political Studies* 35 (2002), 5–34; Gary Goertz, *Social Science Concepts: A User's Guide* (Princeton: Princeton University Press, 2006), chap. 4; Michael Coppedge, Angel Alvarez, and Claudia Maldonado, "Two Persistent Dimensions of Democracy: Contestation and Inclusiveness," *JOP* 70 (2008), 632–47. No datasets exist on the relative democratic-ness of American states over time, and analyses of cross-state variation in democratic governance in the American states are rare. See Kim Quaile Hill, "Democratization and Corruption: Systematic Evidence from the American States," *American Politics Research* 31 (2003), 613–31; Kim Quaile Hill, *Democracy in the Fifty States* (Lincoln: University of Nebraska Press, 1994). Hill does not conceptualize a state's degree (or quality) of democracy beyond the extent of its electoral competitiveness. Also see Ellis Goldberg, Ellis Wibbels, and Eric Mvukiyehe, "Lessons from Strange Cases: Democracy, Development, and the Resource Curse in the U.S. States," *Comparative Political Studies* 41 (2008), 477–514. On measures of state-level party competition, see T. M. Holbrook and Emily Van Dunk, "Electoral Competition in the American States," *APSR* 87 (1993), 955–62.

5. The electoral exclusion of one-half of the population had major spillover effects, such as their absence from juries (jurors were usually chosen from the voter registration rolls). Additionally, women's citizenship was corroded by marriage laws. Generally, see Francisco O. Ramirez, Yasemin Soysal, and Suzanne Shanahan, "The Changing Logic of Political Citizenship: Cross-National Acquisition of Women's Suffrage Rights, 1890 to 1990," *ASR* 62 (1997), 735–45. On voting, marriage, and jury service in the United States, see Gretchen Ritter, *The Constitution as Social Design: Gender as Civic Membership in the American Constitutional Order* (Stanford: Stanford University Press, 2006), chaps. 2, 3, and 4, respectively. Women who married men ineligible for naturalization, such as those declared by public officials as being not-white, often lost their citizenship. See Martha Gardner, *The Qualities of a Citizen: Women, Immigration, and Citizenship, 1870–1965* (Princeton: Princeton University Press, 2005), chap. 8. Also see Eileen McDonagh, "Political Citizenship and Democratization: The Gender Paradox," *APSR* 96 (2002), 535–52.

6. Additionally, several states refused to allow Native Americans to vote through the 1950s. Laughlin McDonald, "Federal Oversight of Elections and Partisan Realignment," in Richard M. Valelly, ed., *The Voting Rights Act: Securing the Ballot* (Washington, D.C.: Congressional Quarterly Press, 2006), 162–63. For incisive analyses of anti-democratic politics in both traditional "machines" (generally on the East Coast and the Midwest) and allegedly "reform" governments (generally in the Southwest and West) in twentieth-century urban America, see Jessica Trounstine, *Political Monopolies in American Cities: The Rise and Fall of Bosses and Reformers* (Chicago: University of Chicago Press, 2008), and Amy Bridges, *Morning Glories: Municipal Reform in the Southwest* (Princeton: Princeton University Press, 1999). On electoral fraud outside the South, see Gary W. Cox and J. Morgan Kousser, "Turnout and Rural Corruption: New York as a Test Case," *AJPS* 25 (1981), 646–63; Peter H. Argersinger, "New Perspectives on Election Fraud in the Gilded Age," *Political Science Quarterly* 100 (1985–86), 669–87; Richard F. Bensel, *The American Ballot Box in the Mid-Nineteenth Century* (New York: Cambridge University Press, 2004). New York authorities attacked Jewish American voting in 1908 by forcing would-be registrants to register on Saturdays and high holy days. For this and other instances of suffrage restriction outside the South, see Alexander Keyssar, *The Right to Vote: The Contested History of Democracy in the United States* (New York: Basic Books, 2000), 126; Tabatha Abu El-Haj, "Changing the People: Legal Regulation and American Democracy," *New York University Law Review* 86 (2011), 1–68; Robert Justin Goldstein, *Political Repression in Modern America: From 1870 to 1976* (Urbana: University of Illinois Press, 2001 [1978]).

7. Michael R. West, *The Education of Booker T. Washington: American Democracy and the Idea of Race Relations* (New York: Columbia University Press, 2006), 13 and 230, fn. 19. Robert Dahl termed the American South a "dual system," a "kind of polyarchy for whites and hegemony for blacks" (*Polyarchy*, 28). George M. Frederickson, *The Black Image in the White Mind: The Debate on Afro-American Character and Destiny, 1817–1914* (New York: Harper & Row, 1987 [1971]), 43–64, 90–96, and 256–82; Kenneth P. Vickery, "'Herrenvolk Democracy' and Egalitarianism in South Africa and the U.S. South," *Comparative Studies in Society and History* 1 (1974), 309–28. An interpretation closer to mine appears in Rueschemeyer, Stephens, and Stephens, *Capitalist Development and Democracy*, 122–32.

8. Robert D. Mitchell, "The Colonial Origins of Anglo-America," in Robert D. Mitchell and Paul A. Groves, eds., *North America: The Historical Geography of a Changing Continent* (Totowa, N.J.: Rowman and Littlefield, 1987), 102. On colony charters and southern state constitutions (and the "proto-constitution" quotation), see Akhil Reed Amar, *America's Constitution: A Biography* (New York: Random House, 2005), 249, 22; G. Alan Tarr, *Understanding State Constitutions* (Princeton: Princeton University Press, 1998), chap. 4; Don E. Fehrenbacher, *Sectional Crisis and Southern Constitutionalism* (Baton Rouge: Louisiana State University Press, 1995), xvii. On antebellum southern politics, see William J. Cooper, Jr., *Liberty and Slavery: Southern Politics to 1860* (Baton Rouge: Louisiana State University Press, 2000 [1983]). On antebellum black voting (and much more), see Hanes Walton, Jr., Sherman C. Puckett, and Donald R. Deskins, *The African American Electorate: A Statistical History*, vol. 1 (Washington, D.C.: Congressional Quarterly Press, 2012), chaps. 4 and 6–7.

9. On the centrality of questions of labor supply to the South, see D. W. Meinig, *The Shaping of America: A Geographical Perspective on 500 Years of History*,

vol. 1: *Atlantic America, 1492–1800* (New Haven: Yale University Press, 1986), 145–50; Russell R. Menard, "Transitions to African Slavery in British America, 1630–1730: Barbados, Virginia, and South Carolina," *Indian Historical Review* 15 (1988), 33–49. The emergence of sharp divisions by race was gradual and seems to have been contingent in part on the demise of the supply of European indentured servants. On interracial social relations before this occurred, see David Brion Davis, *Inhuman Bondage: The Rise and Fall of Slavery in the New World* (New York: Oxford University Press, 2006), 131; Ira Berlin, "Time, Space, and the Evolution of Afro-American Society on British Mainland North America," *AHR* 85 (1980), 69; Barbara Jeanne Fields, *Slavery and Freedom on the Middle Ground: Maryland during the Nineteenth Century* (New Haven: Yale University Press, 1985). Indeed, racial categories themselves were quite supple. Authorities classified some individuals of African descent as "white" on the basis of their "good character" (Davis, *Inhuman Bondage*, 138). On coerced labor by European settlers, including indentured servitude, see Christopher Tomlins, "Reconsidering Indentured Servitude: European Migration and the Early American Labor Force, 1600–1775," *Labor History* 42 (2001), 5–43; Seymour Drescher, "White Atlantic? The Choice for African Slave Labor in the Plantation Americas," in David Eltis, Frank D. Lewis, and Kenneth L. Sokoloff, eds., *Slavery in the Development of the Americas* (New York: Cambridge University Press, 2004), 31–69. Also see Robert J. Steinfeld, *The Invention of Free Labor: The Employment Relation in English & American Law and Culture, 1350–1870* (Chapel Hill: University of North Carolina Press, 1991), chap. 7; Karen Orren, *Belated Feudalism: Labor, Law, and Liberal Development in the United States* (New York: Cambridge University Press, 1991), chaps. 1–3; Davis, *Inhuman Bondage*, 124.

10. On this economic divergence, see Wright, *Slavery and American Economic Development*, 61, and Wright, *Old South, New South*, chap. 2.

11. Northeastern Brazil, where sugar and coffee dominated, was unsurprisingly brutal. There, planters employed restrictions on laborers' mobility, debt peonage, and various forms of physical coercion to keep "their" workers on the land. The opposite holds true for the cultivation of coffee. When dominant crops were grown by "independent smallholders, more broad-based and equitable patterns of political growth usually followed." Jeffry A. Frieden, *Global Capitalism: Its Fall and Rise in the Twentieth Century* (New York: W. W. Norton & Company, 2006), 98–102. On cotton's labor requirements, see Wright, *Slavery and American Economic Development*, 87.

12. Sean Wilentz, *The Rise of American Democracy* (New York: W. W. Norton, 2005), 733–34; Clement Eaton, *The Freedom-of-Thought Struggle in the Old South*, rev. ed. (New York: Harper, 1964 [1940]).

13. The increasing repression of slaves soon regulated slaveowners' own property rights as states began preventing manumission. Davis, *Inhuman Bondage*, chap. 10; Thomas D. Morris, *Southern Slavery and the Law, 1619–1860* (Chapel Hill: University of North Carolina Press, 1996) chaps. 18–19.

14. Michael Kent Curtis, *Free Speech, "The People's Darling Privilege": Struggles for Freedom of Expression in American History* (Durham, N.C.: Duke University Press, 2000), 273–76; Don E. Fehrenbacher, *The Dred Scott Case: Its Significance in American Law and Politics* (New York: Oxford University Press, 1978), 35. On the gag rules, see John A. Aldrich, *Why Parties? The Origins and Transformation of Party Politics in America* (Chicago: University of Chicago Press, 1995), chaps. 4–5; William W. Freehling,

The Road to Disunion: Secessionists at Bay, 1776–1860 (New York: Oxford University Press, 1990), 308–25. If Daniel P. Carpenter is right, and abolitionists' petitions to Congress also served as instruments of political mobilization, then their suppression had additional downstream undemocratic consequences. Carpenter, "The Petition as a Recruitment Device: Evidence from the Abolitionists' Congressional Campaign," unpublished manuscript in the author's possession (November 2003).

15. Davis, *Inhuman Bondage*, 474, fn. 28; David Grimstead, *American Mobbing, 1828–1861: Toward Civil War* (New York: Oxford University Press, 1998), chaps. 3–5. Also see Leonard L. Richards, *The Slave Power: The Free North and Southern Domination, 1780–1860* (Baton Rouge: Louisiana State University Press, 2000). "Arc of southern unfreedom" appears in Amar, *America's Constitution*, 371–72. The treatment of free blacks outside the South was not substantially better than that of their southern counterparts. Several northern states extended voting rights to black men but then later revoked them. See James Oliver Horton and Lois E. Horton, *In Hope of Liberty: Culture, Community and Protest among Northern Free Blacks, 1700–1860* (New York: Oxford University Press, 1998); Leon Litwack, *North of Slavery: The Negro in the Free States, 1790–1860* (Chicago: University of Chicago Press, 1965); Patrick Rael, *Black Identity and Black Protest in the Antebellum North* (Chapel Hill: University of North Carolina Press, 2002). For an analysis of restrictions on free blacks' freedom of movement, see Kunal Parker, "Citizenship and Immigration Law, 1800–1924: Resolutions of Membership and Territory," in Michael Grossberg and Christopher L. Tomlins, eds., *Cambridge History of Law in America*, vol. 2: *The Long Nineteenth Century* (New York: Cambridge University Press, 2008), 168–203. On antebellum black voting rights outside the South, see Keyssar, *The Right to Vote*, 349–53, table A4.

16. Frederickson, *Black Image in the White Mind*, 43–64, 90–96. On the Confederate States of America, see Bensel, *Yankee Leviathan*, chap. 3; George C. Rable, *The Confederate Republic: A Revolution Against Politics* (Chapel Hill: University of North Carolina Press, 2007); Stephanie McCurry, *Confederate Reckoning: Power and Politics in the Civil War South* (Cambridge: Harvard University Press, 2012).

17. Eric Foner, *Reconstruction: America's Unfinished Revolution, 1863–1877* (New York: Harper & Row, 2002 [1988]), and Foner, "Reconstruction and the Crisis of Free Labor," in Foner, *Politics and Ideology in the Age of the Civil War* (New York: Oxford University Press, 1980), 97–127; W.E.B. Du Bois, *Black Reconstruction in America, 1860–1880* (New York: Free Press, 1998 [1935]). This account draws on the work of Eric Foner, W.E.B. Du Bois, C. Vann Woodward, Richard M. Valelly, Richard F. Bensel, J. Morgan Kousser, Heather Cox Richardson, and others. For a similar account of the demise of Reconstruction and the eventual imposition of enclave rule that emphasizes the importance of Supreme Court jurisprudence, see Gibson, *Boundary Control*, chap. 3. Also see Rogers M. Smith, "Legitimating Reconstruction: The Limits of Legalism," *Yale Law Journal* 108 (1999), 2039–275.

18. On black political mobilizations, see Steven Hahn, *A Nation under Our Feet: Black Political Struggles in the Rural South from Slavery to the Great Migration* (Cambridge: Harvard University Press, 2003), chap. 4; Richard M. Valelly, *The Two Reconstructions: The Struggle for Black Empowerment* (Chicago: University of Chicago Press, 2004), chap. 2, especially 73, table 2.1 (on black voter registration estimates), 75, and 88–89, table 4.2 (on newspapers). On black officeholding and legislative behavior,

see Valelly, *The Two Reconstructions*, 5, 78, 96, and 278, fn. 68; Michael D. Cobb and Jeffery A. Jenkins, "Race and the Representation of Blacks' Interests during Reconstruction," *Political Research Quarterly* 54 (2001), 181–204.

19. For a rich new study of southern constitutionalism, see Paul Herron, "State Constitutional Development in the American South, 1806–1902," Ph.D. diss., Brandeis University (2014). Also see Eric Biber, "The Price of Admission: Causes, Effects, and Patterns of Conditions Imposed on States Entering the Union," *American Journal of Legal History* 46 (2004), 119–208; Michael Les Benedict, "The Problem of Constitutionalism and Constitutional Liberty in the Reconstruction South," in Kermit L. Hall and James W. Ely, Jr., eds., *An Uncertain Tradition: Constitutionalism and the History of the South* (Athens: University of Georgia Press, 1989), 241–42.

20. On declining troop levels, see Valelly, *The Two Reconstructions*, 94–95 and table 4.3. South Carolina's Klan insurgency and state and national counterinsurgency campaigns are recounted in Richard Zuczek, *State of Rebellion: Reconstruction in South Carolina* (Columbia: University of South Carolina Press, 1996). On the Freedmen's Bureau, see Paul A. Cimbala and Randall M. Miller, eds., *The Freedmen's Bureau and Reconstruction: Reconsiderations* (Bronx, N.Y.: Fordham University Press, 1999). From 1865 to 1868, Valelly estimates, whites murdered 1 percent of all black men aged fifteen to forty-nine. For discussions of political violence, Valelly, *The Two Reconstructions*, 91, 93–96; Herbert Shapiro, *White Violence and Black Response: From Reconstruction to Montgomery* (Amherst: University of Massachusetts Press, 1988); George C. Rable, *But There Was No Peace: The Role of Violence in the Politics of Reconstruction* (Athens: University of Georgia Press, 1984). A former Klansmen testifying in a federal court in South Carolina admitted that the Klan sought "to advance the conservative party and put down the radical party . . . by killing, and whipping, and crowding out men from the ballot-boxes." Stewart E. Tolnay and E. M. Beck, *Festival of Violence: An Analysis of Southern Lynchings, 1882–1930* (Urbana: University of Illinois Press, 1995), 8. On Louisiana and New Orleans, see Valelly, *The Two Reconstructions*, 116–17; James Keith Hogue, *Uncivil War: Five New Orleans Street Battles and the Rise and Fall of Radical Reconstruction* (Baton Rouge: Louisiana State University Press, 2006).

21. By 1876 fewer than one thousand troops remained (excluding those garrisoned in west Texas to suppress still-present but declining Indian threats). See Bensel, *Yankee Leviathan*, 388; Woodward, *Origins of the New South*; Pekka Hämäläinen, *The Comanche Empire* (New Haven: Yale University Press, 2008), 321–61. In 1877, as federal troops departed the region, some of them were quickly dispatched to subdue striking railroad workers in the West. "The 'Southern question,' a Virginia newspaper observed, had been put to rest. Now, the "trust question" and "the relation of labor and capital" would preoccupy national politics. William E. Forbath, "Politics, State-Building, and the Courts, 1870–1920," in Grossberg and Tomlins, *Cambridge History of Law in America*, 2:643. After the Compromise, southern Democrats quickly capitalized on the withdrawal with additional suffrage restriction and electoral violence. Valelly, *The Two Reconstructions*, 49; Vincent P. De Santis, "Rutherford B. Hayes and the Removal of the Troops and the End of Reconstruction," in J. Morgan Kousser and James M. McPherson, eds., *Region, Race, and Reconstruction: Essays in Honor of C. Vann Woodward* (New York: Oxford University Press, 1982), 417–50.

22. Still, blacks outside the South clearly benefited from the Fifteenth Amendment and national legislation such as the 1875 Civil Rights Act, which helped secure black suffrage and other rights that had until then been unreliable at best. Richard M. Valelly, "National Parties and Racial Disenfranchisement," in Paul E. Peterson, ed., *Classifying by Race* (Princeton: Princeton University Press, 1995), 192; *U.S. v. Reese*, 92 U.S. 214, 217 (1875); Michael Les Benedict, "Preserving the Constitution: The Conservative Basis of Radical Reconstruction," *JAH* 61 (1974), 65–90; Valelly, *The Two Reconstructions*, 100–102; J. Morgan Kousser, "What Light Does the Civil Rights Act of 1875 Shed on the Civil Rights Act of 1964?," in Bernard Grofman, ed., *Legacies of the 1964 Civil Rights Act* (Charlottesville: University Press of Virginia, 2000), 38.

23. On the need for a restructuring of the southern political economy, see Foner, "Reconstruction and the Crisis of Free Labor"; Bensel, *Yankee Leviathan*. Bensel also emphasizes northern Republican coalitional fissures traceable to the conflicting interests of different economic sectors—including the new class of finance capitalists. Heather Cox Richardson shows how northern newspapers interpreted the "black over white" Reconstruction government of South Carolina as the worrisome future of northern state governments if the reins of power were handed over to wage earners. See Richardson, *The Death of Reconstruction: Race, Labor, and Politics in the Post-Civil War North, 1865–1901* (Cambridge: Harvard University Press, 2001), chap. 3.

24. White farm operators involved in cotton production increased from 10 percent in 1860 to 60 percent in 1880. Stanley L. Engerman, *Slavery, Emancipation, and Freedom: Comparative Perspectives* (Baton Rouge: Louisiana State University Press, 2007), 57–61.

25. Pamela Brandwein, *Rethinking the Judicial Settlement of Reconstruction* (New York: Cambridge University Press, 2011). Faced with plummeting earnings on the world market for commodities, especially cotton, southern farmers faced constant debt burdens (cotton prices declined 58 percent from 1873 to 1896). Frieden, *Global Capitalism*, 8, 16.

26. Even in 1880, black men voted at about the same rates in nine southern states as whites vote today (about 60 percent). Kousser, *Shaping of Southern Politics*, 14–16.

27. On the work of the Department of Justice, see Valelly, *The Two Reconstructions*, 65–68, tables 3.7–3.9. For a comprehensive analysis of election contests in the U.S. House, see Jeffery A. Jenkins, "Partisanship and Contested Election Cases in the House of Representatives, 1789–2002," *SAPD* 18 (2005), 112–35, especially 130, table 9, and 131–32. From 1877 to 1897, eighty southern elections were contested in the U.S. House. Consistent with Valelly, Jenkins finds that contested elections declined sharply after Republicans no longer perceived the need for combatting "the Democratic-sanctioned fraud, corruption, and violence" in the South (at 135).

28. Valelly, *The Two Reconstructions*, 121; Vincent P. De Santis, "Republican Efforts to 'Crack' the Democratic South," *Review of Politics* 14 (1952), 254; Sarah A. Binder and Steven S. Smith, *Politics or Principle? Filibustering in the United States Senate* (Washington, D.C.: Brookings Institution, 1997), 129–35. As Kousser shows, its failure at that time was critical. Even if it passed later, it would have constituted a much weaker interference in southern affairs. "By 1903, every Southern state had enacted legislation limiting the vote. No longer would a Lodge bill guarantee fair elections by allowing federal supervisors to observe the registration of voters and

guard against fraud at the polls," as literacy requirements and the poll tax would have blocked their registration. Kousser, *Shaping of Southern Politics*, 32–33.

29. The proportion of U.S. House seats from the South relative to other regions declined from 19 percent in 1894 to 13 percent in 1896. Conversely, a savvy Republican statehood agenda for the West "helped to make the South superfluous to Republican interests." Valelly, "National Parties and Racial Disenfranchisement," 207–8, table 8.6. Also see Charles Stewart III and Barry R. Weingast, "Stacking the Senate, Changing the Nation: Republican Rotten Boroughs, Statehood Politics, and American Political Development," *SAPD* 6 (1992), 223–71; Kousser, *Shaping Southern Politics*, 32; "Republican Party Platform of 1896," Jun. 16, 1896, Gerhard Peters and John T. Woolley, *The American Presidency Project* (hereafter *TAPP*), accessed online: http://www.presidency.ucsb.edu/ws/?pid=29629.

30. Jerry M. Cooper, *The Rise of the National Guard: The Evolution of the American Militia, 1865–1920* (Lincoln: University of Nebraska Press, 1997), 147–48. Judging the costs of the "riot and bloodshed" that accompanied the suppression of opposition parties to be too high, Mississippi Democrats sought a "permanent disfranchisement." Kirwan, *Revolt of the Rednecks*, 58, 49.

31. John D. Hicks, *The Populist Revolt: A History of the Farmers' Alliance and the People's Party* (Lincoln: University of Nebraska Press, 1961 [1931]); Saloutos, *Farmer Movements in the South*; Norman Pollack, ed., *The Populist Mind* (Indianapolis: Bobbs-Merrill Company, 1967); Kousser, *Shaping Southern Politics*, 34–39; Robert C. McMath, Jr., *American Populism: A Social History* (New York: Hill and Wang, 1993). On election results, see Kousser, *Shaping of Southern Politics*, 11, 13, 27 (table 1.3), 28 (table 1.4), 39, 246. Observing the repression of his party, Georgia's Populist leader Tom Watson—once a champion of biracial alliances—concluded that Populist success first required black disfranchisement. He later became a leader of Georgia's Ku Klux Klan. C. Vann Woodward, *Tom Watson: Agrarian Rebel* (New York: Oxford University Press, 1938).

32. Philip Wood (*Southern Capitalism*, 108) argues that improvements in equal treatment by law enforcement had a clear political-economic dimension: it improved black agricultural laborers' fates, since law enforcement officers implemented coercive labor policies such as peonage. In the words of a prominent Wilmington Democrat, Reverend Peyton H. Hoge, "We have taken a city." See 1898 Wilmington Race Riot Commission, *Final Report* (May 31, 2006), Appendix N: Timeline, accessed online: http://www.history.ncdcr.gov/1898-wrrc/report/AppdxN.pdf; David S. Cecelski and Timothy B. Tyson, eds., *Democracy Betrayed: The Wilmington Race Riot of 1898 and Its Legacy* (Chapel Hill: University of North Carolina Press, 1998); Kent Redding, *Making Race, Making Power: North Carolina's Road to Disfranchisement* (Urbana: University of Illinois Press, 2003). On the policy consequences of the state's transition to authoritarian rule, see J. Morgan Kousser, "Progressivism for Middle-Class Whites Only: The Distribution of Taxation and Expenditures for Education in North Carolina, 1880–1910," *JSH* 46 (1980), 169–94. Valelly, *The Two Reconstructions*, 131–32.

33. On parties as tools of intense policy demanders, see Kathleen Bawn, Martin Cohen, David Karol, Seth Masket, Hans Noel, and John Zaller, "A Theory of Political Parties: Groups, Policy Demands and Nominations in American Politics," *Perspectives on Politics* 10 (2012), 571–97. Kousser writes, "[E]ach state became in effect

a laboratory for testing one device or another. Indeed, the cross-fertilization and coordination between the movements to restrict the suffrage in the southern states amounted to a public conspiracy." Fraud was especially prevalent in majority-black counties; there, officials beholden to planters stuffed ballot boxes to offset anti-Democrat voting in majority-white counties. Kousser, *Shaping of Southern Politics*, 11, 39–40, 49–50, 78, 83, 131, 246. Eight states popularly ratified new constitutions or constitutional amendments, but did so with already-restricted electorates and usually with rigged voting. Three others crafted new constitutions and declared them law without ratification. Kousser, *Shaping of Southern Politics*, 83. Kousser elaborates on his argument in "The Undermining of the First Reconstruction: Lessons for the Second," in Chandler Davidson, ed., *Minority Vote Dilution* (Washington, D.C.: Howard University Press, 1984), 27–46, and "The Voting Rights Act and the Two Reconstructions," in Bernard Grofman and Chandler Davidson, eds., *Controversies in Minority Voting: The Voting Rights Act in Perspective* (Washington, D.C.: Brookings Institution, 1992), 135–76. In *Struggle for Mastery: Disfranchisement in the South, 1888–1908* (Chapel Hill: University of North Carolina Press, 2000), Michael Perman emphasizes suffrage restriction via constitution-writing. Kousser suggests that earlier suffrage restriction via statute was critical, and describes an evidentiary bias in using statements at these conventions in making inferences about politicians' motives (since disfranchisers were more circumspect in calling for aiming restrictions at poorer whites at conventions than in other settings). See Kousser, "Review of Michael Perman's *Struggle Over Mastery*," *Journal of Interdisciplinary History* 34 (2003), 109. Five states—including four of the five Deep South states—held constitutional conventions, only a few of which were popularly ratified; others modified constitutions via referenda. Virginia's new Constitution was drafted and went into effect without popular ratification in 1902. Kousser, *Shaping of Southern Politics*, 83.

34. Kousser, *Shaping of Southern Politics*, 6, 8, 40. Kousser's claims regarding the causal effects of suffrage restriction have been corroborated by others, including Kent Redding and David R. James, "Estimating Levels and Modeling Determinants of Black and White Voter Turnout in the South: 1880 to 1912," *Historical Methods* 34 (2001), 141–59. Kousser argues that, in contrast to V. O. Key's finding, suffrage restriction by statute, state constitution, party rule, and informal institutions did not merely ratify ongoing changes but were critically important themselves. Kousser, *Shaping of Southern Politics*, 3; Key, *Southern Politics*, 533. On the constitutions, see Tarr, *Understanding State Constitutions*, 131; Herron, "State Constitutional Development"; Amy Bridges, "Managing the Periphery in the Gilded Age: Writing Constitutions for the Western States," *SAPD* 22 (2008), 32–58. On suffrage restriction and other obstacles to anti-Democrats in Dallas, see Patrick G. Williams, "Suffrage Restriction in Post-Reconstruction Texas: Urban Politics and the Specter of the Commune," *JSH* 68 (2002), 31–64; Alicia E. Rodriquez, "Disfranchisement in Dallas: The Democratic Party and the Suppression of Independent Political Challenges in Dallas, Texas, 1891–1894," *Southwestern Historical Quarterly* 108 (2004), 42–64. These efforts may have worked; David Mayhew describes the Dallas' Citizens Charter Association as "probably as close as anything can get [in American politics] to an executive committee of a ruling class." Mayhew, *Placing Parties*, 241.

35. Key, *Southern Politics*, 20. By 1903 most southern states used the primary; by 1915, all did. Kousser, *Shaping of Southern Politics*, 72–82; Woodward, *Origins of the*

New South, chap. 12. While defeated as an independent political force, southern populists did exert enough influence working with their nonsouthern counterparts in Congress and through their impact on some Democratic politicians to shape the main contours of the Progressive Era expansion of the federal government. These included the creation of the income tax, banking and currency reforms, road development, regulation of railroad and shipping sectors, and support for agricultural vocational education. Elizabeth Sanders, *Roots of Reform: Farmers, Workers, and the American State, 1877–1917* (Chicago: University of Chicago Press, 1999), chap. 1.

36. Key, *Southern Politics*, 280–85.

37. Before 1928, the share of blacks in the eleven southern delegations to national Republican conventions ranged from 10 to 21 percent; by 1932, this was down to 6 percent, which for decades it never approached. Richard B. Sherman, *The Republican Party and Black America: From McKinley to Hoover, 1896–1933* (Charlottesville: University Press of Virginia, 1973), 230–56; Gregory B. Sampson, "The Rise of the 'New' Republican Party in South Carolina, 1948–1974: A Case Study of Political Change in a Deep South State," Ph.D. diss., University of North Carolina-Chapel Hill (1984), 174–75 (hereafter "Sampson"); George B. Tindall, *Emergence of the New South, 1913–1945* (Baton Rouge: Louisiana State University Press, 1968), 541–42. Party leaders liked to keep these parties as small as possible in order to maintain control over greater patronage.

38. Only in those states where there was a durable (if anemic) Republican party did Democratic parties acknowledge and attempt, generally successfully, to reduce the electoral costs of factionalism. Key, *Southern Politics*, chap. 19. Republicans often sold positions to Democrats. Alexander Heard interview with a prominent Mississippi state party official, Alexander Heard Papers, Special Collections, Jane and Alexander Heard Library, Vanderbilt University (hereafter "Heard Papers"); Neil R. McMillen, "Perry Howard, Boss of Black-and-Tan Republicanism in Mississippi, 1924–1960," *JSH* 48 (1982), 205–24. On southern Republicans, see Allan P. Sindler, "The Unsolid South: A Challenge to the Democratic National Party," in Alan F. Westin, ed., *The Uses of Power: 7 Cases in American Politics* (New York: Harcourt Brace & World, Inc., 1962), 250; Daniel J. Galvin, *Presidential Party Building: Dwight D. Eisenhower to George W. Bush* (Princeton: Princeton University Press, 2010), 31; Key, *Southern Politics*, 286–97 and 647; Hanes Walton, Jr., *Black Republicans: The Politics of the Black and Tans* (Metuchen, N.J.: Scarecrow Press, 1975); Alexander Heard, *A Two-Party South?* (Chapel Hill: University of North Carolina Press, 1952), 108.

39. Woodward, *Origins of the New South*, 22; Kousser, *Shaping of Southern Politics*, 8.

40. Nor would southern white publics have accepted such a politics. With some exceptions—usually in Virginia and South Carolina—Democrats preferred popular democratic controls. On Virginia, see Woodward, *Origins of the New South*, 347. Key writes that the state party was "merely a holding company for a congeries of transient squabbling factions, most of which fail by far to meet the standards of permanence, cohesiveness, and responsibility that characterize the … party.… [T]he South as a whole has developed no system … of political organization and leadership adequate to cope with its problems" (*Southern Politics*, 387, 16, 4).

41. As Kousser writes, "Negro domination threatened until all partisan opposition was eliminated. Not only black, but potential white dissent had to be eradicated. From such thinking arose violence, intimidation, gerrymandering, fraud, and

curtailment of the suffrage. Even after almost every Negro ceased voting, Democrats instantly charged any partisan adversary with racial treason. The expression "white man's party" became popular dogma" (*Shaping of Southern Politics*, 38).

42. Key, *Southern Politics*, 646, 666. As Key writes of North Carolina's "oligarchs," their "interests, which are often the interests of the state, are served without prompting" (*Southern Politics*, 211). Also see Dewey W. Grantham, *The Life and Death of the Solid South: A Political History* (Lexington: University Press of Kentucky, 1988), 193.

43. Katherine S. Newman and Rourke L. O'Brien, *Taxing the Poor: Doing Damage to the Truly Disadvantaged* (Berkeley: University of California Press, 2011), chap. 1.

44. Patron-client relations has been defined as a private relationship of reciprocal, dyadic exchange between actors "of unequal power and status." Robert R. Kaufman, "The Patron-Client Concept and Macro-Politics: Prospects and Problems," *Comparative Studies in Society and History* 16 (1974), 285; Lee J. Alston, "Race Etiquette in the South: The Role of Tenancy," *Research in Economic History* 10 (1986), 199–211. White workers were also subjects of different types of paternalism; see Jacquelyn Dowd Hall, James Leloudis, Robert Korstad, Mary Murphy, Lu Ann Jones, and Christopher B. Daly, *Like a Family: The Making of a Southern Cotton Mill World* (Chapel Hill: University of North Carolina Press, 1987); Michelle Brattain, *The Politics of Whiteness: Race, Workers, and Culture in the Modern South* (Princeton: Princeton University Press, 2001), chaps. 1–2.

45. Lee J. Alston and Joseph P. Ferrie, *Southern Paternalism and the American Welfare State: Economics, Politics, and Institutions in the South, 1865–1965* (New York: Cambridge University Press, 1999). Also see the elegiac account of an institution then in its twilight, William Alexander Percy's *Lanterns on the Levee: Recollections of a Planter's Son* (New York: Knopf, 1941). As Texas's experience demonstrated, enclave rulers had no principled objection to federal involvement in labor markets. On the Bracero program—a Mexico-U.S. agreement from the early 1940s to the early 1960s that established a reliable flow of agricultural laborers, ultimately totaling more than five million, from Mexico into the Southwest—see Wayne A. Grove, "The Mexican Farm Labor Program, 1942–1964: Government-Administered Labor Market Insurance for Farmers," *Agricultural History* 70 (1996), 311.

46. In the words of James Bryce, "One road only has in the past led into democracy, viz., the wish to be rid of tangible evils." See *Modern Democracies*, vol. 2 (New York: Macmillan, 1922), 602, quoted in Rustow, "Transitions to Democracy," 354; Rueschemeyer, Stephens, and Stephens, *Capitalist Development and Democracy*, 52. Here, southern planters resembled oligarchs in other predominantly agrarian polities who relied "on extra-economic coercion of labor by the state for the realization of income superior to those possible under more liberal, market-based arrangements," and whose coercion of labor "entails gross violations of fundamental liberal rights of association, speech, free movement, self-ownership, due process, and equality before the law." Wood, *Forging Democracy from Below*, 6–8.

47. An attorney with a small law practice, V. O. Key's father also owned farms worked by tenant farmers and chaired his west Texas county's Democratic party. Andrew M. Lucker, *V. O. Key, Jr.: The Quintessential Political Scientist* (New York: Peter Lang Publishing, 2001), 7–8. The quotation appears in Jasper Shannon, *Toward a New Politics in the South* (Knoxville: University of Tennessee Press, 1949), 43–44. For broader discussions, see Waldner, "Democracy and Dictatorship in the Post-Colonial

World"; Dogan and Higley, "Elites, Crises, and Regimes in Comparative Analysis"; Robert A. Dahl, *Who Governs? Democracy and Power in an American City* (New Haven: Yale University Press, 1961), 90; Mayhew, *Placing Parties in American Politics*, 4.

48. Cobb, "Beyond Planters and Industrialists," 56.

49. Quotation appears in Cobb, "Beyond Planters and Industrialists," 57, 59, 65, fn. 45, 64. Also see Tindall, *The Emergence of the New South*, 106.

50. Bruce J. Schulman, *From Cotton Belt to Sunbelt: Federal Policy, Economic Development, and the Transformation of the South, 1938–1980* (New York: Oxford University Press, 1991), ix.

51. John Egerton, *Speak Now Against the Day: The Generation Before the Civil Rights Movement in the South* (Chapel Hill: University of North Carolina Press, 1995), 20–21.

52. Tariff revenues were used for federal spending that occurred almost completely outside the South (on, for example, Union veterans' pensions and military spending). Richard F. Bensel, *Sectionalism and American Political Development, 1800–1980* (Madison: University of Wisconsin Press, 1984), 62–69; Bensel, *The Political Economy of American Industrialization, 1877–1900* (New York: Cambridge University Press, 2000), chap. 7; Woodward, *Origins of the New South*, chaps. 7 and 11; Lance E. Davis and John Legler, "The Government in the American Economy, 1815–1902: A Quantitative Study," *Journal of Economic History* 26 (1966), 517, fn. 8 (hereafter *JEH*). By the 1930s southern elites' preferences for free trade and access to Europe had not changed, but the international environment had. When their European trading partners were imperiled, southern politicians changed course and provided key votes for Roosevelt's internationalist agenda and rearmament. See Peter Trubowitz, *Defining the National Interest: Conflict and Change in American Foreign Policy* (Chicago: University of Chicago Press, 1998), chap. 3; Jeff Frieden, "Sectoral Conflict and Foreign Economic Policy, 1914–1940," *International Organization* 42 (1988), 83–90; Douglas A. Irwin, *Peddling Protectionism: Smoot-Hawley and the Great Depression* (Princeton: Princeton University Press, 2011), chap. 1.

53. Key likened the behavior of these politicians to the "erraticism of Mexican generals of an earlier day" (*Southern Politics*, 305).

54. Often what were labeled, then and now, as riots were armed clashes during an election campaign. Many others resembled Eastern European pogroms than riots in that they amounted to waves of one-sided, white-on-black killings and the destruction of black property conducted by bands of whites. See Gunnar Myrdal, *An American Dilemma: The Negro Problem and Modern Democracy* (New York: Harper & Row, 1996 [1944]), 566.

55. On the Sunday closest to Lincoln's birthday, some of Charleston's black and white parishioners would worship together. See Cobb, "Beyond Planters and Industrialists," 57; Dewey W. Grantham, *Southern Progressivism: The Reconciliation of Progress and Tradition* (Knoxville: University of Tennessee Press, 1983); Kousser, *Shaping of Southern Politics*, 230. Efforts to fine-tune Jim Crow in order to maintain political and social order are richly detailed and analyzed in Kimberley Johnson, *Reforming Jim Crow: Southern Politics and State in the Age before Brown* (New York: Oxford University Press, 2010). Also see Jack Temple Kirby, *Darkness at the Dawning: Race and Reform in the Progressive South* (Philadelphia: J. B. Lippincott Company, 1972), 4; William A. Link, *The Paradox of Southern Progressivism, 1880–1930* (Chapel Hill:

University of North Carolina Press, 1997), 257–58; Paul Harvey, *Freedom's Coming: Religious Culture and the Shaping of the South from the Civil War through the Civil Rights Era* (Chapel Hill: University of North Carolina Press, 2005), 78; William D. Smyth, "Segregation in Charleston in the 1950s: A Decade of Transition," *South Carolina Historical Magazine* 92 (1991), 121 (hereafter *SCHM*). On violence in the World War I era, see William M. Tuttle, *Race Riot: Chicago in the Red Summer of 1919* (Urbana: University of Illinois Press, 1970). Fissures emerged among white progressives and liberals in the 1940s over whether segregation itself should be attacked (see chapter 4).

56. Brian Kelley, *Race, Class, and Power in the Alabama Coalfields, 1908–1921* (Urbana: University of Illinois Press, 2001), 14–15; Nan Elizabeth Woodruff, *American Congo: The African American Freedom Struggle in the Delta* (Cambridge: Harvard University Press, 2003), 162–97 (on the Southern Tenant Farmers' Union).

57. Gerald Friedman, "The Political Economy of Early Southern Unionism: Race, Politics, and Labor in the South, 1880–1953," *JEH* 60 (2000), 384–413; Bryant Simon, "Rethinking Why There Are So Few Unions in the South," *GHQ* 81 (1997), 465–84. Given the combination of intense competition and a high share of labor costs among all operating expenses, mill owners were particularly opposed to unionization, as they could not pass on the higher costs to consumers. Thomas E. Terrill, "The Lower Right Hand Corner: The American South," *Reviews in American History* 15 (1987), 652; Janet Irons, *Testing the New Deal: The General Textile Strike of 1934 in the American South* (Urbana: University of Illinois Press, 2000); Wood, *Southern Capitalism*, 92; Robin D. G. Kelley, *Hammer and Hoe: Alabama Communists During the Great Depression* (Chapel Hill: University of North Carolina Press, 1990); Robert R. Korstad, *Civil Rights Unionism: Tobacco Workers and the Struggle for Democracy in the Mid-20th Century South* (Chapel Hill: University of North Carolina Press, 2003).

58. For instance, see Thomas Krueger, *And Promises to Keep: The Southern Conference for Human Welfare, 1938–1948* (Nashville: Vanderbilt University Press, 1967). For historian Morton Sosna, a white individual had to oppose Jim Crow and suffrage restriction in order to merit the label "southern liberal." Morton Sosna, *In Search of the Silent South: Southern Liberals and the Race Issue* (New York: Columbia University Press, 1977), viii. For an excellent analysis of postwar southern liberalism, see Tony Badger, "Fatalism, Not Gradualism: Race and the Crisis of Southern Liberalism, 1945–1965," in Brian Ward and Tony Badger, eds., *The Making of Martin Luther King and the Civil Rights Movement* (New York: New York University Press, 1996), 67–95. Also see David L. Chappell, *A Stone of Hope: Prophetic Religion and the Death of Jim Crow* (Chapel Hill: University of North Carolina Press, 2004), 42–43; Walter A. Jackson, "White Liberal Intellectuals, Civil Rights, and Gradualism, 1954–1960," in Ward and Badger, *Making of Martin Luther King*, 96–114.

59. During the drafting of the Articles of Confederation, South Carolina's delegate vowed that the confederation would "end" if it were even "debated, whether … slaves are property." Jack N. Rakove, *The Beginnings of National Politics: An Interpretive History of the Continental Congress* (Baltimore: Johns Hopkins University Press, 1982), 161. By the 1820s, the region's dominant politicians succeeded in converting a central state at first ambivalent about safeguarding slavery into its staunch defender. Don E. Fehrenbacher, *The Slaveholding Republic: An Account of the United States Government's Relations to Slavery*, completed and edited by Ward M. McAfee (New York: Oxford

University Press, 2001). But see Paul Finkelman, "Slavery and the Constitutional Convention: Making a Covenant with Death," in Richard Beeman, Stephen Botein, and Edward C. Carter III, eds., *Beyond Confederation: Origins of the Constitution and American National Identity* (Chapel Hill: University of North Carolina Press, 1987), 188–225; David Waldstreicher, *Slavery's Constitution: From Revolution to Ratification* (New York: Hill and Wang, 2008).

60. Unlike the constitutional protection granted states, cities' boundaries and political institutions can be changed; their very existence can be legally terminated. As urbanization and law regarding cities developed in the late nineteenth century, the doctrine of cities as the "creatures" of the states developed. In addition to lacking constitutional protections, cities' political autonomy has been stymied by their vulnerability to competition with other cities for desirable residents, firms, and capital. Gerald E. Frug, "The City as a Legal Concept," *Harvard Law Review* 93 (1980), 1057–154; Paul E. Peterson, *City Limits* (Chicago: University of Chicago Press, 1981).

61. *Plessy v. Ferguson*, 163 U. S. 537 (1896). *Plessy* also delegated to states the authority of determining racial categories and applying them. Lucas A. Powe, Jr., *The Warren Court and American Politics* (Cambridge: Harvard University Press, 2000), 21. Disfranchising provisions in state constitutions reflected likely federal judicial interpretations of the Fourteenth and Fifteenth Amendments. Fortunately for enclave founders, the Supreme Court aided and abetted such provisions in *Williams v. Mississippi* 170 U.S. 213 (1898). Here, the Court affirmed Mississippi's jury system, which was limited to registered voters, by cynically accepting Mississippi suffrage restriction as racially neutral. Five years later, the Court even more forcefully assisted southern rulers in *Giles v. Harris* (Holmes is quoted at 189 U.S. 488, 1903). See J. Morgan Kousser, *Colorblind Injustice: Minority Voting Rights and the Undoing of the Second Reconstruction* (Chapel Hill: University of North Carolina Press, 1999), 319–23. The "special constitutional status" quotation appears in William E. Forbath, "Constitutional Change and the Politics of History," *Yale Law Journal* 108 (1998–99), 1924. Richard H. Pildes, "Democracy, Anti-Democracy, and the Canon," *Constitutional Commentary* 17 (2000), 296.

62. *Buchanan v. Warley* (245 U.S. 60, 1917) invalidated racist municipal zoning ordinances; still, *Corrigan v. Buckley* (271 U.S. 323, 1926) upheld restrictive residential covenants. See Michael Jones-Correa, "The Origins and Diffusion of Racial Restrictive Covenants," *Political Science Quarterly* 115 (2000), 541–68. On peonage and vagrancy laws, see Aziz Z. Huq, "Peonage and Contractual Liberty," *Columbia Law Review* 101 (2001), 351–91. The Court affirmed the poll tax in *Breedlove v. Suttles*, 302 U. S. 277 (1937), and while it struck down an unsubtle version of the grandfather clause in 1915, it allowed an easy workaround to stand until 1939 (*Lane v. Wilson*, 307 U. S. 268). Manfred Berg, *"The Ticket to Freedom": The NAACP and the Struggle for Black Political Integration* (Gainesville: University Press of Florida, 2005), 73, 85–86.

63. *Luther v. Borden* (48 U.S. 1, 1849). Article IV, Section 4, Clause 1 reads, "The United States shall guarantee to every State in this Union a Republican Form of Government." For the framers (and, presumably, the ratifiers), "republican" seemed to have been synonymous with the modern-day usage of "democratic." Amar, *America's Constitution*, 276–80; also see William E. Wiecek, *The Guarantee Clause of the U.S. Constitution* (Ithaca: Cornell University Press, 1972), 156–65; Alexander Hamilton, James Madison, and John Jay, *The Federalist*, ed. by J. R. Pole (Indianapolis: Hackett,

1995 [1788]), No. 43, 237–39. Black activists invoked it during and after the foundings of enclave rule, and in his famous dissent in *Plessy v. Ferguson* (163 U.S. 563–64,
1896), Associate Justice John Marshall Harlan argued that Louisiana's 1890 Separate
Cars Act violated the Clause. These and other invocations never gained any traction.
The clause may be one among several elements of the Constitution that have only
"normative or aspirational force." John Ferejohn, Jack N. Rakove, and Jonathan Riley,
"Editor's Introduction," in John Ferejohn, Jack N. Rakove, and Jonathan Riley, eds.,
Constitutional Culture and Democratic Rule (New York: Cambridge University Press,
2001), 12–13.

64. See Valelly, *The Two Reconstructions*, 146–47, 132; Sherman, *The Republican
Party and Black America*, 18, 75–77, cited in Berg, *"The Ticket to Freedom,"* 13 and 28–
30; Joseph C. Manning, "Suffrage Conditions in Democratic and Republican States
Compared," *Crisis* 4 (Oct. 1912), 304–8; W.E.B. Du Bois, "Reduced Representation in
Congress" and "The Election and Democracy," *Crisis* 21 (Feb. 1921), 149–50, 156–60;
NYT, May 7, 1921; Kousser, *Shaping of Southern Politics*, 33, fn. 35; "Republican Party
Platform of 1904," Jun. 21, 1904, *TAPP*, accessed online: http://www.presidency.ucsb
.edu/ws/?pid=29631.

65. Peter H. Argersinger, "The Transformation of American Politics: Political
Institutions and Public Policy, 1865–1910," in Byron E. Shafer and Anthony J. Badger, eds., *Contesting Democracy: Substance & Structure in American Political History,
1775–2000* (Lawrence: University Press of Kansas, 2001), 133; Peter H. Argersinger, " 'A
Place on the Ballot': Fusion Politics and Antifusion Laws," *AHR* 85 (1980), 287–306.
A 1918 survey revealed that "the theory that every man has a natural right to vote
no longer commands the support of students of political science." Kousser, *Shaping
of Southern Politics*, 57, 250–57; also see Kirk Harold Porter, *A History of Suffrage in
the United States* (Chicago: University of Chicago Press, 1918). On urban reformers'
penchant for shrinking electorates, see Bridges, *Morning Glories*; Trounstine, *Political
Monopolies*, 5–8. Generally, see Eileen McDonagh, "The 'Welfare Rights State' and the
'Civil Rights State': Policy Paradox and State Building in the Progressive Era," *SAPD*
7 (1993), 225–74; Elisabeth S. Clemens, *The People's Lobby: Organizational Innovation
and the Rise of Interest Group Politics in the United States, 1890–1925* (Chicago: University of Chicago Press, 1997).

66. See, e.g., William Howard Taft: "Inaugural Address," March 4, 1909. *TAPP*,
http://www.presidency.ucsb.edu/ws/?pid=25830; Valelly, *The Two Reconstructions*, 134.
At the 1912 convention, Progressive Party delegates refused to back a "mild" plank
opposing racist discrimination, and party leaders blocked the participation of southern black delegates. Richard B. Sherman, *The Republican Party and Black America:
From McKinley to Hoover, 1896–1933* (Charlottesville: University Press of Virginia,
1973), 104–9; Berg, *"The Ticket to Freedom,"* 44; Sidney M. Milkis, *Theodore Roosevelt,
the Progressive Party, and the Transformation of American Democracy* (Lawrence: University of Kansas Press, 2009), chap. 4.

67. Woodrow Wilson, *Division and Reunion, 1829–1889* (New York: Longmans,
1898), 290; Woodrow Wilson, "The States and the Federal Government," *North American Review* 187 (1908), 684.

68. On the "solid South" in the Senate, see Key, *Southern Politics*, chaps. 16–17. During the New and Fair Deals, southerners chaired one-half of all House committees.
Ira Katznelson, Kim Geiger, and Daniel Kryder, "Limiting Liberalism: The Southern

Veto in Congress, 1933–1950," *Political Science Quarterly* 108 (1993), 284. Except for five years of interruptions, the House Speaker hailed from a southern district from 1931 to 1961. See Polsby, *How Congress Evolves*, 221.

69. Charles O. Jones, "Joseph G. Cannon and Howard W. Smith: An Essay on the Limits of Leadership in the House of Representatives," *JOP* 30 (1968), 617–46.

70. Kousser, "The Voting Rights Act and Two Reconstructions," 150–51; Jeffery A. Jenkins, Justin Peck, and Vesla M. Weaver, "Between Reconstructions: Congressional Action on Civil Rights, 1891–1940," *SAPD* 34 (2010), 57–89. "Chairs derived their power from controlling agendas, managing bills on the floor, distributing benefits to members, and using procedures to limit debate," and "party leaders deferred" to them. Julian E. Zelizer, *On Capitol Hill: The Struggle for Reform Congress and Its Consequences, 1948–2000* (New York: Cambridge University Press, 2004), 17. Also see Nelson Polsby, Miriam Gallaher, and Barry S. Rundquist, "The Growth of the Seniority System in the U.S. House of Representatives," *APSR* 63 (1969), 787–807; Kathryn Pearson and Eric Schickler, "Discharge Petitions, Agenda Control, and the Congressional Committee System, 1927–1976," *JOP* 71 (2009), 1239; Eric Schickler and Kathryn Pearson, "Agenda Control, Majority Party Power, and the House Committee on Rules, 1937–52," *Legislative Studies Quarterly* 34 (2009), 455–91; Gary W. Cox and Mathew D. McCubbins, "Agenda Power in the U.S. House of Representatives, 1877–1986," in David W. Brady and Mathew McCubbins, eds., *Party, Process, and Political Change in Congress: New Perspectives on the History of Congress* (Palo Alto: Stanford University Press, 2002), 107–45. David R. Mayhew argues that the conservative coalition of northern Republicans and southern Democrats was rarely an enacting coalition as opposed to a negative force blocking legislation. Mayhew, *Divided We Govern: Party Control, Lawmaking, and Investigations, 1946–2002*, 2nd ed. (New Haven: Yale University Press, 2005), 127, table 5.6. The "Gettysburg" quotation appears in William S. White, *Citadel: The Story of the U.S. Senate* (New York: Harper & Brothers, 1956), 68. As Caro and others note, this knowledge of arcane rules was possible in part because of southern officeholders' seniority, and desirable given the perceived inability of southern members to ascend to the presidency. See Robert Caro, *The Years of Lyndon Johnson*, vol. 3: *Master of the Senate* (New York: Knopf, 2002), chaps. 1–3.

71. U.S. Congress, Commission on Industrial Relations, *Final Report*, vol. 6: *The Land Question and the Condition of Agricultural Labor* (Washington, D.C.: U.S. Government Printing Office, 1916), 87; on peonage hearings, see Pete Daniel, *The Shadow of Slavery: Peonage in the South, 1901–1969* (New York: Oxford University Press, 1972).

72. The most tangible monument to this inflow of federal spending, the Tennessee Valley Authority, spanned very poor portions of eight southern states. Before its establishment, only 2 percent of farms in this area were electrified. Jean Edward Smith, *FDR* (New York: Random House, 2007), 324–25. A thirteen-state "South" (including Kentucky and Oklahoma) earned barely half of the national per capita income. Schulman, *Cotton Belt to Sunbelt*, ix.

73. "Some Comparisons of Rank, Percentage, and Number of Electrified Farms by States," Rural Electrification Administration, U.S. Dept. of Agriculture. Appended to a letter from REA Administrator Harry Slattery to Russell, Jan. 7, 1941. Folder 3, Box 356, Series 6–2b, Richard B. Russell Papers, Richard B. Russell Library for Political Research and Studies, University of Georgia, Athens (hereafter RBRL).

74. Walter White, *A Man Called White* (New York: Ayer, 1948), 168–70; George C. Rable, "The South and the Politics of Antilynching Legislation, 1920–1940," *JSH* 51 (1985), 201–20. Roll-call analyses of the "Solid South" in Congress include Katznelson and Mulroy, "Was the South Pivotal?"; and Katznelson, Geiger, and Kryder, "Limiting Liberalism." Also see Farhang and Katznelson, "The Southern Imposition." Argentine President Juan Peron's relationship with rural bosses parallels President Franklin D. Roosevelt's ties to southern barons during the New Deal. Edward L. Gibson, "The Populist Road to Market Reform: Policy and Electoral Coalitions in Mexico and Argentina," *World Politics* 49 (1997), 367.

75. During Reconstruction, young Woodrow "Tommy" Wilson lived for four years in Columbia, South Carolina, where a black state legislator represented the Wilson family. John Milton Cooper, Jr., *Woodrow Wilson: A Biography* (New York: Vintage Books, 2009), 24. The District's Reconstruction period, during which it had home rule and banned segregated public accommodations, is chronicled in Kate T. Masur, *An Example for All the Land: Emancipation and the Struggle over Equality in Washington, D.C.* (Chapel Hill: University of North Carolina Press, 2010).

76. Federal civilian employment reached barely 25,000 on the eve of the Civil War, more than 150,000 by the time of enclave rule, and by the time Wilson entered the White House it had more than doubled again to almost 400,000. Ronald N. Johnson and Gary D. Libecap, *The Federal Civil Service System and the Problem of Bureaucracy: The Economics and Politics of Institutional Change* (Chicago: University of Chicago Press, 1994), 17, table 2.1.

77. In the words of Wilson's new head of internal revenue in Georgia, "There is no Government position for negroes in the South. A negro's place is in the cornfields." Quoted in Smith, *FDR*, 662, fn. 6. For the best treatment of this overshadowed event, see Desmond King, *Separate and Unequal: Black Americans and the U.S. Federal Government*, rev. ed. (New York: Oxford University Press, 2007 [1995]).

78. Aldrich, *Why Parties?* 116, 124. Established in 1848, the Democratic National Committee (DNC) lacked autonomous preferences or the capacities to act upon them. Developed solely to organize the upcoming presidential nominating convention, between elections it had no clear purpose. Second, its chairman had no external power base. During years in which the party held the presidency, presidents, eager to replace it with a more effective campaign organization, ran roughshod over the organization. Third, the national committee's governance reflected the shadow existence of a "national party" generally. The DNC comprised two committee persons from each state, and was responsible for approving the Call sent out before each presidential convention. This confederal structure suggested a weak holding company for state party interests. The DNC lacked capacity to do much more than service the states' requests for federal employment patronage. Sidney M. Milkis, *The President and the Parties: The Transformation of the American Party System since the New Deal* (New York: Oxford University Press, 1993); Bernard C. Hennessey and Cornelius P. Cotter, *Politics Without Power: The National Party Committees* (New York: Atherton Press, 1964); Philip A. Klinkner, *The Losing Parties: Out-Party National Committees, 1956–1993* (New Haven: Yale University Press, 1994).

79. David Burner, *The Politics of Provincialism: The Democratic Party in Transition, 1918–1932* (Cambridge: Harvard University Press, 1968), 120–21; *NYT*, Jun. 18, 1924; Lee N. Allen, "The McAdoo Campaign for the Presidential Nomination in 1924,"

JSH 29 (1963), 217; "The Klan and the Democrats, *Literary Digest* 81 (Jun. 14, 1924), 12–13.

80. Malapportionment was a "self-referencing" institution in that it allowed those who benefited from it to protect it (any change in apportionment would have to emerge from the (malapportioned) legislature). See Gary Miller, "Rational Choice and Dysfunctional Institutions," *Governance* 13 (2000), 539. It was a nation-wide phenomenon by the 1940s, but the three worst offenders included Alabama, Florida, and Georgia. Hill, *Democracy in the Fifty States*, 33.

81. Associate Justice Felix Frankfurter famously articulated the doctrine in *Cole-grove v. Green*, 328 U.S. 549 (1946), at 552–56.

82. For evidence of urban delegations' substantial influence in state legislatures despite malapportionment, see Scott Allard, Nancy Burns, and Gerald Gamm, "Representing Urban Interests: The Local Politics of State Legislatures," *SAPD* 12 (1998), 267–302; Margaret Weir, "States, Race, and the Decline of New Deal Liberalism," *SAPD* 19 (2005), 160–64. But see Gerald Gamm and Thad Kousser, "No Strength in Numbers: The Failure of Big-City Bills in American State Legislatures, 1880–2000," *APSR* 107 (2013), 663–78. Quotation appears in H. L. Mencken, *On Politics: A Carnival of Buncombe* (Baltimore: Johns Hopkins University Press, 2006 [1956]), 164.

83. On educational spending, see Kousser, "Progressivism"; Pamela Barnhouse Walters, David R. James, and Holly J. McCammon, "Citizenship and Public Schools: Accounting for Racial Inequality in Education in the Pre- and Post-Disfranchisement South," *ASR* 62 (1997), 34–52; Suresh Naidu, "Suffrage, Schooling, and Sorting in the Post-Bellum U.S. South," Working Paper No. 18129, National Bureau of Economic Research (June 2012); Kousser, *Shaping of Southern Politics*, 229.

84. Wright, *Sharing the Prize*, chaps. 2 and 4 (especially p. 124).

85. While the "one-drop rule" may have reigned supreme culturally by the late nineteenth century in most of the South, it was rarely codified in law before the 1910s. By 1940 seven states—four of them in the ex-Confederacy, including Georgia—defined blacks as those with "one drop" of African blood. Paul Finkelman, "The Color of Law" (review of Andrew Kull, *The Color-Blind Constitution*), *Northwestern University Law Review* 87 (1993), 954, fn. 95 and 955; F. James Davis, *Who Is Black? One Nation's Definition*, 2nd ed. (University Park: Penn State University Press, 1991), 77; Scott Leon Washington, "Hypodescent: A History of the Crystallization of the One-Drop Rule in the United States, 1880–1940," Ph.D. diss., Princeton University (2011), table 3.1, pp. 166, 178, 182; Pauli Murray, *States' Laws on Race and Color* (Athens: University of Georgia Press, 1997 [1950]), 90, 237, 406; William Graham Sumner, *Folkways: A Study of the Sociological Importance of Usages, Manners, Customs, Mores, and Morals* (Boston: Ginn and Company, 1940 [1906]); chap. 214 of the *Mississippi Laws* (1920), 307; Paul Finkelman, "Exploring Southern Legal History," *North Carolina Law Review* 64 (1985–86), 85; Woodward, *Strange Career of Jim Crow*, 103–4, 109, 139. Some historians, such as Howard N. Rabinowitz, have criticized Woodward's claim about both the relatively late timing and contingency of racial segregation; for a defense, see John W. Cell, *The Highest Stage of White Supremacy: The Origins of Segregation in South Africa and the American South* (New York: Cambridge University Press, 1982). Rabinowitz, *Race Relations in the Urban South, 1865–1890* (New York: Oxford University Press, 1978).

86. Sex among black men and white women remained a source of great anxiety among both races, as well as a useful electoral appeal for Democratic politicians. During the founding of enclave rule, Democrats vowed to save white womanhood. Mississippi governor James K. Vardaman argued that, if necessary, "every Negro in the state will be lynched . . . to maintain white supremacy." Neil R. McMillen, *Dark Journey: Black Mississippians in the Age of Crow* (Urbana: University of Illinois Press, 1990), 224. See Glenda Gilmore, *Gender and Jim Crow: Women and the Politics of White Supremacy in North Carolina, 1896–1920* (Chapel Hill: University of North Carolina Press, 1996); Michele Mitchell, *Righteous Propagation: African Americans and the Politics of Racial Destiny after Reconstruction* (Chapel Hill: University of North Carolina Press, 2004); Stephen Kantrowitz, *Ben Tillman and the Reconstruction of White Supremacy* (Chapel Hill: University of North Carolina Press, 2000); Bryant Simon, "The Appeal of Cole Blease of South Carolina: Race, Class, and Sex in the New South," *JSH* 62 (1996), 57–86; Woodward, *Strange Career of Jim Crow*, 116–18. See Peggy Pascoe, "Miscegenation Law, Court Cases, and Ideologies of 'Race' in Twentieth-Century America," *JAH* 83 (1996), 49; Julie Novkov, *Racial Union: Law, Intimacy, and the White State in Alabama, 1865–1954* (Ann Arbor: University of Michigan Press, 2008). By the end of World War II, thirty-one states—including all southern states—criminalized interracial marriage. The Supreme Court invalidated criminalization of interracial marriage in 1967. See Peter Wallenstein, "Race, Marriage, and the Supreme Court from *Pace v. Alabama* (1883) to *Loving v. Virginia* (1967)," *Journal of Supreme Court History* 2 (1998), 65–86.

87. Jennifer Rittenhouse, *Growing Up Jim Crow: The Racial Socialization of Black and White Southern Children, 1890–1940* (Chapel Hill: University of North Carolina Press, 2006), 81. Also see Kristina DuRocher, *Raising Racists: The Socialization of White Children in the Jim Crow South* (Lexington: University Press of Kentucky, 2011), chap. 1; McMillen, *Dark Journey*, 11 and 24–25. As Georgia white dissident writer Lillian Smith suggested, "We [whites] felt worthless and weak when confronted by Authorities who had cheapened nearly all that we held dear, except our skin color. . . . In the Land of Epidermis, every one of us was a little king." *Killers of the Dream* (New York: W. W. Norton, 1994 [1949]), 90.

88. Davis, *Inhuman Bondage*, 272. On the emergence of different racist ideologies, see Alden T. Vaughan, *Roots of American Racism: Essays on the Colonial Experience* (New York: Oxford University Press, 1995); Frederickson, *The Black Image in the White Mind*; Barbara J. Fields, "Ideology and Race in American History," in Kousser and McPherson, *Region, Race, and Reconstruction*, 143–77, and Fields, "Slavery, Race, and Ideology in the United States of America," *New Left Review* 181 (1990), 99; Marek D. Steedman, "How Was Race Constructed in the New South?" *Du Bois Review* 5 (2008), 49–67. On the importance of self-reinforcing dynamics in perpetuating social norms and ideologies, see Pierson, *Politics in Time*, 39–40.

89. Farmers and farmworkers—and especially tenants and sharecroppers—were not just poor but usually had little cash on hand. One dollar in 1900 was about one-fifth of the monthly income of most southerners. "Without the poll tax, which preceded the legalized white primary in nearly every southern state, Republicans and Populists or their successors would have remained a threat *even if blacks had been excluded from Democratic primaries.*" Kousser, *Shaping of Southern Politics*, 63–68. Also see J. Morgan Kousser, "Poll Tax," in Richard Rose, ed., *International Encyclopedia*

of Elections (Washington, D.C.: Congressional Quarterly Press, 2000), 208–9. For a comparison of differences in the poll tax across states, see Walton, Puckett, and Deskins, *The African American Electorate: A Statistical History*, 1:330, table 17.3. On Park, see Gary May, *Bending Toward Justice: The Voting Rights Act and the Transformation of American Democracy* (New York: Basic Books, 2013), xiii (dollar estimates calculated using the "historic standard of living" metric at www.measuringworth.com).

90. Kousser shows that Populists demanded the Australian ballot, and then it was used against them. Also see Hicks, *Populist Revolt*, 443; Valelly, *The Two Reconstructions*, 127; Alan Ware, "Anti-Partism and Party Control of Political Reform in the United States: The Case of the Australian Ballot," *British Journal of Political Science* 30 (2000), 7–9; Richard L. McCormick, *The Party Period and Public Policy: American Politics from the Age of Jackson to the Progressive Era* (New York: Oxford University Press, 1986), 179; Kousser, *Shaping of Southern Politics*, 8, 38–39, 55, 57–59, fn. 30, 161; the Louisiana applicant is quoted in *South Carolina v. Katzenbach*, 383 U.S. 301 (1966), at 313, fn. 12. Georgia employed a grandfather clause, but Mississippi and South Carolina did not. Walton, Puckett, and Deskins, *The African American Electorate: A Statistical History*, 1:329.

91. Key, *Southern Politics*, 432, 438–42, 446; Heard, *A Two-Party South?* 76. Steven Levitsky and Lucan A. Way, "Why Democracy Needs a Level Playing Field," *Journal of Democracy* 21 (2010), 57–58, 60.

92. Egerton, *Speak Now Against the Day*; Patricia Sullivan, *Days of Hope: Race and Democracy in the New Deal Era* (Chapel Hill: University of North Carolina Press, 1996); Tindall, *Emergence of the New South*, 525; Albert O. Hirschman, "Exit, Voice, and the Fate of the German Democratic Republic," *World Politics* 45 (1993), 184; Woodruff, *American Congo*, 125. Authoritarian polities "cannot and do not tolerate independent organizations, [since] as long as no collective alternatives are available, individual attitudes toward the regime matter little for its stability." Przeworski, *Democracy and the Market*, 54. In a region of suffrage restriction, juries, which were filled only by registered voters, could hardly serve as schoolhouses of democracy, as de Tocqueville thought (*Democracy in America*, 1:262–63).

93. McMillen, *Dark Journey*, 174; Woodruff, *American Congo*, 107, 118; James R. Grossman, *Land of Hope* (Chicago: University of Chicago Press, 1989), 92–97; Virginius Dabney, *Below the Potomac: A Book about the New South* (New York: D. Appleton-Century Company, Inc., 1942), 129. Black Pullman porters on southbound trains smuggled and then surreptitiously distributed the *Defender* and *The Negro World*. Mary G. Rolinson, *Grassroots Garveyism: The Universal Negro Improvement Association in the Rural South, 1920–1927* (Chapel Hill: University of North Carolina Press, 2007), 76.

94. Coercion need not result in damage to body or property; rather, the threat of the use of force to compel assent usually suffices. Atmospheres of fear often coincide with low levels of violence; thus, numbers of violent events underestimate coercion. For helpful discussions, see J. Morgan Kousser, "Forum: Revisiting *A Festival of Violence*," *Historical Methods* 31 (1998), 171–75; U.S. Commission on Civil Rights, *Political Participation* (Washington, D.C.: U.S. Government Printing Office, 1968), 127; and Lester M. Salamon and Stephen Van Evera, "Fear, Apathy, and Discrimination," *APSR* 67 (1973), 1288–306. The Deep South, led by Georgia and South Carolina, accounted for about two-thirds of all state executions of southern blacks. Tolnay and Beck, *Festival of Violence*, 100–101.

95. Christian Davenport, *State Repression and the Domestic Democratic Peace* (New York: Cambridge University Press, 2007), chap. 4. On coercion as foundational for political authority, see Gianfranco Poggi, *The State* (Stanford: Stanford University Press, 1990), 6–11.

96. During the bloody industrial conflicts of the 1920s and 1930s, law enforcement and privately financed militias together repressed striking workers. Wood, *Southern Capitalism*, 86–91.

97. Tampa's establishment organized the assassination of those seeking to organize cigar factory workers, as well as other killings. However, such events could spin out of control; disorder following a 1927 lynching resulted in the use of five hundred National Guardsmen, several deaths, and damaging publicity. Robert P. Ingalls, "Lynching and Establishment Violence in Tampa, 1858–1935," *JSH* 53 (1987), 630–32, 642.

98. Jeffrey Herbst, *States and Power in Africa: Comparative Lessons in Authority and Control* (Princeton: Princeton University Press, 2000). In 1919 a mob attacked the white national secretary of the NAACP in Austin, Texas. Authorities, including the governor, publicly voiced their approval. Rolinson, *Grassroots Garveyism*, 90. During World War I, several southern governors successfully requested federal troops to suppress armed bands of war deserters; often, local authorities were unable or unwilling to do so themselves. Jeanette Keith, "The Politics of Southern Draft Resistance, 1917–1918: Class, Race, and Conscription in the Rural South," *JAH* 87 (2001), 1336.

99. In 1899 in Georgia's Newnan County, a crowd of about two thousand watched the torture, immolation, and mutilation of a black man; families traveled from Atlanta on special excursion trains arranged for the event. More than twenty years later, a white mob burned to death thirty black Floridians after one attempted to vote. Numan V. Bartley, *The Creation of Modern Georgia* (Athens: University of Georgia Press, 1990), 140; Michael J. Klarman, "Race and Rights," in Michael Grossberg and Christopher Tomlins, eds., *Cambridge History of Law in America*, vol. 3: *The Twentieth Century and After (1920–)* (New York: Cambridge University Press, 2008), 405. Generally, see Amy Louise Wood, *Lynching and Spectacle: Witnessing Racial Violence in America, 1890–1940* (Chapel Hill: University of North Carolina Press, 2009).

100. Simon, "Appeal of Cole Blease," 61. Mississippi gubernatorial candidate James K. Vardaman considered a white man's participation in lynch mobs as almost a civic duty, but as governor halted several lynchings. In his white supremacist and at times eliminationist demagoguery, Vardaman was inspired in part by South Carolina's "Pitchfork Ben" Tillman. McMillen, *Dark Journey*, 224; William F. Holmes, *The White Chief: James Kimble Vardaman* (Baton Rouge: Louisiana State University Press, 1970), 86, 109, 132–34.

101. Lynchings—often occurring during moments of declining economic fortune for white farmers, and often justified as defenses of white womanhood—illuminate the economic and gender anxieties bound up in much white-on-black violence. Jacquelyn Dowd Hall, *Revolt against Chivalry: Jesse Daniel Ames and the Women's Campaign against Lynching* (New York: Columbia University Press, 1977), 129–57; Tolnay and Beck, *Festival of Violence*. States instituted harsher penalties for law enforcement officials who acquiesced to lynch mobs, and provided these officials with radio-equipped patrol cars and teletype machines. From the late 1910s

until the 1930s, the percentage of attempted lynchings thwarted by authorities more than doubled, to 84 percent. Still, law enforcement officials participated in almost one-half of all lynchings in the early 1930s. Tolnay and Beck, *Festival of Violence*, 203; Arthur F. Raper, *The Tragedy of Lynching* (Chapel Hill: University of North Carolina Press, 1933), Part Seven ("Foiling the Mob"); Michal R. Belknap, *Federal Law and Southern Order: Racial Violence and Constitutional Conflict in the Post-Brown South*, 2nd ed. (Athens: University of Georgia Press, 1995), 9; Leonard D. White, *Trends in Public Administration* (New York: McGraw-Hill, 1933), 125–28.

102. When black leaders began credibly to demand policy benefits in exchange for black votes in municipal elections in the late 1940s, they usually first called for the hiring of black police officers in order to reduce capricious white violence against blacks. Southern Regional Council, "Unequal Badge" (draft report, 1958), Southern Regional Council Papers, Atlanta University Center Library. On the signs affixed to black churches, see Kevin M. Kruse, *White Flight: Atlanta and the Making of Modern Conservatism* (Princeton: Princeton University Press, 2007), 24.

103. Georgian Ellis Arnall, one of the South's most racially liberal governors, declared on the campaign stump in 1942, "Any nigger who tried to enter [the University of Georgia] would not be in existence next day." Harold P. Henderson, *The Politics of Change in Georgia: A Political Biography of Ellis Arnall* (Athens: University of Georgia Press, 1991), 139.

104. On peonage, see Daniel, *Shadow of Slavery*. On legal attacks and publicity campaigns against peonage by the NAACP and the Civil Rights Section of the Department of Justice, see Risa L. Goluboff, *The Lost Promise of Civil Rights* (Cambridge: Harvard University Press, 2010). On the convict lease system see Matthew J. Mancini, *One Dies, Get Another: Convict Leasing in the American South, 1866–1928* (Columbia: University of South Carolina Press, 1996). Chain gangs eventually became more valued to authorities than the leasing of prisoners to private firms as the "good roads" movement emerged during the 1910s and 1920s.

105. Woodward, *Origins of the New South*, 51. See Paul M. Gaston, *The New South Creed* (New York: Knopf, 1970); David W. Blight, *Race and Reunion: The Civil War in American Memory* (Cambridge: Harvard University Press, 2002), 98–139; David W. Blight, *American Oracle: The Civil War in the Civil Rights Era* (Cambridge: Harvard University Press, 2011); W. Fitzhugh Brundage, *The Southern Past: A Clash of Race and Memory* (Cambridge: Harvard University Press, 2005). On conflicts over how to remember Reconstruction, see Du Bois, *Black Reconstruction in America*, chap. 17; Bruce E. Baker, *What Reconstruction Meant: Historical Memory in the American South* (Charlottesville: University of Virginia Press, 2009); Gaines M. Foster, *Ghosts of the Confederacy: Defeat, the Lost Cause, and the Emergence of the New South, 1865–1913* (New York: Oxford University Press, 1988); Fred Arthur Bailey, "The Textbooks of the 'Lost Cause': Censorship and the Creation of Southern State Histories," *GHQ* 75 (1991), 507–33; Catherine W. Bishir, "Landmarks of Power: Building a Southern Past, 1885–1915," *Southern Cultures* 1 (1993), 5–45. For blacks' challenges to the emerging, state-sponsored version of Reconstruction, see Dorothy Sterling, ed., *The Trouble They Seen: The Story of Reconstruction in the Words of African Americans* (New York: Da Capo Press, 1994); Kathleen Ann Clark, *Defining Moments: African American Commemoration and Political Culture in the South, 1863–1913* (Chapel Hill: University of North Carolina Press, 2009). On the production of collective memory, see Jeffrey K.

Olick, Vered Vinitsky-Seroussi, and Daniel Levy, eds., *The Collective Memory Reader* (New York: Oxford University Press, 2011).

106. "Even if in reality the South until this day remains much of a political oligarchy—where, however, the individual oligarchs are often changing—this oligarchy always has to appeal to the common white man as an equal and as the ultimate arbiter of political affairs." Myrdal, *An American Dilemma*, 458–60, 462. See the excellent new study by Devin Caughey, "Congress, Public Opinion, and Representation in the One-Party South, 1930s–1960s," Ph.D. diss., University of California-Berkeley (2012). Even in the limiting cases of Nazi Germany and the Soviet Union, rulers won substantial popular consent in part through the mechanism of elections. Robert Gellately, *Backing Hitler: Coercion and Consent in Nazi Germany* (New York: Oxford University Press, 2001), chap. 1; Wendy Z. Goldman, *Terror and Democracy in the Age of Stalin: The Social Dynamics of Repression* (New York: Cambridge University Press, 2007); and Ralph Jessen and Hedwig Richter, eds., *Voting for Hitler and Stalin: Elections Under 20th-Century Dictatorships* (Chicago: University of Chicago Press, 2011).

107. On one estimate, by requiring additional personnel, weaponry, and insurance, shipboard revolts drove up the costs of the slave trade, thereby reducing the number of Africans brought to the Americas by about one million. David Eltis, *The Rise of African Slavery in the Americas* (New York: Cambridge University Press, 2000), 157–60; Davis, *Inhuman Bondage*, 93, 151. On black politics during the Revolutionary and Civil Wars, Sylvia R. Frey, *Water from the Rock: Black Resistance in a Revolutionary Age* (Princeton: Princeton University Press, 1991); Douglas R. Egerton, *Death or Liberty: African Americans and Revolutionary America* (New York: Oxford University Press, 2009); James Oakes, *Freedom National: The Destruction of Slavery in the United States, 1861–1865* (New York: W. W. Norton, 2012); Foner, *Reconstruction*; Steven Hahn, *The Political Worlds of Slavery and Freedom* (Cambridge: Harvard University Press, 2009), chaps. 1–2.

108. J. Morgan Kousser, "Separate but Not Equal: The Supreme Court's First Decision on Racial Discrimination in Schools," *JSH* 46 (1980), 17–44; August Meier and Elliott Rudwick, "The Boycott Movement Against Jim Crow Streetcars in the South, 1900–1906," *JAH* 55 (1969), 756–75. Du Bois called on black southerners to lift once more "that awful weapon of self-defense" during the pogroms of 1919's "Red Summer." W. Fitzhugh Brundage, "The Darien 'Insurrection' of 1899: Black Protest during the Nadir of Race Relations," *GHQ* 74 (1990), 234–53. Also see Elsa Barkley Brown, "Negotiating and Transforming the Public Sphere: African American Political Life in the Transition from Slavery to Freedom," in Jane Dailey, Glenda Elizabeth Gilmore, and Bryant Simon, eds., *Jumpin' Jim Crow: Southern Politics from Civil War to Civil Rights* (Princeton: Princeton University Press, 2000), 28–66.

109. In economically depressed communities and those hardest hit with white-on-black violence, blacks established clubs to discuss and raise funds for a planned emigration to Liberia. Thirty-two southern Democratic members of Congress hopped aboard by proposing to fund a mass departure. Mitchell, *Righteous Propagation*, chap. 1.

110. Blacks exited the Deep South in great numbers. In Georgia and South Carolina, the largest outflows occurred in the 1920s, and the 1940s in Mississippi. Cohen, *At Freedom's Edge*, 295. Robert Higgs, "The Boll Weevil, the Cotton Economy, and Black Migration, 1910–1930," *Agricultural History* 50 (1976), 335–50; Richard H. Steckel,

"The African American Population of the United States, 1790–1920," in Michael R. Haines and Richard H. Steckel, eds., *A Population History of North America* (New York: Cambridge University Press, 2000), 466; Susan B. Carter, Scott S. Gartner, Michael R. Haines, Alan L. Olmstead, Richard Sutch, and Gavin Wright, eds., *Historical Statistics of the United States: Millennial Edition,* vol. 1 (New York: Cambridge University Press, 2006), Ac142 and Ac206–413 (hereafter *Historical Statistics*); Stewart E. Tolnay and E. M. Beck, "Racial Violence and Black Migration in the South, 1910 to 1930," *ASR* 57 (1992), 103–16.

111. One of the country's most important black papers, the *Chicago Defender,* beckoned black southerners with a weekly siren song. "I beg you, my brother, to leave the benighted land. . . . Get out of the South. . . . Come north then, all you folks, both good and bad. . . . *The Defender* says come." David M. Kennedy, *Over Here: The First World War and American Society* (New York: Oxford University Press, 1980), 280–83; Woodruff, *American Congo,* 58–59.

112. Stewart E. Tolnay, "The African American 'Great Migration' and Beyond," *Annual Review of Sociology* 29 (2003), 209–32. Before 1940 the regional gap in quality of life for blacks increased as better-educated blacks were much more likely to move North. After World War II, this pattern changed, and better-educated southern-born blacks moved to southern cities.

113. James N. Gregory, *The Southern Diaspora: How the Great Migrations of Black and White Southerners Transformed America* (Chapel Hill: University of North Carolina Press, 2005), chap. 7; Wright, *Sharing the Prize,* 18.

114. Walton, *Black Republicans,* chap. 3; Key, *Southern Politics,* 286–91; Valelly, *The Two Reconstructions,* 154; Ralph J. Bunche, *The Political Status of the Negro in the Age of FDR,* ed. Dewey W. Grantham (Chicago: University of Chicago Press, 1973 [1940]), 429.

115. Adolph L. Reed, Jr., *W.E.B. Du Bois and American Political Thought: Fabianism and the Color Line* (New York: Oxford University Press, 1997), 59–60; also see West, *Education of Booker T. Washington.* In Washington's famous 1895 speech, he urged accommodation by blacks and whites to enclave rule: "In all things that are purely social we can be as separate as the fingers, yet one as the hand in all things essential to mutual progress." Booker T. Washington, "The Manuscript Version of the Atlanta [Cotton States and International] Exposition Address," in Louis R. Harlan, ed., *The Booker T. Washington Papers,* vol. 3: *1889–95* (Urbana: University of Illinois Press, 1974 [Sept. 18, 1895]), 585. Washington secretly helped fund some of the lawsuits challenging southern suffrage restriction. R. Volney Riser, *Defying Disfranchisement: Black Voting Rights Activism in the Jim Crow South, 1890–1908* (Baton Rouge: Louisiana State University Press, 2010).

116. On the emergence of the term, see Julie Novkov, "Bringing the States Back In: Understanding Legal Subordination and Identity through Political Development," *Polity* 40 (2008), 33, fn. 28.

117. James D. Anderson, *The Education of Blacks in the South, 1860–1935* (Chapel Hill: University of North Carolina Press, 1988), especially chaps. 2–3.

118. Kevin K. Gaines, *Uplifting the Race: Black Leadership, Politics, and Culture in the Twentieth Century* (Chapel Hill: University of North Carolina Press, 1996). For a deft account of the intellectual consequences of this brokerage model, see Adolph Reed, Jr., "The Study of Black Politics and the Practice of Black Politics:

Their Historical Relation and Evolution," in Ian Shapiro, Rogers M. Smith, and Tarek E. Masoud, eds., *Problems and Methods in the Study of Politics* (New York: Cambridge University Press, 2004), 106–43. Myrdal, *An American Dilemma* and Bunche, *Political Status* discuss the effects of Jim Crow on black associational life. Women in black club and church networks secured impressive gains. Evelyn Brooks Higginbotham, *Righteous Discontents: The Women's Movement in Black Baptist Churches, 1880–1920* (Cambridge: Harvard University Press, 1994); Linda Gordon, "Black and White Visions of Welfare: Women's Welfare Activism: 1890–1945," *JAH* 78 (1991), 559–90; Leslie Brown, *Upbuilding Black Durham: Gender, Class, and Black Community Development in the Jim Crow South* (Chapel Hill: University of North Carolina Press, 2008). On southern elites' legal assault on large fraternal associations, see Theda Skocpol, Ariane Liazos, and Marshall Ganz, *What a Mighty Power We Can Be: African American Fraternal Groups and the Struggle for Racial Equality* (Princeton: Princeton University Press, 2006), chap. 6.

119. Adam Fairclough, *To Redeem the Soul of America: The Southern Christian Leadership Conference* (Athens: University of Georgia Press, 2001 [1987]), 14. On the political place of southern black preachers in the 1930s, see Benjamin E. Mays and Joseph W. Nicholson, *The Negro's Church* (New York: Russell & Russell, 1969 [1933]), chaps. 4, 13, 14 (based on an analysis of sermons), and Myrdal, *An American Dilemma*, 867–78; Harvey, *Freedom's Coming*, 62.

120. Here, nonviolent direct action refers to public confrontations between protesters and the targets of their efforts to persuade, convert, or otherwise secure social change. Direct action is not to be conflated with "civil disobedience"; after all, much of the direct action undertaken by groups such as CORE involved lawful attempts to win compliance of local authorities and firms with recent federal judicial rulings. August Meier and Elliott Rudwick, *CORE: A Study in the Civil Rights Movement, 1942–1968* (New York: Oxford University Press, 1973), 12–13; Meier and Rudwick, "The Origins of Nonviolent Direct Action in Afro-American Protest: A Note on Historical Discontinuities," in Meier and Rudwick, *Along the Color Line: Explorations in the Black Experience* (Urbana: University of Illinois Press, 2002 [1976]), 307–404.

121. Judith Stein, " 'Of Mr. Booker T. Washington and Others': The Political Economy of Racism in the United States," *Science and Society* 108 (1974–75), 424.

122. Woodruff, *American Congo*. Also see the contributions in Eric Arnesen, ed., *The Black Worker: Race, Labor, and Civil Rights since Emancipation* (Urbana: University of Illinois Press, 2007). Additionally, black men's service in wars, from the Spanish-American War to World War I (in which 100,000 served overseas), provided some opportunities for advancement, especially by workers back home in what were now tighter labor markets and better-paying war-related factory positions. But World War I offered no ramp to black progress. Whereas firms outside the South hired blacks for the first time and continued to employ them after the war, southern firms often hired but then fired them at war's end. Wright, *Sharing the Prize*, chap. 1. Tindall, *Emergence of the New South*, 33–69; William Jordan, " 'The Damnable Dilemma': African-American Accommodations and Protest during World War I," *JAH* 81 (1995), 1562–83. Generally, see Christopher Parker, *Fighting for Democracy: Black Veterans and the Struggle against White Supremacy in the South* (Princeton: Princeton University Press, 2009), chap. 1.

123. Berg, *"The Ticket to Freedom,"* 51.

124. Woodruff, *American Congo*, 117; "Location of UNIA Divisions and Chapters," in Robert A. Hill and Blair, eds., *The Marcus Garvey and Universal Negro Improvement Association Papers*, vol. 7: *November 1927—August 1940* (Berkeley: University of California Press, 1987), 986–96; Rolinson, *Grassroots Garveyism*, 4, 90, 117, fn. 16, 163.

125. For a discussion of feigned deference, see James C. Scott, *Domination and the Arts of Resistance: Hidden Transcripts* (New Haven: Yale University Press, 1990), 24; William H. Chafe, Raymond Gains, and Robert Korstad, eds., *Remembering Jim Crow: African Americans Tell About Life in the Segregated South* (New York: New Press), chap. 6; Hahn, *A Nation under Our Feet*; Robin D. G. Kelley, " 'We Are Not What We Seem': Rethinking Black Working-Class Opposition in the Jim Crow South," *JAH* 80 (1993), 75–112. Adolph Reed criticizes scholars' emphasis on "infrapolitics." See his "Why Is There No Black Political Movement?" in Reed, *Class Notes: Posing as Politics and Other Thoughts on the American Scene* (New York: New Press, 1995), 3–4.

126. The usual periodization of what is often considered the "civil rights period" spans from 1954 (*Brown*) to 1965 (Voting Rights Act). This approach underappreciates the importance of the attack on one-party rule by the central state and national party, and obscures the substantial conflict among rulers and their opponents for a decade before *Brown* as well as after. Recently, many historians have aimed to replace this brief periodization with a "long civil rights movement" that stretches even further back. See Jacquelyn Dowd Hall, "The Long Civil Rights Movement and the Political Uses of the Past," *JAH* 91 (2005), 1233–63; Robert Korstad and Nelson Lichtenstein, "Opportunities Found and Lost: Labor, Radicals, and the Early Civil Rights Movement," *JAH* 75 (1988), 786–811; Nelson Lichtenstein, "Recasting the Movement and Reframing the Law in Risa Goluboff's *The Lost Promise of Civil Rights*," *Law and Social Inquiry* 35 (2010), 243–60; Judith Stein, "Why American Historians Embrace the 'Long Civil Rights Movement,' " *American Communist History* 11 (2012), 55–58; Eric Arnesen, "Reconsidering the 'Long Civil Rights Movement,'" *Historically Speaking* (2009), 31–34. And a new generation of historians have brought the period forward into the 1970s and 1980s, thereby revealing the amount of political contestation occurring well after the landmark legislation of the mid-1960s, and illuminating the continued high stakes for ordinary southerners on all sides as politicians continued to adapt to changing conditions—particularly at the local level. See J. Todd Moye, *Let the People Decide: Black Freedom and White Resistance Movements in Sunflower County, Mississippi, 1945–1986* (Chapel Hill: University of North Carolina Press, 2004); Kent B. Germany, *New Orleans after the Promises: Poverty, Citizenship, and the Search for the Great Society* (Athens: University of Georgia Press, 2007); and the excellent synthesis by Timothy J. Minchin and John A. Salmond, *After the Dream: Black and White Southerners since 1965* (Lexington: University Press of Kentucky, 2011).

127. This support first manifested itself not in roll-call voting, but in other activities, such as discharge petition signings, floor speeches, and bill sponsorship. Eric Schickler, Kathryn Pearson, and Brian Feinstein, "Congressional Parties and Civil Rights Politics from 1933 to 1972," *JOP* 72 (2010), 673. On emerging differences in voting patterns, see David Karol, *Party Position Change in American Politics: Coalition Management* (New York: Cambridge University Press, 2009), chap. 4.

128. And, as Key (*Southern Politics*, 9) writes, "[O]n the fundamental issue, only the federal government was to be feared." The narratives point out these secular changes to provide readers with evidence to challenge my arguments.

129. Leslie W. Dunbar, "The Changing Mind of the South: The Exposed Nerve," *JOP* 26 (1964), 14. The landmark reapportionment cases were *Baker v. Carr*, 369 U.S. 186 (1962), and *Reynolds v. Sims*, 377 U.S. 533 (1964). For an excellent analysis of their consequences, see Stephen Ansolabehere and James M. Snyder, Jr., *The End of Inequality: One Person, One Vote, and the Transformation of American Politics* (New York: W. W. Norton, 2008).

Chapter Three:
Deep South Enclaves on the Eve of the Transition

1. In Alabama, Louisiana, and Florida, the share of blacks in 1900 ranged from 44 to 47 percent. For a discussion of the normative democratic implications of these demographics, see Gabriel J. Chin and Randy Wagner, "The Tyranny of the Minority: Jim Crow and the Counter-Majoritarian Difficulty," *Harvard Civil Rights-Civil Liberties Review* 43 (2008), 65–125.

2. More than three-quarters of the country's blacks still lived in the South in 1940. Bureau of the Census, U.S. Department of Commerce, *Statistical Abstract of the United States, 1940* (Washington, D.C.: Government Printing Office, 1941), 16 and 19.

3. The upcountry included the mountainous counties to the northwest. The lowcountry featured a flat, often swampy area extending seventy miles inland, the fertile inner coastal plain, and the Pine Barrens. Two counties on the fall line are counted as both upcountry and lowcountry. Edgar, *South Carolina*, 588, fn. 12, and 589, fn. 18. This study follows historians' spelling conventions regarding these regions.

4. Edgar, *South Carolina*, chap. 3; Davis, *Inhuman Bondage*, 126, 104, 114–15, 196; Meinig, *The Shaping of America*, 1:165–71 ("tiny white oligarchy" quotation at 171). On Barbados, see Richard S. Dunn, *Sugar and Slaves: The Rise of the Planter Class in the English West Indies, 1624–1713* (Chapel Hill: University of North Carolina Press, 2000 [1972]), 110–16. On John Locke's role, see Robert M. Weir, " 'Shaftesbury's Darling': British Settlement in the Carolinas at the Close of the Seventeenth Century," in Nicholas Canny, ed., *The Oxford History of the British Empire*, vol. 1 (New York: Oxford University Press, 1998), 375–97.

5. South Carolina differed from the very conservative settlements in Virginia by lacking much of the paternalism of the latter. Philip D. Morgan, *Slave Counterpoint: Black Culture in the Eighteenth-Century Chesapeake and Lowcountry* (Chapel Hill: University of North Carolina Press, 1998); Robert Olwell, *Masters, Slaves, and Subjects: The Culture of Power in the South Carolina Low Country, 1740–1790* (Ithaca: Cornell University Press, 1998).

6. Meinig, *The Shaping of America*, 1 (quotation at 185); Peter A. Coclanis, "Global Perspectives on the Early Economic History of South Carolina," *SCHM* 106 (2005), 130–46. Officials divided South Carolina from the topographically and economically very different North Carolina in 1712. Forty percent of slaves brought to mainland North America arrived in Charleston. Davis, *Inhuman Bondage*, 136, 178.

7. Davis, *Inhuman Bondage*, 188, 192. Coclanis, "Global Perspectives," 140, 142. The threats posed by living in majority-slave areas were real. The Stono rebellion of

1739 and lowcountry revolts, including the Denmark Vesey plot uncovered in 1822, helped convince South Carolina's elites to restrict by statute the movement and assembly of slaves. Later they improved the training of those charged with repressing slave revolts by establishing The Citadel. Edgar, *South Carolina: A History*, 339; John Hope Franklin, *The Militant South, 1800–1861* (Cambridge: Harvard University Press, 1956), 78–79. In the Stono Rebellion, about sixty slaves torched plantations and almost captured the state's Lieutenant Governor. See Peter H. Wood, *Black Majority: Negroes in Colonial South Carolina from 1670 through the Stono Rebellion* (New York: Norton, 1974). For a revisionist perspective on the Vesey plot, see Michael P. Johnson, "Denmark Vesey and His Co-Conspirators," *William and Mary Quarterly* 58 (2001), 915–76.

8. On the emergence of the upcountry's planters and their role in reducing sectional conflict within the state, see Rachel N. Klein, *Unification of a Slave State: The Rise of the Planter Class in the South Carolina Backcountry, 1760–1808* (Chapel Hill: University of North Carolina Press, 1990).

9. Peter A. Coclanis, "Bitter Harvest: The South Carolina Lowcountry in Historical Perspective," *JEH* 45 (1985), 257, 259, 251.

10. Richard P. Stone, "Making a Modern State: The Politics of Economic Development in South Carolina, 1938–1962," Ph.D. diss., University of Georgia (1996), pp. 1, 16; David L. Carlton, "Unbalanced Growth and Industrialization: The Case of South Carolina," in Winfred B. Moore, Joseph F. Tripp, and Lyon G. Tyler, Jr., eds., *Developing Dixie: Modernization in a Traditional Society* (New York: Greenwood Press, 1988), 121.

11. *South Carolina: A Handbook* (Columbia, S.C.: Department of Agriculture, Commerce and Industries and Clemson College, 1927), 102–3; Philip G. Grose, *South Carolina at the Brink: Robert McNair and the Politics of Civil Rights* (Columbia: University of South Carolina Press, 2006), 32–33. By 1930 fully one-quarter of individuals born in South Carolina lived outside the state (almost 90 percent of them black).

12. Edgar, *South Carolina*, 161. Coclanis, "Bitter Harvest," 251; Lacy K. Ford, "Rednecks and Merchants: Economic Development and Social Tensions in the South Carolina Upcountry, 1865–1900," *JAH* 71 (1984), 294–318. Peter A. Coclanis and Lacy K. Ford, "The South Carolina Economy Reconstructed and Reconsidered: Structure, Output, and Performance, 1670–1985," in Moore, Tripp, and Tyler, *Developing Dixie*, 102 and 105; Carlton, "Unbalanced Growth and Industrialization," 114. From 1880 to 1930, textile's share of the state's manufacturing earnings increased from 16 to 59 percent. Bureau of the Census, *Statistical Abstract, 1940*, 3, tables 5–6, and 57, table 63.

13. Robert V. Haynes, "The Formation of the Territory," and William K. Scarborough, "Heartland of the Cotton Kingdom," both in Richard A. McLemore, ed., *A History of Mississippi*, vol. 1 (Hattiesburg: University Press of Mississippi, 1973), 174–216 and 310–51, respectively; Adam Rothman, *Slave Country: American Expansion and the Origins of the Deep South* (Cambridge: Harvard University Press, 2005).

14. The Delta is actually a flat alluvial plain formed by the two river systems. Cobb, *Most Southern Place on Earth*; Robert L. Brandfon, *Cotton Kingdom of the New South: A History of the Yazoo Mississippi Delta from Reconstruction to the Twentieth Century* (Cambridge: Harvard University Press, 1967). On the eve of the Civil War, only one-third of Delta plantations could afford slaves. Carville Earle, "Regional

Economic Development West of the Appalachians, 1815–1860," in Mitchell and Groves, *North America*, 191. Until the late nineteenth century, more than 90 percent of the state remained forested. Arthell Kelley, "The Geography," in McLemore, *A History of Mississippi*, 1:15.

15. Bartley, *The New South*, chaps. 1–2.

16. Carter, et al., *Historical Statistics*, 1:276, table Aa4305–4401.

17. The temptation of the riches in neighboring South Carolina were obvious to Georgia's settlers, and they soon began smuggling slaves into the colony. Davis, *Inhuman Bondage*, 136; Meinig, *The Shaping of America*, 1:181.

18. The area south of the Black Belt is often divided into two subregions: the Wiregrass and coastal plain. Peggy G. Hargis and Patrick M. Horan, "The "Low-Country Advantage" for African Americans in Georgia, 1880–1930," *Journal of Interdisciplinary History* 28 (1997), 35, fig. 1. On race and labor politics in the carpet tufting and textile industries in the towns of north Georgia, see Douglas Flamming, *Creating the Modern South: Millhands and Managers in Dalton, Georgia, 1884–1984* (Chapel Hill: University of North Carolina Press, 1992); Brattain, *The Politics of Whiteness*. At about 59,000 square miles in size, Georgia is about twice as large as South Carolina (30,500), and one-quarter larger than Mississippi (46,000). Also see Numan V. Bartley, *From Thurmond to Wallace: Political Tendencies in Georgia, 1948–1968* (Baltimore: Johns Hopkins University Press, 1970), chap. 2.

19. Atlanta, the region's largest city by 1940 (about 200,000), was about one-third black. Savannah was second-largest at about 100,000 (nearly half of whom were black), and Macon and Columbus both reached 50,000 by then. Campbell Gibson and Kay Jung, "Historical Census Statistics on Population Totals by Race, 1790 to 1990, and by Hispanic Origin, 1970 to 1990, for Large Cities and Other Urban Places in the United States," Population Division Working Paper No. 76 (Washington, D.C.: Bureau of the Census, Feb. 2005), 46–47, table 11; Carter, et al., *Historical Statistics*, 1:217, table Aa3097–3197.

20. Bartley, *Creation of Modern Georgia*, 183. In 1937, Georgia earned $27 million from manufacturing, compared to $8 million for Mississippi and $17 million for South Carolina. Bureau of the Census, *Statistical Abstract, 1940*; Harriet L. Herring, *Southern Industry and Regional Development* (Chapel Hill: University of North Carolina Press, 1940), 9.

21. By 1940 the share of majority-black counties among all counties ranged from 30 percent in Georgia to 48 percent in South Carolina (with Mississippi at 43 percent). Calculated from U.S. Department of Commerce, *Negroes in the United States, 1920–1932* (Washington, D.C.: Government Printing Office, 1935), 72, table 6.

22. In 1920 the ratio of the voting power of Georgia's tiny Echols County to Atlanta's Fulton County was sixteen to one; in 1960 it reached ninety-nine to one, dwarfing the worst malapportionment nationally. James C. Bonner, "Legislative Apportionment and County Unit Voting in Georgia Since 1877," *GHQ* 47 (1963), 371, 360. Donald O. Bushman and William R. Stanley, "State Senate Reapportionment in the Southeast," *Annals of the Association of American Geographers* 61 (1971), 657; Bryant Simon, "The Devaluation of the Vote: Legislative Apportionment and Inequality in South Carolina, 1890–1962," *SCHM* 97 (1996), 45–59; Eric C. Clark, "Legislative Apportionment in the 1890 Constitutional Convention," *Journal of Mississippi History* 42 (1980), 299–300 (hereafter *JMH*). The state constitutions of Georgia and Mississippi

made legislative reapportionment optional, rather than mandatory as in the other nine southern states. George H. Haynes, "Representation in State Legislatures, III: The Southern States," *Annals of the American Academy of Political and Social Science* 16 (1900), 117.

23. On state constitutional revision, Elmer E. Cornwell, Jr., "The American Constitutional Tradition: Its Impact and Development," and Morton Keller, "The Politics of State Constitutional Revision, 1820–1930," both in Kermit L. Hall, Harold M. Hyman, and Leon V. Sigal, eds., *The Constitutional Convention as an Amending Device* (Washington, D.C.: American Historical Association and American Political Science Association, 1981), 1–36 and 67–86, respectively; John J. Dinan, *The American State Constitutional Tradition* (Lawrence: University Press of Kansas, 2006), chap. 2.

24. Tarr, *Understanding State Constitutions,* 131. Coleman B. Ransome, *The Office of Governor in the South* (Bureau of Public Administration, University of Alabama, 1951); Cortez A. M. Ewing, "Southern Governors," *JOP* 10 (1948), 385–409; Hugh Heclo, *Modern Social Politics* (New Haven: Yale University Press, 1974), 305 (on "puzzling"); Burr Blackburn, "State Programs of Public Welfare in the South," *Social Forces* 1 (1922), 6–11; Elna C. Green, ed., *The New Deal and Beyond: Social Welfare in the South since 1930* (Athens: University of Georgia Press, 2003); Harry C. Evans, *The American Poorfarm and Its Inmates* (Detroit: The Maccabees, 1926), 1–20; Kirk H. Porter, *County and Township Government in the United States* (New York: Macmillan, 1922).

25. Key makes this argument (*Southern Politics,* 305–8), and Gerald Gamm and Thad Kousser confirm it in "Broad Bills or Particularistic Policy? Historical Patterns in American State Legislatures," *APSR* 104 (2010), 151–70.

26. Jon C. Teaford, *Rise of the States: Evolution of American State Government* (Baltimore: Johns Hopkins University Press, 2002), 124–26. In a period during which most states were centralizing their authority, there was a minor movement to establish greater home rule for cities, but it bypassed the Deep South. White, *Trends in Public Administration,* 131–34.

27. Teaford, *Rise of the States,* 33–35, 96–97; White, *Trends in Public Administration,* 104–5. Politicians converted authority over road location and state contracting and employment into political capital. Highway commissioners were often chosen by the legislature or popularly elected; governors, of course, preferred the power to appoint them.

28. In 1933, as hundreds of municipalities and more than one-half of the state's counties declared bankruptcy, the state assumed control over key local tasks, such as roads maintenance. It soon dominated local governments in school finance. Teaford, *Rise of the States.* James C. Cobb details Mississippi's Balance Agriculture with Industry (BAWI) program in *The Selling of the South: The Southern Crusade for Industrial Development,* 2nd ed. (Urbana: University of Illinois Press, 1993), chap. 2; Roger D. Tate, "Easing the Burden: The Era of Depression and New Deal in Mississippi," Ph.D. diss., University of Tennessee (1982), pp. 184–86.

29. As a leading white paper editorialized, "Nobody charges that the colored man is deprived of his vote on account of his color but on account of his politics." Kousser, *Shaping of Southern Politics,* 85, 88, 145; William J. Cooper, Jr., *The Conservative Regime: South Carolina, 1877–1890* (Baltimore: Johns Hopkins Press, 1991 [1968]), 98; Charles J. Holden, *Into the Great Maelstrom: Conservatives in Post-Civil War South Carolina* (Columbia: University of South Carolina Press, 2002) chap. 3.

30. Woodward, *Tom Watson*, 371. As Tillman said five years after the Constitution, "We have done our level best [to disfranchise blacks]. . . . [W]e have scratched our heads to find out how we could eliminate the last one of them. We stuffed ballot boxes. We shot them. We are not ashamed of it." Omar H. Ali, "Standing Guard at the Door of Liberty: Black Populism in South Carolina, 1886–1895," *SCHM* 107 (2006), 203.

31. After the convention, some black South Carolinians met in Columbia to discuss a mass exodus to another state as a protest and as a means of punishing landowners with the loss of workers. Riser, *Defying Disfranchisement*, 30–31.

32. James Lowell Underwood, "African American Founding Fathers: The Making of the South Carolina Constitution of 1868," in James Lowell Underwood and W. Lewis Burke, Jr., eds., *At Freedom's Door: African American Founding Fathers and Lawyers in Reconstruction South Carolina* (Columbia: University of South Carolina Press, 2000), 1–35; Thomas C. Holt, *Black Over White: Negro Political Leadership in South Carolina during Reconstruction* (Urbana: University of Illinois Press, 1977), 96; James L. Underwood, *The Constitution of South Carolina*, vol. 2: *The Journey Toward Local Self-Government* (Columbia: University of South Carolina Press, 1989), 49 and 69; Kousser, *Shaping of Southern Politics*, 147–52; Cooper, *The Conservative Regime*.

33. "By 1933 the variations from county to county were so great that . . . only 15 of 46 counties conformed to the classic [governance] format of a Board composed of one supervisor and two commissioners." Underwood, *Constitution of South Carolina*, 2:93.

34. Kantrowitz, *Ben Tillman*, 215 and passim; Edgar, *South Carolina*, chap. 19; George B. Tindall, "The Campaign for the Disfranchisement of Negroes in South Carolina," *JSH* 15 (1949), 217, 226; Underwood, *Constitution of South Carolina*, 2:79, 93; Columbus Andrews, *Administrative County Government in South Carolina* (Chapel Hill: University of North Carolina Press, 1933), 34–38. As with suffrage restriction, before 1895 the state made some moves toward the goal of centralization through statutory changes.

35. Heard interview with a lowcountry county election official, Heard Papers. Hollings quoted in James L. Underwood, *The Constitution of South Carolina*, vol. 1: *The Relationship of the Legislative, Executive, and Judicial Branches* (Columbia: University of South Carolina Press, 1994), 91.

36. Hollings noted that "the prohibition against a second consecutive term" perhaps made sense in states with a stronger governor's office and a weaker legislature, "but the case is different in South Carolina. We have the weakest of powers. . . . There is no highway patronage to dispense as there is in . . . Georgia. The governor's so-called cabinet runs on their own." Underwood, *Constitution of South Carolina*, 1:86, and chaps. 2–3 (quotation at 18).

37. Underwood, *Constitution of South Carolina*, 2:93–98; Andrews, *Administrative County Government*, 40–41. David D. Wallace, *The South Carolina Constitution of 1895* (Columbia: University of South Carolina Press, 1927), 25; James K. Coleman, *State Administration in South Carolina* (New York: Columbia University Press, 1935).

38. Walter B. Edgar, *A History of Santee-Cooper, 1934–1984* (Columbia: R. L. Bryan, 1984). State employees were beholden to Brown, who capitalized on several kickback schemes. Heard interviews with senior state legislators, Heard Papers. Underwood's description of local government in South Carolina during the seventeenth

and eighteenth centuries fit well the paradox of South Carolina's centralization in the twentieth century: "The system somehow managed to combine excessive localism and lack of coordination with excessive centralization and lack of flexibility." Underwood, *Constitution of South Carolina*, 2:12.

39. In 1941, Barnwell County could boast of Blatt, Brown, Governor Joseph E. Harley, and Winchester "Win" Smith (chair of the General Assembly's Ways and Means Committee). Other practices locked in rural dominance of the legislature. For instance, Blatt placed only one legislator per county on House committees, which meant that members from small, rural counties usually dominated them. Grose, *South Carolina at the Brink*, 12, 53, 71.

40. Upcountry politicians secured only a four-year gubernatorial term (and no successive terms). *Columbia State*, Jan. 16, 1935 (hereafter *CS*). Anthony B. Miller, "Palmetto Politician: The Early Political Career of Olin D. Johnston, 1896–1945," Ph.D. diss., University of North Carolina-Chapel Hill (1976), p. 19.

41. Because of its relatively liberal suffrage requirements and the number of offices that were popularly elected, Mississippi's 1832 constitution "was recognized by contemporaries . . . as being the most democratic in the entire South, or, as far as political democracy for whites was concerned, in the entire Union." Winbourne Magruder Drake, "The Constitutional Convention of 1832," *JSH* 23 (1957), 368.

42. Kousser, *Shaping of Southern Politics*, 139–40; Kirwan, *Revolt of the Rednecks*, 18–19, 22–23.

43. William C. Harris, *The Day of the Carpetbagger: Republican Reconstruction in Mississippi* (Baton Rouge: Louisiana State University Press, 1979).

44. In Mississippi, a convention required merely a majority of both chambers, not a popular referendum. On the convention, also see Kirwan, *Revolt of the Rednecks*, 58–64; Holmes, *The White Chief*, 35; Stephen Cresswell, *Rednecks, Redeemers, and Race: Mississippi after Reconstruction, 1877–1917* (Jackson: University Press of Mississippi, 2006); Timothy B. Smith, *James Z. George: Mississippi's Great Commoner* (Jackson: University Press of Mississippi, 2012), chap. 17. On the apportionment changes, Kirwan, *Revolt of the Rednecks*, 79; Cobb, *Most Southern Place on Earth*, 88–89. Woodward summarized the convention in this way: Rather than effectively redress the malapportionment that motivated Hills counties leaders to agree to the convention and black disfranchisement, it "actually perpetuated and solidified the power of the Black-Belt oligarchy. Its work was therefore doubly undemocratic: it disfranchised the race that composed a majority of the population, and it delivered a large majority of whites into the control of [Black Belt whites]." Mississippi's newspapers strongly opposed the disfranchisement provision as "a fraud and a disgrace," and so convention leaders viewed popular ratification as "unnecessary and inexpedient" and simply declared the new constitution ratified. Woodward, *Origins of the New South*, 341; Vernon Wharton, *The Negro in Mississippi* (Chapel Hill: University of North Carolina Press, 1947), 213–14.

45. Kousser, *Shaping of Southern Politics*, 145, table 6.3.

46. Local officials remained basically uninterested in state politics, except insofar as state budgets affected them. Heard interview with a Mississippi political scientist, Heard Papers. Institute for Government Research, *Report on a Survey of the Organization and Administration of State and County Government in Mississippi* (Washington, D.C.: Brookings Institution, 1932), 622, 627, 720, 739. The Brookings

study recommended a sharp centralization of political authority in the executive branch. Heard interview with a prominent Mississippi attorney, Heard Papers. Also see Charles N. Fortenberry, *A Guidebook of the Board of Supervisors* (Bureau of Public Administration, University of Mississippi, 1948), and Dana B. Brammer, *A Manual for Mississippi County Supervisors* (Bureau of Governmental Research, University of Mississippi, 1966). Also see Charles N. Fortenberry, *A Guidebook of the Chancery Clerk* (Bureau of Public Administration, University of Mississippi, 1949).

47. Counties dispersed authority across five "beats," or districts, each overseen by a supervisor. Supervisors established patronage bases at the district level. Heard interviews with a prominent Mississippi attorney, a journalist, and politicians, Heard Papers.

48. Traditionally, the governor hailed from outside the Delta. Still, Deltan campaign donations proved critical in the Hills counties, and helped make for pliant governors. Robert B. Highsaw and Charles N. Fortenberry, *The Government and Administration of Mississippi* (New York: Thomas Y. Crowell, 1954), 69; Heard interviews with a Mississippi political scientist and several Mississippi legislators, Heard Papers.

49. Legislators backing a constitutional convention mentioned these issues, not racial disfranchisement. Kirwan, *Revolt of the Rednecks*, 79–84. President Benjamin Harrison's call for the protection of black voting rights, combined with the 1888 Republican takeover of Congress, helped conservatives control Mississippi's constitutional convention in the name of disfranchisement. McMillen, *Dark Journey*, 41.

50. The constitution allowed for reapportionment after each decennial census, but the Delta-controlled legislature demurred for seven decades. The more heavily populated "white" counties proposed to apportion the House by voting population, not actual population. Solons from the majority-black Delta opposed this so fiercely that they seriously contemplated secession. The eventual apportionment left sixty-nine "black county" members, and sixty-four from "white counties." Albert D. Kirwan, "Apportionment in the Mississippi Constitution of 1890," *JSH* 14 (1948), 235–37, 241–45.

51. Walter Sillers, the son of a prominent planter, served in the House for forty-nine years (including twenty-one as Speaker). Thomas R. Melton, "Walter Sillers and National Politics," *JMH* 39 (1977), 213; Tate, "Easing the Burden," 23; Elbert R. Hilliard, "The Legislative Career of Fielding Wright," *JMH* (1979), 13; Heard interview with a Mississippi state election official, Heard Papers. Charles N. Fortenberry and F. Glenn Abney, "Mississippi: Unreconstructed and Unredeemed," in William C. Havard, ed., *The Changing Politics of the South* (Baton Rouge: Louisiana State University Press, 1972), 520.

52. Thomas E. Kynerd, *Administrative Reorganization of Mississippi Government: A Study in Politics* (Jackson: University Press of Mississippi, 1978), 45–60, 98–99, 123; Tate, "Easing the Burden," 48; Daniel C. Vogt, "Government Reform, the 1890 Constitution, and Mike Conner," *JMH* (1986), 54; *Jackson Daily News*, Feb. 1, 1934 (hereafter *JDN*); Glenn K. Brown, "Walter Sillers, Jr., and Martin S. Conner: A Study in Mississippi Political Relationships," M.A. thesis, Mississippi State University (1984), p. 58.

53. See Paul A. Cimbala, *Under the Guardianship of the Nation: The Freedmen's Bureau and the Reconstruction of Georgia, 1865–1870* (Athens: University of Georgia Press, 1997); Edmund L. Drago, *Black Politicians and Reconstruction in Georgia: A Splendid Failure* (Baton Rouge: Louisiana State University Press, 1982).

54. Kousser, *Shaping of Southern Politics*, 209–23. But see Ellen Garrison, "Reactionaries or Reformers? Membership and Leadership of the Georgia Constitutional Convention of 1877," *GHQ* 90 (2006), 505–24.

55. Bartley, *Creation of Modern Georgia*, 68–70, 74, 154; Albert B. Saye, *A Constitutional History of Georgia, 1732–1968* (Athens: University of Georgia Press, 1971), 286–87, 304–7; Melvin C. Hughes, *County Government in Georgia* (Athens: University of Georgia Press, 1944), 39. Amended more than three hundred times, mostly for local matters, the constitution provided substantial local autonomy. The constitution required the fifty-four senate districts to rotate among its counties every two years. Since most counties were small (figure 3.3), urban representation diminished further.

56. Kousser, *Shaping of Southern Politics*, 223; Clarence A. Bacote, "The Negro in Georgia Politics, 1880–1908," Ph.D. diss., University of Chicago (1955), pp. 421, 499–500. Bartley, *Creation of Modern Georgia*, 152–53. With the passage of suffrage restriction, one politician remarked proudly, "Georgia has taken out a splendid insurance policy for the future by eliminating, as far as possible under federal limitations, the negro vote" as a factor in the future. "Whatever divisions are yet to come, whatever issues are yet to be met, we will . . . settle them on a white basis." Laughlin McDonald, *A Voting Rights Odyssey: Black Enfranchisement in Georgia* (New York: Cambridge University Press, 2003), 42.

57. Hughes, *County Government in Georgia*, 20–24, 40–43, 166–67. Even by the late 1940s, "sixty percent of the bills introduced" dealt with local issues. Tarleton Collier, "Georgia: Paradise of Oligarchy," in Robert S. Allen, ed., *Our Sovereign State* (New York: Vanguard Press, 1949), 155.

58. Ballots were often numbered so that a voter's name could be matched with her ballot. Those failing to vote as instructed would find that the roads around their farms remained unpaved. William Anderson, *The Wild Man from Sugar Creek: The Political Career of Eugene Talmadge* (Baton Rouge: Louisiana State University Press, 1975), 16; Joseph L. Bernd, *Grass Roots Politics in Georgia: The County Unit System and the Importance of the Individual Voting Community in Bi-factional Elections, 1942–1954* (Atlanta: Emory University, 1960); *Atlanta Constitution*, Dec. 15, 1947 (hereafter *AC*). *AJ*, Mar. 4, Apr. 4, 11, 16, 1948. Bunche, *Political Status*, 162. Joseph L. Bernd, "Georgia: Static and Dynamic," in Havard, *Changing Politics*, 299–300. In the 1940s one legislator noted, "We've never had an honest vote in Georgia." Key men often controlled which candidate captured a county, as well as its election procedures. Kytle and Mackay, *Who Runs Georgia?* 112, 17, 82, 4.

59. Bernd, "Georgia: Static and Dynamic," 321; White, *Trends in Public Administration*, 182–87.

60. Holland, *The Direct Primary in Georgia* (Urbana: University of Illinois Press, 1949), 44–45; Kytle and Mackay, *Who Runs Georgia?* 49. Powerful Atlanta law firms represented large corporations and mediated political dealings between corporation officers and county "bosses." Georgia Power, the state's largest utility and most influential enterprise, extended its influence by propping up financially shaky county newspapers by paying in advance for large advertisement runs. Its executive, Fred Wilson, allegedly decided the outcome of four gubernatorial elections and chose the House clerk, secretary of the Senate, and chairs of key committees. On one estimate, he "owned" fifty legislators. Kytle and Mackay, *Who Runs Georgia?* 43–48. The Senate, not a prestigious institution, featured two known illiterates in the 1940s.

61. Holland, *Direct Primary in Georgia*; Albert B. Saye, "Georgia's County Unit System of Elections," *JOP* 12 (1950), 93–106. First used in 1876 to apportion delegates to party conventions, the system became law in 1917 and applied to all statewide offices and some legislative nominations.

62. Key, *Southern Politics*, 106. Rural Georgia peaked in population in 1920, after which urbanization increased. From 1930 to 1940, urban counties increased in population by 20 percent, while rural counties increased by only 2 percent. Thus, over time the political impact of the system grew. Hughes, *County Government in Georgia*, 170.

63. Bernd, *Grass Roots Politics*; Kytle and Mackay, *Who Runs Georgia?* chap. 1. Estimates of "buyable" counties ranged from twenty to fifty. Heard interviews with a leading Georgia journalist and an unsuccessful gubernatorial candidate, Heard Papers. Kytle and Mackay, *Who Runs Georgia?* 76–84. Georgia outpaced all southern enclaves but Louisiana in its rampant corruption.

64. Heard interview with a Talmadgeite legislator and strategist, Heard Papers.

65. Some Democrats referred to their party as "The Democracy" since the antebellum period. Paula H. Baker, *Affairs of Party: The Political Culture of Northern Democrats in the Mid-Nineteenth Century* (Ithaca: Cornell University Press, 1983), 19.

66. Raymond Tatalovich, "'Friends and Neighbors' Voting: Mississippi, 1943–73," *JOP* 35 (1973), 730–36.

67. Tammy Harden Galloway, "'Tribune of the Masses and a Champion of the People': Eugene Talmadge and the Three-Dollar Tag," *GHQ* 79 (1995), 673–84.

68. Leo Troy, "The Growth of Union Membership in the South, 1939–1953," *Southern Economic Journal* 24 (1958), 409, table 1 and 413, table 4.

69. Measuring the degree of factionalism by patterns of voting over several gubernatorial elections, Key ranked Georgia, Mississippi, and South Carolina as third, eighth, and tenth most factionalized in the eleven-state South. *Southern Politics*, 17.

70. David L. Carlton, *Mill and Town in South Carolina, 1880–1920* (Baton Rouge: Louisiana State University, 1982); Hall et al., *Like a Family*; Bryant Simon, *A Fabric of Defeat: The Politics of South Carolina Millhands, 1910–1948* (Chapel Hill: University of North Carolina Press, 1996).

71. Simon, *Fabric of Defeat*, 4, 53.

72. David L. Carlton, "The State and the Worker in the South: A Lesson from South Carolina," and Thomas E. Terrill, "'No Union for Me': Southern Textile Workers and Organized Labor," both in David R. Chesnutt and Clyde N. Wilson, eds., *The Meaning of South Carolina History: Essays in Honor of George C. Rogers, Jr.* (Columbia: University of South Carolina Press, 1991), 202–13 and 186–201, respectively.

73. At least half of the state's forty-six senators represented lowcountry counties.

74. At $65 million, the 1929 Highway Bond Act represented more than seven times the state's 1928 budget and helped pave much of the unpaved lowcountry. Simon, *Fabric of Defeat*, 73; Edgar, *South Carolina*, 491; Miller, "Palmetto Politician," 26–29. By 1950, the Highway Commission was "virtually autonomous." Its members, one from each of the state's fourteen judicial districts, were elected by their relevant county delegations. Each commissioner received a discretionary fund at the time of $100,000 per year to pave roads as he saw fit in his district—"a potential gold mine of political favors." Philip G. Grose, *Looking for Utopia: The Life and Times of John C. West* (Columbia: University of South Carolina Press, 2011), 67.

75. John E. Huss, *Senator for the South: A Biography of Olin D. Johnston* (Garden City, N.Y.: Doubleday, 1961), 64–72; Underwood, *Constitution of South Carolina*, 1:51–52. The national ridicule that followed such events embarrassed leading state politicians. *NYT*, Oct. 29, Nov. 3, and Dec. 8, 1935; Miller, "Palmetto Politician," 223; Simon, *Fabric of Defeat*, 151–66, 169; Key, *Southern Politics*, 305.

76. Edgar, *South Carolina*, 103, 123–24. John H. Moore, *The South Carolina Highway Department, 1917–1987* (Columbia: University of South Carolina Press, 1987); David Robertson, *Sly and Able: A Political Biography of James F. Byrnes* (New York: Norton, 1994). Carlton, "Unbalanced Growth and Industrialization," 122.

77. *CS*, Jan. 13, 1937; John K. Cauthen, *Speaker Blatt: His Challenges Were Greater* (Columbia: University of South Carolina Press, 1965), 104. For the rest of Johnston's career, the Barnwell Ring supported him. As U.S. senator he was always a loyal New Dealer. William D. Workman, Jr., *Bishop from Barnwell: The Political Life and Times of Senator Edgar A. Brown* (Columbia, S.C.: R. L. Bryan, 1963), 46–47; *NYT*, Jun. 2, 1944; Huss, *Senator for the South*.

78. Delta politicians were most likely to oppose high spending and statewide prohibition. On the 1903 primary statute, Kirwan, *Revolt of the Rednecks*, 122–35.

79. Section 3107, Mississippi Code (1942).

80. Mississippi Code 1930, Sec. 5866; Heard interview with a party official, Heard Papers. By law, all parties were forced to use primaries to nominate candidates; however, the state financed only the Democratic primary. Heard, *A Two-Party South?* 106–7.

81. Delta politicians dominated precinct meetings that selected county convention delegates. Heard interviews with a state election official, state legislators, and a prominent Delta planter, Heard Papers.

82. Delta counties financed one-third of the council's operating budget. Nan E. Woodruff, "Mississippi Delta Planters and Debates over Mechanization, Labor and Civil Rights in the 1940s," *JSH* 60 (1994), 273, 264, fn. 2, 279; Cobb, *Most Southern Place*, 200; Heard interview with a prominent black politician, Heard Papers.

83. BAWI and related efforts moved low-wage light manufacturing and processing plants to Hills and Piney Woods counties, and left Delta labor markets undisturbed. Southern Mississippi politicians tried and failed to force a reapportionment of the legislature. Holmes, *White Chief*, 200.

84. Heard interview with black protest leader in South Carolina, Jan. 20, 1948, Heard Papers; Heard interviews with a Mississippi union leader and a leading newspaper editor, Heard Papers. Willson Whitman, "Tupelo: Feudalism and TVA," *The Nation* 148 (Dec. 31, 1938), 12–14; John R. Skates, "A Southern Editor Views the National Scene: Frederick Sullens and the Jackson, Mississippi, *Daily News*," Ph.D. diss., Mississippi State University (1965).

85. Brown, "Sillers and Conner," 32; Robert L. Brown, "A Revival of Conservatism in Mississippi Politics: The Administration of Henry L. Whitfield, 1924–1927," M.A. thesis, University of Mississippi (1962).

86. Philip A. Grant, Jr., "The Mississippi Congressional Delegation and the Formation of the Conservative Coalition, 1937–1940," *JMH* 50 (1988), 27; Shefter, *Political Parties and the State*, 7.

87. Moreover, the county-unit system bred high levels of electoral corruption; this made control of party machinery—particularly the state party executive committee and county executive committees—much more significant than in other states.

88. For evidence of the role of county bosses in solidifying factional conflict in Georgia, see Charles S. Bullock III and Jessica L. McClellan, "The County Boss in Statewide Elections: A Multivariate Analysis of Georgia's Bifactional Politics," *Politics and Policy* 32 (2004), 740–55.

89. Anderson, *Wild Man*, 17–18; Heard interview with a leading Georgia party strategist and legislator, Heard Papers.

90. Anderson, *Wild Man*, 110; Stephen G. N. Tuck, *Beyond Atlanta: The Struggle for Racial Equality in Georgia, 1940–1980* (Athens: University of Georgia Press, 2001), 18; *NYT*, Sep. 18, 22, and 25, 1934; The Citizens' Fact-Finding Movement of Georgia, *Georgia Facts in Figures: A Source Book* (Athens: University of Georgia Press, 1946), 105; Drew Pearson, "Washington Merry-Go-Round," *Lodi News-Sentinel* (Aug. 14, 1946). Also see John E. Allen, "Eugene Talmadge and the Great Textile Strike in Georgia, September 1934," in Gary M. Fink and Merl E. Reed, eds., *Essays in Southern Labor History: Selected Papers, Southern Labor History Conference, 1976* (Westport, Conn.: Greenwood Press, 1977), 224–43.

91. During a 1931 investigation of his embezzlement of state funds, Talmadge pleaded, "Yeah, it's true. I stole, but I stole for you, the dirt farmers!" Anderson, *Wild Man*, 60, 75; Sarah McCulloh Lemmon, "The Public Career of Eugene Talmadge: 1926–1936," Ph.D. diss., University of North Carolina-Chapel Hill (1952).

92. In 1947 the League of Women Voters had thirteen local branches and a total membership of about 3,700; only two branches were in two-unit counties. Kytle and Mackay, *Who Runs Georgia?* 54.

93. Henderson, *Politics of Change in Georgia*. In the 1940s, Atlanta progressives in state and federal courts challenged the constitutional validity of the county-unit system. Evidence from more than one dozen elite interviews conducted in the 1940s suggests that the vast majority of anti-Talmadge politicians and activists preferred the maintenance of one-party rule, the white primary, and Jim Crow laws and norms. Kytle and Mackay, *Who Runs Georgia?*

94. Indeed, the only gubernatorial elections a non-Talmadge candidate won from the early 1930s until the 1960s occurred when anti-Talmadge groups converged on a single primary challenger.

95. The adoption of civil-service reforms in 1939 and restrictions on spending at the ward level by aldermen made an electoral coalition based on patronage even more unlikely. Clarence N. Stone, *Regime Politics: Governing Atlanta, 1946–1988* (Lawrence: University of Kansas Press, 1989), chap. 2.

96. In Hartsfield's first year in office, the city was still forced to pay its employees in scrip. Stone, *Regime Politics*, chaps. 2–3; Harold H. Martin, *William Berry Hartsfield: Mayor of Atlanta* (Atlanta: University of Georgia Press, 2010 [1978]). Georgia was still "dry" at the time, and more than one-third of the city's police force was reported to have been on the take. Egerton, *Speak Now Against the Day*, 5–6.

97. *NYT*, Feb. 18, 21–28, Mar. 1–2 and 15, 1936. During Talmadge's "dictatorship," his opponents alleged that, among other things, the "National Guard . . . is in physical control of the State Capitol." Rumors circulated that Talmadge employed more than one hundred plainclothes National Guardsmen at campaign events. Anderson, *Wild Man*, 160–61, 164; on other episodes, *AJ*, Dec. 12, 1940; Sullivan, *Days of Hope*, 156; Heard interview with a prominent "good government" activist, Heard Papers.

98. Other powerful senators included South Carolina's Ellison D. "Cotton Ed" Smith (chair of the Agriculture Committee), and U.S. House member John Rankin (D-MS), cosponsor of the mammoth Tennessee Valley Authority legislation, who headed the "public power bloc" in the House. Zelizer, *On Capitol Hill*, 23–24.

99. Finley, *Delaying the Dream*, 2, 5. Hilliard, "Legislative Career of Wright," 19–21; Tate, "Easing the Burden," 186; "Revolution in Mississippi," *Coronet Magazine* 26 (May 1949), 78–82; Kytle and Mackay, *Who Runs Georgia?* 52; Heard interviews with a prominent Mississippi legislator and a newspaper editor, Heard Papers. The papers of federal officeholders are remarkable for the absence of correspondence related to intraparty politics.

100. Edwin Amenta, *When Movements Matter: The Townsend Plan and the Rise of Social Security* (Princeton: Princeton University Press, 2006), 122–23.

101. McAdam, *Political Process*, 45–47. Similarly, Kenneth Andrews defines movement infrastructure as the "combination of leaders, indigenous resources, and local organizations." Kenneth T. Andrews, *Freedom Is a Constant Struggle: The Mississippi Civil Rights Movement and Its Legacy* (Chicago: University of Chicago Press, 2004), 5–6.

102. David J. Garrow, *Protest at Selma: Martin Luther King, Jr., and the Voting Rights Act of 1965* (New Haven: Yale University Press, 1978), 7. Estimates of voter registration and turnout by race are notoriously unreliable, especially for earlier periods. Jack Walker, "Negro Voting in Atlanta: 1953–1961," *Phylon* 24 (1963), 380, table 1; Berg, "*The Ticket to Freedom*," 140–41.

103. On estimates in cities and towns, Paul Lewinson, *Race, Class, and Party: A History of Negro Suffrage and White Politics in the South* (New York: Russell & Russell, 1963 [1932]), 218–21.

104. Berg, "*The Ticket to Freedom*," 22, 39, 109; Patricia Sullivan, *Lift Every Voice: The NAACP and the Making of the Civil Rights Movement* (New York: New Press, 2009); Charles Flint Kellogg, *NAACP: A History of the National Association for the Advancement of Colored People*, vol. 1 (Baltimore: Johns Hopkins University Press, 1967), 117–37. National-level NAACP branch and membership data through 1950 are taken from R. Williams to Gloster Current, Association's Membership from 1912 to 1950," Jun. 15, 1954, Series II, Part A, Box 202, in Randolph Boehm, August Meier, and John H. Bracey, Jr., eds., *Papers of the NAACP* (Bethesda, Md: University Publications of America, 1987), microfilm (hereafter NAACP Papers), cited in Berg, "*The Ticket to Freedom*," table 1, p. 23. NAACP membership and branch data are tricky. Different sources within the organization offer widely varying figures. I have attempted to use the most reliable data, which are reports of the number of branches in each state that have generated enough membership dues to be considered in good standing by the national office. These figures are often lower than those reported by state-level activists themselves.

105. The national office required that chartered branches collect a $1 annual membership fee from at least fifty members. The sharp decline in black disposable income greatly weakened overall membership levels and cost many branches their status as chartered branches in good standing. Berg, "*The Ticket to Freedom*," 56.

106. Levi Byrd, from rural Chesterfield County, built the state Conference of Branches. Peter F. Lau, "Freedom Road Territory: The Politics of Civil Rights Struggle in South Carolina During the Jim Crow Era," Ph.D. diss., Rutgers University

(2001), pp. 97–98, 160, 173; Ervin D. Hoffman, "The Genesis of the Modern Movement for Equal Rights in South Carolina, 1930–1939," *Journal of Negro History* 44 (1959), 346–59 (hereafter *JNH*).

107. Tuck, *Beyond Atlanta*, 29 and 44; Heard interview with a prominent black Democratic activist, Heard Papers.

108. Berg, *"The Ticket to Freedom,"* 110.

109. Valelly, *The Two Reconstructions*, 169.

110. Kenneth H. Williams, "Mississippi and Civil Rights, 1945–1954," Ph.D. diss., Mississippi State University (1985), pp. 35, 13; Andrew A. Workman, "The Rejection of Accommodation by Mississippi's Black Public Elite, 1946–1954," M.A. thesis, University of North Carolina, Chapel Hill (1988), chap. 1; Neil R. McMillen, "The Migration and Black Protest in Jim Crow Mississippi," in Alferdteen Harrison, ed., *Black Exodus* (Jackson: University Press of Mississippi, 1991), 83–99.

111. Berg, *"The Ticket to Freedom,"* 110.

112. Herbert S. Parmet, *The Democrats: The Years After FDR* (New York: Oxford University Press, 1976), 26.

113. The *Atlanta Daily World* was the country's highest-circulation black daily from the mid-1930s to the early 1960s. It endorsed Republican presidential candidates through the 1980s.

114. Bond referenda were not part of Democratic primaries and thus lay beyond the clutches of the white primary, and were the major way the city financed new expenditures on schooling. They required the support of two-thirds of all *registered* residents. Thus, black voter registration drives conducted just before a referendum were enough to win promises for additional spending on black education (including the 1921 promise to build the city's first black high school). Stone, *Regime Politics*, chap. 2; C. A. Bacote, "The Negro in Atlanta Politics," *Phylon* 16 (1955), 333–50; John Dittmer, *Black Georgia in the Progressive Era* (Urbana: University of Illinois Press, 1977). Stone, *Regime Politics*, 12. Black Savannah, perhaps surpassing Atlanta in the degree of its black organization and protest, procured less discriminatory policies even before the abolition of the white primary. In the 1940s, the city led the South in per capita black voter registration, NAACP membership, and voting turnout. This mobilization helped secure black police officers and improvements in parks and other black spaces. Tuck, *Beyond Atlanta*, 46–49. Similarly, Charleston's branch focused on voter registration, in part to influence bond issues, which were decided outside the ambit of the white-only primary. Edwin A. Harleston, Report of Charleston, South Carolina Branch, Report of Branches (Jun. 28, 1919), Tenth Anniversary Conference of the NAACP, Reel 8, Box 2, Series B, Group I, Part I, NAACP Papers.

115. Dittmer, *Black Georgia in the Progressive Era*, 124–30.

116. Kruse, *White Flight*, 14. Herbert T. Jenkins, *Forty Years on the Force, 1932–1972* (Atlanta: Center for Research in Social Change, Emory University, 1973); Steven Weisenburger, "The Columbians, Inc.: A Chapter of Racial Hatred from the Post–World War II South," *JSH* 69 (2003), 821–60.

117. In 1930 the number of blacks per black professional ranged from 132 in Georgia to 193 in South Carolina to 199 in Mississippi. Calculation based on data in U.S. Department of Commerce, *Negroes in the United States*, 293, table 12.

118. On South Carolina, see W. Lewis Burke and William C. Hine, "The South Carolina State College Law School," in W. Lewis Burke and Belinda F. Gergel, eds.,

Matthew J. Perry: The Man, His Times, and His Legacy (Columbia: University of South Carolina Press, 2004), 17, 26, and tables 1 and 2, pp. 40–41; W. Lewis Burke, "Killing, Cheating, Legislating, and Lying: A History of Voting Rights in South Carolina after the Civil War," *South Carolina Law Review* 57 (2005–2006), 875–76. Even by 1947 only seven black attorneys serviced Atlanta, Macon, and Savannah. Since much racial reform had to be pursued county by county, Georgia's high number of jurisdictions, combined with the fact that most of its professionals resided in a few cities, meant that the state's capacity for black protest could easily be overestimated. Williams, "Mississippi and Civil Rights," 32; J. Clay Smith, Jr., *Emancipation: The Making of the Black Lawyer, 1844–1944* (Philadelphia: University of Pennsylvania Press, 1993), 20; Irvin C. Mollison, "Negro Lawyers in Mississippi," *JNH* 15 (1930), 38–71. Black lawyers had to pursue their studies in out-of-state schools and faced severe discrimination from state bars. The NAACP's national office only occasionally assisted affiliated blacks at the state and local levels. Complaints of mistreatment and other issues would arrive at a local branch, which would then contact the organization's national secretariat. Its legal department would decide whether to assist a legal case. Given the huge number of complaints and the national office's paltry financial and personnel resources, it would usually decide to help out only in those instances in which there was a good reason to be hopeful of winning a case or furthering an ongoing legal challenge. Moreover, the national office would only provide assistance to local litigants and branch officials who were not thought to face bodily harm or other reprisals, or if the local community committed significant support, financial and otherwise. Dittmer, *Local People*, 29–30. On the importance of a "support structure" for fostering successful legal mobilization, see Charles R. Epp, *The Rights Revolution: Lawyers, Activists, and Supreme Courts in Comparative Perspective* (Chicago: University of Chicago Press, 1998), chaps. 1–4.

119. Alston and Ferrie, *Southern Paternalism and the American Welfare State*; Leon F. Litwack, *Trouble in Mind: Black Southerners in the Age of Jim Crow* (New York: Vintage, 1998).

120. Bureau of the Census, *United States Census of Agriculture, 1945*, vol. 2: *General Report* (Washington, D.C.: U.S. Government Printing Office, 1947), chap. 3 ("Color and Tenure of Farm Operator"). Another indicator supports this one. In terms of the share of blacks among a state's agricultural workers, by 1930 Deep South enclaves began to diverge. Mississippi and South Carolina were at 65 percent and 62 percent, respectively, but after being higher, Georgia's share had declined to 46 percent. Anderson, *Education of Blacks*, 45, table 2.2.

121. McAdam, *Political Process*, 46. Twenty-seven percent were illiterate, as compared to 23 percent in Mississippi and 20 percent in Georgia. The national average for blacks was 16 percent, compared to an overall national average of 4 percent. U.S. Bureau of the Census, *Statistical Abstract, 1930* (Washington, D.C.: U.S. Government Printing Office, 1931), table no. 49, 55.

122. While Mississippi's rate of educational attainment was superior to that of Georgia and South Carolina in 1900, by 1940 it ranked last among the three. (To be fair, the differences were not large.) In 1900, the share of black and white 10- to 14-year-olds attending school for Georgia, Mississippi, and South Carolina were 46 percent and 70 percent, 53 and 75 percent, and 45 and 64 percent, respectively. Anderson, *The*

Education of Blacks, table 5.1, 151. By 1940, 89 percent of black Georgian 14-year-olds attended school, compared to 83 and 91 percent of these in Mississippi and South Carolina, respectively. Anderson, *The Education of Blacks,* table 5.6, 182. Discrepancies in the share of blacks aged 15–19 attending school were starker. Mississippi's share of just 9 percent was by far the lowest in the South. Anderson, *The Education of Blacks,* 160, table 5.3, and 237, table 6.6. To proxy for a critical mass of well-educated blacks in the 1950s and 1960s, we can look at the number of black college and professional students in each state in 1935. For Georgia, Mississippi, and South Carolina, the totals were 2,319, 687, and 1,813, respectively. Anderson, *The Education of Blacks,* 275, table 7.2.

123. Fairclough, *To Redeem the Soul of America,* 194–95; on black ministers in Mississippi, see Dittmer, *Local People,* 75; Harvey, *Freedom's Coming,* 191.

Chapter Four:
Suffrage Restriction under Attack, 1944–47

1. The epigraphs in this chapter are from W.E.B. Du Bois, "The Negro Citizen," in Charles S. Johnson, ed., *The Negro in American Civilization: A Study of Negro Life and Race Relations in the Light of Social Research* (New York: H. Holt, 1930), 467, 469 (emphasis added); Langston Hughes, "The Fun of Being Black," in *The Langston Hughes Reader* (New York: G. Braziller, 1958), 490; Robert A. Garson, *The Democratic Party and the Politics of Sectionalism, 1941–1948* (Baton Rouge: Louisiana State University Press, 1974), 177; U.S. Senate, *Hearings Before the Special Committee to Investigate Senatorial Campaign Expenditures,* 79th Congress, Dec. 2–5, 1946, convened in Jackson (Washington, D.C.: U.S. Government Printing Office, 1947), 90.

2. 321 U.S. 649 (1944). Beyond the work of specialists, the case has been completely forgotten. Since 1963, it has not been mentioned in the *American Political Science Review,* and it has never been referred to in the *American Historical Review.* C. Vann Woodward, did not mention the ruling in his important essay, "The 'New Reconstruction' in the South," *Commentary* 21 (1956), 501–8. Important studies of the white primary litigation include Darlene Clark Hine's pioneering work, *Black Victory: The Rise and Fall of the White Primary in Texas* (New York: Kraus-Thomson, 1979); Charles L. Zelden, *The Battle for the Black Ballot: Smith v. Allwright and the Defeat of the Texas All-White Primary* (Lawrence: University Press of Kansas, 2004). Also see Michael J. Klarman, *From Jim Crow to Civil Rights: The Supreme Court and the Struggle for Racial Equality* (New York: Oxford University Press, 2004), chaps. 4–5; Berg, *"The Ticket to Freedom,"* chap. 3; Kevin J. McMahon, *Reconsidering Roosevelt on Race: How the Presidency Paved the Road to Brown* (Chicago: University of Chicago Press, 2004), 150–56; Valelly, *The Two Reconstructions,* 159–61.

3. Since South Carolina was the first to respond to *Smith v. Allwright,* the narratives are most easily read in this order.

4. Kirwan, *Revolt of the Rednecks,* 122–35; Stephen Ansolabehere, John Mark Hansen, Shigeo Hirano, and James M. Snyder, Jr., "More Democracy: The Direct Primary and Competition in U. S. Elections," *SAPD* 24 (2010), 190–205.

5. The white primary was established by South Carolina in 1896, Arkansas in 1897, Georgia in 1898, Florida and Tennessee in 1901, Alabama and Mississippi

in 1902, Texas and Virginia in 1904, Louisiana in 1906, and North Carolina in 1915. Valelly, *The Two Reconstructions*, 157; Key, *Southern Politics*, 620.

6. Garrow, *Protest at Selma*, 6–7. In the early 1930s, drawing on *Nixon v. Herndon* (273 U.S. 536, 1927) (see below), federal district courts in Florida and Virginia struck down these states' white primaries because the states paid for them. Nonetheless, because of onerous poll tax requirements and other devices, black voter registration hardly rose; in fact, rural whites plainly ignored the court rulings. On occasion, the Justice Department investigated county and state election boards for failure to register black voters. Michael J. Klarman, "The White Primary Rulings: A Case Study in the Consequences of Supreme Court Decisionmaking," *Florida State University Law Review* 29 (2001), 60. In 1942, the Justice Department indicted members of the South Carolina State Election Board for failing to register a qualified black in the 1940 general election; the jury acquitted. Steven F. Lawson, *Black Ballots: Voting Rights in the South, 1944–1969* (New York: Columbia University Press, 1976), 117.

7. This was the first (and only) white primary established by statute, rather than by party regulation. Donald S. Strong, "The Rise of Negro Voting in Texas," *APSR* 42 (1948), 511; Lawson, *Black Ballots*, 25. On San Antonio's machine politics, see Hine, *Black Victory*, 152–57; Judith Kaaz Doyle, "Maury Maverick and Racial Politics in San Antonio, Texas, 1938–1941," *JSH* 53 (1987), 194–224; Walton, Puckett, and Deskins, *The African American Electorate: A Statistical History*, 2:463–66.

8. The statute provided that all eligible voters swearing their fealty to the state Democratic party could vote in its primaries, but "in no event shall a negro be eligible to participate." *Nixon v. Herndon*, 273 U.S. 536 (1927); Berg, "The Ticket to Freedom," 78–79. In 1927, Texas's Attorney General, Dan Moody, admitted in oral argument that his office had "known nothing about existence of the suit until he found it on that day's assignment." Such a cavalier attitude suggested a quite confident authoritarian enclave. Twenty years later, it would not behave so lackadaisically. *NYT*, Mar. 8, 1927.

9. *Nixon v. Condon* (286 U.S. 73, 1932). The "state action" doctrine held that protections afforded individuals in the Constitution restricted coercion undertaken by public authorities and state institutions, not that undertaken by private actors. Thus, if the fingerprints of the state were not discovered in jurists' forensic analysis of violations of, say due process or voting rights, protections in the Fourteenth and Fifteenth Amendments could not be invoked to redress wrongs committed by private actors. Associate Justice Joseph Bradley enunciated the doctrine in the *Civil Rights Cases* (109 U.S. 3 [1883]). For an important revisionist interpretation of this doctrine, and more generally the constitutional politics of Reconstruction and its aftermath, see Brandwein, *Rethinking the Judicial Settlement of Reconstruction*.

10. In *Grovey v. Townsend*, 295 U.S. 45 (1935), the Court approved the statute even though the primary clearly implicated state action. For example, state law required that parties hold primaries, that the machinery of state election law be used in primary elections, and that parties allow for absentee voting, among other regulations. While Texas's primary elections had been mandated by the state, the party financed them privately; since the state did not furnish or count the ballots used in primary elections, in a sense they remained private affairs. The furious national office thought that a decade of progress had been erased by its intemperate Texas state branch. This discussion relies especially on the indispensable study by Berg, "The

Ticket to Freedom," chap. 3 ("defeat in disguise" at 81); also see Klarman, "The White Primary Rulings," 58; Key, *Southern Politics,* 290. On the use of the "public utilities" metaphor, see Leon Epstein, *Political Parties in the American Mold* (Madison: University of Wisconsin Press, 1986), chap. 6.

11. Berg, *"The Ticket to Freedom,"* 87.

12. *Newberry v. United States,* 256 U.S. 232 (1941).

13. 61 Sup. Ct. 1031 (1941). The case considered whether the federal government was authorized to punish fraud committed in a Louisiana congressional election. Thus, a primary was considered to be, under Article I, Section 4 of the Constitution, an "election." In 1939 the DOJ's new Civil Rights Section pursued *Classic* as an attack on *Newberry,* which, if successful, would pave the way to a much stronger attack on the white primary. On *U.S. v. Classic,* see Robert K. Carr, *Federal Protection of Civil Rights: Quest for a Sword* (Ithaca: Cornell University Press, 1947), 85–94.

14. Klarman, "The White Primary Rulings," 63, quoting *U.S. v. Classic,* 313 U.S. at 318. Others disagreed, or surmised that even if jurists employed *Classic* to overturn *Grovey,* such a ruling would apply only to Texas's white primary. After all, the government's brief and argument in *Classic* differentiated *Grovey* from *Classic* and suggested they raised distinct issues, as Justice Owen Roberts argued in his unanimous opinion in *Grovey* and in his lone, angry dissent in *Smith v. Allwright,* 321 U.S. 649 (1944), at 670. Berg, *"The Ticket to Freedom,"* 89; Mark V. Tushnet, *Making Civil Rights Law: Thurgood Marshall and the Supreme Court, 1956–1961* (New York: Oxford University Press, 1996), 103–5.

15. Several leftist groups submitted amicus briefs, including the American Civil Liberties Union, the National Lawyer's Guild, and the Workers' Defense League. The Southern Conference for Human Welfare (SCHW) collected hundreds of signatures in the South in support of the white primary's abolition. Hine, *Black Victory,* 212–13; Krueger, *And Promises to Keep,* 128.

16. Supreme Court of the United States, Transcript of Record, *Lonnie E. Smith, Petitioner, vs. S. E. Allwright, Election Judge and James E. Liuzza, Associate Election Judge, 48th Precinct of Harris County, Texas,* No. 51, October Term, 1943.

17. Lawson, *Black Ballots,* 43 and 363, fn. 81. While they waited for the ruling, a large conference of leading black protest organizations in New York City demanded that northern candidates seeking black votes must support black suffrage, including the abolition of the white primary. Candidates would also have to have "clearly demonstrated opposition to and departure from the prevailing anti-Negro traditions." Garson, *The Democratic Party,* 71.

18. (321 U.S. (1944)), at 664.

19. (321 U.S. (1944)), at 666.

20. One remaining member of the Court, Associate Justice Owen Roberts, had written the court's opinion in *Grovey;* the other was Chief Justice Harlan Fiske Stone, the author of *Classic.* Berg, *"The Ticket to Freedom,"* 90. Roberts was "incredulous that his nine-year-old precedent was being discarded." Powe, *The Warren Court,* 11.

21. Staffers in the new Civil Rights Division, housed in the DOJ's Criminal Division, sympathized with the NAACP's position, but they (or the White House) perceived the political costs of supporting it as too high. The administration's only supportive act was an article by a Justice staffer endorsing the NAACP's core argu-

ment. Lawson, *Black Ballots*, 42; Fred G. Folsom, Jr., "Federal Elections and the 'White Primary,'" *Columbia Law Review* 43 (1943), 1026–35; Valelly, *The Two Reconstructions*, 160–61. The DOJ's new Civil Rights Section is discussed in Maria Ponomarenko, "The Department of Justice and the Limits of the New Deal State, 1933–1945," Ph.D. diss., Stanford University (2010). On Roosevelt's refusal to endorse black reenfranchisement, see "Delicate Aspect," *Time* magazine (Sep. 19, 1938); Valelly, *The Two Reconstructions*, 153. Klarman ("White Primary Rulings," 64) writes that the Court's members "must have" felt tempted to act on suffrage restriction, as they "cannot have failed to observe the tension between" war abroad and Jim Crow at home, but provides no evidence that jurists perceived such an imperative. McMahon (*Reconsidering Roosevelt*, 142) acknowledges that there is no evidence to suggest that Roosevelt's Supreme Court choices were made with racial equality in mind. For the argument that it was actually the collapse of Weimar Germany that spurred the Court to focus greater attention on the protection of minority rights, see David M. Bixby, "The Roosevelt Court, Democratic Ideology, and Minority Rights: Another Look at *United States v. Classic*," *Yale Law Journal* 90 (1981), 741–79. Also see Mary L. Dudziak, "Making Law, Making War, Making America," in Tomlins and Grossberg, *Cambridge History of Law in America*, 3:711–12. For the broader literature on the relationship between America's wars and their impact on struggles for racial equality, see Phillip A. Klinkner and Rogers Smith, *The Unsteady March: The Rise and Decline of Racial Equality in the United States* (Chicago: University of Chicago Press, 1999); Daniel T. Kryder, *Divided Arsenal: Race and the American State during World War II* (New York: Cambridge University Press, 2000); Kevin M. Kruse and Stephen Tuck, eds., *The Fog of War: The Second World War and the Civil Rights Movement* (New York: Oxford University Press, 2012). On wartime mobilization policies, see Kryder, *Divided Arsenal*; Paul A. C. Koistinen, *Arsenal of World War II: The Political Economy of American Warfare, 1940–1945* (Lawrence: University Press of Kansas, 2004).

22. "The South: Time Bomb," *Time* magazine (Apr. 17, 1944), 20–21.

23. The decision, he claimed, "accentuates a political problem for the Democratic national candidates in the forthcoming campaign." If white southern voters stayed on the sidelines, Republicans could win "several border states" and thus the election. *NYT*, Apr. 4 and Jun. 13, 1944.

24. Justice Department staffers concluded that the ruling would apply to any cases of racial discrimination in any primary. *Washington Post*, Apr. 5, 1944 (hereafter *WP*). Attorney General Francis Biddle asked his staff to explore its implications, and NAACP attorneys prompted him to consider a federal role in enforcing the ruling. But Jonathan Daniels, Roosevelt's point man on race relations, concluded that such action "would translate impotent rumblings against the New Deal into actual revolt at the polls." Lawson, *Black Ballots*, 47; Garson, *The Democratic Party*, 127. Besides the significant evidentiary barriers facing prosecutors, pursuing such cases would be politically suicidal for many federal assistant attorneys, most of whom entertained political ambitions. Klarman, "The White Primary Rulings," 98. On the view of the Justice Department, prosecutors would have to demonstrate that officials had *willfully* deprived blacks of voting rights. Berg, "*The Ticket to Freedom*," 90.

25. Hine, *Black Victory*, 212–17; *Chicago Defender*, Jun. 24, 1944. William H. Hastie, "Appraisal of *Smith v. Allwright*," *Law Guild Review* 5 (1945), 65–72; Du Bois, "A Chronicle of Race Relations," *Phylon* 5 (1944), 166.

26. North Carolina, Tennessee, and Virginia lacked a statewide white primary. *NYT*, Apr. 9, 1944; James O. Farmer, Jr., "The End of the White Primary in South Carolina," M.A. thesis, University of South Carolina (1969).

27. Even the South's most liberal white politician, Senator Claude Pepper of Florida, expressed defiance. Claiming that the decision applied only to Texas, he remarked that the "South will allow nothing to impair white supremacy." *WP*, Apr. 5, 1944; *NYT*, Jul. 25 and Apr. 4–5, 1944; Farmer, "End of White Primary," 10.

28. Key, *Southern Politics*, 669. Texas authorities offered no official state-level resistance, nor much spontaneous or organized resistance at county or municipal levels. Efforts to deregulate the party (see later discussion) foundered on a severe intraparty split over loyalty toward the national party, and a pivotal legislator's own electoral dependence on black voters. By 1946 about 14 percent of eligible blacks voted in the Democratic primary. Afterward, some noted improved attitudes and responsiveness on the part of office-seekers and officials. Blacks served as delegates at county conventions and secured positions as party election administrators. Strong, "Rise of Negro Voting," 512, 521.

29. In Virginia, the statewide white primary had already been invalidated by federal courts, and the party did not officially forbid black participation in meetings or at the polls. By 1948 black candidates competed for several state legislative seats, and black Richmond captured a city council seat.

30. Klarman, "The White Primary Rulings," 69.

31. In *Davis v. Schnell*, 81 F. Supp. 872 (1949), a federal court invalidated the amendment, finding that it led to arbitrary application and thus violated the equal protection clause of the Fourteenth Amendment. Quotations appear in William D. Barnard, *Dixiecrats and Democrats: Alabama Politics, 1942–1950* (Tuscaloosa: University of Alabama Press, 1974), 69 and Parmet, *The Democrats*, 28, respectively. Also see Key, *Southern Politics*, 571; George E. Sims, *The Little Man's Big Friend: James E. Folsom in Alabama Politics, 1946–1958* (Tuscaloosa: University of Alabama Press, 2003), 163–64; Robert J. Norrell, "Labor at the Ballot Box: Alabama Politics from the New Deal to the Dixiecrat Movement," *JSH* 57 (1991), 201–34; Scotty E. Kirkland, "Mobile and the Boswell Amendment," *Alabama Review* 65 (2012), 205–49.

32. Cooper, *Conservative Regime*, 98–103; Herbert Aptheker, "South Carolina Poll Tax, 1737–1895," *JNH* 31 (1946), 131–39; Tindall, "Campaign for Disfranchisement"; Laughlin McDonald, "An Aristocracy of Voters: The Disfranchisement of Blacks in South Carolina," *South Carolina Law Review* 37 (1986), 557–82; Heard interview with the head of a state agency, Heard Papers. The direct, white-only primary emerged first in 1888, and was solidified by 1915.

33. Whites guided by a progressive social reform ethos and a paternalistic strain of white supremacy considered blacks generally unfit for the exercise of suffrage. Tindall, *Emergence of the New South*. Only a few upcountry labor unions supported black voter registration drives. Hoffman, "Genesis of Modern Movement"; Heard interview with leading black activist, Heard Papers.

34. Miller, "Palmetto Politician," 360–61; *CS*, Apr. 23 and May 18 and 21, 1942. Besides seeking to tamp down growing black unrest and political restiveness, many well-to-do whites revealed a centuries-old mistrust of universal *white* male suffrage. South Carolina's lowcountry laid claim to the South's most well-developed opposition to majority rule and self-government. John D. Stark, *Damned Upcountryman:*

William Watts Ball, A Study in American Conservativism (Durham, N.C.: Duke University Press, 1968).

35. Some blacks in Columbia and in upcountry towns registered and voted for Roosevelt in the 1936 general election, increasing their typical vote in Columbia sevenfold (up to about seven hundred). Heard interview with leading black activist, Heard Papers; *NYT*, Aug. 23, 1936. The state party postponed consideration of limited suffrage until 1944 because of the war. Farmer, "End of White Primary," 16; *Christian Science Monitor*, Sep. 22, 1942 (hereafter *CSM*).

36. *Grovey* advanced an interpretation that party activities, including nominations via popular elections, lay outside the scope of constitutional protection as long as the state did not regulate these activities.

37. The state's judges—chosen by the General Assembly, not by popular election—rarely challenged the General Assembly, which often picked them from their own ranks.

38. V. O. Key, untitled memo dated May 5, 1948, Papers of V. O. Key, Heard Papers.

39. The Senate chose to table the bills and take note of further challenges to the primary; when none occurred, it postponed deregulation indefinitely. *CNC*, Apr. 3, 1935.

40. Voters had to "produce written statements from 'ten reputable white men' who swore that the would-be voter had . . . voted the Democratic ticket continuously" since 1876. Farmer, "End of White Primary," 20; Lewinson, *Race, Class, and Party*, 154; Alan Ware, *The American Direct Primary* (New York: Cambridge University Press, 2002), 104; *CS*, Jun. 12, 1938.

41. Demonstrating his bona fides, he later remarked, "Did you know that a nigger can't vote in our primary? One stroke of your Governor's pen made white supremacy safe forever." Miller, "Palmetto Politician," 293, 302–3.

42. Smith was by then the Senate's most senior member, having served since 1909.

43. After all, almost all of the state's low-skilled nonagricultural employment before the war—in the textile mills of the upcountry (by statute) and the shipping jobs around Charleston—were safely racially segregated.

44. In a speech to the state's Home Guard, Johnston warned, "If any outsiders come into our state and agitate social equality among races, I shall deem it my duty to call upon you men to expel them from our state. . . . I call upon you . . . to publicize in your communities this so we may avoid any trouble, so that everybody may know how we feel about this matter." In 1943, Johnston investigated rumors that blacks had assembled weapons caches throughout the state. The Negro Citizens' Committee interpreted the speech as "an appeal to racial hatred." Miller, "Palmetto Politician," 400.

45. State Representative John D. Long secured the passage of an angry resolution that called on the "damned agitators of the North to leave the South alone," and restated "our belief in and our allegiance to established white supremacy." *WP*, Mar. 1, 1944.

46. Smith backed the SDP idea. Miller, "Palmetto Politician," 272; *Anderson Independent*, Dec. 10, 1943.

47. *CR*, Apr. 22, 1948; Sampson, pp. 184–85.

48. A white woman showed up at the offices of the *Lighthouse & Informer*, McCray's newspaper, handed over her pension check in the amount of five dollars,

and suggested that the party be open to whites. She got her wish, as the name was changed to the Progressive Democratic Party. The announcement was covered in white news media. Miles S. Richards, "The Progressive Democrats in Chicago, July 1944," *SCHM* 102 (2001), 225.

49. Hanes R. Walton, Jr., *Black Political Parties: An Historical and Political Analysis* (New York: Free Press, 1972), 69–77, 80–81. Since many NAACP leaders remained affiliated with (and often leaders of) the Republican party, and because the NAACP was required to remain nonpartisan, it could not organize these clubs. In 1942, Charleston NAACP leader Arthur J. Clement called for the formation of a black political party, but others considered this impractical. Instead, the black community would focus on voter registration and a lawsuit against the white primary. The NAACP and black leaders formed the Negro Citizens Committee to raise money and publicize a campaign against the white primary. Miles S. Richards, "Osceola E. McKaine and the Struggle for Black Civil Rights, 1917–1946," Ph.D. diss., University of South Carolina (1994), p. 162. Kerstyn M. Haram, "The Palmetto Leader's Mission to End Lynching in South Carolina: Black Agency and the Black Press in Columbia, 1925–1940," *SCHM* 107 (2006), 310–33.

50. Two party subcommittees studied the issue and in September 1942 recommended the repeal of the state primary laws. The SDEC promptly adopted the report. Miller, "Palmetto Politician," 411–12. *House Journal* (1943), 38; *CS*, Jan. 13, 20, 1943.

51. *CS*, Feb. 10, 1943; Miller "Palmetto Politician," 414.

52. Because this legislation was developed before the Court had even granted certiorari for *Smith*, debate was limited and attracted little attention. The legislature interpreted *Classic* to hold that the statement of the two criteria triggering the state action doctrine was mere obiter dicta, and thus that deregulation would survive judicial scrutiny. This interpretation was a reasonable one, but *Smith* proved it mistaken. Key, *Southern Politics*, 620.

53. *CS*, Apr. 4 and 6–7, 1944. Ball wrote that to "retain [the primary] and admit 300,000 Negro men and women to vote in it would make South Carolina uninhabitable by decent white people." *CNC*, Apr. 4, 1944. Senator Smith backed this recommendation. Miller, "Palmetto Politician," 419.

54. If the proposed new laws and repeals should fail, "we South Carolinians will use the necessary methods to retain white supremacy in our primaries and to safeguard the homes and happiness of our people." *WP*, Apr. 14, 1944; *NYT*, Apr. 15, 1944.

55. Black activist Osceola McKaine considered his closing lines "a threat of violence upon Negroes—an open invitation to the Klan to get busy." Richards, "Osceola E. McKaine," 165.

56. Former interim governor Richard Jefferies earned so much money after returning to the Senate and serving as general counsel for the state's Public Service Authority that he rejected overtures to seek another term as governor. Miller, "Palmetto Politician," 353.

57. Some viewed any action as futile; one doubted whether evasion was possible when "the Supreme Court are smarter than we are." Miller, "Palmetto Politician," 424.

58. In Ball's words, unless the state "conduct[s] primaries as gentlemen conduct elections in the colleges, the white man's party as a voluntary association similar to literary societies or congregations of churches . . . will be afflicted with internal

combustion and blow up." Tinsley E. Yarbrough, *A Passion for Justice: J. Waties Waring and Civil Rights* (New York: Oxford University Press, 1987), 62. Some legislators complained that they had less than three weeks to consider a plan of action before precinct meetings; then the state party convention would convene and new party rules would have to be adopted. Heard interviews with Democratic officials, Heard Papers; Farmer, "End of White Primary," 40.

59. James McBride Dabbs (*CS*, Apr. 21, 1944); Howard Odum (*CS*, Apr. 30, 1944); *Newsweek* (May 1, 1944), 33.

60. Legendary black Republican, columnist, organizer of the state's chapter of the Southern Conference on Human Welfare, and NAACP secretary, Modjeska Simkins, told Alexander Heard that their white allies could be counted on one hand. At the 1944 special session, not a single person testified against the deregulation plan. Heard interview with Simkins, Jan. 19, 1948, Heard Papers. (According to Heard's transcription, his interview with Simkins, unlike others, can be identified by name.) Also see Oral History Interviews with Modjeska Simkins, Nov. 15, 1974, and May 11, 1990, Southern Oral History Program (hereafter SOHP), accessed online: http://docsouth.unc.edu/sohp/G-0056-2/menu.html and http://docsouth.unc.edu/sohp/A-0356/menu.html.

61. From 1940 to 1943 the organization helped enroll scores of blacks in Columbia so that they could attempt to vote in Democratic primaries, but were rebuffed each time by county officials. Walton, *Black Political Parties*, 71.

62. Richards, "The Progressive Democrats in Chicago, July 1944."

63. James Hinton, head of state conference of the NAACP and "an unswerving Republican partisan," "strongly endorsed the PDP." Richards, "The Progressive Democrats in Chicago, July 1944," 226–27.

64. *CS*, Sep. 10–24, 1944; Richards, "The Progressive Democrats in Chicago," 237. On the importance of the NAACP statewide network in helping create the PDP, see Barbara A. Woods, "Modjeska Simkins and the South Carolina Conference of the NAACP, 1939–1957," in Vicki L. Crawford, Jacquelyn Anne Rouse, and Barbara A. Woods, eds., *Women in the Civil Rights Movement: Trailblazers and Torchbearers 1941–1965* (Bloomington: Indiana University Press, 1993), 85–97.

65. Radio address quoted in Richards, "Osceola E. McKaine," 199.

66. Much chicanery ensued. State election officials denied poll-watcher positions to Republicans and PDP members; with the nonsecret ballot still in place, precinct managers could easily destroy ballots of minor parties. Some six thousand may have voted for McKaine, almost double the number officially allotted to him. For the vote estimate of 3,200, see Wim Roefs, "Leading the Civil Rights Vanguard in South Carolina: John McCray and the *Lighthouse and Informer*, 1939–1954," in Charles M. Payne and Adam Green, eds., *Time Longer than Rope: A Century of African American Activism, 1850–1950* (New York: New York University Press, 2003), 476.

67. Heard interview with the editor of a leading South Carolina newspaper, Heard Papers.

68. *CSM*, Jun. 3, 1947; *NYT*, Jul. 13 and 20, 1947, and Dec. 31, 1947; *NYT*, Apr. 20, 1948. In *Elmore v. Rice* (72 F. Supp. 528, S.C., 1947), Waring held that party officials managing the election machinery were "election officers of the state de facto if not de jure, and as such must observe the limitations of the Constitution." Moreover,

"political parties have become in effect state institutions, governmental agencies through which sovereign power is exercised by the people."

69. One-party politics "disfranchised for every practical purpose everybody who didn't go along with the national ... party," and suppressed "disagreements among white[s] ... concerning ... state affairs." *Columbia Record*, Apr. 26, 1948 (hereafter *CR*).

70. In 1962, Workman became the state's first viable Republican U.S. Senate candidate in the twentieth century (see chap. 10). On educational restrictions, *CNC*, Jul. 25, 1948.

71. *WP*, May 21, 1948.

72. The oath required party voters to back state party principles, including social and educational segregation, "states' rights," opposition to the FEPC, and so on.

73. Party leaders threatened to disallow votes from counties that kept open their enrollment books past the executive committee's deadline. *NYT*, Jun. 13 and 28, 1948.

74. *CS*, Aug. 8, 1948; Yarbrough, *A Passion for Justice*, 81. However, in Columbia's municipal elections, with a black voting-age population of at least 10,000, only forty-seven blacks voted. *CR*, May 15, 1948; Key, *Southern Politics*, 628–29.

75. Under Thurmond, the state's Department of Education hired a black educator as a staffer. *WP*, Jul. 18 and Dec. 22, 1948; *CSM*, Jan. 13, Mar. 29, and May 28, 1949; *CSM*, Jan. 4, 1950; *NYT*, Mar. 5, 1950.

76. *NYT*, Jul. 20, 1947.

77. Walton, *Black Political Parties*, 72–73.

78. In the 1946 general election, voters—as usual, in plain sight of all those at the polling precinct—had to choose one of six different ballots for federal office representing six parties or factions.

79. Chester M. Morgan, *Redneck Liberal: Theodore G. Bilbo and the New Deal* (Baton Rouge: Louisiana State University Press, 1985), 228; Tate, "Easing the Burden," 191–92. The National Urban League editorialized, "Down in Mississippi they are afraid of democracy ... [S]ocial justice and labor exploitation have not been ... confined to the Negro. . . . In a world that sees Democracy waging a bitter fight to survive the onslaughts of authoritarian principles of government, Mississippi, a component part of the great Democracy of the West, moves toward repudiations of its basic principles." "Text Books in Mississippi," *Opportunity* 18 (1940), 99–100.

80. Erle Johnston, *Politics: Mississippi Style* (Forest, Miss.: Lake Harbor, 1993), 58; Tate, "Easing the Burden," 191; Morgan, *Redneck Liberal*, 226; *JDN*, May 23, 1940.

81. The Jackson branch of the NAACP sought help from the national office in order to sue the state Democratic party for its white primary in 1944. Klarman, "White Primary Rulings," 75; Dittmer, *Local People*, 29–30, 32.

82. A prominent black activist of voting rights estimated 78,000 in his interview with Heard, Jun. 21, 1947, Heard Papers. Workman, "Rejection of Accommodation," 26 and 51. Martha Swain, "The Mississippi Delta Goes to War, 1941–1942," *JMH* (1995), 335–52; Nan E. Woodruff, "Pick or Fight: The Emergency Farm Labor Programs in the Arkansas and Mississippi Deltas during World War II," *Agricultural History* 64 (1990), 74–80. An editor and publisher of one of Mississippi's more politically moderate newspapers shared such fears in his interview with Heard, Heard Papers. Delta planters' influence in federal manpower agencies and on draft boards allowed them to secure a de facto "work or fight" policy during the war. For interview and survey evidence regarding young blacks' views on social norms from the Mississippi Delta's

Indianola County, see Hortense Powdermaker, *After Freedom: A Cultural Study of the Deep South* (New York: Viking, 1939).

83. Kryder, *Divided Arsenal*, chap. 5; Dittmer, *Local People*, 17. In 1942 white crowds lynched three black men, and Governor Johnson called out two National Guard companies to find a suspect in the shooting death of a sheriff. *WP*, Oct. 19, 1942.

84. In Jackson, uniformed white policemen attacked black vets. Remarkably, after complaints by black groups, Jackson's Mayor Speed dismissed two white officers. Williams, "Mississippi and Civil Rights," 43, 46.

85. The only significant change occurred in 1935, when the Corrupt Practices Act strengthened the poll tax. The act required that the poll tax be paid each year, rather than once for two years' tax. Heard interview with Mississippi party official, Heard Papers.

86. *WP*, Apr. 6, 1944; Stetson Kennedy, *Southern Exposure* (Garden City, N.Y.: Doubleday, 1946), 115. The state's most important columnist, Frederick Sullens, wrote that the Court's decision placed "white supremacy in peril." Dittmer, *Local People*, 26.

87. All political observers considered these elections highly unimportant, especially relative to elections for county offices. Heard interviews with Mississippi journalists, Heard Papers.

88. As late as 1946 the secretary of state's office had not issued a charter of incorporation to a Klan organization. Acting Governor Fielding Wright professed surprise when he heard of Department of Justice plans to investigate the Klan in Mississippi; he claimed he thought it had been dead since 1923. Black leaders also believed there was no organized Klan in the state, nor any similar organization. *Memphis Commercial-Appeal*, Aug. 2, 1946 (hereafter *MCA*); Heard interviews with black activists, Heard Papers.

89. Workman, "Rejection of Accommodation," 32. Difficulties in finding an attorney from outside Mississippi who had passed the state bar stymied the national NAACP's efforts to support indigenous activism. Williams, "Mississippi and Civil Rights," 63–64.

90. Workman, "Rejection of Accommodation," 33–34.

91. Williams, "Mississippi and Civil Rights," 66; *Chicago Defender*, Mar. 2, 1946.

92. *JDN*, May 18–19 and 30, 1946; *WP*, Dec. 6, 1946; *NYT*, Dec. 8, 1946.

93. Williams, "Mississippi and Civil Rights," 71–73; Harry Wright, "A Survey of Veterans Services for Negro Voters in Mississippi," *New South* 2 (1947), 10. Black veterans capitalized on their campus presence, especially at Jackson State University, which was home to a chapter of the interracial, liberal American Veterans Committee (AVC). The South featured twenty chapters of the AVC, which condemned Jim Crow. Jennifer E. Brooks, "Winning the Peace: Georgia Veterans and the Struggle to Define the Political Legacy of World War II," *JSH* 68 (2000), 576.

94. He warned that "if we don't change these laws some day when they address the gentleman from Sharkey [his hometown] and he rises from his seat he'll be black as coal." *JDN*, Feb. 23, 1946; *MCA*, Apr. 9, 1946.

95. On other occasions, Wright argued that reliably hostile circuit clerks would ensure that black veterans would fail registrars' constitutional interpretation test. *Jackson Clarion-Ledger*, Apr. 9, 1946 (hereafter *JCL*); *MCA*, Apr. 21 and Jun. 9, 1946.

96. Heard interviews with a Democratic politician and a prominent black activist of voting rights, Heard Papers; *JCL*, Apr. 11, 1946; *JDN*, Dec. 8, 1946.

97. Bilbo said, "You and I know what's the best way to keep the nigger from voting. You do it the night before the election. I don't have to tell you any more than that. Red-blooded men know what I mean." Whites who helped blacks vote "should be horse-whipped, tarred and feathered and chased out of the state." Dittmer, *Local People*, 2; Williams, "Mississippi and Civil Rights," 75. U.S. Representative John Rankin seconded Bilbo's threats, asking "law-abiding blacks" not to vote in his (predominantly white) district. *WP*, Jul. 2, 1946. Earlier, Rankin warned that black voting had helped defeat right-wing U.S. House members Martin Dies (D-TX) and Joe Starnes (D-AL). *WP*, Apr. 10, 1946.

98. Sidney Hillman, chair of the CIO's Political Action Committee, called on Truman to "suppres[s] this defiance of the law of the land" in order to avoid "a reign of terror in Mississippi and other states where effort is being made to circumvent the Supreme Court decision." Berg, *"The Ticket to Freedom,"* 149.

99. Bilbo's comments, as well as a flogging incident in Rankin County, prompted the Justice Department to announce an investigation to ascertain whether federal laws had been violated, but it dispatched no investigators to the state. Williams, "Mississippi and Civil Rights," pp. 78–79; *NYT*, Jun 25, 1946; *WP*, Jun. 25, 1946.

100. Section 3129 of the Mississippi Code (1942). *JDN*, Jun. 23 and Apr. 19, 1946; Johnston, *Politics: Mississippi Style*, 80.

101. Newspaperman Erle Johnston worried that "Bilbo is not a champion of white supremacy. He is a menace to it. His wild remarks, and their effects, tend to offset the good work being done by those who understand the situation and seek to do something about it intelligently." Johnston, *Politics: Mississippi Style*, 81.

102. Johnston, *Politics: Mississippi Style*, 83.

103. Before the primary, the relatively tolerant Gulf Coast town of Pass Christian, lobbied by white and black veterans, ruled that blacks be allowed to vote. Williams, "Mississippi and Civil Rights," 76; *NYT*, Jun. 9, 1946; *JDN*, Jun. 5, 1946.

104. These included elite negotiations between conservative whites and "accommodationist" blacks that resulted in agreements (later broken) to allow some blacks to vote (Natchez); blacks' choosing not to vote (Greenwood); and a party leader's (fulfilled) agreement with black activists to employ county law enforcement to protect black voters (Clarksdale). Williams, "Mississippi and Civil Rights," 83, citing *New Orleans Times-Picayune*, Jul. 3, 1946; *WP*, Dec. 5, 1946; Heard interview with black activist, Heard Papers. On violence at the hands of law enforcement officials, *NYT*, Jun. 25, 1946; *WP*, Jun. 25, 1946.

105. William D. McCain, "Theodore Gilmore Bilbo and the Mississippi Delta," *JMH* 31 (1969), 23.

106. Investigators gathered information in twenty-two (of eighty-two) counties from some 450 individuals. They noted the key role of circuit clerks in disqualifying blacks, and of many other public officials in intimidating blacks from voting. Williams, "Mississippi and Civil Rights," 93.

107. *Hearings before the Special Committee to Investigate Senatorial Campaign Expenditures*, U.S. Senate, 79th Congress, Dec. 2–5, 1946, Mississippi (Washington, D.C.: U.S. Government Printing Office, 1947). Blacks attempting to vote were beaten in and out of police custody in Gulfport, and white men stood guard around the town's Western Union office to prevent their informing the NAACP or others. In Canton, law enforcement officials deputized "a popular white farmer . . . for the

sole purpose of harassing and beating blacks with a huge club if they tried to vote." Williams, "Mississippi and Civil Rights," 84, 86. Historian Charles Payne calls the participation at the hearings "perhaps the most significant act of public defiance from Negroes the state had seen in decades." Payne, *I've Got the Light of Freedom*, 24–25; Dittmer, *Local People*, 3. On black veterans' leadership role in attacking enclave rule during the 1940s, see Parker, *Fighting for Democracy*, chap. 3.

108. *WP*, Dec. 6, 1946; *NYT*, Dec. 8, 1946.

109. *JDN*, Dec. 10, 1946.

110. Williams, "Mississippi and Civil Rights," 66–67; *NYT*, Dec. 22, 1946. All office-holders and party functionaries interviewed by Heard in the summer of 1947 made this clear.

111. Williams, "Mississippi and Civil Rights," 107; *NYT*, Mar. 4, 1947; *JDN*, Jan. 8, 1947.

112. Kirwan, *Revolt of the Rednecks*. As noted earlier, for many Delta counties, unofficial circles of planters basically determined state legislative nominations.

113. One legislator opposed an earlier call because he feared changing what was then still a "Yankee-proof constitution"; another "warned that changes in the franchise sections of the constitution could lead to 'negro police officers' in Jackson again." Vogt, "Government Reform," 54; *JDN*, Jan. 31 and Feb. 1, 1934.

114. Workman, "Rejection of Accommodation," 53; *NYT*, Mar. 5, 1947.

115. One senator referred to secure black voting rights in Texas and Louisiana. The Senate amended the oath bill by a slim margin; records feature only yea votes, and do not distinguish among those absent, abstaining, or opposing.

116. The House rejected the Senate amendment that allowed for appeals to state courts for those whose registration was rejected, and the Senate approved this version. The House did accept the Senate amendment that primary voters be merely "in accord" with the party's principles. In the final version, those who had voted in the past three primaries were exempted. Lying was punishable under perjury laws. *NYT*, Mar. 15, 1947.

117. "Mississippi's Joke," declared the *Washington Post* (Aug. 8, 1947). However, as this chapter demonstrates, it was not unique to Mississippi. Key, *Southern Politics*, 642.

118. Judge Herbert Holmes, Address Delivered Before State Democratic Executive Committee, Jackson, May 14, 1947, Heard Papers. Other principles included opposition to the establishment of a permanent FEPC; opposition to anti-poll tax and antilynching legislation; and a commitment to support the party's nominees in the general election. The party also opposed "lynching, mob rule, and other forms of violence and lawlessness," and favored "adequate state laws to deal with and suppress such crimes."

119. Besides seeking to avoid handing legal adversaries ammunition about white supremacist motives, harsher rhetoric, as Bilbo showed, brought greater attention to the enclave. *CSM*, May 15, 1947; *JDN*, May 14, 1947.

120. Heard interview with Mississippi State Democratic Executive Committee official, Heard Papers; Key, *Southern Politics*, 642.

121. Heard, American Veterans Committee public meeting on black voting held June 23, 1947, Central Methodist Church (Jackson), Heard Papers.

122. McMillen, "Perry Howard, Boss of Black-and-Tan Republicanism in Mississippi, 1924–1960."

123. *Jackson Advocate*, May 24, 1947; Heard interviews with leading black activists, Heard Papers. Williams, "Mississippi and Civil Rights," 114–17.

124. Heard interview with a leading black activist, Heard Papers. Holmes concurred; *JDN*, Aug. 4, 1947.

125. *JDN*, Aug. 4, 1947; *CSM*, Aug. 5, 1947; *WP*, Aug. 5, 1947; *NYT*, Aug. 6, 1947; *Los Angeles Times*, Aug. 6, 1947 (hereafter *LAT*).

126. U.S. Attorney General Tom Clark asked the department's Criminal Division to investigate whether Mississippi's new primary statutes violated federal law. Instances of infringements on black voting appear in Williams, "Mississippi and Civil Rights," 120; *JDN*, Aug. 6, 1947; *NYT*, Aug. 7, 1947.

127. Kenneth Toler, longtime statehouse correspondent for the *Memphis Commercial-Appeal*, wrote that party officials and candidates agreed to disfranchise black voters while avoiding white supremacist rhetoric. *MCA*, Sep. 20, 1947; *JDN*, Sep. 21, Nov. 4, 1947; Williams, "Mississippi and Civil Rights," 127; *NYT*, Nov. 6, 1947.

128. Key (*Southern Politics*, 642) interprets the failed ratification vote as reflecting the moderate streak of Mississippi's voters. However, a state constitutional amendment's ratification required a majority of those voting for any elections on a ballot, not a majority of those voting on the amendment. Voters traditionally did not bother to vote on constitutional amendment questions unless there was a great deal of campaign discourse about it.

129. The rule stated that all "white voters . . . who desire to align themselves with the Democratic party and who will . . . pledge themselves to support the nominees of *The Democratic Party*, are hereby declared entitled to vote therein." Holland, *Direct Primary in Georgia*, 54. After various changes, rulers restored it in 1908 in party rules.

130. The "whole purpose of the white primary was . . . to flatter white labor to accept public testimony of its superiority instead of higher wages and social legislation. . . . The white primary was to bribe white labor by giving it a public badge of superiority." Du Bois, "Georgia: Invisible Empire State," 63–67.

131. Rather, numbered ballots matched voters' names on lists maintained by county executive committees. By the 1940s state law allowed counties to choose among three ballot types. As in South Carolina, few of the state's 159 counties used a secret ballot. The state developed a statewide secret ballot in 1949. Bernd, "Georgia: Static and Dynamic," 299–300.

132. Although the state's electoral administration was highly decentralized, Georgia's rulers—unlike those in Mississippi—had a much better estimate of black registration levels since poll tax records, forwarded to the secretary of state, categorized payments by race.

133. Lewinson, *Race, Class, and Party*; Ralph Wardlaw, "Negro Suffrage in Georgia, 1867–1930," Phelps-Stokes Fellowship Studies No. 11, *Bulletin of the University of Georgia* 33 (1932).

134. Heard's interviews with Georgia politicians in 1947 make clear that the state's federal officeholders had little impact on state legislative and gubernatorial elections; conversely, courthouse rings, as well as voters, showed little interest in federal elections.

135. Talmadge had won 132 of 150 counties in 1940. Arnall was assisted greatly by Talmadge's clumsy attempt to invoke threats to white supremacy. Just before the race began, he forced University of Georgia (UGA) regents to fire administrators

who supported the construction of a biracial demonstration teaching school. The regents then fired several others, launched investigations of the funders, and banned twenty-three subversive books. Several units in the UGA system lost their accreditation. Talmadge's pardon racket also attracted great, negative publicity.

136. "Exit Gene Talmadge," *Time* magazine (Sep. 21, 1942).

137. Talmadge called himself "the champion of white supremacy in Georgia." *AJ*, Aug. 18, 1942. During the campaign, Talmadge instructed Highway Patrol officers to stop and search all blacks on roads after 9:00 p.m. On the stump, Arnall stated that the "sun would not set" on blacks who tried to enroll in a white school in his native Coweta County. Sullivan, *Days of Hope*, 156; Henderson, *Politics of Change in Georgia*, 139.

138. *Pittsburgh Courier*, Sep. 19, 1942, and *Chicago Defender*, Sep. 19, 1942. National white media echoed this enthusiasm (e.g., *Time* magazine, Sep. 21, 1942).

139. See Tim S. R. Boyd, *Georgia Democrats, the Civil Rights Movement, and the Shaping of the New South* (Gainesville: University Press of Florida, 2012), 42–43. On "good government" reformers and late-1940s union politics, see Jennifer E. Brooks, *Defining the Peace: World War II Veterans, Race, and the Remaking of the Southern Political Tradition* (Chapel Hill: University of North Carolina Press, 2004), chaps. 4 and 5, respectively. Kytle and Mackay's *Who Runs Georgia?* embodies an economic liberalism more often found outside the South.

140. Legislation implementing the Soldiers' Voting Act passed unanimously during a special session in January 1944, and Talmadge forces expressed little concern that it would endanger white-only politics. Garson, *The Democratic Party*, 44, and chapter 5 in this current volume. In 1941 the party's executive committee (SDEC) encouraged counties to use secret ballots.

141. The commission focused mainly on furthering home rule for counties and state governmental reform (e.g., additional constitutional boards, corrections and civil service reform, reapportionment, etc.). Most commissioners, including Arnall, preferred to delete any constitutional or statutory regulations concerning primaries, leaving them unregulated and encouraging even greater levels of electoral corruption. Thus, immediately after *Smith*, Arnall effectively endorsed South Carolina's deregulation plan, seeming to think that statutes or party rules concerning fraud could survive judicial scrutiny. In later meetings, the commission called for retaining the poll tax, but did not recommend that all counties must use a secret ballot. *AJ*, May 29, 1944. "Good government" advocates, such as the League of Women Voters, had lost again. The League opposed the poll tax, but not the white primary.

142. *NYT*, May 11, 1944, and Jun. 8 and 10, 1944. In the party's view, *Smith v. Allwright* did not apply to Georgia.

143. *CSM*, Jun. 24, 1944. In January 1944, a special session passed enabling legislation for the Soldiers' Voting Act.

144. *CSM*, Aug. 25, 1944.

145. In 1940, Talmadge warned against electoral fraud in primaries committed by local officials, and soon signed the law. Proceedings of the Georgia Democratic State Party Convention, Macon (Oct. 2, 1940), vol. 1, Box 1, 73–74, Papers of the Georgia State Democratic Party Executive Committee, RBRL. On signing the law, he declared that if "you don't contest a few elections, it gives unscrupulous people a chance to get in control." *Georgia Laws* (1941), 432 and passim.

146. Governor Ellis Arnall, "Message of the Governor to the General Assembly of Georgia," Jan. 9, 1945, Executive Minutes, Arnall Papers, Georgia Department of Archives and History, Atlanta.

147. In 1945 Arnall, protecting his racist flank, asserted that the party was a voluntary association and could exclude blacks from the "white Democratic primary." *AJ*, Jun. 27, 1945; Henderson, *Politics of Change in Georgia*, 143.

148. These were Alabama, Arkansas, Mississippi, South Carolina (only used in general elections), Tennessee, Texas, and Virginia. "Then There Were Seven," *Time magazine* (Feb. 12, 1945). Roosevelt is quoted in Lawson, *Black Ballots*, 57.

149. Kousser, "Poll Tax"; Sarah Wilkerson-Freeman, "The Second Battle for Woman Suffrage: Alabama White Women, the Poll Tax, and V.O. Key's Master Narrative of *Southern Politics*," *JSH* 68 (2002), 333–74; Johnson, *Reforming Jim Crow*, chap. 4; Glenda E. Gilmore, *Defying Dixie: The Radical Roots of Civil Rights, 1919–1950* (New York: W. W. Norton, 2008), 336–45. On the view of the poll tax's effects, see *Newsweek*, Nov. 30, 1942, 37, cited in Finley, *Delaying the Dream*, 59. Congress passed the Twenty-Fourth Amendment—banning the use of the poll tax in national elections—in 1962 and it was ratified within two years. The Supreme Court in 1966 invalidated the use of the poll tax at any level on constitutional grounds (specifically, the equal protection clause of the Fourteenth Amendment) in *Harper v. Virginia State Board of Education* (383 U.S. 663, 1966).

150. In January 1946, Harris (with help from Talmadge and Rivers forces) again killed the constitutional amendment. Collier, "Georgia: Paradise of Oligarchy," 136; Kytle and Mackay, *Who Runs Georgia?* 164. Later, he became a leading writer and strategist for the state's white supremacist forces, and president of the White Citizens' Councils of America. Numan V. Bartley, *The Rise of Massive Resistance: Race and Politics in the South During the 1950s* (Baton Rouge: Louisiana State University Press, 1969), 192.

151. While Georgia law did not require the holding of a primary, the court ruled that "whenever a political party holds a primary in the State, it is by law an integral part of the election machinery." *Chapman v. King*, 154 F.2d 460 (Mar. 6, 1946). The U.S. Supreme Court quickly denied certiorari, leaving the Fifth Circuit's ruling as law.

152. The *Atlanta Journal* and the *Macon Telegraph* backed the decision. *AJ*, Oct. 13, 1945. Chapter 3 in this volume described the Georgia governor's relatively greater control over state party machinery. *NYT*, Jan. 13, 1946. On the same date, the committee's counterparts in Alabama ruled similarly, but also adopted a resolution backing a constitutional amendment requiring an additional requirement that registrants be able to "understand and explain" parts of the federal Constitution (the "Alabama Plan").

153. Harris boasted that the state's cat-and-mouse game with the courts would "go on *ad infinitum!*" Kennedy, *Southern Exposure*, 123. Arnall signaled his agreement with Gross's speech. *AC*, Mar. 29, 1946. Typically, U.S. Senator Richard Russell—soon to become the South's key congressional strategist—announced that the decision whether to attempt to protect the white primary was best left to the state party and the legislature. *NYT*, Apr. 2, 1946.

154. Arnall pleaded, "Let's be honest about it. Let's not run from the quacks who would confuse the issue. Let's not be afraid of the demagogues." A *Washington Post* reporter thought he had a good chance to become a Democratic presidential can-

didate. *WP*, Jun. 30, 1946; Ellis Gibbs Arnall, *Shore Dimly Seen* (Philadelphia: J. B. Lippincott, 1946), 59–60; *CSM*, May 4, 1946; *AC*, Apr. 5, 1946.

155. In the late 1940s, students performed a sit-in of the city's segregated buses. Boyd, *Georgia Democrats*, 49; Tuck, *Beyond Atlanta*, 24–25, 41, 44, 48–54, and 97; Fairclough, *To Redeem the Soul of America*, 413.

156. In 1949, the bipartisan Atlanta Negro Voters League was established. It allowed its members to support any presidential candidates, but agreed to back Democratic candidates in statewide primaries. This and other voter leagues were alliances among many groups, including NAACP branches, unions, church groups, fraternal and sororal lodges, etc. Unlike NAACP branches, such voter leagues could endorse candidates. And in areas where the "NAACP" label endangered those bearing it, voter leagues could take on registration and turnout activities while inviting less harassment. Berg, *"The Ticket to Freedom,"* 148.

157. Atlanta's NAACP leaders included Walden (Democrat, attorney), John Wesley Dobbs (Republican, postmaster), Ruby Blackburn (key in voter registration drives; former beautician); John H. Calhoun (Republican, Dobbs's assistant); Grace Towns Hamilton (executive director, Atlanta branch of the National Urban League). Walden, known as "The Colonel," was already sixty-one in 1946 (thus almost seventy at the time of *Brown*). The state's most prominent black attorney, he started citizenship schools in 1932 when he headed the Atlanta branch. He would soon develop a reputation among younger activists as insufficiently militant. Ruby Hurley, regional director of the NAACP for the Southeast, once asked him to be removed from handling the state's civil rights cases. Tuck, *Beyond Atlanta*, 97. The most nuanced portrait of Walden and other leading figures in black Atlanta is Tomiko Brown-Nagin, *Courage to Dissent: Atlanta and the Long History of the Civil Rights Movement* (New York: Oxford University Press, 2012).

158. Heard interviews with prominent Atlanta-based black activists, Heard Papers; Walker, "Negro Voting in Atlanta," 380, table 1. Heavy turnout in effectively all-black precincts helped white liberal Helen Mankin win a congressional seat in a 1946 special election. Bacote, "Negro in Atlanta Politics," 344–49. The (white) Committee for Georgia, affiliated with the progressive Southern Committee on Human Welfare, helped finance field workers in all counties to spur black voter registration and campaign against Talmadge. The state's CIO also participated. Heard interview with white female civic group leader, Heard Papers; Karen J. Ferguson, *Black Politics in New Deal Atlanta* (Chapel Hill: University of North Carolina Press, 2002). One year later, Mankin lost a primary for the seat to Judge James C. Davis, rumored to have close ties to the Klan. Depending (quietly) on black voters, she was later mocked by Gene Talmadge as the "belle of [black Atlanta's] Ashby Street." Lorraine Nelson Spritzer, *The Belle of Ashby Street: Helen Douglas Mankin and Georgia Politics* (Athens: University of Georgia Press, 1982).

159. Joseph L. Bernd, "White Supremacy and the Disfranchisement of Blacks in Georgia, 1946," *GHQ* 64 (1982), 492–513, and Bernd, *Grass Roots Politics in Georgia*; Tuck, *Beyond Atlanta*, 66; Brooks, "Winning the Peace," 567, 570. For the accepted estimate of 85,000 black votes, *AC*, Jul. 18–20, 1946.

160. *The Statesman*, Jul. 11, 1946 (the official Talmadge organ).

161. The *Atlanta Constitution* noted that South Carolina did not face the dilemma of repealing a county-unit system (Jun. 7, 1946).

162. *AC*, Jun. 16, 1946; McDonald, *A Voting Rights Odyssey*; James C. Cobb, "Politics in a New South City: Augusta, Georgia, 1946–1971," Ph.D. diss., University of Georgia (1975); James C. Cobb, "Colonel Effingham Crushes the Crackers: Political Reform in Postwar Augusta," *South Atlantic Quarterly* 78 (1979), 507–19; Brooks, "Winning the Peace," 571–76. The black vote in Augusta would have split between independents and the Cracker Party were it not for Harris's race baiting. About four thousand blacks voted, about 90 percent for independent candidates. Kytle and Mackay, *Who Runs Georgia?* 172–73.

163. Carmichael was a former state legislator, economically conservative, and a "good-government" Atlantan. Kytle and Mackay, *Who Runs Georgia?* 256–57; Philip Scranton, ed., *The Second Wave: Southern Industrialization from the 1940s to the 1970s* (Athens: University of Georgia Press, 2001), chaps. 1–2; *WP*, Jul. 14, 1946.

164. *Chicago Defender*, Jul. 20, 1946.

165. *NYT*, Jul. 16, 1946.

166. April 18 and 25, 1946. Common grounds for challenges included failure to meet state and/or county residency requirements (of one year, and six months, respectively); lacking "good character" or failure to "understand the duties and obligations of citizens," illiteracy, and inability to "understand and give a reasonable interpretation" of the state or federal constitutions. Bernd, "White Supremacy," 495–97.

167. Joseph L. Bernd and Lynwood M. Holland, "Recent Restrictions upon Negro Suffrage: The Case of Georgia," *JOP* 21 (1959), 489; William L. Belvin, Jr., "The Georgia Gubernatorial Primary of 1946," *GHQ* 50 (1966), 37–53.

168. Other tactics included outright refusal to allow blacks to vote (in at least five counties), slowdowns at black polling places, and ballot-stuffing. In Savannah, Talmadge supporters blocked more than 5,000 blacks from the polls, a margin that easily decided the county's vote. A. T. Walden's organization in Fulton County and the Committee for Georgia in several other counties successfully used attorneys to challenge purges of black voters through a "slow down" of litigation. Heard interview with white female civic group leader, Heard Papers. On Savannah—the site of much election activity by moderate white returning veterans and black veterans—see Brooks, "Winning the Peace," 569; Bernd, "White Supremacy," 502, 503, 500. Walton, Puckett, and Deskins, *The African American Electorate: A Statistical History*, 2:496–97.

169. Garson, *The Democratic Party*, 199. In Taylor County, whites murdered the county's sole black voter.

170. Wallace H. Warren, " 'The Best People in Town Won't Talk': The Moore's Ford Lynching of 1946 and Its Cover-Up," in John C. Inscoe, ed., *Georgia in Black and White: Explorations in the Race Relations of a Southern State, 1865–1950* (Athens: University of Georgia Press, 1994), 266–83; Kruse, *White Flight*, 24.

171. He also accused Talmadge of attempting to bribe county sheriffs for their election-day support by promising to place all 159 of them on the payroll of the Georgia Bureau of Investigation. *AC*, Jun. 7, 1946.

172. Through careful analysis of declassified FBI affidavits, Joseph Bernd concluded that suffrage restriction efforts altered the likely outcome in twenty counties, totaling fifty-six county-unit votes, and Carmichael would have been nominated. By his analysis of precinct-level returns, 98 percent of the approximately 85,000 black voters backed Carmichael (thus confirming white supremacists' fears about the power of blacks' "bloc voting"). Bernd, "White Supremacy," 502. The coordina-

tion failure took a huge toll on the anti-Talmadge faction. According to the *Atlanta Journal*, 90 percent of Rivers' support would have gone to Carmichael, and the unit votes from Rivers' counties, plus those of other close counties, would have secured Carmichael's victory.

173. Supporting the notion that Georgia's factional conflict during this period did *not* map directly onto sectional differences, by one count, 116 newspapers opposed Talmadge and 9 supported him. *Columbus Ledger*, Jul. 18, 1946. The vast majority of these papers were in "two-unit" counties. Drew Pearson called the election "the most alarming political development in the Nation," and called Talmadge—who used radio appeals and corporate support, and had in previous terms called out the state militia seventeen times—"the most Hitlerian Governor since Huey Long." *WP*, Jul. 24, 1946. The *Chicago Defender* had been confident of Carmichael's victory, calling "white supremacy" "a whiplash to goad Mississippi primitives into violence in that state's recent primary." In contrast, "Georgia is more representative of what the South thinks than retarded Mississippi. . . . Georgia has made great strides toward democracy under . . . Arnall." *Chicago Defender*, Jul. 20, 1946.

174. U.S. House member Eugene Cox—the state's leading racist demagogue in Congress—accused Arnall and the "opposition" of encouraging black primary voting in order to "destroy White supremacy." Convention minutes, 16 (Macon, Oct. 1946). State Democratic Executive Committee Papers, RBRL (hereafter SDEC Papers). Talmadge argued that "bloc voting" indicated blacks' incapacity for full citizenship. He also urged the continuation of voter purge efforts. Convention minutes, 35 and 113–15, SDEC Papers.

175. As Gene Talmadge's health worsened after the primary, his backers launched a write-in campaign for his son Herman in the general election. By law, the legislature would choose between the top two vote-getters, but Herman finished third. Later, the Talmadge's home county of Telfair discovered that fifty-eight votes had been placed in the "wrong envelope," and Herman was selected. Henderson, *Politics of Change in Georgia*, 178.

176. Kytle and Mackay, *Who Runs Georgia?* 61. Legislators introduced an alternative proposal that would not change state regulation of primaries but would require applicants with less than a high-school degree to pass an education test based upon interpreting the U.S. Constitution. The state NAACP financed a legal challenge to the law. *NYT*, Jan. 29 and Feb. 22, 1947.

177. "We . . . call upon all true Democrats in Georgia to join with us in the reorganization of the party so that it may once again become the respected instrument through which the will of the people may be honestly expressed, and constitutional Democratic government restored to our state." *NYT*, Feb. 27, 1947.

178. All legislation passed during Talmadge's tenure would have to be resubmitted for his signature or vetoed.

179. *CSM*, Mar. 25, 1947. He also claimed to have helped draft the white primary bill, and pledged to appoint only those devoted to it and the county-unit system.

180. Some counties already segregated ballots by race. Heard interview with leading Talmadgeite legislator, Heard Papers.

181. Many House members from two-unit counties opposed by black voters voted against the white primary bill and against the constitutional amendment to extend the county-unit system to general elections, because of their allegiance to

Thompson. Heard interviews with a Talmadgeite legislator and a newspaper editor, Heard Papers.

182. Technically, Talmadge was an independent in the 1946 gubernatorial general election who challenged the party nominee, his father. Thus, Thompson forces labeled Talmadge-loyalist Jim Peters and other members of the state executive committee as "bolters" from the Democratic party, and formed their own state Democratic executive committee. Representative William Morris would serve as party chair, and he, in conjunction with Governor Melvin Thompson, would name the other sixty executive committee members. Rulers maintained a few options: First, if those with no schooling whatsoever were barred from voting, fewer than 11 percent of the black voting-age population would be barred from voting, and only about 2.5 percent of whites would be barred. If the minimum educational requirement were set at six years of schooling, about 60 percent of the black voting-age population and 26 percent of the white voting-age population would be barred from voting. Estimates used in the debate held that about 750,000 Georgians over the age of twenty-five lacked at least a seventh-grade education, but these were about equally distributed by race. Observers wondered "how much sacrifice of white votes the Talmadge faithful was willing [to accept] to make. . . . state elections" white-only. *AJ*, Apr. 17 and 30, 1947.

183. Meanwhile, the Thompson party met and set rules for *its* primary. It did not develop a new educational requirement, but merely noted the constitutional provision that all registrants must be able to read and write.

184. Also, all primary candidates would be required to pledge their support to the party's nominees in the general election, and all primary polling places would be segregated by race. *WP*, Aug. 9, 1947; *CNC*, Sep. 21, 1947; *NYT*, Sep. 23, 1947; *Jacksonville Times-Union*, Dec. 18, 1947; *The Statesman*, Jan. 8, 1948.

185. House Speaker Fred Hand did "not dismiss the possibility of a second party." Interview with Fred Hand in Kytle and Mackay, *Who Runs Georgia?* 234–37.

186. He advised Talmadge to advocate the white primary through the 1948 election regardless of a court ruling on the South Carolina plan. By arguing that the ruling had no immediate effect on Georgia, the faction could buy time until the next election. Interview with Fred Hand in Kytle and Mackay, *Who Runs Georgia?* 234–37.

187. Representative Bob Elliott wished "the niggers and the unions and those white folks you talk about would start another party." Interview with Representative Robert Elliott in Kytle and Mackay, *Who Runs Georgia?* 245.

188. Interviews with Representatives Robert Elliott and Roy Harris in Kytle and Mackay, *Who Runs Georgia?* 242–45, 259–64.

189. *Smith v. Allwright* left its mark on a difficult debate that continues today: whether and how to limit parties' autonomy over their own affairs. See *Terry v. Adams*, 345 U.S. 461 (1953); Hine, *Black Victory*, 27–29; Daniel Hays Lowenstein, "Associational Rights of Major Political Parties: A Skeptical Inquiry," *Texas Law Review* 71 (1993), 1741–92; Ellen D. Katz, "Resurrecting the White Primary," *University of Pennsylvania Law Review* 153 (2005), 325–92. Legal scholarship on the regulation of parties has developed rapidly, as litigants and scholars debate the rights of parties to restrict participation in "their" primaries to their own members. See Nathaniel Persily, "Toward a Functional Defense of Political Party Autonomy," *NYU Law Review* 76 (2001), 750–824; Samuel Issacharoff, Pamela S. Karlan, and Richard H. Pildes, *The Law of De-*

mocracy: Legal Structure of the Political Process, 4th ed. (New York: Foundation Press, 2012); Epstein, *Political Parties*, chap 6.

CHAPTER FIVE:
Southern Enclaves and the National Party, 1947–48

1. The epigraphs in this chapter are from Du Bois, "The Negro Citizen," 467, 469; *NYT*, Jun. 30, 1947; Russell to Thurmond, Feb. 17, 1948, Thurmond File, Civil Rights Material, Papers of Richard B. Russell, RBRL; Bartley, *The New South*, 79.

2. "Timeline for the 1947–1949 Freedom Train," accessed online: http://www .freedomtrain.org/freedom-train-timeline.htm; Wendy L. Wall, *Inventing the "American Way": The Politics of Consensus from the New Deal to the Civil Rights Movement* (New York: Oxford University Press, 2008), chap. 7; Dittmer, *Local People*, 20; *NYT*, Nov. 20 and Dec. 25, 1947; *Atlanta Daily World*, Nov. 20, 1947; *Chicago Defender*, Jan. 3, 1948; Stuart J. Little, "The Freedom Train: Citizenship and Postwar Political Culture, 1946–1949," *American Studies* 34 (1993), 35–67; Eric Foner, *The Story of American Freedom* (New York: W. W. Norton, 1998), 249–52.

3. "Democratic Party Platform of 1928," Jun. 26, 1928. *TAPP*, accessed online: http://www.presidency.ucsb.edu/ws/?pid=29594. For a discussion of the reemergence of states' rights discourse outside the South, see Michael Kammen, "The Revival of States' Rights in American Political Culture, ca. 1918–1938: Reflections on the Ambiguities of Ideological Constitutionalism," in Kammen, ed., *Sovereignty and Liberty: Constitutional Discourse in American Culture* (Madison: University of Wisconsin Press, 1988), 157–88. Generally see Forrest McDonald, *States' Rights and the Union: Imperium in Imperio, 1776–1876* (Lawrence: University Press of Kansas, 2000).

4. Southern governors occasionally worked together to promote regional interests, as when its firms faced much higher freight rates than their nonsouthern counterparts in the 1930s and 1940s. H. C. Nixon, "The Southern Governors' Conference as a Pressure Group," *JOP* 6 (1944), 338–45; Robert A. Lively, "The South and Freight Rates: Political Settlement of an Economic Argument," *JSH* 14 (1948), 357–84; National Emergency Council, *Report on Economic Conditions of the South* (Washington, D.C.: Government Printing Office, 1938), 58–59.

5. One elector in Tennessee in December broke ranks and voted for Dixiecrat electors. Because of a technicality, Alabama's ballot in November did not list the Truman-Barkley ticket, so voters still loyal to the national party had to write in their names. Sindler, "The Unsolid South," 245.

6. David McCullough, *Truman* (New York: Simon & Schuster, 1992), 713.

7. Prominent contemporaneous postmortems include Richard Hofstadter, "From Calhoun to Dixiecrats," *Social Research* 16 (1949), 135–50; Emile B. Ader, "Why the Dixiecrats Failed," *JOP* 5 (1953), 356–69. Also see Heard, *A Two-Party South?* Key, *Southern Politics*, chap. 15; and Key, *Politics, Parties, and Pressure Groups*, 5th ed. (New York: Crowell, 1964), 265–67. Important revisionist accounts include Garson, *The Democratic Party*; and Kari Frederickson, *The Dixiecrat Revolt and the End of the Solid South, 1932–1968* (Chapel Hill: University of North Carolina Press, 2001).

8. Over the seventeen presidential elections held from 1880 through 1944, the eleven southern states together voted 187 times; in 179 cases, they backed the

Democratic ticket. Six of the eight defections to the Republican ticket occurred in 1928, when national Democrats nominated New York Governor Al Smith, a Catholic "wet."

9. Wright, *Old South, New South*, 236–38; Pete Daniel, *Breaking the Land: The Transformation of Cotton, Tobacco, and Rice Cultures since 1880* (Urbana: University of Illinois Press, 1985), chap. 1.

10. Wright, *Old South, New South*, chap. 7; Cobb, "Beyond Planters and Industrialists." By 1936 Sen. James Byrnes claimed that New Deal programs brought $242 million into South Carolina, which paid only about $10 million in federal taxes. Grose, *South Carolina at the Brink*, 39.

11. Wright, *Sharing the Prize*, chap. 2; Dewey Grantham, *Southern Progressivism: The Reconciliation of Progress and Tradition* (Knoxville: University of Tennessee Press, 1983); James T. Patterson, *The New Deal and the States: Federalism in Transition* (Princeton: Princeton University Press, 1969).

12. The antilynching bill would empower federal authorities to bring charges against local officials who failed to halt lynchings. George H. Gallup, *Gallup Poll: Public Opinion, 1935–1971*, vol. 1 (New York: Random House, 1972), 48; Virginius Dabney, "Dixie Rejects Lynching," *The Nation* (Nov. 27, 1937), 579–80; Rable, "Politics of Antilynching Legislation." Southern officeholders' effects on federal policymaking extended well beyond South-specific policies. For discussions of southern imprints on Social Security, Aid to Dependent Children, and a host of other policies, see, e.g., Robert C. Lieberman, *Shifting the Color Line: Race and the American Welfare State* (Cambridge: Harvard University Press, 1998); Ira Katznelson, *When Affirmative Action Was White: An Untold Story of Racial Inequality in Twentieth-Century America* (New York: Norton, 2005); John Brueggemann, "Racial Considerations and Social Policy in the 1930s," *Social Science History* 26 (2002), 139–77.

13. Alan Brinkley, *Voices of Protest: Huey Long, Father Coughlin, and the Great Depression* (New York: Vintage, 1983).

14. The party reestablished the two-thirds rule, and all other convention procedures, prior to each convention. In 1932, Roosevelt backers worked to build a coalition to repeal the rule, which could be changed by a simple majority of the floor upon recommendation of the Convention's Rules Committee. Southern delegations, while favoring Roosevelt as the party's nominee, opposed any changes. Eventually, the Rules Committee called for the 1936 convention to consider repeal again. Harold F. Bass, Jr., "Presidential Party Leadership and Party Reform: Franklin D. Roosevelt and the Abrogation of the Two-Thirds Rule," *Presidential Studies Quarterly* 18 (1988), 303–17; Paul T. David, Ralph M. Goldman, and Richard C. Bain, *The Politics of National Party Conventions* (Washington, D.C.: Brookings Institution, 1960), 209; *NYT*, Dec. 5, 1935; *NYT*, Jan. 6, 19, and Feb. 28, 1936; James A. Farley, *Jim Farley's Story: The Roosevelt Years* (New York: McGraw-Hill, 1948), 58; *NYT Magazine*, Aug. 10, 1958.

15. Subsequent delegate reapportionment did not benefit the region. Before 1936 the eleven southern states claimed 22 percent of all delegates. In 1948 they had 24 percent. Interview with James A. Farley (Nov. 2, 1968), p. 24, Oral history Collection, Lyndon Baines Johnson Presidential Library, Austin, Texas (hereafter LBJL); Bass, "Presidential Party Leadership," 309, 317, fn. 63.

16. Roosevelt confidant and South Carolina Senator James F. "Jimmy" Byrnes later expressed his shock and dismay that Roosevelt privately backed repeal. James

F. Byrnes, *All in One Lifetime* (New York: Harper, 1958), 94. *NYT*, Jun. 23 and 26, 1936. Some prominent southern politicians did support the change, including Senator Josiah Bailey (D-NC), Senate Majority Leader Joe Robinson (D-AK), and Representative Doughton (D-NC), chair of House Ways and Means. See Sean J. Savage, *Roosevelt: The Party Leader, 1932–1945* (Lexington: University Press of Kentucky, 1991), 122, citing Schlesinger, *The Age of Roosevelt*, vol. 3: *The Politics of Upheaval, 1935–1936* (New York: Houghton Mifflin & Co., 1960), 581. Rep. Eugene E. Cox (D-GA) attempted to restore the rule at the 1944 convention, but by then only one-fifth of all delegates hailed from the South (suggesting that the change was perhaps more symbolic than substantive).

17. Garson, *The Democratic Party*, 7. In presidential elections from 1916 through 1928, the southern share of the national party's electoral vote ranged from 45.5 percent to 92.6 percent. From 1932 through 1948, it ranged from 23.7 percent to 29.4 percent. Heard, *A Two-Party South?* 18.

18. Mitchell had left the Republican party in 1932. Savage, *Roosevelt*, 95, 120; Louise Overacker, "Presidential Campaign Funds, 1944," *APSR* 39 (1945), 901; Nancy J. Weiss, *Farewell to the Party of Lincoln: Black Politics in the Age of F.D.R.* (Princeton: Princeton University Press, 1983), 286–95; Howard Sitkoff, *A New Deal for Blacks: The Emergence of Civil Rights as a National Issue*, 30th anniversary ed. (New York: Oxford University Press, 2008 [1978]), 93.

19. Hanes Walton, Jr., and C. Vernon Gray, "Black Politics at the National Republican and Democratic Conventions, 1868–1972," *Phylon* 36 (1975), 269. Smith later marched out of the convention hall, boarded a train, and returned home. *Time* magazine (Aug. 7, 1944) described Smith as "a conscientious objector to the twentieth century." This view, while typical, was unfair. First, Smith had backed almost all major New Deal programs. Second, there was nothing unmodern about his support of white supremacy, state-mandated segregation, or suffrage restriction. *CS*, Jun. 28–29, 1936; *NYT*, Jun. 25 and 27, 1936. Smith is quoted in Walter B. Edgar, *South Carolina in the Modern Age* (Columbia: University of South Carolina Press, 1992), 148.

20. For example, historian Jean Edward Smith claims that Henry Wallace's vice-presidential nomination in 1940 almost failed (it succeeded thanks to a speech by Eleanor Roosevelt), and that, had it failed, FDR would not have run for a third term. Also, the final Gallup poll of the campaign gave Roosevelt only a four-point lead. *FDR*, 462, 479.

21. Savage, *Roosevelt*, 117; Everett Carll Ladd, Jr. with Charles D. Hadley, *Transformations of the American Party System*, 2nd ed. (New York: W. W. Norton, 1978), 59.

22. The largest landowners dominated local AAA committees as well as the AAA's key rulemaking body, the U. S. Department of Agriculture's Cotton Section. Woodruff, "Mississippi Delta Planters," 264; Warren Whatley, "Labor for the Picking: The New Deal in the South," *JEH* 43 (1983), 910–11; Richard Lowitt, "Henry A. Wallace and the 1935 Purge in the Department of Agriculture," *Agricultural History* 53 (1979), 607–21; Lawrence J. Nelson, *King Cotton's Advocate: Oscar G. Johnston and the New Deal* (Knoxville: University of Tennessee Press, 1999). As mechanization reduced labor demand, Mississippi Delta planters began supporting the recruitment of agricultural support and processing industries. Cobb, "Beyond Planters and Industrialists," 63; Wright, *Old South, New South*, 236.

23. Garson, *The Democratic Party*, 10–11; George Brown Tindall, *The Disruption of the Solid South* (Athens: University of Georgia Press, 1972), 31. Southern influence in Congress helped prevent the extension of the minimum wage to farmworkers until 1967. Jonathan Grossman, "Fair Labor Standards Act of 1938: Maximum Struggle for a Minimum Wage," *Monthly Labor Review* 101 (1978), 29. Marc Linder, "Farm Workers and the Fair Labor Standards Act: Racial Discrimination in the New Deal," *Texas Law Review* 65 (1987), 1135–387. Low turnout among the region's working-class whites allowed southern House members' to oppose the legislation more vigorously. Robert K. Fleck, "Democratic Opposition to the Fair Labor Standards Act of 1938," *JEH* 62 (2002), 25–54.

24. Jasper Berry Shannon, "Presidential Politics in the South—1938," Parts I and II, *JOP* 1 (1939), 146–70 and 278–300, respectively. Luther H. Zeigler, Jr., "Senator Walter George's 1938 Campaign," *GHQ* 43 (1959), 333–52. In *Roosevelt's Purge: How FDR Fought to Change the Democratic Party* (Cambridge: Harvard University Press, 2010), Susan Dunn interprets the purge as much more decisive, organized, and important than I do here. When he traveled to South Carolina to support Olin Johnston's bid to unseat "Cotton Ed" Smith, Roosevelt refused even to endorse Johnston by name. Southern voters did not punish the president; more than one-half of all southern votes in 1938 Democratic congressional primaries were won by the more liberal candidate, despite its being a very conservative year, as Eric Schickler and Devin Caughey demonstrate in "Public Opinion, Organized Labor, and the Limits of New Deal Liberalism, 1936–1945," *SAPD* 25 (2011), 162–89; Franklin D. Roosevelt, "Remarks at Greenville, South Carolina," Aug. 11, 1938, *TAPP*, accessed online: http://www.presidency.ucsb.edu/ws/?pid=15522.

25. National Emergency Council, *Report on Economic Conditions of the South*. Milkis, *President and the Parties*, 83–97.

26. White southern reformers are profiled in Egerton, *Speak Now*; Sullivan, *Days of Hope*; and Krueger, *And Promises to Keep*.

27. Sullivan, *Days of Hope*, chaps. 2 and 5; Sitkoff, *A New Deal for Blacks*, 58–60.

28. Garson, *The Democratic Party*, 11–12. Uninstructed delegates were free to back whomever they wished, as opposed to those compelled to vote for the nomination of the candidate preferred in advance by the state party.

29. The War Labor Board hurt textile owners' wage advantage, for example. Moreover, the president's use of executive authority to manipulate wage levels meant that the region's congressional influence might not be a sufficient safeguard. Garson, *The Democratic Party*, 17. See Kryder, *Divided Arsenal*, 53–66; Jervis Anderson, *A. Philip Randolph: A Biographical Portrait* (Berkeley: University of California Press, 1986), 256–58; Cornelius L. Bynum, *A. Philip Randolph and the Struggle for Civil Rights* (Urbana: University of Illinois Press, 2010), chap. 9. Also see Hugh Davis Graham, *The Civil Rights Era: Origins and Development of National Policy, 1960–1972* (New York: Oxford University Press, 1990), 47–73.

30. Merl E. Reed, *Seedtime for the Civil Rights Movement: The President's Committee on Fair Employment Practice, 1941–1946* (Baton Rouge: Louisiana State University Press, 1991). But, as Kryder shows, the committee's first chair, Mississippian Mark Ethridge, viewed it as "a valuable forum for strategic and symbolic gestures that might actually weaken black militants." *Divided Arsenal*, 76. On this view, some southern authorities may have conceived of even those new institutions that seemed

to challenge enclave stability as manipulable "safety valves" analogous to the manner in which South Carolina's paternalist whites backed highly limited black suffrage (see chapter 4). These hopes dissipated after three days of FEPC hearings in Birmingham in June 1942. There, blacks and white labor leaders testified, and the committee ordered a shipyard to alter its discriminatory hiring practices. Garson, *The Democratic Party*, 24.

31. Garson, *The Democratic Party*, 42; Finley, *Delaying the Dream*, 17, 33.

32. Garson, *The Democratic Party*, 45; *NYT*, Dec. 8, 1943; *WP*, Dec. 8, 1943. In December 1942, Alabama governor Frank Dixon threatened the possibility of the formation of an independent southern party. *NYT*, Dec. 12, 1942.

33. Garson, *The Democratic Party*, 28, 35–36. These programs included the Civilian Conservation Corps, the Works Progress Administration, and the National Youth Administration. On the investigations, see Eric Schickler, *Disjointed Pluralism: Institutional Innovation and the Development of the U.S. Congress* (Princeton: Princeton University Press, 2001), chap. 5.

34. Garson, *The Democratic Party*, 28–29. These dislocations included the rapid, disorderly growth of small towns and cities due to manpower training and munitions industries. Wright, *Old South, New South* and Kryder, *Divided Arsenal*, detail labor shortages. Howard W. Odum, *Race and Rumors of Race: The American South in the Early Forties* (Baltimore: Johns Hopkins University Press, 1997 [1943]) surveys race rumors and white middle-class perceptions of increasing black assertiveness in challenging social norms. Also see Kelley, "Not What We Seem."

35. Alabama state party chair Gessner McCorvey reported that a "rising tide of indignation . . . is sweeping over the South as a result of the orders and regulations coming out of Washington dealing with the negro question down here. . . . President Roosevelt and his wife have done more towards upsetting and disturbing the friendly relations heretofore existing between the white people and the colored people of the South than" all others in McCorvey's lifetime. Garson, *The Democratic Party*, 27.

36. By one measure, the sixteen-state South contributed 38 percent of the party's campaign funds in 1936, compared to 29 percent by the (much wealthier) Northeast, 15 percent by the Midwest, and 6 percent by the West. Contributions from Texas oilmen, totaling more than $200,000, outmatched those of all western states combined. Louise Overacker, "Campaign Funds in the Presidential Election of 1936," *APSR* 31 (1937), 495–96; Michael J. Webber and G. William Domhoff, "Myth and Reality in Business Support for Democrats and Republicans in the 1936 Presidential Election," *APSR* 90 (1996), 830.

37. On Roosevelt, Alan Brinkley, "The New Deal and Southern Politics," in James C. Cobb and Michael V. Namarato, eds., *The New Deal and the South* (Oxford: University of Mississippi Press, 1984), 97–116.

38. Charles S. Johnson et al., *To Stem This Tide: A Survey of Racial Tension Areas in the United States* (Boston: Pilgrim Press, 1943); Robert A. Hill, ed., *The FBI's RACON: Racial Conditions in the United States during World War II* (Boston: Northeastern University Press, 1995).

39. The *Jackson Daily News* declared, "It is blood on your hands, Mrs. Eleanor Roosevelt." Kryder, *Divided Arsenal*, 226 and passim. Fred Sullens quoted in Skates, "Southern Editor." Some gun dealers had begun to refuse to sell to blacks. Garson, *The Democratic Party*, 86, 89.

40. On the "White Cabinet," Kryder, *Divided Arsenal*, 226–30. Those groups opposed to FDR were "in general . . . the same groups which organized the anti-Roosevelt 'Jeffersonian Democrats' in 1936 and the 'Willkie Clubs' in 1940." Garson, *The Democratic Party*, 89. See Neil McMillen, ed., *Remaking Dixie: The Impact of World War II on the American South* (Jackson: University Press of Mississippi, 1997).

41. In a Gallup survey of southern Democratic (and presumably white) voters, 81 percent backed Roosevelt, and only 5 percent of those opposing him referred to the "race" issue. George Gallup, "The Gallup Poll: Prospects for New Party in South Are Weighted in Special Survey," *WP*, Aug. 7, 1943, 5. The survey polled the eleven southern states and Kentucky and Oklahoma; *WP*, Jul. 7, 1943. Most of those opposing Roosevelt mentioned the growing size of the federal government and federal economic regulation. George Gallup, "The Gallup Poll: 85 Percent for Roosevelt," *WP*, Dec. 24, 1943, 13; Garson, *The Democratic Party*, 98–102.

42. *NYT*, Aug. 1, 5, and 8, 1943. That summer, the party finances issue arose again, as Georgia, Louisiana, and South Carolina announced their refusal to release funds. *WP*, Jun. 17, 1943; *NYT*, Jun. 16–17, 1943.

43. Some southern Democrats sought to convince Virginia senator Harry Byrd to serve as their stalking horse. The Byrd-for-President Committee featured many of the same financial backers as some early 1930s right-wing southern efforts to blunt the New Deal, as well as the subsequent Dixiecrat movement. Some southern U.S. Senate primaries had been interpreted as referenda on the New Deal and Roosevelt. In May, surprisingly decisive renominations of pro–New Deal senators Lister Hill (Alabama) and Claude Pepper (Florida) were interpreted as destroying any hope of a southern bolt from Roosevelt. *WP*, May 4 and Jul. 31, 1944; *NYT*, May 4, 1944.

44. Texas' third-party slate of electors won 11.8 percent of the vote. Sindler, "The Unsolid South," 239; Dunn, *Roosevelt's Purge*, 240; "Democratic Party Platform of 1944," Jul. 19, 1944. *TAPP*, accessed online: http://www.presidency.ucsb.edu/ws/index .php?pid=29598; "Republican Party Platform of 1944," Jun. 26, 1944. *TAPP*, accessed online: http://www.presidency.ucsb.edu/ws/index.php?pid=25835.

45. *LAT*, Jun. 21, 1944, Aug. 2, 1944; Garson, *The Democratic Party*, 128. Generally, southern elites and activists backing anti-Roosevelt movements did not themselves hold elected office, which is understandable given Roosevelt's continued popularity in the region.

46. Texas Democrats split into two conventions for the first time since 1892. The original convention sent an uninstructed delegation and declared that Texas electors should not vote for the national party nominees unless the platform rejected anti-segregation laws, and rejected *Smith v. Allwright*. Texas's pro-FDR faction lost and withdrew to name its own delegates. *CSM*, May 24, 1944; *NYT*, Jul. 21, 1944.

47. Truman quoted in Frederickson, *The Dixiecrat Revolt*, 38; Garson, *The Democratic Party*, 160. Harry S. Truman, "Special Message to the Congress Presenting a 21-Point Program for the Reconversion Period," Sep. 6, 1945, *TAPP*, accessed online: http://www.presidency.ucsb.edu/ws/index.php?pid=12359; Sean J. Savage, *Truman and the Democratic Party* (Lexington: University Press of Kentucky, 1997), 92–94.

48. The standard view of the distribution of voters and position-taking on "race" issues between the major parties holds that before 1964, the Republican lawmakers and activists were more likely than their Democratic counterparts to back race reforms. The realignment of race and party is thought to have occurred suddenly in

the mid-1960s and was brought about by the strategic choices of legislators, presidential candidates, and other party leaders. This conventional wisdom is summed up in the masterwork by Edward G. Carmines and James A. Stimson, *Issue Evolution: Race and the Transformation of American Politics* (Princeton: Princeton University Press, 1989). For further discussion and critiques, see Anthony S. Chen, Robert Mickey, and Robert P. Van Houweling, "Explaining the Contemporary Alignment of Race and Party: Evidence from California's 1946 Ballot Initiative on Fair Employment," *SAPD* 22 (2008), 204–28.

49. See Schickler, Pearson, and Feinstein, "Congressional Parties and Civil Rights Politics," 672–89; Pearson and Schickler, "Discharge Petitions, Agenda Control, and the Congressional Committee System," 1238–56. Also see Jenkins, Peck, and Weaver, "Between Reconstructions." For a comparison of Republican and Democratic legislators with respect to their voting behavior, see Karol, *Party Position Change in American Politics*, chap. 4.

50. Platforms in twenty-two of thirty-nine states outside the South are examined in Brian D. Feinstein and Eric Schickler, "Platforms and Partners: The Civil Rights Realignment Reconsidered," *SAPD* 22 (2008), 1–31. The authors compare state party position-taking on five issues: fair employment, fair housing, desegregation of public accommodations, desegregation of educational institutions, and voting rights.

51. On the liberal coalition of blacks, Jews, labor, and others, see Christopher A. Baylor, "First to the Party: The Group Origins of the Partisan Transformation on Civil Rights, 1940–1960," *SAPD* 27 (2013), 1–31; David Plotke, *Building a Democratic Political Order: Reshaping American Liberalism in the 1930s and 1940s* (New York: Cambridge University Press, 1996); James Foster, *The Union Politic: The CIO Political Action Committee* (Columbia: University of Missouri Press, 1975); J. David Greenstone, *Labor in American Politics* (Chicago: University of Chicago Press, 1969). For an illuminating analysis of this coalition at work at the state level outside the South, see Anthony S. Chen, *The Fifth Freedom: Jobs, Politics, and Civil Rights in the United States, 1941–1972* (Princeton: Princeton University Press, 2009). Also see Eric Schickler, "New Deal Liberalism and Racial Liberalism in the Mass Public, 1937–1968," *Perspectives on Politics* 11 (2013), 89.

52. *Morgan v. Virginia*, 328 U.S. 373 (1946). The ruling has been called a "paper tiger" because its reasoning and scope left it not very useful to those organizations, such as the Congress on Racial Equality, who sought to secure compliance with it. Raymond Arsenault, *Freedom Riders: 1961 and the Struggle for Racial Justice* (New York: Oxford University Press, 2006), 21.

53. The CIO framed its intervention partly as a democratization effort. During 1945–46, more than 10 percent of U.S. workers participated in one of five thousand work stoppages. Barbara Griffith, *The Crisis of American Labor* (Philadelphia: Temple University Press, 1988); Zieger, *The CIO*, chap. 8 and 432, fn. 47; F. Ray Marshall, *Labor in the South* (Cambridge: Harvard University Press, 1967), 254–69; Richard Yeselson, "Fortress Unionism," *Democracy: A Journal of Ideas* 29 (2013), 71–72; *NYT*, Sep. 3, 1946.

54. *WP*, Jul. 27–31, 1946. An incident of police brutality involving a uniformed black veteran in South Carolina garnered national publicity, including four radio addresses by Orson Welles. Kari Frederickson, " 'The Slowest State' and 'Most Backward Community': Racial Violence in South Carolina and Federal Civil Rights Legislation, 1946–1948," *SCHM* 98 (1997), 182; McCullough, *Truman*, 589.

55. White, *A Man Called White*, 330–31. Walter White "warned that Negroes were so pessimistic about governmental protection that they might soon resort to 'armed resistance.'" White reported that Truman was visibly upset and exclaimed, "My God! I had no idea it was as terrible as that! We've got to do something!" Truman adviser David Niles suggested that the president establish a special committee to investigate black civil rights and suggest policy responses. Garson, *The Democratic Party*, 201; Frederickson, "The Slowest State," 185.

56. Harry S. Truman, "Address Before the National Association for the Advancement of Colored People," Jun. 29, 1947. *TAPP*, accessed online: http://www .presidency.ucsb.edu/ws/index.php?pid=12686. His speech was also broadcast nationwide via radio. Black leaders were impressed that Truman reiterated his commitment. White, *A Man Called White*, 348–49. Blacks outside the South, the vast majority in cities, had generally reliable access to the polls, and by organizing politically won municipal and then state laws banning discrimination in public accommodations and employment. Lizabeth Cohen, *A Consumers' Republic: The Politics of Mass Consumption in Postwar America* (New York: Knopf, 2003), chap. 4; Sugrue, *Sweet Land of Liberty*, chap. 5.

57. James Rowe memo to Budget Bureau director James Webb, Sep. 18, 1947. "As always, the South can be considered safely Democratic. And in formulating national policy, it can be safely ignored." Garson, *The Democratic Party*, 228, 231; Alonzo L. Hamby, *Man of the People: A Life of Harry S. Truman* (New York: Oxford University Press, 1995), 431.

58. The black vote in California, Illinois, Michigan, New York, and Ohio was thought to be pivotal, and Wallace was expected to win much of it—especially in New York. Savage, *Truman and the Democratic Party*, 120; Parmet, *The Democrats*, 78.

59. Savage, *Truman and the Democratic Party*, 133; Garson, *The Democratic Party*, chaps. 8–9.

60. "It is not Russia," Du Bois wrote, "that threatens the United States but Mississippi, not Stalin and Molotov but Bilbo and Rankin." W.E.B. Du Bois, ed., *An Appeal to the World: A Statement on the Denial of Human Rights to Minorities in the Case of Citizens of Negro Descent in the United States of America and an Appeal to the United Nations for Redress* (New York: NAACP, 1947). Quoted in Berg, "*The Ticket to Freedom*," 121, 125.

61. As Oona A. Hathaway writes, southern lawmakers "feared that the Genocide Convention and International Covenant on Civil and Political Rights could be used to justify an antilynching bill or to supersede and invalidate segregation laws" and other pillars of enclave rule. Hathaway, "Treaties' End: The Past, Present, and Future of International Lawmaking in the United States," *Yale Law Journal* 117 (2008), 1240–41; also see Mary L. Dudziak, *Cold War Civil Rights: Race and the Image of American Democracy* (Princeton: Princeton University Press, 2000), 43–44, 63–64. On black Americans' growing attention to the global color line, U.S. foreign policy, and the possible use of intergovernmental organizations such as the United Nations, see Penny M. Von Eschen, *Race Against Empire: Black Americans and Anticolonialism, 1937–1957* (Ithaca: Cornell University Press, 1997); Brenda Gayle Plummer, *Rising Wind: Black Americans and U.S. Foreign Affairs, 1935–1960* (Chapel Hill: University of North Carolina Press, 1996); Carol Anderson, *Eyes Off the Prize: The United Nations and the African American Struggle for Human Rights, 1944–1955* (New York: Cambridge

University Press, 2003), 180 and passim; Samuel Moyn, *The Last Utopia: Human Rights in History* (Cambridge: Harvard University Press, 2010), chap. 3.

62. For those traveling southward, upon reaching the District of Columbia blacks left "democratic practices behind." The President's Committee on Civil Rights, *To Secure These Rights* (New York: Simon and Schuster, 1947), 89; *Time* magazine, Apr. 24, 1950; Harry S. Truman, "Statement by the President Making Public a Report by the Civil Rights Committee," Oct. 29, 1947. *TAPP*, accessed online: http://www.presidency.ucsb.edu/ws/index.php?pid=12780. On federal civil rights commissions, see Azza Salama Layton, *International Politics and Civil Rights Policies in the United States, 1941–1960* (New York: Cambridge University Press, 2000), chap. 3.

63. Harry S. Truman, "Executive Order 9980—Regulations Governing Fair Employment Practices within the Federal Establishment," Jul. 26, 1948. *TAPP*, accessed online: http://www.presidency.ucsb.edu/ws/?pid=78208. There had been minor revisions of white-only staffing in federal departments during the Roosevelt years, but this varied by cabinet secretary. Ponomarenko, "The Department of Justice and the Limits of the New Deal State," 253–54; Sitkoff, *A New Deal for Blacks*, 50; Harry S. Truman, "Executive Order 9981—Establishing the President's Committee on Equality of Treatment and Opportunity in the Armed Services," Jul. 26, 1948. *TAPP*, accessed online: http://www.presidency.ucsb.edu/ws/?pid=60737; Jon E. Taylor, *Freedom to Serve: Truman, Civil Rights, and Executive Order 9981* (New York: Routledge, 2013), 97. In March 1948, A. Philip Randolph warned the Senate Armed Services Committee that he would begin a civil disobedience campaign if the military were not soon desegregated. Bynum, *A. Philip Randolph and the Struggle for Civil Rights*, 186–99; Berman, *The Politics of Civil Rights in the Truman Administration*, 116–18. Under Truman the DNC also began to desegregate its staff. Savage, *Truman and the Democratic Party*, 60.

64. Hamby, *The Man of the People*, 435.

65. Sindler, "The Unsolid South," 241–42.

66. For Democrats in North Carolina, Tennessee, and Virginia, who faced small but nontrivial Republican state parties, the threat of allowing their state Democratic Party conventions to be split by the Dixiecrats meant backing the Dixiecrats could imperil Democrats in state legislative elections. Savage, *Truman and the Democratic Party*, 124.

67. Parmet, *The Democrats*, 82.

68. Sampson, p. 10.

69. Many firms signed on because of Truman's opposition to the Taft-Hartley Act (which passed due to strong southern backing), his support for a higher minimum wage, and his failure to support the states in their standoff with the federal government over access to tidelands oil. Here, both the Southern States Industrial Council—claiming some "five thousand member businesses"—and state-level business groups led the way. Bartley, *The New South*, 83; Kennedy, *Southern Exposure*. Savage, *Truman and the Democratic Party*, 122, 124; Key, *Southern Politics*, 331; Goldberg, Wibbels, and Mvukiyehe, "Lessons from Strange Cases," 502 (on the tidelands oil dispute). Indeed, white moderates and liberals in Alabama attacked the states' righters as lackeys of oil tycoons. For the States' Rights platform, *NYT*, Jul. 18, 1948. The Taft-Hartley Act (officially the Labor Management Relations Act of 1947) narrowed the set of permitted strike tactics and weakened unions' bargaining power vis-à-vis

firms by restricting so-called "closed shops" and by encouraging states to pass "right to work" statutes that prohibited unions and firms from negotiating agreements that permitted unions to fire workers who refused to pay union dues. On southern Democrats' critical support for the act, see Mayhew, *Divided We Govern*, table 5.6, 127.

70. Party machinery decided how electors were chosen and instructed, while state legislatures set ballot regulation.

71. From 1900 to 1944, Republican presidential candidates never polled higher than 7 percent. In 1944, seven counties generated fewer than ten Republican votes. Donald Fowler, *Presidential Voting in South Carolina* (Columbia: University of South Carolina Press, 1966), 14.

72. Stone, "Making a Modern State," 66, 72; Grose, *South Carolina at the Brink*, 39.

73. He defended his position partly on the basis of large cost-of-living differentials across U.S. regions, and suggested that South Carolinians could subsist on $.50 per day. *WP*, Aug. 5, 1937; *NYT*, Aug. 12, 22, 1938. Given the New Deal's popularity, even Smith claimed that he supported "80 percent" of New Deal legislation. *CS*, Jun. 16, 1938.

74. In the late 1930s, Byrnes began to decry northern blacks' influence in the national party. In opposing federal antilynching legislation, he argued that it would "inspire ill-feeling between sections, inspire race hatred in the South and destroy the Democratic Party." Echoing remarks by Johnston, he warned that were the law to pass, southern governors would no longer be responsible for preventing racial violence. Roosevelt appointed Byrnes to the U.S. Supreme Court in 1941, and then to the War Munitions Board. Miller, "Palmetto Politician," 281; *WP*, Jan. 12, 1938. DNC chair Ed Flynn persuaded Roosevelt not to choose him as running mate. As an ex-Catholic who had clashed with labor during the war and blacks throughout his career, Byrnes, Flynn thought, was quite a political liability. Smith, *FDR*, 618, 629; Miles S. Richards, ed., "Notes and Documents: James F. Byrnes on the Democratic Party Nomination for Vice President, July 1944," *SCHM* 109 (2008), 295–305.

75. They cited a "disregard for state's rights and attempts to cram down the throats of the South the antilynching bill for political purposes." *CSM*, May 31, 1938; *WP*, Aug. 30, 1938; *CS*, May 20, 1938; *CNC*, May 19, 1938.

76. In June 1943, the party's executive committee refused a DNC request for financial (and "moral") support for the 1944 national campaign. National party loyalists in the upcountry took up some of the slack. *NYT*, Jun. 16–17, 1943. Some held out hope that Roosevelt would choose Byrnes, then serving as war mobilization director, as his vice presidential running mate in 1944.

77. Miller, "Palmetto Politician," 430; *CS* and *CR*, May 17–18, 1944.

78. Smith backed the idea, as reported in the *Anderson Independent*, Dec. 10, 1943. Letter from Ball to Breedin, Oct. 4, 1944, in Farmer, "End of White Primary," 49. The SDP was, predictably, strongest in the lowcountry. Its defeat at the convention left the "party" in tatters. Besides their traditional antipathy to the Republican party, Dewey's racial liberalism prevented these dissenters from turning to the Republican party as a political vehicle in 1944 or 1948.

79. *NYT*, Jul. 13, 1944. The party convention reconvened for only ten minutes, during which Senator Edgar Brown secured backing for the national ticket and a slate of pro-Roosevelt electors. Hard-core white supremacists failed to change the party's name to the "White Man's Party of South Carolina." Also, the party instructed

delegates to the National Convention to oppose interference in the poll tax, in segregation, and in law enforcement, and voiced strong opposition to Wallace's renomination. *CSM*, May 19, 1944. In both 1940 and 1944, South Carolina's presidential ballot listed slates of "Independent" electors pledged to Republican nominee Wendell Willkie and to Sen. Harry F. Byrd (D-VA), respectively. These won 3 percent and about 7.5 percent. Both slates outpaced the Republican ticket. Sampson, p. 200.

80. The state's Preparedness for Peace Commission recommended the reorganization of state agencies, a restructured tax system to increase the state's fiscal capacity. While the Barnwell Ring blocked a constitutional convention, Thurmond did win passage of the Budget and Control Board in 1950. Although it eventually extended its activities to personnel, purchasing, administering the state retirement system, and so on, its major task was to devise an annual state budget. More powerful governors, as in Georgia, exerted influence through their agenda-setting power in budgeting. Still, South Carolina's governors became stronger because of the Board, which became "virtually the only semblance of central authority" in a weak, scattered, and fragmented executive branch. Grose, *South Carolina at the Brink*, 151; Underwood, *The Constitution of South Carolina*, 1: chap. 7; Stone, "Making a Modern State," 164–65 and 230–34; Cole Blease Graham, Jr. and William V. Moore, *South Carolina Politics and Government* (Lincoln: University of Nebraska Press, 1994), 149.

81. Joseph Crespino, *Strom Thurmond's America* (New York: Hill and Wang, 2012), 35, 55; *Chicago Defender*, Feb. 8 and May 8, 1947, and March 26, 1949.

82. *NYT*, May 18, 1947. Surprising observers, the members of the crowd were indicted (but later acquitted). Rebecca West, "Opera in Greenville," *New Yorker* (Jun. 14, 1947), 31–65; Frederickson, "The Slowest State," 188–202. Frank E. Jordan, Jr., *The Primary State: A History of the Democratic Party in South Carolina, 1896–1962* (Columbia, self-published, 1967). On Thurmond's ambitions and his relations with Barnwell Ring leaders, see Key, *Southern Politics*, 150.

83. Wright remained upset at their caution and refused to serve on the committee. Bartley, *The New South*, 88. Governors from Georgia, Florida, and Tennessee made clear they would oppose a bolt. Frederickson, *The Dixiecrat Revolt*, 77–80.

84. Alabama party leaders acted over the objections of its populist and racially moderate governor, Jim Folsom.

85. Frederickson, *The Dixiecrat Revolt*, 80.

86. Savage, *Truman and the Democratic Party*, 123; Garson, *The Democratic Party*, 250.

87. Those in Greenwood and Jasper moved earliest, and Dorchester and Beaufort quickly followed. Garson, *The Democratic Party*, 250, 256, fn. 89.

88. Frederickson, *The Dixiecrat Revolt*, 113.

89. Frederickson, *The Dixiecrat Revolt*, 128–29; Savage, *Truman and the Democratic Party*, 134. Credentials challenges were typically "resolved on the basis of political expediency"—whatever hurt the ticket less. Sindler, "The Unsolid South," 250.

90. The *Columbia Record* (Aug. 17, 1948) criticized the Dixiecrat move, and argued that an effective white southern protest would require meaningful two-party competition. *CS*, Aug. 17, 1948.

91. Baskin declared that the party was "not severing ties with the national party." *CR*, Sep. 2, 1948. In an attempt to avoid a divorce, the executive committee declined to raise funds for the States' Rights movement.

92. These included Florence, Greenville, Anderson, Dillon, and Oconee. *CR*, Sep. 1, 1948.

93. Generally see Ruth C. Silva, "State Law on the Nomination, Election, and Instruction of Presidential Electors," *APSR* 42 (1948), 523–29.

94. *CR*, Sep. 2, 1948.

95. Sampson, pp. 208–9, Tables A-8 and A-9; Frederickson, *The Dixiecrat Revolt*, 180; Fowler, *Presidential Voting*; *NYT*, Sep. 13, 1948. Because the state had still not adopted the secret ballot, any voter choosing the national party ticket would have to select a ballot from that stack, and thus publicly signal a lack of support for the state's governor and the States' Rights ticket. As chapter 4 demonstrates, the party-state's failure to adopt a secret ballot was a residue of its response to *Smith v. Allwright*.

96. Truman backers controlled only three counties. *CS*, Aug. 10, 1949; Frederickson, *The Dixiecrat Revolt*, 194.

97. This break occurred in July 1949, after a Byrnes speech attacked Truman. Truman returned a copy with "Et tu, Brute?" scrawled at the bottom. *WP*, Mar. 12, Apr. 20, 1950.

98. *NYT*, Jul. 12, 1950. The PDP and black voters defeated Thurmond in Marion County, thought to be a Thurmond stronghold. *CS*, Jul. 13, 1950. Thurmond charged that Johnston was "pro-Negro."

99. Byrnes remarked that "as long as I was a Democrat with a full understanding that I was a Democrat, then I'd stay a Democrat." *NYT*, Nov. 5 and 12, 1951, and Aug. 24, 1952.

100. *NYT*, Apr. 17, 1952; *CSM*, Aug. 14, 1952.

101. In 1948, National Democrats, South Carolina Democrats (Dixiecrats), and Republicans all printed and distributed their own ballots. The state finally established a secret ballot in 1950 for any party offering presidential candidates. The South Carolina Democratic party was certified, but no "national" Democratic party was also certified, because the law "provide[d] that organized parties which conducted primaries in 1948 shall have exclusive right to the party label and no party with a substantially similar name can be certified." Of course, the Democratic party was the only party to hold a primary in 1948. These complexities resulted in political reforms meant to enable the state's voters to split their tickets.

102. The "Brown-Robinson Resolution," in Excerpts from Minutes of the State Convention of the Democratic Party of South Carolina, Columbia, Aug. 6, 1952, Workman Papers, South Carolina Political Collections, University of South Carolina, Columbia (hereafter Workman Papers); Sampson, pp. 226–32.

103. In late October, "a county-by-county survey by newspapers and radio stations in the state gave 46 per cent of the vote to General Eisenhower." *NYT*, Oct. 26, 1952.

104. Byrnes warned South Carolina whites about blacks' "bloc voting," claiming that "this bloc will cast 70,000 to 75,000 votes [in 1954], and there will be white politicians willing to enter into secret political trades with the officers of the NAACP. . . . The only way to defeat a group voting as a bloc is to form another bloc." William D. Workman, Jr., untitled manuscript (Nov. 1953), 1953 file, Workman Papers; *NYT*, Aug. 14, Dec. 5, 1952. Until 1952, the largest grouping of state Republicans kept its rules secret and strove not to enroll new members, which would mean sharing patronage spoils with a larger group of claimants. Sampson, pp. 226–30, 690–91, 696.

105. In 1936 officials from Mississippi and South Carolina bet one another a donkey that their state would be more devoted to Roosevelt. South Carolina won, 98.6 percent to 97.1 percent. In this year, about 14 percent of Mississippi's voting-age population voted (the national average was 57 percent). Martha H. Swain, *Pat Harrison: The New Deal Years* (Jackson: University of Mississippi Press, 1978), 146; Secretary of State, *Mississippi Blue Book, 1939–1941* (Jackson, 1941), 338.

106. Tate, "Easing the Burden," 201.

107. An American Institute of Public Opinion survey found two-thirds support in Mississippi. Tate, "Easing the Burden," 163; Morgan, *Redneck Liberal*, 237.

108. Over Harold Ickes's opposition, Harry Hopkins helped protect Harrison's control of patronage. Baruch, a South Carolina–born Wall Street financier, reportedly "owned" several senators during the 1920s and 1930s through his campaign donations. Tate, "Easing the Burden," 161, 170.

109. Morgan, *Redneck Liberal*, 146; Tate, "Easing the Burden," 165.

110. *NYT*, Aug. 5, 1943; *JCL*, Aug. 22, 1943.

111. Murphee quoted in Tate, "Easing the Burden," 199. Heard interviews with Weaver Gore and Allen Bridgforth, Heard Papers; Fred B. Smith, "Address to the 1944 Mississippi Democratic Party Convention," 22, Heard Papers.

112. "Conservative leaders, largely business and professional men and planters, were able to frighten away any effective opposition in the convention by raising the issue of white supremacy." *NYT*, May 30, Jun. 4 and 11, 1944.

113. *NYT*, Jun. 25 and Aug. 12, 1944. Later, the SDEC required electors to back the national ticket unless the national party's positions on white supremacy worsened by November.

114. *WP*, Nov. 3, 1944; Erle Johnston, *Mississippi's Defiant Years, 1953–1973: An Interpretive Documentary with Personal Experiences* (Forest, Miss.: Lake Harbor, 1990), 76; *NYT*, Jul. 9, 1944.

115. Some considered using southern electors to swing the election to any other candidate in order to reestablish the region's influence. Others argued that anti-FDR forces were no longer motivated to capture the state party since Roosevelt and Wallace were gone. Heard interview with a state party official, Heard Papers.

116. Melton, "Walter Sillers," 217.

117. These included workers' compensation, conservation measures, government reorganization, and improved systems of education finance. *MCA*, Apr. 11, 1948; William F. Winter, "New Directions in Politics, 1948–1956," in Richard A. McLemore, ed., *A History of Mississippi*, vol. 2 (Hattiesburg: University Press of Mississippi, 1973), 142.

118. *JCL*, Jan. 4, 1948; Tate, "Easing the Burden," 175. Tate notes that labor unrest in the textile mills of Representative John Rankin's hometown of Tupelo reinforced his hostility to organized labor.

119. Winter, "New Directions in Politics," 141; Dunn, *Roosevelt's Purge*, 244; Interview with William F. Winter (May 21, 1991), John C. Stennis Oral History Project, Mississippi State University, p. 6 and passim.

120. With few exceptions, the state's federal officeholders strongly backed the speech. Melton, "Walter Sillers," 217; *JDN*, Jan. 21, 1948. He later claimed to have seen a transcript of Truman's upcoming speech. *JDN*, Feb. 18, 1948. Richard D. Chesteen, " 'Mississippi Is Gone Home!' A Study of the 1948 Mississippi States' Rights Bolt," *JMH* 32 (1970), 48; Williams, "Mississippi and Civil Rights," 137.

121. *NYT*, Jan. 30, 1948; Williams, "Mississippi and Civil Rights," 138; *JCL*, Jan. 26, 1948. But the *Clarion-Ledger* voiced skepticism about the rush to back Wright without a clearer understanding of rulers' options.

122. Holmes wrote, "If we can get as many as six or eight southern states together, then I would favor holding a separate convention and nominating our own candidates." Williams, "Mississippi and Civil Rights," 140; Chesteen, "Mississippi Is Gone Home," 49; *JDN*, Feb. 3, 1948; *JCL, NYT*, Feb. 12, 1948.

123. Stennis pleaded that bolting should be a last resort, and suggested that the state party hold a statewide election of presidential electors who would attend the National Convention as "free agents." Chesteen, " 'Mississippi Is Gone Home,' " 51; Frederickson, *The Dixiecrat Revolt*, 83.

124. *JCL*, Feb. 12, 1948; Workman, "Rejection of Accommodation," 64.

125. Chesteen, "Mississippi Is Gone Home," 53. Wright told the state's white citizens that the "present leadership of our party ... [is] pledged to invade our state and others and destroy those principles and rights reserved to the states under the Constitution." He urged States' Righters to overtake the usually sparsely attended county conventions. *MCA*, Mar. 21, 1948; *Newsweek*, Oct. 25, 1948.

126. Chesteen, "Mississippi Is Gone Home," 54; *JDN*, Mar. 2 and 16, 1948. Also, state law criminalized the printing or dissemination of arguments backing social equality or racial intermarriage. *MCA*, May 9, 1948.

127. J. E. Johnson, former chair of the Committee of One Hundred, refused to back segregation despite a private meeting with the governor, who promised to soften his rhetoric in exchange for Johnson's support. *MCA*, May 9, 1948; *Jackson Advocate*, May 15, 1948; Williams, "Mississippi and Civil Rights," 57; Frederickson, *The Dixiecrat Revolt*, 885; Workman, "Rejection of Accommodation," 58.

128. Phil Mullens, editor of the *Oxford Eagle* and a state legislator, filed a loyalist slate with election officials even as he denounced Truman's civil rights platform. *JCL*, Mar. 26, 1948; Key, *Southern Politics*, 340; *JDN*, Aug. 2, 1948; *MCA*, Aug. 25, 1948.

129. Eastland declared, "The only weapon we have is to withhold electoral votes.... We must make politicians bid for us.... If you do not remain independent, both the candidates ... will ... be preaching racial and social equality. We must keep the reins on." Johnston, *Mississippi's Defiant Years*, 95.

130. The party's sample ballot warned voters that "a vote for Truman electors is a direct order to our Congressmen and Senators from Mississippi to vote for passage of Truman's so-called civil rights program in the next Congress.... [O]ur way of life in the South will be gone for ever." Chesteen, "Mississippi Is Gone Home," 57; States' Rights Scrapbook, Subject File, Mississippi Department of Archives and History, Jackson (hereafter MDAH).

131. In a warning to the South, the Credentials Committee issued a minority report that "urged that the Mississippi delegation not be seated because of the nature of its restricted credentials." It received 503 votes on the floor, just 115 shy of passage. Sindler, "The Unsolid South," 244.

132. *JDN*, Jul. 14, 1948. Mississippi's delegation was seated by a fifteen-to-eleven margin. Frederickson, *The Dixiecrat Revolt*, 128–29; Melton, "Walter Sillers," 219; Richard C. Bain, *Convention Decisions and Voting Records* (Washington, D.C.: Brookings Institution, 1960), 273; Winter recalled that Stennis "attempted to dissuade the state convention from going that route in a very courageous position." Interview with

William F. Winter, John C. Stennis Oral History Project, Mississippi State University, May 21, 1991. On the walkout, *NYT*, Jul. 16, 1948; Key, *Southern Politics*, 340; Bartley, *Rise of Massive Resistance*, 34.

133. Bernard Cosman, *Five States for Goldwater* (Tuscaloosa: University of Alabama Press, 1966).

134. Professors even threatened to block the graduation of students who attended a loyalist rally. *JCL*, Jun. 19, 1949; *JDN*, Jul. 14, Aug. 16 and 23–24, 1949; *NYT*, Jul. 16, 1949.

135. *NYT*, May 11, 1950, and Aug. 19, 1952. Wright's support of the national ticket angered Sillers, who endorsed Eisenhower, even while swearing fealty to the state party's principles. Melton, "Walter Sillers," 223; Sindler, "The Unsolid South," 250.

136. Bartley, *The Rise of Massive Resistance*, 49; Tami J. Friedman, "Exploiting the North-South Differential: Corporate Power, Southern Politics, and the Decline of Organized Labor after World War II," *JAH* 95 (2008), 331.

137. William H. Simpson, "The 'Loyalist Democrats' of Mississippi: Challenge to a White Majority, 1965–1972," M.A. thesis, University of Southern Mississippi (1974), pp. 21–23.

138. In December 1935, Talmadge sought to lead a regional movement to block Roosevelt's nomination. Only about 3,500—mostly Georgia farmers—attended a "Grass Roots Convention" in Macon meant to galvanize his bid, and observers roundly assailed it as a failure. *NYT*, Jan. 30, 1936; Anderson, *Wild Man*, 139–40, 149; James. C. Cobb, "Not Gone, But Forgotten: Eugene Talmadge and the 1938 Purge Campaign," *GHQ* 59 (1975), 197–209. "The Southern Committee to Uphold the Constitution," a motley crew of conservatives including Texas oilman John Henry Kirby (also a Huey Long backer), the Du Ponts, and the chairman of Coca-Cola, funded the convention. Several of these bankrolled efforts to block Roosevelt's renomination in 1940 and 1944.

139. These tactics included the illegal removal of a strong Roosevelt supporter as Georgia's committeeman to the national party. *NYT*, May 31, Aug. 26, and Nov. 24, 1935. Unless the Talmadge-controlled party held a presidential primary, the DNC would back a loyalist rump convention and hold its own primary in Georgia, and back a separate Georgia delegation. DNC chair Jim Farley organized its members of Congress to back Roosevelt and a preferential primary. *CSM*, Jun. 23, 1936; *NYT*, Jan. 26, Jun. 23, 28, 1936.

140. Roosevelt targeted George because of his high stature in the Senate; he thought George a much more formidable Senate opponent than Talmadge. Anderson, *Wild Man*, 175.

141. Holland, *Direct Primary in Georgia*, 77. By summer 1940, Talmadge changed course and pledged his support to Roosevelt. Party rules required him to make such a pledge or else he would legally forfeit the Democratic gubernatorial nomination he had just won.

142. That summer, Georgia's SDEC chair, Lon Duckworth, declared that it would not raise funds for the 1944 campaign unless national leaders "quit dealing with Republicans and Willkieites in Georgia" and the DNC "changed its policies in Georgia." *WP*, Jun. 17, 1943.

143. In late 1946, Arnall broke with Wallace over foreign policy, but supported Truman. Henderson, *The Politics of Change in Georgia*, 155–57.

144. Interview with banker Malcolm Bryan, in Kytle and Mackay, *Who Runs Georgia?* 102.

145. Heard interview with Talmadgeite legislator and strategist, Heard Papers; Kytle and Mackay, *Who Runs Georgia?* 94. This was a special election for the second half of the late Gene Talmadge's four-year (1947–51) term. Arnall, Herman Talmadge, and then Thompson served from 1947 to 1949 (see chapter 4).

146. *NYT*, Feb. 7, 1948. "The South demands and expects . . . greater participation in fixing [party] policies . . . , in writing its platform, and in selecting its candidates." *WP*, Feb. 13, 1948; *Augusta Courier*, Feb. 9, 1948.

147. *Morris v. Peters*, 203 Ga. 350 (Feb. 23, 1948). *AJ*, Jan. 11, 1948; *WP*, Feb. 24, 1948. A prominent Talmadgeite believed that the state Supreme Court gauged the support for Talmadge's candidacy and then ruled accordingly. Candler to Peters, Feb. 25, 1948, Box 3, SDEC Papers, RBRL. Bernd, "Georgia: Static and Dynamic," 314.

148. *AJ*, Feb. 29, 1948. Leading white supremacist Roy Harris proposed that the 1948 convention empower the SDEC to choose the party's presidential electors. Harris to Talmadge and Peters, May 22, 1948, Box 3, SDEC Papers, RBRL. The 1946 convention had adjourned but not recessed. Bill Murphy to William Mann, Apr. 2, 1948. Box 3, SDEC Papers, RBRL.

149. The "delegation should take no position for the time being and should be left uninstructed and let everybody guess. . . . [T]he best thing to do is to wait until the delegation gets to Philadelphia . . . because it is better to be seated first." Harris to Talmadge and Peters, May 22, 1948. Peters believed that a party resolution should "be based entirely on the Civil Rights Program" rather than on Truman. Young Herman thought that Truman should be denounced. Peters to Harris, May 24, 1948, and Peters to Frank M. Dixon, May 20, 1948, Box 3, SDEC Papers, RBRL.

150. The delegation remained at the convention but did not participate in it.

151. Russell was awarded 263 votes, including all of the delegates from the nine southern state delegations that remained. All but four of Georgia's delegates backed him. *NYT*, Jul. 3, 1948. The four were famed Atlanta newspaperman Ralph McGill and three labor representatives still angry with Russell for supporting the Taft-Hartley Act. Gilbert C. Fite, *Richard B. Russell, Jr., Senator from Georgia* (Chapel Hill: University of North Carolina Press, 1991), 240; Clive Webb, "Charles Bloch, Jewish White Supremacist," *GHQ* 83 (1999), 267–92.

152. Alabama elites acknowledged that a third party would alienate thousands of anti-Truman voters seeking to maintain ties to the national party. Wilkinson to Peters, May 17, 1948, Box 3, SDEC Papers, RBRL.

153. For example, Heard interview with prominent Atlanta newspaperman, Heard Papers.

154. Arnall did publicly reconcile with his on-again, off-again rival Rivers, thereby keeping him from dividing the anti-Talmadge vote. Henderson, *Ellis Arnall*, 64, 209. Arnall reflected later that "Herman had pulled everybody so far to the right that there was no way I could have won." Egerton, *Speak Now*, 521; *AJ*, Mar. 28 and May 26, 1948.

155. Fite, *Richard B. Russell, Jr.*, 199, 209. For example, in the summer of 1948, Russell and South Carolina senator Burnet Maybank fought in vain to block Truman's forthcoming executive order integrating the armed forces. *NYT*, May 28, Jun. 2 and 10, 1948; Russell to Thurmond, Feb. 17, 1948, Thurmond Files, Civil Rights Material, Russell Papers, RBRL.

156. By March 1948, he described himself as the "chairman of the Senate group opposing this civil rights stuff." *NYT*, Mar. 20, 1948. Given a diversity of views on Truman's nomination and his responsibility to maintain unity, he refused to support his renomination.

157. "The Governors of the several southern States are closer to the people and have more control over the party machinery than [their] members of Congress. . . . It is my opinion that we should in all events maintain the Democratic party at the State and local levels." Russell to Thurmond, Feb. 17, 1948, Thurmond File, Civil Rights Material, Russell Papers, RBRL; *NYT*, Oct. 29, 1948; Frederickson, *The Dixiecrat Revolt*, 167.

158. *AC*, Aug. 1, 1948. Henderson, *Politics of Change in Georgia*, 210–12. Proceedings of the State Convention, Macon, Jul. 2, 1948, Box 3, SDEC Papers, RBRL.

159. *NYT*, Sep. 9, 1948. The Klan endorsed Talmadge, and pledged 100,000 Klan votes for him. *NYT*, Aug. 15, 1948. John E. Holliman letter to Peters, Jul. 28, 1948, Box 3, SDEC Papers, RBRL; *NYT*, Sep. 12, 1948; Elliott to Peters, Jul. 3, 1948, Box 3, SDEC Papers, RBRL.

160. Tuck, *Beyond Atlanta*, 75.

161. Various correspondence, Box 1, Vol. 2, 1948, SDEC Papers, RBRL. Talmadge was a distant cousin of Thurmond.

162. Peters to Whipple, Sep. 17, 1948, and Peters to Spalding, Sep. 17, 1948, both in Box 3, SDEC Papers, RBRL.

163. *Macon Telegraph*, Sep. 16, 1948.

164. Elliott to Peters, Talmadge and others, Sep. 21, 1948, Box 3, SDEC Papers, RBRL.

165. Thompson argued that "all the candidates for election on any ticket should be required to let the people know in advance . . . for whom they will vote in the Electoral College." He then called a special session to pass legislation permitting the names of all candidates of all parties to appear on the November ballot but that would also bar unpledged electors. Then, if Talmadge-chosen electors did not pledge their support for Truman, anti-Talmadge forces would, by petition, place a pro-Truman slate of electors on the ballot. *Macon Telegraph*, Sep. 16, 1948; *AC*, Sep. 30, 1948.

166. Boyd, *Georgia Democrats*, 72; Bartley, *From Thurmond to Wallace*, table 2–9, 32.

167. Peters declined to comment on the national ticket, and the silence of Talmadge and Peters aided Truman workers in rural counties. *NYT*, Oct. 22, 1948; Frederickson, *The Dixiecrat Revolt*, 166–67. Unsurprisingly, Talmadge dominated the vote in these counties. Bernd, "Georgia: Static and Dynamic," 318; Heard, *A Two-Party South?* 26.

168. The election would fill a standard, four-year gubernatorial term (1951–55). Thompson accused Roy Harris of stealing fifty counties from him, while Harris thought "it wasn't more than thirty-five." M. E. Thompson interview with Gene-Gabriel Moore, in Harold P. Henderson and Gary L. Roberts, eds., *Georgia Governors in an Age of Change from Ellis Arnall to George Busbee* (Athens: University of Georgia Press, 1988), 72.

169. Meanwhile, in January 1949, Russell introduced legislation to subsidize the outmigration of southern blacks, since, he claimed, pro-civil rights whites outside the South should be delighted to assist blacks themselves in their home states. Again,

party leaders' correspondence is remarkable for its failure to mention the names of Russell or Senator Walter George. Fite, *Richard B. Russell, Jr.*, 245–50; Vol. 1 (1950), Box 4, SDEC Papers, RBRL.

170. Few thought that Russell could win the presidential nomination, but he gradually developed such a hope. Others believed that Russell's candidacy would result in a more acceptable national ticket and party platform. Fite, *Richard B. Russell, Jr.*, 273–79. *NYT*, Feb. 4, 1952.

171. Sean J. Savage, "To Purge or Not to Purge: Hamlet Harry and the Dixiecrats, 1948–1952," *Presidential Studies Quarterly* 27 (1997), 780–85; *NYT*, Aug. 25, 1949. As Truman remarked, "The Democratic party is a national party, and not a sectional party any more. The tail no longer wags the dog." Harry S. Truman, "Remarks at a Dinner Honoring William Boyle," Aug. 24, 1949. *TAPP*, accessed online: http://www.presidency.ucsb.edu/ws/?pid=13283. In 1948 the Democrats retook the U.S. House, and more than sixty new non-southern Democratic members took office, many of them unlikely to support enclave prerogatives. Savage, *Truman and the Democratic Party*, 149–51; Donald R. McCoy and Richard T. Ruetten, *Quest and Response: Minority Rights and the Truman Administration* (Lawrence: University Press of Kansas, 1973), 184. Savage uses a thirteen-state "South" (the eleven plus Oklahoma and Kentucky).

172. Stymied by southern Democrats, Republicans, and many non-southern Democrats—as well as congressional leaders such as House Speaker Sam Rayburn (D-TX)—Truman failed to secure his top legislative objectives, from national health insurance to race reforms to federal aid for elementary and secondary school education to the repeal of Taft-Hartley. The House did pass legislation providing for a permanent FEPC and abolishing the poll tax, but both died in the Senate with the help of the filibuster. The one major piece of domestic policy legislation Truman won was the 1949 Housing Act, which southern Democrats defanged. Alexander von Hoffman, "A Study in Contradictions: The Origins and Legacy of the Housing Act of 1949," *Housing Policy Debate* 11 (2000), 299–326. William C. Berman, *The Politics of Civil Rights in the Truman Administration* (Columbus: Ohio State University Press, 1970), 137–81.

173. Thomas J. Sugrue, "All Politics Is Local: The Persistence of Localism in Twentieth-Century America," in Meg Jacobs, William J. Novak, and Julian E. Zelizer, eds., *The Democratic Experiment: New Directions in American Political History* (Princeton: Princeton University Press, 2003), 311.

174. My analysis here is indebted to an excellent essay by Allan P. Sindler, "The Unsolid South" (quotation at 247).

175. After Thurmond's exit from the DNC, the newly appointed member from South Carolina, Senator Burnet Maybank, disputed the party's authority to remove members. Taking a "states' rights" view of the organization of the Democratic party, Maybank argued that DNC members could be expelled only by the states that appointed them. Savage, "To Purge or Not to Purge," 783–85; *NYT*, Aug. 25, 1949.

176. Sindler, "The Unsolid South," 265; Parmet, *The Democrats*, 100–101.

177. Sindler, "The Unsolid South," 247; Savage, *Truman and the Democratic Party*, 194–96; "Democratic Party Platform of 1952," Jul. 21, 1952, *TAPP*, accessed online: http://www.presidency.ucsb.edu/ws/?pid=29600.

PROLOGUE TO PART THREE:
Brown, Massive Resistance, and Campus Crises, 1950–63

1. Epigraphs in this prologue are from Woodward, *Strange Career*, 159; Broadus Mitchell, "Preface," in Howard H. Quint, *Profile in Black and White: A Frank Portrait of South Carolina* (Washington, D.C.: Public Affairs Press, 1958), iii–iv; and Harold C. Fleming, "Resistance Movements and Racial Desegregation," *Annals of the American Academy of Political and Social Science* 304 (1956), 52.

2. The ruling sprang from black protest nationwide and would have national implications. In 1954 seventeen states required segregated schools, and four others (and the District of Columbia) permitted districts to segregate them. Almost 39 percent of America's primary and secondary students attended schools in segregated districts. James T. Patterson, *"Brown v. Board of Education": A Civil Rights Milestone and Its Troubled Legacy* (New York: Oxford University Press, 2002), xvi.

3. *Brown v. Board of Education of Topeka, Kansas*, 347 U.S. 483 (1954). Robert B. McKay, "Segregation and Public Recreation," *Virginia Law Review* 40 (1954), 697–731.

4. Southern Education Reporting Service, *Statistical Summary of School Segregation-Desegregation in the Southern and Border States* (Nashville, May 1961), 3.

5. It has been commonplace since the 1970s for white southern politicians to dismiss their speech acts during the ancien régime as mere cheap talk, pandering, and so on. Scholars often agree with them. Whatever these politicians' true preferences or the constraints upon them, their words often had huge consequences, whether as signals to democratizers at home and abroad about their prospects for success, as setting parameters of policy debate, or in shaping citizens' expectations about their regime's goals and longevity. Elite position-taking should be taken seriously as often highly important behavior, whatever the retrospective self-justifications now on offer.

6. Alternative approaches emphasize elite preferences and quality of leadership. See, for example, Sproat, "Firm Flexibility," 166; Synnott, "Federalism Vindicated."

7. Bartley, *Rise of Massive Resistance*, 223.

8. Had the South been more industrialized by the early 1940s, and featured better skilled workers, it would have benefited much more from surges in defense spending. Schulman, *From Cotton Belt to Sunbelt*, 92–93, 112–16, 133, 140–42; David L. Carlton, "The American South and the U.S. Defense Economy: A Historical Review," in David L. Carlton and Peter A. Coclanis, *The South, the Nation, and the World: Perspectives on Southern Economic Development* (Charlottesville: University of Virginia Press, 2003), 151–62; Fred Bateman and Jason E. Taylor, "The New Deal at War: Alphabet Agencies' Expenditure Patterns, 1940–1945," *Explorations in Economic History* 40 (2003), 251–77; Fred Bateman, Jaime Ros, and Jason E. Taylor, "Did New Deal and World War II Public Capital Investments Facilitate a 'Big Push' in the American South?" *Journal of Institutional and Theoretical Economics* 165 (2009), 307–41.

9. Bateman et al., "Did New Deal and World War II Public Capital Investments Facilitate a 'Big Push' in the American South?" 317, 334.

10. Cobb, *Selling of the South*, 102; F. Ray Marshall, *Labor in the South* (Cambridge: Harvard University Press, 1967), 102, 115, 330. In 1958 North Carolina authorities and

firm owners broke the back of textile organizing with the help of the state police, National Guard, and pliant state judges. Wood, *Southern Capitalism*, 160–61.

11. But this figure does exaggerate the pace of change somewhat, since some of this increase is due to the Census Bureau's redefinition of "rural" and "urban" before 1960. Boyd, *Georgia Democrats*, 28 and 264, fn. 15.

12. Carlton, "The American South and the U.S. Defense Economy," 154.

13. At the end of the 1957, the number of active duty military personnel and civilian employees numbered about 108,000 in Georgia, 69,000 in South Carolina, and 24,000 in Mississippi. "Number of DOD Military and Civilian Personnel Stationed Within the Continental United States, and Annual Payrolls, by State of Duty Location," Department of Defense (May 8, 1958), Folder 3, Box 30, Subseries A.2, Series 6, Russell Papers, RBRL.

14. Jack Temple Kirby, *Rural Worlds Lost: The American South, 1920–1960* (Baton Rouge: Louisiana State University Press, 1986), 276; Sampson, p. 63.

15. Craig Heinicke and Wayne A. Grove, "Better Opportunities or Worse? The Demise of Cotton Harvest Labor, 1949–1964," *JEH* 63 (2003), 736–67; Heinicke and Grove, "Labor Markets, Regional Diversity, and Cotton Harvest Mechanization in the Post–World War II United States," *Social Science History* 29 (2005), 269–97; Heinicke and Grove, "'Machinery Has Completely Taken Over'": The Diffusion of the Mechanical Cotton Picker, 1949–1964," *Journal of Interdisciplinary History* 39 (2008), 65–96; Wright, *Sharing the Prize*, 69–70.

16. James Street, *The New Revolution in the Cotton Economy: Mechanization and Its Consequences* (Chapel Hill: University of North Carolina Press, 1957), 133; Bureau of the Census, *Historical Statistics of the United States, Colonial Times to 1970*, Bicentennial ed., Part 1 (Washington, D.C.: Government Printing Office, 1975), Series K, 109–53 (data are for 1954). In 1954 there remained about 160,000 black sharecroppers in the South, compared to about 300,000 in 1940. The number of white sharecroppers had fallen by 56 percent since 1940 (from about one-quarter million to about 100,000). Alston and Ferrie, *Southern Paternalism and the American Welfare State*, 2, 11.

17. Lassiter, *The Silent Majority*, 24.

18. In areas such as transportation, courts first struck down policy arrangements for failing to meet the "equal" requirement of the *Plessy* doctrine, and then invalidated the entire doctrine.

19. White supremacists linked token desegregation to "mongrelization." Mississippi state circuit judge Tom P. Brady powerfully articulated these fears, and their political implications, in *Black Monday* (Brookhaven, Miss.: n.p., 1954), the bible of the White Citizens' Council (WCC) movement.

20. Robert A. Margo, *Race and Schooling in the South, 1880–1950: An Economic History* (Chicago: University of Chicago Press, 1990); Wright, *Sharing the Prize*, chaps. 1 and 5.

21. This share increased from 1 percent in 1930 to 86 percent by 1936. State and local governments could not afford to pay their employees, including teachers. In rural Alabama, 81 percent of children faced shuttered schools. Georgia closed more than one thousand, affecting more than 170,000 students. Generally, "The great loser of the 1930s was local government." Teaford, *Rise of the States*, 125 (quotation at 121); Smith, *FDR*, 289; Patterson, *The New Deal and the States*, 195.

22. Woodward, *Strange Career*, 140. In *Missouri ex rel. Gaines v. Canada*, 305 U.S. 337 (1938), the Court required Missouri to provide blacks with a law school of equal quality or begin admitting black students to the state's law school, thus invalidating the practice of subsidizing black students' attendance of out-of-state schools. The decision's narrow scope, state intransigence, and legal difficulties blunted its impact. Patterson, *Brown v. Board*, chap. 1. On *Gaines* and the NAACP's litigation strategy generally, see Tushnet, *The NAACP's Legal Strategy against Segregated Education, 1925–1950*.

23. Tighter postwar labor markets also increased salaries. Margo, *Race and Schooling in the South*, 65.

24. *Sweatt v. Painter*, 339 U.S. 629 (1950). Southern attorneys general filed amicus briefs defending "separate but equal," but were countered by the U.S. Attorney General and many law professors associated with the NAACP. Patterson, *Brown v. Board*, 5. The Court decided similarly regarding the University of Oklahoma law school in *McLaurin v. Board of Regents*, 339 U.S. 637 (1950).

25. Bartley, *Rise of Massive Resistance*, 39, 37. After 1950, Walter F. Murphy writes, court-watchers agreed that, "given the climate of judicial—as well as national—opinion, the 'separate but equal' formula was doomed." Murphy, *Congress and the Court* (Chicago: University of Chicago Press, 1962), 80.

26. Woodward, *Strange Career*, 145.

27. Most light industries were situated in and around small towns in the rural South, not in cities. Cobb, "Beyond Planters and Industrialists," 45–68.

28. By 1953, blacks enrolled in two dozen formerly segregated universities at the graduate level and ten as undergraduates "on a token basis." Woodward, *Strange Career*, 143, 145.

29. The solicitor general's office and many Department of Justice officials supported the petitioners and filed an amicus brief on the behalf of the NAACP, whose counsel argued that *Sweatt* and *McLaurin* required the invalidation of "separate but equal." Many southern Eisenhower supporters were furious. Eisenhower confided to South Carolina's Governor James Byrnes that race relations would improve only community by community; imposing federal authority would damage the federal-state balance in police powers. But he also doubted the long-term viability of "separate but equal" given its "extraordinary expenditures." Attorney General Herbert Brownell sought to persuade Byrnes that "under our doctrine [desegregation] would take a period of years, and he wouldn't have to 'declare war,' so to speak." Five months before the ruling, Eisenhower hoped that the Court would remain consistent with "past decisions." Michael S. Mayer, "With Much Deliberation and Some Speed," *JSH* 52 (1986), 46–50, 56, 59; Jim Newton, *Eisenhower: The White House Years* (New York: Doubleday, 2011), 174, 116–17; Dwight D. Eisenhower, *The Eisenhower Diaries*, ed. by Robert H. Ferrell (New York: W. W. Norton, 1981), 246; Robert F. Burk, *The Eisenhower Administration and Black Civil Rights* (Knoxville: University of Tennessee Press, 1984), 93–98; Sampson, p. 244. Many of Eisenhower's actions belied his stated ambivalence about the use of the state to secure racial equality. He appointed Brownell attorney general, despite knowing the latter's position as an advocate for race reforms. And he appointed to the Federal Fifth District (seated in New Orleans and charged with overseeing the most of the Deep South) several strong protectors

of civil rights. Finally, he enforced Truman's (until-then unimplemented) order to desegregate the U.S. military, and desegregated elements of the District of Columbia. The Fifth Circuit judges are profiled in Jack Bass, *Unlikely Heroes* (Tuscaloosa: University of Alabama Press, 1990).

30. Scholars have recently debated whether and how U.S. foreign policy objectives affected judges' thinking or that of the Eisenhower administration. See Dudziak, *Cold War Civil Rights*; Thomas Borstelmann, *The Cold War and the Color Line: American Race Relations in the Global Arena* (Cambridge: Harvard University Press, 2001); Layton, *International Politics and Civil Rights Policies in the United States, 1941–1960*; Desmond King, *The Liberty of Strangers: Making the American Nation* (New York: Oxford University Press, 2005), chap. 7.

31. Patterson, *Brown v. Board*, chaps. 1–2. The Court asked other attorneys general to do so. Alabama, Georgia, Louisiana, and Mississippi refused, claiming the ruling did not cover their state or that it was illegitimate.

32. Woodward, *Strange Career*, 149–50. Eisenhower thought *Brown* impeded racial progress and that "it is just plain nuts" to think that "you can do these things by force." Mayer, "With Much Deliberation," 60–61.

33. Elizabeth Jacoway, "*Brown* and the Road to Reunion," *JSH* 70 (2004), 305.

34. After Justice Jackson died, Eisenhower nominated John Harlan, the grandson of *Plessy*'s dissenter; southern senators delayed his confirmation. Mayer, "With Much Deliberation," 62–63.

35. Kluger, *Simple Justice*, 651, 675; Mayer, "With Much Deliberation," 63–66, 69. The federal government asked for a "flexible" remedy. Bartley, *Rise of Massive Resistance*, 59.

36. Acceptable reasons included "problems related to administration, arising from the physical condition of the school plant, the school transportation system, personnel, revision of school districts and attendance areas into compact units to achieve a system of determining admission to the public schools on a nonracial basis, and revision of local laws and regulations which may be necessary." *Brown v. Board of Education*, 349 U.S. 294 (1955), at 300–301; Philip Elman, "The Solicitor General's Office, Justice Frankfurter, and Civil Rights Litigation, 1946–1960: An Oral History," *Harvard Law Review* 100 (1987), 817–52.

37. Klarman, *From Jim Crow to Civil Rights*, chap. 6.

38. *Briggs v. Elliott*, 132 F. Supp. 776, 777 (1955). The case outlined an implementation order for school officials in lowcountry Clarendon County. Patterson, *Brown v. Board*, 85, 91; *Southern School News* (Aug. 1955), 6 (hereafter *SSN*); Woodward, *Strange Career*, 153. The behavior of many of these judges betrayed such confidence. Jack W. Peltason, *Fifty-eight Lonely Men: Southern Federal Judges and School Desegregation* (Urbana: University of Illinois Press, 1961).

39. Klarman, *From Jim Crow to Civil Rights*, 314; J. Harvie Wilkinson III, *From "Brown" to "Bakke": The Supreme Court and School Integration, 1954–1978* (New York: Oxford University Press, 1978), chap. 4.

40. Robert Carter and Thurgood Marshall, "The Meaning and Significance of the Supreme Court Decree," *Journal of Negro Education* 24 (1955), 397–404 (hereafter *JNE*); *SSN*, Jun. 8, 1955, p. 5.

41. Jo Ann Gibson Robinson, *The Montgomery Bus Boycott and the Women Who Started It: The Memoir of Jo Ann Gibson Robinson* (Knoxville: University of Tennes-

see Press, 1987); Morris, *Origins of the Civil Rights Movement*, chap. 3. The U.S. Supreme Court in December 1956 unanimously invalidated the city's bus segregation ordinance in *Gayle v. Browder* (352 U.S. 903). For evidence that *Brown* helped inspire the bus boycott, see David J. Garrow, "Hopelessly Hollow History: Revisionist Devaluing of *Brown v. Board* of Education," *Virginia Law Review* 80 (1994), 151–60. J. Mills Thornton discusses the boycotters' sensible reasons not to attack segregation head-on from the beginning in "Challenge and Response in the Montgomery Bus Boycott of 1955–1956," *Alabama Review* 33 (1980), 163–235.

42. *SSN*, Mar. 1956; Woodward, *Strange Career*, 154. This bus boycott came 113 years after agitation in Boston to secure a state ordinance banning segregated railway cars. The ordinance did not pass, but railway firms acquiesced. Kousser, "What Light Does the Civil Rights Act of 1875 Shed on the Civil Rights Act of 1964?" 35.

43. Joseph J. Thorndike, "The Sometimes Sordid Level of Race and Segregation," in Matthew D. Lassiter and Andrew B. Lewis, eds., *The Moderates' Dilemma: Massive Resistance to School Desegregation in Virginia* (Charlottesville: University of Virginia Press, 1998), 51–71.

44. Bartley, *The New South*, 188 (emphasis added).

45. Recently scholars have debated whether *Brown* may have delayed race reforms by inducing a white supremacist backlash that disrupted gradual change under way in the early 1950s. The evidence of ongoing reforms in the pre-*Brown* era is not persuasive, while the evidence of repression throughout the 1940s and early 1950s is impressive. For the "backlash" thesis, see Michael J. Klarman, "How *Brown* Changed Race Relations: The Backlash Thesis," *JAH* 81 (1994), 81–118. For helpful critiques, see Tony Badger, "*Brown* and Backlash," in Clive Webb, ed., *Massive Resistance: Southern Opposition to the Second Reconstruction* (New York: Oxford University Press, 2005), 39–55; also see Daniel T. Kryder and Robert Mickey, "The Politics of Backlash: Consequences of a Metaphor," unpublished paper in author's possession. On the red-baiting of moderate southern candidates in 1950, see Savage, *Truman and the Democratic Party*, 171–75.

46. The "Declaration of Constitutional Principles" featured the names of nineteen of twenty-two southern senators and 77 of 105 southern House members. Bartley, *Rise of Massive Resistance*, 116–17. At this time, Sen. James Eastland (D-MS) told Mississippi whites, "You are not required to obey any court which passes out such a ruling—you are obligated to defy it." Klarman, *From Jim Crow to Civil Rights*, 413.

47. The "Declaration of Constitutional Principles" included the names of nineteen of twenty-two southern senators and seventy-seven of 105 southern House members. Tony Badger, "Southerners Who Refused to Sign the Southern Manifesto," *Historical Journal* 42 (1999), 517–34 (quotations at 517).

48. U.S. Senator Harry Byrd (D-VA), the state's longtime party leader, was exceptional as a southern federal officeholder who directed his state's massive resistance. By 1956 even he had grown detached from state-level policymaking. Matthew D. Lassiter and Andrew B. Lewis, "Massive Resistance Revisited: Virginia's White Moderates and the Byrd Organization," in Lassiter and Lewis, *The Moderates' Dilemma*, 11.

49. Neil R. McMillen, *The Citizens' Council: Organized Resistance to the Second Reconstruction, 1954–1964* (Urbana: University of Illinois Press, 1971), chap. 2. Quotation is in Payne, *I've Got the Light of Freedom*, 34–35.

50. Besides the all-male White Citizens' Councils (WCCs), they formed about fifty other such organizations. Southern Regional Council, *Special Report: Pro-Segregation Groups in the South* (Atlanta: Southern Regional Council, 1956); Bartley, *Rise of Massive Resistance*, 83. Sparked by the Montgomery boycott and the University of Alabama crisis, WCCs peaked in the summer of 1956 at about one-quarter million. The Klan suffered from attacks as a "subversive" organization by the federal government and state attorneys general. Fleming, "Resistance Movements," 45.

51. White politicians and media of all persuasions complained that "the North" refused to report the "southern" perspective. Some states financed speakers' bureaus and hosted northern journalists.

52. James N. Wallace, "Whites Boycott Whites Thought to Support Integration of Schools," *Wall Street Journal*, Mar. 9, 1956, pp. 1, 9 (hereafter *WSJ*).

53. *WP*, Jul. 10, 1949.

54. Quoted in David Cunningham, *There's Something Happening Here: The New Left, the Klan, and FBI Counterintelligence* (Berkeley: University of California Press, 2004), 123. Eisenhower criticized their tactics (characterizing them in part as "unwarranted economic pressures") in the written version of his 1956 State of the Union address. Dwight D. Eisenhower, "Annual Message to the Congress on the State of the Union," Jan. 5, 1956, *TAPP*, accessed online: http://www.presidency.ucsb.edu/ws/?pid=10593. In 1962, ten of the FBI's 6,030 special agents were black. Allan Lichtman, "The Federal Assault Against Voting Discrimination in the Deep South, 1957–1967," *JNH* 54 (1969), 349. A spate of bombings in southern cities during the late 1950s worried and embarrassed many southern whites. More than twenty cities shared intelligence in a "Southern Conference on Bombing" to fight the trend. Some tensions emerged between law enforcement personnel and elected officials, as the former were often quick to request federal assistance unwanted by the latter. Belknap, *Federal Law and Southern Order*, 54–55 and 57; *CNC*, Jan. 24, 1959.

55. As Woodward (*Strange Career*, 165–66) described the moment, "All over the South, the lights of reason and tolerance and moderation began to go out under the resistance demand for conformity.... During 1957, 1958 and 1959, a fever of rebellion and malaise of fear spread over the region.... Words began to shift their significance and lose their common meaning. A 'moderate' became a man who dared open his mouth, an 'extremist' one who favored eventual compliance with the law, and 'compliance' took on the connotations of treason." McMillen, *The Citizens' Council*, 337.

56. "The absence of a genuine liberal alternative on the race issue was a signal void in southern politics." Bartley, *Rise of Massive Resistance*, 25.

57. Przeworski, *Democracy and the Market*, 54.

58. Lassiter and Lewis, "Massive Resistance Revisited," 9, 1. "In a few cases, white[s] believed to hold unorthodox racial views have been 'advised' by ... neighbors to move; and a small but growing number of white ministers have lost their pulpits." Fleming, "Resistance Movements," 49. Just before *Brown*, the Atlanta-based Southern Regional Council, riven by a dispute among its white members over whether to oppose Jim Crow and suffrage restriction head-on, sided with its liberal members and announced that enclave rule was itself immoral and dedicated itself to Jim Crow's death. "Toward the South of the Future: A Statement of Policy and Aims of the Southern Regional Council," *New South* 6 (1951), 1–2.

59. Gene Roberts and Hank Klibanoff, *The Race Beat: The Press, the Civil Rights Struggle, and the Awakening of a Nation* (New York: Knopf, 2006), 212.

60. For instance, the office of Alabama's attorney general gathered the names and addresses of all of the state's NAACP members in an effort to suppress the organization. Citing the Fourteenth Amendment's Due Process Clause, the U.S. Supreme Court barred this practice in *N.A.A.C.P. v. Patterson*, 357 U.S. 449 (1958). Of course, for much of the 1950s the South was not greatly out of step with the United States in launching these attacks, as a review of the executive branch's Domestic Security program, the activities of the House Un-American Affairs Committee, the criminal sanctions for the Communist Party, and the Supreme Court's approval of most of these initiatives makes clear. Powe, *The Warren Court*, 15–16.

61. Regionwide efforts produced the biggest gains, especially those directed by unsung NAACP officials Kelly Alexander, John M. Brooks, and W. C. Patton. Berg, *"The Ticket to Freedom,"* 143, 153–57, 163, 189.

62. Bartley, *The Rise of Massive Resistance*, 212–24; Almicar Shabazz, *Advancing Democracy: African Americans and the Struggle for Access and Equity in Higher Education in Texas* (Chapel Hill: University of North Carolina Press, 2004), chap. 5; Morris, *Origins of the Civil Rights Movement*, 33; Valelly, *The Two Reconstructions*, 178–81.

63. Conversely, black school desegregation efforts were much bolder in the Outer South. There, the national NAACP devoted most of its resources, with Virginia leading the way. Lassiter and Lewis, *The Moderates' Dilemma*, 5.

64. Federal Bureau of Investigation, *The Communist Party and the Negro, 1953–1956* (Washington, D.C., 1956), Document Number CK3100376980, Declassified Documents Reference System; Jeff Woods, *Black Struggle, Red Scare: Segregation and Anti-Communism in the South, 1948–1968* (Baton Rouge: Louisiana State University Press, 2004); Sarah Hart Brown, "Congressional Anti-Communism and the Segregationist South: From New Orleans to Atlanta, 1954–1958," *GHQ* 80 (1996), 745–816, and "Communism, Anti-Communism, and Massive Resistance: The Civil Rights Congress in Southern Perspective," in Glenn Feldman, ed., *Before "Brown": Civil Rights and White Backlash in the Modern South* (Tuscaloosa: University of Alabama Press, 2004), 170–97. On anticommunism in the Outer South, see George Lewis, *The White South and the Red Menace: Segregationists, Anticommunism, and Massive Resistance, 1945–1965* (Gainesville: University of Florida Press, 2004). Southern authorities' fears about communist infiltration had a long pedigree. For discussions of the NAACP's own anticommunism, see Manfred Berg, "Black Civil Rights and Liberal Anticommunism in the Early Cold War," *JAH* 94 (2007), 75–96; Eric Arnesen, "Civil Rights and the Cold War at Home: Postwar Activism, Anticommunism, and the Decline of the Left," *American Communist History* 11 (2012), 5–44.

65. Valelly, *The Two Reconstructions*, 178–81; Klarman, *From Jim Crow to Civil Rights*, chap. 7.

66. These and other estimates are cited in Valelly, *The Two Reconstructions*, 296, fn. 67.

67. Berg, *"The Ticket to Freedom,"* 162–63.

68. In 1956, pollsters found that about four-fifths of southern whites disapproved of desegregation; some 90 percent did so in the Deep South. Bartley, *Rise of Massive Resistance*, 276–77; David L. Chappell, "The Divided Mind of Southern

Segregationists," *GHQ* 82 (1998), 45–72. By the mid-1950s, southern Baptists and southern Presbyterians backed desegregation by majority votes of their delegates at regional meetings. Chappell, *A Stone of Hope*, 5. On the Baptists' resolution, "which squared *Brown v. Board of Education* with the scriptural teaching," see Mark Newman, *Getting Right with God: Southern Baptists and Desegregation, 1945–1995* (Tuscaloosa: University of Alabama Press, 2001), chap. 2 (quotation at 24) and chaps. 4–9. Newman documents substantial variation in Baptist ministers' treatment of segregation.

69. Florida, North Carolina, Tennessee, and Texas took this path. Lassiter, *The Silent Majority*, 29–30. There were important exceptions. As noted earlier, much of the intellectual and political leadership for massive resistance originated in Virginia, where politicians triggered school-closing laws and local authorities kept schools in Prince Edward County closed for several years. Even after federal courts struck down such laws, hardliners called for continued massive resistance. Lassiter and Lewis, "Massive Resistance Revisited," 2–3; Amy E. Murrell, "The 'Impossible' Prince Edward Case," in Lassiter and Lewis, *The Moderates' Dilemma*, 134–67.

70. Donald R. Green and Warren E. Gauerke, *If the Schools Are Closed . . . A Critical Analysis of the Private School Plan* (Atlanta: Southern Regional Council, 1959).

71. Politicians advocating "moderation" often argued that such defiance would invite additional unwanted federal supervision. One opponent to moderates, U.S. Representative John Bell Williams (D-MS), viewed moderation as akin to "a little bit of pregnancy." Bartley, *Rise of Massive Resistance*, 247.

72. Lassiter and Lewis, "Massive Resistance Revisited," 9 and 1. For much of the 1950s, most officeholders sincerely believed that almost all blacks—including black teachers and administrators—favored continued segregation. A review of private correspondence of white politicians and other evidence presented in chapters 6–8 supports this inference.

73. *SSN*, Jan. 6, 1955, p. 14.

74. Lassiter and Crespino, "Introduction," in Lassiter and Crespino, *The Myth of Southern Exceptionalism*, 3. Also see Hirsch, *Making the Second Ghetto*, and Sugrue, *Sweet Land of Liberty*.

75. Its primary agency, the FBI, traditionally handled investigations, not enforcement, of federal judicial rulings. Other armed federal agents, ranging from the Border Patrol to the U.S. Marshals service to officers of the Internal Revenue Service (IRS), were not trained or equipped to manage crowd disturbances. Clayton D. Laurie and Ronald H. Cole, *The Role of Federal Military Forces in Domestic Disorders, 1877–1945* (Washington, D.C.: Center of Military History, U.S. Army, 1997).

76. Elizabeth Jacoway, "Taken by Surprise: Little Rock Business Leaders and Desegregation," in Jacoway and David R. Colburn, eds., *Southern Businessmen and Desegregation* (Baton Rouge: Louisiana State University Press, 1982), 15–41. Roy Reed, *Faubus* (Fayetteville: University of Arkansas Press, 1997). Richard E. Neustadt, *Presidential Power and the Modern Presidents: The Politics of Leadership from Roosevelt to Reagan* (New York: Free Press, 1990), 20, 25–26.

77. In a ruling signed by all nine justices, the Court held that *Brown* "can neither be nullified openly and directly by state legislators or state executive or judicial officers nor nullified indirectly by them through evasive schemes for segregation." *Cooper v. Aaron* (358 U.S. 1, 1958).

78. Woodward, *Strange Career*, 17; Cobb, *Selling of the South*, 126. Little Rock averaged five new major plants per year from 1950 to 1957, but landed none from 1958 through 1961. James C. Cobb, *Industrialization and Southern Society, 1877–1984* (Lexington: University Press of Kentucky, 1984), 110–11. However, as Gavin Wright points out, many Little Rock "moderates" who owned and operated downtown retail outlets and favored open schools met sit-in protests in 1960 and 1961 with their own massive resistance. Wright, *Sharing the Prize*, 158.

79. Clotfelter, *After "Brown,"* 24.

80. Compare Thornton, *Dividing Lines*, 126, and Bartley, *The New South*, 220.

81. Roberts and Klibanoff, *The Race Beat*, 143–83.

82. Earl Black and Merle Black, *The Vital South: How Presidents Are Elected* (Cambridge: Harvard University Press, 1992), 176–89.

83. This discussion draws heavily on Galvin, *Presidential Party Building*, 50–65.

84. Contested races for U.S. House seats increased from 34 to 42 from 1952 to 1956. *WP*, Sep. 8, 1958.

85. The national party put a different southerner on the ticket, Sen. Estes Kefauver (D-TN). Parmet, *The Democrats*, 125, 133–34; Dunn, *Roosevelt's Purge*, 254.

86. Gibson, *Boundary Control*, 6, 25, 31–33. Also see John H. Kessel, *The Goldwater Coalition: Republican Strategies in 1964* (Indianapolis: Bobbs-Merrill, 1968), 39–40. Black vote estimate appears in Francis M. Wilhoit, *The Politics of Massive Resistance* (New York: George Braziller, 1973), 53. On Florida, *WSJ*, Oct. 1, 1958.

87. Southern Republicans and other anti-Democrats had been angered a few years earlier because *Brown* occurred on Eisenhower's watch. Making matters worse, it was championed by his nominee for Chief Justice, and featured an amicus brief siding with the NAACP penned by the president's own attorney general, Herbert Brownell.

88. Galvin, *Presidential Party Building*, 64–65; *WP*, Oct. 17, 1957, and Sep. 8, 1958; *WSJ*, Oct. 1, 1958; Parmet, *The Democrats*, 182; Louis M. Seagull, *Southern Republicanism* (New York: John Wiley and Sons, 1975), chaps. 1 and 7.

89. Many white southerners were unaware of these sudden changes, since campus administrators followed a "rule [of] little or no publicity." Guy B. Johnson, "Racial Integration in Southern Higher Education," *Social Forces* 34 (1956), 309, 312.

90. Teaford, *Rise of the States*, 37.

91. Richard A. Easterlin, "Growth and Composition of the American Population in the Twentieth Century," in Michael R. Haines and Richard H. Steckel, eds., *A Population History of North America* (New York: Cambridge University Press, 2000), 645.

CHAPTER SIX:
Mississippi and the Battle of Oxford

1. On black education during the Jim Crow era, McMillen, *Dark Journey*, 72–108.

2. Clotfelter, *After Brown*, 16 (one-room school data are for the 1944–45 school year). Black communities often provided buildings where local authorities refused to do so. Teachers' salary figures are for 1948. Leander L. Boykin, "The Status and

Trends of Differentials Between White and Negro Teachers' Salaries in the Southern States, 1900–1946," *JNE* 18 (1949), 40–47; Michael Fultz, "Teacher Training and African American Education in the South, 1900–1940," *JNE* 64 (1995), 198–99. Deltan racial disparities were even worse; Sunflower County, home to Senator James Eastland and the birthplace of the White Citizens' Councils, spent $183 for each white student and $38 per black student. B. R. Brazeal, "Some Problems in the Desegregation of Higher Education in the 'Hard Core' States," *JNE* 27 (1958), 364.

3. A member, Alcee Johnson, was son of the chair of the Committee of One Hundred, which brought together black elites from each of the state's eighty-two counties. Considered relatively accommodationist and cautious tactically, the committee after *Smith v. Allwright* was superseded by the NAACP and other organizations. The MATCS became the Mississippi Teachers Association in 1951 as part of this growing militancy. Workman, "Rejection of Accommodation," 70.

4. In fact, a council report stressed the importance of black human capital in shaping the region's fate. Robert Baker Highsaw, *The Delta Looks Forward: An Inventory of Natural and Human Resources* (Stoneville, Miss.: Delta Council, 1949). On expectations about the advent of mechanization, Cobb, *Most Southern Place*, chaps. 7–8.

5. See Crespino, *In Search of Another Country*, as well as Crespino, "Strategic Accommodation: Civil Rights Opponents in Mississippi and Their Impact on American Racial Politics, 1953–1972," Ph.D. diss., Stanford University (2003), p. 71.

6. This trend of improved state planning and administrative capacities held nationwide, involving both the professionalization of legislatures and state agencies. Teaford, *Rise of the States*, chap. 7.

7. The legislature did not endorse the concept of salary equalization. Governor Tom Bailey, closely linked to the legislature's Deltan leadership, also called on greater funding for black junior colleges and the state's two four-year black colleges. Workman, "Rejection of Accommodation," 30; E. S. Bishop, "A Program of Equalization," *Mississippi Educational Journal* 22 (Dec. 1945), 142–48.

8. The legislature admitted that monies earmarked for salary equalization never reached black teachers in many counties. Harry S. Ashmore, *The Negro and the Schools* (Chapel Hill: University of North Carolina Press, 1954); Workman, "Rejection of Accommodation," 51, 63; *JCL*, Feb. 24, 1950.

9. Wright later spoke to the MATCS annual convention but did not depart substantially from his radio address. Black leaders answered him with a detailed list of demands for improving black education. *Jackson Advocate*, May 15, 1948; Williams, "Mississippi and Civil Rights," 154; Workman, "Rejection of Accommodation," 58–60. Soon, black Southern Regional Council (SRC) member Ruby Lyles publicly criticized segregation but—following SRC policy—vowed that it could not yet be toppled. "Address by Governor Fielding L. Wright," *Mississippi Educational Journal* 25 (1949), 122–28.

10. Workman, "Rejection of Accommodation," 62. The *Jackson Daily News*'s rabidly white supremacist Fred Sullens called low levels of spending on black education "a public scandal." *New South* 4 (Oct. 1949).

11. *JCL*, Nov. 6, 1951; *Jackson Advocate*, Apr. 14, 1951; Workman, "Rejection of Accommodation." A 1953 boycott of gas stations that failed to provide washrooms for

blacks was successful. Aaron Henry with Constance Curry, *Aaron Henry: The Fire Ever Burning* (Jackson: University Press of Mississippi, 2000), 80.

12. Workman, "Rejection of Accommodation," 54, 72.

13. *NYT*, Jul. 29, 1951; Reid S. Derr, "The Triumph of Progressivism: Governor Paul B. Johnson, Jr., and Mississippi in the 1960s," Ph.D. diss., University of Southern Mississippi (1994), pp. 41–44; Johnston, *Mississippi's Defiant Years*, xv; Williams, "Mississippi and Civil Rights," 161; *NYT*, Jul. 29, 1951. During his second term, White continued to push his industrialization agenda. Oral history with William Joel Blass (Mar. 26, 1977), Civil Rights in Mississippi Digital Archive, McCain Library and Archives, University of Southern Mississippi, Hattiesburg (hereafter CRMDA).

14. Percy Greene agreed, and claimed that a majority of the Mound Bayou audience backed the governor's plan. J. D. Boyd, the MTA's conservative president, also promised the governor that most black teachers supported him. Workman, "Rejection of Accommodation," 73–74; *JCL*, Nov. 14, 1952, Nov. 6, 1953. Greene was an informant for Mississippi's State Sovereignty Commission. Julian Williams, "Percy Greene and the Mississippi Sovereignty Commission," *Journalism History* 28 (2002), 66–72.

15. The state NAACP conference criticized Boyd and other backers of voluntary segregation, but "most black leaders … maintained their silence." Workman, "Rejection of Accommodation," 74.

16. In his inaugural address, he called for a study committee to recommend new policies regarding black and white education. Yasuhiro Katagiri, *The Mississippi State Sovereignty Commission: Civil Rights and States' Rights* (Jackson: University Press of Mississippi, 2001), xxvi.

17. To White, racial educational disparities added "just that much more fuel to the fire"; the "most we can hope to salvage from a court decision would be a holding that we can separately educate the races provided [equalization]." "It may well be that our acknowledged failure in the past in this regard is the cause of our present emergency." *JDN*, Nov. 3, 1953; *JCL*, Nov. 4, 1953; Skates, "Southern Editor."

18. By 1952 the white-to-black ratio in teachers' pay had been reduced to 3.3. Katagiri, *Mississippi State Sovereignty Commission*, xxvii. As debate continued, a conference of black leaders in Jackson declared their support for desegregation, while NAACP leaders criticized those blacks backing the equalization legislation. *JDN*, Nov. 7, 1953.

19. The plan was estimated to cost eventually some $120 million, the brunt of which would be spent on the construction of new black schools. *NYT*, Dec. 14, 1953; Williams, "Mississippi and Civil Rights," 36. The new State Education Finance Commission would oversee the plan. During the next session, Sillers finally backed the introduction of new taxes to fund the equalization plan, but only appropriated school funds for one year. Since the state legislature held biennial sessions, this move guaranteed a special session after the expected Supreme Court ruling. *JCL*, Jan. 24, 1954; *NYT*, May 2, 1954.

20. The committee—first proposed by Sillers—had a membership of twenty-five (thirteen ex-officio) leading state politicians and judges, and later two full-time attorneys. Chaired by the governor, the vice chair was the House Speaker, whom all expected to be Sillers long into the future.

21. *SSN*, Feb. 3, 1955, p. 9. In Governor White's words, if the central state invalidated the state's use of its police powers, "the last vestige of sovereignty is gone." *SSN*, Apr. 7, 1955, p. 5.

22. Williams, "Mississippi and Civil Rights," 37.

23. Charles C. Bolton, "Mississippi's School Equalization Program, 1945–1954: 'A Last Gasp to Maintain a Segregated Educational System,'" *JSH* 66 (2000), 781–814. From 1954 to 1955, the ratio of black to white school spending rose from 48 to 73 percent. Workman, "The Deep South," 93.

24. In an editorial entitled "Blood on the Marble Steps," he called May 17 "a black day of tragedy for the South . . . [The ruling] is the worst thing that has happened to the South since the . . . Reconstruction days. It is even worse. It means racial strife of the bitterest sort. It can conceivably lead to bloodshed and loss of life . . . Mississippi cannot and will not try to abide by such a decision. Mississippi will never consent to placing white and Negro children in the same public schools. The white people and the thinking Negro people did not want that to happen." Johnston, *Mississippi's Defiant Years*, 3 (and Sullens quoted at xiv–xv); *JDN*, May 18, 1954; *Greenville Delta Democrat-Times*, May 18, 1954. Hodding Carter III, *The South Strikes Back* (Garden City, N.Y.: Doubleday, 1959), 25.

25. *Jackson Daily News* reporters wrote that the "consensus among the school men was that schools in Mississippi will be affected little, if any, by the Court decision—at least in [the] foreseeable future." Many school superintendents concurred. Johnston, *Mississippi's Defiant Years*, 21–22.

26. He later remarked, "I didn't ask that we resist [*Brown*]. In other words, it amounted to the equivalent of seeking compliance or pointing out the advantages of not wasting energy resisting compliance." Interview with Frank E. Smith, Center for Oral History and Cultural Heritage, McCain Library, University of Southern Mississippi, Aug. 27, 1993, p. 2. See Dennis J. Mitchell, *Mississippi Liberal: A Biography of Frank E. Smith* (Jackson: University Press of Mississippi, 2001).

27. Ten days after the ruling, Eastland launched an attack on the Senate floor: "Let me make this very clear. The South will retain segregation." *JDN*, May 18, 1954. His office distributed 135,000 copies of the speech. Interview with Frank E. Smith, 56; Johnston, *Mississippi's Defiant Years*, 16–20. From 1956 to 1977, Eastland chaired the Senate Subcommittee on Internal Security, the Senate's counterpart to the House Un-American Affairs Committee.

28. Two months before *Brown*, he believed that "there are many counties in Mississippi . . . in which the white people and the colored people could meet and work out a plan satisfactory for both . . . [which] would perhaps work for 15 or 20 or 25 years." Writing to Governor White, U. S. Senator John Stennis worried about the counterproductive nature of open defiance. In his view, "[Georgia Governor Herman] Talmadge is making a severe mistake in advertising his non-compliance." Crespino, *In Search of Another Country*, 18.

29. Among these was shutting down the public school system. Harvey McGehee, chief justice of the state Supreme Court, offered that the state should consider ways to secure black leaders' commitment to voluntary segregation. The *Jackson Daily News* reported that both McGehee and Governor White thought that "95 percent" of the state's blacks supported segregation. *JCL*, May 19–20, 1954; Workman, "Rejection of Accommodation," 76.

30. Dittmer, *Local People*, 41 and 44 (Dittmer's NAACP data differ from those in table 3.3, which I report here). *JDN*, May 29 and Sep. 26, 1954.

31. Walton, Puckett, and Deskins, *The African American Electorate: A Statistical History*, 2:505–6.

32. The legislature's few race liberals shared this expectation. Interview with William Joel Blass, Mar. 26, 1977, CRMDA. They convinced White to invite black leaders in order to legitimize the meeting and eventual policies, and assured him that 95 percent of participants would be supportive. Black newspaperman Percy Greene claimed the meeting portended regular elite dialogue. *JDN*, Jul. 18, 1954.

33. *JDN*, Jul. 11 and 18, 1954.

34. *JCL*, Jul. 8, 1954. William A. Bender, "Desegregation in the Public Schools in Mississippi," *JNE* 24 (1955), 287–92. Dittmer (*Local People*, 38–39) argues that NAACP officials leaned on these leaders beforehand.

35. Charles C. Bolton, *The Hardest Deal of All: The Battle over School Integration in Mississippi, 1870–1980* (Jackson: University Press of Mississippi, 2005), 63–67; Johnston, *Mississippi's Defiant Years*, 39. Crespino, "Strategic Accommodation," 45.

36. T.R.M. Howard, "The Mississippi Negro's Stand on Segregation in the Public Schools of Mississippi," speech given at Governor's Conference, Jul. 30, 1954; and "Statement Issued by Negro Leaders from Every Area of the State of Mississippi," "*The Jackson Declaration," Journal of Human Relations* 3 (1954), 104–10. On Howard, see David T. Beito and Linda Royster Beito, "T.R.M. Howard: Pragmatism over Strict Integrationist Ideology in the Mississippi Delta, 1942–1954," in Feldman, *Before "Brown,"* 68–95.

37. Erle Johnston, *Mississippi's Defiant Years*, 40; *JDN*, Jul. 31, 1954. Katagiri, *Mississippi State Sovereignty Commission*, xxxi; Carter III, *The South Strikes Back*, 36; Henry, *Aaron Henry*, 91.

38. *SSN*, Sep. 1954; the *Jackson Daily News* (Aug. 24 and 31, 1954) then praised the group. In November, the state NAACP conference reaffirmed its position on desegregation and declared that it did not rely on black educators. Erle Johnston, *Mississippi's Defiant Years*, 44, 4. Opening the special session, White angrily denounced the state's black leaders: "No hope can now be predicated upon the cooperation of these men. We can go forward ... with the clear conscience of knowing that we gave them the opportunity to cooperate ... and they spurned the offer. Upon them, not us, must rest full responsibility for rejection." Regarding *Brown*, White insisted that the state was "not to defy" the ruling, but rather would defend itself in the courts, just as the NAACP did in attacking "separate but equal." Workman, "Rejection of Accommodation," 80–81; *SSN*, Oct. 1954.

39. Former legislator William Joel Blass remarked that the caucus "decided things" the night before floor debate. Oral history with William Joel Blass, Mar. 26, 1977, CRMDA. The amendment stated that a two-thirds vote of both chambers could abolish the school system, and by a simple majority they could authorize counties and localities to do so. *SSN*, Oct. 1, 1954, p. 9. The governor threatened that, in the absence of its passage, he would not call an additional session required for the following year's appropriations.

40. *SSN*, Sep. 1954, Oct. 1954, Jan. 1955, Feb. 1955, Apr. 1955. Washington County had recently contributed $10 million to the equalization fund, and received back only $2 million. The state took other largely cosmetic steps to defend segregation.

It criminalized the conspiracy to boycott or "to overthrow or violate the segregation laws of this state through force, violence, threats, intimidation, or otherwise."
And Attorney General James P. Coleman appointed some eleven hundred white
attorneys as "Special Assistant Attorneys General" to help school districts fend off
desegregation suits. Johnston, *Mississippi's Defiant Years*, xiv, 24.

41. *SSN*, Nov. 1954, p. 11; future governor Paul B. Johnson, Jr., quoted in Derr,
"The Triumph of Progressivism," 48. These included continued constitutionally
mandated segregation; pupil assignment; gerrymandering school districts; the use
of police power to quell disorder brought about by integration; and possibly new
statutes. The brochure noted that passage would signal the state's resolve to blacks,
"alien organizations," and other states.

42. Significantly, a number of self-described "pragmatic" segregationists—such
as newspaperman and future Sovereignty Commission official Erle Johnston—
preferred an "honest approach to the Negro people" through "persuasion" to the
"big stick . . . being waved over the heads of Mississippi voters" in the referendum.
SSN, Dec. 1954, p. 8; Johnston, *Mississippi's Defiant Years*, 23.

43. Hills opponents of the amendment "criticized Delta leaders for using school
abolition as a way of avoiding the heavy costs of school equalization that would be
required if majority-black counties were forced to bring black schools on a par with
white schools." Moreover, the "Friends of Segregated Schools" accused Deltans of
placing their own economic interests over segregation. Johnston, *Mississippi's Defiant Years*, 22–24; *SSN*, Jan. 1955, p. 6; Carter III, *The South Strikes Back*, 46–53.

44. As with the previous effort, Eastland backed it strongly. Hodding Carter and
Fred Sullens, on the other hand, opposed it because it would disfranchise whites.
Carter further charged that its proponents sought to maintain planter rule. Wil-
liams, "Mississippi and Civil Rights," 164–65; *NYT*, Feb. 3, 1955.

45. Constitution of the State of Mississippi, Art. 12, sec. 241(a). Carter III, *The
South Strikes Back*, 36–48; McMillen, *The Citizens' Council*, 320–21; Payne, *I've Got the
Light of Freedom*, 35.

46. In Jefferson Davis County, reregistration reduced the number of registered
blacks from 1,221 to seventy. Dittmer, *Local People*, 71.

47. Williams, "Mississippi and Civil Rights," 169; Earl M. Lewis, "The Negro Voter
in Mississippi," *JNE* 26 (1957), 335; *NYT*, Oct. 3, 1955; Berg, *"The Ticket to Freedom,"* 156.

48. Teaford, *Rise of the States*; *SSN*, May 4, 1955, p. 8; *SSN*, Apr. 7, 1955, p. 5.

49. Oral history with William Joel Blass (Mar. 26, 1977), CRMDA.

50. The state did pass the region's first pupil placement law. Here, students could
be individually assigned to schools based on nominally nonracial criteria (such as
psychological, social, or public health considerations) in order for segregated schools
to pass constitutional muster with the Supreme Court. And it criminalized whites'
attendance at public schools in which "colored or Negro" students enrolled. Parents
and teachers, not students, would meet financial or jail penalties. Unlike Georgia,
Mississippi rejected a state Building Authority, which opponents in the Hills counties considered an unwise step toward deregulation. Like other states, Mississippi
also repealed its compulsory attendance laws to prepare for the doomsday option.
Dittmer, *Local People*, 59; *SSN*, May 4, 1955, p. 8.

51. Governor White called it "favorable to Mississippi and the South." Gubernatorial candidate James P. Coleman was "wholly unworried as to any possibility

of desegregation in Mississippi." Party chair Tom J. Tubb called it "a very definite victory. . . . [O]ur local judges know the local situation and it may be one hundred years before it's feasible. We have not reached the point where we are ready for racial integration. . . . We must raise and educate a whole new generation who can accept [integration]." The Delta Council, the partly state-funded pressure group, criticized the ruling and feared that it would lead to "unbearable friction between the races." *SSN*, Jun. 8, 1955, pp. 5, 15.

52. Former governor Wright and other candidates suggested using the state's police powers to defend segregation, while Coleman trumpeted his legal experience. *JCL*, Aug. 4, 1955; Johnston, *Mississippi's Defiant Years*, 29–33; Derr, "The Triumph of Progressivism," 54–59. White endorsed Coleman and worked behind the scenes for him.

53. Anders Walker, *The Ghost of Jim Crow: How Southern Moderates Used "Brown v. Board of Education" to Stall Civil Rights* (New York: Oxford University Press, 2009); Anders Walker, "The Violent Bear It Away: Emmett Till and the Modernization of Law Enforcement in Mississippi," *San Diego Law Review* 46 (2009), 468; Stephen J. Whitfield, *A Death in the Delta: The Story of Emmett Till* (Baltimore: Johns Hopkins University Press, 1991 [1988]).

54. These were Clarksdale, Vicksburg, Natchez, and Yazoo City; 140 signed in Vicksburg, and 42 in Jackson. Local papers published signers' names, after which several asked to have their names removed from the petitions. Brazeal, "Problems in Desegregation," 365.

55. In 1950, Sunflower County was about 68 percent black. Carter III, *The South Strikes Back*, 31; McMillen, *The Citizens' Council*, 18–19. By the summer of 1956, Councils had been founded in sixty-seven of the state's eighty-two counties. Members saw themselves as "the old time town meeting, called to meet any crisis by expressing the will of the people." David Halberstam, "The White Citizens' Councils: Respectable Means for Unrespectable Ends," *Commentary* 22 (1956), 300. About half of the original group in Indianola were farmers. Moye, *Let the People Decide*, 64–65.

56. *SSN*, May 4, 1955, p. 8; Crespino, *In Search of Another Country*, 25.

57. William J. Simmons, president of the Mississippi White Citizens' Council and a close adviser to Governor Ross Barnett, stated that the movement "is much more than a white supremacist group . . . I think it is fundamentally the first real stirrings of a conservative revolt in this country. . . . Some of the people who are attracted to this movement may not be concerned about the Negro." Many members later joined broader conservative movements and the Republican party. In *Black Monday*, state Circuit Judge Tom P. Brady called for "a cold war and an economic boycott" to avoid disorder and violence. Carter III, *The South Strikes Back*, 159–60, 29; Johnston, *Mississippi's Defiant Years*, xv.

58. The Hedermans were very close with Senator James Eastland, and helped him remain a dominant figure in state politics. McMillen, *The Citizens' Council*, 25; author's interview with Wilson F. "Bill" Minor, Aug. 2000. Future governor Paul Johnson joined secretly. Derr, "The Triumph of Progressivism," 50.

59. A state-level organization was created in December 1955. Later, the Councils organized units in each congressional district; representatives from each served on its executive committee, thus defusing criticism that it was Delta-dominated. Hodding Carter, "A Wave of Terror Threatens the South," *Look* (Mar. 22, 1955); *SSN*, Dec.

1955, page number illegible; McMillen, *The Citizens' Council*, 27, fn. 37, and 31; J. Michael Butler, "The Mississippi State Sovereignty Commission and Beach Integration, 1959–1963: A Cotton-Patch Gestapo?" *JSH* 68 (2002), 107–48; Carter III, *The South Strikes Back*, 199.

60. Later, its *Annual Report* claimed that "the idea of solid and unified backing of circuit clerks, sheriffs, and local and state officials in the proper discharge of sworn duties was worked out." The group helped shape parameters of legislative debate. Interview with William Joel Blass (Mar. 26, 1977), CRMDA; Neil R. McMillen, "Development of Civil Rights, 1956–1970," in McLemore, *A History of Mississippi*, 2:159; Carter III, *The South Strikes Back*, 32–33, 123–25, 132–34.

61. White Citizens' Councils openly discussed economic coercion. *SSN*, Sep. 1955, p. 5. David Halberstam called the strategy "an ideal solution" for a group viewing itself as law-abiding. "White Citizens' Councils," 300.

62. Crespino, *In Search of Another Country*, 29.

63. Luders, *The Civil Rights Movement and the Logic of Social Change*, 35; *WSJ*, Mar. 9, 1956; Johnston, *Mississippi's Defiant Years*, 46–47; Carter III, *The South Strikes Back*, 159–60.

64. Halberstam, "White Citizens' Councils," 300. Ten years later, this same motivation would mean calling on communities to comply with court enforcement of new statutes. In both periods, however, the stated rationale was to preserve social order. As chapter 10 demonstrates, white supremacists' efforts to repress black insurgency and maintain order increasingly became riskier.

65. He later wrote that "at none of the meetings was a plan described that would be effective in the fight to preserve segregation, other than massive membership." Johnston, *Mississippi's Defiant Years*, 15; Halberstam, "White Citizens' Councils," 299–301. Governor Coleman also claimed that the Councils successfully vented emotions that otherwise would have encouraged violence. Oral history with James P. Coleman (Nov. 12, 1981 and Feb. 6, 1982), CRMDA.

66. James W. Silver, *Mississippi: The Closed Society*, enlarged ed. (New York: Harcourt, Brace, 1966), 38.

67. McMillen, *The Citizens' Council*, 38, 337; Carter III, *The South Strikes Back*, 189–90; *JDN*, Apr. 25, 1958; Crespino, "Strategic Accommodation," 36–38; Johnston, *Mississippi's Defiant Years*, 80–81; Bartley, *Rise of Massive Resistance*, 197. And, like the grocer in communist Czechoslovakia forced by the Party to display a "Workers of the World Unite" sticker in his shop window, Councils asked local merchants to do likewise with "White Citizens' Councils" stickers. On "surveys" in other states, see Luders, *The Civil Rights Movement and the Logic of Social Change*, 37–38. On the dynamics of preference falsification as a barrier to coordination in authoritarian regimes, see Václav Havel, "The Power of the Powerless," in Havel, *The Power of the Powerless*, ed. by John Keane (London: Hutchinson Books, 1985); Timur Kuran, *Private Truths, Public Lies: The Social Consequences of Preference Falsification* (Cambridge: Harvard University Press, 1997). In a remarkable letter to the editor, famed Georgia writer Lillian Smith concurred, writing that "it is easy to be convinced—because we hear nothing to the contrary—that most Southerners (except ourselves of course) are so loyal to WHITE SUPREMACY, so prejudiced against their fellow Americans, that the only way they can be persuaded to move an inch toward racial democracy is by throwing them the d. y. [damn yankee] as a bone for their hate to gnaw on. It is a

vast, though unintentional, libel against the whole South. Our Southern papers and radio sustain this fiction. We are caught in a trap that we have contrived ourselves." *NYT*, Apr. 4, 1948. Smith's writings earned her several years of surveillance by the FBI, panicked as it was by dissidents of Jim Crow. Will Brantley, "The Surveillance of Georgia Writer and Civil Rights Activist Lillian Smith: Another Story from the Federal Bureau of Investigation," *GHQ* 85 (2001), 59–82.

68. Wroten claims that former House speaker Buddie Newman and former Ways and Means chair Charlie Jacobs "were among those who reinforced the atmosphere in which others felt freer to make threats against me and my wife." Others—including U.S. Senator John Stennis—quietly helped block the most rabid white supremacist legislation and discourse. Joseph E. Wroten interview with Jeff Sainsbury (Mar. 31, 1992), John C. Stennis Oral History Project, Mississippi State University. Brazeal, "Problems in Desegregation," 367; *SSN*, Dec. 1955.

69. In doing so, they support the inference that rulers' similar statements about black support for segregation were sincere, not (merely) cheap talk. Oliver Emmerich worried about the deleterious effects on state politics of ignorant black voters, and "fervently believed that Mississippi blacks preferred their own schools." David R. Davies, "J. Oliver Emmerich and the McComb *Enterprise-Journal*," in Davies, ed., *The Press and Race: Mississippi Journalists Confront the Movement* (Jackson: University Press of Mississippi, 2001), 111–36.

70. *SSN*, Jun. 8, 1955, p. 15; Dittmer, *Local People*, 54–55.

71. Johnston, *Mississippi's Defiant Years*, 48; Dittmer, *Local People*, 51; Workman, "Rejection of Accommodation," 83. Banks refused loans, insurance firms canceled policies, and grand juries indicted leaders on trumped-up charges.

72. Brazeal, "Problems in Desegregation," 368; *SSN*, Dec. 1955.

73. Dittmer, *Local People*, 51, 75, 78; Dittmer, "The Politics of the Mississippi Movement, 1954–1964," in Charles W. Eagles, ed., *The Civil Rights Movement in America* (Jackson: University Press of Mississippi, 1986), 65–94; Michael V. Williams, *Medgar Evers: Mississippi Martyr* (Fayetteville: University of Arkansas Press, 2011).

74. On Delta's Greenwood County, see Payne, *Light of Freedom*, chap. 5; Dittmer, *Local People*, chap. 7.

75. Dittmer, *Local People*, 86–89, 455, fn. 38; Butler, "The Mississippi State Sovereignty Commission and Beach Integration"; James Patterson Smith, "Local Leadership, the Biloxi Beach Riot, and the Origins of the Civil Rights Movement on the Mississippi Gulf Coast, 1959–1964," in Samuel C. Hyde, ed., *Sunbelt Revolution: The Historical Progression of the Civil Rights Struggle in the Gulf South, 1866–2000* (Gainesville: University Press of Florida, 2003), 210–33; *NYT*, Mar. 29–31, 1961 (on nonviolent direct action in Jackson).

76. He always supported racially segregated schooling, and on the NBC television program *Meet the Press* remarked that "no baby born in Mississippi today will live long enough to see integrated schools." When he ran again for governor in 1963, he did so noting that no desegregation had occurred on his watch. Quoted in Johnston, *Mississippi's Defiant Years*, 58; Bill Minor, "Mississippi Schools in Crisis," *New South* 25 (1970), 31–36; Katagiri, *Mississippi State Sovereignty Commission*, 3–4. Frank Smith called Coleman the "closest thing to a moderate that was possible in a governor." Interview with Frank Ellis Smith, Aug. 27, 1993, Stennis Oral History Project, Mississippi State University.

77. Crespino, *In Search of Another Country*, 54–57.

78. "History teaches in a long succession of events that such efforts have always failed, and in failing have brought down terrible penalties upon the heads of those who attempted it." *SSN*, Jan. 1956, p. 6; Crespino, "Strategic Accommodation," 48, citing *JDN*, Dec. 15, 1955.

79. He also vowed that, if judicial rulings affecting Mississippi were forthcoming, he would call a special session and veto the use of the doomsday option pending such rulings. Coleman noted that the state's other Virginia hospitals had long been desegregated. *JDN*, May 8, 1957, quoted in Johnston, *Mississippi's Defiant Years*, 57. Governor White feared the impact of violent repression of black insurgency on efforts to attract capital investment and avoid the federalization of law enforcement. *SSN*, Jan. 1956, p. 6.

80. During the gubernatorial campaign, he accused Paul Johnson of attempting to convert the group into a "political machine," and privately referred to the White Citizens' Councils as the state's "hidden government." Johnston, *Mississippi's Defiant Years*, 55–58; 63–66, 80; *JCL*, Aug. 18, 1955; Katagiri, *Mississippi State Sovereignty Commission*, 24–27; *SSN*, Mar. 1956. On the grounds of avoiding unwanted interference by the federal government, Coleman successfully opposed the banning of the NAACP, as other states did. Dittmer, *Local People*, 59 and fn. 49, 450.

81. Walton, *Black Political Parties*, 68; Carl H. Butler, "The Republican Party of Mississippi Is Emerging as an Important Factor in Mississippi Politics," M.A. thesis, Florida State University (1966), pp. 14, 58–60.

82. He promised to reconvene the convention should at least one-fifth of the delegates or a majority of the executive committee so desire. Carter III, *The South Strikes Back*, 68–70; Bartley, *Rise of Massive Resistance*, 158.

83. Coleman again failed to repeal a 1948 law allowing party members to split their tickets without facing reprisals. Johnston, *Mississippi's Defiant Years*, 64–69; Carter III, *The South Strikes Back*, 97.

84. Crespino, *In Search of Another Country*, chaps. 1 and 4.

85. Dittmer, *Local People*, 60; Sarah Rowe-Sims, "The Mississippi State Sovereignty Commission: An Agency History," *JMH* 61 (1999), 29–58, and Katagiri, *Mississippi State Sovereignty Commission*. For instance, it drafted legislation—clearly aimed at the NAACP—authorizing the attorney general to develop a list of "subversive" organizations. The LEAC also recommended repealing the state's rarely enforced compulsory school attendance law, criminalizing champerty, and requiring teachers to list their recent organizational affiliations.

86. Oral history with Erle Johnston, No. 2 (Aug. 13, 1993), CRMDA.

87. Heard interview with Delta Council official, Heard Papers.

88. Interview with Joseph Wroten (Nov. 4, 1993), Center for Oral History and Cultural Heritage, McCain Library, University of Southern Mississippi, Hattiesburg.

89. Johnston, *Mississippi's Defiant Years*, 49. Future governor William Winter also dissented. Rowe-Sims, "Mississippi State Sovereignty Commission," 39. Interview with Erle Johnston, Aug. 13, 1993, Stennis Oral History Project, 2–3. The final House vote was ninety-one to twenty-three, with twenty-six abstentions; Johnston, *Mississippi's Defiant Years*, 49.

90. National NAACP leader Roy Wilkins called one of them a "traitor." Katagiri, *Mississippi State Sovereignty Commission*, 14, 38–43.

91. *Delta Democrat-Times* (Greenville, Mississippi), Jan. 22, 1958. Fred Miller, publisher of the Mound Bayou *News*, and Reverend J. H. Parker sought SSC funding to develop a statewide organization of blacks to serve as an anti-desegregation counterweight to the NAACP. Zack J. Van Landingham to Director of Mississippi State Sovereignty Commission (MSSC); Memo Regarding Negro Anti-NAACP Organization, Feb. 18, 1959, MSSC Papers, MDAH.

92. Katagiri, *The Mississippi State Sovereignty Commission*, 82–84. Litigation over its directorship dragged on during the first two years. One investigator previously served as administrative assistant to Edgar Hoover. Later, Coleman appointed another—known only to him—to monitor desegregation petition filings around the state. Katagiri, *Mississippi State Sovereignty Commission*, 9–11, 37, 45.

93. Katagiri, *Mississippi State Sovereignty Commission*, 31, 56–61; Dittmer, *Local People*, 79–83; Halberstam, "White Citizens' Councils," 301. Coleman helped defeat a bill allowing local and county governments to fund nonprofit organizations such as the WCCs, and prevented the commission from doing so. Interview with William Joel Blass, CRMDA; Carter III, *The South Strikes Back*, 62–77; Johnston, *Mississippi's Defiant Years*, 79; Carter III, *The South Strikes Back*, 92–93; interview with Joseph Wroten, Mississippi State University.

94. The *Jackson Daily News* complained that Coleman "thwarted the will of a friendly legislature [and] loaded the agency with orders to be anemic on performance concerning integration." *SSN*, May 1958; Katagiri, *Mississippi State Sovereignty Commission*, 31–33. The state terminated funding for the agency in 1973. *NYT*, Apr. 22, 1973.

95. This was a nationwide phenomenon. Until the late 1940s, a quota ceiling of 1 percent was placed on black police officers in Detroit's police department. W. Marvin Dulaney, *Black Police in America* (Bloomington: Indiana University Press, 1996), 12–18, 26. States occasionally mustered "State" or "Home" Guards meant to supplement their National Guards when the latter were depleted by wartime service. Under the command of the governor's adjutant general, they could not be federalized. William H. Riker, *Soldiers of the States: The Role of the National Guard in American Democracy* (Washington, D.C.: Public Affairs Press, 1957).

96. "Among other techniques, authorities [with effective policing] refuse permits, narrow walkways, and concentrate police where demonstrations can occur." William H. Sewell, Jr., "Space in Contentious Politics," in Ronald R. Aminzade et al., *Silence and Voice in the Study of Contentious Politics* (New York: Cambridge University Press, 2001), 58–59, 68–69. Weldon Cooper, "The State Police Movement in the South," *JOP* 1 (1939), 415, 418, 424; Bruce Smith, *Police Systems in the United States* (New York: Harper and Row, 1960), 144–69.

97. Dana B. Brammer and James E. Hurley, *A Study of the Office of the Sheriff in the United States, Southern Region* (Bureau of Government Research, University of Mississippi, 1968), 81–82; Frank D. Day, "State Law Enforcement," in Council of State Governments, *The Book of the States, 1962–1963* (Lexington, Ky.), 435–40. For a sustained discussion of a southern state police force, see Michael Lindsey, *Big Hat Law: The Arkansas State Police, 1935–2000* (Fayetteville: University of Arkansas Press, 2008).

98. By 1930, a public opinion survey suggested a majority of white Mississippians favored repeal. The distribution, sale, and consumption of liquor remained

widespread, especially in the Delta, Gulf Coast, and in private clubs statewide. By 1965, fifty-three of the state's eighty-two counties openly sold liquor. Tom S. Hines, Jr., "Mississippi and the Repeal of Prohibition: A Study of the Controversy Over the Twenty-First Amendment," *JMH* 24 (1962), 3; John R. Skates, Jr., "Fred Sullens and Prohibition," *JMH* 29 (1967), 83–94; Harold D. Holder and Cheryl J. Cherpitel, "The End of U.S. Prohibition: A Case Study of Mississippi," *Contemporary Drug Problems* 23 (1996), 304–13; *WSJ*, Dec. 23, 1965.

99. "Authority migration" is taken from Elisabeth R. Gerber and Ken Kollman, "Introduction: Authority Migration: Defining and Emerging Research Agenda," *PS: Political Science & Politics* (Jul. 2004), 397. Institute for Government Research, *State and County Government in Mississippi*, 816–18. Tate, "Easing the Burden," 48. The Brookings report called for sheriffs to be appointed. Kynerd, *Administrative Reorganization*, 45–60, 98–99, 123. In the late 1940s, Governor Wright failed in a half-hearted attempt to strengthen the executive. In many states, prohibition convinced many states to centralize policing somewhat; legislatures granted state officials, usually the governor, the authority to remove sheriffs and other local officers in order to better enforce prohibition laws. White, *Trends in Public Administration*, 127.

100. The law snuck past "dry" legislators from Hills counties partly because House Speaker Walter Sillers convinced them that the tax was meant for war-rationed items. Oral history with Jesse Boyce Holleman (Aug. 9, 1976), CRMDA; oral history with Charles Marx (Oct. 28, 1976), CRMDA; *NYT*, Apr. 12, 1959; David Cohn, "A Little Prohibition in Mississippi," *Atlantic Monthly* 103 (Jun. 1959), 57–59.

101. When a governor would ask a sheriff to "clean up" his county, the sheriff would agree but also threaten to end liquor sales; the governor then quickly backed off. This dynamic stymied prosecution of Gulf Coast gambling and mafia operations. Oral history with George Saxon (Jun. 3, 1993), CRMDA; *SSN*, Jan. 1956; *SSN*, May-Aug. 1956.

102. For Coleman, this "made the sheriff the king and he could be just as corrupt as he wanted to be—or just as weak as he wanted to be—and feel no fear of the state . . . moving in on him." "The legislature had been careful not to give us anything else." Oral history with James P. Coleman (Nov. 12, 1981, and Feb. 6, 1982), CRMDA.

103. Oral History with James P. Coleman (Nov. 12, 1981 and Feb. 6, 1982), CRMDA.

104. Ibid.

105. Given steady outmigration from the Delta and population growth outside it, Deltan legislators over time benefited even more from malapportionment. As economic power drifted toward urban areas, they had reason to guard it even more carefully.

106. A small air force accompanied the National Guard; the state also had some two hundred armed game wardens. Doyle, *An American Insurrection*, 88, 100, 22; *New South* 4 (Oct. 1949); "Negro Vote in Mississippi," *Ebony* 6 (Nov. 1951), cited in Dittmer, *Local People*, 445, fn. 36.

107. The governor-appointed commissioner of public safety led the Highway Patrol. *The Book of the States, 1943–1944* (Lexington, Ky.: Council of State Governments, 1944), 277; oral history with Charles Marx (Oct. 28, 1976), oral history with Mississippi Highway Patrol Lieutenant Colonel Billie Hughes (Jul. 7, 1993), and oral

history with James P. Coleman (Nov. 12, 1981 and Feb. 6, 1982), all CRMDA. During violent labor strife, the legislature quickly granted the governor but then dissolved a "Gestapo-like" Bureau of Investigation. *WP*, Nov. 12 and 30, 1947, and Feb. 27 and Mar. 2, 1948.

108. In Coleman's words, "Instead of falling into the jaws of the federal courts, I wanted us to write a constitution that would remedy defects—under our control, and by our initiation—rather than having the federal courts do it." Oral history with James P. Coleman (Nov. 12, 1981 and Feb. 6, 1982), CRMDA.

109. Sillers claimed to oppose a convention because it could expose the document's disfranchising devices to attack by federal courts. Interview with George W. Yarbrough, Center for Oral History and Cultural Heritage, McCain Library, University of Southern Mississippi, Feb. 21, 1980; Carter III, *The South Strikes Back*, 85–86; oral history with C. B. "Buddie" Newman (Jun. 18, 1992), CRMDA.

110. Nadine Cohodas, *The Band Played Dixie: Race and Liberal Conscience at Ole Miss* (New York: Free Press, 1997).

111. In the 1930s, Bilbo attacked the heads of several colleges, slashed budgets, and fired faculty; only one institution salvaged its accreditation. Brown, "Sillers and Conner," 57; Doyle, *An American Insurrection*, 61.

112. *LAT*, Dec. 13, 1962. As in South Carolina, Mississippi's black activists did not prioritize university desegregation. The analysis below is indebted to the remarkable research by William Doyle in *An American Insurrection*, which draws on declassified FBI files and still-classified records of the Mississippi Highway Patrol.

113. "We must now identify the traitors in our midst! We must eliminate the cowards from our front lines! You did not elect me governor to bargain away your heritage in a smoke-filled hotel room!" *Time* magazine, Sep. 7, 1959, p. 13.

114. Less than halfway through his term, he was booed at a University of Mississippi football game. Silver, *Mississippi: The Closed Society*, 43; Doyle, *An American Insurrection*, 53, 56, 87.

115. Barnett canceled an SSC meeting soon after Johnson's speech because he feared that Johnston would be voted out. Johnston distinguished his status as a "practical segregationist" from "emotional segregationist[s]" and "unyielding resister[s]." Barnett later named Johnston the SSC's director, where he successfully fended off "rather fanatical" board members. Oral history with Erle Johnston, No. 1 (Jul. 30, 1980) and No. 2 (Aug. 13, 1993), CRMDA.

116. Attorney General Robert F. Kennedy complimented Mississippi's law enforcement on this episode. Dittmer, *Local People*, 95; McAdam, "Tactical Innovation," 748. Avoiding the breakdowns of law and order that occurred in Alabama did not mean, of course, that Mississippi complied with the ICC ruling which the Freedom Riders were testing. In several small towns, bus terminals closed or simply ignored the ruling. Arsenault, *Freedom Riders*, 459.

117. McMillen, "Development of Civil Rights," 159.

118. Doyle, *An American Insurrection*, 61.

119. Bureau of the Census, *1964 Statistical Abstracts* (Washington, D.C.: Government Printing Office, 1964), 133; Carter et al., *Historical Statistics*, 1:505 and 507, table Ac53–205.

120. *WSJ*, Sep. 26, 1962.

121. Carter III, *The South Strikes Back*, 189–90. Susan Weill, "'In a Madhouse's Din': Civil Rights Coverage by Mississippi's Daily Press, 1948–1968," Ph.D. diss., University of Southern Mississippi (1998), pp. 167–68.

122. He blustered, "There is no case in history where the Caucasian race has survived social integration.... We will not drink from the cup of genocide." Doyle, *An American Insurrection*, 65.

123. *Saturday Evening Post*, Nov. 10, 1962.

124. Walter Lord, *The Past That Would Not Die* (New York: Harper and Row, 1965), 143; Jonathan Rosenberg and Zachary Karabell, eds., *Kennedy, Johnson, and the Quest for Justice: The Civil Rights Tapes* (New York: Norton, 2003). Attorney General Robert F. Kennedy had about twenty conversations with Barnett in the last two weeks of September; the president became more involved on September 29. By that date, Barnett "wanted an even larger show of federal force" before allowing Meredith to register. Timothy Naftali and Philip Zelikow, *John F. Kennedy: The Presidential Recordings: The Great Crises*, Vol. 2: *(September—October 21, 1962)* (New York: W. W. Norton, 2001), 224–25; Nick Bryant, *The Bystander: John F. Kennedy and the Struggle for Black Equality* (New York: Basic Books, 2006), chap. 20.

125. In April 1963, Lee Harvey Oswald attempted to kill Walker at his Dallas home. He was considered an extremist by none other than Mississippi White Citizens' Council President William Simmons. Clive Webb profiles Walker in *Rabble Rousers: The American Far Right in the Civil Rights Era* (Athens: University of Georgia Press, 2010), 141–50. In Oxford, Walker announced that he had been on the "wrong side" at Little Rock. Rick Perlstein, *Before the Storm: Barry Goldwater and the Unmaking of the American Consensus* (New York: Hill and Wang, 2001), 118–19; Crespino, *In Search of Another Country*, 79.

126. Lord, *Past That Would Not Die*, 191; Doyle, *An American Insurrection*, 114–15.

127. Efforts since the early 1950s to professionalize the service from a patronage operation into a service covered by civil service laws had failed, in large part due to opposition by the Senate Committee on Government Operations, whose members fought to maintain their hold on this source of patronage. Rather than keep order in situations of mass disorder, marshals usually served subpoenas, sold real estate pursuant to court order, made arrests, and transported prisoners. See "Appointment of U.S. Marshals," 2–4, Deputy Attorney General Nicholas Katzenbach to S. A. Andretta, May 9, 1962, James J. P. McShane to Herbert E. Hoffman, Aug. 27, 1964, and Statement of Barefoot Sanders (Assistant Deputy Attorney General), Subcommittee No. 5, House Judiciary Committee, on H.R. 16575 (Appointment of United States Marshals by the Attorney General), Aug. 31, 1966, all in Administrative History of the Department of Justice, Box 10, Administrative Histories, LBJL; Lichtman, "The Federal Assault Against Voting Discrimination in the Deep South," 349, 362.

128. In a typical excerpt, Barnett pleaded, "Please let us treat what we say as confidential.... I am sorry about the misunderstanding last night. I am extremely hurt over it really. I didn't know I was violating any agreement. Please understand me ... please let's not have a fuss about what we talked about.... I hope you will consider my position here." Doyle, *An American Insurrection*, 122.

129. Two expected bloodshed, one of whom, future House Speaker Buddie Newman, revised his last will and testament. Doyle, *An American Insurrection*, 129 and 193; Robert Massie, "What Next in Mississippi," *Saturday Evening Post*, Nov. 10, 1962, p. 23.

130. Lieutenant Governor Paul B. Johnson's diary, quoted in Derr, "The Triumph of Progressivism," 123.

131. Six years later, sheriffs' offices lacked basic telecommunications infrastructure. Brammer and Hurley, *Office of Sheriff*, table 35, 103.

132. That the marshals chose to "occupy" the Lyceum was especially unfortunate, since it was the university's most sacred ground. From its steps the University Grays departed for war, and twice it served as a Confederate war hospital. Oral history with Hugh H. Clegg (Oct. 1, 1975), CRMDA.

133. Doyle, *An American Insurrection*, 221–23.

134. Federal officials placed Walker under psychiatric examination. *NYT*, Oct. 3, 1962. Doyle, *An American Insurrection*, 278–80, 148, 171.

135. Weill, "'In a Madhouse's Din,'" 141; Doyle, *An American Insurrection*, 289; *CSM*, May 9, 1963. Of eight students who dined with Meredith, none remained in school by June. *NYT*, Jun. 9, 1963.

136. The slogan "Kennedy's Hungary" framed many Mississippi license plates after the riot. Thomas Borstelmann, "'Hedging Our Bets and Buying Time': John Kennedy and Racial Revolutions in the American South and Southern Africa," *Diplomatic History* 24 (2000), 445. CORE immediately announced plans to boycott products of industrial firms that relocated to Mississippi. *WSJ*, Oct. 3, 1962; Dittmer, *Local People*, 138.

137. *NYT*, Oct. 3, 1962; *WSJ*, Oct. 3, 1962. Prominent Jackson business executive Billy Mounger, whose insurance firm owned both of Jackson's leading television and radio outlets, WLBT-TV and WJDX, delivered a mea culpa for not speaking up earlier for the cause of "law and order" and peaceful compliance. Doyle, *An American Insurrection*, 260; Steven D. Classen, *Watching Jim Crow: The Struggles Over Mississippi TV, 1955–1969* (Durham, N.C.: Duke University Press, 2004).

138. *WSJ*, Oct. 3, 1962. As Crespino shows, the Sovereignty Commission monitored the meeting and developed a "List of Moderates." Crespino, *In Search of Another Country*, 292, fn. 69, citing file 3–9–1–70, MSSC Papers, MDAH. Doyle, *An American Insurrection*, 260. Silver, *Mississippi: The Closed Society*, 127; General Investigating Committee, *A Report of the Mississippi State Legislature Concerning the Occupation of the Campus of the University of Mississippi, September 30, 1962, by the Department of Justice of the United States* (Jackson: State of Mississippi, 1963).

139. Dittmer, *Local People*, 197; Silver, *Mississippi: The Closed Society*, 75; Wright, *Old South, New South*, 302, fn. 42; *WSJ*, Jun. 10, 1963. Days after the battle, officials at a conference of southern governors remained concerned about violence in those states still maintaining segregated universities, such as Alabama and South Carolina. *NYT*, Oct. 3, 1962.

140. E.g., "The insurrection … was the inevitable response of the closed society of Mississippi to a law outside itself." Silver, *Mississippi: The Closed Society*, 3.

CHAPTER SEVEN:
South Carolina Navigates the Clemson Crisis

1. About $12 was spent annually per white student, and $1.25 per black student. Frances Simkins, "Race Legislation in South Carolina since 1865," *South Atlantic*

Quarterly 20 (1921), 170. In 1941 the legislature discovered that nineteen of the state's forty-six counties lacked a black high school, and that the state provided white students with 1,644 buses, compared to eight for blacks. Grace Graham, "Negro Education Progresses in South Carolina," *Social Forces* 30 (1952), 429–38.

2. Maxie Myron Cox, "1963—The Year of Decision: Desegregation in South Carolina," Ph.D. diss., University of South Carolina (1996), chap. 1. William D. Smyth, "Segregation in Charleston in the 1950s: A Decade of Transition," *SCHM* 92 (1991), 99–123. Jack Bass and Walter De Vries interview with Charleston politician Gedney Howe, Bass and De Vries project, Southern History Collection, University of North Carolina, Chapel Hill (hereafter SHC); *SSN*, Sep., 1954, p. 12.

3. Egerton notes that *Brown v. Board* should have been named *DeLaine v. Clarendon County*, since DeLaine was most responsible for making this, the first of *Brown*'s five cases, a reality. In Summerton, there were 298 white and 2,259 black students. In Clarendon County, blacks outnumbered whites by about three to one. In 1951 total expenditures for white and black school systems were $282,950 and $395,329, respectively. Black facilities were in terrible shape, and NAACP litigators welcomed the inclusion of *Briggs v. Elliott*, since Clarendon represented a typical Black Belt county. Arsonists torched his home and church, and he shot at a carload of white men approaching his house. Persistently harassed, DeLaine fled the state after a warrant was issued for his arrest. Today, Clarendon still maintains two effectively separate systems. Grose, *South Carolina at the Brink*, 67; Egerton, *Speak Now Against the Day*, 609; Alan Richard, "The Heat of Summerton," *The Nation* (May 3, 2004), 32–35. See Orville Vernon Burton, Beatrice Burton, and Simon Appleford, "Seeds in Unlikely Soil: The *Briggs v. Elliott* School Segregation Case," in Moore and Burton, *Toward the Meeting of the Waters*, 176–200; Sampson, table 2.18, p. 103.

4. The NAACP appealed the decision, as Governor James Byrnes applauded it. The Eastern District Federal Court panel included Waring; George Bell Timmerman, Sr., a respected judge and father of soon-to-be governor George Bell Timmerman, Jr.; and John J. Parker, whom the NAACP blocked from ascending to the Supreme Court in the 1930s. Kenneth W. Goings, *The NAACP Comes of Age* (Bloomington: University of Indiana Press, 1990). Appellees' brief quoted in Quint, *Profile*, 14. Eisenhower again considered Parker to replace Chief Justice Vinson in fall 1953. Mayer, "With Much Deliberation," 51. David W. Southern, "Beyond Jim Crow Liberalism: Judge Waring's Fight against Segregation in South Carolina, 1942–52," *JNH* 66 (1981), 215; *NYT*, May 29, 1951.

5. Quint, *Profile*, 14–16.

6. Bartley, *Rise of Massive Resistance*, 44; *CS*, *NYT*, Jan. 17, 1951. Before the 1950 gubernatorial election, the state's lower chamber created a committee to investigate a sales tax to pay for education. Its authorizing resolution declared that the "mandate of the Federal Courts in regard to existing school problems in South Carolina requires the institution of a program for permanent improvements in our schools." Increased spending on education would also mean centralizing education policy. Byrnes endorsed the move. *SSN*, Sep. 1954, p. 12.

7. *NYT*, Mar. 17, 1951; *SSN*, Oct. 1, 1954, p. 1; Byrnes quoted in Quint, *Profile*, 16; *NYT*, Mar. 19, 1951, Jun. 25, 1951, and Jul. 10, 1951.

8. Grose, *South Carolina at the Brink*, 118–21.

9. The plan went into effect on July 1, 1951. Soon the state had allocated more than $124 million for school construction or repair, two-thirds of which went to black schools. *SSN*, Sep. 3, 1954, p. 12. Senator Marian Gressette credits Rembert Dennis, Richard M. Jeffries, and himself with the idea, which was carried by a special legislative committee to study the matter in the spring and summer of 1950. Byrnes, after his gubernatorial victory in November, supported the committee's recommendations. Marion Gressette, quoted in Grose, *South Carolina at the Brink*, 69 and fn. 21, 306–7. When the state embarked on its massive increase in spending on black schools, it also centralized the school system. By 1960 the number of one- and two-teacher schools was cut from 1,434 to 16. The number of accredited high schools in the state almost doubled in less than ten years. But district school superintendents typically viewed their job as overseeing only white schools; still-underfunded black schools operated fairly autonomously. Grose, *South Carolina at the Brink*, 127; Stone, "Making a Modern State," 298–99.

10. Sproat, "Firm Flexibility," 167. The Committee was comprised of five senators, five members of the General Assembly, and five private citizens. Serving in the Senate from 1936 until 1984, Gressette's political influence continued long after the massive resistance period. As chair of the Judiciary Committee, he shaped the state's adjustments to the Civil Rights and Voting Rights Acts, reapportionment, and other federal challenges.

11. The governor, lieutenant governor (as president pro tempore of the Senate), and longtime House Speaker and Barnwell Ring politician Sol Blatt chose the members. In 1951, it lapsed into a "stand-by" role until *Brown*'s announcement. Bass and De Vries interview with Gedney Howe, SHC; *SSN*, Sep. 3, 1954, p. 12.

12. *SSN*, Sep. 3, 1954, p. 12. In 1956, in the midst of desegregation suits regarding public beaches and parks, the General Assembly broadened the Gressette Committee's mandate to consider "all phases of segregation" in order to improve strategizing. *SSN*, Apr. 1956, p. 12; *NYT*, May 27, 1951. The state also created the Educational Finance Commission to oversee the plan.

13. The state's constitution stated that "separate schools shall be provided for children of the white and colored races, and no child of either race shall ever be permitted to attend a school provided for children of the other race" (Section 5, Article XI, Constitution of South Carolina of 1895).

14. The margin was 68 percent to 32 percent. Quint, *Profile*, 17. Bruce H. Kalk, *The Origins of the Southern Strategy: Two-Party Competition in South Carolina, 1950–1972* (Lexington, Mass.: Lexington Books, 2001); Bartley, *Rise of Massive Resistance*, 45; Interview with Robert E. McNair, Feb. 2, 1983, Governor McNair Oral History Project, Part 15, 16, South Carolina Political Collections, Columbia (hereafter SCPC).

15. Sproat, "Firm Flexibility," 166.

16. *SSN*, Sep. 3, 1954, p. 12. Workman, "The Deep South," 96. The commission's director reported that the equalization program would be complete in two years. *SSN*, Oct. 1, 1954, p. 12.

17. The (white) South Carolina Education Association, and many white PTAs, opposed the ruling, and the (black) Palmetto Education Association backed it. *SSN*, Dec. 1954, p. 13; *SSN*, Dec. 1955, p. 6. After conferring privately with representatives of teachers and parent groups of both races—as well as newly formed white

supremacist organizations—the Gressette Committee agreed with Byrnes that, in the absence of an implementation decree, the state need not call a special session to respond. *SSN*, Sep. 3, 1954, p. 12.

18. *CNC*, May 30, 1954.

19. Lander, *A History of South Carolina*, 194–95; Henry Savage, Jr., *Seeds of Time* (New York: Henry Holt, 1959), 267.

20. Gressette declared that the committee would remain "in more or less continuous session." *SSN*, Jan. 6, 1955, p. 13. Quint, *Profile*, 33. Papers also endorsed "voluntary segregation." *CNC*, Dec. 3, 1954; *CR*, Nov. 26, 1954.

21. The *Columbia State* called on the region to "hold the line" in resisting desegregation. Most papers continued to oppose the rulings. *SSN*, Oct. 1955, page number illegible; *SSN*, Jun. 8, 1955, p. 11. The *Florence Morning News'* editor, Jack O'Dowd, wrote that "the Southland is feeding itself large doses of self-delusion and false hope." *SSN*, Mar. 1956, page number illegible.

22. Thomas R. Waring, the aristocratic editor of the *Charleston News and Courier* and nephew of Charleston's recently ostracized Judge Waties Waring, summed up the establishment's view in "The Southern Case Against Desegregation," *Harper's* 212 (1956), 39–45, describing White Citizens' Councils as "protective organizations" seeking "to combat the lawless element" represented by the Klan. He also likened *Brown* to Prohibition—a poorly enforced and ultimately rescinded social experiment—and noted that responsible white leaders feared the violence of the "grass roots."

23. Senator Gressette noted that "thousands of Negroes are on our side. . . . [We should] encourage the members of the Negro race with these views, so that they may . . . discourage the few whites and colored, from within and without the state, who advocate integration." *SSN*, Oct. 1955. Workman chastised those who thought most blacks preferred segregation, including Governor Timmerman, Lieutenant Governor Ernest Hollings, Gressette, and Waring; Quint, *Profile*, 77.

24. Bass and De Vries interview with Gedney Howe, SHC; *SSN*, Jan. 6, 1955, p. 14.

25. Brown helped engineer loyalists' takeover of several top party positions at the 1954 convention. In 1956, he deterred many key defections to Eisenhower. Workman, *Bishop from Barnwell*, 178–84.

26. Grose, *South Carolina at the Brink*, 99.

27. Grose, *Looking for Utopia*, 84–85; Nadine Cohodas, *Strom Thurmond and the Politics of Change* (Macon, Ga.: Mercer University Press, 1993); Jack Bass and Marilyn W. Thompson, *Strom: The Complicated Personal and Political Life of Strom Thurmond* (New York: Public Affairs, 2005). In naming a black Charleston doctor to the state's Advisory Hospital Council, Thurmond made the century's first black appointment at a state agency. Cassandra Maxwell Birnie, "Race and Politics in Georgia and South Carolina," *Phylon* 13 (1952), 238. Brown successfully challenged Baskin as party chair in 1952 in an effort to repair relations with the national party, and then helped engineer the loyalists' takeover of top party positions at the 1954 convention. Workman, *Bishop from Barnwell*, chap. 12, p. 178.

28. Huss, *Senator for the South*, 133. Johnston ran unopposed in 1956.

29. The plan was absurd on its face, and Bates objected to the plan as likely to lead to some desegregation, which was more than voters preferred.

30. Grose, *Looking for Utopia*, 77.

31. Inaugural Address, Jan. 17, 1955, reprinted in *CS*, Jan. 18, 1955; Bass and De Vries interview with Gedney Howe, SHC; Quint, *Profile*, 96, 116–24.

32. He called integration "contrary to the divine order of things. Only an evil mind could conceive it. Only a foolish mind can accept it." In a televised speech, Timmerman vowed that there "shall be no compulsory racial mixing in our schools," castigated the NAACP, and asked "every responsible Negro to repudiate [its] false leadership . . . and its alien white sponsors. . . . It is the duty of every responsible white person to see to it that no harm comes to innocent southern Negroes." *SSN*, Apr. 7, 1955, p. 13; *SSN*, Dec. 1955, p. 6; *CNC*, Jul. 30, 1956; *SSN*, Aug. 1956, p. 9.

33. *SSN*, Jun. 8, 1955, pp. 6, 11. Black parents filed in Charleston, Beaufort, Greenville, Florence, Richland, Spartanburg, and other counties. *SSN*, Sep. 1955, p. 6; Workman, "The Deep South," 127.

34. *SSN*, Sep. 1955, p. 6; these included Clarendon, Calhoun, and Colleton. *SSN*, Jun. 8, 1955, p. 11.

35. Timmerman signed the bill but expected parents to continue to send their children to school; educators disagreed on its likely effects, but few legislators opposed the move. Future governor Robert McNair first proposed the legislation. *SSN*, Sep. 3, 1954, p. 12; *SSN*, Mar. 3, 1955, p. 14; *SSN*, Jun. 8, 1955, p. 11. *CNC*, May 28, 1955.

36. *SSN*, Apr. 1956, p. 12. The state centralized education policymaking—financial and administrative authority migrated upward to the state, and from local to county- and district-level officials. In 1956 the state also authorized law enforcement officers to administer pupil transfers.

37. *SSN*, Apr. 1956, p. 12, and Jan. 1956, p. 5. The resolution was entitled, "A Joint Resolution Condemning and Protesting the Usurpation and Encroachment on the Reserved Powers of the States by the Supreme Court of the United States, Calling upon the States and Congress to Prevent This and Other Encroachment by the Central Government and Declaring the Intention of South Carolina to Exercise All Powers Reserved to It, to Protect Its Sovereignty and the Rights of Its People." The NAACP's James Hinton protested the resolution, and demanded (unsuccessfully) that blacks be allowed input before any action was taken.

38. Some worried that federal authorities would respond by closing Fort Jackson, which played a significant role in Columbia's economy. Andrew H. Myers, *Black, White, and Olive Drab: Racial Integration at Fort Jackson, South Carolina, and the Civil Rights Movement* (Charlottesville, Va.: University of Virginia Press, 2006).

39. *SSN*, Apr. 1957, p. 9; *SSN*, Jul. 1957, p. 4. On some segregation issues, practices had not yet been state mandated.

40. Epitomizing the pattern of other desegregation battles, lower courts dropped a suit concerning the desegregation of Edisto Beach because the state had already closed the park. State appropriations later limited public funding to segregated parks. The state operated twenty-two parks, all segregated; five were for use by blacks. *SSN*, Apr. 7, 1955, p. 13. After the ruling, a suit to desegregate Edisto Beach Park commenced. *SSN*, Jun. 8, 1955, pp. 11, 23; *SSN*, Dec. 1955, p. 6; *CS*, Jul. 26, 1957. Earlier legislation clarified that state appropriations to parks required their racial segregation (HB 1896). *SSN*, May 1956, p. 14. The Fourth Circuit affirmed (*SSN*, Nov. 1956, p. 13). On appropriations, see *SSN*, Jul. 1957, p. 4.

41. In district court, Judge Timmerman had initially dismissed the suit in part by arguing that "education and personality is [*sic*] not developed on a city bus." *SSN*, Jun. 8, 1955, pp. 11, 23; *SSN*, May 1956, p. 14; *SSN*, Dec. 1956, p. 2; *SSN*, Jan. 1957, p. 3. A Columbia city attorney hesitated "to put anything in writing about 'desegregation' in the Richland County Public Library as we certainly do not want it advertised that the Main Library welcomes . . . both races at all times." James F. Dreher letter to Workman, Nov. 2, 1959, Desegregation Folder, Workman Papers.

42. John Bartlow Martin, *The Deep South Says "Never"* (New York: Ballantine Books, 1957), 67–68; *CNC*, Jul. 1, 1956. The state's AFL affiliate publicly opposed them. Quint, *Profile*, 48–52.

43. James W. Vander Zanden, "The Southern White Resistance Movement to Integration," Ph.D. diss., University of North Carolina, Chapel Hill (1957), p. 130. *SSN*, Sep. 1955, p. 6; McMillen, *The Citizens' Council*, 74–75. William Bagwell, *School Desegregation in the Carolinas: Two Case Studies* (Columbia: University of South Carolina Press, 1972), 143; *SSN*, Aug. 1957, p. 13.

44. Lieutenant Governor Ernest "Fritz" Hollings hinted at his disapproval of economic coercion.

45. *SSN*, Mar. 1956, page number illegible. Praising the organization, Hollings remarked that he was "glad that responsible spokesmen for the movement say they do not use organized economic pressure as a weapon against anyone. . . . The organization of pressures is full of dangers." Fleming, "Resistance Movements," 49; *SSN*, Oct. 1955, page number illegible. These efforts occurred in the lowcountry, where many signers depended on white landowners for employment. *CS*, Sep. 16, 1955; Quint, *Profile*; *SSN*, May 1956, p. 14.

46. *SSN*, Sep. 1955, p. 6; McMillen, *The Citizens' Council*, 210. Quint discusses successful efforts in lowcountry towns (*Profile*, 51–52). Orangeburg's NAACP coordinated the removal of petitioners' names, encouraging those "most vulnerable" to economic reprisals to remove their names. Twenty-six were left. W. E. Solomon, "The Problem of Segregation in South Carolina," *JNE* 25 (1956), 320; Fleming, "Resistance Movements," 49; Workman, "The Deep South," 103; Vander Zanden, "Southern White Resistance Movement," 129. *SSN*, May 1956, p. 14; William C. Hine, "Civil Rights and Campus Wrongs: South Carolina State College Students Protest, 1955–1968," *SCHM* 97 (1996), 310–31; Workman, "The Deep South," 103; *SSN*, Dec. 1955; McMillen, *The Citizens' Council*, 211–13; John W. White, "The White Citizens' Councils of Orangeburg County, South Carolina," in Moore and Burton, *Toward the Meeting of the Waters*, 261–73; Meier and Rudwick, *CORE*, 87. On the biracial food drive, see *SSN*, Apr. 1956, p. 12. On SLED, see I. A. Newby, *Black Carolinians: A History of Blacks in South Carolina from 1895 to 1968* (Columbia: University of South Carolina Press, 1973), 346–49.

47. *SSN*, Mar. 1956, page number illegible; *SSN*, Oct. 1955, page number illegible; and *SSN*, Jan. 1956, p. 5; South Carolina Senate *Journal* (1956), 248–49. The rally coincided with a push to double its membership of 20,000. Fleming, "Resistance Movements," 49; *SSN*, May 1956, p. 14.

48. *SSN*, Sep. 1955, p. 6. The *News and Courier* published the names of all such signers of the three petitions filed in the Charleston area. *SSN*, Oct. 1955, page number illegible; Quint, *Profile*, 48, 98, 152. In 1956, it published a pamphlet of thirty-two editorials that seemed to mix sincere preferences and strategic position-taking in

order to increase the expected costs—for statewide politicians and courts alike—of *Brown*'s implementation.

49. Workman, "The Deep South," 100; *SSN*, Sep. 1955, p. 6.

50. The Committee of fifty-two included Farley Smith (son of U.S. Senator "Cotton Ed" Smith), who assumed leadership of the White Citizens' Council state organization. Quint, *Profile*, 38–54; McMillen, *The Citizens' Council*, 77–78; *SSN*, Jan. 1956, p. 5. Jenkins criticized the White House for playing "dirty politics" with potential appointees linked to the Councils. *SSN*, May 1956, p. 14.

51. Quint, *Profile*, chap. 4, and p. 39; Bartley, *Rise of Massive Resistance*, 207. Crowds at two rallies exceeded one thousand (*SSN*, Sep. 1955, pp. 7, 16). In June, White Citizens' Council officials claimed fifty-seven local branches had enrolled some 55,000 members. They decried the Klan and claimed to deter its growth. *SSN*, Jul. 1957, p. 4. *SSN*, Jun. 1956, page number illegible; *SSN*, Nov. 1956, p. 13; *SSN*, Jan. 1957, p. 3; *SSN*, Feb. 1957, p. 11. A cross-burning in Orangeburg County attracted whites from neighboring states. *SSN*, Jan. 1956, p. 5. Federal judge Ashton Williams declared that "no progress can be made unless and until both Klan and the NAACP are wholly eliminated from the picture." *SSN*, Oct. 1955, page number illegible.

52. Carlton, "State and Worker"; Terrill, "No Union for Me"; Simon, *A Fabric of Defeat*.

53. The state's James McBride Dabbs, a well-known academic, clergyman, and writer, served as president of the Southern Regional Council (1958–63). In his April 1963 "Letter from Birmingham Jail," Martin Luther King, Jr. singled out Dabbs as one of a few true southern white allies of the movement, in contrast to the "moderates" the letter assailed. The YWCA provided the only setting for interracial meetings with meal facilities "until the 1960s." Bagwell, *School Desegregation*, 151.

54. Workman, "The Deep South," 108; *SSN*, Apr. 7, 1955, p. 13; *SSN*, May 1956, p. 14. After AFL president George Meany called for banning school aid to southern states that refused to comply with *Brown*, the state's affiliate had even less room to maneuver on the issue. Red-baited and now race-baited, AFL-CIO affiliates in Rock Hill faced opposition in 1957 from a white supremacist "labor" organization. White Citizens' Councils often attacked labor. *WSJ*, Feb. 6, 1957.

55. Quint, *Profile*, chap. 10.

56. Often, however, groups of ministers advocated "freedom of conscience and speech" independent of the state's segregation policy, or issued proclamations declaring Christianity to be silent on the issue. *SSN*, Oct. 1955; *SSN*, Dec. 1955, p. 6; *SSN*, May 1956, p. 14.

57. *SSN*, Aug. 1957, p. 13; *SSN*, Dec. 1957, p. 6; Quint, *Profile*, 173; Reverend Ralph E. Cousins et al., *South Carolinians Speak: A Moderate Approach to Race Relations* (n.p., 1957), vi; *Chicago Defender*, Nov. 21, 1957. An all-white jury acquitted the defendants, all Klan members, of the bombing. *SSN*, Aug. 1958, p. 5. Also see Timothy Tyson, "Dynamite and 'The Silent South': A Story from the Second Reconstruction in South Carolina," in Dailey, Gilmore, and Simon, *Jumpin' Jim Crow*, 275–97.

58. *SSN*, Jan. 1956, p. 5. Southern "resistance . . . is not whole-hearted resistance . . . because it is not really hopeful; it is not so much actual resistance as the enactment of a role of resistance." Joseph Margolis, AAUP Winter 1957–58 *Bulletin*; *SSN*, Feb. 1958, p. 7.

59. House Bill 2289 requested that the State Library Board remove texts "antagonistic and inimical to state traditions." Solomon, "Problem of Segregation," 319; *SSN*, Apr. 1956, p. 12; Preston Valien, "The Status of Educational Desegregation, 1956," *JNE* 25 (1956), 360. *SSN*, Apr. 1957, p. 9; *SSN*, May 1957, p. 3. It also considered labeling blood by race. Legislators crafted and passed most "race" bills quietly, with little fanfare. *Rock Hill Evening Herald*, Jun. 26, 1957. As U.S. paratroopers prepared to deploy to Little Rock, Governor Timmerman resigned his U.S. Naval Reserve commission in protest. Lander, *History of South Carolina*, 204–5.

60. *SSN*, Aug. 1956, p. 9; *SSN*, Sep. 1956, p. 2; *SSN*, Feb. 1957, p. 11; *SSN*, Jul. 1957, p. 4.

61. For example, American Friends Service Committee, Southeastern Office, *Intimidation, Reprisal, and Violence in the South's Racial Crisis* (High Point, N.C.: Southeastern Office, American Friends Service Committee, Dept. of Racial and Cultural Relations, National Council of the Churches of Christ in the United States of America, and Southern Regional Council, 1959). Bagwell, *School Desegregation*, 147.

62. Bagwell, *School Desegregation*, 149–50, discusses Greenville in this context. Hollings continued Timmerman's refusal to cooperate with the commission, noting that to do so would "support . . . a commission in violation of fundamental constitutional principles. . . . We have good race relations [and] law and order . . . I would suggest the use of the Federal Bureau of Investigation as South Carolina's 'advisory committee.'" Governor Ernest F. Hollings, Dec. 29, 1959, U.S. Commission on Civil Rights File, Workman Papers; *SSN*, Feb. 1960.

63. Callison stated, "Our own people were agitating the strife which is now going on, we could be more patient, but when it comes from without by meddlers who are playing directly in the hands of communism, . . . our patience may become exhausted and . . . God knows what the results will be." The resolution noted that the U.S. House Committee on Un-American Activities linked fifty-three "subversives" to the NAACP. *SSN*, Jan. 1956, p. 5; *SSN*, Dec. 1955, p. 6. *CR*, Oct. 11, 1955; Quint, *Profile*, 109.

64. Bartley, *The New South*, 218.

65. The bill would "protect our Negro citizens and colored public employees . . . from the intimidation and coercion of the NAACP, as well as to limit its activities against the best interests of our white citizens." According to its preamble, the NAACP was "wholly incompatible with the peace, tranquility, and progress that all citizens have a right to enjoy." Lau, "Freedom Road Territory."

66. *SSN*, May 1957, p. 3. *CSM*, Jun. 22, 1957. On federal rulings on the constitutionality of legislation proscribing NAACP membership for public employees. Workman, "The Deep South," 104–5. *SSN*, May 1957, p. 3.

67. *SSN*, Sep. 1955, p. 6; preamble quoted in *SSN*, Apr. 1956, p. 12. The *Florence Morning News* and the *Anderson Independent* criticized them. Quint, *Profile*, 112. After he and his staff had their cars driven off the road, among other threats and harassments, Jack O'Dowd, the *Morning News'* editor, was later forced to resign, and left the state. He wrote, "Our Southland is becoming a place where non-concurrence with the established orthodoxy is cause for rejection and social ostracism." "The Status of Educational Desegregation, 1956," 362; *SSN*, Aug. 1957, p. 13; Grose, *Looking for Utopia*, 90.

68. Some of the teachers resigned first. *SSN*, Oct. 1956, p. 2; *SSN*, Feb. 1957, p. 10. Authorities elsewhere fired many black teachers—including famed activist Septima Clark—who refused to deny their membership in the organization.

69. In the common law tradition, "barratry" involved the sponsorship or encouragement of unnecessary litigation by third parties. Virginia enacted similar legislation, which the NAACP soon challenged. This offense included inciting quarrels to disturb the peace in courts or elsewhere. Also see Murphy, "The South Counterattacks," 371–90.

70. *SSN*, Mar. 1957, page number illegible. Guilty parties would be barred permanently from practicing law, and the law would ban organizations found to be inciting litigation. Senator John C. West, later the state's most racially progressive governor of the transition period, introduced the legislation. *SSN*, Feb. 1957, p. 11. NAACP president James Hinton quickly denounced it.

71. Faculty had issued a resolution championing freedom of thought and the NAACP. *SSN*, Oct. 1955; *SSN*, Apr. 1956. Brazeal, "Problems in Desegregation," 369–70; Quint, *Profile*, 118–24. The move sparked lawsuits to integrate state universities.

72. Bartley, *The New South*, 221; Quint, *Profile*, 87; *SSN*, Apr. 1957, p. 9. Laurens County (which required registration of those involved in "civil rights" organizations) and Abbeville County made exceptions for those employed in hazardous work. *SSN*, Jul. 1957, p. 4; Bartley, *Rise of Massive Resistance*, 214.

73. As discussed in chapter 2, in capturing the degree of coercion in a polity, it is vitally important to distinguish reports of physical violence from widespread fears of physical coercion plaguing many black communities.

74. Since "Congress of Racial Equality" was thought to be too radical and likely to spark repression, in South Carolina "CORE" stood for "Committee on Registration Education." Meier and Rudwick, *CORE*, 80–87.

75. Walton and Gray, "Black Politics at the National Republican and Democratic Conventions," 275.

76. *Anderson Independent*, Aug. 28, 1956.

77. *SSN*, Jun. 1957, p. 11; *SSN*, Aug. 1957, p. 13. By the mid-1950s, white suburban growth left Charleston's schools 65 percent black; *WP*, Aug. 7, 1957.

78. Grose, *South Carolina at the Brink*, 182–83.

79. Sproat, "Firm Flexibility," 167; Stone, "Making a Modern State," pp. 445–47. Bass and De Vries interview with Earle Morris, SHC. This latter claim is disputed later.

80. *SSN*, Apr. 1957, p. 9; *SSN*, Jul. 1957, p. 4.

81. Quint, *Profile*, 115. The legislation—passed unanimously by the Senate—empowered the governor to declare that danger exists. *CS*, Mar. 15 and Jun. 19, 1957.

82. Michael S. Hindus, *Prison and Plantation: Crime, Justice and Authority in Massachusetts and South Carolina, 1767–1878* (Chapel Hill: University of North Carolina Press, 1980).

83. Roger K. Hux, "The Ku Klux Klan and Collective Violence in Horry County, South Carolina," *SCHM* 85 (1984), 211–19; Lau, "Freedom Road Territory," p. 137.

84. Most millhands participated in the South's 1934 textile strike. Clashes between workers and guards resulted in several deaths. Governor Blackwood declared martial law and ordered the state militia to "shoot to kill." Incoming governor Johnston declared a "state of insurrection" in two upcountry counties. *NYT*, Jun. 20, 1935; Miller, "Palmetto Politician," pp. 101, 175–77.

85. Formed in 1893 to enforce liquor laws, the unpopular, reckless force in response, Tillman had to deploy the state militia. Operating intermittently, the Johnston reestablished the constabulary in 1935 to enforce all state laws. Edgar, *South Carolina*, 441–43; Miller, "Palmetto Politician," p. 237; Heard interview with prominent South Carolina legislator, Heard Papers.

86. The constabulary was weak enough that governors called on the federal government for assistance in dealing with (often Klan-related) disturbances. *NYT*, Jan. 15, 1940.

87. *CNC*, Apr. 21, 1938, May 22, 1938, Jan. 22, 1947; Miller, "Palmetto Politician," 137–38, 425, fn. 30; Stone, "Making a Modern State," 238; Heard interview with prominent white political observer of South Carolina, Heard Papers; Hollings quoted in Luders, "The Politics of Exclusion," 208.

88. The highly respected Strom provided a steady hand in his thirty-one-year tenure as director. Daniel E. Harmon, "SLED," *Sandlapper: The Magazine of South Carolina* (winter 2004), 22.

89. Grose, *South Carolina at the Brink*, 205.

90. Quint, *Profile*, 38–47; *NYT*, Aug. 30, 1951.

91. For this reason, it is not surprising that the SHP was slower in reforming its treatment of blacks and its hiring practices. Luders, "The Politics of Exclusion," 208; William J. Mathias and Michael G. Smith, "The South Carolina Highway Patrol: The First Half Century, 1930–1980," *Proceedings of the S. C. Historical Association* (2000), 15. No blacks applied until 1965; four joined by 1971. More than fifty municipalities passed anti-masking statutes in the late 1940s and early 1950s. Belknap, *Federal Law and Southern Order*, 23; William D. Workman, Jr., "Klan Again on the March," *NYT*, Dec. 3, 1950.

92. Cox, "1963—Year of Decision," 300. Vander Zanden ("Southern White Resistance Movement," 131) reports monthly rallies of at least one thousand spectators in the first half of 1956. *SSN*, Oct. 1956, p. 2; *Charleston Herald*, Sep. 27, 1957. State denial of organization charters to Klans disrupted their organization and resources. *SSN*, Mar., 1957 (page number illegible), *SSN*, Apr., 1957 (page number illegible), *SSN*, May, 1957, p. 3.

93. The year 1960 featured a wave of Klan cross-burnings across the upcountry and Pee Dee regions; for Hollings's very high estimate, see Luders, "The Politics of Exclusion," 206, fn. 26, quoting Hollings interview with Marcia G. Synnott interview (Jul. 8, 1980). On SLED surveillance of biracial student groups, see Dan T. Carter, "Coming Home to Carolina," Keynote Address at the 66th Annual Meeting of the University South Caroliniana Society, Apr. 27, 2002, accessed online: http://library.sc.edu/socar/index.html.

94. See chapter 10 in this volume.

95. *SSN*, Feb. 1958; *CR*, Oct. 9, 1962, quoted in Cox, "1963—Year of Decision," p. 1.

96. Stone, "Making a Modern State," pp. 84–85, 93; South Carolina State Planning Board, *The Fiscal System of South Carolina* (Columbia: State of South Carolina, 1939).

97. The plant was shared by Aiken, South Carolina, and Augusta, Georgia. Kari Frederickson, "The Cold War at the Grassroots: Militarization and Modernization in South Carolina," in Lassiter and Crespino, *The Myth of Southern Exceptionalism*, 190–209; Ernest M. Lander, Jr., *A History of South Carolina, 1865–1960* (Chapel Hill: University of North Carolina Press, 1960), 214; Grose, *South Carolina at the Brink*, 107,

86–87; Sampson, p. 85; Stone, "Making a Modern State," 480 (on textiles' share of industrial jobs).

98. Sampson, pp. 85, 113–14, table 2.22.

99. My guide through this maddening period is the political scientist Gregory Sampson, author of a tremendous study on the topic. Gregory B. Sampson, "The Rise of the 'New' Republican Party in South Carolina, 1948–1974: A Case Study of Political Change in a Deep South State," Ph.D. diss., University of North Carolina-Chapel Hill (1984), especially chaps. 5–7 and 9.

100. NYT, Oct. 18, 1957; WP, Oct. 18, 1957. SSN, Aug. 1957, p. 13; SSN, Oct. 1957, 15.

101. Sampson, p. 329, fn. 86; Parmet, The Democrats, 186.

102. At least in this case, ecological analysis is safe. Ward 9 in Columbia and in Charleston were almost entirely black, so inferences drawn from precinct-level data can be trusted. On Eisenhower's loss of metro whites in the Deep South, see Black and Black, The Vital South, chap. 6; Bartley, Rise of Massive Resistance, 162.

103. Sampson, p. 696.

104. James Duffy, "In GOP We Trust," unpublished memoir, SCPC; F. Clifton White with William J. Gill, Suite 3505: The Story of the Draft Goldwater Movement (New Rochelle, N.Y.: Arlington House, 1967), 21, 39; Perlstein, Before the Storm, 154. Milton Friedman saluted Spartanburg in a radio broadcast of his "Free to Choose" series. Wood, Southern Capitalism, 95. Republican leaders from the North included upcountry textile giant Roger Milliken, Greg Shorey, Constance Armitage, and Dabney Barnes. Kalk, Origins of Southern Strategy, 33, 38.

105. Kalk, Origins of Southern Strategy, 35–36, 44, 52. SSN, Apr. 1958, p. 14; Republican Platform, Republican Party File, Workman Papers.

106. For a fascinating account, see Perlstein, Before the Storm (on Milliken's ideology, 154).

107. Sampson, pp. 748, 751.

108. In categorizing Deep South politicians, AC editor Ralph McGill grouped Hollings with Mississippi's Ross Barnett. LAT, Jun. 4, 1961.

109. He had urged his speechwriters to avoid "Citizens Councils talk." Hollings letter to Workman, Apr. 21, 1958, Workman Papers. The inaugural address did not depart from white racial orthodoxy. Unlike Mississippi's James Coleman, Hollings praised the White Citizens' Councils.

110. Charles Daniel, head of the enormous Daniel International Construction Corporation in Greenville, chastised state officials and the state's bankers for delaying the modernization of the South Carolina economy. This modernization, he argued, required better-trained black workers and integrated labor markets, and that meant a higher sales tax, bond initiatives, and so on. Stone, "Making a Modern State," pp. 242–70; Bagwell, School Desegregation, 166–67; Claude R. Canup and William D. Workman, Jr., Charles E. Daniel: His Philosophy and Legacy (Columbia, S.C.: R. L. Bryan, 1981), 183–84; Cobb, Selling of the South, 79; SSN, Aug. 1961, p. 13.

111. Jordan, The Primary State, 48–49.

112. NYT, Mar. 16 and Jun. 13, 1960; Kalk, Origins of Southern Strategy, 42.

113. Stone, "Making a Modern State," pp. 505–9; Bass and De Vries, Transformation of Southern Politics, 250–51.

114. As with the 1948 Dixiecrat vote, support for independent elector and Republican slates in 1952 and 1956 centered in Black Belt counties and wealthy urban

precincts. Kalk, *Origins of Southern Strategy*, 9 and 29–30. Lowcountry legislators had recently passed a House resolution denouncing U.S. interference with South Africa's apartheid regime. Bagwell, *School Desegregation*, 159.

115. Stone, "Making a Modern State," p. 455. In 1960 the state remained predominantly rural; no city had a population larger than 100,000, and only three over 50,000. Chester Bain, "South Carolina: Partisan Prelude," in Havard, *The Changing Politics*, 590; Luders, "The Politics of Exclusion," p. 198; Neal R. Peirce, *The Deep South States of America: People, Politics, and Power in the Seven Deep South States* (New York: Norton, 1974), 411.

116. Just weeks before Gantt's arrival, Hollings traveled to Milan to discuss South Carolina's economic ties with the European Common Market. *NYT*, Dec. 12, 1962.

117. From 1940 to 1965, white workers filled more than 90 percent of the state's manufacturing jobs, and its textile mills remained effectively white-only by law. Although the law was repealed in 1960, only with the enforcement of the Civil Rights Act did blacks desegregate the mills, which boosted black incomes in the state. Wright, "Civil Rights Revolution," 280.

118. Sproat, "Firm Flexibility," 166. White Citizens' Council leader Farley Smith called on Hollings to join Barnett in Oxford, but Hollings refused. McMillan, "Integration with Dignity," 17–18, 20; Peirce, *Deep South States*, 394. Cox, "1963—Year of Decision," p. 24.

119. Perlstein, *Before the Storm*, 169; Russell Merritt, "The Senatorial Election of 1962 and the Rise of Two-Party Politics in South Carolina," *SCHM* 98 (1997), 281–301. Workman later claimed that Council leaders understood that violence was both legally and politically counterproductive in defending segregation. Workman, *Bishop from Barnwell*, 301; William D. Workman, Jr. *The Case for the South* (New York: Devin-Adair, 1960). Workman's vote tally was inflated by the fact that Johnston did not begin campaigning until October 10 (Sampson, p. 352). Observing higher rates of black voter registration in the early 1960s, as well as state data that the black failure rate on the selective service exam for draftees was 75 percent—mostly because of functional illiteracy—Workman suggested to Senator Strom Thurmond that Selective Service test results be used as "requirements for voting." Workman to Thurmond aide Harry Dent, Mar. 8, 1963, Workman Papers. For a later report, see Hubert M. Clements, Jack A. Duncan, and Richard E. Hardy, *The Unfit Majority: A Research Study of the Rehabilitation of Selective Service Rejectees in South Carolina* (Columbia: South Carolina Vocational Rehabilitation Department, October, 1967), 8.

120. Kalk, *Origins of Southern Strategy*, 35. And future governor John West later recalled that tensions had become so high that if "Hollings had said, 'Go to war,' the legislature would have done just that.... The state could have gone either way." Herbert Hartsook interview with Governor John West, quoted in Badger, "From Defiance to Moderation," 14; West in *CNC*, Aug. 10, 2003. Sen. Edgar Brown pointed to the relatively greater freedom of business leaders to speak in support of compliance. Workman, *Bishop from Barnwell*, 299.

121. Cox, "1963—Year of Decision," pp. 19–20, citing interview with Hollings. The marshals service had been roundly (but wrongly) pilloried for instigating crowd violence at Oxford. Doyle, *An American Insurrection*.

122. Earlier, Justice Department civil rights troubleshooter Burke Marshall approved of the state's law enforcement plans. Suggesting that federal intervention would not be necessary, Marshall wrote, "We have no intention of interfering in local matters where men such as yourself exert sufficient leadership that a crisis can be averted without publicity and without federal formal intervention of any sort at all." Quoted in Synnott, "Federalism Vindicated," 304–5.

123. Strom recalled, "We tried to write out a plan and improve on every mistake they made [so that] when Harvey Gantt came to Clemson, you could hear a pin drop." Oral history with Pete Strom, quoted in Grose, *South Carolina at the Brink*, 321–22, fn. 17; Luders, "The Politics of Exclusion," 213.

124. Hollings approved "The Advanced Plan of Law Enforcement, Maintenance of Student Discipline and Arrangements for the Press" in January. Synnott, "Federalism Vindicated," 316, fn. 43; Cox, "1963—Year of Decision," pp. 19–20, 40; Luders, "The Politics of Exclusion," p. 213, fn. 39. Letter from U.S. House member William J. B. Dorn to President Kennedy, Jan. 25, 1963, in Eisiminger, *Integration with Dignity*, 69. Governor Donald Russell, a Byrnes protégé and former president of the USC, took office on Jan. 22.

125. The *Charleston News and Courier* supported Senator Brown's strong declaration that Clemson "will not tolerate violence." A survey of newspapers found that almost all opposed a violent defense of Clemson. Cox, "1963—Year of Decision," p. 27.

126. "Not only must we insure law and order at Clemson College, but we must preserve and protect the good name of South Carolina." Quoted in Cox, "1963—Year of Decision," p. 37.

127. One scholar suggests that the quiet organization of elite support for a strategic accommodation "caught potential opposition by surprise," and that important white supremacist leaders misread Hollings's intentions. Cox, "1963—Year of Decision," pp. 22, 24. The group included Hollings, dean of the State Senate and Clemson trustee Edgar Brown, Clemson president Robert Edwards (a former textile manufacturer), Wayne Freeman (editor of the *Greenville News* and staunch segregationist who served on the Gressette Committee), John Cauthen (the state's leading textile lobbyist), and Charles Daniel. Sproat, "Firm Flexibility," 170.

128. Politicians later denied these allegations. McMillan, "Integration with Dignity," 20; Cox, "1963—Year of Decision," p. 60. Red Bethea was similarly contacted about investment in his home county of Dillon. Peirce, *Deep South States*, 394. On Edwards, see Cobb, *Selling of the South*, 258–59. On Calhoun County's economic situation, Sampson, p. 135, table 2.28.

129. Governor Ernest F. Hollings, "Address to the General Assembly of South Carolina" (Jan. 9, 1963), "Digital Collection: Fritz Hollings: In His Own Words," SCPC, accessed online: http://www.sc.edu/library/digital/collections/hollings.html.

130. *Florence* (S.C.) *Morning News*, Jan. 10, 1963; *NYT*, Jan. 15, 1963. Briefly protected by a security detail, Gantt faced no major problems at Clemson.

131. For example, *NYT*, Jan. 30, 1963; *CSM* lauded the "Triumph of Quite Voices," Jan. 22, 1963. McMillan, "Integration with Dignity," 16–21.

132. *NYT*, Apr. 4, 1963; Synnott, "Federalism Vindicated," 306. The cash value of prime contracts to South Carolina firms increased 600 percent from 1960 to 1968. Bureau of the Census, *Statistical Abstract*, various years. Synnott, "Federalism Vindicated," 295. *Pittsburgh Courier*, Feb. 16, 1963.

133. Gantt quoted in Jack Bass and Jack Nelson, *The Orangeburg Massacre*, 2nd ed. (Macon, Ga.: Mercer University Press, 1984 [1970]), 16. In the early 1970s, even South Carolina Senator Strom Thurmond endorsed the culturalist account of South Carolina's transition while butchering a famous quotation from Martin Luther King, Jr.: "It's not the color of people that count but the manners of people that really counts." Sampson, p. 603.

134. Synnott argues that Mississippi and South Carolina parted company on massive resistance "by the 1950s." "Federalism Vindicated," 292–318.

135. Had Timmerman had the opportunity to defy court-ordered school desegregation, the state might have headed "down the road Alabama and Mississippi were traveling at the time to ultimate civil disorder." However, no cases in the state reached fruition during his term. Sproat, "Firm Flexibility," 5. I. A. Newby emphasizes the state's fortunate timing in *Black South Carolinians*.

CHAPTER EIGHT:
Georgia's Massive Resistance and the Crisis at Athens

1. *SSN*, Sep. 1954, p. 5.

2. Harold P. Henderson, *Ernest Vandiver: Governor of Georgia* (Athens: University of Georgia Press, 2000), 17–19. As a share of per capita income, school spending was 2.6 percent, close to the national average of 2.8 percent. Ashmore, *The Negro and the School*, 115, 144–45.

3. In 1947 the legislature acknowledged severe racial disparities. R. O. Johnson, "Desegregation of Public Education in Georgia," *JNE* 24 (1955), 234–35. Aaron Brown, "The Education of Negroes in Georgia," *JNE* 16 (1947), 347–53, and "Negro Higher and Professional Education in Georgia," *JNE* 17 (1948), 280–88; William H. Brown, "Financial Support of Secondary Education for Negroes in Georgia," *JNE* 21 (1952), 478–83.

4. *SSN*, Sep. 1954, p. 5. Consolidation meant, as elsewhere, fewer administrative jobs.

5. Henderson, *Ernest Vandiver*, 24. Talmadge convinced his attorney general to rule him eligible to run again. Henderson, *Ellis Arnall*, 214–15. Correspondence among Talmadge, party chair Jim Peters, Roy Harris, and Bob Elliott, SDEC Papers, RBRL. Ellis Arnall refused to run after Thompson announced his bid. Henderson, *Ellis Arnall*, 216.

6. Thompson interview with Gene-Gabriel Moore in Henderson and Roberts, *Georgia Governors*, 72.

7. Roy Harris convinced the state party convention to declare *Sweatt* and *McLaurin* null and void in Georgia. Boyd, *Georgia Democrats*, 84.

8. From 1946 to 1954, the state's share of total school spending increased from 55 to 72 percent, as total spending rose from $19.2 million to $83.6 million. Henderson, *Ernest Vandiver*, 25; "Inaugural Address," Talmadge Papers, RBRL. The planned target for 1956 called for the reduction of 2,310 black schools to 511. R. O. Johnson, "Desegregation of Public Education," 232. *SSN*, Sep. 1954, p. 5. Bartley, *Creation of Modern Georgia*, 42–43.

9. The *Atlanta Journal* backed these equalization suits. *NYT*, May 1 and Aug. 14, 1949; *NYT*, Oct. 30, 1949.

10. Floyd Hunter, *Community Power Structure: A Study of Decision Makers* (Chapel Hill: University of North Carolina Press, 1953), 130–32; Ferguson, *Black Politics in New Deal Atlanta*; Tuck, *Beyond Atlanta*, 97, 100. Some two hundred black parents joined to sue Atlanta school officials. Also in 1950, blacks in Irwin County sued for equalization of school facilities.

11. Although Walden helped file a suit charging that Atlanta's state-mandated racially segregated schools were unconstitutional, he did not pursue the case. Rather, he used the threat of the suit as leverage in calling for reducing educational spending disparities by race. The NAACP dropped the case, *Aaron v. Cook*, in 1956. Opposed by almost the entire political class, including white moderate newspaper editor Ralph McGill, it had been the first such suit in the urban South. In response to it, Roy Harris proposed the private school option. Thomas V. O'Brien, "The Dog That Didn't Bark: *Aaron v. Cook* and the NAACP Strategy in Georgia before Brown," *JNH* 84 (1999), 79–88.

12. In 1949, after complaints from county party officials about the confusing ballot alternatives, the state adopted a mandatory secret ballot. Bernd, "Georgia: State and Dynamic," 299.

13. The Amendment required potential registrants to "understand and explain" the state constitution to the satisfaction of county boards of registrars. In *Davis v. Schnell*, 81 F. Supp. 872 (1949), the court ruled that the amendment led to arbitrary application and nonobjective evaluation. The Boswell Amendment—and disfranchisement devices more generally—split Alabama's ruling party along sectional and class lines. Many south Georgia politicians fought the device, fearing it would work as Alabama's rulers intended it to by disfranchising poorer whites likely to support a different faction.

14. *NYT*, Jan. 19, 1949; Re-Registration Act files, SDEC Papers, RBRL.

15. Blacks sued in state court, but the state Supreme Court upheld the law as nondiscriminatory in late 1949. *Franklin v. Harper*, 205 Ga. 779 (1949).

16. Olive H. Shadgett, *Voter Registration in Georgia* (Athens, Ga.: Bureau of Public Administration, 1955). Shadgett's influential survey hastened the law's repeal. Bernd and Holland, "Recent Restrictions," 497; Bernd, "Georgia: Static and Dynamic," 319; *CSM*, Jan. 4, 1950.

17. *Georgia Laws, 1949*, 528–532; Bernd, "Georgia: Static and Dynamic," 321; *CSM*, Mar. 29, 1949.

18. In 1952, Governor Talmadge still owned *The Statesman*, which employed two aides who were also on the state payroll. Other state workers "volunteered" on the campaign for the 1952 amendment, and "failure to help wouldn't affect their jobs." *Thomasville (Georgia) Times-Enterprise*, Sep. 24, 1952.

19. The pro-amendment pamphlet, "Your Stake in the County-Unit System," stated that the amendment would prevent "mixed schools," corrupt politics, organized crime, and blacks' control of state politics. It also featured pages of photographs of black men dancing with white women. This was not a typical arid debate about institutional change. Talmadgeite legal expert Charles Bloch defended the system from its critics by agreeing with them: "I defy [them] to point out ... the word 'democracy' in the Constitution!" Boyd, *Georgia Democrats*, 76–77 (and quotation at 39).

20. *Thomasville* (Georgia) *Press*, Oct. 17, 1952; Boyd, *Georgia Democrats*, 79–80.

21. In Atlanta opposition to the amendment and income were highly correlated; poorer and working-class whites were much more likely to back it. Bartley, *From Thurmond to Wallace*, table 3–1, 41.

22. File No. 12, Box 16, Series VI: Political, Russell Papers, RBRL. Many voters reportedly did not understand the proposed amendment. Bernd, "Georgia: Static and Dynamic," 323.

23. As discussed in chapter 3, party rules empowered the gubernatorial nominee to choose most members of the party's executive committee, giving the governor greater control of party machinery than those in other southern enclaves.

24. McDonald, *A Voting Rights Odyssey*.

25. Bartley, *Rise of Massive Resistance*, 37.

26. *NYT*, Jan. 19, 1954 and Nov. 17, 1953.

27. Leading white supremacists imagined the broader implications of the ruling, among which "racial intermarriage" was primus inter pares. On school segregation strategy discussions, Folders 7 and 12, Box 2, Papers of Herman E. Talmadge, RBRL.

28. However, other organizations—including groups of Atlanta churchwomen and the state's League of Women Voters—helped repeal these resolutions.

29. Bartley, *Rise of Massive Resistance*, 46; Jeff Roche, *Restructured Resistance: The Sibley Commission and the Politics of Desegregation in Georgia* (Athens: University of Georgia Press, 1998), 24; *Augusta Courier*, May 24, 1954; *The Statesman* (Hapeville, Georgia), Aug. 12, 1954. "THE PEOPLE" edited the paper, while Talmadge served as associate editor; Valien, "Status of Educational Desegregation," 360.

30. *Rome News-Tribune*, Oct. 6, 1954; Lassiter, *The Silent Majority*, 54–58.

31. *You and Segregation* (Birmingham: Vulcan, 1955); Robert W. Dubay, "Marvin Griffin and the Politics of the Stump," in Henderson and Roberts, *Georgia Governors*, 110; Peirce, *Deep South States*, 132; Bartley, *Rise of Massive Resistance*, 54–55, fn. 21. *SSN*, Nov., Oct., Dec. 1954, Jan. 1955; *Augusta Courier* (various issues, Nov.–Dec. 1954); Bernd, "Georgia: Static and Dynamic," 328–29; Bartley, *Rise of Massive Resistance*, 69.

32. *NYT*, Jun. 26, 1954; *Augusta Courier*, Aug. 23, 1954. Griffin called for large county school boards that would sort students by race. After receiving much criticism, he backed Talmadge's private school plan. *SSN*, Oct. 1, 1954, p. 6. To one observer, "Never in Georgia history had so many stolen so much." Dubay, "Marvin Griffin," 108. Soon after his departure, the state attorney general sought indictments for his kickback schemes.

33. Dubay, "Marvin Griffin," 109. His skirmishes with the Atlanta press began during the late 1930s, when he played a key role in Governor E. D. Rivers' more outrageous and illegal antics. *SSN*, Nov. 1955 (page number illegible), *SSN*, Dec. 1955 (page number illegible). Attorney General Cook called members of the Commission on Interracial Cooperation dupes of "the more sinister elements manipulating the Southern Regional Council." Johnson, "Desegregation of Public Education," 243. Valien, "Status of Educational Desegregation," 360.

34. At the time, Harris published a widely circulated white-supremacist broadsheet, the *Augusta Courier*. *SSN*, Sep. 1955, p. 16; *AC*, Sep. 24, 1955. Old Talmadge hands, in particular Roy Harris, helped build the Georgia States' Rights Council. McMillen, *The Citizens' Council*, 82.

35. In fact, controlling for sentiment, Georgia should have produced many more councils than other Deep South states since it had 159 counties.

36. Southern Regional Council, *Special Report: Segregation Groups in the South*; McMillen, *The Citizens' Council*, 85, 80–81. This inference is supported by Bartley, *Rise of Massive Resistance*, 103.

37. *NYT*, Jan. 21, May 1, and Jun. 24, 1949; *WP*, May 5, 1949; *CSM*, Feb. 5, 1949. For example, Attorney General Eugene Cook, "The Ugly Truth About the NAACP," before the 55th Annual Convention of the Peace Officers Association of Georgia (1955), Box 49, Folder 1, Vandiver Papers, RBRL.

38. Boyd, *Georgia Democrats*, 93.

39. Georgia's Highway Patrol—created in 1937 but rendered ineffective given local- and county-level opposition to a powerful state agency interfering with their police powers—still lacked sufficient bureaucratic autonomy to function as a professional and effective organization. Officially, the board of the Department of Public Safety chose the Patrol's director, but the governor's preference usually carried the day. Henderson, *Ernest Vandiver*, 53–54, 92; Dubay, "Marvin Griffin," 112; Woods, *Black Struggle, Red Scare*, 92–93, 105.

40. Aimee I. Horton, *The Highlander Folk School: A History of Its Major Programs, 1932–1961* (Brooklyn, N.Y.: Carson Publications, 1989).

41. *AC*, Dec. 8 and Dec. 10, 1952. A 1957 affair tarnished the commission's political legitimacy. When the commission acquired the unregulated capacity to wiretap, Vandiver, then lieutenant governor, warned of a "state Gestapo." *AC*, Oct. 30–31, 1957; Henderson, *Ernest Vandiver*, 57–58; Bartley, *Rise of Massive Resistance*, 222–23, fn. 56; *AJ*, Aug. 1, 1958; Dubay, "Marvin Griffin," 111.

42. Additionally, the governor could close any public facility or halt any activity harmful to public order. "The Act authorizes and empowers the Governor to 'take such measures and to do all and every act and thing which he may deem necessary in order to prevent overt threats of violence or violence.'" *Opinions of Attorney General Eugene Cook* 4:11 (Dec. 15, 1957), 1, Georgia Department of Archives and History, Atlanta.

43. Henderson, *Ernest Vandiver*, 137; McDonald, *A Voting Rights Odyssey*, 67; Boyd, *Georgia Democrats*, 95.

44. "Number of VOTING Delegates to which Branches are Entitled on Basis of Paid-Up Membership" (Jun. 11, 1957), Part 25, Series A, Supplement 2, Reel 5, NAACP Papers. Note that 1956 data do not appear in table 3.3 because they were not reliable for all three states.

45. *SSN*, Sep. 1955, Dec. 1955, Dec. 1956, and Feb. 1958. The state's first desegregation suit was filed in 1958. Atlanta academic Brailsford R. Brazeal authored a series of confidential memos for the Southern Regional Council that analyzed black mobilization efforts in several Georgia counties. Southern Regional Council Papers, Special Collections, Atlanta University Center Library; Tuck, *Beyond Atlanta*, 75, 81–82, 99; Adam Fairclough, *Race and Democracy: The Civil Rights Struggle in Louisiana, 1915–1972* (Athens: University of Georgia Press, 1995), 135.

46. For accounts of this accommodation in Atlanta, see Ronald H. Bayor, *Race and the Shaping of Twentieth-Century Atlanta* (Chapel Hill: University of North Carolina Press, 1996); Hunter, *Community Power Structure*; Stone, *Regime Politics*.

47. *Atlanta Daily World*, Dec. 9, 1945. The 1960 presidential election and sit-ins increased white registration. Clarence A. Bacote, "The Negro Voter in Georgia Politics,"

JNE 26 (1957), 308–11, 316; Walker, "Negro Voting in Atlanta," 380; M. Kent Jennings, *Community Influentials* (New York: Glencoe, 1964). Prior to his appeals to black voters, Hartsfield tacked to standard white supremacist positions, but privately told leaders of black organizations that that would change should black support become pivotal for him. Martin, *William Berry Hartsfield*, 46; Bradley R. Rice, "The Battle of Buckhead: The Plan of Improvement and Atlanta's Last Big Annexation," *Atlanta Historical Journal* 25 (1981), 5–22.

48. Bacote, "Negro in Atlanta Politics," 349–50. These officers could not arrest whites. Mayor Hartsfield often used them as stage props; in full regalia, they flanked him on the dais in speeches before black audiences. Martin, *William Berry Hartsfield*, 51. In 1951, the city hosted the NAACP's national annual convention, and Hartsfield greeted its delegates. Recent Nobel Prize laureate Ralph Bunche castigated the city's Jim Crow restrictions. "History in Georgia," *Time* magazine (Jul. 9, 1951); Boyd, *Georgia Democrats*, 96–100; Stone, *Regime Politics*, 31.

49. In 1957, Hartsfield won reelection thanks to capturing 97 percent of the black vote, as well as 70 percent of affluent whites. His opponent, successful restaurateur and white supremacist activist (and eventual governor) Lester Maddox, captured about two-thirds of working-class white Atlantans. Lassiter, *The Silent Majority*, 50, 59. The centralization of the city's school administration up to the state legislature and governor's office meant Hartsfield had little to offer his black coalition partners.

50. Bayor, *Race and the Shaping of Twentieth-Century Atlanta*, 7 (table 1) and 18 (table 2).

51. The number of Macon registrants fell from 3,750 to 1,600 over this period. Walton, Puckett, and Deskins, *The African American Electorate: A Statistical History*, 2:499, table 23.6.

52. Tuck, *Beyond Atlanta*, 79.

53. Atlanta and Savannah membership plunged after the violent 1946 election. Tuck, *Beyond Atlanta*, 6, 73–75, 85. Valuable here are B. R. Brazeal's remarkable county-level reports on black politics commissioned and circulated privately by the Southern Regional Council. Southern Regional Council Papers, Special Collections, Atlanta University Center Library.

54. Boyd, *Georgia Democrats*, 94.

55. Henderson, *Ernest Vandiver*, 82. He later joined the call for Eisenhower's impeachment.

56. William T. Bodenhamer, Baptist minister, leader in the Georgia States' Rights Council, ran "a blisteringly racist" campaign in 1958 while challenging Ernest Vandiver. Bodenhamer captured about one-quarter of the vote in south Georgia and the Black Belt, compared to only 7.8 percent in north Georgia (and 5.8 percent in Atlanta's Fulton County). Bartley, *From Thurmond to Wallace*, 32, table 2–9; *SSN*, Sep. and Oct. 1958.

57. Robert A. Pratt, *We Shall Not Be Moved: The Desegregation of the University of Georgia* (Athens: University of Georgia Press, 2002), 67. In deciding, Vandiver did not consult with Senators Richard Russell or Herman Talmadge. This fact reinforces a finding made throughout this study—federal officeholders had surprisingly little influence on enclave politics. Henderson, *Ernest Vandiver*, 81.

58. These included Roy Harris, Bob Elliott, and Carter Pittman, a leader of Georgia's States' Rights Council. Henderson, *Ernest Vandiver*, 84. Vandiver later admitted

that he would have won easily without this rhetorical excess. Pratt, *We Shall Not Be Moved*, 149.

59. *AJ*, Jan. 13–15, 1959; Pratt, *We Shall Not Be Moved*, 107. His most defiant advisers included brother-in-law Bobby Russell and Peter Zach Geer, the next lieutenant governor.

60. *AC*, Jan. 6, 1959; Henderson, *Ernest Vandiver*, 89. Georgia featured two school-closing laws—the first, signed in 1956, required the governor to close all desegregated schools. A 1959 law authorized the governor to close schools in a variety of contexts. Southern Regional Council, *A Report on School Desegregation, 1960–1961* (Atlanta: SRC, 1961), 32.

61. Hartsfield likened school closings to a bond forfeiture by the city. Atlanta agreed to desegregate one grade per year. Henderson, *Ernest Vandiver*, 105, 107, 111; Lassiter, *The Silent Majority*, 77.

62. *Atlanta Journal-Constitution*, Jan. 17, 1960; Henderson, *Ernest Vandiver*, 113; Boyd, *Georgia Democrats*, 95; Lassiter, *The Silent Majority*, 79.

63. Roche, *Restructured Resistance*.

64. The Commission's official name was General Assembly Committee on Schools. Roche, *Restructured Resistance*. Lassiter, *The Silent Majority*, chap. 2; Paul E. Mertz, "'Mind Changing Time All Over Georgia': HOPE, Inc., and School Desegregation, 1958–1961," *GHQ* 77 (1993), 41–61. Lassiter (53) notes that HOPE was led by upper-middle-class women, especially those living in Buckhead, an affluent neighborhood that had just a few years before been annexed by the city. Were it not for this annexation, he writes, "the city's confrontation with Georgia's massive resistance program would have been markedly different." On splits between north and south Georgia, see Lassiter, *The Silent Majority*, 81.

65. These included Coke, Ford, General Motors, Trust Company Bank, and Georgia Power. Lassiter, *The Silent Majority*, 71 and 76.

66. Fairclough, *Race and Democracy*, 234–64.

67. Lassiter, *The Silent Majority*, 84 and 87.

68. Roche, *Restructured Resistance*, 181; S. Ernest Vandiver, "Vandiver Takes the Middle Road," in Henderson and Roberts, *Georgia Governors*, 161.

69. *AC*, Jun. 22, 1957. In 1957 the suit was dismissed on a technicality. Roy Harris endorsed (the threat of) exactly this kind of violence. Both a leading white supremacist political strategist and a member of UGA's Board of Regents, he urged that "the negroes . . . consider . . . when the time comes for the white and negro children to attend the same schools, there is [*sic*] going to be a lot of people killed in this state. If that day ever comes, we will have bloodshed, race riots, and a race war, and the most terrible time this state has ever known." Quoted in Pratt, *We Shall Not Be Moved*, 61.

70. Henderson, *Ernest Vandiver*, 122; *WP*, May 10, 1961. Pratt, *We Shall Not Be Moved*, 108; Lassiter, *The Silent Majority*, 88. The exceptions were Frank Twitty and Carl Sanders, his House and Senate floor leaders, respectively. Kennedy eventually rejected Vandiver's nomination after the latter's public opposition to the desegregation of the armed forces and to interracial marriage in Brazil and the United States. *WP*, Jan. 29, 1961.

71. Charles Pyles, "S. Ernest Vandiver and the Politics of Change," in Henderson and Roberts, *Georgia Governors*, 152; *AC*, Feb. 21, 1958.

72. "The peaceful demonstrations for first-class citizenship which have recently taken place in many parts of this country are a signal to all of us to make good at long last the guarantees of our Constitution." "Democratic Party Platform of 1960," Jul. 11, 1960, *TAPP*, accessed online: http://www.presidency.ucsb.edu/ws/?pid=29602.

73. Henderson, *Ernest Vandiver*, 126. Malcolm Bryan, president of the Atlanta Federal Reserve, in a speech to the Atlanta Rotary Club, quoted in Cobb, *Selling of the South*, 130.

74. Black police from Atlanta guarded Holmes's residence. Pratt, *We Shall Not Be Moved*, 79–83.

75. Section 8 (a) of the 1956 General Appropriations Act provided state monies only to "racially segregated units" in public universities; Section 8 (d) terminated appropriations to desegregated public schools of higher education. Following the recommendation of the Sibley Commission, Vandiver also called for a constitutional amendment prohibiting the forced attendance of white students at mixed schools, as well as a tuition-grant program for white schools and the devolution of the power to close schools to the district level. *NYT*, Jan. 25, 1961; Pratt, *We Shall Not Be Moved*, 134, 88–89, 108–9.

76. One law student boasted that Hunter and Holmes would "receive the same greeting Autherine Lucy got at the University of Alabama." *AJ*, Jan. 15, 1961. FBI documents suggest that students invited Klansmen—and Roy Harris—to help them destabilize the campus. Indeed, a Klan-led conflagration would likely have been quite bloody, for Klansmen had advocated killing blacks involved in desegregation. Cohen, "G-Men in Georgia," 524–25, fn. 29.

77. Athens was a center of Klan activity in northern Georgia, and the surrounding Clarke County was home to a Klavern of some four hundred dues-paying members. In 1964 Klan members murdered a black army officer in Athens. Bill Shipp, *Murder at Broad River Bridge* (Atlanta: Peachtree Publishers, 1981); Pratt, *We Shall Not Be Moved*, 100, 103.

78. Student planners admitted to these communications during FBI interrogations. The politician was likely Lieutenant Governor Garland Byrd. Cohen, "G-Men in Georgia," 521, fn. 22.

79. Cohen, "G-Men in Georgia," 517–21; *Augusta Chronicle*, Jan. 12, 1961; Calvin Trillin, *An Education in Georgia: Charlayne Hunter, Hamilton Holmes, and the Integration of the University of Georgia* (Athens: University of Georgia Press, 1991 [1964]), 53.

80. Atlanta broadcaster Ray Moore recalled that Vandiver's office—as well as university officials—certainly knew in advance that it would occur that night. That day, planners "bragg[ed] about the promises of help and immunity they had received from legislators. Some students got dates for the basketball game and the riot afterward." Trillin, *An Education*, 52. Morehouse College faculty described the state's role as "planned negligence." Henderson, *Ernest Vandiver*, 138, 150–51; Pratt, *We Shall Not Be Moved*, 101–6; *AC*, Jan. 19, 1961.

81. By 1960, the total population of the eight largest counties—worth a total of 48 of the 206 unit votes needed to win a statewide election—was about 1.6 million, and for the first time was larger (by almost 350,000) than the total population of Georgians living in the 121 smallest counties—worth 242 unit votes. Louis T. Rigdon II, *Georgia's County Unit System* (Decatur: Selective Books, 1961), 40.

82. The virulence with which students defended white supremacy surprised faculty at the time and historians afterwards. Robert Cohen, " 'Two, Four, Six, Eight, We Don't Want to Integrate': White Student Attitudes toward the University of Georgia's Desegregation," *GHQ* 80 (1996), 616–45. Cohen relied on scores of student essays written soon after the riot. *AJ* quoted in *CSM*, Jan. 17, 1961. *Time* magazine summed up national coverage in "Shame in Georgia" (Jan. 20, 1961), 44; Lassiter, *The Silent Majority*, 89. Editorial cartoonists mocked the state.

83. Lassiter, *The Silent Majority*, 90–91; Harvey K. Newman, *Southern Hospitality: Tourism and the Growth of Atlanta* (Tuscaloosa: University of Alabama Press, 1999).

84. President John F. Kennedy, "The President's News Conference," August 30, 1961. *TAPP*, accessed online: http://www.presidency.ucsb.edu/ws/?pid=8294; Lassiter, *The Silent Majority*, 96–99, 105; *NYT*, Aug. 27, 28, and 31, 1961.

85. Lassiter, *The Silent Majority*, 68.

CHAPTER NINE:
The Civil and Voting Rights Acts and National Party Reform, 1964–72

1. The epigraphs in this chapter are from William Faulkner, Annual Meeting of the Southern Historians Association, Nov. 1955, in Egerton, *Speak Now*, 619; Marcia G. Synnott, "Desegregation in South Carolina, 1950–1963: Sometime Between 'Now and Never,'" in Winfred B. Moore and Joseph F. Tripp, eds., *Looking South* (Westport, Conn.: Greenwood, 1989), 59; John Lewis, *Walking with the Wind: A Memoir of the Movement* (New York: Simon & Schuster, 1998), 221 (quotation is from the original draft of his speech at the March on Washington for Jobs and Freedom); Jack Bass and Walter De Vries, *The Transformation of Southern Politics* (New York: Basic Books, 1976), 407.

2. An adviser to Mississippi governor Paul B. Johnson, Jr. (1964–68), in Derr, "The Triumph of Progressivism," 432.

3. Fairclough, *To Redeem the Soul of America*, 135, 141; Clayborne Carson, *In Struggle: SNCC and the Black Awakening of the 1960s* (Cambridge: Harvard University Press, 1995), 90.

4. There was a rapid takeoff of advertising spending by state development boards. Mississippi's 1964 spending doubled that of its neighbors. Cobb, *Selling of the South*, 70, 91–94.

5. Tony Badger, "Review Essay: Segregation and the Southern Business Elite," *Journal of American Studies* 18 (1984), 105–9; Jacoway and Colburn, *Southern Businessmen and Desegregation*.

6. Wright, *Sharing the Prize*, 79.

7. For example, assessments of the quality and safety of public schools influenced firms' decisions to relocate employees and their families to southern enclaves. Cobb, *Selling of the South*.

8. In 1968, Atlanta's Maynard Jackson, a black challenger to U.S. Senator Herman Talmadge, told a crowd of poorer whites that "Talmadge promised segregation

as a reward for your poverty, pain, and suffering, and he can't even deliver that." Bartley, *From Thurmond to Wallace*, 94.

9. Historian Tony Badger rightly notes that the state's leadership "had given people the drinks in the first place." Badger, "From Defiance to Moderation," 13.

10. Dan T. Carter, *The Politics of Rage: George Wallace, the Origins of the New Conservativism, and the Transformation of American Politics* (Baton Rouge: Louisiana State University Press, 1995).

11. Vote on House Resolution 7152, Civil Rights Act of 1964, Jul. 2, 1964 (88th Congress), accessed online: https://www.govtrack.us/congress/votes/88-1964/h182. David B. Filvaroff and Raymond E. Wolfinger, "The Origin and Enactment of the Civil Rights Act of 1964," in Grofman, *Legacies of the 1964 Civil Rights Act*, 9–32. The Civil Rights Acts of 1957 and 1960 are discussed later in this chapter.

12. Wright, *Sharing the Prize*, 84. The constitutionality of the Title II's reliance on the Commerce Clause was affirmed later that year in *Heart of Atlanta Motel Inc. v. United States*, 379 U.S. 241 (1964). Johnson quoted in Minchin and Salmond, *After the Dream*, 16.

13. Bayard Rustin, "From Protest to Politics: The Future of the Civil Rights Movement," *Commentary* 39 (1965), 25.

14. Gary Orfield, *The Reconstruction of Southern Education: The Schools and the 1964 Civil Rights Act* (New York: Wiley-Interscience, 1969).

15. On President John F. Kennedy's efforts to delay the Commission's hearings and reports, which brought to light embarrassing facts that resulted in unwelcome public pressure on the White House, see Richard Reeves, *President Kennedy: Profile of Power* (New York: Simon and Schuster, 1994), 467–70.

16. Wright, *Sharing the Prize*, 113; James J. Heckman and Brook S. Paymer, "Determining the Impact of Federal Antidiscriminatory Policy on the Economic Status of Blacks: A Study of South Carolina," *American Economic Review* 79 (1989), 138–77. On the effects of similar laws at the state level outside the South, see William J. Collins, "The Labor Market Impact of State-Level Anti-Discrimination Laws, 1940–1960," *Industrial and Labor Relations Review* 56 (2003), 244–72.

17. In 1964–65, the NAACP generated more than one-third of all charges received by the EEOC. Minchin and Salmond, *After the Dream*, 51; Ken Bode, "Unions Divided," *The New Republic*, Oct. 15, 1977, p. 21 (hereafter *TNR*).

18. U.S. Commission on Civil Rights, *Federal Efforts to Eradicate Employment Discrimination in State and Local Governments: An Assessment of the U.S. Department of Justice's Employment Litigation Section* (Washington, D.C.: Government Printing Office, 2001); U.S. Commission on Civil Rights, *For ALL the People. . . . By ALL the People: A Report on Equal Opportunity in State and Local Government* (Washington, D.C.: Government Printing Office, 1969); George P. Sape and Thomas J. Hart, "Title VII Reconsidered: The Equal Employment Opportunity Act of 1972," *George Washington Law Review* 40 (1972), 824–89; Donna L. Kohansky, "The Coverage of Appointees of State and Local Elected Officials Under the Equal Employment Opportunity Act of 1972 and Congressional Power to Enforce and the Fourteenth Amendment," *Georgetown Law Journal* 65 (1976–77), 809–36; Sean Farhang, *The Litigation State: Public Regulation and Private Lawsuits in the United States* (Princeton: Princeton University Press, 2010), 131–47; Graham, *The Civil Rights Era*, chap. 17. On its passage and

southern Democrats' long opposition to it, see Chen, *The Fifth Freedom*, 202–10. The DOJ began twenty-two suits against southern state and local governments by 1974. Minchin and Salmond, *After the Dream*, 159.

19. The need to desegregate southern law enforcement was a primary motivation of those pushing for this legislation as well as liberals in Congress. Senator Jacob Javits (R-NY), *Congressional Record* (May 3, 1967), 11,510; U.S. Commission on Civil Rights, *Law Enforcement: A Report on Equal Protection in the South* (Washington, D.C.: Government Printing Office, 1970). This was of course a longstanding demand by blacks. Myrdal, *An American Dilemma*, 103. The South's law enforcement apparatus would be reformed through carrots as well. The DOJ's Law Enforcement Assistance Administration offered block grants to communities for training and other purposes. U.S. Commission on Civil Rights, *Federal Civil Rights Enforcement Effort* (Washington, D.C.: Government Printing Office, 1970), 948.

20. U.S. Commission on Civil Rights, *Federal Civil Rights Enforcement Effort*, 937–51; Bertram J. Levine, *Resolving Racial Conflict: The Community Relations Service and Civil Rights, 1964–1989* (Columbia: University of Missouri Press, 2005). Democrats had recently called for something similar. "Democratic Party Platform of 1960," Jul. 11, 1960. *TAPP*, accessed online: http://www.presidency.ucsb.edu/ws/?pid=29602.

21. From 1962 to 1970, the number of federal categorical grant programs increased from 160 to 530. Hugh Davis Graham, "The Civil Rights Act and the American Regulatory State," in Bernard Grofman, ed., *Legacies of the 1964 Civil Rights Act* (Charlottesville: University Press of Virginia, 2000), 43–64; James L. Sundquist with David W. Davis, *Making Federalism Work: A Study of Program Coordination at the Community Level* (Washington, D.C.: Brookings Institution, 1969), 2.

22. U.S. Commission on Civil Rights, *Title VI. . . . One Year After: A Survey of Desegregation of Health and Welfare Services in the South* (Washington, D.C.: Government Printing Office, 1966); Gary Orfield, "The 1964 Civil Rights Act and American Education," in Grofman, *Legacies of the 1964 Civil Rights Act*, 101. Also see Orfield, *The Reconstruction of Southern Education*; Jerome T. Murphy, "The Education Bureaucracies Implement Novel Policy: The Politics of Title I of ESEA, 1965–1972," in Allan P. Sindler, ed., *Policy and Politics in America: Six Case Studies* (Boston: Little, Brown and Company, 1973), 160–98; Elizabeth Cascio, Nora Gordon, Ethan Lewis, and Sarah Reber, "Paying for Progress: Conditional Grants and the Desegregation of Southern Public Schools," *Quarterly Journal of Economics* 125 (2010), 445–82. Another important federal "pass-through" program which influenced the behavior of southern school districts' desegregation policies was the National School Lunch Act of 1948. Susan Levine, *School Lunch Politics: The Surprising History of America's Favorite Welfare Program* (Princeton: Princeton University Press, 2008), chaps. 6–7.

23. The Fifth Circuit played a crucial role in transforming the DHEW's voluntary guidelines into the Court's new standards for enforcing *Brown*.

24. See *U.S. v. Jefferson County Board of Education*, 372 F. 2d 836 (Fifth Circuit, 1966). The DHEW had fewer options with respect to pressuring all-white colleges and universities, as reflected in the much slower pace in their desegregation. Minchin and Salmond, *After the Dream*, 69–70, 123; Peter Wallenstein, ed., *Higher Education and the Civil Rights Movement: White Supremacy, Black Southerners, and College Campuses* (Gainesville: University Press of Florida, 2008).

25. See U.S. Commission on Civil Rights, *Equal Opportunity in Hospitals and Health Facilities: Civil Rights Policies Under the Hill-Burton Program* (Washington, D.C.: U.S. Government Printing Office, 1965); Karen Kruse Thomas, "The Hill-Burton Act and Civil Rights: Expanding Hospital Care for Black Southerners, 1939–1960," *JSH* 72 (2006), 823–70; Administrative History of the Department of Health, Education, and Welfare During the Johnson Administration, 1963–1969, Administrative History Papers, LBJL; Jill Quadagno, "Promoting Civil Rights Through the Welfare State: How Medicare Integrated Southern Hospitals," *Social Problems* 47 (2000), 68–89; Douglas Almond, Kenneth Chay, and Michael Greenstone, "The Civil Rights Act of 1964, Hospital Desegregation and Black Infant Mortality in Mississippi," (unpublished manuscript in author's possession dated March 2008; Christopher Bonastia, "The Historical Trajectory of Civil Rights Enforcement in Health Care," *JPH* 18 (2006), 362–86; David Barton Smith, *Health Care Divided: Race and Healing a Nation* (Ann Arbor: University of Michigan Press, 1999), chap. 5.

26. DHEW Administrative History, part 2, box 2, Administrative Histories, LBJL; Minchin and Salmond, *After the Dream*, 35; U.S. Commission on Civil Rights, *Federal Civil Rights Enforcement Effort*, 555. By 1969, as U.S. Commission on Civil Rights wrote, what was needed was "not so much new laws . . . as . . . strengthened capacity." U.S. Commission on Civil Rights, *Jobs and Civil Rights: The Role of the Federal Government in Promoting Equal Opportunity in Employment and Training* (Washington, D.C.: Government Printing Office, 1969), cited in Minchin and Salmond, *After the Dream*, 2. Hanes Walton, Jr., *When the Marching Stopped: The Politics of Civil Rights Regulatory Agencies* (Albany: State University of New York Press, 1988), chaps. 2–3; Tyson King-Meadows, *When the Letter Betrays the Spirit: Voting Rights Enforcement and African American Participation from Lyndon Johnson to Barack Obama* (Lanham, Md.: Lexington Books, 2011).

27. The Economic Opportunity Act, passed in June, 1964, created the OEO. Six of ten members of Georgia's House delegation voted for it on final passage, as did one of the six representatives from South Carolina. All of Mississippi's representatives opposed it. Almost immediately, community action agencies, and the OEO itself, were on the defensive. In the 1966 midterms, forty-five House incumbents who had backed the program lost their seats. U.S. House, Vote on S. 2642, (Aug. 8, 1964), accessed online: https://www.govtrack.us/congress/votes/88-1964/h201; U.S. House, Vote on House Resolution 12633 (Sep. 22, 1964), accessed online: https://www.govtrack.us/congress/votes/88-1964/h227; Parmet, *The Democrats*, 243. For illuminating studies of the War on Poverty in the South, see Susan Youngblood Ashmore, *Carry It On: The War on Poverty and the Civil Rights Movement in Alabama* (Athens: University of Georgia Press, 2008); Germany, *New Orleans After the Promises*; William S. Clayson, *Freedom Is Not Enough: The War on Poverty and the Civil Rights Movement in Texas* (Austin: University of Texas Press, 2010).

28. Sidney M. Milkis, "Remaking Government Institutions in the 1970s: Participatory Democracy and the Triumph of Administrative Politics," *JPH* 10 (1998), 51–74; Richard M. Flanagan, "Lyndon Johnson, Community Action, and the Management of the Administrative State," *Presidential Studies Quarterly* 31 (2001), 585–608; Michael L. Gillette, *Launching the War on Poverty: An Oral History* (New York: Oxford University Press, 2010), 318–28; Peter K. Eisinger, "The Community Action Program and the Development of Black Political Leadership," Discussion Paper No. 493–78

(Madison: Institute for Research on Poverty, University of Wisconsin, 1978); James A. Morone, *The Democratic Wish: Popular Participation and the Limits of American Government* (New York: Basic Books, 1990), chap. 6.

29. See Administrative History of the Office of Economic Opportunity during the Johnson Administration, 1963–1969, 66–86, Administrative History Papers, LBJL; Dittmer, *Local People*, chap. 16; Maris A. Vinoskis, *The Birth of Head Start: Preschool Education Policies in the Kennedy and Johnson Administrations* (Chicago: University of Chicago Press, 2005), 95–99; David C. Carter, *The Music Has Gone Out of the Movement: Civil Rights and the Johnson Administration, 1965–1968* (Chapel Hill: University of North Carolina Press, 2009), chaps. 2 and 5.

30. Bureau of the Census, *1970 Statistical Abstracts* (Washington, D.C.: Government Printing Office, 1970), 332, table 508.

31. Ibid., 86, table 124.

32. The 1957 Act authorized the U.S. Attorney General to bring civil and criminal charges against local election officials for denying equal access to voter registration. The 1960 Act enhanced the DOJ's capacity to file such cases, but very few were filed. Also see Daniel M. Berman, *A Bill Becomes a Law: The Civil Rights Act of 1960* (New York: Macmillan, 1962); Caro, *Master of the Senate*; Sundquist, *Politics and Policy*, 222–50; Brian K. Landsberg, *Free At Last to Vote: The Alabama Origins of the 1965 Voting Rights Act* (Lawrence: University Press of Kansas, 2007), chap. 7.

33. May, *Bending Toward Justice*, 48–51.

34. Stephen Tuck, "Making the Voting Rights Act," in Valelly, *Voting Rights Act*, 78; Garrow, *Protest at Selma*, 399; May, *Bending Toward Justice*, 82, 92, 95; Taylor Branch, *Pillar of Fire: America in the King Years, 1963–65* (New York: Simon & Schuster, 1998), 575–600.

35. David Alan Horowitz, "White Southerners' Alienation and Civil Rights: The Response to Corporate Liberalism, 1956–1965," *JSH* 54 (1988), 184–85; Garrow, *Protest at Selma*, 157; U.S. Senate, Vote on Conference Report of S. 1564 (the Voting Rights Act), Aug. 3, 1965 (89th Congress), accessed online: https://www.govtrack.us /congress/votes/89-1965/s178; U.S. House of Representatives, Vote on Conference Report of S. 1564 (the Voting Rights Act), Aug. 3, 1965 (89th Congress), accessed online: https://www.govtrack.us/congress/votes/89-1965/h107.

36. Voting included "all acts necessary to make a vote effective in any election, including registration." Section 14 (c) (1).

37. Section 10 of the Act also directed the DOJ to sue the four states still using a poll tax in any elections, and it quickly filed suits against Alabama, Mississippi, Texas, and Virginia. In March 1966, federal courts invalidated those in Alabama and Texas. In January, 1964, the Twenty-Fourth Amendment (never ratified by any Deep South state) eliminated the use of the poll tax in federal elections. Bruce Ackerman and Jennifer Nou, "Canonizing the Civil Rights Revolution: The People and the Poll Tax," *Northwestern University Law Review* 103 (2009), 63–148. Mississippi was the only state to vote on but reject ratification. Walton, Puckett, and Deskins, *The African American Electorate: A Statistical History*, 2:476–77. Sections 4 through 9 are temporary. They were renewed for an additional five years in 1970, seven years in 1975, twenty-five years in 1982, and twenty-five years in 2006.

38. For counties with larger shares of blacks, the use of so-called literacy tests was by the early 1960s most responsible for dampening black voter registration.

Onerous residency requirements disfranchised greater shares of whites than blacks. James E. Alt, "The Impact of the Voting Rights Act on Black and White Voter Registration in the South," in Chandler Davidson and Bernard Grofman, eds., *Quiet Revolution: The Impact of the Voting Rights Act, 1965–1990* (Princeton: Princeton University Press, 1994), 353–54. Later, the coverage formula was extended to include any jurisdiction in which a test or device appeared and in which the share of registrants fell below 50 percent of the voting-age population in 1968 or 1972.

39. Richard H. Pildes, "Introduction," in David L. Epstein, Richard H. Pildes, Rodolfo O. de la Garza, and Sharyn O'Halloran, eds., *The Future of the Voting Rights Act* (New York: Russell Sage Foundation, 2006), xii. Associate Justice Hugo L. Black invoked the still-dormant Guarantee Clause in support of his constitutional objections to Section 5. The Court upheld the law in *South Carolina v. Katzenbach*, 383 U. S. 301 (1966), at 359–60.

40. U.S. Commission on Civil Rights, *The Voting Rights Act: Ten Years After* (Washington, D.C.: Government Printing Office, 1975), 25, 28.

41. Mack H. Jones, "The Voting Rights Act as an Intervention Strategy for Social Change: Symbolism or Substance?" in Lorn S. Foster, ed., *The Voting Rights Act: Consequences and Implications* (New York: Praeger, 1985), 63–84.

42. May, *Bending Toward Justice*, 172; Howard Ball, Dale Krane, and Thomas P. Lauth, *Compromised Compliance: Implementation of the 1965 Voting Rights Act* (Westport, Conn.: Greenwood Press, 1982), 56. Steven F. Lawson, *In Pursuit of Power: Southern Blacks & Electoral Politics, 1965–1982* (New York: Columbia University Press, 1985), 29.

43. Katzenbach to President Johnson, April 26, 1966, Box 31, White House Central Files Ex PL/ST 1, LBJL. Katzenbach, who led federal marshals at Oxford, served as deputy attorney general from 1962 to 1965, and as attorney general from 1965 until October 1966.

44. Katzenbach called on nongovernmental organizations to publicize voter registration locations and educate blacks about their political rights. On freedom schools, see Len Holt, *The Summer That Didn't End: The Story of the Mississippi Civil Rights Project of 1964* (New York: Da Capo Press, 1992).

45. U.S. Commission on Civil Rights, *The Voting Rights Act: The First Months* (Washington, D.C.: Government Printing Office, 1966). Quoted in James C. Harvey, *Black Civil Rights during the Johnson Administration* (Jackson: University Press of Mississippi, 1973), 159; Christopher Hunter, *The Shameful Blight: The Survival of Racial Discrimination in Voting in the South* (Washington, D.C.: Washington Research Project, 1972), 28.

46. In planning stages, DOJ staff had recommended that examiners be sent immediately to Allendale and Williamsburg counties in South Carolina's lowcountry, to be followed by Charleston and Clarendon counties, and then Calhoun, McCormick, and Lexington counties. In these latter three counties, black voter registration amounted to just 13 percent of the black voting-age population. However, examiners in the first two years were sent only to Clarendon and Dorchester counties. Stephen J. Pollak to John Doar, Memo regarding Counties in which Examiners Are to Be Sent and Time Schedule, Jul. 18, 1965, and Doar to Katzenbach, Jul. 22, 1965, p. 8, both in Ex FG 135, Box 184, WHCF, LBJL; Hunter, *Shameful Blight*, 57, 87.

47. By the end of April 1966, examiners had registered more than 35,000 blacks in twenty-three Mississippi counties, compared to about 4,500 blacks in two South

Carolina counties. Two years later, barely one hundred more blacks had been registered by examiners in South Carolina, compared to an additional 23,000 in Mississippi. Macy to President Johnson, Apr. 25, 1966, and Apr. 25, 1968, both in Ex HU 2–7, Box 55, WHCF, LBJL. South Carolina, joined by Alabama, Louisiana, Mississippi, and Virginia, unsuccessfully challenged the constitutional validity of the act; the suit had the air of perfunctory position-taking about it. *South Carolina v. Katzenbach*, 383 U.S. 301 (1966). As long as local officials seemed to act fairly, large racial disparities in registration did not suffice as evidence of discrimination. Lawson, *In Pursuit of Power*, 23. County officials were expected to take "affirmative steps" to compensate for past discrimination. Southern Regional Council, *Special Report: The Effects of Federal Examiners and Organized Registration Campaigns on Negro Voter Registration in the South, Autumn 1970* (Atlanta: SRC, 1970).

48. Ball et al., *Compromised Compliance*, 56; L. Thorne McCarty and Russell B. Stevenson, "The Voting Rights Act of 1965: An Evaluation," *Harvard Civil Rights-Civil Liberties Law Review* 3 (1967), 371.

49. The vast majority of examiners were deployed before 1972.

50. U.S. Commission on Civil Rights, *Political Participation*, 173; Lawson, *In Pursuit of Power*, 21, 82, and 308, fn. 18; Hunter, *Shameful Blight*, 7.

51. Alt, "The Impact of the Voting Rights Act," 368–69; Lawson, *In Pursuit of Power*, 34; Garrow, *Protest at Selma*, 185–90; Minchin and Salmond, *After the Dream*, 30.

52. Very few observers were black, which lessened their effectiveness in reassuring black communities that voting was safe and that their vote would be fairly counted. The fact that they were often present only on election eve weakened their effects, since there was insufficient time to publicize their presence. U.S. Commission on Civil Rights, *The Voting Rights Act: Ten Years After*, 36; U.S. Commission on Civil Rights, *Political Participation*, 157–62.

53. Valelly, *The Two Reconstructions*, 200; John Lewis and Archie E. Allen, "Black Voter Registration Efforts in the South," *Notre Dame Law Review* 48 (1972–1973), 105–32; Drew S. Days III and Lani Guinier, "Enforcement of Section 5 of the Voting Rights Act," in Davidson, *Minority Vote Dilution*, 169–70.

54. Discussion of data appears in Valelly, *The Two Reconstructions*, 304, fn. 33.

55. From 1962 to 1964, VEP drives registered more than 550,000 blacks. However, almost 400,000 of those were Texans. In Georgia, about 60,000 blacks were registered (among the state's total black registration of 240,000), and in South Carolina about 32,000 of the state's 127,000 registered blacks. Efforts in Mississippi, cut off early because of bad results, did not reach 4,000, and the state's total black registration remained below 7 percent, at about 29,000. Press Release, Southern Regional Council, Aug. 3, 1964 (Atlanta, Georgia), Table III; Pat Watters and Reese Cleghorn, *Climbing Jacob's Ladder: The Arrival of Negroes in Southern Politics* (New York: Harcourt, Brace and World, 1967); Meier and Rudwick, *CORE*, 175–76; Reeves, *President Kennedy*, chap. 10; Richard J. Timpone, "Mass Mobilization or Government Intervention? The Growth of Black Registration in the South," *JOP* 57 (1995), 425–42. From 1965 to 1969, a second wave of VEP drives bankrolled almost five hundred separate voter registration and citizenship education programs. Minchin and Salmond, *After the Dream*, 28, 71; Valelly, *The Two Reconstructions*, 206.

56. By 1968, Mississippi's blacks led the Deep South in voter registration; in 1976 and 1986, they led all southern blacks. Lawson, *In Pursuit of Power*, 297.

57. U.S. Commission on Civil Rights, *Political Participation*, 155–56. In terms of the number of available offices, Georgia and its 159 counties offered the greatest opportunity among these states for electing black candidates. In demographic terms, Mississippi (37 percent) had the greatest share of blacks, compared to 26 percent for Georgia and 31 percent for South Carolina in 1970. By 1965, about 15 percent of Georgia's counties remained majority-black, compared to about one-third of those in Mississippi and South Carolina. By 1970, South Carolina had the highest proportion of majority-black counties (28 percent).

58. Hunter, *Shameful Blight*, 60–61, table 3.1, and p. 65, table 3.2.

59. James L. Sundquist, *Politics and Policy: The Eisenhower, Kennedy, and Johnson Years* (Washington, D.C.: Brookings Institution, 1968); Polsby, *How Congress Evolves*.

60. May, *Bending Toward Justice*, 152.

61. Before the Voting Rights Act, they had given priority to these states when preparing lawsuits against county election officials. Lawson, *In Pursuit of Power*, 21, 82, and 308, fn. 18.

62. *NYT*, Oct. 28, 1962.

63. McCarty and Stevenson, "The Voting Rights Act of 1965," 412. Data are drawn from the Civil Rights Division of the Department of Justice in late 1967. Lurleen Wallace, wife of outgoing governor George Wallace, ran for and won a gubernatorial race in 1966. In that year, her vote total almost doubled that of her husband's in 1962 (of course, nearly all newly enfranchised blacks opposed her). Observers pointed to an impressive series of voter registration drives undertaken by Wallace forces. May, *Bending Toward Justice*, 183; Carter, *Days of Rage*, 287; Peyton McCrary, Jerome A. Grey, Edward Still, and Huey L. Perry, "Alabama," in Davidson and Grofman, *Quiet Revolution*, 39; Minchin and Salmond, *After the Dream*, 31.

64. Memorandum, John W. Macy, Jr. to President Johnson, Aug. 31, 1965, HU 2–7, WHCF, LBJL.

65. Harold W. Stanley, *Voter Mobilization and the Politics of Race: The South and Universal Suffrage, 1952–1984* (New York: Praeger, 1987), chaps. 1–3.

66. In the predominantly rural, majority-black counties of all three states, black potential voters remained vulnerable to intimidation and physical and economic coercion. Whites exploited the standard pressure points: employment, credit, housing, access to federal welfare disbursements, and life and limb. U.S. Commission on Civil Rights, *The Voting Rights Act: The First Months*, 154, 138–39, 171–72. Hunter, *The Shameful Blight*, catalogues scores of such episodes.

67. On at-large districting as the "cornerstone" of vote dilution, see Peyton McCrary, "Bringing Equality to Power: How the Federal Courts Transformed the Electoral Structure of Southern Politics, 1960–1990," *University of Pennsylvania Journal of Constitutional Law* 5 (2003), 669. In all states, counties changed offices from elective to appointive as the black share of the electorate increased. Davidson and Grofman, *Quiet Revolution*.

68. Hunter, *Shameful Blight*, 139.

69. On capacity, see Ball et al., *Compromised Compliance*, 140–43; J. Morgan Kousser, "The Strange, Ironic Career of Section 5 of the Voting Rights Act, 1965–2007," *Texas Law Review* 86 (2008), 681; *Allen v. State Board of Elections of Mississippi*, 393 U. S. 544 (1969). Kousser notes that the U.S. Commission on Civil Rights' important 1968 report, *Political Participation*, flagged dilution practices as the primary obstacle

facing black electoral influence. Kousser, "The Strange, Ironic Career of Section 5," fn. 22, 673 and 674. Covered states submitted for review only 255 statutory changes through 1970; in the next five years, this number increased to 5,337. Valelly, *The Two Reconstructions*, 215.

70. Valelly, *The Two Reconstructions*, 208; William J. Crotty, *Decision for the Democrats: Reforming the Party Structure* (Baltimore: Johns Hopkins University Press, 1978), 44, 73–74.

71. Fairclough, *To Redeem the Soul of America*, 61–62.

72. Meier and Rudwick, *CORE*, 101, 144. While some younger activists criticized as insufficiently militant the voter registration drives of the NAACP and others, they quickly came to see such drives, especially in the rural Deep South, as dangerous enough to earn the label "direct action." Escorting registration applicants to county courthouses was the most dangerous component of such drives. COFO, "Overview of the Political Program," (no date, 1966), Jan Hillegas Collection, Jackson, Miss.

73. Meier and Rudwick, *CORE*, 415; Carson, *In Struggle*, 304.

74. SNCC, "Summary of SNCC Staff," 1964, Reel 1, frame 630, SNCC Papers. In a characteristic field report from Orangeburg, SNCC staffer Reginald Robinson reported that the NAACP has "given me nothing but the run around," and had refused to permit the town's local NAACP branch to work with SNCC. Robinson, "Field Report: Orangeburg, S.C.," Feb. 23, 1963, Reel 40, frame 542, SNCC Papers; also see SNCC, "Current Field Work, Spring 1963," Reel 17, SNCC Papers.

75. Clayborne Carson, "SNCC and the Albany Movement," *Journal of Southwest Georgia History* 2 (1984), 15–25. In summer 1965, SNCC based seventeen workers in Georgia, but almost all held administrative posts in Atlanta. *NYT*, Aug. 1, 1965; Tuck, *Beyond Atlanta*, 115–27. By 1966, only one-third of SNCC staffers remained in the rural South. Carson, *In Struggle*, 281.

76. Meier and Rudwick, *CORE*, 12–13 (quotation here), 415, 169, 261.

77. Meier and Rudwick, *CORE*, 88–90, 112–14, 117, 164–66, 217; Everett C. Ladd, *Negro Political Leadership in the South* (Ithaca: Cornell University Press, 1966), 109. On Atlanta, Len Holt, "Field Report" (May 24, 1960), Series 5, Reel 40, vol. 334, p. 509, CORE Papers.

78. Luders, *The Civil Rights Movement and the Logic of Social Change*, 23.

79. Tuck, *Beyond Atlanta*, 149; David J. Garrow, *Bearing the Cross: Martin Luther King, Jr., and the Southern Christian Leadership Conference* (New York: William Morrow, 1986), chap. 4. Also see Charles D. Hadley, "The Transformation of the Role of Black Ministers and Black Political Organizations in Louisiana Politics," in Laurence W. Moreland, Robert P. Steed, and Tod A. Baker, eds., *Blacks in Southern Politics* (New York: Praeger, 1987), 133–48; Morris, *Origins of the Civil Rights Movement*, 23.

80. Particularly for black clergy who were not financially dependent of local whites, involvement in militant protest was difficult. Even in the SCLC's massive Birmingham project in 1963, only twenty of more than two hundred local black clergy supported the effort. Fairclough, *To Redeem the Soul of America*, 35, 194–95. On black ministers in Mississippi, see Dittmer, *Local People*, 75; Harvey, *Freedom's Coming*, 191.

81. Fairclough, *To Redeem the Soul of America*, 91, 206, 95.

82. For example, Part 26, Series A, Selected Branch Files: The South, 1940–55, Reel 9, frame 919, NAACP Papers.

83. For example, Medgar Evers to Roy Wilkins, Gloster Current, and Ruby Hurley, "Special Report on the Operation of Other Civil Rights Organizations in the State of Mississippi," Oct. 12, 1961, Reel 15, p. 16, NAACP Papers.

84. Bob Moses to SNCC Executive Committee, (no date, 1963), p. 2, Reel 40, frame 0004, SNCC Papers; SNCC, "Current Field Work, Spring 1963," Reel 17, SNCC Papers.

85. Such parties or proto-parties sprang up in several southern states during the 1960s. See Walton, *Black Political Parties*.

86. Of course, whether the national party controlled Congress and/or the White House greatly affected its ability to issue (or threaten) reprisals to rebellious state parties.

87. *Newsweek*, Jul. 27, 1964. Mississippi Republican party chair Wirt Yerger accused the White House of fomenting racial disturbances to aid his reelection bid. On the RNC's 1963 conference in Denver, Robert D. Novak, *The Agony of the GOP, 1964* (New York: Macmillan, 1965), 179.

88. Paul Tillett, ed., *Inside Politics: The National Conventions, 1960* (Dobbs Ferry, N.Y.: Oceana, 1962), 53–83; White with Gill, *Suite 3305*, 163–65, 203, 218–24; *NYT*, Jul. 25, 1960; Perlstein, *Before the Storm*, 215, 371–72, 379–84; *NYT*, Jul. 15, 1964. Cosman, *Five States for Goldwater*.

89. Lewis Chester, Geoffrey Hodgson, and Bruce Page, *An American Melodrama: The Presidential Campaign of 1968* (New York: Viking, 1969), 190.

90. Crotty, *Decision for the Democrats*, 14, 276–77, fn. 19. Eventually the national party required that blacks "have the opportunity to participate fully in party affairs," but did not require their presence in state delegations. Still, observers saw the rules as spelling the end of the party's "lily white" delegations. *NYT*, Jan. 9 and 13, 1968; *WP*, Jul. 8, 1968.

91. Valelly, *The Two Reconstructions*, 209.

92. John R. Schmidt and Wayne W. Whalen, "Credentials Contests at the 1968 and 1972 Democratic National Conventions," *Harvard Law Review* 82 (1969), 1450–54.

93. Byron E. Shafer, *Quiet Revolution: The Struggle for the Democratic Party and the Shaping of Post-Reform Politics* (New York: Russell Sage Foundation, 1983), 161–68, 541.

94. George McGovern and then Donald Fraser chaired the DNC's Commission on Party Structure and Delegate Selection. The reforms have been alternately celebrated and criticized for altering presidential nominations and for changing the relationship between levels of the party. Probably the most important consequence of the reforms—the quick move from delegate selection by convention to the use of primaries—was completely unanticipated by reformers. Crotty, *Decision for the Democrats*, 5–6; Shafer, *Quiet Revolution*; Nelson Polsby, *Consequences of Party Reform* (Oxford: Oxford University Press, 1983); Howard Reiter, *Selecting the President: The Nominating Process in Transition* (Philadelphia: University of Pennsylvania Press, 1985); Marty Cohen, David Karol, Hans Noel, and John Zaller, *The Party Decides: Presidential Nominations Before and After Reform* (Chicago: University of Chicago Press, 2008). Also see Jeffrey S. Walz and John Comer, "State Responses to National Democratic Party Reform," *Political Research Quarterly* 52 (1999), 189–208; Scott R. Meinke, Jeffrey K. Staton, and Steven T. Wuhs, "State Delegate Selection Rules for Presidential Nominations, 1972–2000," *JOP* 68 (2006), 180–93.

95. Crotty, *Decision for the Democrats*, 203. The share of black delegates at Democratic conventions increased from fewer than 3 percent in 1964, to 15 percent in 1972, to one-fifth in 2004.

96. Valelly, *The Two Reconstructions*, 210.

CHAPTER TEN:

Harnessing the Revolution? Three Paths Out of Dixie

1. Governor Paul B. Johnson, Jr., quoted in Derr, "The Triumph of Progressivism," 452; *JDN*, Jan. 30, 1965.

2. Since the mid-1960s, political actors and observers have constructed a "Mississippi exceptionalism." On this view, differences in degrees of political tumult and violence among southern states constitute differences in kind. Because Mississippi was the "worst" southern state, its democratization experience is retrospectively explained as inevitable given the state's "nature." This approach serves the interests of politicians of other southern states, past and present, who continue, as V. O. Key noted in 1949, to "thank God for Mississippi" (*Southern Politics*, 229). An exceptional Mississippi highlights their successes, while their failures pale by comparison. Joseph Crespino, "Mississippi as Metaphor: Civil Rights, the South, and the Nation in the Historical Imagination," in Lassiter and Crespino, *The Myth of Southern Exceptionalism*, 99–120.

3. Here I do not minimize the countless injustices, small and large, that characterized enclave rule, or suggest that the external interventions that arrived in the state one century after the end of the Civil War were excessive. Rather, the breaches of Mississippi "sovereignty" described here were vastly greater than those experienced by other enclaves. Stated another way, interventions in Georgia, South Carolina, and elsewhere can safely be interpreted as much too small given these enclaves' previous track record and token compliance.

4. Barnett appointed the "moderate" Erle Johnston director of the State Sovereignty Commission, just one year after his public conflict with the White Citizens' Councils. Under his direction, the SSC played an important "troubleshooting" role at the community level (discussed later).

5. A photograph of Johnson confronting the leader of the federal marshals at Oxford helped his "Stand Tall with Paul" campaign. His main opposition in the primary was former Governor Coleman. Johnson successfully exploited Coleman's support of the Kennedy administration. Oral history with Pete Johnson (Jan. 26, 1993), CRMDA; oral history with Erle Johnston, No. 2 (Aug. 13, 1993), CRMDA; Derr, "The Triumph of Progressivism," 194, 159–60; Johnston, *Politics: Mississippi Style*, 154; Butler, "The Republican Party in Mississippi," 66.

6. Johnson, traveling frequently to encourage capital investment and firm relocation, worried greatly about the state's image. The state's spending on advertising for its state development programs in 1964 more than doubled that of its Deep South neighbors. Derr, "The Triumph of Progressivism," 212; Cobb, *Selling of the South*, 91.

7. "Ours is a state in transition . . . the Mississippi economy is not divisible by political party or faction, or even by race, color or creed." Avoiding any talk of

defiance, he insisted that "we are Americans as well as Mississippians. . . . Hate, or prejudice, or ignorance will not lead Mississippi while I sit in the governor's chair." *NYT*, Jan. 22, 1964; Derr, "The Triumph of Progressivism," 189, 225–31. Mississippi journalist Bill Minor termed this Johnson's "rejoin the Union speech." *New Orleans Times-Picayune*, Jan. 26, 1964; oral history with Ken Fairly (Jul. 7, 1993), CRMDA. Later he vowed that the state would "have no more Ole Miss invasions nor future Birmingham visitations. I shall so protect your vital interests in such a manner that no President can find an excuse for federal troops to put their feet on Mississippi soil."

8. Charles Sallis and John Quincy Adams, "Desegregation in Jackson, Mississippi," in Jacoway and Colburn, *Southern Businessmen and Desegregation*, 236–56; *NYT*, Jul. 6, 1964; Dittmer, *Local People*, 275–76; Joseph Luders, "Civil Rights Success and the Politics of Racial Violence," *Polity* 37 (2005), 124.

9. Mississippi Republican Party, "Summary of Public Opinion in Mississippi in Regard to the Negro Issue" (unpublished, 1964), cited in Butler, "The Republican Party in Mississippi," 78–79.

10. Mississippians for Public Education, "A Time to Speak" (brochure), no date, Constance Curry Papers, Manuscript, Archives, and Rare Book Library, Emory University (accessed online: Online Manuscript Resources in Southern Women's History); Dittmer, *Local People*, 228, 353–62.

11. Cobb, *Most Southern Place*, chap. 11.

12. Oral history with Ken Fairly (Jul. 7, 1993), CRMDA; Crespino, "Strategic Accommodation," p. 160. The most important short-term impact of Oxford was a heightened "white resistance to COFO activity in the Delta and throughout the state." Dittmer, *Local People*, 138.

13. Oral history with Ken Fairly (Jul. 7, 1993), CRMDA. Data on Klan support are notoriously unreliable. On journalist Bill Minor's estimate, 5,000 Mississippians joined Klan organizations by the summer of 1964. Large numbers of white industrial workers lived in Natchez and other towns in southwest Mississippi and Klan recruiters in nearby Louisiana targeted them in membership drives. Dittmer, *Local People*, 138, 216–17, and 476, fn. 7.

14. Derr, "Triumph of Progressivism," 368–71; oral history with Jesse Boyce Holleman (Aug. 9, 1976), CRMDA. About five out of some 275 patrolmen were thought to have joined the Klan.

15. Dittmer, *Local People*, 138, 175.

16. On the Holmes County movement, Andrews, *Freedom Is a Constant Struggle*, chap. 4; Spencer D. Wood, "The Roots of Black Power: Land, Civil Society, and the State in the Mississippi Delta, 1935–1968," Ph.D. diss., University of Wisconsin-Madison (2006).

17. *JCL*, Jan. 4, 1964; Hodding Carter, "Invasion Imminent," *Greenville Delta Democrat-Times*, Jun. 17, 1964. "The sheriffs stick together for mutual protection and are jointly so powerful that governors and legislators tiptoe around them." Reese Cleghorn, "The Two Faces of Sheriff Rainey," *NYT Magazine* (Feb. 21, 1965), 11; Derr, "Triumph of Progressivism," 210–11. During its then-longest legislative session, Mississippi passed statutes facilitating the suppression of white supremacist groups advocating or committing violence, as well as criminalizing tactics employed by black protest workers. Jerry DeMuth, " 'Criminal Syndicalism' in Mississippi," *Texas Observer* 56 (Nov. 13, 1964).

18. Derr, "The Triumph of Progressivism," 262–63.

19. It also monitored gun sales in the southwest of the state. Unlike patrolmen, investigators could serve warrants and make arrests in any jurisdiction once authorized by the governor. The Bureau of Investigation of the MHP focused on the southwest counties, while the Sovereignty Commission monitored both COFO and white supremacists. The state also created several anti-riot squads. Oral history with George Saxon (Jun. 3, 1993), CRMDA. Oral history with Ken Fairly (Jul. 7, 1993), CRMDA. This warrant of authority to the governor had to be renewed every four years. All involved understood that "civil rights disturbances" motivated the legislation. Oral history with Charles Marx (Oct. 28, 1976), CRMDA; Derr, "Triumph of Progressivism," 200–201, 253, 262–63, 467; Johnston, *Mississippi's Defiant Years*, 237–39.

20. The state's willingness and capacity to suppress white crowd violence became painfully clear to whites in crowd disturbances in Grenada. There, some whites—tears streaming down their faces, brows twisted with incredulity—spat and cursed at officers, calling them "Paul Johnson's niggers." Oral history with Ken Fairly (Jul. 7, 1993), CRMDA; oral history with Charles Marx (Oct. 28, 1976), CRMDA; oral history with Lt. Col. Billie Hughes (Jul. 7, 1993), CRMDA.

21. Derr, "Triumph of Progressivism," 400–409, 425.

22. *NYT*, Nov. 25, 1984.

23. Crespino, *In Search of Another Country*, chap. 4, offers an original and convincing reinterpretation of the commission along these lines.

24. Ibid.

25. The tax code referred to whiskey as "tangible personal property, the sale of which is prohibited by law." Bill Minor, *New Orleans Times-Picayune*, Mar. 13, 1955.

26. Within one year, more than fifty of eighty-two counties legalized liquor. Derr, "The Triumph of Progressivism," 502–5; oral history with C. B. "Buddie" Newman (Jun. 18, 1992), CRMDA; Belknap, *Federal Law and Southern Order*, 138–39, 233–40; Johnston, *Politics: Mississippi Style*, 167–73; Robert Canzoneri, *"I Do So Politely": A Voice from the South* (Boston: Houghton Mifflin, 1965), 115–21; *WSJ*, Feb. 18, 1966.

27. Oral history with Lieutenant Colonel Billie Hughes (Jul. 7, 1993), CRMDA.

28. The U.S. Commission on Civil Rights offered an institutional account of Mississippi's law enforcement problems. It noted that six of its eleven recommendations regarding state and local law enforcement in Mississippi echoed those made by the exhaustive Brookings report (see chapter 11 in this volume). *Law Enforcement*, chap. 5, esp. 97–99. The report drew on data from Alabama, Florida, Georgia, and Mississippi.

29. Payne, *Light of Freedom*; Dittmer, *Local People*, chaps. 5–6, 120. CORE's national office insisted that its workers have their own territory, so COFO set aside the state's Fourth Congressional District in central Mississippi.

30. Neil R. McMillen, "Black Enfranchisement in Mississippi: Federal Enforcement and Black Protest in the 1960s," *JSH* 43 (1977), 360–64.

31. Quoted in Payne, *I've Got the Light of Freedom*, 317.

32. Immediately after Oxford, county officials withheld food relief from recipients and fired farmworkers because of their civil rights activism. This coercion backfired, as food distribution efforts facilitated SNCC's rural outreach to register voters. Dittmer, *Local People*, 128, 144–45; Carson, *In Struggle*, 80.

33. Dittmer, *Local People*, 244, 251. Only 1,600 blacks were registered, most in just one county. McMillen, "Black Enfranchisement in Mississippi."

34. Woodward, *Strange Career*, 186.

35. Crespino, *In Search of Another Country*, 116; Seth Cagin and Philip Dray, *We Are Not Afraid: The Story of Goodman, Schwerner, and Chaney and the Civil Rights Campaign in Mississippi* (New York: Scribner, 1988). The FBI agreed to treat the case as a kidnapping, and 153 agents entered the state. Two hundred U.S. Marines and four hundred sailors joined local, state, and federal investigators in the search for the missing three. Derr, "The Triumph of Progressivism," 292–94; Cunningham, *There's Something Happening Here*, 72. In late 1967 an all-white jury convicted Deputy Sheriff Cecil Price and six others of violating the civil rights of those they murdered. Dittmer, *Local People*, 418.

36. Dittmer, *Local People*, 55.

37. Derr, "The Triumph of Progressivism," 425. In *Before the Storm* (212–14), Rick Perlstein captures how national establishment media biased their coverage of southern and nonsouthern disturbances, and the political consequences of this bias. In 1963, he notes, national press wrongly interpreted massive civil rights boycotts and demonstrations targeting local injustices in northern cities as sympathy rallies for protests in Birmingham.

38. C. L. Sulzberger, "The Foreign Policy of Mississippi," *NYT*, Oct. 3, 1962. Reinhold Niebuhr wrote, "Justice in Mississippi is corrupted to such a degree that without aid from the outside it is doomed." Preface to Council of Federated Organizations, ed., *Mississippi Black Paper: Fifty-Seven Negro and White Citizens' Testimony of Police Brutality, the Breakdown of Law and Order, and the Corruption of Justice in Mississippi* (New York: Random House, 1965).

39. *NYT*, Dec. 18, 20, 1964; *WSJ*, Feb. 2, 1965; Derr, "The Triumph of Progressivism," 363; *LAT*, Dec. 14, 1964.

40. According to Evers, in response to a demand that Mississippi receive examiners in every county, President Johnson asserted, "I'm going to send in enough to show that we will come if they don't give you the support that you want." In Gibson's terms, these democratizers overcame rulers' monopoly on linkages to the central state by forging their own. Transcript, Charles Evers Oral History Interview I, Apr. 3, 1974, by Joe B. Frantz, Internet Copy, LBJL; Crespino, *In Search of Another Country*, 161.

41. The state also faced the most DOJ lawsuits in the years preceding the Voting Rights Act; by August 1965, sixty of its eighty-two county registrars had suits pending against them. *WP*, Jul. 2 and Sep. 1, 1965; oral history with Brad Dye (Sep. 20, 1993), CRMDA; Derr, "The Triumph of Progressivism," 486–87; Lawson, *In Pursuit of Power*, 21, 82, and 308, fn. 18.

42. Watters and Cleghorn, *Climbing Jacob's Ladder*, 262; transcript, Andrew J. Young, Jr., Oral history Interview I, Jun. 18, 1970, by Thomas H. Baker, 18–19, LBJL.

43. Southern Regional Council, *Special Report: Effects of Federal Examiners*.

44. *CSM*, Apr. 26, 1966; *NYT*, Nov. 17, 1966. Lawson, *In Pursuit of Power*, 297.

45. Lawson, *In Pursuit of Power*, 177–83; Bass and De Vries, *Transformation of Southern Politics*, 185–88.

46. Traditionally, each county was divided into five "beats," or precincts. Each precinct elected its own supervisor to the board. With the advent of substantial black voting, majority-black precincts would be able to elect many black supervisors. HB 223, *Mississippi Laws*, 1966, chap. 290; Frank Parker, *Black Votes Count: Politi-*

cal Empowerment in Mississippi after 1965 (Chapel Hill: University of North Carolina Press, 1991). In 1962, before black voting began in earnest, the state required cities to use at-large elections for their city councils, and banned single-shot voting and required winners to receive majorities. The state Senate justified the law as a tool for reducing black electoral power.

47. Bass and De Vries, *Transformation of Southern Politics*, 188; Cobb, *Most Southern Place*, chap. 11.

48. White House adviser Lee C. White to President Johnson, Jul. 16, 1964, Box 2, White House Central Files, Ex HU 2, LBJL; *NYT*, Jul. 6, 1964; Weill, "In a Madhouse's Din," p. 201; Sallis and Adams, "Desegregation in Jackson, Mississippi", *JCL*, Jul. 4 and 7, 1964; *JDN*, Jul. 9, 1964. In some spaces, such as hotels, the city desegregated more quickly than other southern cities.

49. The legislature would not be reapportioned until 1967.

50. In McComb, whose violence and disorder had been widely publicized nationally, national insurance firms ordered local agents to sell additional coverage, and the city's largest manufacturer began shipping its products from Louisiana "to avoid the 'made in McComb' stigma." Dittmer, *Local People*, 309–10; Hodding Carter, *So the Heffners Left McComb* (Garden City, N. Y.: Doubleday & Company, Inc., 1965), 135–36. The statement is in U.S. Commission on Civil Rights, *Hearings in Jackson, Mississippi*, held Feb. 16–20, 1965 (Washington, D.C.: Government Printing Office, 1965); *CSM*, Feb. 15, 1965; *WP*, Feb. 20, 1965. On Stennis, Crespino, *In Search of Another Country*, 131. Official concern about the state's image was most evident in politicians' extensive cooperation with the U.S. Commission on Civil Rights, which held hearings in Jackson. McMillen, "Development of Civil Rights," 154–76.

51. Jackson's mayor formed a biracial committee that issued a majority report denouncing the Highway Patrol; the mayor fired Jackson's police chief. Governor Williams called on the MHP to withhold its cooperation with the Davis Committee, and Williams said that its own "complete and impartial investigation" blamed the protesters. Stephan Lesher, "Jackson State, A Year After," *NYT Magazine* (Mar. 21, 1971), 48–62; oral history with Charles Marx (Oct. 28, 1976), CRMDA; Bill Minor, *New Orleans Times-Picayune*, May 24, 1970; Tim Spofford, *Lynch Street: The May 1970 Slayings at Jackson State College* (Kent, Ohio: Kent State University Press, 1988).

52. Having peaked in population in 1930 at about one million, black Mississippi by 1970 had declined to its lowest level since the 1890s. Carter et al., *Historical Statistics* 1: 505 and 507, table Ac53–205.

53. Dittmer, *Local People*, 384. In 1966 the state's producers took in almost $40 million (just shy of $300 million in 2013 dollars).

54. Cobb, *Most Southern Place on Earth*, 255–56. On the FLSA reform, see Linda C. Majka and Theo J. Majka, *Farm Workers, Agribusiness, and the State* (Philadelphia: Temple University Press, 1982), 260. On the tour, one U.S. senator said conditions "bordered on genocide." On the hunger tour, *LAT*, May 9, 1967; Dittmer, *Local People*, 364, 383–86; *NYT*, Apr. 24 and 30, 1967; John Dittmer, *The Good Doctors: The Medical Committee for Human Rights and the Struggle for Social Justice in Health Care* (New York: Bloomsbury Press, 2009), 230–31. Mississippi Republicans angrily rebutted charges of hunger and famine in a pamphlet entitled, "Are They Deliberately Starving Negroes in Mississippi?" Clippings File, Republican Party, MDAH.

55. Oral history with James P. Coleman (Nov. 12, 1981 and Feb. 6, 1982), CRMDA; *NYT*, Jul. 20, 1961; Jeff Broadwater interview with William E. Winter, Center for Oral History and Cultural Heritage, McCain Library, University of Southern Mississippi, 21.

56. Organizers had hoped for a turnout of 200,000, which would have amounted to about 40 percent of the state's voting-age population. Voters "elected" the NAACP's Aaron Henry governor, and awarded the lieutenant governor's office to white Tougaloo College chaplain Reverend Ed King. The Freedom Vote was also a conscious effort to develop new networks to help expand COFO's presence in southern Mississippi. In some respects, though, the election disappointed organizers. More than two-thirds of votes came from just eight counties; in twenty-five counties, fewer than one hundred ballots were collected in each. For Bob Moses, the exercise confirmed that the state's blacks would not secure the suffrage "until the equivalent of an army is sent here." Joseph A. Sinsheimer, "The Freedom Vote of 1963: New Strategies of Racial Protest in Mississippi," *JSH* 55 (1989), 217–44; Dittmer, *Local People*, 200–205; Andrews, *Freedom Is a Constant Struggle*, 52–53; Payne, *I've Got the Light of Freedom*, 424.

57. Dittmer, *Local People*, 237.

58. Ibid., 273; Johnston, *Mississippi's Defiant Years*, 263–73; *NYT*, Jul. 20, 27, Aug. 13, 1964. Johnson refused to go to Atlantic City.

59. Kay Mills, *This Little Light of Mine: The Life of Fannie Lou Hamer* (New York: Penguin, 1993); Dittmer, *Local People*, 290; Perlstein, *Before the Storm*, 404; *LAT*, Aug. 26, 1964.

60. The MFDP was not allowed to name its two delegates, who sat with the Alaska delegation. *NYT*, Aug. 23, 1964; *LAT*, Aug. 23, 1964; *WP*, Aug. 23, 1964.

61. For one party leader, the episode in Atlantic City meant that the national party would be dead "for the next 100 years." *NYT*, Aug. 26, 1964; *WP*, Aug. 28, 1964; Derr, "The Triumph of Progressivism," 352–53.

62. In 1967 he asked that his seniority be restored. House liberals in the caucus defeated him. He said afterward that he would not switch to the Republican party, but would remain "a Mississippi Democrat." He then entered the gubernatorial race, announcing that he would fight for a Wallace delegation to Chicago. *WP*, Jan. 24, 1967; *NYT*, Feb. 2 and 12, 1967.

63. Claude Ramsay, the racially liberal head of the state's AFL-CIO affiliate, helped found the MDC. In the early 1960s, labor's power in Mississippi had been declining; it had been unable to block the popular ratification of a "right to work" state constitutional amendment. Ramsay saw blacks as key players in labor's growth. Labor itself remained weakly incorporated into the state Democratic party; the AFL-CIO actually endorsed Republican nominee Rubel Phillips in 1963. Charles N. Fortenberry and F. Glenn Abney, "Mississippi: Unreconstructed and Unredeemed," in Havard, *Changing Politics*, 504–7, 517; Alan Draper, *Conflict of Interest: Organized Labor and the Civil Rights Movement in the South* (Ithaca: Cornell University Press, 1994), chap. 6; Winkeljohn, "The Political Career of Rubel Phillips," 44.

64. Ramsay quoted in John C. Topping, Jr., John R. Lazarek, and William H. Linder, *Southern Republicanism and the New South* (Cambridge: Ripon Society, 1966), 78. Also see Simpson, "The 'Loyalist Democrats' of Mississippi," 53–54; Walton, *Black Political Parties*, 170–71.

65. Dittmer, *Local People*, 370–82.

66. *NYT*, Oct. 5 and 9, 1965; *WP*, Jun. 17, 1966.

67. Dittmer, *Local People*, 349.

68. Simpson, "The 'Loyalist Democrats' of Mississippi," 58–60.

69. At a meeting of the party's executive committee, a member proposed that it go on record as having "no objection" to the incorporation of black members, but the proposal failed. Governor Williams warned that such a resolution would "do serious damage" to the regulars. Jack H. Young et al., *Brief Submitted by the Loyal Democrats of Mississippi*, Subcommittee on Credentials of the Democratic National Committee, 1968), 21–22. General Civil Rights Collection, Tougaloo College Archives, Mississippi Digital Library, accessed online: http://collections.msdiglib.org /cdm/compoundobject/collection/tougaloo/id/757/rec/16.

70. *LAT*, Jan. 17, 1968; *NYT*, Jan. 17, 1968.

71. Quoted in Simpson, "The 'Loyalist Democrats' of Mississippi," 91. *WP*, Aug. 20, 1968. *NYT*, Jul. 23 and Aug. 20, 1968. Aaron Henry, Hodding Carter III, and Charles Evers held the chief leadership positions. *LAT*, Aug. 26, 1968; *NYT*, Aug. 23 and 28, 1968. The *New York Times*'s editors noted that the case "points up the growing power of the national convention as something more than just a meeting of fifty autonomous state parties."

72. *NYT*, Sep. 6, 1968. Evans and Novak called the regulars "a floating, partyless mass." *WP*, Nov. 14, 1968. Fortenberry and Abney, "Mississippi," 523–24. Bass and De Vries, *Transformation of Southern Politics*, 207.

73. Most national party leaders were concerned by the fact that only five members of the loyalists' executive committee of fifteen were white. But the liberal reformers prioritized ascriptive representation. National reform leader Donald Fraser lauded the "state party's efforts to bring true democracy to Mississippi." *NYT*, Jun. 5, 1969, Feb. 28, 1972.

74. Ken Bode, "Turning Sour: Democratic Party Reform," *TNR* 165 (July 10, 1971), 20.

75. Simpson, "The 'Loyalist Democrats' of Mississippi," 126–27; Bode, "Loyalists vs. Regulars," 6–17.

76. Henry and others demanded a fifty-fifty split by race for the delegation to Miami, the state party's executive committee, as well as compliance with McGovern-Fraser reforms and loyalty to the national ticket. Simpson, "The 'Loyalist Democrats' of Mississippi," 117, 130, 136–37, 140, 147, 164; Lawson, *In Pursuit of Power*, 198–200; Parker, *Black Votes Count*, 300. Loyalist Hodding Carter III remarked, "I hate to see … the entry of federal courts into the question of purely party politics" (in Simpson, "The 'Loyalist Democrats' of Mississippi," 145). Fannie Lou Hamer served on the national party's Platform Committee.

77. Henry became co-chair of a new state party executive committee of one hundred, with blacks occupying twenty-seven seats. In 1978, Henry met with Sen. Eastland to discuss the latter's upcoming reelection bid. Eastland was elected in 1942, one quarter-century before black voting became important in the state's elections. When told that his prospects for electoral support from the state's blacks were "poor at best" and that he had "a master-servant philosophy with regard to blacks," Eastland, Henry recalls, "just burst into tears." Henry offered to introduce him to black groups, but Eastland soon announced his retirement. Bass and De

Vries, *Transformation of Southern Politics*, 203; *NYT*, Jun. 15 and Dec. 30, 1975, Jan. 25, 1976; Howell Raines, "Revolution in South: Blacks at the Polls and in Office," *NYT* (Apr. 3, 1978), A1; Simpson, "The 'Loyalist Democrats' of Mississippi," 120, 124.

78. In 1964, Holmes County, which was 72 percent black, had voted almost 97 percent for Goldwater. Only an impressive voter mobilization drive that relied on the county's Freedom Party and NAACP networks helped Clark win a slim victory. From 1992 to 2003, he served as the chamber's speaker pro tempore. Cosman, *Five States for Goldwater;* Dittmer, *Local People*, 416.

79. Sixty-seven of seventy-four candidates for the powerful office of county supervisor were unsuccessful, despite the fact that almost all of them ran in majority-black counties. Lester M. Salamon, "Mississippi Post-Mortem: The 1971 Elections," *New South* 27 (1972), 43–47; "Black Power, Municipal Style," *Commonweal* 90 (Aug. 8, 1969), 477–78; Emilye Crosby, *A Little Taste of Freedom: The Black Freedom Struggle in Claiborne County, Mississippi* (Chapel Hill: University of North Carolina Press, 2005), chaps. 6–14. Statewide, black voter registration dipped from almost 68 percent of the black voting-age population at the end of 1970 to below 60 percent just one year later. Twenty-six counties required voters to reregister in 1971, and many black voters who worried about economic reprisals did not reregister. Simpson, "The 'Loyalist Democrats' of Mississippi," 115, fn. 13; "Black Politics," *TNR* 165 (Jul. 17, 1971), 13.

80. Federal courts enjoined the law in 1970, and the U.S. attorney general blocked it under the Voting Rights Act's pre-clearance provisions in 1974. Quotation appears in Simpson, "The 'Loyalist Democrats' of Mississippi," 114. Also see U.S. Commission on Civil Rights, *The Voting Rights Act: Ten Years After*, 273–74; Parker, *Black Votes Count*, 62; *NYT*, Mar. 24 and Apr. 28, 1971; Hunter, *Shameful Blight*, 139–43.

81. E. C. Foster, "A Time of Challenge: Afro-Mississippi Political Developments since 1965," *JNH* 68 (1983), 190. Freedom Democrats and loyalists also filed challenges to block the seating in the Democratic House Caucus of the state's Democratic members on the grounds that they were not true Democrats. A similar 1970 challenge, reflecting a more liberal Caucus and greater impatience with the regulars, drew significant support. *WP*, Dec. 17, 1970; *NYT*, Jan. 20, 1971. Walton, *Black Political Parties*, 105–13.

82. *NYT*, Jun. 30 and Jul. 1, 1965; Butler, "The Republican Party of Mississippi," 68, 79–80.

83. Citing ruling party harassment of Republican campaign workers, threats to bankers backing the Republican ticket by the state's bank comptroller, and the intimidation facing state employees to back the Democratic ticket, Phillips complained, "They are treating my workers like niggers." Sinsheimer, "Freedom Vote of 1963," 242; Billy B. Hathorn, "Challenging the Status Quo: Rubel Lex Phillips and the Mississippi Republican Party, 1963–1967," *JMH* 47 (1985), 240–65; *NYT*, Nov. 8, 1964. Topping, Lazarek, and Linder, *Southern Republicanism*, 79. *NYT*, Dec. 3, 1969; Crespino, *In Search of Another Country*, 217–18.

84. Republicans lost the three state legislative seats they had captured, and won only one of 57 local races. *JCL*, Oct. 28 and Nov. 1, 1967; *NYT*, Oct. 4 and Nov. 5, 1967; *WP*, Nov. 5, 1967; *Time* magazine, Oct. 13, 1967; Winkeljohn, "The Political Career of Rubel Phillips," 70–81, 99, 104–6; Robert Sherrill, *Gothic Politics in the Deep South: Stars of the New Confederacy* (New York: Grossman Publishers, 1968), 382; "Document labeled 'Restricted,' concerning the instruction of Poll Watchers in Jackson,

Mississippi, and support for or against the political views of civil rights activist Law-rence Guyot," Erle Johnston Papers, McCain Library, University of Southern Missis-sippi. Hathorn, "Challenging the Status Quo," 262; *Time* magazine, Nov. 17, 1967, 29. Fortenberry and Abney, "Mississippi," 500.

85. Eastland had championed many of Nixon's judicial nominees. Rubel Phil-lips publicly backed Eastland. Still, signs of the emergence of Mississippi Repub-licans were apparent. The Democratic presidential candidate had failed to win a plurality of the state's vote for the fourth straight election, and Trent Lott and Thad Cochran won two of the state's congressional races as Republicans. Clarke Reed asked Carmichael to run because only James Meredith (!) sought the Republican nomination to oppose Eastland, and if Meredith had been on the ticket, the Repub-lican House candidates would have lost badly. *WP*, Oct. 1, 1972; *NYT*, Oct. 1, 1972.

86. Dittmer, *Local People*, 424.

87. Hine, "Civil Rights and Campus Wrongs," 311. Edgar, *South Carolina: A His-tory*, chap. 22, and Sproat, "Firm Flexibility," articulate the "integration with dignity" thesis. The aristocratic claim appears in Newby, *Black Carolinians*, 373.

88. The value of prime contracts to South Carolina firms increased 600 percent from 1960 to 1968. Annual data appear in Bureau of the Census, *Statistical Abstract*, various years.

89. South Carolina whites considered the university's initial desegregation "one of the most heinous acts of Reconstruction." Edgar, *South Carolina: A History*, 392. USC, unlike the University of North Carolina, was not an incubator for dissidents and reformers or a refuge of interracial cooperation. Black activists viewed its lead-ership as by equal measures reactionary and timid. Heard interview with a PDP official, Jan. 19, 1948, Heard Papers; Henry H. Lesesne, *A History of the University of South Carolina* (Columbia: University of South Carolina Press, 2001), chap. 5.

90. This incident recalls Governor Olin Johnson's mustering of the State Guard in 1943 to intimidate Klansmen during a period of wild rumors of armed black revolts (see chapter 4). By 1970, the state's formerly white colleges enrolled tiny num-bers of blacks and featured substantial racial hostility. *SSN*, Sep. 1963, pp. 22–23; Cox, "1963—Year of Decision," pp. 91, 94; Bass and De Vries interview with James Redfern, SHC. Subsequent college desegregations also occurred peacefully.

91. "A cotton mill town with a chip on its shoulder," Rock Hill was home to many organized white supremacists. Arsenault, *Freedom Riders*, 121–23 (quotation at 121). According to Hollings, "When Martin Luther King marched in . . . we had black policemen policing the streets and the incidents, and when one of them stepped out of line there was a black policeman leading him into the paddy wagon and they threw away their cameras. They said this isn't what we want, and they went on down to Montgomery." Oral history with Hollings, in Luders, "The Politics of Exclu-sion," 209. *NYT*, Mar. 7, May 11 and 31, Jun. 31, 1961.

92. In the late 1960s the FBI's COINTELPRO infiltrated and weakened growing Klans in Columbia. Cunningham, *There's Something Happening Here*, 314, fn. 17 and 150.

93. For instance, historian I. A. Newby argues that South Carolina's NAACP dominated the state's black protest, and "determined the course the movements took, channeling them into cautious, limited programs in pursuit of moderate, prag-matic objectives." Newby, *Black Carolinians*, 278.

94. Events data are analyzed in Joseph Luders, "Countermovements, the State, and the Intensity of Racial Contention in the American South," in Jack A. Goldstone, ed., *States, Parties, and Social Movements* (New York: Cambridge University Press, 2003), 27–44; and Luders, "The Politics of Exclusion," 218. Law enforcement detained more than three hundred demonstrators in Rock Hill in a chicken stockade. Hine, "Civil Rights and Campus Wrongs," 320, 324–31. *NYT*, Feb. 9, 1961; Arsenault, *Freedom Riders*, 88.

95. The manipulation of polling hours and precinct locations continued throughout the 1970s. Former White Citizens' Council leader Micah Jenkins later pushed for such a change in Charleston County. Cohodas, *Strom Thurmond*, 426–27; Orville Vernon Burton, Terence R. Finnegan, Peyton McCrary, and James W. Loewen, "South Carolina," in Davidson and Grofman, *Quiet Revolution*, 191, 200–202; Bass and De Vries, *Transformation of Southern Politics*, 271.

96. *Stevenson v. West*, 413 U.S. 902 (1973); U.S. Commission on Civil Rights, *The Voting Rights Act: Ten Years After*, 219. The politically weaker House reapportioned in 1974.

97. E.g., Carson, *In Struggle*. Meier and Rudwick discuss efforts by CORE workers in the 1950s to register voters in *CORE*, 80–90, 175–76, 333.

98. In 1967, the NAACP's Roy Wilkins claimed that, unlike other Deep South states, the state had "been going steady along an unheralded course . . . away from the glare [of] the racial spotlight. . . . On the race question South Carolina . . . already has caught and passed many a Northern community." "South Carolina's Progress in Race Relations Is Sound," *LAT*, Mar. 6, 1967.

99. Synnott, "Federalism Vindicated," 296; Badger, "From Defiance to Moderation," 15.

100. Bagwell, *School Desegregation*, 159.

101. The city conducted a disorderly but nondeadly token school desegregation in 1963. Fifteen years after *Brown*, barely 1 percent of black students in Clarendon County attended schools with whites. The situation had not changed by the mid-1990s. Cox, "1963—Year of Decision," pp. 186, 194.

102. *NYT*, Feb. 9, 10, 1968.

103. These included White Citizens' Council leaders such as Farley Smith (son of the infamous Senator "Cotton Ed" Smith) and Micah Jenkins, both active in independent elector movements for Eisenhower and Nixon. Workman was not the favored candidate of the upcountry, antistatist wing of the party. Benefiting from Oxford, Workman netted a surprising 43 percent of the vote—the most successful Republican bid since Reconstruction. Perlstein, *Before the Storm*, 59; Merritt, "The Senatorial Election of 1962 and the Rise of Two-Party Politics in South Carolina"; Bass and De Vries interview with Workman, SHC.

104. McMillan, "Integration with Dignity," 18; Kalk, *Origins of Southern Strategy*, 36–37.

105. Sampson, pp. 758, 741–42.

106. Only three of Nixon's eighteen counties lay above the fall line. Kalk, *Origins of Southern Strategy*, 41–42; *NYT*, Nov. 24, 1963. By 1960, Byrnes and some prominent White Citizens' Council leaders campaigned for the actual Republican ticket. Other well-known segregationists sponsored a "Democrats for Nixon-Lodge" campaign, given the stigma still attached to the Republican label and their own Democratic

affiliation. The national party blocked access to federal patronage to its leader, U.S. House member Albert Watson. *NYT*, May 26, 1965.

107. State Electoral Commission, *Report to the General Assembly* (Columbia: State of South Carolina, 1968).

108. Sampson, pp. 547–48, fn. 101. In 1963, at a public barbecue for incoming governor Donald Russell, NAACP field director Newman was photographed in a receiving line as he shook hands with the new governor, whom Hollings had successfully "out-segged" in the 1958 gubernatorial primary. In 1966 Russell faced Hollings in the party's U.S. Senate primary. Capturing the bizarre nature of black incorporation in South Carolina, Newman gave the photograph to Hollings and suggested that he use it to "out-seg" Russell again; he did so, and won. On the photograph episode, see Badger, "From Defiance to Moderation," 11. This reception was the state's "first racially integrated public occasion … since Reconstruction." Historian Walter Edgar, *Greenville News*, Nov. 25, 2002.

109. Sampson, pp. 464–65.

110. Workman, "Long Distance Conversation with Harry Dent and Sen. Strom Thurmond," Workman Papers. Two of Thurmond's top aides, Harry Dent, and another aide J. Fred Buzhardt believed his "days were numbered if he remained a Democrat," and pushed him to switch for this reason. Sampson, p. 422, fn. 68. For a similar argument about the importance of race and evolving primary electorates in the mid-1960s, see David W. Brady, John A. Ferejohn, and Jeremy C. Pope, "Congress and Civil Rights Policy: An Examination of Endogenous Preferences," in Ira Katznelson and Barry R. Weingast, eds., *Preferences and Situations: Points of Intersection Between Historical and Rational Choice Institutionalism* (New York: Russell Sage Foundation, 2005), 76.

111. Sampson, pp. 454–55. Barry Goldwater had urged Thurmond to switch parties, and a survey of voters supported this advice. In his announcement, he said that if Democrats won election, "freedom as we know it in this country is doomed." Perlstein, *Before the Storm*, 431. Thurmond maneuvered to install his confidant Harry Dent as party chair. In 1966, campaigning on themes of white supremacy, "law and order," and antisocialism, Thurmond won reelection easily, but lost black precincts by Goldwater-like margins. Kalk, *Origins of Southern Strategy*, 68–70.

112. Sampson, pp. 486–87, 491.

113. Kalk, *Origins of Southern Strategy*, 66, 90, 122.

114. Quoted in Minchin and Salmond, *After the Prize*, 77.

115. Reeves, *President Nixon*, 117.

116. Philip G. Grose, Jr., "Briefing Given to Nixon on Columbia School Fight," *CS* (date unknown), 1968; Richard Reeves, *President Nixon: Alone in the White House* (New York: Simon & Schuster, 2001), 171–72.

117. According to Gary Orfield, "The Nixon administration virtually stopped administrative enforcement of the 1964 Civil Rights Act within American schools, but the federal courts ordered its resumption and struggled for fifteen years to enforce a succession of orders. Nixon fired Leon Panetta, the official enforcing the school desegregation standards, and denounced mandatory school desegregation; he privately often urged his chief of staff, H. R. Haldeman, to stir up the busing issue for political purposes." Orfield, "The 1964 Civil Rights Act and American Education," 94; Leon E. Panetta and Peter Gall, *Bring Us Together: The Nixon Team and the Civil Rights Program* (Philadelphia: J. B. Lippincott, 1971).

118. In his inaugural address, McNair said, "I intend to use all of the authority and influence at my command to see that the good name of our state is not tarnished, either by infringement of human rights, or by flagrant disregard of law and order." Bass and Nelson, *The Orangeburg Massacre*, 2.

119. Blacks comprised 14 percent of the state's delegation. West, McNair, and most other delegates backed eventual Democratic presidential nominee Hubert Humphrey. Meanwhile, more than 70 percent of the state's voters (and a much greater share of South Carolina whites) voted against the Democratic party (for either Nixon or Wallace). Grose, *Looking for Utopia*, 148; Sampson, p. 548.

120. Brown considered some of the SERC's directives as "obnoxious" and likely counterproductive; what is more telling about the odyssey of South Carolina Democrats since the Dixiecrat revolt is the simple fact that he participated on the punitive party council. *NYT*, Feb. 17, 1967. Crotty, *Decision for the Democrats*, 203; Sampson, p. 585.

121. Robert Sherrill, "Sen. Ernest Hollings: Education of a Conservative," *The Nation* (Aug. 16, 1971), 105–9; Jean Dreze and Amartya Sen, *Hunger and Public Action* (New York: Oxford University Press, 1989); Bureau of the Census, *1970 Statistical Abstracts*, 86, table 124.

122. *NYT*, Feb. 7, 1971; Ernest F. Hollings, *The Case Against Hunger: A Demand for National Policy* (New York: Cowles, 1970). Thurmond—not incorrectly—called Hollings's sudden interest in hunger a craven bid for black votes. *NYT*, Feb. 15, 1969. The renewal of the Voting Rights Act in 1970 was the first civil rights bill in three decades *not* subject to a southern filibuster. As Senator Ernest "Fritz" Hollings admitted, "I'm not going back to my state and explain a filibuster against black voters." Lawson, *In Pursuit of Power*, 159–60.

123. McNair assumed office after Governor Donald Russell moved to the U.S. Senate, and later won reelection. Grose, *South Carolina at the Brink*, 103, 9.

124. Grose, *South Carolina at the Brink*, 143; Sampson, p. 453.

125. Sampson, pp. 551–54.

126. Many state politicians continued to dissent from the consensus position within the ruling party to back industrialization and the modernization of the state's workforce. The reinstatement of South Carolina's compulsory school attendance law occasioned the most intense filibuster during McNair's tenure as governor. Interview with Robert E. McNair, Feb. 2, 1983, Governor McNair Oral History Project, Part 15, p. 16, SCPC.

127. The name is courtesy of SNCC President H. Rap Brown.

128. Orangeburg was also home to the private (black) Claflin College.

129. Fritz Hamer, "Review of Philip G. Grose, *South Carolina at the Brink: Robert McNair and the Politics of Civil Rights*," H-Net Reviews (Jan. 2007), accessed online: http://www.h-net.org/reviews/showpdf.php?id=12812.

130. *NYT*, Oct. 20, 1963. The spokesman of the local chapter of the John Birch Society owned and operated WDIX, the local radio station. On the town's desegregation, see Steven A. Davis, *National Register of Historic Places Multiple Property Document* (Washington, D.C.: National Park Service, United States Department of the Interior, Jun. 24, 1996), Section E. Sellers had told students beforehand that desegregation was "an irrelevant issue" and that they should not waste their time with a demonstration at a bowling alley. Cleveland Sellers with Robert Terrell,

The River of No Return: The Autobiography of a Black Militant and the Life and Death of SNCC (Jackson: University of Mississippi Press, 1990), 205–22; Grose, *South Carolina at the Brink*, chap. 10. Bass and Nelson, *The Orangeburg Massacre*, 8–10, 101, and passim; *NYT*, Oct. 22, 1985. The state did not issue a formal apology for the shooting deaths until 2003.

131. Grose, *South Carolina at the Brink*, 167.

132. This account relies on Leon Fink and Brian Greenberg, *Upheaval in the Quiet Zone: A History of Hospital Workers' Union, Local 1199* (Urbana: University of Illinois Press, 1989), chap. 7; Leon Fink, "Union Power, Soul Power: The Story of 1199B and Labor's Search for a Southern Strategy," *Southern Changes* 5 (1983), 9–20; Grose, *South Carolina at the Brink*, chap. 11; Interview with Robert E. McNair (May 16, 1983), Part 21 (Tape 22), pp. 1–16. On the South's much better known public sector strike, see Michael K. Honey, *Going Down Jericho Road: The Memphis Strike, Martin Luther King's Last Campaign* (New York: Norton, 2007). The strike also departed from what historian Stephen O'Neill calls "a weak black protest tradition in Charleston. . . . A new, more demanding black leadership emerged to supplement [or even] supplant an older conservative elite that had, under the old system, forged close political ties with the city's white elite." See O'Neill, "From the Shadow of Slavery: The Civil Rights Years in Charleston," Ph.D. diss., University of Virginia (1994), pp. 4–5 and chap. 5; Oral history Interview with Mary Moultrie (Jul. 28, 1982), conducted by Jean-Claude Bouffard, Jean-Claude Bouffard Civil Rights Interviews, Avery Research Center, Charleston accessed online: http://lcdl.library.cofc.edu/lcdl/catalog/lcdl:23397; interview with William Saunders, conducted by Kieran Taylor and Jennifer Dixon (Jun. 17, 2008), SOHP; Jack Bass and Alice Cabaniss, "Strike at Charleston," *New South* 24 (1969), 35–44; Robert H. Zieger, *For Jobs and Freedom: Race and Labor in America Since 1865* (Lexington: University Press of Kentucky, 2007), 195–98. Moultrie had been trained at the Highlander Folk School.

133. The state's right-to-work ordinance had no bearing on public sector workers. By 1969, public sector unions had secured positive statutory rights in most U.S. states. Henry S. Farber, "The Evolution of Public Sector Bargaining Laws," Henry S. Farber, in Richard B. Freeman and Casey Ichniowski, eds., *When Public Sector Workers Unionize* (Chicago: University of Chicago Press, 1988), 129–68.

134. Kalk, *Origins of the Southern Strategy*, 93; Sampson, p. 111, table 2.21. The networks used to develop all of these protests relied in part on the still-extant connections among participants of the "citizenship schools" of the 1950s and 1960s.

135. Lassiter, *The Silent Majority*, 247; *JCL*, Nov. 8 and Dec. 11, 1969.

136. Grose, *South Carolina at the Brink*, 278. As Lassiter argues, "The center held in Greenville, thanks to favorable racial demographics in a countywide school system, a comprehensive busing plan that kept most white students in their current facilities, preemptive action by local civic and business leaders determined to avoid disorder and defiance, and a silent majority of white families who looked to the future and maintained their allegiance to public education." Lassiter, *The Silent Majority*, 257; *NYT*, Jan. 28, 1970.

137. *NYT*, Feb. 18 and Mar. 4, 1970; *WP*, Feb. 18, 1970; Grose, *South Carolina at the Brink*, 279–81. A similar attack on black schoolchildren occurred in Grenada, Mississippi in 1966. Dittmer, *Local People*, 403. Later that fall, McNair blamed Watson after another spate of school violence—this time a large riot between black and white

high school students in Columbia that Watson's own campaign aides may have fomented. Grose, *Looking for Utopia*, 154.

138. Grose, *Looking for Utopia*; Bass and De Vries interview with John C. West, SHC; Gordon E. Harvey, *A Question of Justice: New South Governors and Education, 1968–1976* (Tuscaloosa: University of Alabama Press, 2002), 178; Randy Sanders, *Mighty Peculiar Elections: The New South Gubernatorial Campaigns of 1970 and the Changing Politics of Race* (Baton Rouge: Louisiana State University Press, 2002), 113–45.

139. In the 1968 presidential election, in a real departure from previous patterns, only five of the state's fifteen majority-black counties featured voting rates for registered voters below the state average. Bain, "South Carolina: Partisan Prelude," 613, 633.

140. Upon taking office, Governor West appointed one of the UCP's leaders, James Clyburn, to his staff, and later named him the state's human affairs commissioner. Clyburn, now a Democratic member of Congress, is the state's most powerful black politician. On Republican funding, author's interview with former Democratic state party chair Don Fowler, Columbia, Apr. 2000; Billy B. Hathorn, "The Changing Politics of Race: Congressman Albert William Watson and the Republican Party, 1965–1970," *SCHM* 89 (1988), 233.

141. Walton, *Black Political Parties*, and Walton, "The National Democratic Party of Alabama and Party Failure in America," in Kay Lawson and Peter H. Merkl, eds., *When Parties Fail: Emerging Alternative Organizations* (Princeton: Princeton University Press, 1988), 365–88. In this sense, the UCP's dilemmas recalled those faced by women's suffrage organizations in the 1920s and 1930s, as detailed by Anna Harvey, *Votes without Leverage: Women in American Electoral Politics, 1920–1970* (New York: Cambridge University Press, 1998).

142. *NYT*, Jan. 10, 1971; Sampson, pp. 564–65. By summer 1972 blacks had filled the influential party posts of executive director and vice-chair. Folder 48, Box 2; Folder 103, Box 3; Folder 148, Box 5, all in Papers of the State Democratic Party, SCPC.

143. Grose, *South Carolina at the Brink*, 290; Reg Murphy and Hal Gulliver, *The Southern Strategy* (New York: Scribner's, 1971), 171–72; *NYT*, Aug. 27 and Nov. 1, 1970. Harvey, *A Question of Justice*, 178, fn. 10. After several years of failing to develop usable party machinery for contesting general elections, by 1966 South Carolina Democrats seemed shaken by the growth of the state's Republican party in presidential elections. In one sign that they had begun to respond effectively, they departed from decades-long practice by having gubernatorial nominees in 1966 and 1970 who did not face challengers in the primary. Sampson, p. 671.

144. "We can, and we shall, in the next four years, eliminate from our government any vestige of discrimination because of race, creed, sex, religion, or any other barrier to fairness for all citizens." "We pledge to minority groups no special status other than full-fledged responsibility in a government that is totally color-blind. . . . The politics of race and divisiveness fortunately have been soundly repudiated in South Carolina." "The time has arrived when South Carolina . . . must break loose and break free from the vicious cycle of ignorance, illiteracy, and poverty which has retarded us throughout our history." Thurmond responded, quite reasonably, that "Democrats have been in power here all these years, and if there is any discrimination, they could have eliminated it. I thought [it] had been eliminated." *CSM*, Jan. 23, 1971; *NYT*, Jan. 20, 1971.

145. Underwood, *Constitution of South Carolina*, 2: chaps. 4–7. These efforts culminated in the 1975 Home Rule Act, which ended the one-to-one apportionment of senators and counties.

146. Bass and De Vries, *Transformation of Southern Politics*, 213, 263; Peirce, *Deep South States*, 414; "Accomplishments of West Administration," 2, West File, Workman Papers. *NYT*, Jan. 20, Apr. 25 and 30, 1971, and Jul. 2, 1972; Murphy and Gulliver, *The Southern Strategy*, 170–72, 158–63; *CSM*, Jan. 23, 1971; Grose, *South Carolina at the Brink*, 173; Eugene N. Zeigler, Jr., *When Conscience and Power Meet: A Memoir* (Columbia: University of South Carolina Press, 2008), chap. 28.

147. In 1968, Robert Coles and Harry Huge wrote that "no southern state can match South Carolina's ability to resist the claims of black people without becoming an object of national scorn." Coles and Huge, "Strom Thurmond Country: The Way It Is in South Carolina," *TNR* (Nov. 30, 1968), 19.

148. On appointments, author's interview with Don Fowler. Office Files, Papers of the Democratic Party, SCPC; on the state Senate, Burton et al., "South Carolina," 203–4.

149. Author's interview with Don Fowler; Bass and De Vries interview with former Lieutenant Governor Earle Morris, SHC.

150. According to the Ranney index—a commonly used metric for estimating the degree of multi-party competition)—South Carolina until 1963 was the region's least competitive state. By 1974, it was the Deep South's most competitive. Sampson, pp. 21–22 and table 1–1, 23; Bass and De Vries, *Transformation of Southern Politics*, 511.

151. The state had four Standard Metropolitan Statistical Areas (defined as one or more central counties featuring a core population, plus outlying counties, which total at least 50,000): Atlanta, Augusta, Columbus, and Macon. The latter two lay below the fall line. From 1950 to 1960 the largest eight counties grew by 27 percent, while the smallest 121 counties declined by 4 percent. U.S. Bureau of the Census, *Statistical Abstract, 1960* (Washington, D.C.: U.S. Government Printing Office, 1961), table 9, 14; Rigdon, *Georgia's County Unit System*, 15; Lassiter, *The Silent Majority*, 54.

152. By the mid-1950s more than one-third of black Georgians—those most likely to register and to vote—lived in the five largest metro counties, and thus had negligible impact on statewide elections because of the county-unit system, and precious little representation in the highly malapportioned House and Senate. These were Fulton (Atlanta), Chatham (Savannah), Muscogee (Columbus), Richmond (Augusta), and Bibb (Macon). Rigdon, *Georgia's County Unit System*, 40.

153. McCrary, "Bringing Equality to Power," 677, fn. 59.

154. Bartley, *From Thurmond to Wallace*, 47–56.

155. Bartley, *From Thurmond to Wallace*, 15–33; Boyd, *Georgia Democrats*, 47. Georgia lost momentum in its manufacturing growth during the 1950s. The presence of a robust white supremacist impulse could be a point of vulnerability for south Georgia. In 1955, the South Carolina Development Board, seeking to help lure a nitrogen plant to the state, sent the target firm a copy of Roy Harris's *Augusta Courier*, Georgia's leading white supremacist broadsheet, to point out "the unstable political and economic climate in the neighboring state." Cobb, *Selling of the South*, 159, 70.

156. The Atlanta-based Southern Regional Council distributed thousands of "Leadership Reports" to local leaders encouraging them to be "heroes" and oversee peaceful desegregations. Cobb, *Selling of the South*, 129.

157. Some business interests blamed the dip in the state's manufacturing growth on the county-unit system. Cobb, *Selling of the South*, 159–61.

158. Forty-nine percent of Georgia's population lived in the eighteen largest counties by 1960. Bartley, *From Thurmond to Wallace*, 15.

159. In 1960, for example, future moderate governor Carl Sanders continued to sing in the Talmadgeite chorus for the system's preservation, arguing that without it, control of the state government would be lost to "pressure groups or bloc votes." The system allowed the state, he claimed, to keep "liberals and radicals from taking over." All involved in state politics understood that the "bloc vote" was code for urban black voters. Atlanta's electorate was then about 30 percent black. McDonald, *A Voting Rights Odyssey*, 83; on the coded use of "bloc vote," see p. 92.

160. *Colegrove v. Green*, 328 U. S. 549 (1946), at 556 (discussed in chapter 2).

161. *Sanders v. Gray*, 203 F. Supp. 158 (Apr. 28, 1962). The U.S. Supreme Court affirmed. In the majority opinion, Justice William O. Douglas used for the first time the phrase "one person, one vote" while arguing that the Fourteenth Amendment's equal protection clause required legislative districts be roughly equal in size (*Gray v. Sanders*, 372 U.S. 368 (1963)). Before the court ruled, Governor Vandiver asked the General Assembly to preempt an unfavorable decision by reforming the system. Henderson, *Ernest Vandiver*, 160–67. Bernd, "Georgia: Static and Dynamic," 302, 331, 362. On the benefits of reapportionment for non-southern Democrats across the country, see Gary W. Cox and Jonathan N. Katz, *Elbridge Gerry's Salamander: The Electoral Consequences of the Reapportionment Revolution* (New York: Cambridge University Press, 2002), chap. 4.

162. Data published by the National Municipal League and reprinted in Arthur L. Goldberg, "The Statistics of Malapportionment," *Yale Law Journal* 72 (1962), Appendix A, 100–1.

163. In 1962 two Republican senatorial candidates in the Atlanta area—one running against a well-known black Democrat, Leroy Johnson—and another running against a white Democrat—were black. *CSM*, Nov. 2, 1962. Johnson later aligned himself with Lester Maddox—a further demonstration of the incomplete incorporation of blacks in north Georgia's Democratic circles. *NYT*, Apr. 3, 1978.

164. The demise of the county-unit system emboldened urban interests and "good government" advocates to lower the legal barriers to county consolidation. Although no counties disappeared from the state map, the threat of consolidation helped permanently weaken the lobby of county commissioners. Bernd, "Georgia: Static and Dynamic," 302, 331, 362; *WSJ*, Jun. 17, 1963; *CSM*, Aug. 8, 1963.

165. Primarily because of Vandiver's personal antipathy for the year's main white supremacist candidate, former governor Marvin Griffin, he persuaded the party to require that the nominee receive a majority of votes cast. Vandiver assumed that Griffin would lose a runoff election. Peyton McCrary and Steven F. Lawson, "Race and Reapportionment, 1962: The Case of Georgia Senate Redistricting," *JPH* 12 (2000), 299–300.

166. A centerpiece of Griffin's campaign was his promise to jail Martin Luther King. James F. Cook, "Carl Sanders and the Politics of the Future," in Henderson and Roberts, *Georgia Governors*, 170–71.

167. After the Sibley Commission recommended defusing the state's "doomsday device," Arnall announced that he would not run and cleared the way for Sanders to challenge Griffin. Henderson, *Politics of Change in Georgia*, 221.

168. James F. Cook, *Carl Sanders: Spokesman of the New South* (Macon, Ga.: Mercer University Press, 1993), 93; Murphy and Gulliver, *Southern Strategy*, 184. Sanders opposed desegregation, but said, "I won't cause you and your state to be spread across the headlines all over the nation and cause you embarrassment." Cobb, *Selling of the South*, 141.

169. Sanders received over 70 percent of the urban vote, which comprised 42 percent of the state's turnout. Griffin's urban voters were working-class voters who—in the case of Atlanta—had backed Lester Maddox's mayoral campaigns of the late 1950s. Cook, *Carl Sanders*, 89–91; McCrary and Lawson, "Race and Reapportionment, 1962," 301–2. While Sanders won both the popular vote and what would have been the county-unit vote, evidence suggests that the invalidation of the county-unit system demobilized voters in "two-unit" counties. Bernd, "Georgia: Static and Dynamic," 335–36; Boyd, *Georgia Democrats*, 118.

170. Boyd, *Georgia Democrats*, 120.

171. Bartley, *From Thurmond to Wallace*, 9, table 1–4, and 11.

172. Ibid.

173. Of course, not all federal intervention was unwelcome; many Atlanta politicians backed lawsuits in federal court to overcome the county-unit system.

174. Atlanta's leaders had cultivated the city's image since the 1940s, and Mayor Hartsfield began touting it as "the city too busy to hate" in the 1950s. Stone, *Regime Politics*, 27; Hornsby, "A City That Was Too Busy to Hate."

175. Seymour Freedgood, "Life in Buckhead," *Fortune* 64 (1961), 108–9; Claude Sitton, "Atlanta's Example: Good Sense and Dignity," *NYT Magazine* (May 6, 1962), 22, 123, 128; Frederick Allen, *Atlanta Rising: The Invention of an International City, 1946–1996* (Athens, Ga.: Longstreet Press, 1996).

176. Staring down protesters, Maddox brandished a pistol and then closed his well-known restaurant rather than desegregating it. Bruce Galphin, *The Riddle of Lester Maddox* (Atlanta: Camelot, 1968); Lester G. Maddox, *Speaking Out: The Autobiography of Lester Garfield Maddox* (Garden City, N.Y.: Doubleday, 1975). Bernd, "Georgia: Static and Dynamic," 357; Bartley, *From Thurmond to Wallace*, chap. 3.

177. Grady-Willis, *Challenging U.S. Apartheid*, 26–29. Chafe argues that this dynamic between protesters and those empowered by city authorities to negotiate on their behalf was a common one in southern cities. Chafe, *Civilities and Civil Rights*, 155.

178. White supremacist leaders long disparaged Atlanta; Roy Harris called it the state's "Achilles heel" in the defense of segregation. Pratt, *We Shall Not Be Moved*, 64. Sitton, "Atlanta's Example," 22, 123, 128. Cobb, *Selling of the South*, 147.

179. Alton Hornsby, Jr., "A City That Was Too Busy to Hate," in Jacoway and Colburn, *Businessmen and Desegregation*, 121–32. Firms in Atlanta were not exceptional in this regard. Even in Little Rock, which was supposed to have generated so many valuable lessons for southern officials and whose political institutions by 1959 were controlled by "business moderates," downtown firms responded to sit-ins with intransigence. Wright, *Sharing the Prize*, 81.

180. Tuck, *Beyond Atlanta*, 112, 115–17; David Levering Lewis, *King: A Biography* (Urbana: University of Illinois Press, 1970), 233–35. One of King's top lieutenants concluded that "SCLC's activities in Atlanta were a waste of time." Fairclough, *To Redeem the Soul of America*, 176–77.

181. Ivan Allen, Jr., with Paul Hemphill, *Mayor: Notes on the Sixties* (New York: Simon and Schuster, 1971); Bartley, *From Thurmond to Wallace*, 47; Lassiter, *The Silent Majority*, 109–10; Kruse, *White Flight*, 3–5.

182. Quoted in Trillin, *An Education in Georgia*, 8. Young and others organized the Atlanta Committee for Cooperative Action to provide an alternative to the city's "old guard," but it failed to gain traction. NAACP regional director Ruby Hurley called for the city's NAACP branch to be moved away from Auburn Avenue—the heart of the city's black establishment—because this proximity damaged prospects for a "vibrant branch." Tuck, *Beyond Atlanta*, 100, 105, 120, 125. On the old guard, see Jack Walker, "The Functions of Disunity: Negro Leadership in a Southern City," *JNE* 32 (1963), 227–36, and Walker, "Protest and Negotiation: A Case Study of Negro Leadership in Atlanta, Georgia," *Midwest Journal of Political Science* 7 (1963), 99–124.

183. Two Atlanta-area U.S. House members had been among only a handful of southern members who voted in favor of the legislation. Watters and Cleghorn, *Climbing Jacob's Ladder*, 262.

184. Of course, there were crowd disturbances in the city, including demonstrations in the black neighborhood of Summerhill that Maddox would draw on to defeat Ellis Arnall in the Democratic gubernatorial primary of 1966. And in 1964 a large George Wallace rally in Atlanta turned violent. During a speech by Ross Barnett, three black SNCC members walked near the rally. Cries of "Kill 'em!" broke out throughout the crowd, and soon white men crashed metal folding chairs and placards over their heads. *WP*, Jul. 5, 1964. Elsewhere in north Georgia, there were significant racial clashes, including race riots in Rome, a hardscrabble manufacturing town in northwest Georgia, and substantial white-on-black violence in Athens. However, these events had little impact on north Georgia's reputation or led to greater federal oversight or black protest interventions in the region. On Rome, see Brattain, *The Politics of Whiteness*, epilogue.

185. This was "an induced riot involving a few susceptible Negroes," reported the *New York Times*. Quoted in David Andrew Harmon, *Beneath the Image of the Civil Rights Movement and Race Relations: Atlanta, Georgia, 1946–1981* (New York: Routledge, 1996), 206; Carson, *In Struggle*, 226–27, chap. 13, 238. Winston A. Grady-Willis attempts to rehabilitate the Atlanta project appears in *Challenging U.S. Apartheid: Atlanta and Black Struggles for Human Rights, 1960–1977* (Durham, N.C.: Duke University Press, 2006), chap. 4. Also see Stone, *Regime Politics*, chap. 6.

186. Because of the extraordinary leadership of local NAACP president W. W. Law, Savannah—not Atlanta—featured the most effective civil rights movement in the state, securing more extensive policy gains and doing so earlier than Atlanta or other cities. Savannah's NAACP and black voter registration growth in the 1940s was the most impressive in the entire South. Unlike those in the rest of the state, Savannah blacks sustained the substantive victories emanating from this electoral influence throughout the 1950s and beyond. But even Savannah suffered from a shortage of black attorneys willing to work with the NAACP. In 1953, for the first time a black attorney outside Atlanta accepted civil rights cases. Rome, Brunswick, and Macon also featured effective local movements. Tuck, *Beyond Atlanta*, 97, 45–51, 139–40 (quotation at 126–27).

187. For an insightful discussion, see Boyd, *Georgia Democrats*, 123.

188. Boyd, *Georgia Democrats*, 125.

189. Bartley, *From Thurmond to Wallace*, table 3–6, 51.

190. McCrary, "Bringing Equality to Power," 682. A county court judge ruled that the Senate had to maintain single-member districts, and so Leroy Johnson was able to desegregate the Senate in 1963. Observers interpreted the appointments as attempts to "checkmate Republican efforts" to attract black voters. *WP*, May 14, 1963.

191. By requiring a candidate to win a majority of the vote, a black candidate would not be able to benefit from a divided white electorate. Before the 1964 legislation, about two-thirds of counties had used a plurality system. Kousser, *Colorblind Injustice*, 200; McDonald, *A Voting Rights Odyssey*, 93, 101–2. Federal courts invalidated Sanders-supported efforts to use at-large senatorial districts to block the election of black senators from the Atlanta area. Laughlin McDonald, Michael B. Binford, and Ken Johnson, "Georgia," in Davidson and Grofman, *Quiet Revolution*, 74–75, 411; McCrary and Lawson, "Race and Reapportionment, 1962," 296–98, 303–8.

192. However, at the close of Jackson's first term, the city's sanitation workers—who had backed him in 1969—went on strike. He fired about two thousand of them. Significantly, in an indication of how politically demobilized black Atlanta had become, his actions were met with little dissent from the city's black establishment and he easily won reelection. Joseph A. McCartin, "Managing Discontent: The Life and Career of Leamon Hood, Black Public Employee Union Activist," in Arnesen, *The Black Worker*, 271–300; Bayor, *Race and the Shaping of Twentieth-Century Atlanta*, 44–45; Adolph Reed, Jr., "Demobilization in the New Black Political Regime: Ideological Capitulation and Radical Failure in the Postsegregation Era," in Michael P. Smith and Joe R. Feagin, eds., *The Bubbling Cauldron: Race, Ethnicity, and the Urban Crisis* (Minneapolis: University of Minnesota Press, 1995), 196; Bartley, *From Thurmond to Wallace*, 98–99, 101. On the mayoral tenures of Maynard Jackson and Andrew Young (1974–1981 and 1982–1990, respectively), see Larry Keating, *Race, Class, and Urban Expansion* (Philadelphia: Temple University Press, 2001), 78–87.

193. Lassiter, *The Silent Majority*, 108. A comprehensive school desegregation plan would have to include the city's suburbs; however, black leaders helped defeat annexation efforts because it would dilute their electoral influence. Bayor, *Race and the Shaping of Twentieth-Century Atlanta*, 85–92.

194. For example, the region received no federal registrars or election observers, despite standard complaints about election chicanery.

195. James C. Cobb, "Yesterday's Liberalism: Business Boosters and Civil Rights in Augusta, Georgia," in Jacoway and Colburn, *Southern Businessmen and Desegregation*, 151–69.

196. In 1970, highway patrolmen shot six blacks; all died, and seventy-five others were injured. *LAT*, May 13–14, 1970; *CSM*, May 16 and 27, 1970. Governor Lester Maddox eventually deployed one thousand National Guard troops and 150 highway patrolmen, blamed events on a "Communist conspiracy," and then met with hometown celebrity and local radio station owner James Brown to call for peace and an end to looting. The National Guard deployment secured order. The disturbances prompted white civic and business leaders to consider long-rejected black demands.

197. Quoted in Lawson, *In Pursuit of Power*, 214, 308, fn. 18; U.S. Commission on Civil Rights, *Political Participation*, 169.

198. Transcript, Andrew J. Young, Jr., Oral history Interview I, Jun. 18, 1970, by Thomas H. Baker, LBJ Library (Austin), pp. 18–19.

199. In thirty-four other counties, black voter registration was below 10 percent. In 1972, blacks held fewer than 2 percent of all elected officials in Georgia, but they comprised 26 percent of the state's electorate. By late 1974, more than 9 percent of state legislators were black. McDonald, *A Voting Rights Odyssey*, 10, 130, 215, 217.

200. Mary S. Lawson, "C. B. King," *New Georgia Encyclopedia*, accessed online: http://www.georgiaencyclopedia.org/nge/Article.jsp?id=h-1100.

201. Quoted in Fairclough, *To Redeem the Soul of America*, 61. Eventually, the King-centric civil rights historiography would label the Albany movement a failure, given the refusal of local authorities to accept an omnibus desegregation demand. However, taking a longer view, the movement laid the groundwork for blacks' eventual takeover of many of the city's offices. If anything, the introduction of King and the SCLC into negotiations with city officials seems to have been counterproductive to ongoing demonstrations, boycotts, and other actions by indigenous groups. Lawrence J. Hanks, *The Struggle for Black Political Empowerment in Three Georgia Counties* (Knoxville: University of Tennessee Press, 1987); Tuck, *Beyond Atlanta*, 147–57; Fairclough, *To Redeem the Soul of America*, 56–57, 106; Paul D. Bolster, "Civil Rights Movements in Twentieth-Century Georgia," Ph.D. diss., University of Georgia (1972), pp. 255–84; Barkan, "Legal Control of the Southern Civil Rights Movement"; Thornton, *Dividing Lines*.

202. Fairclough, *To Redeem the Soul of America*, 87.

203. Bolster, "Civil Rights Movements in Twentieth-Century Georgia," pp. 301–15; Fairclough, *To Redeem the Soul of America*, 264; Branch, *Parting the Waters*, 529–38; Garrow, *Bearing the Cross*, 173–82; Carson, *In Struggle*, 56–60; Morris, *Origins of the Civil Rights Movement*, 239–42.

204. McDonald, *A Voting Rights Odyssey*, 117; Carson, "SNCC and the Albany Movement," 15–25; Tuck, *Beyond Atlanta*, chap. 5; William B. Williford, *Americus Through the Years: The Story of a Georgia Town and Its People, 1832–1975* (Atlanta: Cherokee, 1975); *NYT*, Aug. 1, 1965.

205. E.g., Claude Sitton, *NYT*, Jul. 27, 1962.

206. In 1965, as a member of Congress, Callaway testified against the Voting Rights Act. Before, he had run for election calling to attempt to secure the repeal of civil rights laws. *NYT*, Nov. 19, 1961; McDonald, *A Voting Rights Odyssey*, 9 and 114. Callaway endorsed Goldwater in 1964.

207. Quoted in Lester G. Maddox, "A Chance for Truth," in Henderson and Roberts, *Georgia Governors*, 213. Bartley, *From Thurmond to Wallace*, table 5-1, 69, 77. Arnall's support of the national Democratic party hurt him in 1966. His campaign also suffered from black demonstrations and crowd disturbances in the black neighborhood of Summerhill in Atlanta just prior to the primary. During the campaign, Maddox promised to chase Martin Luther King from the state. His write-in bid was supported by the state's two largest black voter organizations (Georgia Voter League and the Association of Democratic Clubs). In another attempt to prevent Maddox's election and avoid a return to massive resistance, establishment Democrats—including white moderates, hard-core segregationists, and some leading older black elites—organized "Democrats for Callaway." Boyd, *Georgia Democrats*, 174–76.

208. The vote was 182 to 66. Nine of the eleven black legislators refused to vote. At the time, Republicans held 29 of 259 seats in the General Assembly. Democratic legislators worried that a Callaway administration would open the door to

Republican appointments, the "purging" of Democrats, and more contested general elections. Murphy and Gulliver, *The Southern Strategy*, 174. *NYT*, Sep. 29, 1966.

209. Henderson, *Politics of Change in Georgia*, 237; Bradley R. Rice, "Lester Maddox and the Politics of Populism," in Henderson and Roberts, *Georgia Governors*, 197; U.S. Commission on Civil Rights, *The Voting Rights Act: The First Months*, 60. In 1966, U.S. House member Charles Weltner—the only Deep South supporter of the Voting Rights Act—quit his reelection bid on the grounds that he could not uphold an oath to back Democratic candidates (i.e., Maddox). Right-wing Republicans replaced Weltner and Mackay, "the only two progressive members of Georgia's congressional delegation." Bartley, *From Thurmond to Wallace*, 79–81; Boyd, *Georgia Democrats*, 167.

210. Boyd, *Georgia Democrats*, 180. Because of the election's delayed result, for the first time in decades, the legislature, not the governor, chose its leadership and committee chairs. Also, given Maddox's disinterest in legislative politics, this drift continued. By the time Carter—a highly activist executive—took office, "the power and influence of particular legislative leaders had grown tremendously, and they zealously protected and defended that independence." Author's interview with Charles C. Bullock, Athens, Aug. 2001; Gary M. Fink, "Jimmy Carter and the Politics of Transition," in Henderson and Roberts, *Georgia Governors*, 234–35.

211. After King's assassination, he called in state troopers to guard the capitol, and instructed them to "shoot . . . down" protesters and "stack them up" if need be. Rice, "Lester Maddox," 204.

212. Maddox's executive secretary resigned, charging that the governor refused to appoint blacks. Rice, "Lester Maddox," 201–6, 209.

213. *WP*, Jun. 9, 1963; *NYT*, Jul. 29, 1964; Cook, "Carl Sanders and the Politics of the Future," 181. *NYT*, Aug. 27, 1964. South Georgia politicians supporting Goldwater included Marvin Griffin, Roy Harris, and James Gray.

214. The regular party chose seven blacks (three delegates and four alternates) for its 107-member delegation, which had forty-three votes (forty-one delegates plus two DNC members).

215. The Forum's challenge drew great sympathy from nonsouthern delegates, who nominated Bond for vice president. Party chair Gray threatened to refuse to certify the presence of the national ticket on the state ballot. The Forum cited Gray's 1964 support for Goldwater, and Maddox's likely support for George Wallace in the upcoming election. Many white regulars refused to be seated in any delegation involving Bond, whose early, outspoken opposition to the Vietnam War made him highly controversial. *NYT*, Dec. 10, 1967, and Jul. 25, Aug. 11, 17, 22–31, 1968; *LAT*, Aug. 27–28, 1968; *CSM*, Aug. 25–26 and Sep. 4, 1968; *WP*, Sep. 17, 1968; Rice, "Lester Maddox," 205;

216. Bartley, *From Thurmond to Wallace*, tables 6–2 and 6–7, 84, 93, 95; *AJ*, Nov. 3, 1968; Boyd, *Georgia Democrats*, 195–99.

217. *NYT*, Aug. 28, 1968.

218. Boyd, *Georgia Democrats*, 201. Later, Jimmy Carter slammed the party reforms, as well as McGovern, whom he painted as a radical who "alone among all the candidates refuses to promise equal treatment under federal law for the southern states." This position-taking was quite ironic because Carter would go on to receive his party's presidential nomination in large part because of the delegate selection

rules unleashed by the McGovern-Fraser commission. Office of Governor Jimmy Carter, Press Release, May 25, 1972; Nelson W. Polsby, *Consequences of Party Reform* (New York: Oxford University Press, 1983).

219. Boyd, *Georgia Democrats*, 207.

220. In a display of the increasing voting strength of rural black Georgia, fewer than one-half of his support came from cities. *CSM*, Dec. 19, 1969; Hanes Walton, Jr., *The Native Son Presidential Candidate: The Carter Vote in Georgia* (New York: Praeger, 1992).

221. Sanders, *Mighty Peculiar Elections*, 146–69; Boyd, *Georgia Democrats*, 143–54; Murphy and Gulliver, *Southern Strategy*, 190–97; Bass and De Vries, *Transformation of Southern Politics*, 211–14; Lassiter, *The Silent Majority*, 270.

222. Jimmy Carter, Inaugural Address (Atlanta), Jan. 12, 1971; *NYT*, Jan. 17, 1971; *CSM*, Jan. 15, 1971. *Time* magazine featured a cover portrait of Carter (Mar. 31, 1971). *WP*, Jun. 2 and 6, 1972; *NYT*, Jun. 5, 1972; *NYT*, Jul. 2, 1972; Fink, "Jimmy Carter," 237–38.

223. The number of state agencies was reduced from 278 to twenty-two. Carter also pursued education reform (especially a statewide kindergarten program), public health programs, criminal justice and penal reform, judicial reform, ecological reform, budgetary reform, and consumer protection regulations. Gary M. Fink, *Prelude to the Presidency: The Political Character and Legislative Leadership Style of Governor Jimmy Carter* (Westport, Conn.: Greenwood Press, 1980).

224. The number of black state employees increased from 4,850 to 6,684. Fink, "Jimmy Carter," 240; Fink, *Prelude to the Presidency*, 15. Henderson, *Ernest Vandiver*, 150–51; Cook, "Carl Sanders and the Politics of the Future," 179; Jimmy Carter interview with Gary L. Roberts, in Henderson and Carter, *Georgia Governors*, 251; Bass and De Vries, *Transformation of Southern Politics*, 145. The state's all-white Bureau of Investigation was not decoupled from the power of county sheriffs and professionalized until the Carter years. The dismantling of racist law enforcement at the local level did not occur quickly, either. In 1974, Atlanta mayor Maynard Jackson began a protracted conflict with the city's white power brokers in attempting to reform the city's police department. Stone, *Regime Politics*, 88–92.

225. *NYT*, Jan. 5, 1974; *Memphis Tri-State Defender*, Mar. 9, 1974. At the unveiling, Georgia's National Guard band played "We Shall Overcome."

226. However, political observers agreed that Carter's tenure was mediocre at best. He did a poor job of forging political coalitions, alienated would-be allies, and left office with very low popularity. His national reputation as a racial moderate would carry him up through presidential politics. Fink, *Prelude to the Presidency*, 170–72; Fink, "Jimmy Carter," 243–48.

227. Carter cooperated well with House majority leader—and future two-term governor—George Busbee, and other House Democrats. However, Maddox cobbled together a Senate faction only two votes short of a veto on all of Carter's legislation. The Senate then had fifty-six members; twenty-two voted against the administration, and another five "usually voted with" Maddox. Fink, "Jimmy Carter," 235–37; Fink, *Prelude to the Presidency*, 27, 121.

228. The state finally secured a new one in 1983. In 1963, under Sanders's leadership, the state convened yet another Constitutional Revision Commission. Dominated by Sanders's appointees, it drafted a new constitution, and the General Assem-

bly approved it. However, since the General Assembly was malapportioned when it approved the constitution, federal courts temporarily blocked a popular referendum needed to ratify it, and the moment passed.

229. Minchin and Salmond, *After the Dream*, 83, 153; Wright, *Sharing the Prize*, 150.

230. David W. Rhode, *Parties and Leaders in the Postreform House* (Chicago: University of Chicago Press, 1991), table 1.1 (at 15), 45–46.

231. For an interpretation of Thurmond as less a museum piece of an "old" South than a national politician on the leading edge of the New Right, see Crespino, *Strom Thurmond's America*.

232. Orfield, "The 1964 Civil Rights Act and American Education," 112–13.

233. Charles M. Payne, " 'The Whole United States Is Southern!' *Brown v. Board* and the Mystification of Race," *JAH* 91 (2004), 83–91.

CHAPTER ELEVEN:
Legacies and Lessons of the Democratized South

1. Arguments relying on such mechanisms must specify the relative importance of the legacy vis-à-vis more temporally proximate causal forces, as well as its duration. On "historical causes," see Arthur Stinchcombe, *Constructing Social Theories* (New York: Harcourt, Brace and World, 1968), 103–18.

2. Mahoney, "Path Dependence in Historical Sociology," 515. On specifying the "mechanisms of reproduction" of such legacies, see Thelen, "Historical Institutionalism in Comparative Politics," 391, and Collier and Collier, *Shaping the Political Arena*, 31–34. Generally, see Pierson, *Politics in Time*.

3. For example, Shafer and Johnston, *End of Southern Exceptionalism*.

4. Charles S. Bullock III and Mark J. Rozell, "Introduction," in Bullock and Rozell, eds., *The New Politics of the Old South* (New York: Rowman and Littlefield, 1998), 13. John C. Kuzenski, "South Carolina: The Heart of GOP Realignment in the South," in ibid., 25–48.

5. In 1995 the election of Republican governor Kirk Fordice failed to provide coattails for other Republican statewide candidates, all of whom lost. David A. Breaux, Don E. Slabach, and Daye Dearing, "Mississippi: A Synthesis of Race, Region, and Republicanism," in Bullock and Rozell, *New Politics*; also, Stephen D. Shaffer and Latarsha Horne, "The End of Regionalism? Revisiting V. O. Key's Delta versus Hills Sectionalism in Mississippi Politics," *American Review of Politics* 19 (1998), 97–114.

6. Charles S. Bullock III, "Regional Realignment from an Officeholding Perspective," *JOP* 50 (1988), 571. Kevin P. Phillips, *The Emerging Republican Majority* (New Rochelle, N.Y.: Arlington House, 1969); Richard Nadeau and Harold W. Stanley, "Class Polarization in Partisanship Among Native Southern Whites, 1952–1990," *AJPS* 37 (1993), 900–919; Charles D. Hadley, "Dual Partisan Identification in the South," *JOP* 47 (1985), 254–68; James M. Glaser, *Race, Campaign Politics, and the Realignment in the South* (New Haven: Yale University Press, 1996); A. J. Barghothi, Elisha Carol Savchak, and Ann O'M. Bowman, "Candidate Quality and the Election of Republican Governors in the South, 1950–2004," *American Politics Research* 38 (2010), 563–85. On slow-changing "partisan imagery" in the South, see Donald

Green, Bradley Palmquist, and Eric Schickler, *Partisan Hearts & Minds: Political Parties and the Social Identities of Voters* (New Haven: Yale University Press, 2002), 141.

7. D. Stephen Voss and David Lublin, "Racial Redistricting and Realignment in Southern State Legislatures," *AJPS* 44 (2000), 792–810.

8. Black and Black, *Politics and Society*. On the mechanism of replacement with reference to generational change and elite turnover, Pierson, *Politics in Time*, 90.

9. For a complementary analytic account, James M. Snyder, Jr. and Michael Ting, "An Informational Rationale for Political Parties," *AJPS* 46 (2002), 90–110. Generally, Aldrich, *Why Parties?*

10. Nicholas A. Valentino and David O. Sears, "Old Times There Are Not Forgotten: Race and Partisan Realignment in the Contemporary South," *AJPS* 49 (2005), 672–88; Stephen Ansolabehere, Nathaniel Persily and Charles Stewart III, "Regional Differences in Racial Polarization in the 2012 Presidential Election," *Harvard Law Review Forum* 126 (2013), 205–20.

11. For support of this perspective, see, for example, Glaser, *Race*.

12. David T. Canon, "The Emergence of the Republican Party in the South, from 1964 to 1988," in Allen D. Hertzke and Ronald M. Peters, eds., *The Atomistic Congress: An Interpretation of Congressional Change* (Armonk, N.Y.: M. E. Sharpe, 1991), 73–105; David T. Canon, Matthew M. Schousen, and Patrick J. Sellers, "The Supply Side of Congressional Redistricting: Race and Strategic Politicians, 1972–1992," *JOP* 58 (1996), 846–62.

13. The appellation "racial conservatism" is a curious but widespread one. A less polite and more accurate term for such attitudes and appeals is "racial resentment." Donald R. Kinder and Lynn M. Sanders, *Divided by Color: Racial Politics and Democratic Ideals* (Chicago: University of Chicago Press, 1996).

14. A Republican won the governorship in 1974, but this was due to a set of random events that did not foster additional Republican gains. On Thurmond, Kalk, *Origins of Southern Strategy*.

15. For a bill of particulars, see Burton et al., "South Carolina," 191–232.

16. In 1995, its party chair during the 1960s, Don Fowler, served as chair of the DNC.

17. Glen T. Broach and Lee Bandy, "South Carolina: A Decade of Rapid Republican Ascent," in Alexander P. Lamis, ed., *Southern Politics in the 1990s* (Baton Rouge: Louisiana State University Press, 1999), 51, 62, 71.

18. In an Aiken County exit poll during the 1994 Republican primary, 78 percent of Republican identifiers thought "we have gone too far in pushing equal rights in this country." Alexander P. Lamis, "The Two-Party South: From the 1960s to the 1990s," in Lamis, *Southern Politics in the 1990s*, 6; John J. Brady, *Bad Boy: The Life and Politics of Lee Atwater* (New York: Perseus Books, 1996); Glen T. Broach and Lee Bandy, "South Carolina: A Decade of Rapid Republican Ascent," in Lamis, *Southern Politics*, 51, 62, 71; *NYT*, Jan. 22, 1995.

19. Alexander P. Lamis, *The Two-Party South*, 2nd ed. (New York: Oxford University Press, 1990).

20. Charles Evers and Andrew Szanton, *Have No Fear: The Charles Evers Story* (New York: John Wiley & Sons, 1997), 286; Foster, "A Time of Challenge," 191.

21. On his first campaign trip after winning the Republican nomination in 1980, Ronald Reagan flew to Philadelphia—where white supremacist activists and law en-

forcement officials coordinated in the murder of three civil rights workers in 1964—and famously declared to an almost all-white crowd at the Neshoba County Fair, "I believe in states' rights." He promised to "restore to states and local governments the powers that properly belong to them." *NYT*, Aug. 4, 1980; *LAT*, Jan. 20, 1989. Completing a bizarre circle, in 1984, Trent Lott declared that the "spirit of Jefferson Davis" now animated the Republican Party! Stephen D. Shaffer, David E. Sturrock, David A. Breaux, and Bill Minor, "Mississippi: From Pariah to Pacesetter?" in Lamis, *Southern Politics in the 1990s*, 250.

22. For example, time-series analysis of state legislative and gubernatorial elections, as compared to congressional and presidential voting, is needed to test the party brand name argument sketched here.

23. On the capital accumulation strategies of state elites in North Carolina, see Wood, *Southern Capitalism*.

24. Robert J. Barro and Xavier Sala-i-Martin, "Convergence Across States and Regions," *Brooking Papers on Economic Activity* 1 (1991), 107–82; Paul M. Romer, "The Origins of Endogenous Growth," *Journal of Economic Perspectives* 8 (1994), 3–22; Paul Krugman, *Geography and Trade* (Cambridge: MIT Press, 1991); Wright, "Civil Rights Revolution"; Mancur Olson, "The South Will Fall Again: The South as Leader and Laggard in Economic Growth," *Southern Economic Journal* 49 (1983), 917–32; Scranton, *The Second Wave*.

25. It is also worth considering whether the variables prized by economists themselves are partly endogenous on southern states' different democratic transitions. For instance, both partisan and economic change in the South is thought to be influenced by the influx of nonnative whites to the region. In 1950, Deep South enclaves contained an identical share of nonsouthern-born whites (3–4 percent)—this was one-half that of Outer South states. But in 1980, Georgia and South Carolina reached 12 percent, while Mississippi only 8 percent. By this time, nonsoutherners had bypassed the "vast majority" of southern counties. Black and Black, *Politics and Society*, 13–16, 19.

26. Declines in private investment in South Africa were caused by potential investors' perceptions of instability. Wood, *Forging Democracy from Below*, 151–52 and chap. 6. It is likely that these reputations might be more damaging to subnational political jurisdictions, since they are less able to erect barriers to capital flight than sovereign states.

27. Personal communication with historian James C. Cobb, Apr. 3, 2006 (Atlanta). Timothy J. Bartik, "Business Location Decisions in the United States: Estimates of the Effects of Unionization, Taxes, and Other Characteristics of States," *Journal of Business & Economic Studies* 3 (1985), 14–22; Cletus C. Coughlin, Joseph V. Terza, and Vachira Arromdee, "State Characteristics and the Location of Foreign Direct Investment within the United States," *Review of Economics and Statistics* 73 (1991), 675–83; James R. Hines, Jr., "Altered States: Taxes and the Location of Foreign Direct Investment in the United States," *American Economic Review* 86 (1996), 1076–94; Paul Brace, "The Changing Context of State Political Economy," *JOP* 53 (1991), 297–317.

28. The state has been viciously antiunion since the 1930s. In fact, upcountry mill owners recruited Bob Jones from Tennessee to preach against unions. Mark T. Dalhouse, *Island in a Lake of Fire: Bob Jones University, Fundamentalism, and the Separatist Movement* (Athens: University of Georgia Press, 1996).

29. South Carolina lost 300,000 textile jobs from 1979 to 1985. Cobb, *Selling of the South*, 267; the drive for foreign direct investment is not universally shared; state leaders have often taken steps to keep foreign—or U.S.—companies out of counties with unionized workers. For example, mill owners opposed Michelin's move into Greenville because it paid higher wages than mills. Edgar, *South Carolina: A History*, 532; Coclanis and Ford, "South Carolina Economy," 106.

30. Bethany Lamar Baskin interview with William E. Winter (Apr. 28, 1992), 23 (John C. Stennis Oral History Project, Mississippi State University Libraries, accessed online: http://digital.library.msstate.edu/cdm/ref/collection/jcsi/id/921.

31. Matthew L. Wald, "Mississippi Extends Hospitality to Nuclear Power," *NYT*, Jan. 27, 2005; Robert D. Bullard, *Dumping in Dixie: Race, Class, and Environmental Quality* (Boulder, Colo.: Westview Press, 1990). On the contemporary Delta, Arthur G. Cosby, Mitchell W. Bracken, T. David Mason, and Eunice R. McCullough, eds., *A Social and Economic Portrait of the Mississippi Delta* (Starkville: Social Science Research Center, Mississippi State University, 1992); Larry Doolittle and Jerry Davis, *Social and Economic Change in the Mississippi Delta: An Update of Portrait Data* (Starkville: Social Science Research Center, Mississippi State University, 1996).

32. Two-thirds of UGA's total enrollment hailed from ten of Georgia's counties; 60 percent of the 2006 class came from within one hundred miles of Atlanta. *Athens Banner-Herald*, Sep. 4, 2002.

33. Some econometric evidence exists for the positive effects of such missions on foreign direct investment. Timothy J. Wilkinson and Lance Eliot Brouthers, "Trade Shows, Trade Missions and State Governments: Increasing FDI and High-Tech Exports," *Journal of International Business Studies* 31 (2000), 725–34.

34. Wright, "Civil Rights Revolution," 285 (emphasis added). Of course, robust causal inferences about cross-state variation in the trends presented above require finely grained data on economic investments before, during, and after the democratic transitions, as well as data on human capital, technology, infrastructure, and so on. Such inferences also require evidence of the decision-making of potential investors.

35. Valelly, *The Two Reconstructions*, 182. Chappell calls the South's democratization "astonishingly nonviolent," the final round of segregationist violence of the 1950s and 1960s resembling "more an expression of desperation than determination." Chappell, *A Stone of Hope*, 2.

36. Florida, Georgia, Louisiana, North Carolina, and Virginia all adopted new constitutions; Arkansas and Texas designed new constitutions that voters ultimately rejected. Tarr, *Understanding State Constitutions*.

37. Carles Boix, "Setting the Rules of the Game: The Choice of Electoral Systems in Advanced Democracies," *APSR* 93 (1999), 609–24.

38. Anna Grzymała-Busse, *Rebuilding Leviathan: Party Competition and State Exploitation in Post-Communist Democracies* (New York: Cambridge University Press, 2007).

39. Among a mushrooming literature, see Jon Elster, *Closing the Books: Transitional Justice in Historical Perspective* (New York: Cambridge University Press, 2004), Martha Minow, *Between Vengeance and Forgiveness: Facing History After Genocide and Mass Violence* (Cambridge: Harvard University Press, 1999), and Sanford Levinson, *Written in Stone: Public Monuments in Changing Societies* (Durham, N.C.: Duke Uni-

versity Press, 1998); Marguerite Feitlowiz, *Lexicon of Terror: Argentina and the Legacies of Torture* (New York: Oxford University Press, 1998).

40. Black resistance to "Dixie" and the Confederate flag began in earnest with school desegregation, as black high school band members boycotted the song, black college students desecrated the flag, and so on. *NYT*, Feb. 26, 1969. The often-painful disclosure of surveillance files in eastern Germany and Mississippi are discussed in Timothy Garton Ash, *The File: A Personal History* (New York: Random House, 1997); David Oshinsky and Richard Rubin, "Should the Mississippi Files Have Been Reopened?" *NYT Magazine* (Aug. 30, 1998), 30–32; and Peter Maas, "The Secrets of Mississippi: Post-Authoritarian Shock in the South," *New Republic* 219 (Dec. 21, 1998), 21–25. Also controversial are the adoption of state holidays for Martin Luther King, Jr., and for Confederate soldiers, representations of enclave rule in high school textbooks, etc.

41. In Mississippi, crusading journalist Jerry Mitchell has helped relaunch successful prosecutions, including the murder of Medgar Evers (*JCL*, Sep. 3, 2005). More than three decades after the Orangeburg Massacre in South Carolina, the state's governor issued a formal apology (*CS*, Feb. 9, 2003).

42. Outcomes of gubernatorial elections in Georgia, Mississippi, and South Carolina have been significantly affected by candidates' positions on the flag—in all cases, candidates supporting the removal of flags bearing Confederate elements have either lost or escaped with a narrow victory. J. Michael Martinez, William D. Richardson, and Ron McNinch-Su, eds., *Confederate Symbols in the Contemporary South* (Gainesville: University of Florida Press, 2000); Vincent L. Hutchings, Hanes Walton, Jr., and Andrea Benjamin, "Heritage or Hate: Race, Gender, Partisanship & the Georgia State Flag Controversy," paper presented at the 2005 APSA Meetings, Washington, D.C.

43. Bryce, *Modern Democracies*, 602. Also see Guillermo O'Donnell, "Human Development, Human Rights, and Democracy," in O'Donnell, Jorge Vargas Culell, and Osvaldo M. Iazzetta, eds., *The Quality of Democracy: Theory and Applications* (Notre Dame, Ind.: University of Notre Dame Press, 2004), 9–92.

44. William R. Keech, *The Impact of Negro Voting: The Role of the Vote in the Quest for Equality* (Chicago: Rand McNally, 1968); James W. Button, *Blacks and Social Change: The Impact of the Civil Rights Movement in Southern Communities* (Princeton: Princeton University Press, 1989).

45. The election of black authorities in Atlanta has been a boon to black public sector employment. Peter K. Eisinger, "Black Employment in Municipal Jobs: The Impact of Black Political Power," *APSR* 76 (1982), 380–92. In the private sector, the desegregation of South Carolina's textile mills has been one of the greatest victories won by South Carolina's blacks. James J. Heckman and Brook S. Payner, "Determining the Impact of Federal Antidiscrimination Policy on the Economic Status of Blacks," *American Economic Review* 79 (1989), 138–77; Gavin Wright, "The Economics of Civil Rights," Citadel Conference on the Civil Rights Movement in South Carolina (Mar. 5–8, 2003), Charleston; Timothy J. Minchin, *Hiring the Black Worker: The Racial Integration of the Southern Textile Industry, 1960–1980* (Chapel Hill: University of North Carolina Press, 1999).

46. Earl Black, *Southern Governors and Civil Rights: Racial Segregation as a Campaign Issue in the Second Reconstruction* (Cambridge: Harvard University Press, 1976).

47. Harvey, *A Question of Justice*, 3. The share of per capita personal incomes in the non-metro South relative to the non-South has been stagnant for more than three decades, and still amounts only to about 70 percent of non-metro non-South levels. Wright, "Civil Rights Revolution," 283. Donald Tomaskovic-Devey and Vincent J. Roscigno, "Uneven Development and Local Inequality in the U.S. South: The Role of Outside Investment, Landed Elites, and Racial Dynamics," *Sociological Forum* 12 (1997), 565–597; Kenny Johnson and Marilyn Scurlock, "The Climate for Workers: Where Does the South Stand?" *Southern Changes* 8 (1986), 3–15; Cobb, *Selling of the South*, 264, 272; Wright, "Civil Rights Revolution"; Wright, *Old South, New South*, chap. 7; Schulman, *Cotton Belt to Sunbelt*; Charles E. Menifield and Stephen D. Shaffer, eds., *Politics in the New South: Representation of African Americans in Southern State Legislatures* (New York: SUNY Press, 2005).

48. Dahl, *Polyarchy*, 54; Robinson, "Economic Development and Democracy," 508–11. Wood accounts for the meager political-economic gains in El Salvador and South Africa in terms of their particular democratization paths and the legacies of oligarchic rule. *Forging Democracy from Below*, 209–11. For a complementary explanation, Alexander, *Sources of Democratic Consolidation*. The structural dependence of democratic states on capital reinforces this result. Adam Przeworski and Michael Wallerstein, "Structural Dependence of the State on Capital," *APSR* 82 (1988), 11–29; William Roberts Clark, Matt Golder, and Sona Nadenichek Golder, *Comparative Politics* (Washington, D.C.: Congressional Quarterly Press, 2008); Stephen L. Elkin, "Pluralism in Its Place: State and Regime in Liberal Democracy," in Roger Benjamin and Elkin, eds., *The Democratic State* (Lawrence: University of Kansas Press, 1985), 179–211.

49. Key, *Southern Politics*, 670; Reinhard Bendix, *Nation-Building and Citizenship: Studies of Our Changing Social Order* (New York: Transaction Publishers, 1996 [1964]).

50. Brazil's authoritarian enclaves include its second most populous state, Minas Gerais, Amazonia, and several states in the northeast. Argentina's include rural provinces in the northwest, as well as some in the center. O'Donnell, "On the State," 1359. Cornelius, "Subnational Politics and Democratization," and Snyder, "After the State Withdraws." Personal communication with Alejandro Poire, executive director, Office of Political Parties, Mexican Federal Election Institute (Mar. 1, 2005).

51. Guillermo A. O'Donnell, *Counterpoints: Selected Essays on Authoritarianism and Democratization* (Notre Dame, Ind.: University of Notre Dame Press, 1999).

52. Snyder, "Scaling Down," 93–110, offers a similar view. Also, Edward L. Gibson, ed., *Federalism and Democracy in Latin America* (Baltimore: Johns Hopkins University Press, 1994). Riker articulated one of the dark sides of federalism—the perpetuation of stable pockets of injustice. *Federalism*, 155. For another call for a hemispheric U.S. South, Richard Tardanico and Mark B. Rosenberg, eds., *Poverty or Development: Global Restructuring and Regional Transformations in the U.S. South and the Mexican South* (New York: Routledge, 2000).

53. On the decline in outsized ambition, see Ira Katznelson, "Structure and Configuration in Comparative Politics," in Mark Irving Lichbach and Alan S. Zuckerman, eds., *Comparative Politics: Rationality: Culture, and Structure* (New York: Cambridge University Press, 1997), 81–112; Katznelson, "The Doleful Dance of Politics and Policy: Can Historical Institutionalism Make a Difference?" *APSR* 92 (1998), 191–98;

and Pierson, *Politics in Time*, 4–6. Also see Gerring, "APD from a Methodological Point of View."

54. Farhang and Katznelson, "The Southern Imposition"; Katznelson, *When Affirmative Action Was White*; Lieberman, *Shifting the Color Line*; Bensel, *Yankee Leviathan*; Korstad and Lichtenstein, "Opportunities Found and Lost.

55. Douglas, *Jim Crow Moves North*, is part of a growing literature concerning racial battles over policies, neighborhoods, and citizenship outside the South since at least the Great Migration. Also see Thomas J. Sugrue, *The Origins of the Urban Crisis: Race and Equality in Postwar Detroit* (Princeton: Princeton University Press, 1996).

56. Keyssar, *The Right to Vote*. Keyssar notes many moments when lawmakers "tightened the belt of democracy." *The Right to Vote*, 316–324. Shefter, *Political Parties and the State*, chap. 6.

57. Christopher Uggen, Sarah Shannon, and Jeff Manza, *State-Level Estimates of Felon Disenfranchisement in the United States, 2010* (New York: The Sentencing Project, 2012); Keith G. Bentele and Erin E. O'Brien, "Jim Crow 2.0? Why States Consider and Adopt Restrictive Voter Access Policies," *Perspectives on Politics* 11 (2013), 1088–116; Nicholas Stephanopolous, "The South after Shelby County," *Supreme Court Review* (2013), pp. 55–134.

58. Rogers M. Smith, *Civic Ideals: Conflicting Visions of Citizenship in U.S. History* (New Haven: Yale University Press, 1997). On the legal canon's blind spots, Pildes, "Democracy, Anti-Democracy, and the Canon"; James Morone, *Hellfire Nation: The Politics of Sin in American History* (New Haven: Yale University Press, 2003).

59. New efforts to periodize U.S. political history with race at the foreground include Desmond S. King and Rogers M. Smith, "Racial Orders in American Political Development," *APSR* 99 (2005), 75–92. Gonzalez and King argue that the United States did not become fully democratic until the Voting Rights Act, but they make this argument only with reference to black suffrage, not by reckoning with the features of southern enclaves ensnaring whites and blacks alike. Francisco E. Gonzalez and Desmond King, "The State and Democratization: The United States in Comparative Perspective," *British Journal of Political Science* 34 (2004), 193–210.

60. Valelly, *The Two Reconstructions*, chap. 1. King and coauthors have gone further and placed American democratization in cross-national perspective. Desmond King, Robert C. Lieberman, Gretchen Ritter, and Laurence Whitehead, eds., *Democratization in America: The United States as a Democratizing Nation* (Baltimore: Johns Hopkins University Press, 2009).

61. Bensel, *The Political Economy of American Industrialization*. Of course, on Bensel's view, the maintenance of democratic rule outside the South remains puzzling.

62. Some scholars have made the leap. For example, Rebecca J. Scott, *Degrees of Freedom: Louisiana and Cuba after Slavery* (Cambridge: Harvard University Press, 2005); Peter Kolchin, *A Sphinx on the American Land: The Nineteenth-Century South in Comparative Perspective* (Baton Rouge: Louisiana State University Press, 2003); Anthony W. Marx, *Making Race and Nation: A Comparison of the United States, South Africa, and Brazil* (New York: Cambridge University Press, 1998).

63. I thank a reviewer for suggesting this phrasing.

64. The current moral panic over and calls for policy responses to "voter fraud" is unsurprising given the hypercompetitive partisan landscape. And it raises parallels to fierce fights over contested elections during Redemption. Justin Levitt, *The Truth about Voter Fraud* (New York: Brennan Center for Justice at NYU Law School, 2007); James and Lawson, "Political Economy of Voting Rights Enforcement."

65. For William H. Riker, "Federalism is an impediment to the freedom of everybody except segregationist whites in the South." *Federalism: Origin, Operation, Significance* (Boston: Little, Brown, 1964), 144. On the view outlined here, federalism is anything but an engine of the South's democratization. For this suggestion, see Richard P. Young and Jerome S. Burstein, "Federalism and the Demise of Prescriptive Racism in the United States," *SAPD* 9 (1995), 1–54.

66. The Staple Singers "I'll Take You There" (music and lyrics by Alvertis Isbell [ASCAP, 1972]); William Faulkner, *Requiem for a Nun* (New York: Random House, 1951), 92.

Index

PRINCETON STUDIES IN AMERICAN POLITICS
HISTORICAL, INTERNATIONAL, AND COMPARATIVE PERSPECTIVES

SERIES EDITORS
Ira Katznelson, Eric Schickler, Martin Shefter, and Theda Skocpol

Printed in the USA
CPSIA information can be obtained
at www.ICGtesting.com
JSHW021215161223
53887JS00002B/4